People Migrations in Europe and America: Nation Building Prehistory to 1913

FOR COLLEGE HISTORY COURSES

SECULAR - THEOLOGICAL - GENEALOGICAL

A comprehensive chronological history based not on opinions of the author, but on reliable ancient and modern historical resources and eye witness accounts, all carefully documented.

Permissions to use copyrighted materials are available on request. Most maps and quotations are from very old publications. All are documented using super-scripted references to the Bibliography of 172 books and articles.

© 2016 first edition. ISBN see back cover

Research and Correlation by:

Barbara Nemeth M.I. Macdonald

Myrtle Ida Schneider Macdonald

101 45875 Cheam Avenue, Chilliwack, B.C., V2P 1N7, Canada.

(604) 795-6390 E-mail: schmac@shaw.ca

Suggestions for a second edition are welcomed.

Self published, assisted by Soda 8, CreateSpace-Amazon and Bookow

People Migrations in Europe and America: Nation-Building Prehistory to 1913

Resources for College History Courses and Family Genealogies

D e d i c a t i o n:

to daughter Evelyn and late son Timothy

grandchildren,

great grandchildren,

Sister Cora, Brother Walter, nieces, nephews,

cousins,

friends,

students,

professors and mentors:

Here is precious information from the past of high relevance for our future.

People Migrations in Europe and America

ACKNOWLEDGMENTS

Credit is due to the multicultural pioneer community Vegreville, Alberta, where the author was born in 1921 and grew up, with a splendid start in appreciation of ethnic backgrounds. Before the railway came in 1905 the first settlers were land hungry Catholic and Baptist Americans; French from Quebec who had first tried to settle in the USA; and Loyalists from Ontario (previously from Pennsylvania). Next by train came English, Welsh and Irish, many varied Slavic peoples, diverse German speaking groups and enough Jews to have a Synagogue. Orphaned youths from England were adopted into her family. Neighboring farmers came to her father for his advice in fluent English, German or Russian. A succession of District Agriculturists, Home Economists and Health Nurses, Music and Drama Festivals, Agricultural and School Fairs, Women's Institute, Farmers Clubs, Rural School Boards, Telephone Companies, Wheat Pool, and many different churches, all stimulated and enriched knowledge. Like her parents she appreciates many faiths and life styles. Her mother's education was elementary but she was an avid reader of weekly and monthly periodicals: *Western Producer, Country Guide, Winnipeg Free Press* and *Vegreville Observer.* Hunger for learning was catching. Every 6 miles there was a one room school. Her grades 2 to 8 school teacher Wilhemina Tierney, had a Loyalist mother and Scottish father, and she made history live. The author drove a horse and buggy or sleigh 6 miles to high school. She liked all subjects especially history. As a nursing student at University of Alberta she saw differences in the history of nurses and doctors. She was inspired by Phoebe's hospice work in Rome, referred to by St. Paul. She was pleased there were two women co-translators of St. Jerome's Latin Vulgate Bible [25].

The author's parents were examples of neighborliness, pioneer spirit, innovation and industriousness, and in 1955 were honored as *a Master Farm Family.* They asked her never to undervalue the contribution of **Moravians** to the world. Throughout the 600 years since 1415 their significance was great, but overlooked. Likewise few people realize that **Huguenots** (French Protestants) were major world explorers, ship builders, artisans and silk producers.

The author thanks her professors in graduate studies at McGill University for both multidisciplinary and systems approaches. They helped her gain skill in *Participant Observation, Grounded Theory* and *Library Research* which she has continued to apply since. In 1971 she was granted the Master of Science, Applied in Nursing and Research with a minor in Social Sciences (Anthropology, Sociology and Social-Psychology).

Through working in six provinces across Canada she has enjoyed many friends with roots back to French protestants. Likewise her perspective was enriched by work with indigenous peoples in Canada and in four countries overseas (India, Pakistan, Thailand and Lesotho). The advocacy group for justice *Ten Days for World Development,* helped her appreciate the conditions and potential of nomads and other under-privileged peoples. She is grateful for insights from travel in Europe, Africa, Australia, New Zealand, China, Burma and Pacific Islands.

She thanks members of her extended family for genealogies that contain insight into history. Their patience in waiting for her family history[40] to be published is appreciated, since that work was put on hold while this history was being compiled, as a background for genealogy. The author is grateful to the Rev. Kurt Vitt [71] for information about pioneer leader Andreas Lilge (her maternal grandfather's older half brother) and to William G. Brese for resources from Moravian historical societies in Edmonton, Alberta [73; 84; 109] and Europe [51;56]. Thanks are due to government archives in Warsaw, Poland and Zhytomir, Ukraine for vital statistics and data regarding land purchase and census.

Gratitude is due to Ron Neuman, author[85] and founding editor of the periodical *Wandering Volhynians,* and Ewald Wuschke, long term editor. Often by phone Wuschke answered questions to match up disparate bits of information. That stretched perspective. Genealogists Jerry Frank, Howard Krushel and Harvey Heinz helped.

Dr. Samuel Marx, son of Moravian missionaries in Ladakh, Kashmir, served in Honduras with his wife, the author's nursing classmate Grace (Hoppe) B.Sc. 1945. Her parents were pioneers in Bruderfeld [pp 170-71], now called Millwoods, within Edmonton city limits. They informed her of the genius and world-wide influence of **educator Comenius** [pp 76-77], and recommended the out-of-print book by J. Taylor Hamilton, *A History of the Moravian Church or Unitas Fratrum, during the 17th to 19th Centuries* [57].

Librarians at Fraser Valley Regional Library were helpful in a variety of ways. Often after a long search of other libraries, they located rare books, such as that by Hamilton. They also helped her download the history of J.E. Hutton about the followers of **John Wyclife** and **Jan Hus**, back to the thirteenth century [134] [pp 39-41, 52-53]. **Presbyterian** friends Rev. Dr. John Ross and his wife Kay and others provided **Calvinist** and **Reformed** history [p 59].

The author wants her sister, brother, daughter and family and her late son's family to know she is grateful for their support, patience and timely advice during the long years it took to write this book. She thanks computer technicians Joe, Donna, Chuck, Scott, Mary, Edwin, Steven and Roanan. She is grateful to cousin Joan for earlier valuable draft copies, to Anglican Rev. John Sovereign for copies and encouragement, and to choir members Henry, Gail, Margaret and Rowland with Elena for proof reading and other great help.

People Migrations in Europe and America

PREFACE

Why This History of People Migrations in Europe and America Was Written

A major reason for correlating the histories of European countries, and later of America, was to stimulate awareness of waves of migration back and forth, through the centuries. Because national boundaries kept changing, nation-building is best studied as a **systems analysis** to avoid regional bias. This is an unusually broad approach that includes simultaneous events in the whole of Europe and America.

The author has assembled this **history of Europe and America to be comprehensive yet concise**. It covers several millenniums until 1913. Human interest bits featuring ethnic, social, political and religious movements, are interwoven **to correct insularity** and **to awaken the interest of students bored with history**. Content is arranged **to appeal to a broad spectrum of interest** & **academic disciplines**. Academics and students around the world can benefit from this nationally interrelated study of history. Although the author is Canadian, through this book, people throughout the Americas and Europe can gain fresh appreciation of their own history and that of other nations and cultures. Peace-keeping Canadians often have the function of promoting mutual understanding and tolerance.

This work fills in serious gaps in the history of important people groups. For example, few people know that educated **Huguenots** (French Protestants) were scattered during the Inquisition to England, Prussia, the West Indies, Acadia (Canada), northeastern America and South Africa, and that they established industries such as silk production, viniculture and ship-building. Few historians are aware that **Jacques Cartier**, **Samuel de Champlain** and other early explorers were Huguenots. Such significant people-groups should be recognized and appreciated. Horrible blood-baths of Huguenots, Moravians and other nonconformists were under-reported, perhaps because of embarrassment to either church or state. They are reported here in a sensitive manner and briefly. Scholars concerned at present about ***ethnic cleansing*** could benefit from reading this book.

Historians barely mention the **Moravian Church** (Unitas Fratrum=Unity of Brethren=Brüder Gemine), although their influence was great following the martyrdom of Jon Hus in 1415, until modern times. **Educators** can benefit from the scholarly, practical books of Bishop **Comenius** (1592-1670) [p 77]. He added pictures to school books. He reformed **education of boys and girls** in Poland, Sweden, Denmark, Hungary, Romania, Holland and England.

Few **Lutherans** realize how much their church was revived by thousands of **diasporas**, small mid-week fellowships (*Brüder Gemine*) developed by *Moravians* in Europe, the Baltic States and Volhynia (in Russia). Because they refrained from "sheep-stealing" and church-planting, membership statistics were not kept. East Europeans today are aware of the continuing influence of *Brüder Gemine*, but not of the name *Moravian Church*. Moravians are numerous in some West Indian and east and south African countries. Moravian missions began in the West Indies in 1732, Greenland 1733, England 1734, Georgia 1734 and Pennsylvania 1736. During the *Great Awakening* in England, Ireland and the USA their influence was strong. During wars in Europe and later in the American civil war, they did not believe in taking up arms, but their attractively built schools and industries were often occupied as quarters for officers and hospitals from either or both sides. Invading armies in many European wars required horses, great amounts of fodder, food and care of the injured. They conscripted their youths to the sorrow of mothers.

The author's interest in history began in a multiethnic community in a one-room rural school and Vegreville high school. Later at University of Alberta in baccalaureate nursing, a history course brought to life the practices of knights, caring monks, nuns and secular women ministering to travelers, pilgrims, refugees and the sick.

Care Taken to Document Information and Keep it Succinct

References with page numbers are super-scripted within the body of the narrative to ensure accuracy and easy access for busy history professors and students. A bibliography of 172 books and articles was compiled. Generalities and opinions of the author are avoided. Dates are emphasized to ensure accurate correlation of simultaneous events and to enable analysis of interrelationships. **Dates are placed at the left as a visual aid** to facilitate study of history of different countries concurrently. There are many maps but no pictures in the book. Should the reader want to see pictures and study any area or era more thoroughly, the books referred to are available through public and academic libraries. On the world wide web such as in Wikipedia, and British sites there are ongoing historic findings.

Ancestors Migrated Within Europe for Millenniums and Spread Across America

Currently teachers and children are often interested in family roots. So are young adults contemplating parenthood. This study is of real value for many families wanting background regarding the migrations and lifestyle of their ancestors. See web sites about genealogy and family history research [p 183]. Whether your known ancestors were from Great Britain, Scandinavia, the Low Countries, Europe, Russia or Asia you will likely find that they migrated several times. They moved in waves back and forth during the centuries. Tribes and languages were intermingled, assimilated and evolved. Many went extinct. The boundaries of countries kept changing.

Because the author's **paternal ancestors** migrated from around the Baltic Sea to Alsace-Lorraine, to Poland and later to Russia, she decided to explore the histories of all these areas. This took her back before the Roman Empire, through *the Middle Ages, Renaissance, Enlightenment* and 18th to 20th centuries. Her paternal ancestors were Roman Catholic in Alsace west of the Rhine, but in Poland, shocked by actions of priests to produce tears on the image of Mary, they became Lutherans. After they arrived in Canada in 1896, having respected Moravian neighbors in Russia they joined their church built in 1895. The author's **maternal ancestors** have a history of worshiping in the Jon Hus Moravian manner in Bohemia, Poland and Russia. In 1894 her grandfather's half-brother Andreas Lilge, a teacher-lay minister, led 100 families from Russia to homesteads near **Edmonton**, Canada [see chapters 22 and 23].

Since pioneer days in Canada, Catholic and Protestant classmates and neighbors have been friends. Closure of one room schools followed by replacing of local high schools with large consolidated schools, has damaged multicultural harmony. When friendships are uni-ethnic they tend to become cliques and gangs.

Why Chapters about Architecture are Included

Many people today still look down upon other ethnic groups as primitive, especially those who lived long ago. It is helpful and humbling to learn about the skills unlikely people-groups perfected in the past. The author made this study originally because her paternal ancestors were **stone masons** and **sculptors**. She wanted to know what they might have known about architecture. She realized that some were also **black-smiths**. Her father had a forge on his farm in Alberta. Neighbors came for his help to shape hinges, alter tools and sharpen plow shares and axes. She became aware from family histories written by older cousins, that other ancestors were skilled carpenters and **cabinet-makers**. A few made **violins**. Some did complicated **inlays of wood or metal**. These skills go back to **Visigothic** and **Frankish** roots. Several cousins reported how log houses were built with artistic **dovetailed corners**. The author saw log houses so skillfully finished that they did not look rustic. Fretwork arches decorated the verandahs.

Library search provided many references [1]; [6]; [15]; [21]; [23]; [24]; [26]; [31]; [35]; [36]; [37]; [76]; [111]; [137] which indicate that since prehistoric times, Franks, Goths and other Germanic tribes had developed artistic crafts related to metals, wood, leather, gems and sculpture [See pp 8, 9 and 19]. **This is not a family history but the author's family exemplify these skills**, and bring to life abstract concepts. Johann Schneider and son Johann from Alsace-Lorraine, were sent by **Napoleon** to **Warsaw, Poland** about 1805 to repair *the Cathedral of the Decapitation of St. John the Baptist* [69 WV, Vol 3, No 3, pp 10-11, 86], per uncles [86] and an aunt [69]; [40 Part 2, Chapters 2, 6 and 8]. [See pp 33-37; 67-68; 85-86, 91, 133 and 144-6]. Pictures are not included in this book, but many can be found in libraries and on line through the bibliography.

Learning from the Experience and Skills of Elders and Ancestors

There is benefit from exploring and analyzing the circumstances surrounding the migrations of ancestors. They were able to adapt to great changes of climate, feudal, autocratic and self-government, economics and culture. Ingenious survival skills emerged. There is much to admire in three millenniums of innovative pioneers. Techniques and knowledge they acquired, which later became dormant, may be needed in the future [p 182]. The author invites further information and human interest anecdotes.

Myrtle (Schneider) Macdonald, 101 45875 Cheam Ave., Chilliwack BC. V2P 1N7.
Phone: 1-604-795-6390. E-mail: schmac@shaw.ca

People Migrations in Europe & America: Nation-Building Prehistory to 1913

Resources for College History Courses and Family Genealogies

CONTENTS

People Migrations in Europe and America: Introductory Maps:

Map: *The Roman Empire - Greatest Extent, at the Time of Emperor Trajan. AD 117* [154]

The boundaries of the Roman Empire in Europe were the Rhine and Danube Rivers.
The Danube flows from the Alps mountains to the Black Sea (Pontus Euxinus) 1740 miles.

Celtic tribes settled all of Europe. In southern Europe, northern Africa and the middle east there were tribal colonies speaking Proto-Greek, Proto-Anatolian, Mycenaean, Illyrian, Hittite and Semitic dialects. On the internet much ancient history is updated with new discoveries from caves and peat bogs. The prefix Proto is added for prehistoric languages not yet well understood, but thought to have preceded those that have a history. Recently through DNA studies[172], it was found that descendants of Noah's sons spread to all parts of the world:

Shem: Arabs, Jews, Elam-Persians and Assyrians,

Ham: descendants of four sons: north and central Africa, Italia, long faced American Sioux and Algonquins, Lapps, middle and far east Asians, Chinese [Sino], Mongoloid round faced Eskimos, Crees, and most other American tribes, South Sea islanders, Maori and others.

Japheth: descendants of seven sons: Indo-Aryan to India, north Asia and Europe. **Sanskrit, Latin and Greek** are related languages. South Indian Dravidian and south east Asian languages and DNAs have earlier origins.

When tribes settled near different tribes they tended to merge their languages partially or completely. They lost contact with their original tribe so new dialects and cultures evolved. See Chapter One for the circumstances surrounding their moving westward in Europe, driving one another out, as they moved onward. Some were seeking a livelihood from the land. Others were warriors on fleet horses seeking power, who plundered communities and then rushed on to do so in another area. Others went north west, crossed the Baltic and North Seas by ship, and then explored up the rivers, seeking land to occupy. Often wives and children were with them. Most spoke Indo-European languages. There were many Germanic dialects. Compare maps on pp xiii to xviii and Chapters One and Two (pp 1-10) for tribal migrations during the next 400 years.

People Migrations in Europe and America: Introductory Maps:

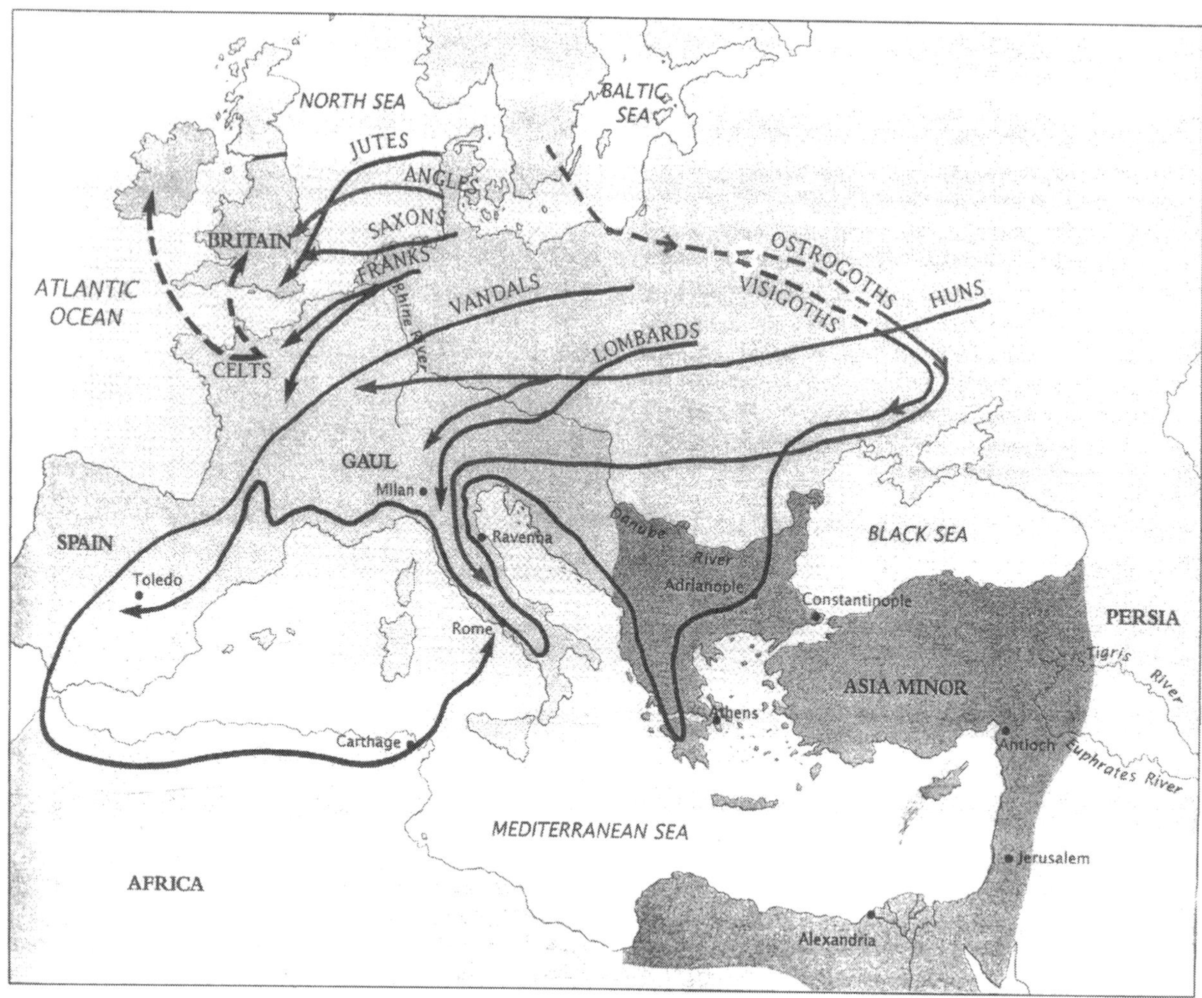

Map: *Early Migrations and Invasions* [25, p 277].

Since prehistory Celts consisting of many tribes, lived in Central Europe. Many Germanic tribes began to invade, pushing the Celts west. The Romans referred to the Celts as Gauls and assimilated them. Some Celts have remained in the north west province still called Breton and in the country of Belgium. Others populated what later was called the British Isles. Their cultures and languages are still live in Ireland, Wales and Scotland.

Celtic words and colloquialisms are common in the French villages of Quebec in Canada. The various dialects that persisted made the learning of French in high schools across Canada difficult. There has been growing uniformity in the past 50 years. Strangely, the author and many other anglophone Canadians understand Parisian French better than Canadian French.

The Acadians in New Brunswick (maritime eastern Canada) speak **other dialects of French**. So do the Métis in western Canada, the descendants of the Voyageurs, fur trader-explorers whose ancestors were Scottish, French and numerous aboriginal tribes. Other Francophones married descendants of Catholic settlers brought by Lord Selkirk to the Red River, now in Manitoba and Wisconsin. Thousands of Canadian French migrated on the Mississippi to New Orleans where their French is sometimes called Cajun (Canadian). Many of them speak a Creole dialect consisting of early French, English and African dialects. Mardis Gras became an important festival.

In prehistoric times Greek and middle east peoples explored the Mediterranean Sea, and some went as far as Denmark and Norway. They built and colonized coastal harbors and actively traded in salt, copper, coal, grain, fruit, silk, wool and spices. DNA similarities of some **Italians** have been found in **Sioux** and **Algonquins** [172].

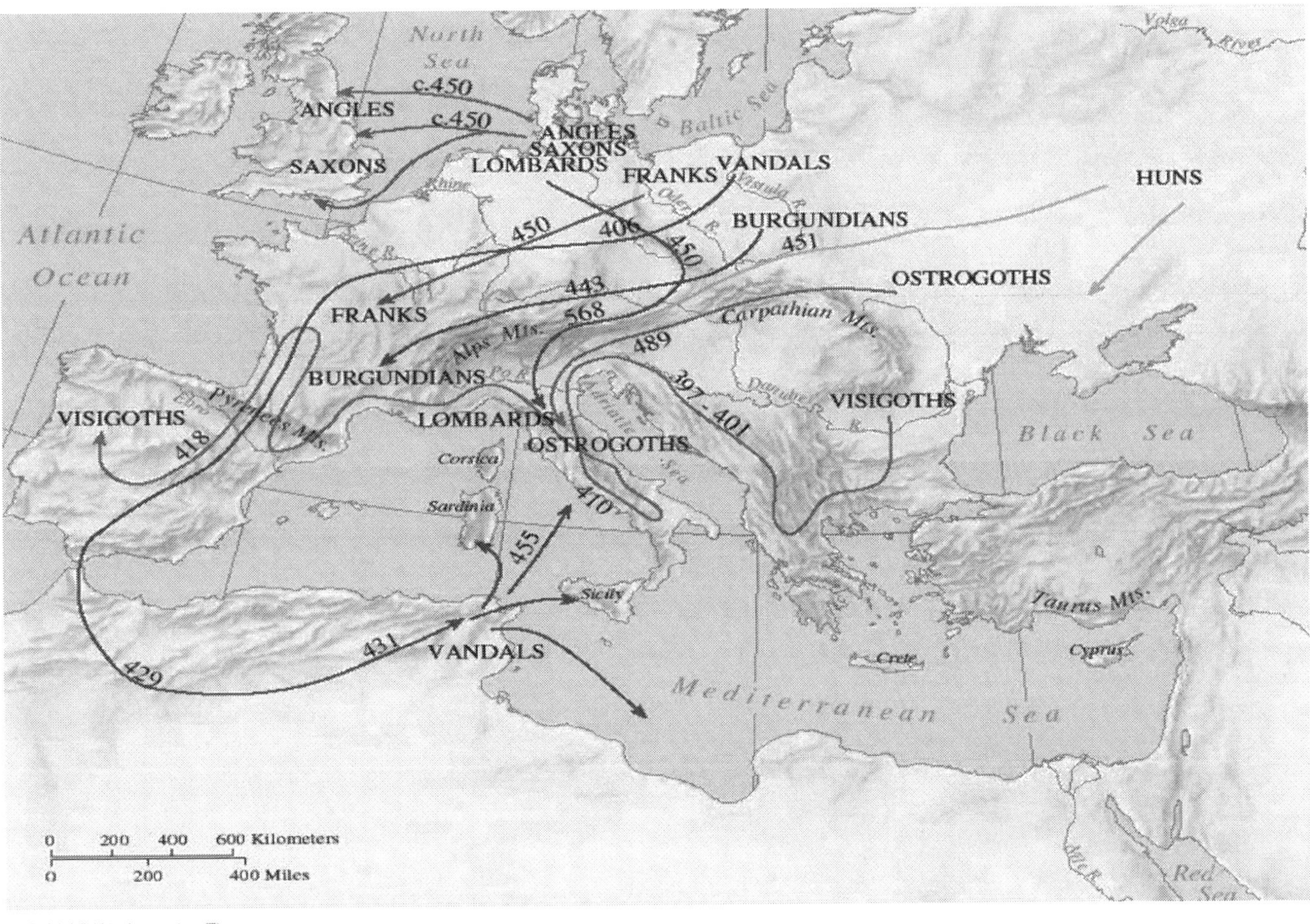

Map: *Migrations by many Germanic Tribes and the Huns in the Third to Fifth Centuries* [9b, p 182].

In prehistoric times **Celts** occupied Europe. Romans called western Europe Gaul. Many northern tribes referred to as, Franks, Germanic, Teutonic, Gothic and Vikings successively moved south & west.

- 180 AD Goths were moving south toward the Black Sea.
- 248-251 the Goths divided into **Ostrogoths** (eastern) & **Visigoths** (western) and crossed the Danube River.
- 250 **Franks** (Norse, Northmen) settled on the Rhine River delta and pushed inland; in 257 invaded Spain.
- Germanic **Alemanni** and **Suebi** (Suevi, Schwabs) occupied east and west of the Rhine and in 258 north Italy.
- 312-337 Emperor Constantine moved the Roman Empire capital from Rome to **Constantinople**.
- 360-470 Mongolian **Huns** on swift horses, invading from Asia, pushed the Germanic tribes west. After 470 they returned to Asia. Gradually various **Slavic tribes** migrated west into Poland and SW into the Balkans. Scythians had an Indo-European Language akin to Persian[136, p 24]. Magog was Scythia in Greek [172].
- 396 Visigoths invaded Greece, in 398 the Balkans and in 401 plundered Rome.
- 400 Germanic **Vandals** began to move west across Gaul and in 406 settled in Spain.
- 416 Visigoths, Alani and Suevi took over southern France and Spain;
- 428 eighty thousand Vandals began to occupy north Africa and in 455 captured Rome.
- 449 **Angles** and **Jutes** settled in Celtic Britain. In 476 **Saxons** drove the Romans from Britain.
- 493-554 Ostrogoth Theodoric captured Ravenna, Italy and founded a prosperous empire.
- 552 Eastern Roman (Byzantine) Emperor Justinian regained control of Ravenna.
- 470 Germanic **Lombards** crossed the Alps and by 568 they controlled most of Italy, but not Ravenna or the Papal estates. Lombardi dukes ruled much of Italy until 774.

Map: *Franks, East and West Goths, Vandals and The East Roman Empire in 526 AD.*

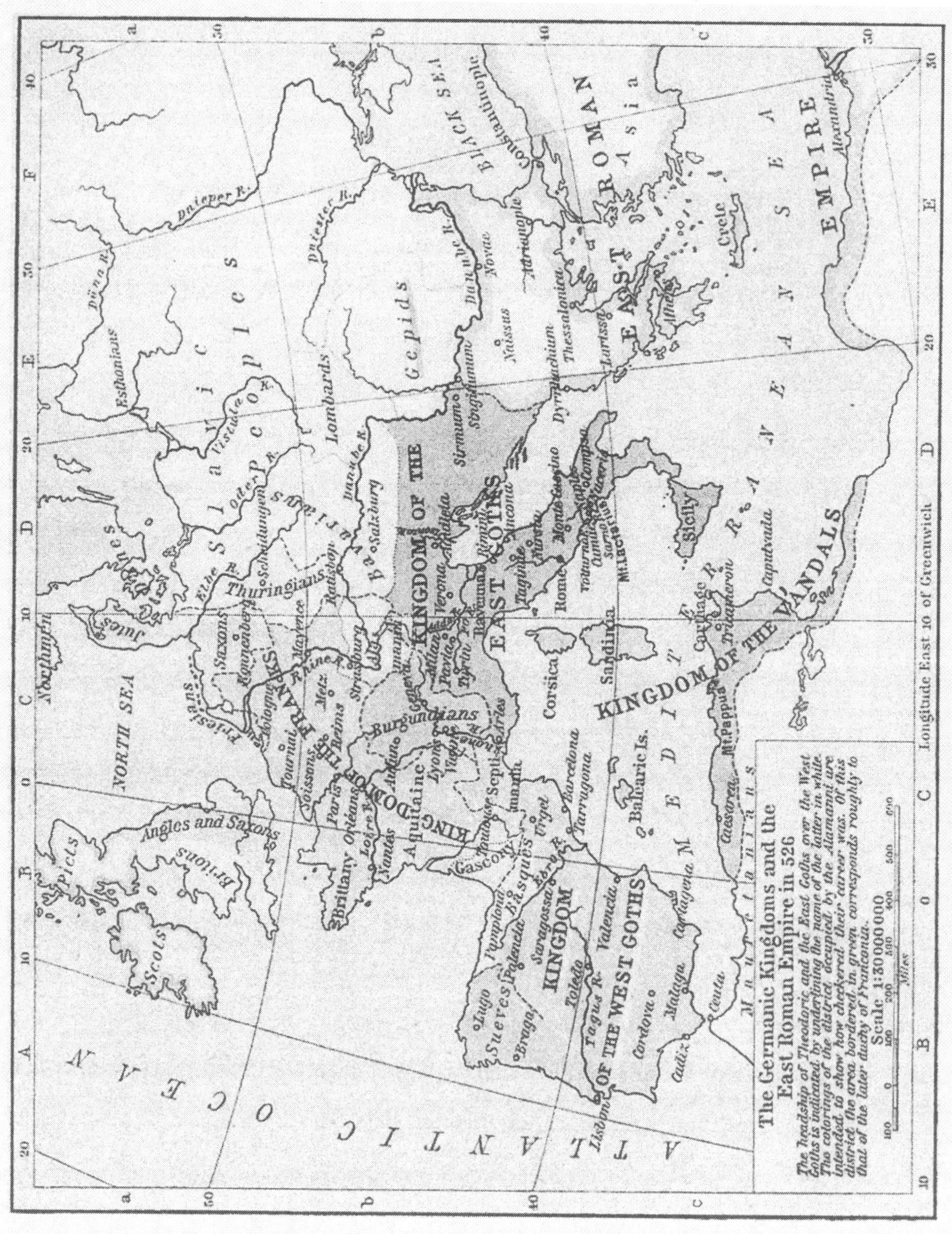

Map: Roman Balkan Provinces in 526 AD

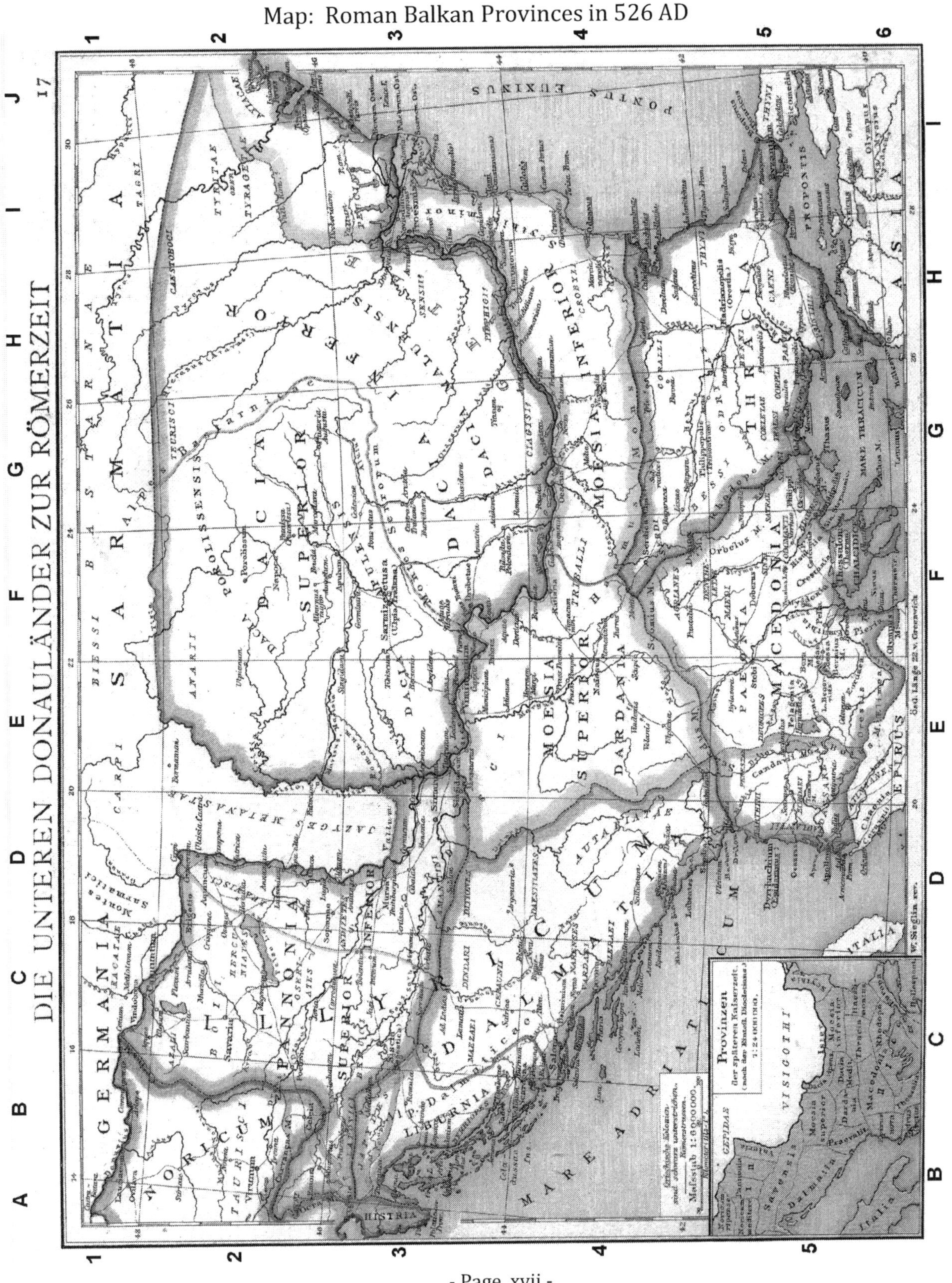

People Migrations in Europe and America: Introductory Maps:

Map: *The Roman Empire in 125 AD during the reign of Hadrian*

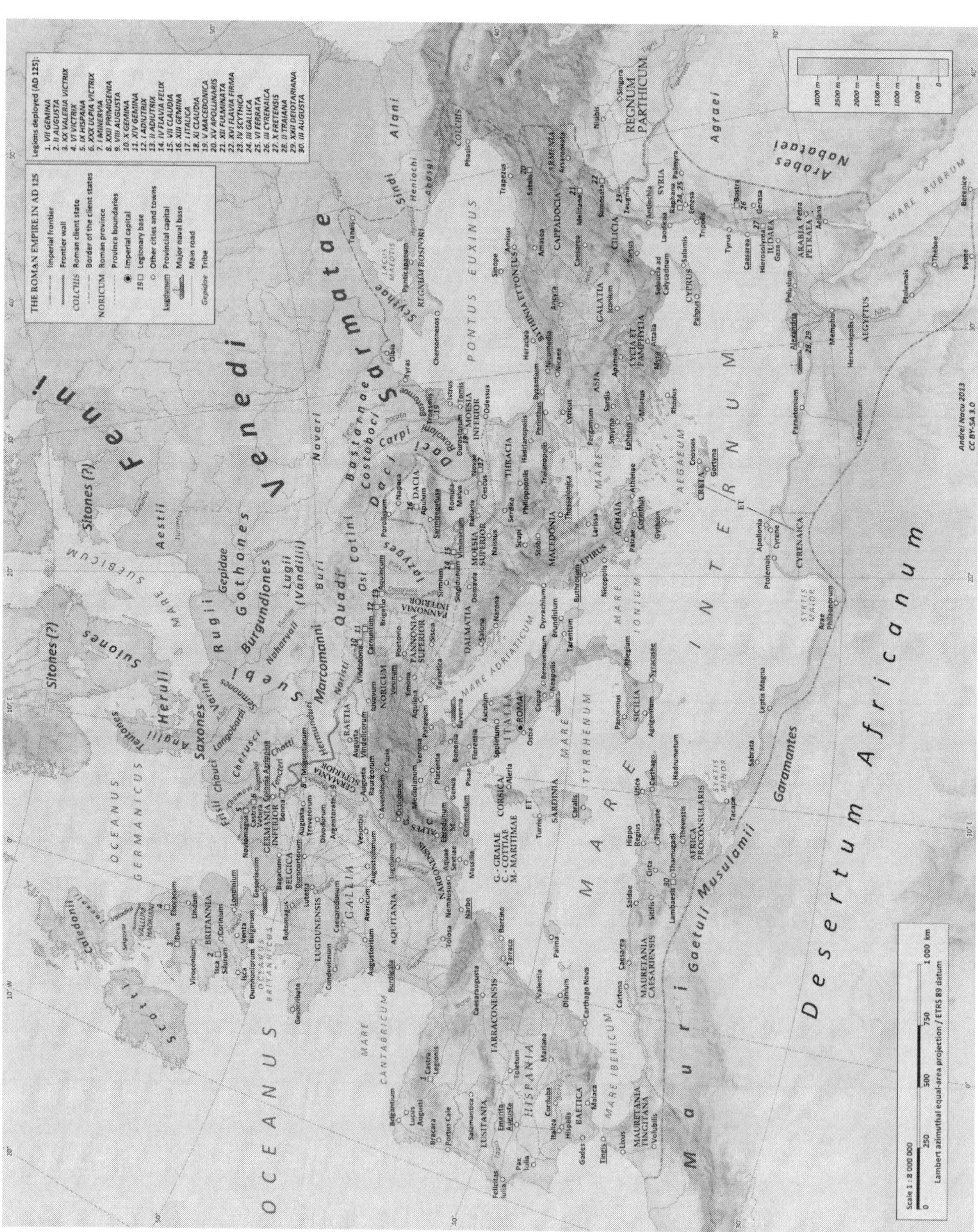

Chapter One

From Prehistory to The Sixth Century AD

Early European Tribes and Nations

When reindeer began to find grass as the ice melted, blue-eyed hunter-gatherers went north in Europe and Asia:
- 3000-2500 BC Indo-European tribes from Babylonia, Iraq & Arabia migrated into Europe: **Celtic** tribes in central & west Europe and **Germanic** tribes **started Scandinavian cultures** around the Baltic Sea.
- 2250 BC Indo-European **Achaean** (Proto-Greek) tribes came to the coastlands and islands surrounding the Agean sea. Other Indo-Europeans from Asia entered the Balkans between the Adriatic and Black Seas. **Illyrian** and other Indo-European tribes settled the entire Balkans (SE Europe), **Italy** and west to the **Rhone** river. Archeologists are finding fine crafts and pictographs from those cultures.
- 2000 BC **Doric** Greek tribes pushed Illyrians N & NW into the rugged mountains and along the Adriatic Sea. Indo-European **Etrusian** and **Italic** tribes settled Italy. 1200 BC Illyrian **Venetians** invaded **Italy**.
- 2000-1450 BC **Minoans** settled Crete. To keep export/import records they invented a script later called Linear A. 100,000 people lived in the city of Knossos; destroyed by a massive volcano or by loss of wealth through competition.
- 1600-1100 BC **Mycenaean** ancestors of the Greeks succeeded the Minoans, developed a flourishing civilization & spread northward to **Thrace**. A new script called Linear B evolved. The key to read both A and B has not been found. Thrace was the legendary birthplace of **Orpheus** and **Spartacus**. About 1000 BC the **Trojan war** took place.
- 750-650 BC **Homer** wrote Greek mythology & the **Iliad** epics. Indo-Europeans from the Black sea populated Moldova, **Drace** & present day Hungary & Slovakia, north of the Danube.
- 1100-800 BC: the Greek **Dark Ages** were a time of stagnation after the skilled Bronze Age Mycenaean, Hittite & Egyptian civilizations were destroyed by **Iron Age** Indo-European **Phrygians**. Some had red hair and blue eyes. **Alphabetic writing, though without vowels, transformed commerce/record-keeping**. Their script on several tablets and inscriptions, had similarities with people/place names in **Armenia** and **Thrace**. Records exist of Kings Gordius (Gordian Knot) and Midas (golden touch).

Developing of Classical Greek Culture

- 1000 BC to 324 AD many rival Greek cities ruled coastland & island sister states around the Agean Sea. Ancient Greeks became literate through the **Phoenicians** & began western civilization.
- 776 the first **Olympic Games** were held. City states were much in conflict with each other yet mathematics, architecture & philosophical scholarship began; **vowels** were added to the alphabet.
City states **Sparta**, **Argos**, **Olympia** and **Corinth** were called **Peloponnesus**.
- 700 BC to 10 AD ancient **Illyria** at its height included the **Adriatic** Dalmacian coastline & mountainous NW Balkans. **Venetians** & **Albanians** are descendants. Phrygian power was broken by Iranian **Cimmerians** fleeing Turkic **Scythians** west to **Pannonia** (map xvii).
- 600-280 BC: Celtic **Boii** pushed **Etrusians** back into Italy, Dacians east & Illyrians to Dalmacia (Albania).
- 600-400BC **Ionians** from islands & coastal near east, began **Athens** & established settlements in Illyria, south Gaul, and trading post **Marseille**. The Italian-French border south of the Alps is 300 miles long. **Phonecians,** masters of the sea, could navigate across the Mediterranean, without hugging the coast.
- 500-449 BC many rival Greek cities fought to hold back **Persian invaders**, while developing politics, philosophy, architecture, sculpture and debate. 620-560 BC ***Aesop's Fables*** evolved and were collected.
- 484-425 **Herodotus** wrote a vast history of legends. Greece was **Hellas** in the Helen of Troy legend [45, p 481].
- 354-342 BC Thracians were assimilated, valued as soldiers, called **Dacians** by Romans, **Getae** by Greeks and later **Vlach** (Wlach) by Goths, meaning foreigner [101, p 14, 264]. Wallachia (**Romania**) expanded west to Pannonia and the Carpathian mountains and east to the Dnieper River in Russia [maps p xv and xvi].

Hellenization of Europe & Mesopatamia

- 359-336 BC Phillip II of **Macedonia**, related ethnically to Greece, Thracia and Phrygia, expanded his territory, colonized Philippi, united Greece and Hellenized the Balkans. **Aristotle** tutored his son:
- 336-323 BC **Alexander the Great** amassed a vast Greek empire[55, pp 584-91] in Asia Minor, Persia (already culturally & architecturally rich), India & Egypt. All spoke Aramaic Greek. Next four generals ruled the empire.
- 300-150 BC General **Ptolemy** & successors built cisterns & huge library in Alexandria, Egypt, home of Greeks & Jews. The Hebrew Old Testament was translated into Greek (Septuagint LXX) by 70 Jewish scholars [16 p 674].
- 229-169 BC **Rome** invaded Thrace & Macedonia. Mountains slowed Balkan occupation [12 Vol 11, p 733].

The Roman Empire

[maps pp xiii, xvi-xviii]

- 146 BC Greece came under Roman rule, but Romans liked Hellenization, so it continued.
- 121 BC Romans calling the Celts Gauls, occupied west of the Rhine. 55 BC Julius Caesar occupied **Britain.**
- 31 BC Romans conquered more of Thrace, and not until 9 BC Illyria & Pannonia [p xvii].
- 33 AD visitors from N Africa, Persia & Europe in Jerusalem became Christians [Acts chap 2].
- By 46 AD Rome had conquered the Balkans and built roads, massive theatres, baths, stadiums, and Roman colonies in Provinces [maps xvii, xviii] all along the south of the Danube River from the Alps, 1740 miles east to the Black Sea, and south in Asia Minor, leaving central Europe undeveloped [p 77-88]. **Romania** was part of Dacia, their ancient dialect similar to Latin. Writing and written records became widespread with the Romans.
- 64 AD a great fire destroyed much of Rome.

Germanic Tribes Migrated West and South from Around the Baltic Sea

- 180 AD Germanic tribes: **Suebi, Vandals, Gepids, Jutes** and **Goths** from south Sweden, Danish Jutland migrated along the **Baltic Sea** and North Sea, and up the **Ems, Oder** & **Vistula** rivers west of present day **Poland** [map xvi]. They took over from Celts and from one another. Jutland (Gottland) perpetuates memory of Goths. In the time of **Julius Caesar** there were Germani Franks raiding and settling west of the Rhine [see xiv, xv]. Caesar described Celts and Germani peoples but decided to focus on the Celts whom they called Gauls. Germani is a Celtic word [1, p 34]. They were called barbarian, since their languages had ba ba sounds.
- 98 AD: Roman Historian **Tacitus** identified in his book *Germania*, the following Germani tribes:
- **Frisii** in the Ems and Rhine River coastlands, who later became the **Flemish** in Belgium.
- **Chauci** at the mouth of the Weser River; **Cherusci** farther south; **Chatti** in what is now **Hesse.**
- **Suebi (Suevi)** later called **Schwabs,** in Thuringia, Saxony, Mecklenburg and Bradenburg areas.
- **Langobardi** later called **Lombards,** settled in central Europe and Italy.
- **Angles** settled in Schleswig. **Saxons** & **Burgundians** who were also Germanic, were not mentioned.
- **Marcomanni** lived along the **Main** River and in the region later named **Bohemia** for the Celtic **Boii.**
- 258 AD: **Alemanni** and **Suebi** conquered north Italy, but were defeated at Milan. Alemanni then settled the east side of the Rhine river in the **Black Forest**, across from **Alsace**, and became the Dutchy of Alamannia. Even today **Germany** is called **Allemagne** in French and **Alemania** in Spanish.

Four Major Language Groups Descended from Germanic Tribes

(maps xiii-xvi)

- 248-251 AD **Goths** from around the Baltic Sea in Scandinavia [5, p 272; 12, Vol 5, p 382], crossed the Danube River.
- 268 & 270 Emperor **Claudius** II drove them back but died. Germanic **Gepidae** had migrated from Sweden to Carpathian mountains Transylvania [map xv]. 270 AD some Roman Legions withdrew from east Europe due to constant invasions by **Goths**. Others retired there. Some Germanic tribes [12 Vol 5, pp 210-215] came south to farm.
- **German**, **English** and the **Scandinavian** languages are Germanic, and also called **Teutonic** or **Teutone.**
- **French** evolved from Germanic **Frank** by assimilating Latin and Gaul (Roman name for Celtic). **Franks (Norse, Northmen)** were several Germanic barbaric tribes who came in fine boats on the North Sea to the marshy lowlands of the **Rhine** River in Brittany, NW Gaul. They raided, gradually acquired territory and settled west of the Rhine [1, Edward James pp 35-38]. They wore knee length breeches, bandage leggings and a leather girdle and belt from which hung an axe, knife, comb, scissors and broad-bladed sword. They had fair hair and blue eyes and many were over 6 feet tall [139, pp 120, 126]. Franks served as **mercenaries** in the armies of both Western and Eastern Roman Empires (Byzantine) so assimilated their Romance languages [pp xiv-vi, 3, 5].
- By 300 AD five Germanic tribes had separately developed into dukedoms: **Alemanni, Franks, Thuringians, Goths,** and **Saxons** [3, pp 251-300]. They had strong tribal rulers, but no sense of German nationalism, so were rivals. They migrated when needing fertile land or when pushed by other invaders.
- 400 **Vandals** a fierce Germanic tribe from the north Baltic area, went west to Spain [p vi; map xiv].

Later Gothic & Slavic Migrations

[maps xiv-xvii]

- By 100 AD Christianity came to Dacia (Romania) by Andrew [16 and 46] Jesus' disciple. The Romanian language was related to Latin (but later the Greek Orthodox church was preferred rather than the Roman Catholic).
- 180 AD Ostrogoths (East) moved south of Sweden into the Crimea, east of the Back Sea.
- Third century AD many Ostrogoths migrated west to the present Romania, Transylvania (S Poland)& Bohemia.
- Turkic **Avars** went west up the Danube. Patzinaks (Petchenegs) invaded Dacia [map p 24].
- Some Ostrogoths ruled **Khazar** a **Jewish state** [WV Vol 2, 89, Sep p 5] [map p 6]. Germanic **Yiddish** language evolved.

- 270 AD the Roman Legions withdrew from the Balkans, because of constant invasions by **Goths**.
- Later **Croats** [12 Vol 2, pp 619-622; 9 Vol 7, pp 336-7] and other **Slavic tribes** began to settle the **Balkans,** SE Europe. Slavic languages were similar, but divided by rugged mountains, numerous dialects and separate nations evolved. For four centuries waves of **various Slavic** peoples settled in the **Balkans** [9 Vol 3, pp 212-214]. Other Slavs settle NE in the **Baltic.**
- Turkic **Bulgarian** tribes settled and assimilated with Slavs. Asian **Huns** invaded in the fifth century [p 4]. Slavic **Serbs** came later [12 Vol 10, p 645], in 6 th and 7 th centuries.
- The **Balkans** are generally described as bounded on the **east** by the Black Sea, on the **north** by the Danube River, on the **west** by the Adriatic Sea, and **south** by Macedonia and Greece. Settlers in the central and east Balkans chose the **Eastern Orthodox church**, and those in the west the **Roman Catholic.** Orthodox **Romania,** north of the Danube extending west into **Pannonia, Transylvania** plateau & **Carpathian** mountains [xv]. Most of Greece is on a peninsula separated from Greek islands by the Agean Sea. Turkey included Asia Minor.

Constantine, First Christian Emperor of Both West and East Roman Empires

Constantine the Great, born about 280 AD, assisted his father **Caesar** fighting in **Gaul** and **Britain** [5, pp 194; 207-233].
- 306-337 AD Constantine succeeded, in 312 became a Christian, felt his new Christian Roman Empire should have a new capital city at Greek **Byzantium** (present-day Istanbul, Turkey) crossroads of Europe and Asia, a natural fortress with protected harbor. Many thousands of skilled artisans built beautiful **Constantinople** for his whole Roman court and government [see p 8], as the centre of the expanding Roman Empire, while Rome became weak. By 500 AD the population grew from 100,000 to nearly one million. Constantine unified a massive empire, reorganized it and established the supremacy of Christianity [9].
- 337 sons of Constantine, **Valentinian** I & **Valens** ruled the huge Roman Empire, including **Carthage,** map xiii.

The Eastern Orthodox Church

- The **Orthodox Church** flourished with its own traditions and style of worship with little contact from the **Roman Catholic Church**. Constantine held a Council to develop the **Nicene Creed**. 200 clergy came, but the Roman Pope sent only two representatives [5, pp 217-223]. See Ecumenical Councils: East & West Rome in Index & Catalogue of Events.
- About 300 AD **Armenia** became a Christian nation. Their alphabet was developed, the Bible translated.
- By 400 in **Georgia** the church was founded [46]. Later Armenia and Georgia became part of Russia [map p 38].
- **Thomas** Jesus' disciple went to south **India** as an apostle. **Syrian Christians** later migrated to India and Orthodox Constantinople kept in touch [117, pp 16-21].
- Goths migrated south in the present **Ukraine** toward Crimea and the Black Sea [5, pp 217] and via the Danube into Thrace. **Goths** became **Arian** Christians, but denied the full divinity of Christ. The **Gnostic** mystical philosophy also was popular. 300 AD the diocese of Thrace [12 Vol 11, p 733] was founded by Aegean (Greek) and east Danube churches.
- 323 Constantine attacked Goths in Thrace south of the Danube River.
- 341 missionary **Wulfila (Ulfilas)** 311-383, was consecrated Bishop by the Eastern Orthodox church, invented the **Gothic alphabet** and translated the Bible into Gothic. Some portions remain. The Gothic language is no longer spoken, but there still are Gothic features and words in the **Crimea** [5, pp 272-278].
- 353-430 Aurelius **Augustine** of **Carthage** became influential theologically until today [16, p 50]. [See p 6.]
- 397 he called a Synod at Carthage when the New Testament Canon (authentic scripture) was settled.
- 382-400 **Jerome** assisted by two women located in Bethlehem translated the **Latin Vulgate Old Testament** from the Hebrew scripture early compiled in Alexandria [16, p 380]. They reviewed and added the New Testament.

The Roman Empire Harassed by Huns, Bulgars and Goths [See maps pp xiv and xv]

- 360 **Huns,** a Mongolian tribe invade Europe [3, p 28-30]. 370 **Bulgars** a Turkic tribe from central Asia, settled on the steppes west of the Volga River, Russia. About 375 AD **Huns** moved into the area **north of the Black Sea** (now south Ukraine) driving the Goths west. Huns were power-hungry not land-hungry. Christian **Ostrogoths** in the province of **Dacia** north of the Danube were persecuted, so Bishop Wulfila was granted permission for them to settle in the Roman province of **Moesia**, now **Bulgaria**, south of the Danube [5, p 274] [map p xvii].
- 383 Wulfila died. Goths split into Ostrogoths & Visigoths, moved on displacing other tribes [15, p 12-13, 3, p 28-30].
- **Visigoths** (west Goths) homeless/restless, were demanding land from **Emperor Valentinian** I. He made a pact to cross the Danube, in exchange to lay down arms and return hostages.
- 378 the Visigoths rebelled at Adrianople because the Romans preoccupied with other strife, were slow to keep their agreement. Emperor **Valens** and 2/3rds of the Roman army [5, pp 272-274; 16, p 12] died.
- In 382 Byzantine Emperor **Theodosius** I (379-395) made a treaty for recruits from Visigoth King **Alaric** for land by the Danube River and Balkan Mountains [5, pp 246]. Then:

Tribal Migrations From Southeast to West Europe

- 396 **Alaric** leading the Visigoths invaded southern Greece, plundered Athens and in 398 the Balkans.
- 395 AD the **Roman Empire divided** into west and east. The east **Byzantine Empire** continued to flourish; Rome (west) became weak. As revenues were drained to the east they became vulnerable to attacks by Vandals, Goths & other land-hungry Germanic barbarians pushed west by **Huns** [13, pp 31-37] who controlled vast territories from the Caspian Sea to Gaul.
- 400 AD **in Western Europe there were three Free Confederacies of Germanic peoples:**

1. **Burgundians** occupied Main River valley, flowing 300 miles from the east, joining the Rhine at Mainz.
2. **Alemanni** in the Black Forest, SE of the Rhine river; in 443 some moved west of the Rhine into **Alsace** [3, p30].
3. **Franks** in Gaul on the Rhine River, with high civil and military positions in the Roman Empire [1, pp 41-44].

- They were invaded successively by Huns, Visogoths, Vandals and other tribes, who moved on. Visogoths migrated to **Aquitaine,** SW **Gaul** (France) & established the Visogothic kingdom [15, pp 4-7, 10-13] [maps xiv- xvi].
- 397 **Bishop Augustine** chaired a Synod at Carthage, N Africa; the authentic New Testament Canon was settled.
- 401 **Visigoths** led by **Alaric, invaded Italy**, plundered and occupied **Rome** for some months, but left.
- About 406 **Vandals** left central Europe, crossed the Rhine River, pillaged Gaul and settled in **Spain**.
- 416 **Visigoths, Alani** and **Suevi** invaded **Spain** and drove the **Vandals** south from the land they held.
- 429 **Vandals** a tribe of 80,000, under **King Gaiseric** crossed over to Carthage and Hippo, **North Africa** settled the fertile lands [95, p 446] and ousted Byzantine rulers. They became wealthy through grain trade [map xvi].
- 430 **Bishop Augustine** was killed in the siege of **Hippo**. His writings ***Confessions*** and ***The City of God*** are still highly valued [25, pp 269;275].
- 439 Vandal King Gaiseric took **Carthage**, N Africa and ruled there until his death 477 [5, p 274-6] [pp xiii-v].
- 408-450 **Theodosius** II East Roman emperor [more below] compiled **laws: *Codex Theodasianus*** [16, p 754].
- 433 Meanwhile along the Danube River **Attila,** ruler of the **Huns**, **sought fame rather than land**, as a warrior, not an administrator [13, p 33]. Roman Commander **Aetius** had been a hostage of the Huns, so knew Attila as a boy, and was not intimidate by him. On light horses the Huns passed near **Paris** and attacked **Orleans.**
- 436 Attila destroyed **Worms** in **Burgundy**, crossed and re-crossed the Rhine River, and suddenly withdrew.
- 441 Theodosius II fought Attila's hordes, bought them off; they rushed past the Adriatric Sea [3, p 28-30] to north Italy.
- 453 Attila was killed; his sons scattered. Some intermarried and assimilated. Fear of Huns kept barbarian mercenaries of mixed loyalties united. Refugees settled **Venice**. Germans were wrongly called Huns in WWII.
- 470 the divided Huns retreated to Russian plains but gave their name to **Hungary** [5, pp 276-278] [see p 14].
- 455 **Vandal Gaiseric** attacking from N. Africa, **sacked Rome.** The Pope unarmed persuaded him to leave. He took precious **relics** from Jerusalem, plus the Roman Empress & daughters as hostages.

The Western Roman Empire Was Vanquished; The Dark Ages Began in 476 AD

- 476 **Emperor Romulus Augustus** was deposed by the **Saxons** [95, p 480]. Italian p**rinces** fled to rural estates, regained influence and were able to choose and demote religious leaders. Bishops free from civil authority, extended their influence to control secular affairs, and made alliances with **Gothics, Franks** and other rivals.
- 454, 480 **Byzantine rulers hired Bulgars** to fight the Ostrogoths invading the Balkans [12 Vol 2, pp 618-622] [maps 6, 20].
- 493-554 **Ostrogoths** ruled north **Italy at Ravenna** [map p xvi], under **King Theodoric** (454-526) and successors. He had grown up in the Roman Imperial court in Constantinople, his wife a sister of Frank king **Clovis**. He drained Po river marshes, stabilized grain prices, repaired aqueducts and walls; built palaces and churches [p 9] and rejuvenated Italy. Ostrogoths influenced Germanic people up the Danube Alps but were rejected by Franks.

The Frank Merovingian Dynasty - Salian Franks 451-750

- The Salian (Salic) Franks spread south along the Rhone, Somme & Loire Rivers, intermarried with Gallo-Romans, and wrote **a law-code**[1, pp 51-58]. In 451 Salian Frank King **Meroveus** assisted Romans against the Huns.
- 457-81 His son King **Childeric** I helped the Romans fight invading **Visigoths** [15, p 24]. In 481 his 25 year old son **Clovis** succeeded.
- 486, ten years after Rome fell, Clovis defeated **Syagrius,** last Roman Governor of Gaul.
- 494-511 **Clovis** founded the **Merovingian Dynasty**. His wife was a French-speaking Christian from **Burgundy**, Rhone valley. Franks settled abandoned Roman estates, converted to Christ, prospered as farmers. Various dialects blended into French.
- 507 **Clovis** defeated **Visigoths** in **Aquitaine**, south Gaul and pushed them south into **Setimania** [1, p 104]. Clovis moved his capital to **Paris**. Unlike the Romans, Clovis began to rule both sides of the Rhine, map xvi. He ruled the **Alamans** who since 443 had lived in **Alsace, Würtemberg** & **Bavaria** [1, pp 84-85].

Migrations of French, Germanic, Celtic and Lombardi Nations

- 511 **Merovingian** Frank rule continued under **Clovis' four sons,** who divided up France. Though divided, Merovingian Frank kingdoms continued to expand/thrive; conquered **Burgundy,** south-central France, and **Bavaria** east of the Rhine. Borders of domains kept changing due to feuding [maps pp xvi, 6 and 20]. These powerful **Salic Frank** kings had assimilated Roman style administration/attitudes. Inter-married with the Gallo-Romans, they spoke Roman-Gallic mixed with Germanic Frank[1, pp 51-77] and gradually lost their original tongue. They ruled north and central Gaul, later named France for the Franks. Their language became French, but accents/dialects varied. It was fashionable for Romans to have a Frankish Germanic name, whether of high or low birth. Historians are unsure whether ancient records/grave findings are Frank, Gaul or Roman [1].
- By 536 Franks had taken over all of Roman Gaul except **Brittany** north & Visigoth **Setimania** south [map xvi].
- East of the Rhine River, in nearby duchies (dukedoms), cultural barriers remained [1, p 104]. Land was 4/5ths forest. **Ripurian** (east) **Franks** and other Germanic peoples were still feuding nomads. They still spoke Germanic Frankish languages [1, pp 88-90] having not been acculturated by the Romans. They pushed back raids of **Huns** and founded five dukedoms: **Bavaria**, **Franconia**, **Swabia**, **Lorraine** and **Saxony**.
- By 586 **Visigoths ruled Spain** until 730 [2], 200 years. Converted to Christ they built Roman style basilicas with dazzling gold embossing and inlay, traditional Visigothic skills [1, pp 82-87] [pp 8, 19]
- 583 **St. Columba** and other early missionaries served west of the Rhine. Not until 720 did **Boniface** the missionary evangelize east of the Rhine [p 11].
- Since 55 BC Romans had controlled and developed **Britain**, inhabited by **Celtic tribes** they called **Britons**.
- About 450 AD **Saxons, Angles** and **Jutes** (Goths) arrived on Britain's shores. Due to overpopulation they sought land all over Britain, and became **Angle-land (Eng-land)** in the 5th-6th centuries [5, pp 66, 118, 149, 194, 207, 281-309]. North Denmark was known as Gotland (Goths-land). The Romans could not keep invaders out because many had been called home to protect Rome from barbarian (Gothic and Vandal) invasions [maps xiv-xviii].
- **Bretons** (Britons) were **Celtic** tribes [pp xiv, xv] pushed from south England, who settled in **Brittany**, NW France.
- North Men (**Normans=Norse=Vikings**) raided/colonized **Ireland**, **Scotland** and rivers of **north France**.
- 500 AD Germanic **Lombards** [map p 6], settled in present Hungary, became **Arian** Christians [p 3] allied with Asian **Avars**, defeated Germanic **Gepids** [maps pp xvi, 6] and intermarried with both tribes.

Roman Emperor Justinian I & Empress Theodora

- 476 the Roman Empire fell in Rome. Roman Emperors ruled Europe, North Africa and Syria from Constantinople [maps p xiv, xv & 6]. Some weak emperors continued to rule in Rome [list in Index/Catalogue under Italy].
- 527-565 **Justinian** I and **his wife Theodora** poured much wealth into building forts, monasteries, hospitals, aqueducts, bridges, & many churches. Theodora rehabilitated prostitutes, built orphanages [5, pp 287-294].
- 533 at **Carthage**, N Africa, Justinian's army defeated **Vandals,** who then gradually scattered. He defeated the **Persians** and **Ostrogoths** gaining much lost territory in the Middle East, Balkans and Italy [25, pp 269; 275]. There were wars with Persians, Turks, Huns, Slavs, Bulgars & Goths. Justinian sorted and **organized old codified Roman law** and wrote ***Digest and Institutes*** (explanations of the law). This significantly influenced the development of legal systems of Western Civilization [18, p 35].
- 537 in Constantinople Justinian dedicated enormous **Hagia Sophia** (**St. Sophia Church**); decorated with mosaics of saints & Bible characters [p 9].
- 558 the dome collapsed in an earthquake; was rebuilt.
- 542 in the **Bubonic Plague** (**Black Death**) over a third of Constantinople, about 300,000 people died. Justinian himself became ill and slowly recovered. Plague spread through Europe in waves for 50 years. A quarter of Europe's population died.
- 552 Justinian **regained control of north Italy from Ostrogoths** [13, p 63; 15, p 40-41] [see pp 3, 4] assisted by Merovingian Franks. Much of **Italy** consisted of Papal Estates, ruled by the Pope [pp 7-10], and city states. Justinian, trying to unite east and west, built **St. Vitale** church in **Ravenna** [18, p 32-35] and **St. Mark's** in **Venice**. Merchant families ruled independent city states. In 565 Justinian the last Latin-speaking emperor died.
- 565-578 **Greek**-speaking **Justin** II; communication with the western Roman Empire became difficult.
- 568 Germanic **Lombards** crossed the Alps into Italy, began a thirty-year war and conquered [15, p 24-25] most of the Ostrogothic Byzantine kingdom except Ravenna. They controlled **Venice** & much of **Italy**, not including the city states and Papal Estates [maps pp 6; 20]. Several Lombardi Dukes united, elected kings, ruled much of **Italy** until 774 [15].
- 578-582 Greek-speaking **Tiberius** II was Emperor in Constantinople; 582-602 **Maurice**.
- 586-730 pushed out of Gaul, the **Visigoths ruled Spain**[2] for 200 years, became Christians, built Roman basilicas with dazzling gold embossing and inlay, traditional Visigothic skills [1, pp 82-87] [pp 8, 13-14, 19].

Gradual Dawn of Hope in The Dark Ages

- About 387-461 **Patrick**, born a Briton, at 16 was captured by Irish raiders, escaped to the continent, studied at Tours; was consecrated a bishop. 432-461 Patrick was a missionary in **Ireland** [16, p 561, 139, p 124].
- 521-597 **Columba**, an Irish missionary with 12 companions established a religious community on the island of **Iona**, west coast of **Scotland**, and went on missionary tours all over Scotland/northern England.
- 543-615 **Columban** another Irish monk, at age 40 in 583, sent as **a missionary** with 12 assistants, spread teachings of Christ throughout Gaul until he was 72 years old. This work did not penetrate east of the Rhine River. The missionaries brought a fresh piety, devotion, relationships with God and enthusiasm. Many cathedrals, abbeys and nunneries became centres of basic and religious education for monks and laymen. Patrick, Columba & Columban were later canonized.
- 529 **Benedict** set up 12 monasteries and wrote the ***Benedictine Rule*** (guidelines) [16, p 85] founding the **Benedictine Monastic Order,** based on moderation, a balance between physical and mental activity and renunciation of both fanaticism and excessive asceticism [map p 10].
- 581 Lombards destroyed Monte Cassino Benedictine monastery, S Italy. Monks escaped to Rome.
- 590-604 **Pope Gregory** generally regarded as the **first Pope,** was a Benedictine monk. He restored civil order in Italy after war, floods, Black Death and anarchy. From the resources of his inherited estates he provided relief and hope for many thousands of starving people of Italy, Spain, Gaul & England [25, pp 316-318].
- 596 **Augustine**[16, p 59] (not related to Bishop Augustine of Hippo) with 40 missionaries was commissioned by Pope Gregory, brought Christianity to large numbers of new believers at **Canterbury, England** [25, pp 316-18].
- By 600 AD missionaries sent to Gaul had set up over 200 monasteries [14, pp 12-13,34] map p 10. ***Benedictine Rule*** (guidelines) was followed in both old and new monasteries all over Europe, bringing civilization/education/ stability/humanity to turbulent warring people. Monastic communities were self sustaining with gardens, orchards, mills, animal husbandry, crafts, industries & libraries. They sheltered the sick & travelers. **Bishops were the real rulers**. Franks became monks, priests & bishops; noble women were **Abbesses** [1, pp 129-137].

Sixth Century Merovingian Rulers

- 558-61 **Chlothar I** a son of Clovis, reunited the four provinces that had been under his brothers [p 4-5]. However,
- 561 Chlothar I died; in 567 his kingdom divided among his four sons became: **Neustria** (France), **Austrasia** (Lorraine, Belgium and east bank of the Rhine River) and **Burgundy** [continued p 11; map p 20].

Map: *Europe in 600* [p 9b, p18]. Notice the settling of west, east and south by Slavs, Avars and Bulgars.

Chapter Two

Greek, Roman, Barbarian and Christian Architecture until 599 AD

Classical Greek Architecture

- The Hellenistic period, which followed the time of Alexander the Great was a time of great construction all over the middle east, including in Alexandria, Egypt, named for him. Much attention was given to city planning. In every town or city a central pavement with fountains was surrounded by porticoes which opened into civic and recreational buildings, including temple, council house, theatre, baths and gymnasium.
- Aramaic, a colloquial Greek was spoken by all middle Easterners.
- Hellenic civilization had great influence on all aspects of Roman, Jewish and Christian history, including literature, philosophy, medicine, politics, culture, sculpture and architecture.
- In private homes an inner court was typical [35]. Rooms opened onto the court where the extended family shared the gardens, baths and facilities.
- Classical architecture gave attention to graceful proportions, symmetry & balance [16, p 46] as in the **Parthenon** built 448-32 BC in **Athens.** Greek temples were located on a hill so that all sides could be seen. They were large or small, and were surrounded by slender tall columns, holding up post-and-lintel roof construction. The columns were topped with three styles of capitals, Doric, Ionic and Corinthian [9 Vol 2, pp 273-4]. Doric capitals were used for the Parthenon. The **Ionic** order was more slender & had a quite different curved base & fluting. Elaborate **Corinthian** capitals were developed later to grace the corners of buildings.
- In France and England in the 17 th century, the simple elegance of Greek architecture was rediscovered and known as Neo-classical Revival.
- In England it was called **Georgian** [See Chap 20, p 143].

Roman Architecture

- The Romans applied many ideas of the Greeks throughout their large empire, but in a robust grandiose scale. They established great engineering feats, such as aqueducts, canals, bridges, stadiums, thermal baths, coliseums, triumphal arches and palaces. Rows of round arches were used in bridge building and for large buildings, for weight-bearing and to allow openings for doors, windows and porticoes. Greek style columns were for ornamental purposes, not for load-bearing. Masonry was of stone, brick, marble and/or mosaic.
- **Basilicas** were very high large buildings, used as a palace, exchange or law court. They consisted of a high rectangular hall (*the nave*), at least twice as long as broad, with the entrance at one end, and a curved raised platform (*the apse*) at the other. Here a throne for an emperor or a seat for a judge or professor was placed, or later in churches, the altar. The roof was usually made of wood, flat or pitched, with a low slope.
- 118-128 AD the **Pantheon** (meaning a temple belonging to all the gods) was built in Rome by Emperor Hadrian, with a central **dome,** 142 feet high. Due to its weight it was placed on 20 foot thick walls [9 Vol 2, p 275]. A large circular opening in the dome allowed light into the interior. Round arches were efficient for distributing weight and they added grace and beauty. Statues of benefactors and deities decorated these buildings.
- The Romans gradually developed the **groin vault**, formed by **intersecting two barrel vaults**. The barrels thus reinforced each other and placed the weight on opposite corners. Only four strong columns were needed to hold up this type of roof [9 Vol 2, p 275]. Other writers [9; 23 Altet, pp 84-94; 24 Edward Norman] describe: "the intersection of two tunnel vaults at right angles". The walls were free for large windows, lattices and doorways. Use of the groin vault roof made it possible to build larger central halls in baths, law courts and covered markets.

Roman Basilica Style Churches

- In the fourth century, throughout the Roman Empire, churches, abbeys and monasteries were built of stone or brick on the Basilica plan, as were law courts and other official buildings.
- 379 in **Milan**, Lombardy, a cathedral was built [42, pp 746-8; 25, pp 264-5]. **Ambrose** was bishop 374 to 397.
- The long high hall was the seating space for the audience or congregation. Along both sides seating space and/or extra rooms were attached, with rows of pillars and arches between them and the main hall. The roofs on these side lean-tos were much lower [12 Vol 5, p 741-2].
- Along the top half of the long hall were small windows cut into the thick stone walls. The walls had to be very thick to bear the great weight of the roof.
- Some churches were built in the shape of a cross to provide seating space for monks and choir.
- Later, a stone or brick/tile dome was sometimes built into the roof. Small domes were built with a barrel or tunnel vault [26, pp 36-46, 72]. These had a long rounded surface.

Places of Worship in the Early Christian Era

- In the early years of Christianity believers worshiped in private homes. Those who were well-to-do built a larger room in their home for worship services. As the number of Christians in Europe grew, churches were built for worship. In southern Gaul they were often built in the same style as Roman basilicas [23 Altet, p 57, 62]. If there was a bishop in residence the church was called a cathedral, meaning bishop's chair.
- As the number of Christians multiplied, churches were built and placed under priests or bishop's assistants.
- In Rome when persecution began, Christians lived and buried their dead in the Catacombs, underground caves. They built a vast network of hundreds of miles [5, pp 202-205, 228-5, p 763] of tunnels and galleries decorated with beautiful paintings, beneath [137, pp 20-21,25, pp 200-4] the city of Rome. Between two and seven million Christians were buried here from the reign of Emperor Tiberius (AD 12-37) until Constantine (323-337).

Construction by Christian Roman Emperor Constantine

- Constantine the Great, born about A.D. 280 (Emperor from 323-337) became a Christian in 312. He was the first emperor to rule in the name of Christ. He built two basilicas for Christian worship in Rome, a church over the traditional burial place of Peter, and a cathedral. There were courtyards at the entrance, for pagans who wished to come to hear the gospel being read. The present St. Peter's was built on this site in the 16th century.
- Constantine built his new capital city of the Roman Empire at **Byzantium**, a small Greek seaport (present-day Istanbul, Turkey). It was a natural fortress with a protected harbor, at the crossroads of Europe and Asia.
- 324-330 within six years, small Byzantium became a metropolis. Thousands of skilled artisans worked on many projects. The streets were decorated with plazas, fountains, mosaics and porticoes. A temple to the fertility goddess Aphrodite was replaced by a basilica, containing statues of the 12 Apostles. An imperial palace, forum, public baths, and an enlarged hippodrome were completed, using marble and bronze taken from pagan buildings. Many pagan Greek and Roman temples were razed and replaced by churches and public buildings. Relics of Andrew, Luke and Timothy were reburied here [5, p 234-5]. Emperor Constantine had his whole court and government take up residence [45, pp 759-760;5, pp 196, 213, 239, 251] in this jewel of a city, reorganizing a tottering empire. Constantinople supplanted Rome as the centre of the Roman Empire [maps xvi and p 6].

Middle East Christian Architecture in the Fourth Century

- About 240 **Gregory** was born in **Armenia**, and when his family were persecuted, he was sent to safety. He later returned as a Christian Apostle but was persecuted.
- About 301 when the king was gravely ill Gregory was instrumental in his healing and conversion, and also of his family and army. The king made Christianity the official language. 315 Gregory became a Bishop, baptized the people and was known as the *Illuminator* of the Armenians. He created an alphabet and translated scripture. He built churches and monasteries [25, pp 196-7].
- In the 4th century Byzantine Christian architecture spread into Greece [35]. Many small cross-shaped churches were built. Some churches had a small dome covering the central room. Waves of barbarians invaded Greece from the north. Alliances were made with Goths and Franks. Later they built many copies not only of the great Byzantine edifices, but also of small cross-shaped Greek churches and the Roman Basilicas.

Architecture of the Visigoths

- The Visigoths (western Goths) migrated south from north Europe and were held back at the Danube River by the Romans for many years. When the Roman Empire became weak Visigoths invaded Italy and lived there for some time. They learned the building methods of the Italians, and added their own impressive skills of gold and jewel inlay. They moved west from Milan into south Gaul (France).
- 507 they were a kingdom in south Gaul and Spain, with capital at **Toulouse.**
- By 587 converted to Christianity, they controlled most of Spain [p 19; map xv].

Architecture of the Ostrogoths (Eastern Goths)

- 493-526 Ostrogothic king Theodoric had grown up in the Roman Imperial court in Constantinople. He established the capital in Ravenna, north Italy. His kingdom south and west from the Danube river included the Alps, SE Gaul (France) and most of Italy. "His wise and just rule gave Italy a period of tranquility and prosperity not enjoyed for centuries"[16]. Throughout Italy he built new palaces, an amphitheatre and churches, and the mausoleum and cathedral of Santo Spirito at Ravenna. Ceilings & walls were decorated [23; 25] with Byzantine style mosaics. The buildings combined Roman basilica and Byzantine style [9, p 276].
- 526-547 outstanding St Vitale church was built in Ravenna [25, pp 288-9]. Until 554 Ostrogoths ruled in Italy.

Byzantine Architecture in the Fifth and Sixth Centuries

- Byzantine churches were built on a circular or polygonal plan, with a small dome and encircling aisle inside.
- Orthodox Churches were built in Constantinople, Armenia, Greece and the Balkans [12 Vol 5, pp 741-2].
- 554-565 the Eastern Roman Emperor, **Justinian** I and his queen **Theodora** [see p 5] were great builders, pouring much wealth into construction. During their reign they constructed forts, monasteries, hospitals, aqueducts, bridges, and many churches, as far away as **Syria** and **Africa**.
- 537 in Constantinople they dedicated the enormous **Hagia Sophia** (St. Sophia Church). Sophia means "holy wisdom". It was 250 by 107 feet, with a dome 180 feet high and 107 feet in diameter, encircled with arched windows, which flooded the interior with light, so that silver, gold and jeweled inlays and chandeliers gleamed. The interior decoration was lavish with more than four acres of mosaic pictures of saints and Bible characters crafted from delicate bits of green, black and rose marble and gold-embossed glass [25, pp 285-7].
- The dome had ribs that rested on four arches, 125 feet tall. The spaces between the ribs were arched vaults.
- 558 there was an earthquake and the dome collapsed. 559 an even higher new dome was built.

Trends in the Fifth and Sixth Centuries and Black Death

- In **Latin western churches**, **images** of Christ, the Virgin Mary and the saints, beautifully sculpted of white marble, stone or clay, decorated the churches and were venerated as part of their worship.
- In **Orthodox eastern churches**, **icons** became an important feature of worship. Worshipers cross themselves, kiss and bow to these paintings, tapestries or mosaics of holy people [36, p 38].
- 541-547 about 300,000 people died from **Bubonic Plague** (**Black Death**), which was over one third of the population of Constantinople [95, p 83].
- The plague killed a quarter of the people of Europe in waves for 50 years.

Wooden Gables of the Franks

- Through the centuries, in Scandinavia and northern Europe, the skills of building wooden roofs with multiple arches were developed. The Franks and several other Germanic tribes brought these ancient skills to western and central Europe. **Wooden fan vaulting** originated from tents, chalets and high gables [26, pp vii, 12-15, 47-66, 174-195], and evolved into highly skilled carpentry and joinery.
- By 400 **Franks held high civil and military positions within the Roman Empire** [12, pp 41-44]. They spread south on the west side of the Rhine, were friendly with Gallo-Romans [1, pp 51-58] and intermarried. Gradually France became a united country with powerful kings who assimilated Roman style administration and attitudes [11, pp 51-77]. They learned Roman masonry building methods mingled with their own.
- 481-511 the reign of **Clovis** united the Franks, forming the **Merovingian Kingdom** which included most of France, including Alamans, living in **Würtemberg** and in **Alsace** since 443 [1, pp 84-85]. His wife was a Christian from **Burgundy**. 508 he moved his capital to **Paris**. Gauls, Romans & Franks converted to Christ.
- 486 the last Roman Governor of Gaul was defeated, 10 years after the fall of Rome.
- Clovis extended his rule across the Rhine over the **Ripuarian Franks**, who still spoke [1, pp 88-90] the Germanic Frank language. He brought Gallo-Roman-Christian culture to them [continued chapter three].
- Clovis' four sons divided up the kingdom and much feuding and intrigue followed [see chapter one, pp 4-5].

Early Medieval Church Growth

- 583-615 **Columban**, an **Irish missionary**, with 12 assistants spread the teachings of Christ throughout Gaul, but not east of the Rhine. They brought fresh piety, devotion and enthusiasm. Some Franks became monks, priests, bishops and missionaries. High ranking Frank women promoted **Nunneries** [1, pp 129-137].
- Many cathedrals, abbeys and nunneries were built of stone with wooden roofs in Roman style, together with Frank and Gaul carpentry and masonry and Frank metal and jewel work [1]. Both stone and wooden arches were beautifully ornamented by the Franks [1, Edward James pp 65, 148-152].
- These Christian buildings became centres of basic and religious education for monks and laymen. Many wooden churches were built.
- 590-604 Pope **Gregory** I, born about 540 is generally regarded as the first Pope [see chap 1, p 6]. He restored civil order after war, Black Death, floods and anarchy.
- Pope Gregory used the resources of his vast papal estates to bring relief to thousands who were starving.
He lived simply. His influence was estblished over the churches of Italy, Spain, Gaul and England.
- By 600 there were more than 200 monasteries and nunneries in Europe.

Anglo-Saxon Rulers were dominant for six hundred years 560-1066

- About 450 Angles, Saxons and Jutes (Danes) began to invade Briton after the Romans left to protect Rome. Written records were not kept. There were three major areas with unity of tribes or kingdoms: north, central and south.
- 590 Augustine & 40 missionaries to England [p 11]; started at Canterbury a former Roman city [p 6];
- 560-615 Ethelbert of Kent became Christian;
- 635 monastary Lindisfame built on Northumbria coast; 752 Cuthred defeated Ethelbald;
- 673-735 **monk Venerable Bede first historian**; 757-786 Cynewulf; 798-821 Cenwulf of Mercia;
- 760 The *Book of Kells* ornate Irish four Gospels [p 11];
- 793 Northmen (Vikings) raids; sacked Lindisfame, Jarrow and Iona; monks carried bones of Bishop Cuthbert to Durham Cathedral;
- 802-839 Egbert of Wessex; 834 Danes invaded: called berserk/werewolves; sacked London, Lison/Cadiz & Piza.
- 839-858 Ethelwulf in York; 851 Danes attacked Canterbury [p12];
- 866-871 Saxon Aethelred I paid tribute coins to Viking king **Harold**;
- 865 Vikings defeated east Mercia; developed kingdom of York; their dialect influenced English language;
- 871-899 **Alfred The Great** Saxon king of Wessex [p 12]; had monthly meetings, law, order, tax, jury and writing; 885 he took London back from Danes; 899-924 Edward;
- 925-940 Saxon Athelstan united Vikings and Saxons; 940-955 Edmund; 955-959 Edwy; 957-975 Edgar;
- 973-1013 Aethelred II paid protection money to Danes;
- 1003-14 Dane Sweyn conquered England/Canterbury; his son:
- 1016-1035 **Canute** the Great: England/Norway/Burgundy/Ireland/Scots; 1045 buried in Winchester Cathedral.
- 1041-1066 **Edward, the Confessor**: son of Aethelred and his mother from Normandy brought Frank culture [p 33]; 1052-65 built **Westminster Abbey** 21; conflict with Harold, Earl of Wessex who had been promised the crown;

Map: ***Monastic Centres in Europe 548 to 1153 AD*** 46b, p10 [See pp 6, 10, 21, 25-26 and Chaps 3, 4 and 6]

Chapter Three - 600 to 999 AD

Early Middle Ages - Fifth To Tenth Centuries

"Middle Ages" is the name given to the period in history from 400-1400 AD. The adjective is "Medieval."

Merovingian Dynasty 500-750 [continued from pp 4-6]

- 584-628 Chlothar II was king of **Neustria (France)**. 612 his counsellor **Arnuf** became Bishop of Metz.
- 613 Chlothar II united **Burgundy** and Neustria [3]. and his **Mayor** was **Pepin**.
- 623 Dagobert I, elder son of Chlothar II became king of **Austrasia** (Lorraine, Belgium & Rhine east bank).
- 629-34 **Dagobert** I succeeded in uniting the whole Frankish kingdom [3]. Arnuf was Bishop; Pepin Mayor.
- 638-657 **Clovis** II, aged 6 years, succeeded; 656-660 **Chlothar** III was king of all Franks.
- 663-673 **Childeric** ruled Austrasia [map 6]. Civil war and anarchy followed his death. Gradually the real leadership of the Franks was by **mayors**, administering both civil government and army.
- 687 **Pepin** the Younger, united the three Frankish kingdoms and became **hereditary Mayor**.
- 691-695 **Clovis** III was king of all the Franks; 695-711 **Childebert** III; 711-716 **Dagobert** III [3];
- 700 **Thuringia** was added to Frankish kingdoms [3] [maps 6 and 20].
- 715 **Charles Martel** became **Mayor** of the Frankish court. 725 he conquered **Bavaria** [3; 167, pp 48-53].
- 716-720 **Chilperic** II ruled Neustria and 719 added all the Frankish kingdoms; 720 **Theodoric** IV.
- 730 the dukedom of **Alemanni**, east of the source of the Rhine, came under Frankish rule.
- 732 Martel in the <u>Battle of Tours</u>, using horsemen with coats of mail and stirrups [139, p 126], stopped **Muslim invasions from Spain**. He rewarded horse-men with **feudal** grants of land (**fiefs**=feudum in Latin) [139, p 126].
- 737-751 **Childeric** III became king of all Franks. 735 Martel conquered **Burgundy**. 739 requested by the Pope, he provided help against **Lombards** from the north, **Greeks** from the east and against **Saracens** (Muslim Arabs) who were invading Italy. [See pp 16-17].
- 741 **Pepin the Short** succeeded his father as Mayor of the Frankish court [3]; 751 he deposed Childeric III.
- 750-768 Pepin the Short was chosen king, ending the Merovingian dynasty [3]. 754 he provided forces who routed invaders from Rome. In 756 Pepin <u>subdued Lombardy</u> to vassal state [3].
- 768-771 Pepin's son **Carloman** succeeded. <u>Papal Estates</u> were created.
- 771 his son Charles (**Charlemagne**) succeeded [167, pp 52; 56].

Missionaries Sent From the British Isles to Central Europe 720-755

- 596 **Augustine** with 40 missionaries, and more later brought Christianity to England; to Cambridge.
- 673-735 the monk **Venerable Bede** recorded life in **Anglo-Saxon England** [139, p 121].
- 583 **Irish** missionaries spread Christianity **west** of the Rhine. Churches and monasteries were established throughout France [map 10], but it was not until 137 years later that:
- 720 led by **Boniface**, Anglo-Saxon missionaries went from **England** to northern and central Europe. They began around the Baltic sea, from where their ancestors had migrated to England three centuries earlier. Next they introduced civilization and religious order throughout **Thuringia, Hesse** and **Bavaria**.
- 746-754 **Boniface** was Archbishop of **Mainz**. 755 he was murdered [16, p 98] and was later canonized. In the eighth century **many Benedictine monasteries** set up **schools** for both peasants and noblemen. They taught crop rotation, stock-breeding, fruit tree cultivation, handicrafts, literacy, art and the copying of books, to discover and preserve ancient knowledge. The <u>wandering barbaric Germanic tribes</u> began to find unity and higher purposes in life than warring for land and power [7, p 7-8; 5, pp 296-297, 300-301].
- 760 the **Book of Kells**, ornately illuminated 680 page Irish version of the four gospels, was created [139, p 125; 3].

Carolingian Dynasty of Frankish Rulers

- 771-814 **Charlemagne (Charles the Great)** 6 feet six (three?) inches tall, Pepin's son, Charles Martel's grandson, ruled **both sides of the Rhine river**. <u>Carol of Carolingian is an alternate spelling of Charles</u> [18, p 39]. He subdued the **Saxons, Holstens** and **Jutes** (later Denmark) and built a fortress at **Hamburg** [167, pp 56-57].
- Many north people (**Norse, Norman** & **Vikings**) needing land, became **raiders** and **pirates** in western Europe and Britian. Charlemagne greatly extended the borders east to the Elbe river and divided the empire into **marches** (marks=districts=counties) administered by a Margrave (Marquis=Count). He personally held court all over his empire. **Marches** were vassals to dukes. In 803 he established **Ostmark** (east March) later called **Austria** (oster=east county) [98, p 8]. In the south he annexed **Lombardy** (northern Italy). He recovered **Bohemia** from **Slavs**; farther east he pushed back **Slavs, Avars** and **Arabs** [7, p 7-19].

- A **feudal system** of government emerged. Military duties and payment of dues came along with possessing a farm. As a result the free status of farmers began to disappear. **Charlemagne** pushed Slavs northeast to the Oder River & established **Magdeburg-Halle Marche**, with a colony of Frank settlers [WV Vol 11, Sep 98, p 11]. **Bavarians** (Boii tribe) ruled from the eastern Alps to Vienna (map 20). **Counts** of the stables (constables) organized transport for both court and military purposes[139, p 126].
- 800 Charlemagne was crowned the **first Holy Roman Emperor** by Pope Leo I, having fulfilled the pope's aim to build a Catholic Roman Empire [165, p 83, 90]. As Protector of the Church, Charlemagne built monasteries, schools and model farms, where the peasants were instructed. He Christianized **Saxons** [WV Vol 11, Sep 98, p 11], built churches, and bishoprics, participated in Ecumencal Councils (of Orthodox and Catholic churches) where the Apostles' Creed evolved, and was promoted in all of rural Europe[165, p 96]. 747 Bishopric of St. Boniface in **Mainz.**
- At **Aachen** (French**: Aix-la-Chapelle**, the **new Athens**) [map p 20] his capital near the Rhine River in Germany. He built a cathedral with Italian marble and a high dome, a warm mineral springs swimming pool, large enough for 100 bathers, a library and a palace with central heating and a 160 foot hall. He founded a **palace school for education in Latin** for both government and church leaders. Any boy who showed promise [15, p 46-49] could attend. The head master was an English monk.
- In a renaissance of traditions from Caesar's Roman Empire he built roads, established stable currency (coinage), and enacted laws to govern all aspects of life. Charlemagne named the upper and lower Rhine districts **Palatinate** after Caesar's seats of power in the seven hills of Rome, the Palatines.
- 814-840 **Ludwig** (**Louis the Pious**) Charlemagne's son, ruled the Holy Roman Empire. [See below p 12-13.] He founded several bishoprics and monasteries where grammar, rhetoric, logic, geometry, music and astronomy were featured. These cathedral schools were the forerunners of universities.
- **The Roman (Latin) Church was gaining power**, after centuries of spiritual, and political weakness.
- **The Eastern (Greek) Orthodox** and Roman Churches had many differences in belief and practice.
- 859 east and west split. **Popes** and **Bishops** in the west; **Patriarchs** and **Metropolitans** in the east [p 13].

New Wave of Raids by Northmen (Norse), Vikings, Danes and Asiatic Tribes

- **Normans** (Northmen, Norse) from NE Europe, raided and settled NW river deltas around the Baltic Sea.
- **Saracens** (**Muslim Arabs**) invaded and traded with southern Italy and Sicily [See p 17].
- Turkic **Avars** raided up the Danube, overran Oster-mark [98, p 8]; Ural Mountain **Magyars** raided [p 14].
- 826 **King Harold** of the **Danes** was baptized at Mainz. He returned home with monk **Ansgar** (801-865) who spread Christianity in Denmark and other parts of Scandinavia [3];[95, p 104].
- 834 **Danes** (Vikings) **i**nvaded Britain. 851 they attacked **Canterbury**. The local people said they were berserk (frenzied like bears with a shirt). They also called them werewolves [139, pp 128-129].
- Danes sacked **London, Lisbon, Cadiz and Pisa**. They had long maneuverable swift ships. The sails were of woven wool cloth with reds stripes or checks. There were 16 (or 32 ?) oarsmen, probably working in shifts. 64 shields were hung over the edge. (Archeologists recently excavated ships, mummies, clothing and artifacts from peat bogs [139, p 129].)
- 860 Vikings landed in **Iceland**; 874 they colonized Iceland [95, p 109]. Some explored **Malta** and **Sicily**.
- 861 Vikings sacked **Cologne**, **Aachen** (Carolingian Capital), **Worms**, **Toulouse** and **Paris** [95, p 107].
- 870 they occupied **East Anglia**. Norse principal deities were Odin (Woden) symbolized by the raven, and Thor, the god of thunder, symbolized by the hammer. Wednesday and Thursday are named for them [139, p 129]. Valhalla was their heaven and Valkyries were Odin's warrior handmaidens.
- Some raiders became Christians; started Christian communities in Sweden, Norway & Denmark [6, p 80].
- 875-899 **King Alfred** ruled Wessex [139, p 121]. In 885 he took London back from the Danes.
- 892 Vikings, short of land in Norway, with their women and children, in 300 ships invaded England and were repulsed. 916 Danes attacked Ireland and in 941 made war on England;
- 899 Alfred the Great of England died, succeeded by his son **Edward**, the Elder 899-924 [95, p 111]. More p 10.]
- 980 Danes attacked Chester and Southampton; in 991 they were defeated in Essex [3].

Charlemange's Large Empire Divided Among Three Grandsons

- 814-840 Charlemange's son **Ludwig I** was strong academically but weak holding together rival tribes.
- 833 Ludwig's sons humiliated their father in public. **Lothar** (eldest son) became Holy Roman **Emperor**. His brothers rebelled, so Ludwig divided the empire with them at the **Treaty of Verdun**:

- 843 the **Treaty of Verdun**, dividing the empire into three dynasties and was signed in two languages: **Romance** [Latin-Gaul, later **French**) and **East Frank** (later **High German**). [Maps 6 & 20].

1. Italian Carolingian dynasty 843-875: son **Lothar** received Aix-la-Chapelle & Rome, Italy, Frisia, Lorraine, Lotharingen (formerly called Austrasia [maps 6, 20] and became Holy Roman Emperor. He died 855.
- 855- 875 son **Lothar** II became king of **Italy** and Holy Roman Emperor [16, p 443] and received **Lorraine** p 18.
- **Charles** received **Provence** & south **Burgundy**.

2. German Carolingian dynasty 843-911: **Louis I** (**Ludwig** the German) became king of most of the area that is now **Germany**; died 876. His son **Carloman** succeeded. 891 **Arnuf von Karten**, drove out the Vikings, and 896-899 was elected King by princes of the five dutchies: **Franconia, Bavaria, Lorraine, Swabia** and **Saxony**; crowned Holy Roman Emperor.
- 899-911 his son **Louis** III was the last Carolingian German king. A Saxon dynasty followed (see p 18).

3. French Carolingian dynasty 843-987: **Charles** II, **the Bald** 843-877, king of Francia Occidentalis (most of Gaul) [95, p 106]; was crowned Holy Roman Emperor; - 877-879 his son **Louis** II the stammerer;
- 879-882 sons **Carloman** ruled south France; **Louis** III North France.
- 881-887 **Charles** III the Fat, of **Swabia** (Alsace) [95, p 110]. 886 **Norsemen** laid seige to Paris [95, p 110]; Charles had a large army but paid the Norse ransom to withdraw. 887 he was deposed.
- 888-898 **Odo** Count of Paris was king of the west Franks. A **league of free farmers** rose up against large landowners, in the midst of **growing anarchy**. 893-922 **Charles** III, the Simple, after five years' civil war.
- 911 Norsemen ravaged towns and monastaries along the north, so Charles III granted large tracts of land along the Seine River to **Norman warlord Rollo**, hoping he could keep out others, and he did, so invasions ended [139, p 136; 95, p 113]; Normans & French intermarried, Christianized; 911 the Treaty of St. Clair-sur-Epte set up the Dukedom of **Normandy**. Rollo (Hrolf the Ganger) became the first **Duke of Orleans** [95, p 113]. 912 baptized and **renamed Robert**, began to dominate the Franks.
- 911 Lorraine transferred allegiance to France when Saxon kings were elected [see p 18].
- 987-996 **Hugh Capet** was elected king of an area around **Paris.** Burgundy SE & Aquitaine SW remained separate, the rest of France ruled by local lords (continued pp 21-22);

Early History of Austria

- 15 BC the landlocked country that became Austria was governed by the Roman Empire because of deposits of iron. Mountainous Austria, drained by the long **Danube River**, rises in the Alps, flows into the **Black Sea**. Local **Celtic** people were invaded by Germanic Bavarians (**Boii**) and both were Romanized.
- 796 **Charlemange** set up Avar March [12 Vol 1, pp 719-720]. For 50 years Austrians struggled with **Magyar** invaders from the Ural mountains, driving them east to Hungary [Hohenstaufen & Premysl Dynasties [pp 14; 27; 29-30; map 31]. They had a unique language spoken also in Finland and Estonia.
- 800-814 Emperor Charlemange was crowned **the first Holy Roman Emperor** [pp 11-12]. He subdued the Bavarians_[9Vol 3, pp 107-112; 96, p 8-9]. He established Oster (east) March, later called OsterReich pronounced Austria. When Turkic **Avars** invaded Charlemange drove them back and Magyars replaced them.
- 936-973 **Otto** I king of Franks and Lombards revived Eastern March p 18;
- 976 **Leopold** I **Babenburg**, Bavaria was Margrave. Until 1246 **Babenburg Dynasty** ruled Austria.

The Eastern Roman Empire - Known as the Byzantine Empire [from p 5; pp 17; 29-30]

- 541, 732 & 746 Bubonic Plague struck Constantinople severely [95, pp 96-97, 84], decimating the population.
- 610-641 Byzantine Emperor **Heraclius** drew together what remained of **Roman** & **Greek civilizations**. He gave land to soldiers; they began to prosper as farmers. 626 he defeated the **Persians** and lost parts of **Syria** to Muslims. In the north he defeated Turkic Avars [167, pp 44-47]. 641-668 **Constans** II Pogonatus was preoccupied with invaders on all sides. 668-685 Constantine IV; weak emperors, but preserved Greek scientific knowledge.
- 674-8 **Saracens** (Arab Muslim armies) besieged Constantinople, and again in 717-718 p 17.
- 680 Asian **Bulgars** invaded the **Balkans**, northern Byzantine empire (**Greece**) [15, p 18]. 697 **Byzantine** Christian **north Africa** was defeated by **Muslims**, many **converted to Islam**. 685-695; 705-711 **Justinian** II;
- 695-698 Leontius; 698-705 Tiberius III; 711- 713 Philippicus; 713-716 Anastasius; 716-717 Theodosius;

- 717-741 **Leo** III forbad worship of icons; 732 **Bubonic plague**. 742-775 **Constantine** V; 748 retook Cyprus from Arabs; 775-780 **Leo** IV; 780-797 10 year old **Constantine** VI and his mother **Irene**, Regent; 790 he began to rule; 797 be was blinded on her orders. 802-810 emperor **Nicephorus** killed by Bulgarians;
- 810-13 **Michael** I; 813-20 **Leo** V Armenian; 820-29 **Michael** II; Arabs conquered Crete; 829-42 **Theophilus**;
- 842-67 **Michael** III Macedonian Dynasty ruled the Byzantine Empire and sent **Cyril** & **Methodius** as missionaries to the Slavs [18, pp 49-50] [p 15]. 867-886 **Basil** I Macedonian Dynasty; in Constantinople commerce and culture centre of the world. 886 son **Leo** VI, the Wise revised Justinian's laws;
- 912-959 **Constantine** VII 8 years old; mother **Zoe** Regent; 927 famine; 959-963 his son **Romanus** II;
- 961 Byzantine forces took back Crete; 963 general **Nicephorus** II married Romanus' widow, co-emperor; took Cyprus from Arabs; 963-969 emperor Theophano recovered Antioch after 300 years' Arab rule.
- 976-1025 **Basel** II emperor 50 years, fought back invading nomadic Asian **Bulgars**. Some soldier-farmers commanded their own armies, ignoring the emperor [8, p 53]. In 988 to put down these rebels he received help from Vladimir of **Kiev**, Russia. Basel's sister married Czar Vladimir; became Christian [p 16]

Slavic and Magyar Migrations and Early Nation-Building in the Balkans [from pp 2-3]

- **Romanians**, descended from ancient **Dacians**, were influenced by Greeks, Romanized and spoke a Latin language, were kept north of the Danube River. The countries called the **Balkans**, south of the Danube River, **include Bulgaria, Macedonia, Serbia, Croatia, Bosnia, Slovenia** and **Albania**. Borders changed greatly during the 3rd to 10th centuries as waves of Asian nomadic tribes on swift horses swept through the Russian steppes into Europe, pushing out settled cultures. **Turkic tribes: Avars** and **Bulgars,** mixed with **Slavs** [15, p 18] and became Slavic-speaking. Some settled in Anatolia, Turkey.
- 681 the **Bulgarian Empire** was founded in the Balkans [55, pp 24, 49, 54, 84-7], from seven tribes [maps xv & 20].
- 689 Byzantine Constantinople troops defeated Slavs in **Thrace**, but were weakened with internal strife.
- Some Turkish **Avar** families migrated west up the **Danube River** 1740 miles from Black Sea to the Alps.
- 796 an Avar feudal March was founded in Salzburg by Charlemagne (Oster March/East Reich/**Austria** [3]) Other tribal leaders also became **Margraves** (Count or Marquis) [see pp 12-13, 29-30; map p 6].
- 864 **Boris** I **Czar** (**Khan**) of Bulgaria and his people became Orthodox Christians [95, p 108; 46, p 92]. Mountain ranges divided the several different **Serb** tribes. About 879 one Serb tribe accepted Byzantine rule and became Orthodox Christians, through **missionaries Cyril** and **Methodius** [12 Vol 10, p 645]. [See p 15]
- 894-927 **Symeon Czar** of **Bulgaria** invaded Thrace [95, p 111, 113]. Nomadic **Magyars**, driven from Russia came for a new homeland. They spoke a unique language related to Finnish and Estonian [55, p 302]. The Byzantines appealed to them to help fight the Bulgars. In 910 Byzantines paid tribute to the Magyars.
- 894-907 **Arpad** led **Magyars** up the Danube, drove out Avars, settled in present Hungary; raided Italy and Alsace [see 30]. Meanwhile 913, 917 Czar Symeon of Bulgaria threatened Byzantine for nonpayment of tribute; named himself Czar of Bulgarians & Greeks, but 924, 926 was defeated by Byzantines and Slavic **Croats**; 927-968 son Czar **Peter** made peace. 925 in NW Balkans the kingdom of **Croatia** was founded. Languages & cultures of west and east Slavs evolved differently, due to rugged mountains [maps pp 20, 24].
- NW Balkan Slavs were Roman Catholic and eastern Slavs Orthodox.
- 940 **Bogomils**, Bulgarian sect, working-class political movement, were denounced heretic by the pope.
- 998 **Hungary** was founded/expanded. 1000-1038 the first king was **Stephen** I (Istvan or Walk), married a Bavarian princess; baptized 997; became patron saint of Hungary [55, pp 277, 305] [pp 28-30; Maps 27, 38]

Early History of Great Moravia and Bohemia; Premsyl Dynasty 818-1306 [maps 20, 31, 38]

- Bohemia is located in central Europe on a plateau. The geographic chart below shows their locations:

		North		
		Poland		
NW	**Saxony**	**BOHEMIA**	**Moravia Slovakia**	*East*
		Austria	**Hungary**	
		South	*South-East*	

- The long **Elbe river** rises in the Carpathian/Tatra mountains of north Bohemia and runs NW through Bohemia & **Saxony** & other German states. It enters the North Sea west of Denmark.

- Bohemia received its name from a **Celtic tribe**, the **Boii**, who were expelled by a Germanic tribe, the **Marcomanni** [See xiii & p 1]. In 5th-8th centuries **Czech, Premysl** & other **Slavic** tribes settled around **Morava** River that flows into the Danube. 800-1306 the **Premysl (Przemzsl) Dynasty** from southern **Poland**, ruled Bohemia and Moravia [map p 31]. They spoke Czech, a Slavic language. There still is a Premysl district in Galicia, south Poland [27, pp 143, 164-5, 214, 232].
- 818-846 **Mojmir Premysl** founded **the state of Moravia**. 833 Ratislav expanded **Great Moravia** west to rule **Bohemia**, north to include southern **Poland** & east into **Slovakia** and north half of **Hungary**. The people became Christians [9 Vol 4, p 188; 10, pp 25-32]. His successor expanded it further [43, p 1]. [maps p 6, 20, 27and 31].
- 862 Moravian ruler **Rostislav** invited Orthodox missionaries **Cyril and Methodius** from Constantinople. They became the ***Apostles of the Slavs***. [see p 14]. Cyril developed the **Cyrillic alphabet**, and translated the Bible into the Old Slavic language. Pope Adrian II allowed sermons in the Slavic language, but after Emperor Charlemange installed a **Swabian bishop**; the apostles were expelled [10, pp 25-32]. 862 Magyars invaded German & Italian territories [95, p 113]. 869-894 Premysl King **Svatopuk** united Slovakia, Moravia and Bohemia [43, p 1].
- 862 Cyril died in Rome [95, p 108]. 870 Prague castle was built; 884 Methodius became Archbishop [9 Vol 7, p 419].
- 896 Magyars drove out Avars, ruled Hungary. 900 Slavic **Czechs** asserted rule over all Bohemian tribes [95, p 112].
- 903-35 **Wenceslas (Vaclav)** I ruled the Moravian empire, was broken up by Magyars in 907 but won back supremacy. Venerated as a saint, 929 Wenceslas I was forced to swear allegiance to Holy Roman Emperor Henry I of Saxony but was murdered by his brother Boleslav, a non-Christian [maps 20, 24, 38].
- 935-967 **Boleslav** I ruled **Bohemia, Moravia**, west **Slovakia**, southern **Poland** and **Silesia**. [more p 29].
- 950 German king **Otto** I became Holy Roman Emperor [10, pp 25-32]. [See p 18].
- 967-999 **Boleslav** II founded Prague Bishopric, built magificent cathedrals, churches and forts [p 35].

NE Europe - the Baltic Sea and Poland

- 400-500 AD migrations of Germanic tribes to the south and west left a vacuum into which Slavic people moved. Slavic ancestors of the Poles migrated west-ward from the marshy areas between the Dnieper and Vistula (Weichsel) rivers [maps xvi, 6, 20, 38]. They were agricultural nomads, moving to new areas when fertility of the land was worn out. Some remained in their old location. Others moved on. They grew barley, millet, rye and oats; beets, onions and garlic; raised sheep, pigs, goats and oxen. To weave cloth they used wool and grew hemp and flax. They worshiped the sun, thunder and many gods. The **Polish** people spoke about 20 Slavic languages. The Vistula flows north from the alpine **Tatra/Carpathian Mountains**, through forests, central plains, rolling hills and swamps into the Baltic Sea.
- Poland has no natural boundaries along the east or west, so there was much migration back and forth.
- In NW Europe, **along the North Sea** there were Germanic tribes who later organized into provinces: Flanders, Netherlands, Hanover, Schleswig/Holstein & Denmark on Jutland peninsula [map 38].
- In NE Europe, **along the Baltic Sea** there were Germanic tribes who later organized into provinces: Mecklenburg, West Prussia, Pomerania, East Prussia, Esthonia, Livonia, Lithuania & Courland (Latvia). These people from both east and west developed similar **Plautdeisch (low German/Teutonic)** languages, but they clashed with one-another for supremacy. Germanic peoples from central Europe were moving east into Poland for more than a 1000 years [per Editor Ewald Wuschke *Wandering Volhynians*]. "They migrated up the rivers, settling for a few decades until overpopulation and/or greener pastures urged them onward south-easterly, to settle in a succession of areas that showed potential to become fertile" [61; 62; WV Vol 11, Sep 98, pp 11-19]. The climate made it possible to have wonderful crops and abundance one year and unexpectedly, famine the next, due to floods, drought or frost. Unlike the Slavic Poles, these Germanic tribes were skilled at draining and diking swamps to grow good hay, so as to fatten cattle to produce milk and cheese [compare pp 173-4]. Sandy forested land became fertile fields for grain, vegetables (especially cabbage, and in the 17th century potatoes), berry bushes and pears, apples and plums. They followed a three-field crop-rotation system, leaving one field fallow in turn. Thus fertility improved.
- Some were artisans who produced the tools and spun cloth required for themselves, and to sell to the tribes there before them. Many Germanic settlers assimilated into the Polish ethnic family [61].
- In **Pomerania** (Pomern or Pomorze) the Slavic **Kashubs** were displaced by Germanic/Nordic settlers, who in turn were called Kashubs. Some migrated south. The author's maternal grandmother Juliana Henkelmann Klammer, was sometimes put down as a Kashub by her Schwab (SW German) husband. Her low German ancestors settled in **Poznan (Posen** in German)[63], the NW province of Poland, home of the **Polanie** tribe [27, p 80].
- 550 **Polanie Slavs** settled in **Galicia** (south Poland) and **Ruthenia (Ukraine)** in east Galicia [3].

- 966-992 **Mieszko 1** (**Mieczyslav**) of the **Piast dynasty founded Poland**. He organized the tribes into a unified whole and was baptized. His wife and many attendants and officials were from **Cologne**. Poland consisted of the provinces of **Poznan** in the NW, **Silesia** in the SW and **Galicia** in the south [61;64].
Pomerania was added to Mieszko's kingdom of Poland, but their Duke married a Danish princess, rebelled and joined a German state. **Mazovia Plains** in central Poland (also spelled **Masowiecki**[27, p 112, 297] or **Mazowsze**[28, p 144]) were added, with headquarters at **Plock** [27, pp 55-6].
- Mieszko I gained independence from the Hapsburg church and built a bishopric at **Gniezno** just northeast of present-day Poznan (Posen) [27, pp 10, 189].
- 992-1025 oldest son **Boleslaw** I (**Boleslaus**) the Brave, succeeded. His capital was at **Gniezno**.
- 994 he conquered **Pomerania** to **access the Baltic Sea.** Bishoprics were: **Krakow** in **Galicia, Wroclaw** in **Silesia**, & **Kolobrzeq** on the **Baltic Sea**.
- 1000 Boleslaw founded Gniezno Archbishopric [pp 27-28; map 38].

Early History of Russia

[Maps pp 31, 37 & 38]

The **Rus were Vikings** (Vargarians, a Germanic tribe) from the **Baltic Sea** in the north, who went via the Dneiper river map xv, to trade in Constantinople. They established powerful cities, **Novgorod** in the north and **Kiev** in the centre. By the late 10th century they were speaking Slavic, using Slavic names [47, p 50; 136, p 24].
- **Saracen** (Muslim) **supremacy in the Mediterranean** meant that **Europeans** who wanted to trade with Constantinople had to travel via rivers flowing into the **Black Sea** to reach Constantinople: in the SW the **Danube**, and in the north, rivers flowing into the **Baltic Sea**. These three river systems were well traveled by Vikings since prehistoric times [See map p 31, 38]. Thus **Saracen** opposition indirectly contributed to the development of Russia. **Kiev** is just south of the confluence of the **Dnieper** and **Desna** rivers, 590 miles (952 km) from the Black Sea. The west bank is high and steep and the east bank wide, low and flat [12].
- 850 **Rurik**, a Vargarian, made himself ruler of **Kiev** [95, p 106]. 862 he founded **Novgorod**, became Grand Prince and established the Russian royal family. They soon settled in towns along the Dnieper river and built up **Kiev**. The princes of **Kiev** ruled **Russia** [8, pp 34-37], controlling all the rivers, from the **Baltic Sea** in the north, the **Black Sea** south, the **Volga** east and **Danube** west, winter and summer.
- Through marriage they assimilated with the Slavs [21, pp 116-132] mingling Germanic & Slavic blood. The ethnic roots of the Rurik Dynasty and the Rus (Ros) may be the same [12 Vol 10, p 244].
- 865 Russian Norse sacked Constantinople [95, p 108].
- 882 **Oleg Rurik** moved the capital to Kiev from Novgorod [95, pp 110, 113]. 907 he laid siege to Byzantine Constantinople and controlled trade routes. 911 Oleg made peace and a commercial treaty with them.
- 941 **Igor**, Prince of Kiev crossed the Black Sea and raided **Bithynia**, north **Turkey** destroying their fleet.
- 945 his widow, **Olga the first Christian Slav ruler**, succeeded [95, p 116]. Ruriks of Kiev raided the Byzantine empire and made a treaty with them. [Compare maps pp 31 and 37 and see Architecture p 37.]
- About 980 **Vladimir** Prince of Kiev, influenced by Orthodox **missionaries Cyril** and **Methodius** went to see Constantinople. Filled with awe in St. Sophia cathedral, he said he felt like he was in heaven.
- 987 **Basil**, Macedonian Dynasty, Emperor of the Byzantine Roman Empire [p 14], when facing rebellion in Constantinople, appealed to Vladimir of Kiev for assistance, who agreed provided he could marry a Byzantine princess. Although he already had several wives and 800 concubines, worried Basel agreed to give him his sister Anna in marriage. Anna refused unless Vladimir accepted Christianity and agreed to have only her as his wife. He agreed and in 988 [47, p 50] Vladimir and his people were baptized. Later all Russia became Christian. Many Russian Orthodox churches were built. He ruled **Halicz, Novgorod** and **Suzdal** [12 Vol 10, p 244] [map 38].
- By 1015 **Vladimir was called Tsar** (Czar) emulating Roman **Caesar** [47, p 50]. He compiled the first Kievan Rus **Law Code**, and formed a hierarchical confederation of Russian cities with a son in charge of each.
- 1147 first written mention of **Moscow** [136, p 80], populated by eastern tribes and later by Ruriks [pp 31; 56].

Islamic Influence – 6 th to 8 th Centuries

- About 570 **Mohammed (Muhammad)** was an **Arab** descended from **Ishmael, Abraham's** son by Egyptian **Hagar**, in the **Quraysh** tribe. He felt disillusioned by the Arabs' polytheistic religion, so tried to bring back the monotheism of Abraham. He rejected the Trinity taught by Christians, and forbade all images, paintings and mosaic murals of saints or historical people.
- His inspirations, written in the Quran (Koran) are in the first person directly from Allah (God).
- 610 he declared himself Prophet; began to conquer the middle east. By 630 all Arabia converted to Islam.

- 632 Mohammed died. Their capital was **Medina** [15, pp 28-31; 37, pp 18-19]. The religion is called **Islam** and members of the faith **Muslims** or **Moslems**, but not Mohammedans.
- 632-644 **Abu Bakr** his father-in-law, was chosen **Caliph** (meaning successor in Arabic); died at age 61.
- 634-644 **Omar** I, Mohammed's advisor, was chosen 3 rd Caliph.
- 635 **Damascus** was acquired. Muslim rule spread in the middle east [pp 13-14; map 38].
- 643 building of the Dome of the Rock in Jerusalem began [3]. Omar was murdered 644 [13, pp 46-54].
- 644-656 4th Caliph **Othman (Uthman)** sorted the Qur'an(Koran) into 114 Sûrahs (chapters) [3], not chronological. He was assassinated. **Saracens** (easterners in Greek) was the term Byzantines used for all Muslims, meaning **pirates** in the west. 649 Saracens raided **Cyprus**, and 655 defeated the Byzantines in a sea battle.
- 654 the 5th Caliph **Ali,** Mohammed's cousin and son-in-law married **Fatima**, his daughter. They have long-term influence [12 Vol 4, pp 697-8] as Shi'ites (Shi'ah).
- 661 Ali and his sons were assassinated. A dispute arose over who was the rightful Caliph (successor) of Mohammed. Islam then divided into two major branches of Islam [16, p 732], **Sunni** and **Shi'ah.**

Sunnis collected **Sunnas** (oral tradition/legends/interpretations/commentaries) ascribed to Muhammed.

Shi'ahs insisted the Caliph must be a descendant of Ali and rejected the Sunna held sacred by Sunnis.

Shi'ah Imams have much authority, but **Sunni Imams**' role is to lead prayer in the Mosque(Musjid).

- 660 the **Omayyad (Umayyad)** dynasty was begun by **Caliph Muawiyah** (Mu'awiya) governor of Syria, son of an administrator under Mohammed, a prominent merchant of the same tribe, **Quraysh.**
- 661-750 the capital was transferred to the thriving city **Damascus**. Despite the Shi'ite/Sunni schism, Islam aided by the Syrian army, quickly spread into **Persia** (Iran), **Arabia**, **Syria** and **Egypt**, assimilating their skills, scholarship and services [12 Vol 12, p 121].
- 684-705 **Abd al-Malik** the greatest **Omayyad**, expanded his rule into central Asia, west **India** and **Spain.** He improved communications in the empire, introduced standard coinage, reorganized the government, completed building the Dome of the Rock [13, p 54] and made **Arabic the only official language**.
- 694 Arabs overran **Armenia.**
- 698 **Saracens** captured **Carthage**, North Africa, <u>a Byzantine city</u>, and from there raided **Italy** [maps 6, 20].
- 705-715 during the rule of **Caliph al-Walid**, Muslims <u>conquered much of the Byzantine Empire</u>, including all of North Africa and converted the **Berbers** to Islam. **Constantinople** remained the Byzantine capital but their empire was much reduced in size [See pp 13-14 and 19].
- 711 Muslim **Moors** of N Africa conquered most of Visigothic **Iberia (Spain)** [12 Vol 2, p 745] maps pp xiii-xv, 6.
- 720 they invaded south France.
- 732 **Charles Martel**, grandfather of Charlemagne, routed the Muslims from France [167, pp 48-52] [see p 11].
- By 750 **Saracens controlled Mediterranean trade routes**, thus hampering world commerce of **Italian** families/city states. To reach Constantinople, Italians traded along the **Danube** and rivers of **Russia** to the **Black Sea**[8, pp 34-37, 55-57]. Rivers of Europe were well known & colonized by **Viking** raiders/traders [map 31].
- 750 the Umayyads were overthrown due to internal unrest. Though people of many cultures were Muslims, only Arabs were allowed to hold office in government. Some escaped to **Spain**; set up a Caliphate in **Cordova.**
- 750-945 the **Abbasids**, descendants of an uncle of Mohammed, were powerful Sunni rulers. With their capital at **Baghdad, Syria** since 762, close to Persia, the Abbasids cultivated the intellectual and cultural heritage of Persia, though considered worldly by Arabs. Persian scholars were interested in **Greek Classics.** During Abbasid rule, works of **Ptolemy, Euclid, Hippocrates** and **Galen.**[13, p 89] were <u>translated into Arabic</u>.
- **Aristotle's philosophy** was applied in all fields of thought. There was <u>a great expansion of knowledge</u> in the sciences, philosophy, arts and literature [47, p 50-53]. Baghdad became one of the greatest cities in the world. **Greek** writings greatly influenced Arabic scientific thought [13]. Prosperity and culture advanced.
- New discoveries by Baghdad scholars were added to <u>medical and mathematical knowledge</u>**.** Vast quantities of literature on law, poetry, philosophy and Koranic commentary were produced in <u>Arabic</u>, the <u>official language</u>, <u>unifying peoples of many languages</u>. **All Muslims were obliged to learn Arabic**, <u>and still are today</u>. Schools for boys were called **Madrassas.**
- 945 the rough tribal **Buyid** family from Northern Persia **conquered Baghdad** but retained **Abbasid Caliphs** as figurehead rulers and until 1055 ruled Baghdad.
- 901-999 the **Samanid** family from central Asia **ruled Persia** but acknowledged the Abbasid Caliphs as spiritual Sunni leaders. Scholars continued to develop medicine, mathematics and astronomy[12 Vol 2, p 745].
- 956 **Seljuk Turks** from central Asia, <u>descendants of the</u> **Great Khan Oghuz,** converted to Sunni Islam and sought to eradicate Shi'ite Islam. They defeated **Afghanistan** and east **Persia** [21, pp 43-67] [maps 20, 24, 38].

- In the 10th century the influence of Baghdad on the vast Muslim empire began to wane. An army could not be raised as before, so **Berber**, **Slav** and **Turkish mercenaries** were hired [13, p 80-81; 12 Vol 1, p 10], but were less loyal.

The Arab Empire split into several smaller Caliphates

The majority of Muslims were and are Sunni, but the major caliphates were Shi'ah.
1. **Persia - the Samanid Caliphate** 901- 999, revived Persian culture. They were Shi'ites, descendants of Ali. 980-1037 a renowned physician and philosopher **Avicenna (Ibn Sina)** wrote medical books that expounded on those of **Greek Physician Galen** 200-130 BC [47, p 52-53]. His medicine and pharmacology text book was translated into Latin, Arabic and Hebrew. These translations, plus his book that added to Aristotle's science & philosophy, were highly influential during the middle ages in Europe and the middle east [9, p 199].
2. **Egypt - the Fatimid Caliphate** 909-1171, Shi'ite descendants of **Mohammed's daughter Fatima** and Ali the 5th Caliph, kept trying to overthrow the Abbasids. By 920 they ruled Tunisa, North Africa, and by 969 the Nile Valley, Sinai, Palestine, Mecca, Medina, Yemen and Syria. In **Cairo** their capital they founded **al-Azhar Seminary** and colleges. Students from afar were trained as instructors of **Shi'ite** and **Ismaili** doctrines, aiming to overthrow Sunni theology. The Caliph was both Emperor and Imam (spiritual head). Red Sea trade with Asia expanded. However the majority of ordinary people **remained Sunni** in outlook [12 Vol 4, pp 697-8; Vol 2, p 745].
3. **Morocco - a Shi'ite Caliphate** [13, p 80-81, 89] governed the Moors, who gave their name to Morocco, descended from Arabs and Berbers. They peopled **Algiers** and **Tunisia** and rule **Spain** from 711 to 1492 [16, pp 504-6].
4. **Spain** - the court in **Cordova** flourished; had a library of 400,000 books [13, p 81-89] [See pp 19-20; map 20].
- 976 the University of Cordova was the most important academic institution in the world [95, p 119] [p 36].
5. **Indian Ocean** - Contact from Europe to the middle and far east was by caravans overland to ports on the Persian Gulf, Arabian Sea and Indian Ocean. Shipbuilding was advanced in the far east [more p 50-52].
- Since Muslims controlled trade routes, churches established in South India by St. Thomas, disciple of Jesus, and Syrian Christians settled in India, lost contact with the Church in Constantinople [117, pp 21-22].

A Saxon Dynasty Ruled Central Europe More than a Century 918-1024

- 899-911 **Louis** III was the last German Carolingian. Electors (leading princes)elected a Saxon [pp 12-13]
- 911-918 Conrad; 918-936 **Saxon Henry** 1 was respected also by Franks along the Mainz River (arises in the east and runs west into the Rhine). He subdued the **Bavarians** and **Swabians** and later the Duke of Lorraine (**Alamans**) and signed a nine-year truce with the **Thuringians** and **Hungarians**. During this time of peace he built massive military fortifications and towns in strategic places, revived old Roman towns and gathered burghers (civilians) into thriving new market towns along the Rhine, Mainz and Danube rivers. Romanesque art and construction flourished [p 20]. Doctrines of Christ & the Old Testament were taught in art and drama.
- Henry I created **Knights**, a new traveling cavalry, with property and status attached to fortifications, in exchange for their loyalty. He bestowed a title on the Duke of **Burgundy**, and in return received a **relic**, the lance used to pierce Jesus' side, as well as a special black and gold banner. This banner began to unify diverse Germanic peoples. Henry I was popular with peasants, burghers, knights and nobles. Henry's son:
- 936-973 **Otto** I crowned by the archbishop at Mainz, in 951 married daughter of king of Burgundy, widow of Lothar King of Italy. Thus he **became king of Franks & Lombards**. He developed good relationships by sending diplomats to every dukedom and endowing bishops and abbots with rich estates. Castles, monasteries and churches were built along the northern and eastern borders. Otto revived the **Eastern March;** gave the title of **Margrave** to the administrator [9, Vol 3, p 111]. **Austria** emerged politically; he also became Duke of **Bavaria**. 955 Otto drove **Magyar** invaders east [p 30] to the area now known as **Hungary.**
- 962 **Otto** I was crowned Holy Roman Emperor by the Pope [p 15] since with his powerful army he restored order among noble **Italian** families of independent cities, vying with each other. Highway travel became safe.
- 973-983 **Otto** II married **Theophano** the highly educated daughter of the **Byzantine Emperor**. She brought Greek culture and science into Germany. 978 at war with Lothair of France, Otto sacked Aix-la Chappelle.
- 982-3 Otto II was defeated by **Saracens** in southern Italy. Their son: Otto III was only three years old; his mother Theophano was Regent. Various other dukedoms ruled in their own regions, until:
- 996-1002 **Otto** III crowned Emperor, made pilgrimage to Rome fearing, like many people that the **end of the world** and the **Day of Judgement** would come in 1000 [7, p 19]. (1000 years later many had similar fears of worldwide catastrophe from failure of computers at midnight Dec 31, 1999!)
- 1002-1024 cousin **Henry** II succeeded - the last king in the Saxon dynasty [Continued p 21].

Chapter Four - 600 to 999 AD

Architecture of The Early Middle Ages

Architecture of the Visigoths

- 401-3 the Visigoths (west Goths)[15, p 296], a Teutonic tribes were living near the Danube River (map xiv).
- 410 they plundered Rome and lived in Italy for some time. There they learned the building methods of the Italians. They added their own impressive skill of **gold and jewel inlay**.
- 507 moving west they established a Gothic kingdom in Toulouse, south Gaul and Castile, Spain (map xvi).
- By 587 they converted to Christianity/intermarried/ assimilated with Celts and Romans [28b, pp 20, 27, 54, 330].

The churches that Visigoths built were in **Roman basilica style**, ornately decorated:

- outside with rows of <u>geometric wheels, flower and bird patterns</u>, and
- inside with elaborate <u>gold & jewel inlaid murals</u>.
- columns carved with <u>scroll-work</u> and <u>topped with capitals</u>, engraved with <u>Bible story heroes</u>, such as Daniel in the lions' den.
- Visigoths controlled most of Spain until 711, when Muslim **Moors** from north Africa took the south [28b, p 20].

Early Medieval Church Growth

- 590-604 **Gregory** I born about 540, is generally regarded as the **first Pope**. He restored civil order after war, the Black Death, floods and anarchy. He used the resources of his vast family estates to bring relief to thousands who were starving. He lived simply. His influence was established over the churches of Italy, Spain, Gaul & England. He sent **Augustine** to Christianize England. He influenced building of monasteries [p 10].
- 859 due to many differences in belief and practice and geographic distance, the church split in two, west and east, the **Roman Catholic Church** <u>using Latin</u> and ruled by the Pope. Priests were expected to be celibate.

The **Byzantine Eastern Church** <u>using Greek</u>, became known as the **Greek Orthodox Church** and had several archbishops called **Metropolitans** or **Patriarchs**, but the chief authority was decentralized in the Synods. Each province had its own autonomous leadership. Clergy were encouraged to marry.

- 381, 451, 553, 680-681 and periodically, Ecumenical Councils were called with east & west representation, to formulate the Creeds (articles of Faith), the use of images and icons, and to take action on heresies.

Early Islamic Influence in the Middle East [Continued from p 17]

- 956 **Seljuk Turks** from central Asia, descendants of the Great Khan Oghuz, converted to Sunni Islam and sought to eradicate Shi'ite Islam. They defeated Afghanistan and east Persia [21, pp 43-67] [maps 20, 24, 38].
- Mohammed, born about 570, in 610 declared himself Prophet and began to conquer the middle east.

In 532 he died. His successors were called **Caliphs**. They spread their rule across **North Africa**, and were invading central and eastern Europe [pp 16-18].

- Muslim places of worship are called **Masjids** (**Mosques**). They were designed as shady arcades or shelters with pillars and arches in Hellenic (Greek) style, and a flat roof, surrounding a large open court. It was essential to have fountains or water spouts (to wash their hands and feet) [83, pp 2-6, 16, 20]. In the arcades there was space to rest, read or get acquainted, and for travelers and camels to spend the night. At one side was a larger prayer hall, with a high raised pulpit [83, p 10]. High towers called **minarets** were built at the four corners. One of them was very tall, slender and contained a narrow spiral stair winding up to the top. Five times a day the **muezzin** (a man with a loud resonant voice) climbed to the top and called the people to prayer. Some would come to the masjid. Others spread a mat anywhere facing east and prostrated in the prescribed prayer ritual.
- **No pictures or statues** of people were allowed, because they were **considered idolatry**. Elaborate flowers and calligraphy from their holy book, the Qur'an (Koran) became more and more beautiful.
- Gradually **Greek** and **Byzantine** architecture and **domes** were included in the building of masjids.

Islamic Architecture and Scholarship in Southern Spain [See p 18; maps xv and 20]

- 711 Muslims (**Moors**) from North Africa conquered Spain; built castles and controlled most of the **Iberian** (**Spanish**) peninsula. Gradually they were driven back. 732 Frank **Charles Martel** saved the rest of western Europe from Muslims conquest. 750 **Granada** [3, p 750] was founded [16, p 298]. 753 the **Emirate of Córdoba** was founded by Abd al Rahman. 785-990 the Great Mosque, Córdoba (**Cordova**) built with cooling fountains [3, p 85];
- 930 became the seat of Arab learning, science and industry. 968 Córdoba University [3, p 118; 13, pp 82-89] founded/ by 976 developed the greatest library and centre of learning in the world, with Greek, Persian, Jewish and Muslim scholars [Continued p 36].

Romanesque Style of Architecture

- About 800 Romanesque architecture was begun in north Italy, based on Ostrogothic architecture [p 5] of **Ravenna**, and modified from ancient Roman basilicas and public buildings. There were elaborate mosaics made of tiny bits of colored marble, inlaid with gold and gems, as well as colorful enameled murals. This combined Greek, Byzantine and Roman art and architecture, as well as the arts and crafts of Frankish tribal heritage, notably stone and metal work inlaid with jewels, as well as vaulted roofing skills [p 9].
- Other innovations such as bell towers and galleries were added.
- See photographs of ancient churches in Altet [23, pp 84-94;148-149], and [24, Edward Norman pp 118-119, 128].
- 771-814 **Charlemagne** ruled most of what is now France & Germany; his ancestors were Germanic Franks.
- 796 be built the outstanding Palatine Chapel at **Aix-la-Chapelle (Aachen)** [23, p 127] [See p 12].
- 800 he was crowned Holy Roman Emperor. He conquered all of Europe. His aim was to revive Roman culture, so he actively encouraged the building of Romanesque Basilicas throughout the empire, adapting the old Roman style [23, pp 127-184 and 223-230]. Under the apse (a semi-circular addition at the front) was a large crypt for graves of important people and the veneration of relics. In the late 10th century 40 new Romanesque cathedrals and churches were built. They were located along rivers, for ease of transportation.
- To seat the monks, the basilica rectangle was made cross-shaped, with a small extension on each side, near the altar end. The monks sat in one side and the choir (also monks) in the other. Many little chapels or altars were added along the sides of the long rectangular nave. At the entrance were vestibules and reception areas for pilgrims/travelers and for segregated **lepers**. Completion of construction took many years [more p 33].
- Many Romanesque churches were built in northern Spain [42b, pp 68-69, 248].

Map: *Europe in 800 AD* [9b, p 184]. Charlemagne's vast empire pushed Slavs and Magyars back to the east, civilized Saxons, Bavarians and Lombards, and kept Muslims in Spain. [Compare maps xv, 6 and 2

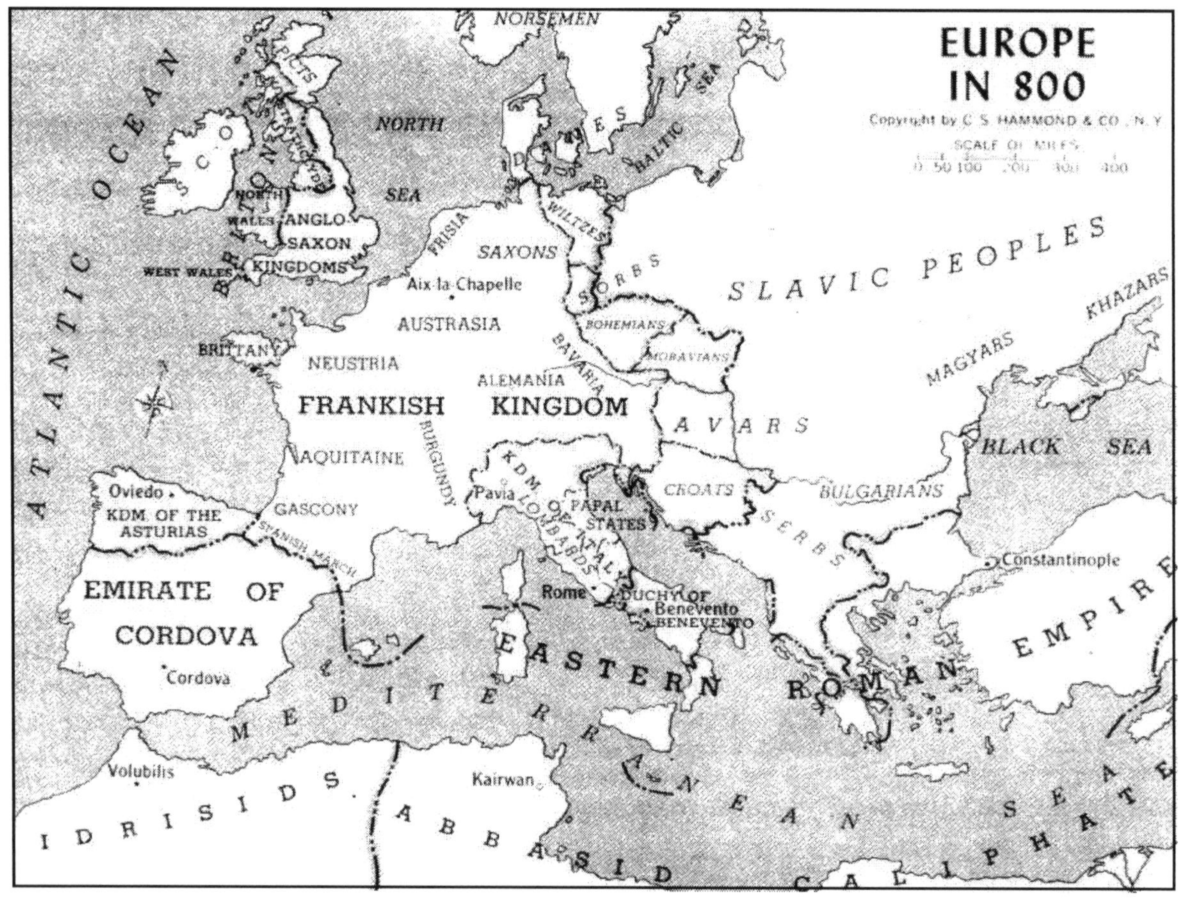

Chapter Five - 1000 to 1299

The Crusades And Middle Ages Migrations

Monastic and Church Reform

- 529 **Benedict** wrote **the *Rule*** on which monastic life in western Europe is based [p 6 & 10]. Every monastery was independent. There was no central governing body. Following of the *Rule* was voluntary. Those monasteries that followed it became centres of devotion, learning, copying of manuscripts and agricultural innovations. They were also places of refuge and of the healing arts.
- As early as the 800's many European noble families founded **monasteries.** Some monks became wealthy and then lax in their discipline. Bishops were often appointed by ruling families and usually were not learned. There were ungodly popes who bought their appointment. Some openly had mistresses and appointed their sons as bishops. There was much corruption [45, pp 774-776]. Church reform was felt necessary by many people.
- 910 a monastery was founded at **Cluny**, province of **Burgundy**, by **Duke William** I of **Aquitaine**, in SW France. Abbot **Odo** was the strong leader who brought about a reform movement that spread to other monasteries. A key to success was its freedom from interference from any lord. Duke William, called **the Pious**, conscientiously surrendered all rights he & his heirs might have had as founder [13, pp 90-91] [maps p 6, 10].
- **Hugh** the Great, summoned Abbot Odo to reform the monastery at Fleury. This in turn became a major centre for reform. Hugh's son Hugh was elected king, who founded the **Capetian Dynasty** [See below p 22].
- By the **late eleventh century** there were over **200 Cluniac houses**. Well administered periodic visits were made to the houses located in ten provinces.
- One key of success in bringing about reform was this built-in supervision. Another means for renewal was that all of the priors met at Cluny annually for a spiritual convocation. Cluny became the centre of a movement to reform the church of laxity, immorality and **Simony** (buying and selling of church office). Thus prestige of monasticism rose high. Its leaders were influential in church & lay affairs. Later with growing wealth, the Cluny Abbey was ornamented richly. This was looked upon by critics as a betrayal of monastic vows of poverty [13, pp 90-81; 122-125] [Map p 10].
- 1098 the **Cistercian Order**, based on early Benedictine rule, was founded by reform-minded **Benedictine** monks in Burgundy. They built a monastery and started a reform movement. By the mid-twelfth century 400 **Cisterian monasteries** were built throughout Europe. [Map: p 10]
- 1002-1024 **Henry** II was the last Saxon king [p 18].

East Franks Ruled by Salian (Salic) West Franks for 100 Years - 1024 to 1125

- 1024-39 **Conrad** II a West **Salian Frank Count**, was elected king by Germanic nobles and freemen, in a ceremony near the Rhine River. In Rome he was crowned **Holy Roman Emperor**. On Knowledge Television Network February 18, 2000 an excellent video entitled *Out of the Dark Ages* showed the lifestyle of the era and Conrad II's actual crown, orb and sword, ornately inlaid with precious stones and pearls, and also believed imbedded with pieces of the cross and a nail from the crucifixion of Christ.
- Conrad II was a very mobile king, touring all over the empire with his government, magistrates, soldiers and their wives and children [pp 5 & 11-13]. He pushed back the border of **Poland**. He added **Bavaria** and **Swabia** to France. He built a Romanesque style Abbey church, the walls still standing today.
- Succeeding kings in this dynasty were **Henry** III, IV and V, his son, grandson and great grandson. All were Holy Roman Emperors. There were power struggles between emperors and popes.
- 1109 Henry V invaded Silesia (SW Poland) but was repulsed [See re Poland pp 27-28].

Norman Conquest of Northern France, England and Southern Italy [See map p 24]

- 911 aggressive Normans (Norse; Northmen) established the **Dukedom of Normandy**, with **Rouen** capital and **Robert** 1 (**Rollo**) as Duke [p 13] in a treaty with the Carolingian king. They soon spoke French [p 27].
- 1010-1189 Normans **Robert** & **Roger** helped Byzantines drive Saracen Arabs from **Italy** and **Sicily** [13, p 119].
- 1089-1154 **Roger** II built up prosperous **Palermo** in Sicily, influenced by **Jewish, Greek** and **Muslim** cultures. He mentored Al-Idrisi the Muslim geographer who wrote *the **Book of Roger*** [pp 23, 32 & 36].
- 1041-1066 English king **Edward the Confessor**; 1052 built Westminster Abbey; dedicated 1065 [16, p 216].
- 1066-1087 **William** I **the Conqueror** from Normandy subjugated and ruled **England**: his son:
- 1087-1100 **William** II **Rufus**; 1078-1300 built the **Tower of London**, basilicas and monasteries; Westminster Abbey was completed in 1245-69 in the finest Gothic style [16, p 330, 812] by Henry III [p 33].

- 1100-1135 **Henry** I a son of William the Conqueror, developed the **English system of justice**. This meant lasting cultural change to England with 70 years of efficient strong rule [13, p 118].
- The **Normans** introduced **feudalism** and knighthood and fought in the Crusades. There they learned how to build massive castles.
- 1135 **Matilda (Maud)** daughter and heir of Henry I married **Geoffrey,** Count of **Anjou (Angevin)**. Thus England inherited the large province of Anjou including the capital city **Angers**, northwest of Paris [map 44].
- 1135-1154 **Stephen** her cousin, usurped the crown, but agreed to appoint as his successor her son Henry of Anjou [16] surnamed **Plantagenet**, meaning broom plant. This dynasty **ruled England until** 1399.
- 1154-1189 **Henry** II Plantagenet of **Anjou**, Duke of Normandy became king of England. He had enlarged the Anjevin Empire by his marriage to **Eleanor, heiress of Aquitaine**, SW France [20, p 56] [map 44]. Her first husband was **Capetian Louis** VII of France (see below).
- Henry II ruled **England, Ireland,** and more than half of **France** for 35 years.
- In Anjou Henry II **built Hospital St. Jean**, and a massive palace [9 Vol 2, pp 129-30, 159-60] and helped build a magnificent cathedral. He made **legal reforms** [49, pp 54-61]. Although he was anti-clerical he appointed as Chancellor, Archbishop **Thomas à Becket**, who later opposed him and was murdered [16].
- Two sons of Henry II and Eleanor became kings of England and much of France, **Richard** I and **John** [p 33].
- 1189-1199 **Richard** I the Lion Heart, also Duke of Aquitaine, **a leading Crusader**, won <u>a treaty from the Muslims</u>, that <u>allowed pilgrims to visit holy places</u>. Though king 10 years he was in England but a few months. Returning from the Crusades he was imprisoned in Austria and Germany 1192-4. [20, pp 56, 64, 118]. [p 24-25]
- 1199-1216 King **John** lost control of Normandy. Then barons demanding a part in decisions, in 1215 forced him to sign the **Magna Charta**. John failed to keep the Angevin Empire united [20, p 56, 64, 118; 16, p 384].
- 1204 **Capetian Philip** II Augustus, acquired **Anjou;** by 1223 took much of France from the English [map 44].
- 1216-1272 **Henry** III, John's son, inherited the crown when he was 9 years old. He built 60 castles, 20 lodges and palaces and **Westminster Abbey**! He received the gift of an elephant, amazing to the English.
- 1258-64 the Barons forced Henry III to hand over government. The **House of Commons** was established. He was imprisoned. 1265 his son **Edward** I took back government leadership.
- 1272-1307 **Edward** I founded **Common Law**, and was **known as the English Justinian**. Parliament became a partnership between [49, pp 54-61, 80-1, 90] the king, his barons, knights from every shire and representatives from towns. <u>Taxation could only be levied with consent of Parliament</u>. He conquered **Wales** and **Scotland** [p 43].

Meanwhile the Capetian Dynasty Ruled France 350 Years - 967 to 1328

- 967-996 **Hugh Capet** descended from Franks, was elected king of a small district around Paris. The rest of France was ruled by powerful local lords. Hugh Capet's descendants became a hereditary monarchy:
- 996-1031 **Robert** II the Pious; 1031-1060 **Henry** I. Each Capetian king had his own son crowned king before his decease, thus <u>ensuring an unbroken succession</u>, and therefore a <u>stable regime</u>. Previously like German kings, French kings were elected. By providing protection and privileges to nobles they gradually came to rule all of France. They were not aggressive but developed basic administrative institutions and a central representative assembly. The towns and merchants prospered.
- The Capetians did **not** gain control of **Aquitaine** (SW), **Burgundy** (SE). **Flanders** and **Brittany** in northern France [9 Vol 2, p 225] [p 43; map p 44].
- Aquitaine was named by the Romans, ruled by the Visigoths for a time and later ruled by Frank Dukes.
- 1071-1126 **William** X, the last Duke of **Aquitaine**, & his daughter **Eleanor** only heir, were **troubadours** (trouvère in French) [16], writing and singing poetry about love, religion & war, in their own language.
- 1137-80 **Capetian Louis** VII Eleanor's first husband, ruled France. Louis and Eleanor, with her ladies, **went on the Second Crusade** to Antioch 1147-49 [13, p 134-5] [p 24]. She learned Byzantine life style and held an elegant court. Since she had no children, Louis arranged for annulment by the pope. Five years later:
- 1152 Eleanor married **Henry Plantagenet**, Count of Anjou, Duke of Normandy.
- 1154 he **became Henry** II **King** of **England** so Aquitaine came under English rule. <u>Thus England ruled more than half of France</u>. Two sons, **Richard** and **John** later ruled England [above and p 33].
- 1180-1223 **Capetian Philip** II **won back Anjou** and much of **France** [20, p 56]. Allied with towns and merchants he organized good administration, modeled by successors. Members of the Capetian royal family of France became Counts of **Anjou, Navarre** and **Provence**. Dukes of **Anjou**, **Burgundy & Brittany** were elected <u>professional rulers</u> of **Hungary**, **Naples** and **Constantinople**.
- 1223-25 **Louis** VIII **of France** invaded England during the reign of **King John** [pp 33 and 43].

- 1226-70 **Capetian Louis** IX devoted to justice and saintly living, was **canonized St. Louis** [12 Vol 2, pp 108-109, 829].
- 1270-85 Capetian **Philip** III died of plague. 1285-1314 Capetian **Philip** IV struggled with Pope Boniface VIII; strengthened the French crown. Clement V was elected pope. **Philip** IV of France won the new pope over by bribery and arranged the pope's coronation in Lyon [49, p 80].
- 1307 **Pope Clement** moved the papal court to **Avignon, France** [49, p 80]. More **Capetian** kings:
- 1314-16 Capetian **Louis** X; 1316 **John** II (Jean); 1316-22 **Philip** V; 1322-8 **Charles** III [12 Vol 4, p 920; Vol 2, p 829];
- 1328-50 Philip **VI** of the **Valois Dynasty,** a cousin of Capetian Phillip II, succeeded the last Capetian.
- 1337 **The Hundred Years' War** began [p 45]. 1589-95 the **House of Bourbon** ruled until the French Revolution but the Capetian name continued: 1774-92 Louis XV1 was jeered a Frank Capet, when guillotined.

The Middle East in the Eleventh Century [See pp 2-3, 5; 13-14 and 16-18]

- 976-1014 **Czar Samuel of Bulgaria** expanding his borders kept **Romanians** north of the Danube River.
- 976-1025 **Byzantine Emperor Basel** II ruled 50 years; invaded by nomadic Bulgarians; Byzantine soldier-farmers began to command their own armies and ignore the emperor [8, p 53]. To put down rebels in 988 Basel II received help from **Prince Vladimir**, ruler of **Kiev, Russia** [Map p 38], friendly since early 900s when Basel's sister married Vladimir, who with his people became Christians. By 1014-18 Basel II gradually defeated the **Bulgars** and they became Christians [18, pp 49-50]; 1018 he ruled Macedonia; recaptured parts of **Syria** and **Iraq** from Muslims; recovered **Armenia** from the **Persians**.
- 1032 **Sicily** was recaptured; 1028-34 **Romanus** III poisoned by Empress Zoe, wife of **Michael** IV;
- 1034-41 **Michael** IV; 1042-54 **Zoe** married **Constantine** IX and was co-emperor; 1056-7 Michael V;
- 1054 Supernova, visible 18 months exploded; 1066 Halley's Comet.
- 1054 the eastern church (**Orthodox - Greek**) divided from the western church (**Roman Catholic - Latin**).
- 1030 **Seljuk Turks**, fierce nomadic horsemen from central Asia, who had **subjugated Persia** (Iran) and **Syria** (Iraq), migrated in large numbers into the middle east [see map p 38]; introduced a new kind of government all over central and south Asia and middle east. Though aggressively holding power, Seljuk Turk warriors, led by **Sultans** [21, pp 43-67], formed partnerships [12, Vol 10, p 621], with a nominal Arab Sunni Caliph.
- By 1055 Seljuk Turks were ruling Baghdad and surrounding areas. For hundreds of years Arabs had allowed Christians to make pilgrimages to holy places in Jerusalem for faith healing and to hunt for relics of Christ and saints (fragments of bones, clothing and the cross) to venerate in shrines and cathedrals.
- 1056-9 **Michael** VI last in **Macedonian Dynasty**; 1057 Army officer **Isaac** I founded **Comnenus Dynasty**:
- 1059-67 **Constantine** X Comnenus; 1067-71 **Romanus** IV Comnenus; 1070 the fierce **Sejuk Turks** overran the Holy Land, imprisoned pilgrims and massacred local Christians. Few escaped. They seized most of **Armenia** and **Anatolia** (central Turkey) from the Byzantine Empire. 1064 Hungarians seized Belgrade.
- 1071 Seljuks defeat Byzantines in Manzikert, Anatolia, east of Constantinople, captured Emperor Romanus, but released him. Loss of a huge army and territory was serious; 1078-81 **Michael** VII Comnenus;
- 1081-1118 **Alexius** I and successors renewed Byzantine strength; wrote to the Pope asking for protection of Constantinople[20, pp 78-90] from Seljuks and unruly **Frank plunderers** and **mercenaries** [20, pp 20-27, 58].
- 909-1171 the **Fatimid Caliphate in Cairo** led a flourishing civilization in **Egypt** and **north Africa**.

The Crusades - 177 Years - 1095-1272

- 1095 **Pope Urban** II responded to Emperor **Alexius Comnenus** by a sermon to a meeting of French (Frankish) clergy and nobility: a call to arms to liberate the Holy Land and Holy Sepulcher and give aid to the Byzantines (Greeks), hoping to reunite Latin and Greek churches. He referred to overpopulation in France, but said rather than fight each other for land in France, they should go for estates in the Holy Land. He promised them remission of sins to earn a place in heaven. Deceived by this false teaching, very large numbers responded, so he advised only those able to bear arms to go; women only with a husband or brother.
- 1118-43 Emperor **John** II **Comnenus** ruled. 1101-54 Norman **Roger** II was Count of **Sicily** [p 21, 32].

First Crusade - 1096-99

All participants had a cross sewn on their clothing: origin of the word "crusade". It took time to find committed noblemen to organize, prepare supplies, recruit soldiers and negotiate for Italian merchant ships.
- Meanwhile 40,000 poor people set out on foot with wagons, led by a Polish knight, **Walter Gottschalk**[70] and **Peter the Hermit,** carrying crosses, swords or clubs.

Some crusaders attacked and robbed **Jews** in Cologne, Mainz, Worms, etc. Many Jews were given asylum in Poland. The Crusaders believed that as the army of God, local inhabitants would/should feed them, and many did willingly. When food was not supplied they stole it [37, pp 32-37, 48-55].

- They arrived at Constantinople where the emperor and cultured people were disgusted by their uncouth uneducated behavior, but ferried them across the sea. Attacked by Turks most died of heat and hunger.
- The well-to-do crusaders traveled via Italy to Constantinople, where relations with the Byzantine Emperor were poor, but he did supply provisions when they agreed to return to him cities of Asia Minor that he had lost to the Turks. Communications were often betrayed. Cities won were lost. Italian merchants brought food, troops, horses and siege equipment. Knights and noblemen rode heavy horses.
- **Saracens** (Arab Muslims) fought the Crusaders, rode light rapid ponies, shot arrows with skill while riding, and used clever strategies. Their scimitars (swords) were short, flexible and razor sharp.
- **Assassins** were a few fanatic Persian Muslim terrorists [37, pp 42-43, 54-55, 66-67], who used hashish [49, p 73].
- In Europe castles and forts had been built of wood. The Crusaders quickly built **mobile wooden siege towers**, on which they attacked massive stone castles [37, pp 60-65, 73, 85-91], gained entrance, conquered with terrible bloodshed, **took Jerusalem** and installed **Godfrey**, **Duke of Lorraine** (Bouillon) as king.
- Both Crusaders and Muslims committed cruel atrocities [13, pp 144-157]. Land was seized by nobleman-crusaders and castles built at **Tripoli** in Lebanon, **Antioch** in Syria, and **Edessa**, now Urfa in Turkey [22, pp 22-35].
- **Military-Religious Orders** formed to protect pilgrims: 1113 **St. John "Hospitaller"**; 1119, **Templars**.

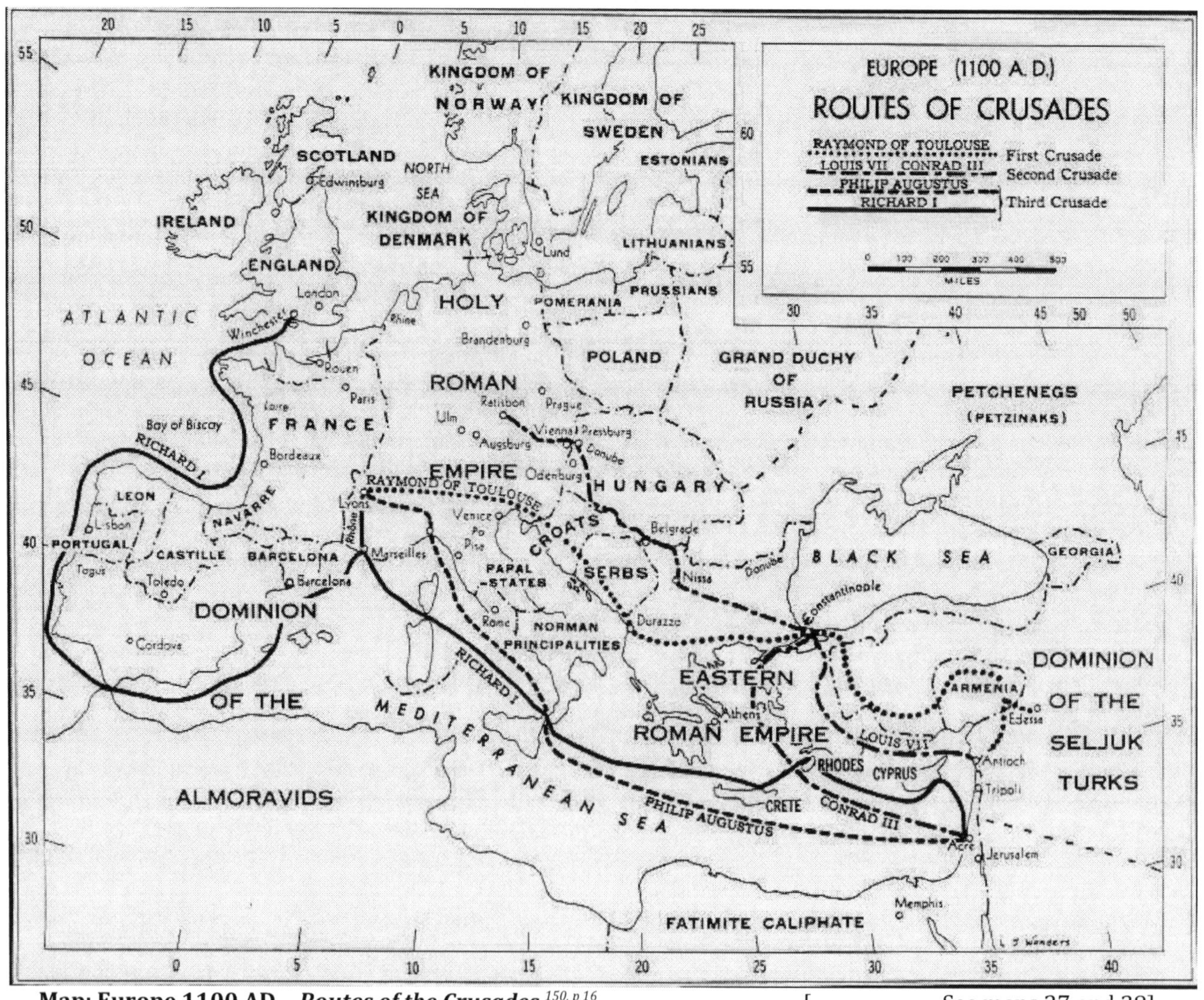

Map: Europe 1100 AD – *Routes of the Crusades* [150, p 16] [See maps 27 and 38]

Second Crusade: 1147-49: was precipitated by the Muslim capture of Edessa in 1144, which merely postponed the fall of Jerusalem. **Louis** VII, king of France, and his queen **Eleanor**, Duchess of **Aquitaine** (southern France) joined this expedition. Europeans learned to dress, bathe, eat fruit and live in a hot climate. She had no children so he arranged with the pope to annul their marriage. She married Henry II of England.
Third Crusade: 1189-92: 1187 Jerusalem fell to **Sultan Saladin:** led by Philip (**France**), Richard the Lion Heart (**England**) son of Henry II & Eleanor [p22, 43] and Frederick Barbarossa (**Germany**). Philip quarreled/ returned to France. Frederick drowned. Richard captured the port of **Acre**, was granted a treaty allowing pilgrims to visit holy places; but returning home was held hostage 2 years in **Austria**. Saladin died 1193.
- 1193-1249 **Al-Malik as-Salih Ayyub** succeeded but he was murdered by **Mamluks** (slave bodyguards).
- 1250-1382 a Turkish **Mamluk dynasty** ruled Egypt and Syria, in a nominal Abbasid regime.
-1190 **Teutonic Knights** were founded in Bremen and Lubeck, Baltic Sea to alleviate suffering in Acre.
Fourth Crusade: 1204: was disabled by the Bubonic Plague [95]. Uneducated **Franks** and **Latins** occupied Greece, took Constantinople, set up a Latin **Romanian** kingdom for 50 years and, believing the Greek mythical story about Aeneas was actual history, looted Byzantine treasures relating to the myth [167, p 70].
From the Byzantines the cruel Crusaders slowly learned merciful treatment of enemies [22, pp 4-22].
Children's Crusade: 1212: About 30,000 boys and girls, mostly preteens, led by a French shepherd boy, convinced unarmed innocence would prevail. Most died en route, or were sold as slaves in Africa [37, pp 80-81].
Sixth Crusade: 1228-29: won Jerusalem back 1228; scholarly Holy Roman Emperor **Frederick** II, could read and write Arabic, negotiated a ten-year truce [49, pp 44-45, 73]. For his other great contributions see pp 26, 27.
Seventh Crusade: 1244: Jerusalem was lost to the Muslims. **Eighth Crusade**-1248-1254: failed.
Ninth Crusade: 1270-1272: was futile. 1291 when **Acre** fell, all Crusaders were evacuated or killed.

1272 The Crusades Ended: Greece remained under the control of European invaders [continued p 32].
- Only the first Crusade was successful. Despite carrying out cruel, misguided warfare, knights who went to the Holy Land learned courtly manners, gentlemanly behavior toward women, first aid and nursing skills, and **a taste for Greek and Arab learning, paving the way for the Revival of Learning.**
- Crusaders seemed unwashed semi-barbarians to cultured Muslims. Banking, decimals, money instead of barter, buying and selling of privilege, and the importing of oriental fruit, silk, cotton, spices, etc., multiplied.
- The Crusades delayed invasion of Europe by the Turks but **earned the scorn of Muslims to this day**.

The Age of Chivalry

- Uncouth, cruel and illiterate Crusader knights and princes gradually became civilized [37, pp 22-29, 38-41, 54-55, 84-85]. Princes, dukes or military leaders would train boys first as **squires** to ride and care for horses, hunt and care for weapons. When they became skilled they were dubbed knights [19, pp 10-37] in a ceremony. Trying to control widespread fighting between rival knights, the church became involved, using the lure of earning a place in heaven by noble good behavior. Noblemen not in a crusade also learned gentle manners, courtesy for ladies and chivalry (archery on horseback).
- With fewer wars knights had tournaments of ritualized combat for entertainment and to hone fighting skills [19, pp 22-23]. On heavy war-horses in heavy armor they charged each other with lances and elaborate rules. Each noble had a coat of arms, registered in the ***Book of Heralds*** [19, pp 18-19].
- The Duke of **Aquitaine** and daughter **Eleanor** were troubadours. She was elegant in the Crusades with first husband Louis VII of France. As Queen she brought folk singing and manners to England [p 22, 24, 43].
- Poets called **troubadours**, composed lyrical poetry to celebrate their love for women, and wrote romances about lovers tested by many separations and adventures. They traveled widely under the patronage of nobles. They sang accompanied by a harp or lute, an instrument played with a bow [19, pp 20-21].
- Arabic harmony with bass & tenor, contrasted with unison singing of traditional Gregorian chants [20, pp 82-89].

Culture, Religion and Education in the Middle Ages

[See Maps pp 10, 20 and 38]

- 1119 the **University of Bologna** was founded; the Medical Faculty in 1150. 1203 in **Siena**;
- 1204 University of **Vicenza** [3] were founded. **Greek philosophy** was studied.
- 1210 **Francis of Assisi**, Italy, started an order in which the monks lived simply, equally as brothers, whether from rich or poor families, imitating Christ. Francis was an artist and poet; saw beauty in nature; traveled about France, Spain and Egypt; developed a chronic eye infection.

- **Franciscans** had thousands of followers; founded houses not monasteries abroad, including in Canterbury, London & Oxford. 1224 the similar order of nuns, the **Poor Clares** was founded.[See pp 10 and 21].
- 1216 in **Spain** the **Dominican Order** was founded by Dominic who realized that ignorance of the clergy was one of the reasons for the spread of heresy. Dominicans toured the large cities of Europe teaching Bible knowledge to refute heresy. They were soon established in the **universities** of Paris and Bologna, Italy.
- 1209 **Cambridge University**, England was established and **Oxford University** in 1249.
- 1214-1292 **Roger Bacon** a Franciscan friar, studied Greek and Arabic science/mathematics; taught in Oxford & Paris; amassed experimental laboratory equipment; invented glasses to correct visual defects [49, p 63]; believed men should use scientific knowledge for power over nature for happier, healthier, longer lives.
- The Crusaders brought back many books and a taste for learning from the middle east. Both Greek and Arabic knowledge added to the intellectual ferment of medieval Europe.
- 1225 Emperor **Frederick** II Hohenstaufen grandson of Barbarosa, **Arabic scholar**, founded the University of **Naples** and **medical school** at **Salerno.** After the Sixth Crusade he negotiated a ten-year truce [p 27].
- In Italy secular men of letters initiated **Humanism** an intellectual movement. Study of human nature emphasized unity and compatibility of truth, S**yncretism**, plus the dignity of man without need of penance. They developed an integrated new body of knowledge. Thus many scholars, feeling freed from old dogma and inspired with confidence in human creative and intellectual ability, began the **Renaissance** [12 Vol 9, p 1020].
- 1254 the **Paris School of Theology** was founded and later called the **Sorbonne**. Church grammar, dogma, logic, arithmetic, geometry, astronomy, music, public speaking and Greek philosophy were taught.
- After 1255 all students were required to read Greek Philosophy of **Aristotle** (384-322 BC). Classics, theology, medicine, law and logic were added to curriculums. This meant learning to read classical Greek, but instruction was in Latin so Boethius' 480-524 Latin translation of **Aristotle** was popular [9 Vol 4,p 186].
- 1225-74 **Thomas Aquinas**, a Benedictine and Dominican studied at University of Naples. He taught philosophy and theology at Rome, Piza, Bologne and Naples emphasizing Aristotle. Aquinas organized know-ledge of his time to reconcile faith with intellect [49, pp 63-71], synthesizing the four sources of knowledge:

Aristotle and other classic Greek sages;
Augustine and other Christian theologians [25, pp 267-271];
Averroes, **Avicenna** and other Islamic scholars; and
Maimonidies, **Solomon ben Yehuda ibn Gabirol** and other Jewish thinkers [9 Vol 2, pp 223-4] [p 36].

- European literature was written in Latin, but people began to write in the languages of their everyday speech. In Provence, southern France, **troubadours** wrote intricate love poetry in their own dialect. Northern French poets wrote songs and poetry to honor exploits of knights. Hardly anyone in Europe could read. Many church officials and monks were barely literate. Ordinary people learned Greek and Roman culture and Bible stories from touring monks, drama groups, troubadours and minstrels [8, p 60-61, 12-13, 16-27].
- 1265-1321 Italian **Dante Alighieri** wrote the influential epic poetic allegory *The Divine Comedy* [49, pp 82-89] which encouraged interest in I**ndividualism**.
- The study of **Roman law** spread to universities. **Legists** (law experts) were appointed advisors to kings.
- 1271 **Marco Polo** about 17 years old, with his merchant father traveled to the court of **Kublai Khan**. Marco was sent by the Khan to China and India [16, p 586]. 1298-9 while a prisoner of the Genoese he wrote about his travels. Marco became a member of the grand council of Venice. Died 1324.

Evolution of the German and French Languages [Continued from pp 4-5]

- Soon after the Franks settled in Gaul, west of the Rhine, they began to assimilate with the Romans and Celtic Gauls. The **Romance language** that emerged consisting of a combination of Latin, Gaul and and several Frank dialects. It became fashionable for Romans to take Frankish names. Gradually the Frank languages evolved into many **French** dialects. Charlemagne spoke French but considered himself German.
- 987 **Hugh Capet** was the first king of France of Frank descent who spoke only French [1, pp 6-8, 28-33, 109-120, 237]. Words of Frank origin still persist in French, especially related to country life, agriculture, colors, government and the military.
- Many Germanic tribes, chiefly Alemanni, Swabish, Norman, Fresian, Burgundian and Visigothic **developed the French language**, but others **developed German dialects**: Anglo-Saxon, Frank, Frisian, Swabish, old High German and Netherlandic.
- By 1100 the first collective name, **Diutisc** (**Deutsch**) was in fashion. A **standard High German evolved** based on **Alemannic** (including several Suebi/Schwab dialects) and **Bavarian**.

Suppression of Religious Freedom: The Inquisition Began

- **Albigenses (Carthari)** in south France read the Bible translated into Latin by Jerome and two ladies; were zealous about self-denial and personal morality; preached against immorality of priests, pilgrimages and worship of saints and images. By 1200 most of the people of S France and N Italy embraced these beliefs.
- 1208 Pope Innocent III ordered a crusade against Albigenses [45, p 785]. It took 100 years to root them out.
- About 1176 **Waldenses** were founded by **Waldo**, a rich merchant who gave his property to the poor and went about southern France and northern Italy preaching from the Bible as the sole rule of life. He rejected the mass, prayers for the dead and purgatory. Large numbers of people believed. Severely persecuted, a few survived in Alpine valleys. Now they are the leading Protestant Church in Italy [45, p 785].
- **Anabaptists** in Germany, Netherlands and Switzerland, in groups not known to each other, were genuinely pious people devoted to the Bible; preferred adult, not infant baptism; taught separation of church and state.
- 1248 the **Inquisition** founded by Pope Innocent IV suppressed heretics (anyone whose beliefs differed from those of the Roman Catholic Church). To counter heresy, **Dominicans** from Toulouse SW France were sent to preach in Italy, Spain, Netherlands, Portugal and overseas [16, p 363] [pp 52-53; 62-63].

Swabian Hohenstaufen Dynasty: Holy Roman Emperors 1125-1254 [from p 13]

- 1138-1152 the German princes elected **Conrad** III, **Duke of Hohenstaufen**, Swabia, as Emperor. **Swabia** (Schwabia) is a southern district near the Rhine and Danube rivers. The **Welf** family ruled Bavaria, east of Swabia. Though closely related, Welfs and Swabians had continual feuds and power struggles.
- 1152-1190 **Frederick** I Swabia, called **Barbarossa** (red beard) an educated descendant of both families, was selected Emperor by German princes; extended his power in Italy. The pope crowned him Holy Roman Emperor. He had **legists** (law school graduates) as advisors, so had conflict with the pope [95 pp 151-8].
- 1190-1197 **Henry** VI was crowned Holy Roman Emperor; built Cathedrals [p 34-35]; married Constance, daughter of **Norman Roger** II of **Sicily** (see pp 21 & 33]. She was mother of Frederick II and regent.
- 1211-50 **Frederick** II Hohenstaufen grandson of Barbarosa, crowned Holy Roman Emperor, inherited **Sicily** and **Naples;** was **educated in Aristotle**, the natural sciences and languages. He studied and **translated Arabic works**, so was able through diplomacy during the Sixth Crusade, to win a ten-year truce from the Sultan of Egypt. This granted access/control of Jerusalem, Bethlehem and Nazareth [pp 25, 26 & 29].
- 1225 he founded the **University of Naples** and endowed a **Medical School at Salerno**. Both men and women students were admitted. Decorations in his palace were of exotic Moslem style fountains and silk hangings [49, pp 44-45, 62-3, 65, 73], and fruit was imported. He had scholars in Melfi codify Norman, Byzantine and Arab laws, appoint judges, control powerful families, collect taxes and develop an efficient state. He struggled years with both pope & Italian city states. 1242 after the Mongol invasion [p 31] he seized the vacant dukedom of **Austria**, leaving nobles to administer his vast German states [p 29]. 1250-54 his son **Conrad** IV ruled. 1250-73 there was no Holy Roman Emperor [95, p173].

Map: ***Europe in 1190 – The Middle Ages*** [46c]

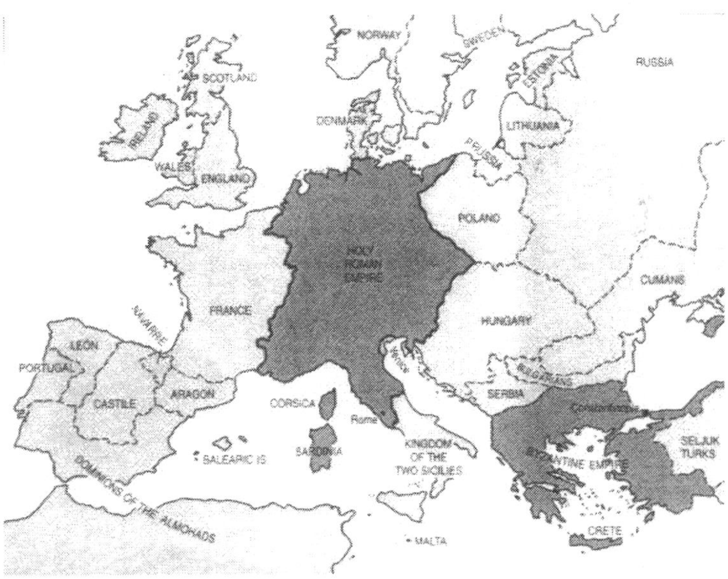

The Founding of Poland as a Nation by the Piast Dynasty [from pp 15-16; map p 38]

- 966-92 **Mieszko I** (Mieczyslav) **Piast Dynasty** unified and founded the country of Poland: **Poznan (Posen** in German) in the NW, **Silesia** in the SW and **Galicia** south. The **Mazovia Plains** in central Poland with headquarters at **Plock** [27, pp 55-6] were added, also spelled **Masowiecki** [27, p 112, 297] or **Mazowsze** [28, p 144].
- Mieszko I gained independence from the German church; capital **Gniezno** near **Poznan** (Posen) [27, pp 10,189].

- 992-1025 oldest son **Boleslaw** I (**Boleslaus**) **the Brave**, succeeded; 994 he conquered **Pomerania** for access to the Baltic Sea; founded a Bishopric at Wroclaw in Silesia.
- 1000 Boleslaw founded **Archbishopric of Gniezno**, with oversight of three bishoprics: **Krakow** in **Galicia**, **Wroclaw** in **Silesia** and **Kolobrzeq** on the **Baltic Sea**. Other churches were built [27], as beautiful as cathedrals. A Benedictine monastary was established in Krakow [28, p 196].
- 1003 Boleslaw extended power into **Bohemia**, **Moravia** [61]; [64]; and probably **Slovakia**, and 1018 into **Kiev**, which ruled much of **Russia**. His son succeeded:
- 1025-33 **Mieszko** II (**Mieczyslav**) inherited power from the **Baltic Sea** to the **Danube River** and much of **Russia**, yet was defeated by German and Russian armies; 6 years' civil war followed. [Maps xvi and 38]:
- 1039-58 **Casimir** I moved the **capital** of Poland to **Krakow** where it remained until 1596 [28, p 144]. The original population was **Vistulan** (**Wislanie**) **Slavs**. The region is called **Malopolska** (Little Poland).
The Vistula River rising south of Krakow [27, p 39, 58-9, 225] flows to the Baltic Sea.
Casimir gained power in central Poland and Silesia.
- 1058-81 Casimir's son **Boleslaw** II **the Bold**, of Poland took **Kiev** 1067 [3], but 1077 while he was in Russia, the Polish nobles rebelled. 1079-1102 **Ladislas** I **Hermann** was king of Poland; abdicated hoping for peace.
- 1102-38 **Boleslaw** III, Wrymouth, recovered **Pomerania,** including seaport **Gdansk** (**Danzig** in German).
- 1109 Germans led by **Holy Roman Emperor Henry** V invaded **Silesia**; were repulsed by Boleslaw [27, p 10].
- 1138 when Boleslaw III died **Poland divided** among his **four sons** which fragmented unity until 1320 [27, p 10]. Duke of **Mazovia** (**Masowiecki**) ruled the central to NE plains, later called **Warsaw** district.

Northern Poland Ruled by Feudal Dukes and Teutonic Knights [Maps pp 6, 38 and 61]

- 1138-1320 Poland remained divided among Slavic and German feudal dukes, noblemen and knights [27, p 10]. With immigration towns & nobility of **Pomerania** (Pomorze)& **Posen** (**Poznan**) were Germanized [12 Vol 9, p 588].
- Germany remained hundreds of independent duchies, states and cities until the 19th century. Because German and Polish kings and states lacked unity [6, pp 76-87], cities along the Baltic Sea in the north joined the **Hanseatic League** and those in the west the **League of Rhenish Towns** (Rhine).
- 1211-1225 the **Third Crusade** against Muslims in Palestine ended, so the **Teutonic Knights** returned to Europe; had possessions in several regions. They were invited to help defend **Hungary**, but after 14 years they came into conflict with **Hungarian King Andrew** II, and were expelled [12 Vol 11, pp 661-2; 98, p 63].
- 1226 **Duke Conrad of Mazovia** (**Masowiecki**) in central and NE Poland, asked the Teutonic Knights for protection from the **native Prus** who were attacking, promising them all the lands they conquered [98, p 63].
- 1230 twelve knights, who were German noblemen, arrived with many armed followers who were skilled farmers, craftsmen and builders.
- They brought more farmers from the **lowlands** of **Schleswig/Holstein**, north **Hanover** & **Mecklenburg**, west of **Poland** [map p 38], who spoke **Plautdeitsch** (**low German**) dialects.
- 1234 Pope Gregory IX commissioned the Teutonic Knights to convert the pagan **Prus** tribe [49, p 45] and he granted them papal land in perpetual tenure [12 Vol 11, pp 661-2]. Also Holy Roman **Emperor Frederick** II (the last Hohenstaufen [p 27] granted them land in the Vistula River delta and ordered them to conquer the **Prus**.
- 1237 the **Knights of the Sword** in **Livonia** and **Latvia** united with the Teutonic Knights [12 Vol 11, pp 661-2].
- 1239-40 **Alexander Nevski** of the Russian **Rurik Dynasty** won access to the Baltic Sea from the **Swedes**; drove the Teutonic Knights from **Novgorod**, NW **Russia**, keeping them out two centuries [20, pp 57-91] [p31].
- 1240-41 **Mongols** (**Tatars** or **Tartars**) from central Asia, led by **Genghis Khan**, invaded and defeated **Russia**, **Poland** and **Hungary**. The cities of **Krakow** (in Galicia) and **Wroclaw** (in Silesia) were destroyed and **Piast Prince Henry** the Pious, the heir to the throne, was killed [27, p 58 and 71]. Rebuilding was quick.
- 1242 occupation and **domination of southern Russia** by the **Golden Horde** began [63]; (Mongols, wearing gold-colored turbans) terrorized Russia. They occupied lands along the north of the Black Sea; demanded tribute; drained Russian economy and delaying their progress for over 200 years [maps p 37].
- After conquering land along the Baltic Sea, **Teutonic Knights** turned SE, under papal authority to conquer heathen Russia and extend the boundaries of Christendom; drive **Turks** from province of **Volhynia** (**Wolinsk** or **Wolinien**), homeland of **Wollin**, a Slavic people, west of Kiev [65] (now north half of **Ukraine**).
- To keep Turks out of Volhynia, knights invited German farm families to develop old estates. Landlords spoke German and Slavic dialects; assimilated as Polish noblemen of feudal estates, with serfs.
- 1261-83 the Knights captured **Estonia**, thus becoming rulers all along the **Baltic Sea** from **West** to **East** Poland and Prussia, exterminating most of the native **Prus** [maps pp 37 and 38].

- The Knights resettled depopulated Prus areas with German farmers, landlords & artisans, building 10,000 villages, allowing democratic village self-government and religious freedom [62; 64; 66; 67] as in their home communities. Towns were granted autonomy; estates were bestowed on German and Polish nobles, but they became vassals to the Teutonic order. Teutonic knights had a monopoly on grain trade [12 Vol 11, pp 661-2].
- Towns and cities were built up by German businessmen and artisans. **Posnan (Posen)** [27, p 80] in the west, and **Gdansk (Danzig)** [27, p 88] on the Baltic Sea thrived [map p 38]. Fine Romanesque and Gothic town halls, cathedrals & churches were constructed in Posen, Plock & other towns, and later by 1400 in **Warsaw**.
- 1276 Teutonic Knights built mammoth **Marienburg (Malbork) fortress** [28, pp 401-479] at the mouth of the Vistula River, in **Pomerania (Pommern** or **Pomorze)** as headquarters for knights and their horses.
- 1293 the **Kingdom of Lithuania** became independent and expanded eastward. It had been created by the Teutonic Knights as a buffer state [49, p 100] [See Map p 38].
- 1138-1320 Poland remained divided among feudal dukes, noblemen and knights [27, p 10] [pp 41-42].

Meanwhile Southern Poland was Influenced by Neighboring Countries

* Poland's SW province of **Galicia**, has a southern boundary of high mountains: Carpathian-Tatra Ranges.
* South of the mountains, from west to east, were **Czechs (Bohemians), Moravians** and **Slovaks**.
* Further south **Austrians, Hungarians** and **Serbs** kept changing boundaries [maps pp 24, 27, 37, 38, 55].

- 1038 **Krakow**, SW **Galicia**, became **capital of Poland** until 1596 [28, p 144]. It was a very old city, producing great wealth from commerce in amber, salt, sulphur, copper and lignite coal. There is magnificent ancient salt architecture deep below ground in **salt mines** [54] by local and **Italian** architects, and even chandeliers of salt.
- In **Italy** Frankish-ruled **Sicily** was being absorbed into the papal estate. Independent **Italian city-states** gained power through commerce. **Florence** became an independent, wealthy republic.
- The **Cistercian monastic order** spreading from Italy, was established in Poland [28, pp 229-9].
- The **eastern half of Galicia** was populated by **Ruthenian (later called Ukranian)** peasants and **Boyars** (nobles) in contact with **Kiev** [27, pp 102-3, 146, 163-5, 233, 236], who built ornate **Orthodox churches**, often of wood.
- **Piast Polish kings** encouraged immigration of Germans to increase productivity of farms, coal mines and textiles in SW Poland: **Silesia (Slask** in Polish, **Slezsko** in Czech and **Schlesien** in German) [12 Vol 10, p 803].

The Polish Premysl Dynasty Ruled Moravia and Bohemia: 800-1306 [from pp 14-15]

- 800-1306 **Premysl(Przemzsl) dynasty** from south **Poland**, ruled Bohemia & Moravia [maps pp 31, 38].
- 862 Magyars attacked; 894 King **Syatopuk** of **Great Moravia** died after adding Bohemia to Greater Moravia.
- 967-999 **Boleslav** II founded Prague Bishopric; built magnificent cathedrals, churches and forts [p 35].
- 1035-1055 **Bretislav** permanently united Bohemia and Moravia; 1140-1173 **Vladislav** ll [3].
- 1197-1280 **Otakar I (Ottokar)** was crowned king of **Bohemia-Moravia**; 1204 recognized by the pope.
- 1212 **Premysl** ruling house received hereditary kingdom status [12 Vol 9, p 677; 59, p15]. 1096-1299 the Crusades.
- 1230-53 King **Wenceslas** l succeeded. 1250-1273 no Holy Roman Emperor was crowned.
- 1253-78 **Ottokar** II Premysl ruled **Bohemia-Moravia**. 1251 **Austria** was added by Austrian nobles.
- 1260 he gained control of **Hungary** [10, p 27; 12, Vol 1, p 766]. His power/wealth derived from **silver mines** [10, p 27].
- 1273 the pope crowned **Ottokar** II Holy Roman Emperor because he was strong and had added to his kingdom **Styria**, **Carinthia** [map p 38](called Istria and Carniola in Austria and Slovenia today). The pope hoped his Holy Roman Emperor status would help the church control the powerful German dukes.
- 1272 German princes selected **Rudolph** I **Habsburg** (Hapsburg) as Emperor, but he was **not** crowned by the pope. 1276 determined to get his way, Rudolf attacked Ottakar II and seized the Austrian provinces.
- 1278 Ottokar II struck back and was killed. 1278-1305 son **Wenceslas (Vaclav)** II, extended rule to two-thirds of Poland [12, Macropedia Vol 25, pp 930-944] [map 31]. 1306 Wenceslas III last Premsyl, was assassinated [p 40]

Early History of Austria and the Rise of the Hapsburg Dynasty [from p 13]

- 975-1246 the house of Babenburg ruled Austria. In 1221 **Vienna (Wein)** received a city charter [96, p 8-9].
- 1246 **Frederick** II the last **Babenburg** ruler died without heir. The Mongol invasion of 1238-1242 of central and east Europe caused panic in Austria, so 1246 **Hohenstaufen Frederick** II, Holy Roman Emperor, seized the vacancy in Austria; left his nobles to administer his numerous German states [p 27]; died 1250.
- 1258 **Ottokar** II **(Otakar)** the **Premysl** king of **Bohemia-Moravia** 1253-1278, was **elected Duke of Austria** by Austrian nobles [12 Vol 1, p 766]. 1260 he also gained control of **Hungary** [10, p 27].

- 1272 **Rudolf, Count of Habsburg** came from his ancestral castle in **Switzerland** [12 Vol 5, p 603]. He was elected Emperor **by German Electors** (rulers of several prominent German states) but **instead:**
- 1273 the **Pope crowned Ottokar** II (king of Bohemia-Moravia) **as Holy Roman Emperor** because he was strong and had added to his kingdom **Styria, Carinthia, Carniola** and **Istria** [35, p 563] (regions belonging to **Austria** and **Slovenia** today) [Map p 38]. The Pope hoped ordaining him as Holy Roman Emperor would help the church control the powerful German dukes. (Repeated here to clarify implications for Austria.)
- 1276 Rudolf of Hapsburg forced Otakar II of Bohemia to submit, leaving him with only Bohemia, Moravia and Hungary. 1278 Ottokar II struck back and was killed. He was succeeded by his son:
- 1278-1305 **Wenceslas (Vaclav)** II extending his rule to include two-thirds of **Poland** [12, Macropedia Vol 25, pp 930-944].
- 1282 Austria passed into the rule of **Rudolf** I **Habsburg (Hapsburg)** after all. Rudolf I bestowed Austria and Stryia on his sons, thus beginning identification of the House of Habsburg with Austria, which gradually gained supremacy throughout Europe. **Habsburgs ruled Austria until** 1918 without interruption [12 Vol 5, p 603]. -
- 1283-1308 **Albert** I **of Habsburg** ruled some of the former domains of Ottokar II [9 Vol 3, pp 107-112].
- 1305 after Wenceslas II died, his son **Wenceslas** III ruled **Bohemia, Hungary** and much of **Poland** for a year and was assassinated. 1306 **Rudolf of Habsburg** invested his descendants with **Bohemia, but** instead:
- 1310-1346 **John, Duke of Luxemburg**, son-in-law of Wenceslas II, was crowned king of Bohemia [p 40].

Early History of Hungary

- 375-470 Asian Huns invaded, are lost from ongoing history, but Hungary is named for them.
- 894 **Magyars** from east of Ural mountains, on fast horses went SW to the Black Sea and Balkans [p 14].
- 896-907 led by **Arpad** they went up the Danube and drove out **Avars**. The unique Magyar language is similar to Finnish and Estonian. They expanded as far as France until 955 [p 18] and invaded Italy.
- 972 Grand **Prince Geza** was converted to Christianity. 977 Stephen, Arpad's great grandson was born.
- 997-1038 **Stephen** was crowned 1000 by envoys sent by the pope. 1038-47 nephew **Peter Orseolo;**
- 1047 **Andrew** I (Andras I) deposed Peter and ruled until 1060; 1060-63 **Béla** I ruled;
- 1063-74 **Solomon ruled**; 1074-8 **Geza** I; succeeded by **Ladislas** I who restored prosperity [95]; [3].
- 1083 King **Stephen** I was canonized and became the patron saint of Hungary.
- 1116 **Coloman**, king of Hungary died after conquering **Croatia** [95]; 1116-1131 **Stephen** II.
- 1141 **Béla** II, the blind king of Hungary, died after taking terrible revenge; 1141-1161 **Geza** II;
- 1173 **Stephen** III died; 1173-1196 **Béla** III; 1196-1204 son **Emeric** ruled; 1203-35 **Andrew** II ruled.
- 1222 the **Golden Bull** (the Hungarian Magna Charta) was forced on Andrew by nobles. This milestone in Hungarian constitutional history, provided rights for nobles, such as relaxed taxes, payment for foreign service, annual parliament [49, p 62], and no imprisonment without trial by an independent judge. However restrictions were placed on foreigners, and Jews were banned from the important offices of treasury, salt and customs [100,p187].
- 1235 **Elizabeth** of Hungary was canonized; died 1231 [3]. 1235-1270 **Béla** IV son of Andrew.
- 1241-43 **Mongol Ogadei**, son of **Genghis Khan** laid Hungary waste, killing half of the population, but retreated. King Béla issued a city charter to **Pest** [100,p187]; began building **Buda** hill fort [55, 278] [map p 38]
- 1270-1272 **Stephen** V ruled; 1272-1301 **Andras** III last of the Arpad Dynasty died; civil war began [p 42].
- 896-1301 Hungary was the principal nation in east-central Europe, a strong independent kingdom.

Mongol and Tatar Oppression of Russia, Poland and Hungary [From pp 16-17, 32, 37]

- 1206 **Temujin** (1162-1227) **united** more than 30 **Mongol** (Mogul) and **Tatar** (Tartar) **nomadic clans in central Asia** and became their **Genghis Khan** (Universal Leader).
- 1215 they captured **Beijing**, China; 1221 invaded India. At his death his empire was the largest the world had ever seen, Pacific Ocean to Dnieper river, Russia [14, pp 38-42, 46] [compare maps pp 38 & 94].
- 1227 the Mogul empire was divided among his four sons, with son **Ogadei** the **Great Khan**.
- 1234 they defeated the last of the **Chin Empire** in **China.**
- 1223-40 Mongols under **Genghiz Khan**, and later **Ogadei**, riding small swift horses in winter on frozen rivers, shooting powerful bows from the saddle, occupied **Georgia**, **Kiev**, **Volga** and much of **Russia** [19, pp 38-39].
Mongols had two types of cavalry, **heavy**: for officers clad in armor, and **light**: of riders with swift horses.
New weaponry was learned from people they conquered: **from Arab Muslims** stone-throwing trebuchets, giant catapults and assault towers to ascend castles [37, pp 44-45, 60-61,73], and **from Chinese**, gunpowder.
- 1222 **Yaroslav** of the **Rurik Dynasty**, when elected **Prince of Novgorod,** transferred his family north.

- After 1228 Yaroslav was away from home and his sons had guardians.
The Rurik people intermarried with Finnish tribes, left the Roman Catholic faith and became Orthodox.
- Sons of the Rurik dynasty traditionally rotated as rulers in four principalities successively, as prestige grew. The highest position was that of Grand Prince of Kiev. It was hard to keep this pattern of succession.
- 1236 **Yaroslav** became the **Grand Duke of Kiev** a large state that ruled all of Russia, and **Alexander** his son, became **Prince of Novgorod,** when 19 years of age [p 19]. Alexander drove the Lithuanians back west.
- **Novgorod** was a free city that **traded furs** with German Hanseatic Leaugue Cities [Maps pp 37, 38]
- **Vladimir-Suzdal**, another Rurik Dynasty branch, ruled east-central Russia, at the source of the mighty Volga River. They traded oriental goods on vessels via the Black and Caspian Seas [20, pp 57-91] [map p 37]
-1238 **Mongols** advanced within 60 miles of Novgorod, near the Baltic Sea. Grand Duke Yaroslav was summoned by the Great Khan to **Karakorum.** He died returning home, possibly from poison.
- 1239 regaining access to the Baltic Sea from the **Swedes**, Alexander earned the **title Nevski**. 1240 he drove the **Teutonic Knights** back west-ward in a batttle that kept them back for two centuries.
-1241 **Mongols** invaded central Europe, shocking people with ruthless speed in any weather. In **Poland** they showered the **Teutonic Knights** with arrows, pretending to retreat, lured them away from their army, and then crushed them [map p 37]. Farther south a large **Hungarian** army panicked and fled, confused by the **Mongols** using surprise attacks, smoke and noise. Suddenly they left when Great Khan Ogadei (Ughetai) died.

Map: *River Route Baltic to Black Sea* [46b]

1242 Mongol families settled in southern Russia and were called the **Golden Horde**, since they wore golden raw silk clothing. Arrows could not penetrate the silk and were pulled out by Chinese surgeons traveling with them [37, pp 44-45]. [See Maps pp 37, 38]. Russians, even in **Novgorod** paid heavy taxes to the Mongols/Tartars [20, pp 106-111, 170-71] annually until the 14th century. The Golden Horde dominated south and central Europe 200 years, but thinking Europe backward did not bother invading.
-1246-47 **Svyatoslav Rurik** Grand Duke.
-1247-52 grandson **Andrew**, and brother:
-1252-63 Alexander Nevski was promoted as Grand Duke to the capital Kiev [49, pp 46-61], and controlled all Russia, but Tartars from the south extracted tribute. To become Grand Duke prince Nevski had to seek a patent from the Mongol Khan. With dignity and meekness, and blessed by the Orthodox Patriarch, Alexander Nevski made five trips on behalf of his people to negotiate better terms with the Great Khan [49, pp 46-51, 53, pp95-115]; later was canonized. 1263 **Daniel,** son of Nevski became Grand Duke and founded the **House of Moscow**, which evolved into a strong principality [12 Vol 8, pp 244, 349]. Moscow was located in the heart of a network of rivers, between dense forests and treeless steppes, at the site of an ancient fortress, on the **Moskova River**, branch of the **Oka** which joins the **Don River** that runs into the Black Sea. Nearby **Volga River** drains into the **Caspian Sea**.- 1264-71 Nevski's brother **Yaroslav**, Grand prince of **Vladimir** to the east, founded the **House of Tver**.
- In new generations, the Houses of Tver and Moscow were rivals [12, p 244] although it was traditional to follow a rotation plan. Small Moscow gained strength by trading furs & avoiding the Tartar Golden Horde. Absorbing **Vladimir-Suzdal** and other states, gradually the **Principality of Moscovy** became dominant [pp 32, 37].

Byzantium Ruled by Bulgars, Serbs, Franks and Ottomans 1000-1299 [pp 21, 23-25]

- 1018-1185 Asian **Bulgarians** in the Byzantine Empire [12 Vol2,pp618-21], had learned Slavic speech [map p 38].
- 1185 the **House of Asen**, the second Bulgarian kingdom began. Orthodox Greek churches were built, and expanding west, **Bulgaria** became the **superpower of the Balkans**, controlling most of present-day **Albania**, half of **Greece**, half of **Romania**, and parts of **Serbia** and **Turkey** [55,pp49,55;42,p129]. [maps xvii Dalmacia; p 38]
- 1169 **Stephan Nemanjic** emerged as a leader of some of the **Serb tribes**, and his dynasty expanded their power. His son became archbishop and was later **canonized St. Sava** by the autocephalous (independent) Serbian Orthodox Church. The **Serbs** seized much of **Macedonia** from the Byzantines [12 Vol 10,pp 645].
- 1118-43 **John** II **Commenus** ruled the Byzantine Empire; 1143-80 Manuel I; 1180-83 Alexius II;
- 1149 after the **Second Crusade, Franks** influenced and ruled the Byzantine Empire in Constantinople.
- 1185-1261 Frank **Baldwin Count of Flanders.** Nephew **Baldwin** II and retinue learned Greek culture.
- 1186-95 **Isaac** II was Byzantine Emperor. Many Byzantine nobles left Constantinople and set up separate Greek states such as Nicea, Thessalonica, Trabzon. Epirus and some Agean Islands [49,p20].
- 1200 in **Fourth Crusade** Constantinople and Romania for 50 years were occupied by **Franks**. They took treasures and manuscripts to Europe which led to interest in Greek Classics. The Bubonic plague killed many.
- 1261 **Michael** VIII Palaeologus, united various Greek districts, drove the **Franks** out of Constantinople; restored the Byzantine Empire until 1453, but preoccupied defending frontiers from **Serbia**, **Bulgaria**, north **Greece** and **Venice**, did not notice the growing prowess and ambition of the **Ottomans** [21c,pp 47-54].
- 1282-1355 the **Great Balkan Empire of Serbs and Greeks** [5,pp272-274] enlarged its borders [pp 42-43].
- 1259-1326 **Osman** (**Uthman in Arabic**, later **Ottoman**) leader of **a tribe newly arrived** in Turkey from **Asia**, crossed the strait into Europe and quickly made conquests. Rough and ruthless they assimilated the genteel ways of Seljuk Turks and Greeks. Their religion combined idolatry, Shamanism and Islam [21d, pp 47-54].
- 1288 the **Ottoman Empire** was founded; 1299 **Osman** had 4000 troops and was beginning to move.

The Middle East and Far East During Second to Ninth Crusades 1147 to 1272 [p 25]

- The Caliphs for their own protection had placed **Mamaluks** (slaves) in administration, mounted guard and the army. After the **Second Crusade** (1147-49) **Saladin** a **Kurdish** (Khurd) general, installed an **Abbasid Caliph** under Mamaluk surveillance in Cairo, Egypt [12Vol 7, pp750-751].
- 1150 then Mamaluk **Saladin made himself Sultan**. His army of Khurds, Arabs and Turks [12 Vol 7, pp750-751] consisted of both slaves and free men [167, pp 66-67]. Then:
- 1171 he overthrew the **Fatimid Dynasty** in Egypt; became **Sultan** of Egypt and **Syria** [12 Vol 2, p745; Vol 7, pp750-751].
- 1187 Jerusalem fell to Sultan Saladin bringing on the **Third Crusade**. **Richard** the Lion Heart, King of **England**, by negotiating, was granted a treaty allowing pilgrims to visit the holy places.
- 1193 Sultan Saladin died. 1193-1249 **Al-Malik as-Salih Ayyub** ruled; was murdered by Mamaluk slaves.
- 1250-1382 the **Mamaluk Dynasty**, with Turkish leadership ruled all middle east nations [p 25].
- 1258 the Muslim capital of **Baghdad**, ruled by the **Abbasid Caliphate was sacked** by a major **Mongol** army from central Asia, under a **Genghis Khan**. He left quickly, but **Baghdad** was left leaderless and **could not rise** again. To administer government the Mamaluks restored a nominal **Abbasid Caliph**.
- 1260 the Mongols also took **Damascus** but **soon withdrew** to Iran and India [167, pp 64-69].
- Grandsons of Genghis continued to expand in the east: 1251 Il-Khan set up an empire in **Persia**, and
- 1280-1368 **Kublai Khan** founded the Yuan dynasty in **Beijing**; ruled all of **China**, **Korea**, **Vietnam** and:
- 1287 ruled **Burma** [20, p 98]. The Mogul empire became so large that it divided into several branches [15, p 266-8].
- 1288 the Islamic **Ottoman Empire** was founded by **Osman** (**Uthman**) 1259-1326 [see above].
- 1290 **Osman** I was awarded the **title Sultan** by the Caliph of Cairo [12 Vol 9, p 6].
- 1301 Byzantine Christian outreach from Constantinople became very difficult. Islamic expansion took in the whole Balkans, up to the Danube River, and started to invade **Hungary**. Many generations of warfare continued.
- As the church in Constantinople weakened, Orthodox Christians looked increasingly to the **Patriarchate of Moscow** for moral leadership. This included Orthodox Christians in **eastern Poland**.

However the **Orthodox Church** in each country was autocephalous (independent).
- The Roman Catholic Church was strong in the western Balkans, Hungary and most of Poland.
- 1382-1517 the **Circassian Mamaluks** ruled **Egypt**. [Continued pp 42-43].

Chapter Six - 1000 to 1299

Norman, Romanesque, Early Gothic, Moorish and Russian Architecture

Architecture in England During the Norman and Plantagenet Dynasties [See pp 21-22]

- 1052 **Edward the Confessor** ruled England for 25 years, 1041-1066 [16, p 812], built **Westminster Abbey**; consecrated it in 1065, a year before the Norman conquest, founded by Benedictines.
- There were other monasteries and churches in Saxon England [12 Vol 5, pp 741-2] [See map p 10].
- 1066 Battle of Hastings, the Norman conquest by the cavalry of **William** I, **the Conqueror.**
- The Normans brought with them prefabricated wooden castles stored in barrels. The pieces were quickly assembled, by forced labor, inside a bailey (stockade) on a hill or mound [111, pp 136-7], sometimes with a moat.
- Soon wooden and stone castles were built all over England as far as Scotland.
- 1066-87 **William** I governed in a system of **feudalism**, with **vassals** indebted to a hierarchy of lords.
- 1085 he commissioned **a census of property** legally held by landowners. An **exchequer** regulated taxes.
- 1150 the **Domesday Book** (or Doomsday) was published, organized by "hundreds" (counties).
- By 1100 over 500 castles were either built or reconstructed with permanent materials.
- c 1100 **Durham** cathedral was built with the first **rib vault roof** [9 Vol 2, p 277] and intersecting diagonal arches.
- 1087-1100 England was ruled by **William** II **Rufus** and
- 1100-1135 **Henry** I developed the **English system of justice**. His heir was his daughter **Maud** (**Matilda**).
- 1135-54 **Stephen**, Maud's nephew usurped the throne [see p 22].
- 1154-89 **Henry** II **of Anjou**, Maud's son, ruled England and much of France [16, pp 532; 72]. He began the **Plantagenet dynasty**. He married **Eleanor,** Duchess and heir of **Aquitaine**, who 1147-49 with her first husband Louis VII of France, was in Constantinople for the **Second Crusade** [pp 22, 25, 43].
- They lived in palaces both in France and England. In Anjou Henry II built **Hospital St. Jean**, massive **Angers palace** [9 Vol 2, pp 129-30, 159-60] and a large part of St. Maurice cathedral.
- He brought **Ireland** under the rule of England [see p 22].

Two of Henry and Queen Eleanor's sons became kings, Richard I and John. Herself a musician, her sons and many returning crusaders, advanced music, poetry, books, classical learning, importing of tropical spices and fruit, and elegant architecture [pp 22, 25-26 and 39].

- 1167 **Oxford University** and 1200 **Cambridge University** were founded [3].
- 1189-1199 **Richard** I, **the Lion Heart** captured Acre in the **Third Crusade** (1189-92) [p 22].
- 1199-1216 **King John** was shamed as the nobles forced him to grant rights through the of Magna Carta.

Gothic style cathedral building began at **Canterbury** 1174, **Lincoln** 1192, **York Minster** 1261, **Exeter** 1280.

- 1220 **Oxford spire** had octagonal dormers on the sides and corner pinnacles at the base [12 Vol 21, pp 40-42].
- 1220-58 **Salisbury Cathedral** had a 460 foot octagonal steeple set on a square tower with corner pinnacles.

Early cathedrals had thick walls and slender windows. **Arabic numerals** marked the rafters [pp 36, 48].

- 1216-1272 **Henry** III succeeded his father King John. He built 60 castles, 20 lodges and palaces.
- 1245-69 he completed **Westminster Abbey** [16, pp 330, 812] with networks of decorative stone tracery in some of the cloister windows. 1264 the barons put him in prison.

  (About 1490 Henry VII added a chapel [16, pp 812] and about 1690 **Christopher Wren** the western towers.
  Until 1547 the **House of Commons** met in the Cloisters and Chapter House [see p 49].)

- 1265-1307 **Edward** I son of Henry III reigned. He conquered **Wales** and **Scotland**. [Continued pp 43-44]

Romanesque Style Cathedrals [continued from p 20]

- Large Roman style basilicas were still being built, with very thick walls and windows few and high.
- 950-1120 the church "at Tournos, France used transverse arches to support a series of barrel vaults".
- 980 **Mainz** cathedral on the Rhine River was begun and rebuilt 1081-1137 [24].
- 1015 construction of **Strasbourg Cathedral** in **Alsace** began. The town was captured by Germans.
- 1088-1121 **Cluny monastery** was ornate Romanesque, 450 feet long with 15 side-wall chapels [p 21].
- In later construction the groin vault was preferred as there was room for high windows and the sanctuary could be long. Early examples are **Worms** (11th century) and **Vezelay** (1104). The arches of the groin vault soared over a long series of square areas where the congregation sat to worship [9, Vol 2, pp 276-7, 288; 137, pp 46,47].
- The churches in **Toulouse** (1080-1120) and **Conques** (1050-1120) had barrel-shaped vaulted roofs with four barrel shapes meeting in a circle, resting on 4 large pillars [9 Vol 2, pp 276-7, 288].
- 1200 the **Freiburg im Breisgau Cathedral** was started in **Romanesque style** [next page]

Increasing Skill in Building Spires

- See above regarding the spire of **Oxford University** and the 460 foot steeple of **Salisbury Cathedral**.
- Earlier spires were wooden [12, Vol 11]. 1200 the **Freiburg im Breisgau Cathedral**, in a free market town in the Frankish-German Dutchy of **Baden-Württemberg**, was started in **Romanesque style** and
- 1270-88 a 117 **metre spire** with delicate open stone tracery, pinnacles and spiral stairway were added. This filigree spire of Freiburg cathedral was admired and copied for other churches.
- 1513 Freiburg cathedral was finished in **Gothic** style [6, Oggins, p 80, 82; 12, Vol 11]. [See below pp 34-35].
- **Cologne** cathedral, begun 1248, and **Ulm** Minster 1377-1494 had Freiburg style spires [6; 12 Vol 21, pp 40-4].

The Cult of Saints and Pilgrimages to Venerate Holy Relics

- 1071 **pilgrimages** to **worship holy relics at distant shrines** and churches became popular. Notable in France were churches St. Martin in **Tours** and St. Sernin in **Toulouse**, and in northwest Spain cathedral **Santiago de Compostela**. They were built in elaborate Romanesque style. Large numbers of pilgrims were accommodated en route in monasteries and abbeys [20, pp 39, 46, 50-3].

Italian and Middle East Architecture

- Eleventh century **St. Mark's Basilica** in **Venice** is cross-shaped [9 Vol 2, p 276-7; 12 Vol 5, pp 741-2]. The walls and **dome** are covered with golden Byzantine mosaics. Small domes were built when larger domes collapsed.
- In southern Europe and the middle east, arches were round. As skill grew, arches became more elaborate. Gothic pointed arches were thought to be barbaric. "The term **Gothic** was coined by . . . Italian writers of the Renaissance who attributed the invention (and what to them was nonclassical ugliness) of medieval architecture to the barbarian Gothic tribes that had destroyed the Roman Empire and its classical culture in the fifth century AD. The term retained its derogatory overtones until the nineteenth century, at which time a positive critical evaluation of Gothic architecture took place;" per Encyclopedia Britannica [12 Vol 5, pp 382-3].
- **Gothic design originated with Franks not Goths**. Goths from Sweden migrated via the Black Sea and Balkans to Italy and Spain [See maps: pp xii and xiii and pp 1, 2]. The architecture of both Visigoths (west Goths) and Ostrogoths (east Goths) had other attractive distinctive features [See pp 8, 9 and 19].

Development of Gothic Style Architecture

- Wooden fan vaulting originated from tents, chalets and high gables [20, pp 70, 87]. Through the centuries in Scandinavia and northern Europe, the skills of building wooden roofs with multiple arches were developed. The arches came to a point at the top. When elaborate wooden arches were added to Romanesque Basilicas, Gothic architecture was born. Later complicated dovetailed vaulted stone roofs, similar to the original wooden ceilings were built [9 Vol 2, pp 287-290; 26, James Acland].
- **Gothic style stone architecture originated in northern France,** of Frankish origin, and was perfected under the **Capetian dynasty** 967-1328 [12 Vol 2, p 629; Vol 4, p 920]. Later, bricks and tiles were used instead of stone.
- Crusaders brought back to Europe knowledge about building castles. They also gained a taste for airy arcades and larger windows to let in light [37, p 85] and lighter weight walls.

To support a heavy roof on a wide church and prevent the outward thrust and collapse of walls:
Four brilliant innovations were developed:

1) Vaulted roofs were designed with strong weight-bearing arched ribs. The spaces in between were light material. This greatly reduced the overall weight of the roof.
2) Ribs of the roof were supported by widely spaced pillars/piers, instead of thick solid walls, to allow light to enter the lower part of the nave.
3) Buttresses were added beside the pillars, and slim flying buttresses outside the building, to help carry both the weight and outward thrust.
4) Round arches were replaced by pointed arches which distributed the thrust to pillars, not in all directions (focused on weight-bearing). In this way the walls could be thinner.

- These discoveries enabled the masons to make larger, taller buildings with more complicated floor plans. Larger windows could be added. Balconies were added inside the sanctuary.
- Two huge towers were built at the entrance. Piers were decorated with pinnacles.
- 1144 the **first Gothic cathedral**, the Abbey Church of **St. Denis** near Paris, was completed [20, pp 62-6].

- 1150-1250 twenty-five **French Gothic cathedrals were built,** in such places as **Amiens**, **Chartres**, **Notre Dame** in Paris, **Reims** and **Strasbourg** [137, pp 48-49].
- All over Europe for **three centuries Gothic Cathedrals were built** and Gothic features were added to basilicas, but **not in Italy** where Gothic architecture was still considered ugly and barbarian.
- In 1225 a bridge was built across the Rhine river. Two great cathedrals were built on the east side of the Rhine River at Baden-Wurttemberg: **Freiberg** Cathedral started Romanesque in 1200, was remodeled and completed 1513 with Gothic towers. Oggins wrote "Freiberg was founded as a free market town in the twelfth century. It's **Munster** (cathedral) took three centuries to complete and has one of the finest spires in the world" [6, Oggins, pp 81-82] [See above pp 33-34].
- It took over a 100 years to build stone-sculptured Gothic churches, due to wars/plague/political instability. The author's paternal ancestors were sculptors and stone masons from the Wurttemberg, Freiberg and Strasbourg area. Napoleon himself invited them to go to Poland about 1805 to repair churches that had deteriorated. Earlier he engaged skilled architects to complete **Milan Cathedral** during his Italian campaign.

Stained Glass Windows

- Colored and stained glass windows with an elaborate network of moldings decorated the Gothic churches. A large circular stained glass window, resembling a rose, was designed for many cathedrals and churches.
- 1237-1276 further work was done to complete **Strasbourg Cathedral** in Alsace, begun 1015. Construction was funded by townspeople. It became a model for religious buildings. See a picture of the nave [24, p 170] showing a Gothic rose window. An essay by **Goethe** praised the master-mason of Strasbourg cathedral [24, p 252]. Artistic ability to craft stained glass windows grew.

Architecture of Prague, Bohemia [See pp 29-30; maps 31, 38]

- 800-1306 the **Premysl (Przemzyl)** dynasty of south **Poland** expanded to rule all of **Bohemia**, **Moravia** and the west part of modern **Hungary**; known as **Great Moravia** and spoke **Czech**, a Slavic language.
- 863 King Ratislav invited Orthodox missionaries Cyril and Methodius. The Bible was translated.
- 870 Prague **Hrad** (castle) [55, p 202] was built and the kingdom consolidated.
- 903-935 **Wenceslas** (Vaclav**)** won supremacy over the **Magyars** in Moravia [55, p 138, 202]; later canonized.
- 926 construction of **St. Vitus Cathedral**, named for a fourth century Sicilian tortured to death in Rome in the pre-Christian Roman era. It is covered with jewels. On the roof there are **Gargoyles** on the rain water spouts. Contains the tombs of St. Vitus and St. Wenceslas [55, p 202]. Enlarged in the 14th century, it dominates castle hill;
- 967-999 Boleslav II founded Prague bishopric.
- 1142 **Basilica St. George** was built in Romanesque style originally as a convent [55, pp 139, 161, 188-193], in the castle courtyard. In 1670 a red baroque facade was added.
- 1233 St. Agnes Convent was founded by princess Agnes, sister of King Wenceslas I [55, p 198].

Eastern Orthodox and Muslim Arts and Architecture [See pp 23 and 32]

- Classical architecture of the Greeks influenced the Eastern Roman Empire and Orthodox church. From the sixth century onwards invading tribes from the north, admired/copied their architecture [pp 8-9].
- 1204 during the fourth Crusade **Franks and Latins occupied Greece**.
- 1270 After the Crusades ended, Greece remained in the control of European invaders. They adapted some aspects of classical Greek architecture in their homelands and stole many relics.
- In southern Europe and the middle east, **arches were round**. Some were **key-shaped**.
- Sometimes **small domes** were added. A few huge domes collapsed from the sheer weight.

"The **Arabs** did not have a building tradition before they conquered the Byzantine and Persian Empires. Initially they used the structures they found in their new territories as mosques. But in time the Caliphs constructed their own religious buildings to rival the Christian churches." [18, p 51 (pp 39 - 53)].

- Tall narrow minarets with a spiral staircase were built at the corners of **mosques** (masjid in Arabic) built or adapted for Muslim worship. Five times a day a call to prayer is made from the top of minarets.
- Muslims developed **a great variety of arch styles:** scalloped, horseshoe, and S-curve.
- Blue ceramic tiles, filigree lattices, semi-precious stone, colored marble and mirror inlay and verses from the Koran in graceful calligraphy, were used to decorate **Muslim tombs** and places of worship.
- All images, both sculptures and paintings of people and animals are forbidden, but floral decorations are allowed. Places of worship are beautifully ornate with mosaics, filigree and porcelain.

- 1058 **Arab Califs** were conquered by **Seljuk Turks**. Damascus capital 661-750, was moved to Baghdad.
- 1258 Mongols under Genghis Khan destroyed Baghdad. Scholars fled to Africa, Spain and Italy.
- 1288 the Turks recovered and founded the Turkish **Ottoman Empire** [See pp 16-18; 32, 43].
- **Sufiism**, a form of **mysticism**, began in Persia & spread throughout Islam among ordinary and educated people, seeking personal spirituality in a whirling dance [80, pp 86-112; 149, pp 128-166; 82, pp 123-6]. Their devotional poetry was and still is admired.

Moorish Muslim Architecture and Scholarship in Spain [See map p 38]

- 711-1236 **Muslim Moors from north Africa** occupied much of Spain; with their **capital at Cordova**, south Spain[42, pp 982-3, 987; 16, p 504, 63]. Moorish **Caliphs** (successors of Mohammed) & **Emirs** (governors, princes) held court in Cordova (**Cordoba**), **the world's foremost centre of culture, art and learning**. Their scholars had learned the Greek classics and were adding new knowledge of medicine, mathematics and science [13, pp 82-89].
- 975-1002 learned **Caliph al Hakam** promoted scholarship; **built up the greatest library** of that day.
- 929-1031 Cordoba Caliphate reached its peak of cultural, scientific & political power but collapsed from civil war with less learned rivals; **Almoravids from Morocco** made invasions into Spain. **Al-Mansur** (Ibn Abi Amir or Almanzor) purged the great library of Cordoba. Destruction continued under his son & rival Muslim Berbers and "Christian" **Castilians**, who sacked the palaces of Cordoba. Great private collections were destroyed/dispersed. Small Christian & Muslim kingdoms then ruled Spain [13, pp 84-89; 28b, pp 26, 782-6].
- 1031 the learned **Umayyad Caliphate** in the middle east collapsed; scholars migrated to Spain and Italy.
- 1085 **Alphonso** VI **of Leon and Castile**, northern Spain, captured **Toledo**, the ancient Visigothic capital, in central Iberian peninsula (Spain). For protection **Sevilla Muslims** hired the **Almoravids,** a fanatical sect of Saharan **Berber** nomads from north Africa, [28b, p 27].
- 1091-1140s **Almoravids**, took over rule of all **Andalucia** (Al-Andalus, southern Spain) [28b, pp 782-6].
- 1160-1173 **Almohads, another Muslim Berber sect** overthrew the Almoravids in Morocco and Spain;
- 1195 they pushed back "Christian" Castile's army. **Seville** was centre of science & scholarship. Almohad built the great mosque in Seville. His successor:
- 1184-99 **Caliph Yacoub Yousouf al Mansour** defeated Portuguese Templars. He added elaborately carved **Giralda tower** to the great mosque [20, pp 70-71]. He protected scientist physician **Averroes** (Abul-ibn-Roshd) who, born 1126 in Cordova [20, pp 70-71] wrote commentaries on **Aristotle** not accepted by Muslims, but studied by Christian philosophers for two centuries [13, pp 86-7; 28b, p 26].
- **Averroes** coauthored a medical encyclopedia with Physician **Abu Marwan ibn Zuhr,** who died 1161,
- 1154 The ***Book of Roger***, written/complied by **cartographer Al-Idrisi** of Palmero who died 1162, was named after **Roger**, **Norman ruler** of **Sicily** and much of **Italy**. Geography of central & south Asia and all of African east & west sea coasts and interior was well known by Arab traders and Al-Idrisi himself.
- 1135-1204 Moses **Maimonides** the **Jewish** doctor and philosopher of Cordova was greatly respected.
- 1221-84 Castillian Christian **King Alfonso, the Learned** was tolerant of Jews and Muslims; had **Arab and Greek science and philosophy translated into Latin**, including much of al-Hakam's great library. This famous Toledo library attracted scholars from Paris, England and eastern Europe.
- Works by Averroes were translated by **Michael Scot** and other westerners [20, p 71] who studied there. From Toledo scholars carried their new knowledge throughout Europe. 1220-58 the cathedral in Salisbury England was built with rafters sorted and numbered with Arabic numerals [p 33].
- 1236 Cordova was conquered by Castile [3, p 170]. The **Great Mosque** at **Cordoba** built 786-965, was converted into a Christian cathedral [9, Vol 2, p 279]. Castile became rich from **wool** production.
- 1240 Philosopher **Ibn al-'Arabi**, a poet and leader of the **Sufi movement** died [82, pp 123-6; 80, pp 101,107-8].
- 1200-1248 renowned herbalist-botanist **Ibn al-Baytar** developed **Pharmacy** textbooks.
- 1248 Sevilla fell to **Ferdinand** III **of Castile** [13, pp 88-89], and was tolerant of Muslims and Jews. Some Muslims and Christians intermarried, but tolerance began to disappear in Spain [p 48, 49].
- 1248-1492 **Nasrid Emirate of Granada** ruled Andalucia from magnificent **Alhambra palace**, an earlier fort restored [20, pp 142-4, 172-5] and gradually expanded [28b, pp 891-2, 887; 83, pp 24-5, 27; 21d, pp 55-7], with pools, fountains & shaded bowers. Refugees, scholars, artisans from all Andalucia and foreign traders stimulated culture & science.
- Muslim power survived while the rulers with political vigilance [28b, pp 20, 26-7] played off Aragon, Castile and Morocco. Later while preoccupied with **mysticism,** literature and the enjoyment of luxurious gardens, led to the lowering of initiative, defenses and downfall.

Russian Architecture

[See p 16 and maps: pp 31, 37 and 38]

- 988 **Tsar Vladimir of Kiev** was baptized in the Greek Orthodox faith when he married Byzantine princess Anna. Filled with awe when he saw St. Sophia cathedral in Constantinople; started to build in Kiev his Cathedral **Domition of the Virgin** [20, pp 37-8] and many churches combining Russian and Byzantine styles.
- 1018-37 his son **Yaroslav the Wise**, built St. Sophia in Kiev with 3 aisles and five domes, later enlarged to nine aisles and thirteen small domes [20, pp 38, 45], decorative rather than essential for roof support [9 Vol 2, p 276].
- 1045-62 St. Sophia in **Novgorod**, NW Russia, was built by **Yaroslav the Wise** taller but with smaller windows and small onion-shaped domes [56, pp 34-43; 20, pp 24-25, 37-8, 45]. He revised Russian Law; died 1054.
- 1113 the Church of St. Nicholas, Novgorod was built with one of the first onion-shaped domes [95, p 143].
- 1125 paintings of the *Virgin of Vladimir* emphasize her motherhood and compassion.
- Late 12th C St. George Cathedral in Yuriev Monastery, Novgorod built by **Master Peter**, **Russian Architect** whose indigenous style was long popular [20, pp 67, 70, 85]; no external ornaments, but many asymmetrical domes.
- By 1200 Kiev had diminished in power because of pressure from all directions: Teutonic Knights in the north, western Slavs pushing east, Muslim Mongol nomad raids in the SE, and civil war among Russians. Both **Novgorod** in the NW and **Vladimir-Suzdal,** at the head of the mighty **Volga River**[20, pp 59, 92-3,] had grown in power. Novgorod was wealthy from **fur trade**.
- Although northerly, Suzdal [p 31, 38] had easy access to the Black Sea so traded with the east and Africa. **Suzdal** churches were a modest compact cube topped with one onion-shaped dome. St. Dmitry in **Vladimir** had one small dome on top of a cone. Outer walls were highly decorated.
- 1166 in **Suzdal** the *Pokrov (Church of the Protection and Intercession of the Virgin)* is a cube decorated with carvings, covered with gold, designed by Prince **Andrey Bogoliubsky**. His palace was more ornate.
- 1183 after a fire in **Vladimir**, the splendid Cathedral of St Dormition was rebuilt by **Vsevolod**, Prince Andrey's brother and successor. It has several high rounded annexes [20, pp 59, 92-3].
- 1194-7 Prince **Vsevolod** also rebuilt the Church of St Dmitry, with complex external carvings [20, pp 67-70].
- 1238 Mongols (Tartars) invaded and sacked Vladimir and several other central Russian cities, including Moscow which was still undeveloped. The unique architecture of Vladimir-Suzdal was never fully revived, but it was a model for later Muscovite princes. [See p 31; 56].
- 1240 Kiev fell to the Mongols. Novogrod was drained of revenue having to pay tribute them [96, p 187].

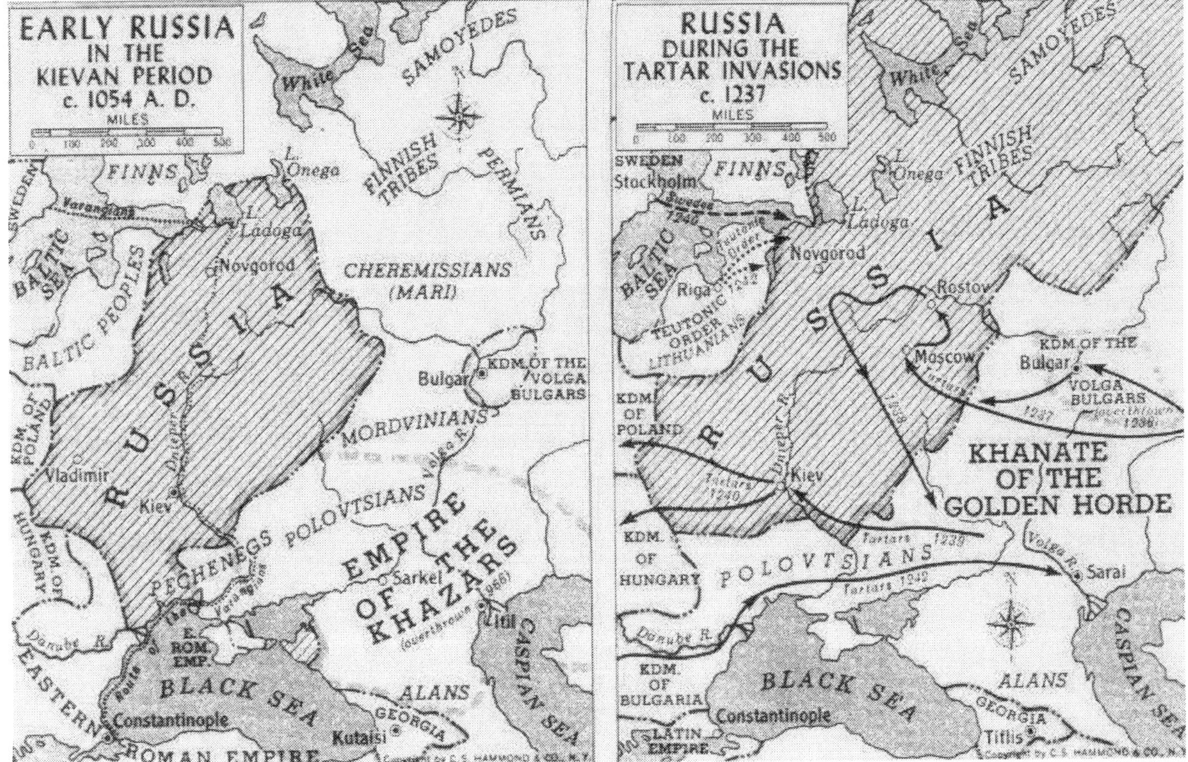

Maps: ***Russia during the Kievan period and Mongol/Tartar Invasions***[96, p 187]

Map: ***Europe, N. Africa & Western Asia*** **–** 1200 AD [150, p 7].

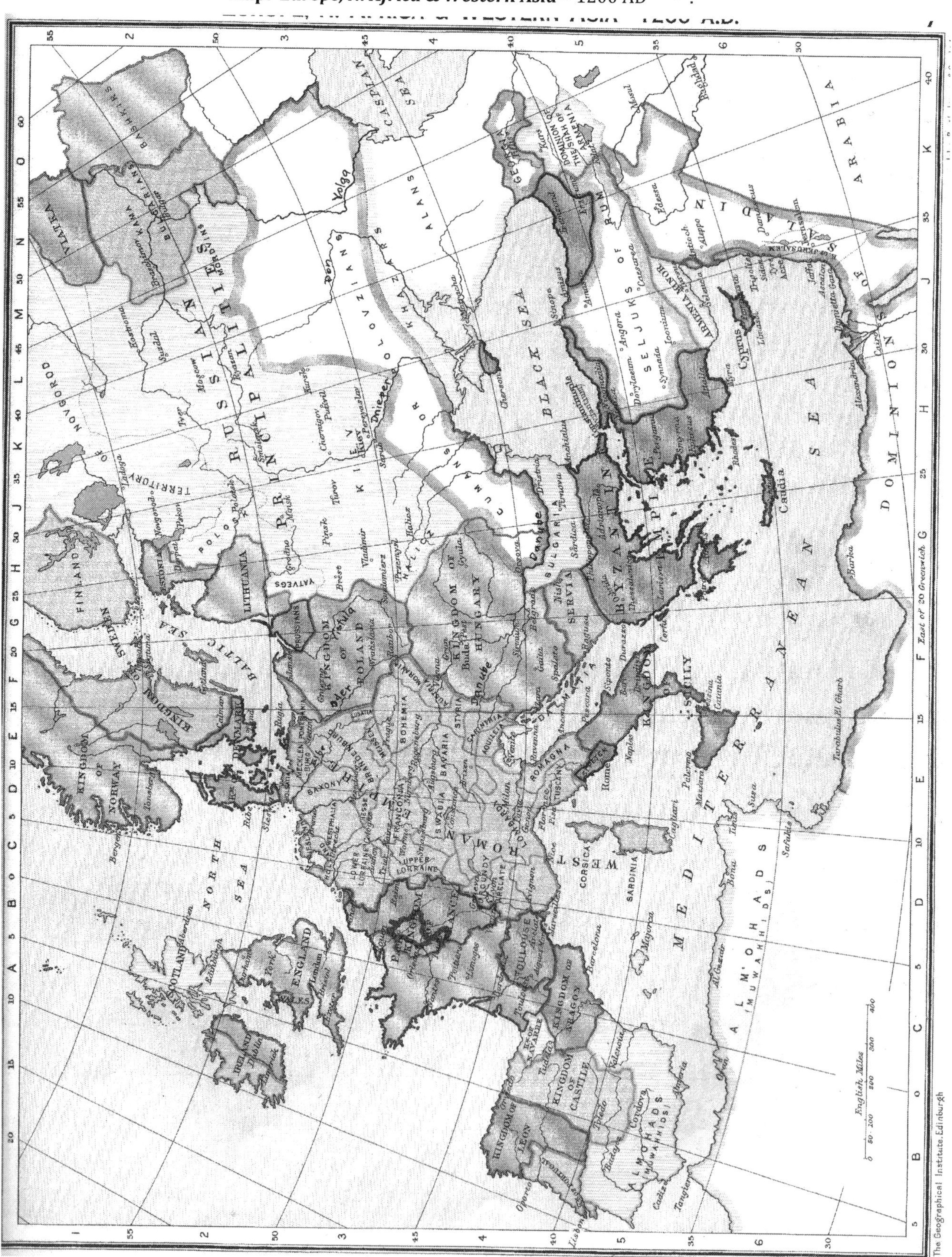

Chapter Seven - 1300 to 1399

Revival of Learning, Black Death, Ottoman Invasions & English in France

European Economy in the Late Middle Ages

- Forests were cleared and opened for very productive farming. Food shortages were largely overcome.
- Plows became heavier, dug deeper and were drawn by horses.
- Improved crop-rotation methods [3]; plantings in spring and fall; improved crop yields. To hold back the sea for agriculture, lands were drained and dikes built, along the North Sea and Italy's Po River delta & valley.
- Political power was centralized, autocratic and increased taxes without consent of the people [8, p 57].
- A voice in government was demanded by peasants in **overpopulated feudal estates, towns and cities.**
- Towns received a charter to protect commerce and industry [3]. **Escaped serfs** got jobs in towns [60, p136].
- **Factories** became larger but wages lower. People from the farms came to work in factories [139, pp 138-145].
- Complicated tools were invented: the crane or windlass to lift heavy loads [111, pp 144, 366]; water and wind-mills to power various machinery, such as a hammer to "full" textiles (pound clay into them to remove grease); treadle looms and spinning wheels; silk production, spinning and weaving; paper making, etc.
- **Craft Guilds** were established by workers of the same trade or craft, in order to set standards, regulate training of apprentices, fix prices, and provide assistance and fellowship between colleagues, levy fines on members who broke the rules, etc. Some guilds secured a charter, and many became powerful and influential enough to become the governing body of their town.
- Homes were beautified with tapestries, mirrors, latticework and glass window panes [111, pp 143, 370].
- Village markets sold local and imported goods. Permanent markets were set up along main roads and trade routes. **Venice** imported Middle East goods. **Genoa**, **Pisa** & **Amalfi** traded with Mediterranean ports.
- Established trade routes by land and sea expanded. Eastern Orthodox church contacts with St. Thomas and Syrian Christians in south **India** [117, pp 16-28] ended, because **Muslims ruled the Indian Ocean.**
- Cities on the North and Baltic seas united as the **Hanseatic League** (Hanses means associations) to protect, develop and regulate foreign trade. Ships were built to carry heavier loads. **Maps** were improved.
- **Canals** and roads were built. Travel became common not only by **merchants** but also **pilgrims** to holy places, often distant. **Stagecoaches** traveled between the major cities all over Europe and the middle east.
- Foreign merchants included Armenians, Jews, Greeks, Germans, Scots and Italians [28, p 245].
- Accounting became easier by changing from **Roman numerals** to the **Arabic numbers** we use today.
- Mathematical concepts of **zero** and **fractions** came from the Arabs.
- Many towns had **clock towers** [111, p 365].
- **Banking** and money-lending began to flourish, spreading from Florence, Italy.

Revival of Learning and Early Years of Renaissance

[Continued from pp 25-26]

- Monks in monasteries copied and studied old manuscripts, became hungry for learning and taught townspeople and children to read and write. Tradesmen and bankers increased their literacy and knowledge.
- Crusaders brought back many books and taste for learning from the middle east. **Ptolemy**'s **Geography** was translated into Latin, stimulating interest in world exploration.
- Universities were founded. Greek Scholars taught in them; students were eager to read the Classics. Literature, philosophy and medical knowledge of ancient Greece and Rome was studied with great ardor.
- Libraries were founded, dictionaries and grammars produced. Mere copying gave way to **free inquiry**.
- 1305-1377 for 70 years the Papal headquarters were in **Avignon** by the Rhone river, southern France.
- The Roman church was in disorder. Wealthy Italians ruled their own domains and fought for supremacy.
- An intellectual movement called **Humanism** initiated by secular men of letters [12 Vol 9, p 1020] first in Italy, spread all over Europe. Individual search for God and study of the Bible were intensified, but most priests and popes of that era lacked education [52, pp 3-6; 98, pp 157-166]. Many people made pilgrimages to shrines [139, pp 150-1] and brought back changes in outlook and culture.

-1329-1384 **John Wycliffe** taught in Oxford, England. He translated the Latin Bible into English. He opposed pilgrimages, images, the papacy, transubstantiation and prayers for the dead [16 pp 5-6, 82, 89].

- 1348 **Bubonic plague** and **civil wars** delayed the Renaissance for 50 years [12 Vol 9, p 1020]. Probably because they lived inland **John Wycliffe** and followers, called **Lollards** survived and spread his teachings in England.

Richard II **of England** born 1366, in his teens married Anne, **sister of Bohemian King Wenceslaus** III.

- Bohemians from Prague studied in Oxford. Wycliffe's teachings spread rapidly in Bohemia.

The Black Death - Bubonic Plague 1347-51 [Bubonic plague hit also in 542; 575-642; 732; 746]

- 1341 the Black Death (Bubonic Plague) broke out in Asia [14, p 48]. It has been documented historically that Bubonic Plague first emerged as a major killer in 1331 in Hopei, northern **China** [95, pp 194, 196-7].
- 1346 the first western cases of plague were in **Georgia** and **Crimea**, southern Russia. The "great dying" reached **Constantinople** in 1347.
- By mid-1348 the plague moved to **Italian coastal** cities, from seaport to seaport in **France** and across central and northern France. By the end of the year it was in Spain, Portugal, southern and central Europe and southern England. It spread throughout the British Isles, Scandinavia, the Hanseatic ports, and up the rivers of Germany and Poland. In Poland only Poznan (Posen) and Prussia were hit hard. South and central Poland, Hungary, Bohemia and the Balkan kingdoms of Serbia and Bulgaria **escaping the plague, flourished economically** and expanded [20, p 148-171]. **Milan** and a few inland parts of Italy, part of Aquitaine, France, and east Germany escaped.
- 1351-3 the plague spread to northern Russia [20, pp 144-5].
- 1347-51 Bubonic Plague killed 33 million people in Europe, a third of the population [49, pp 103-9; 139, 150-1].
- It took a long time to realize that the disease was spread by fleas on rats, in crowded cities and via overland trade routes and ships [14, pp 47-48]. Rich and poor were equally afflicted.
- Great loss of life although devastating, eased the unemployment and overpopulation of Europe [49, pp 103-110].
- Large numbers of serfs escaped from their feudal bonds.
- Coastal towns in England lost half of their population. After the Black Death a large number of peasants found themselves free from their feudal overlord, but landless. Many easily found jobs with wages. Others felt economic difficulties.
- Many clergy died, especially those who were most attentive to care of the sick. Anti-clericalism increased.

Bohemia the Cultural Focus of Europe [pp 29-30; map p 38]

- 1278-1305 **Wenceslas** II, son of Otakar, was king of Bohemia, Poland and Hungary. His son succeeded.
- 1305-1306 **Wenceslas** III, the last of the **Premsyl Dynasty** [map 31], was assassinated 1306.
- 1310-46 **Duke John of Luxemburg** was crowned king and married a daughter of Wenceslaus II.
- 1306-1437 the **house of Luxemburg-Bohemia ruled Bohemia** [9 Vol 4, p 188; 10, p 27].
- 1316 his son was born in Prague and named Wenceslaus for John's father. He studied in Paris under the future pope Clement VI.
- Boy Wenceslaus was renamed **Charles** since he admired Emperor Charlemange (Charles the Great), [10, pp 28-32].
- He learned several languages, lived in Venice and at age 17 was appointed governor of Bohemia-Moravia.
- 1344 the pope approved founding the Archbishopric of Prague, Bohemia, and construction of a Gothic cathedral began [p 47].
- 1347 he was crowned **Charles** IV king of **Bohemia**.
- 1355 the Pope, wanting to limit the power of the Electors, had Charles promise to abandon German political ambitions in Italy [49, p 110], [16, p 219] in exchange for the title Holy Roman Emperor.
- 1356 the ***Golden Bull*** was promulgated to regulate the power/privileges of the Electors to prevent unification, so as to keep Germans divided among rival dukes. Charles IV was their head not politically, but with vast religious sway [map 68].
- Prague became the **capital of Europe** and the **cultural focus of a wealthy empire**, since Charles was Holy Roman Emperor and resided there, many architectural splendors were built [see p 47].
- Contemporaries called the era the "Golden Age". Tourists in Czechoslovakia today can see how advanced civilization was at that time, and learn cultural, political and religious history [10; 42; 43; 44; 56].
- **German** was spoken by the elite; **Czech** was considered the dialect of peasants.
- Europe's trade routes crisscrossed in the south through **Prague** to **Venice**, in the north to the **Baltic Sea**, in the east to **Kiev** & **Constantinople**, and in the northwest to **Flanders**.
- Roads improved. The network of roads fanned out from Prague. The economy thrived.
- 1347-51 the **Bubonic Plague** killed one third of the population in Europe, 33 million [49, pp 103-9], but Bohemia and most of Poland escaped. The rest of Europe was sinking into chaos [10, pp 28-32].
- 1377-1453 England and France were engaged in the mutually destructive **100 Years' War** [pp 43-46]
- Charles IV established 35 new monasteries in Bohemia and Moravia. Many old churches were rebuilt.
- 1348 Emperor Charles IV **founded Charles University at Prague**, the first university in central Europe.
- 1403 **Jan Hus** became Rector [see pp 52-53].

- 1378-1419 king **Wenceslas IV** succeeded his father Charles IV, but the kingdom divided: he ruled the Bohemian part, and
- 1387-1437 his half-brother **Sigismund** inherited rule of the **Hungarian** section; 1410 crowned Holy Roman Emperor; 1415 Sigismund arranged the martyrdom of **Jan Hus** [see p 52].
- **Universities** founded: 1364 **Krakow** Poland; 1356 **Vienna** Austria; 1386 **Heidelburg**; 1388 **Cologne** [63].

French and Italian Rival Popes

- 1305-77 **Papal Headquarters** were in **Avignon** by the Rhone River, **southern France.**
- People were becoming more and more outspoken in their criticism of the morals of the clergy. **Italian** princes and city states were involved in power struggles and for control of Rome.
- Emperor **Charles** IV tried to persuade the Pope to return to Rome.
- Italian mystic **Catherine of Siena** [49, p 120], later canonized, urged the pope to give more attention to winning souls than to recovering earthly possessions.
- 1376 hoping to restore order in Rome, Pope Gregory XI moved his residence back to Rome, but the people blamed him for the riots and wars of the past 70 years, and he died [21d, p 41]. The people of Rome demanded an Italian pope, so church leaders chose the archbishop of Bari, Urban VI, an Italian. He antagonized both the Italians and French.
- Then **anti-pope Clement** VII was elected in Avignon. Urban refused to be deposed;
- 1377-1417 there were **two popes** for 40 years. France, Scotland and some German cities supported Clement, but England, the Holy Roman Empire and many German states favored Urban. Monastic orders were split in their loyalties [Continued p 50].

The Reunited Piast Dynasty Revitalized and Expanded Poland

[Continued pp 27-28]

- 1138 when Boleslav III died Poland was divided among four sons [27, p 10], resulting in disunity until 1320; the Duke of Mazovia (Masowiecki) ruled the central to NE plains, later called Warsaw district.
- 1308 the **Teutonic Knights** seized **Gdansk (Danzig** in German), slew the Christian Polish duke and population, built a castle and rebuilt what is still the Old Town, to provide a safe outpost for the order. The location was on the west side of the **Vistula delta** [28, pp 421-4]. 1309 the Grand Master moved the rest of the Teutonic Knights from Venice to Gdansk; expanded nearby **Marienburg (Malbork)** into a massive fort [28, p 401-3, 415-7]; occupied most land along the Baltic Sea, and became a serious threat to Poland [27, p 10].
- 1320 **Ladislaus** I (**Wladyslaw** I) the Short, reunified Poland; was crowned King. For another 450 years the crown was the symbol of Polish Unity [12 Macropedia Vol 25, pp 930-944].
- 1333-1370 his son **Casimir** III **the Great (Kazimierz** III) **Wielki** was **the last in the Piast Dynasty.**

In the northwest, **Pomerania** was annexed by the Teutonic Knights [27, p 10]. They ruled **Gdansk (Danzig)**, cutting off **Poland's** access to the **Baltic Sea,** and also acquired lands in central and south Germany. At this time German farmers were invited or conscripted by the knights into western Poland.
- German businessmen and artisans also migrated into towns and cities, stimulating their prosperity. Cities thrived, such as in northwest **Poznan (Posen** in German) [27, p 80] to Gdansk in the north [27, p 88].

In the southwest, **Silesia** was taken by Bohemia, which consolidated Poland.

Casimir built more than **50 castles** on hilltops, **like the Chinese wall,** most in **nearby Silesia,** to protect Krakow from Bohemian invasions [28, p 208]; built Gothic churches and 80 monasteries all over Poland.

In the south Casimir **annexed Galicia** from Bohemia.
- In the south **Krakow**, a very old city [28, pp 144;175-203], was capital 1038-1596; produced great wealth from amber, salt, sulfur, copper and lignite coal. **Trade flowed** on roads from Krakow to **Italy**, **Kiev**, **Russia** and **Constantinople**.

In the southeast the **Boyars** (noblemen) were **Ruthenian (Ukranian)**. 1323-40 the Boyars elected **Boleslaw Jeizy** of **Mazovia**, central to NE Poland, to rule. Casimir III united them with **Krakow;** formed a larger **Galicia;** favored Polish nobles; forced the Boyars to Polanize and convert from Orthodox to Roman Catholic. The **Orthodox Church** had many parishes in SE Poland, influenced by **Kiev** [27, pp 163-5, 236].
- Casimir III codified law & created uniform administration [27, p 10]. He supported the development of many cities and towns and a social class of **burghers** and **merchants**.

Religious tolerance lasted for two centuries. **Jewish** refugees were protected [12 Macropedia Vol 25 p 930].

In the northeast **the Knights** 1346 annexed **Estonia** a Finno-Ugic language group [maps 24, 27, 38 and 55].

- Magnificent Romanesque & Gothic town halls, cathedrals & churches were constructed in Posen, Krakow and many towns. 14th C Cathedral ***The Decapitation of St. John the Baptist*** in Warsaw was built[27; 28; 42] (repaired about 1810 by stone mason/sculptor Johann Schneider & son Johann) [40;69, pp 10-11].
- 1347-51 while the **Bubonic Plague** (Black Death) devastated Europe, **only Poznan** (Posen) in northwest and the north Teutonic Knights were hit hard [60, p 75], while the rest of land-locked Poland, **Lithuania**, **Bohemia** and eastern Europe prospered.
- 1362 the port of Gdansk joined the **Hanseatic League** so the knights became wealthy.
- In the northeast 1341-77 **King Olgierd** expanded and modernized **Lithuania** [20, p 148] [map 68].
- In the south 1307-42 Charles Robert of **Anjou** (**Angevin**), a **French** dynasty, was elected to rule **Hungary**.
- 1364 **Krakow** Academy, later renamed Jagiellonian University, was founded. **Italian** architects and craftsmen constructed outstanding **Renaissance arts** and **architecture** there.
- (1135-1413 Angevins surnamed Plantagenet ruled **England** [pp 22 and 43-44]).
- 1342-82 **Louis** I (Lewis) **Anjou**, son of Charles Robert, became king of Hungary and:
- 1370 when Poland's Casimir III, last of the Piast Dynasty died, as he had no heir he had decreed that his throne pass to his nephew Louis I of Hungary, to keep his expanded realm from breaking apart [49,p100].
- 1370-82 **Louis** I **Anjou** the Great, was king of Poland & Hungary [20, p 148] [more p 55; maps pp 38, 55].
- 1384-6 his daughter **Queen Jadwiga** succeeded, married Grand Prince **Ladislaus Jagiello** of **Lithuania**.
- The ruler of Hungary was **Sigismund**, half-brother of Wenceslas IV king of Bohemia [pp 40-41 above].
- 1386-1434 **Wladyslaw** II (**Vladislav** or **Ladislaus**) **Jagiello**, united **Poland**, **Lithuania** & **Kiev**, founding the huge kingdom **Jagellonian Dynasty** who ruled nearly 200 years [60, pp 28-29], including much of **Russia**.
- The **Golden Horde** of Tatars (Moghuls) still occupied much land north of the Black Sea [See p 55].

Golden Eras of Balkan Nations: Hungary, Serbia and Bulgaria [from p 30]

a. Hungary: consists of four regions, two lowland and two mountainous, as follows: Nagy Alford (Great Plain) south and east; Kis Alford (Little Plain) west; Transdanubia, hilly north, west and NE highlands. The Danube flows from Vienna in the NW and makes a right angle turn south in Budapest [maps xvi, 38, 55].
- 896-1301 **Arpad Dynasty**. 1102 king **Koloman** also ruled Illyrian **Croatians**. 1241-3 Mongol destruction.
- 1301 **Andras** III last Arpad died. 1301-5 Wenceslas II ruled **Bohemia**, **Poland** & **Hungary**.
-1307-42 **Charles** I **Robert** of **Anjou** (**Angevin**), a **French** dynasty, was elected to rule **Hungary**. He began to build a new castle to replace the one destroyed by the Mongols in 1241-3 [100, p 153].
- 1342-82 his son **Louis** (Lewis) **Anjou** the Great, expanded Hungarian territory through Romania and Moldova to the **Black Sea** [20, p 148; 100, p 187]; and gained control of many Dalmatian coastal towns (**Adriatric Sea**). **Bosnia** won independence from Hungary [21d, p 64]. 1367 University at Pécs was founded [55, p 410].
- 1366 Byzantine emperor John V asked for help against Ottoman Turks.
- 1382 daughters: **Maria** succeeded Louis the Great in Hungary & Jadwiga in Poland. 1387-1437 Sigismund son of Charles IV of Luxemberg-Bohemia, was king of Hungary. 1389 lengthy war with Ottoman Turks.
- 1396-1456 Muslim Ottomans ruled [21d, p 64] [pp 54 & 64]. Hungary though small overthrew them [map p 68].

b. Serbia (Servia): [Continued from pp 14, 30, 32 and maps p 20 & 38]
- 1282-1321 king Stephen Urosh II **Milutin** founded the Great Empire of Serbs [20, p 148, 170] west of **Bulgaria**.
- 1331-55 **Stephen** Urosh IV **Dushan** assumed the title **Tsar of the Serbs and Greeks** [3].
- 1346 he added **Bulgars** and **Albanians** to his domains, along the Danube River to central Greece [12, Vol 10, pp 645].
- Stephen I had founded an **Orthodox** Patriarchate at Péc, independent of the Patriarch of Constantinople (later part of **Hungary**). National boundaries changed greatly. 1371-89 **Lazar** ruled Serbia [20, p 148].
- 1389-1459 Serbs, allied with Bosnia and Bulgaria, were invaded/defeated by Ottoman Turks [21d], causing mass migrations of Serbs and Kosovos from southern ancestral land, to push NW into Bosnia and Croatia.

c. Bulgaria: [from p 3, 14 and 32; maps: pp 20, 38]
- 1185 brothers **Ivan** and **Peter Asen** were blond haired Turkic **Cumans** [map 38] who helped the Asian Bulgarians push back Byzantines and create the 2nd Bulgarian dynasty with [55b, p 93-95, 99].
- By mid-13th century Bulgaria had become a **superpower** (most of present-day Albania, half of Greece and Romania and parts of Serbia and Turkey), but it fell increasingly under Turkish domination [55b, pp 49-54, 73, 83-4].
- 1277 **Czar Constantine Asen** was killed by a peasant usurper [95, p 179]. 1280 Bulgaria were under **Serbia**, but
- 1396-1878 Bulgaria was occupied by the Ottoman Turks, 500 years [see pp 43 and 54].

The Turkish Ottoman Empire Gained Supremacy [Continued from p 32]

- 1261 Greek Emperor **Michael Palaeologus**, who had united various Greek districts, drove the **Franks** out of the city of Constantinople. His dynasty **restored the Byzantine Empire** and ruled until 1453, but by then had gradually declined [49, p 20]. 1301 destruction of the Byzantine (Orthodox) Constantinople began.
- Orthodox Christians in east European countries looked increasingly to Moscow for moral leadership.
- 1288 the Turkish Ottoman Empire was founded. In 1290 **Osman** I was awarded the title **Sultan** by the Caliph of Cairo and held power all over the middle east [12 Vol 9, p 6]. Successors:
- 1324-60 **Orphan**; 1360-89 **Murad** I 1389-1402 **Bayezid** I, conquered most of Anatolia (now Turkey). Only Constantinople remained free.
- 1345-6 Ottoman Turks crossed into Europe & seized **Thrace, Macedonia** & **Bulgaria** [maps 20, 61 & 68].
- Poland and the Balkan nations (Bulgaria, Serbia and Hungary) were enjoying a golden era of expansion/ power [p 42]. The **Danube River** flows west to east from the Alps 666 miles between Bulgaria on the south shore and Romania on the north, to the **Black Sea.** There were three largely **Romanian-speaking** feudal states: **Transylvania**, **Wallachia** and **Moldavia**. Turkish occupation separated/subjugated them to pay tribute; Transylvania was part of **Hungary** [55, pp 584-9, 639].
- 1389 **Serbia** was defeated at **Kosovo** [12 Vol 9, p 6; Vol 10, p 645] and taken over by the Ottoman Turks [55, pp 25-27; 278]. They resented being moved by Byzantine to the Dinaric mountains to serve as a buffer, as did the coastal Bosnians.
- 1396 OttomanTurks defeated **Hungary** and **Poland** at Nicopolis on the **Danube River** and pushed on to **Vienna**, **Austria** and **Germany** but were repulsed. Long warfare north of the Danube ensued. South of the Danube **Albania, Serbia, Bulgaria** and Byzantine Greece were ruled by **Ottomans** 500 years [pp 38, 68].

The Ottoman Empire Crushed by Mongol Timur [Continued from p 32]

- 1369 **Timur** (**Tamerlane**, meaning **Timur the lame**) of Samarkand, Turkistan (1336-1405) wounded his knee in his teens but developed great prowess on horseback [15, pp 295-6]. As a warrior leader on a grand scale, he subjugated/united many Tartar/Mongol (Mogul) tribes; became the **Great Khan** of Asia, his armies highly mobile over great distances.
- 1380-90 **Timur destroyed the Golden Horde** of Mongols in south Russia, ending their 200 years of oppressive occupation of Russia. He reached **Moscow**, but withdrew [20, p 99, 174]. Muscovites gained power.
- 1402 Timur defeated the **Persians**, **Ottomans**, and the **Mamluks of Egypt** and **Syria** [49, pp 145-153]. (In 1398 he had conquered Delhi. The **Mogul empire in India** lasted from 1526-1853), 327 years [167, pp 67-68].
- Timur scored several victories over the Ottomans, who <u>were so beaten and defeated that they gave up expansion into Europe for 50 years</u> [See p 54 for further expansion into Europe after 1451] [21d, pp 47-70].
- The Mongols did not remain; leaving ruins behind, moved on to conquer other Asian nations [21d, pp 70-103].

English Territory Within France, Scotland and Wales [from pp 22-23, 25 and 33]

- 1154-89 Maud's son Henry II ruling Normandy, Anjou and England, acquired **Aquitaine** in SW France by marrying **Eleanor**, heiress last in the line of the large duchy [map 45]; was in the 2 nd Crusade [pp 22, 24-25].
- Eleanor was mother of kings **Richard** I the Lion Heart 1189-99 [p 25 - 3 rd Crusade], and **John** 1199-1216.
- 1216-1272 **Henry** III, John's son succeeded. 1204 **principality Anjou was conquered** by **Philip** II Capetian king of **France**. Loss of ancestral property in France was never fully accepted by the English.
- 1272-1307 **Edward** I eldest son of Henry III, laid the foundations of **English Common Law**, and was **known as English Justinian**. <u>Parliament</u> began partnership of the King, barons, knights from every shire and leaders from towns [49, pp 54-61, 80-1, 90]; taxation with consent of Parliament. He conquered **Wales** and **Scotland.**
- 1307-27 **Edward** II was first to receive the **title Prince of Wales**. He gained supremacy with **Scotland** and made peace, but **Robert Bruce** revolted/won independence for the Scots from Edward II at **Bannockburn**.
- 1327 Edward II because he was partial to favorites, was deposed and murdered.
- 1314-16 **Capetians** Louis X; John II 1316; Philip V 1316-22; Charles IV the Fair 1322-8 [12 Vol 4, p 920; Vol 2, p 829].
- 1328-50 **Philip** VI **Valois dynasty**, seized the throne of France after the death **of his cousin**, Charles the Fair, **the last Capetian**, who lacked male heirs. Uniting the domains of two dynasties enhanced his power.
- **Philip** VI **Valois** ruler of most of France was a cousin of both Capetians Phillip II and Charles IV; began "diplomatic machinations" with **Scottish nobles**, long allied with France [21d, pp 17-45].
- 1327-77 **Edward** III succeeded his father Edward II, subdued Scotland; 1332 deposed **Robert Bruce;** was recognized overlord by **Edward Baloil**, king of the Scots. Edward III considering Philip VI a usurper, **turned his attention to France;** feared possibility of French military intervention in his domains [49, pp 93-4].

Map: ***English Possessions in France in*** 1180, 1272 & 1180; **Map:** ***English Possessions in*** 1314

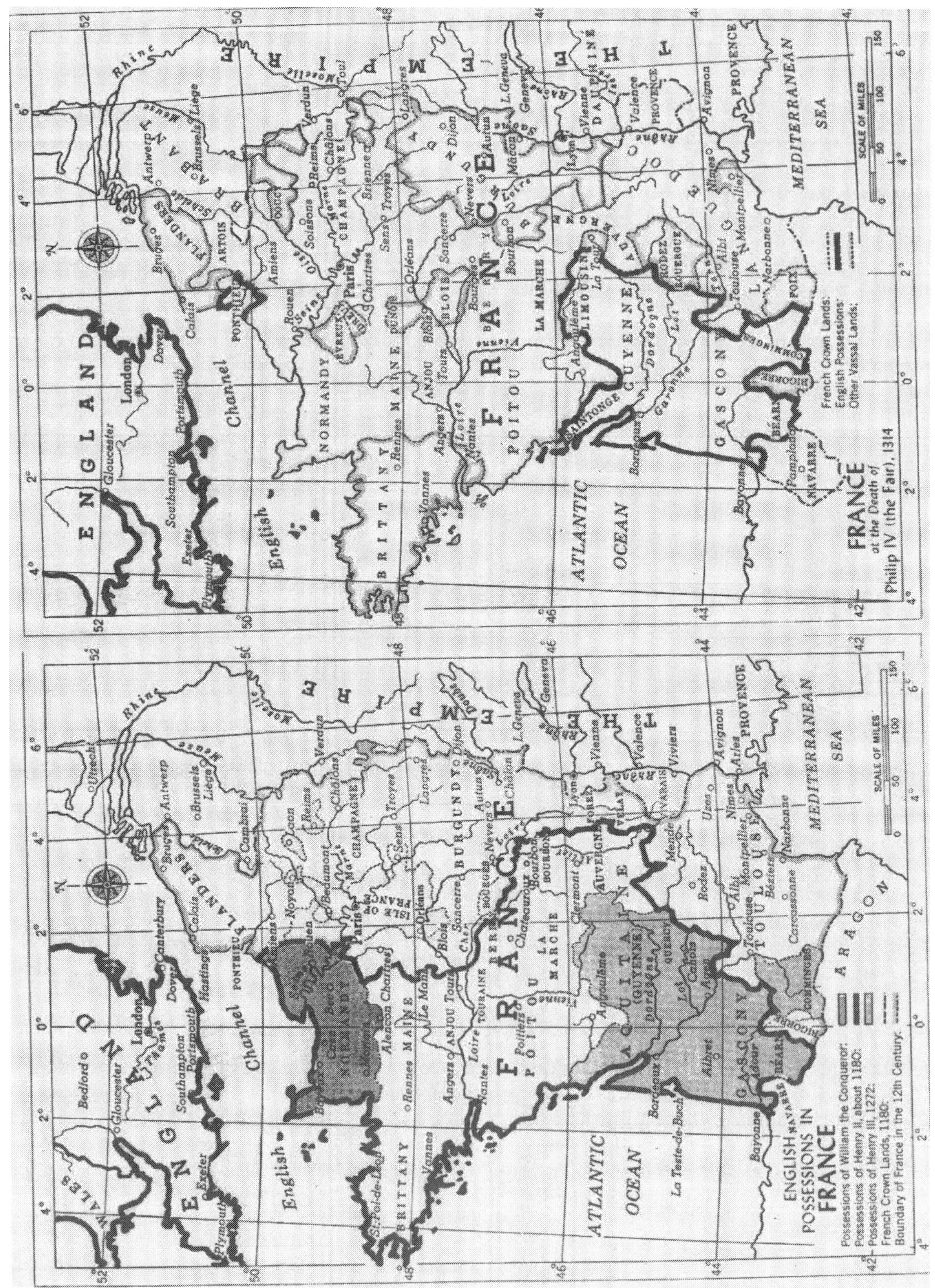

The Hundred Years' War - 1338 to 1453

[Continued from pp 22 & 43.]

- May 1337 **Philip** VI **Valois occupied Aquitaine**, Edward III's possession, English territory since 1152 when Henry II married Eleanor. Then **Edward** III of **England** claimed the throne of France; since **his mother Isabella** was a sister of the last two Capetian Kings, he saw no reason why the throne could not descend through her, the female line [maps p 44]. This triggered the Hundred Years' War [49, pp 91-99; 16, p 349].
- 1339 September Edward III ravaged **northeast France**, but withdrew as winter set in.
- 1340 June, with **long bows** he soundly defeated the French fleet; due to debt could not fund war on land.
- 1342 Phillip took **Brittany**, northwest France. Edward fought back with 12,000 armored knights and men. There was sporadic fighting until Edward had a foothold in **Breton** in 1345.
- Philip confiscated the lands of a powerful Norman Baron, who then turned to Edward for help.
- 1346 Edward arrived and laid waste the countryside in a **drive toward Paris**, so Phillip mobilized a huge cavalry, backed up by men with old-fashioned **crossbows**. At **Crecy**, northeastern France, the opposing forces met in combat. Edward's men with great accuracy with **six-foot longbows** shot and killed most of the French. Much of the flower of French nobility lay dead.
- Edward did not have the funds to proceed south, but turned aside and laid siege on **Calais** for a year, and took it. He returned to England in triumph [49, pp 91-99, 103-9].
- 1347-51 the **Black Death** decimated their populations and changed feudal relationships [49, p 130-6]. Many serfs left the land of their lord and worked in towns.
- 1350-64 **Jean** II (**John**) the Good, succeeded as King of France, when Philip IV Valois died.
- 1350 Edward III began to build **Windsor Castle** near London, England.
- 1355 the **Black Prince**, **Edward Prince of Wales**, Edward III's eldest son, with 6000 men renewed the war and gained much booty. The next summer two English armies raided France, led by the Black Prince and his brother, the **Duke of Lancaster**, planning to link up. King Jean set out to drive a wedge between them. He was defeated and taken hostage for four years, in the tower of London. France was stunned and in disorder.
- 1360 Edward III arranged a peace settlement in which he regained much of France, but not the crown, and a ransom of three million crowns was promised.
- Peace lasted only until 1369 [21d, pp 17-45], as the French king could not agree for long to lose his authority .
- 1305-1375 the **Pope residing in Avignon France**, being pro-French made difficulties for England [49, p 120].
- The **Black Prince** became **Duke of Aquitaine**. He levied high taxes, so the nobles appealed to Charles V the new king of France. The French and English could not agree on treaty terms.
- 1364-1380 **Charles** V ruled France. He named three of his brothers Dukes: of **Berry**, **Burgundy** and **Anjou** (not related to the former house of Anjou) starting new dynasties. (From this line later professional kings were elected to rule other countries.)
- 1369 **Black Prince** renewed fighting against French king Charles V, intending to gain the crown of France [16]. He became ill with a recurring fever, and in 1370 he supervised a battle from his sick-bed, but lost territory. Finally, leaving **John of Gaunt**, **Duke of Lancaster** in charge of the war, he returned to England; died 1376.
- 1377-99 **Richard** II son of the Black Prince [21d, pp 25, 37, 40], became King of Great Britain at 10 years of age.
- 1381 oppressed farm serfs rebelled, led by **Walt Tyler.** Though only 14 years old, Richard went out bravely to talk with them, **averting civil war**, promising to improve conditions; he did so for a time [49, pp 130-135; 60, pp 130-5].
- Richard II **married Bohemian princess Anne**, sister of King **Wenceslas** III; daughter of Emperor **Charles** IV. She and Bohemian scholars at **Oxford**, under **John Wycliffe**, spread Protestant teachings in Bohemia.
Queen Anne's alleged crown [98, p 124]resembles the crown of her ancestor Wenceslaus I [10, p 26]. She was from Prague, Bohemia, a culture with exquisite jewels and architecture [20, pp 160-2] [See pp 35, 47-48].
- 1384 Wycliffe died. His followers the **Lollards** continued to teach, though persecuted.
- 1380-1422 **Charles** VI **Valois** at 12 years of age succeeded his father as king of France. **Two boy kings** Richard II of England and Charles VI of France came together to try to bring about peace. There was initial success which did not last.
- Richard II's court enjoyed many international visitors who influenced **Geoffrey Chaucer**, poet [20, pp 163].
- 1387 Chaucer published **Canterbury Tales** a collection of entertaining poetry, in colloquial English. These enduring, witty satires bringing to life every type of pilgrim and traveler en route to the shrine of Saint **Thomas à Becket**. This and other poems made Chaucer the admired "Father of English Poetry".
- Richard II appointed architects to renew the Great Hall and roof of **Westminster** "an amazing combination of aesthetics and mechanics ....which owes it's existence to the taste and cultural energy of King Richard II" [98, p 103; 20, p 163].

- 1396 to try to bring peace between France and England, Richard II was advised to marry a second time, the six year old daughter of king Charles VI of France [49, pp 135-144; 2c, p 37].
- **Duke of Lancaster**, **John of Gaunt**, had continued the war until 1396. He died 1399. Truce lasted almost 20 years [95, p 207]. However a mood of discontent continued because the English had lost control of much land in France[49, p 129], both south and north. In England unrest escalated. Taxes were high.
- 1399 Richard II was forced to abdicate, and died 1400, probably murdered. The **Plantagenet Dynasty divided** in two, **Lancaster** and **York** [16].
- 1399-1413 **Henry** IV (son of John of Gaunt) seized the throne of England from Richard II, and became the **first of three Lancaster kings**.
- The Hundred Years' War continued until 1453 [Continued p 49]

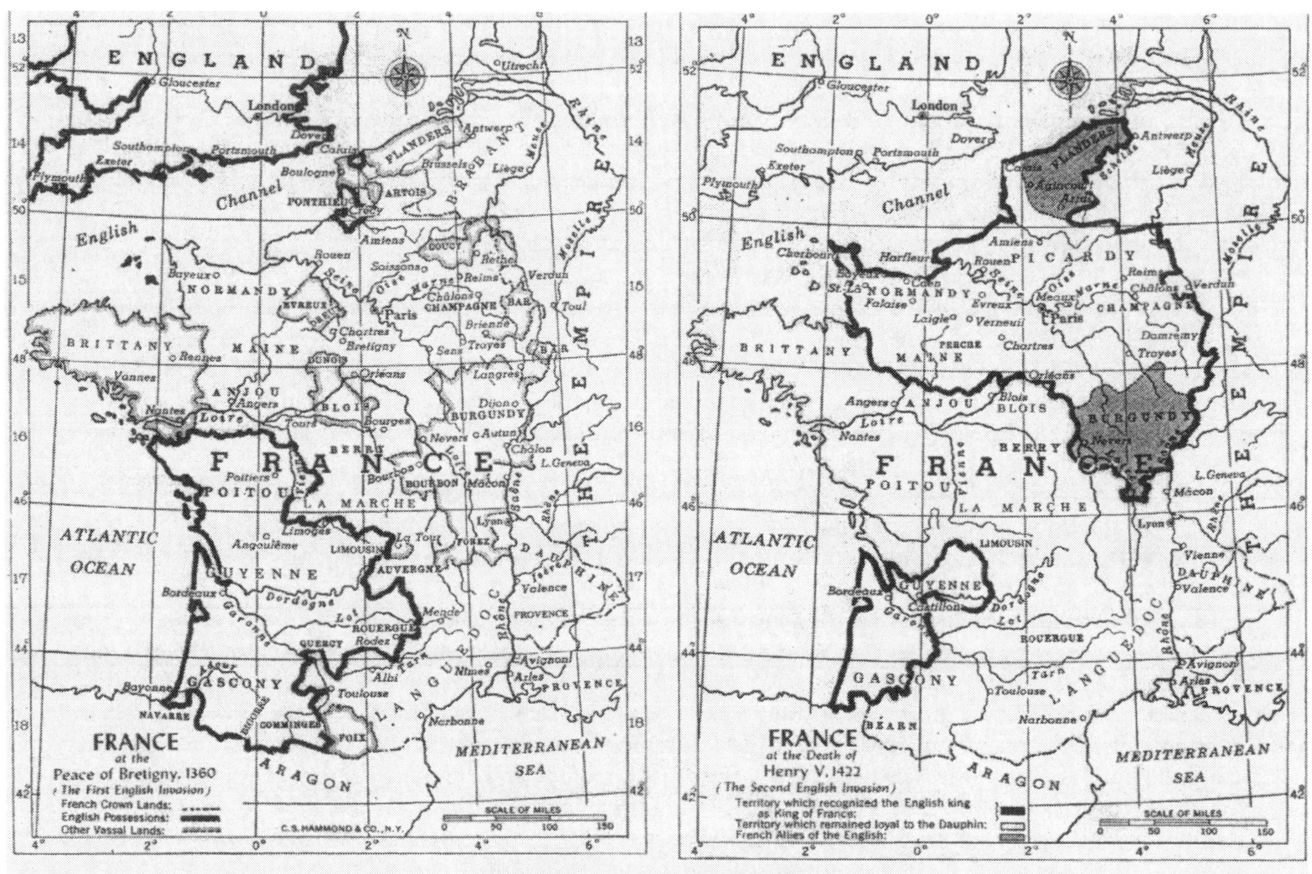

Map: *English Possessions in France in* 1360 *and* 1422 [9b, p 185].

Chapter Eight - 1300 to 1399

Architecture During the Revival of Learning

Architecture of Prague - Cultural Focus of Europe

[from pp 35 and 40]

-1278-1305 **Wenceslas** II was king of Bohemia, Moravia and Hungary. [pp 29-30]
-1305-6 his son **Wenceslas** III, the last of the Premsyl Dynasty was assassinated.
-1310-47 Duke **John of Luxemburg** was **crowned king of Bohemia;** married a daughter of Wenceslas II. The house of Luxemburg-Bohemia ruled Bohemia until 1437 [9, Vol 4, p 188; 10, p 27].
- His son **Charles**, born 1316, **educated in Paris** grew accustomed to the splendor of the French court.
- 1333 at 17 years of age Charles became governor of Bohemia-Moravia. Soon he became concerned about the run-down state of castles and churches.
- 1344 under King John of Luxemburg, the Pope approved founding of the Archbishopric of Prague.
- **Matthias of Arras** was appointed to build a Gothic Cathedral. King John was succeeded by son:
- 1347-78 **Charles** IV was crowned king. 1347-51 the Bubonic plague devastating Europe, spared Bohemia. Prosperity grew from mining and trading in salt and silver.
-1348 Charles IV founded **Charles University** the first university in central Europe. In **a** building spree he updated and added many elaborate new structures [55, p 188].
-1353 Schwabish (Swabish) **Peter Parler** a Gothic architect from Cologne, was engaged [10, p 156; 55, p 140].
-1355 Charles IV was crowned **Holy Roman Emperor**. He renovated the Romanesque castle-palace in an innovative Gothic style with "unusual swirling, interlaced vaulting" [55, p 140,192]. The main hall was large enough for a tournament of horses. Nearby **Basilica St. George** was kept Romanesque inside, but with elaborate updating. Adjoining are the **Diet** (parliament) and the **High Court**. A city wall were built around these massive structures.
- **Prague** capital of **Bohemia**, became the cultural focus of Central Europe; many architectural splendors were built. Because the Holy Roman Emperor Charles IV resided there, Prague became the capital of Europe and of a vast wealthy empire. The era was described by contemporaries as the ***Golden Age***. Europe's trade route roads crisscrossed through Prague.
-1348-1365, 30 km SW of Prague, Charles IV built **Karlstein Castle/Palace** [55, p 213], [10, pp 176-8], to safeguard the crown jewels. In the **Chapel of the Holy Cross** at Karlstein Palace, the lower walls were studded with 2000 large semi-precious stones, and the upper walls were lined with paintings of the saints.
-1357 Parler began to build beautiful Gothic **Charles Bridge** across the wide Vltava (Moldau) River. It is 1500 feet long and 30 feet wide, and has a beautiful Gothic tower at each end, for defense purposes [55, p 203].
-1362-4 **St. Vitus Cathedral** begun in 926 **as a basilica**, was greatly enlarged. It was the first cathedral built with fan vaulting [10, p 155-9]. The bottom level of the sanctuary was quite dark, but through new high windows the cathedral was flooded with light [49, pp 28-31; 148-150, 136]. The remains of fourth century Sicilian martyr St.Vitus were reburied here [55, pp 189-192]. Inside are 21 chapels. "Good" King Wenceslas 903ca - 935, referred to in the English Christmas carol, is venerated as a saint in a chapel bearing his name [55, pp 138, 140, 192]; the lower part of the tomb encrusted with over 1300 pieces of jasper and amethyst; the upper part with paintings of the saint's life.
- On the **west bank** of Moldau river are fourteenth century **Prague Castle** and **St. Vitus cathedral**.
- On the **east bank** are eleventh century **Old Town Hall** [55, pp 160-61] and **Tyn Church**, which in 1380 Parler began building on the site of earlier churches. It has majestic 260 foot twin spires. Here **Jan Hus** heard early Reformation sermons, and became concerned about the need for reform.
-Tourists in Czechoslovakia today wonder at their advanced cultural, political and religious history. Excellent tourist books [42, 43 and 55] contain fascinating information on architecture and history of many towns and cities.
-1380 Peter Parler started building **St. Barbara church** with lovely fan vaulting at **Hutna Hora**, a **silver mining** town.
-In 1399 Parler was buried in St. Vitus Cathedral [10, p 156] [Continued p 85].
-Charles IV established 35 **new monastaries** throughout Bohemia-Moravia and rebuilt many old churches
-1378-1419 **Wenceslaus** IV son of Charles IV ruled Bohemia; his **half-brother Sigismund** ruled Hungary,
-1403 **Jan Hus** a Roman catholic priest, became rector of Charles University. He advocated poverty for clergy and allegiance only to Christ, and he opposed accumulation of power in one man, the Pope.
-1410 **Sigismund** king of Hungary was crowned Holy Roman Emperor [See pp 40-41].
-1412 **Jan Hus was excommunicated** but continued preaching outside the university in **Bethlehem Chapel** which seated 3000 [55, p 197], who enjoyed singing hymns and reading the Bible published in the **Czech** language.
-1415 Hus was **martyred**, bound to a stake and burnt to death [55, p 138-9] by order of Emperor Sigismund.

Construction in Poland by the Reunited Piast Dynasty [See p 41]

-1333-1370 **Casimir** III the Great, of the Piast Dynasty of Poland, built more than 50 **castles on hilltops**, like the Chinese wall, mostly in Silesia, **to protect Krakow** from invasions by princes from the west [28, p 208].

-He built **Gothic town halls** and churches all over Poland. A Basilica was built in **Warsaw**: the **Cathedral of the Decapitation of St. John the Baptist**. [Continued pp 144-146].

-In eastern Poland many **Orthodox style churches** were built [27, pp 163-5, 236]. They had small onion-shaped domes and icons, influenced by Kiev, Russia.

High Gothic and Late Gothic Architecture 1280-1500 [Continued from pp 33- 35]

-1200-1280 **the second phase of Gothic Architecture**, known as **High Gothic**, emphasized achieving height plus rich visual effects, a new architectural style [12 Vol 5, p 383] called **Rayonnant** in France and **Decorated Gothic** in England. Moldings and window tracery became elaborate.

-Pastel colors were used in stained glass to let in more light than the deep colors of previous eras.

-Pinnacles with spires were added on top of piers, or a parapet and corner pinnacles on top of towers.

-Small buttresses were added to some pinnacles.

-Waterspouts with grotesque beasts or birds, called gargoyles, drained rain (evil spirits) off roofs [24, p 64].

-1280 in France the **Flamboyant style** of construction was begun and favored until 1500. Stone tracery in windows looked like flames. Vertical support was reduced to a minimum "allowing an almost continuous expanse of glass and tracery" [12 Vol 5, p 383; Vol 22, pp 123-5]. Churches were either built in this style or completed in it.

-These features are also seen in many **town halls**, **guild halls** and **aristocratic homes**.

-1250-1400 the twin towers at **Lincoln Cathedral** had pinnacles at the four corners [12 Vol 22, pp 115-6]. Windows were of great width and height with elaborate stone tracery.

- 1320 the stone tracery in the nave and west front of **Yorkminster**, appears to flow like flames [12 Vol 5, p 383].

-1375 to 1500 in England **Perpendicular style** of construction was preferred. Examples are **Gloucester Cathedral** and **King's College Chapel, Cambridge** [12, Vol 5, p 383].

-1329-84 John **Wycliffe** taught at Oxford University [See p 39]. Some of his students were Bohemians. **King Richard** II married **Anne**, sister of Bohemian King **Wenceslas** IV, daughter of Emperor Charles IV the great builder. There was interchange of culture, religion and architectural taste [See p 45].

-1377-99 Richard II's court enjoyed a steady stream of international visitors. He appointed architects to renew the **Great Hall** and **roof of Westminster** "an amazing combination of aesthetics and mechanics. . . which owes its existence to the taste and cultural energy of King Richard II" [98, p 103; 20, p 163].

Architecture in Spain [Continued from p 36]

-1236 The Moorish regime of Cordoba and in 1248 of Sevilla, fell to various northern Spanish kingdoms. Muslims fled to **Granada,** ruled by the **Nasrid emirate**, recently founded by Mohammed al-Ahmar.

-1354-91 the dazzling Islamic palace/fort, the **Alhambra** was built at **Granada** [9 Vol 2, p 279; 83, pp 24-5, 27]. Its ornate domed ceilings, delicately sculpted marble courts and fountains delighted courtiers and harem at that time, and visitors ever since [21d, pp 55-7]. Granada was the last stronghold of the Moors [42, p 990-92].

-The **Nasrids** stayed in power by playing off Aragon and Castile against each other. With an influx of traders, artisans and scholars, this dynasty flourished for 250 years [28b, pp 801photo inserts-887, 892].

-Preoccupation with mysticism, passionate literature and luxury of palace gardens led to lowered defenses.

-1492 **Ferdinand of Aragon** and **Isabella of Castille** united (married 1479), defeated the Nasrid Moors.

-Meanwhile Aragon-Castille had absorbed Nazrid culture.

-1499 *the Inquisition* reached Alhambra [3] [See pp 27, 49].

Clocks, Bells and Organs

-1354 a **mechanical clock** was installed in **Strasbourg Cathedral** [3], west of the Rhine River.

-Soon other churches had elaborate clocks.

-Use of bells in churches spread through Europe from the sixth to eleventh centuries.

-Constant clapping caused bells to crack, so the edge was thickened, which also improved the tone.

-By 1400 the **casting of bells** in the present shape with a flared rim, had evolved [9 Vol 3, pp 412-3].

-Tuning of bells began [Continued p 68].

-**Organs** were installed in some churches [12 Vol 8, pp 993-4].

Chapter Nine - 1400 to 1499

Renaissance, Expanding Horizons and Dawn of Reformation

French and English Power Struggles [continued from p 45-46]

-1328-1477 the **Valois Dynasty** held the throne of France, before and well after the Hundred Years War.
-English **John of Gaunt** (Duke of **Lancaster**) continued war until 1396; died 1399. Truce [95, p 207] lasted 20 years. Since the English had lost control of much of France, both south and north [49, p 129] and taxes were high, discontent in England escalated. **Plantagenet Dynasty divided** into two branches **Lancaster** and **York** [16].
-1399 **Richard** II Plantagenet, was forced to abdicate, and died 1400 [continued from p 46 and 48].
-1399-1413 **Henry** IV, John of Gaunt's son, first of three **Lancaster** kings, seized the throne from Richard II.
-1413-22 **Henry** V put down a Protestant **Lollard uprising**. He claimed the throne of France. In 1415 he won a victory in Agincourt and 1420 conquered the whole of Normandy, made easy because of civil war in France.
-1422-71 at one year of age **Henry** VI became king of France and England when his father died. His uncles, Dukes of Beaufort and Gloucester were regents. 1429 under visionary **Joan of Arc** the French started to gain ground [16, p 384]. 1445 Henry Vl married **Margaret of Anjou**, mid-France.
-1453 **The Hundred Years' War ended**; the English holding only Calais across the English Channel [16].
-1453-61 Richard Duke of York was Protector in England because Henry VI went insane, being stressed over defeat in France, and **Lancaster/York quarrels**.
-1455-85 the costly **Wars of Roses** in England followed. The Houses of York and Lancaster fought in England with heavy slow horses and armor [95]. Richard Duke of York was killed after defeating the Lancasters. His son Edward of York of York succeeded, although Henry VI lived (insane) until 1471.
-1461-1483 King **Edward** IV reigned well for 22 years [60, pp 111-117], settled disorder and avoided foreign wars.
-Meanwhile 1467-77 Duke **Charles the Bold of Burgundy** in 1468 married **Margaret, sister of Edward** IV of England, considered treason by the French [95, p 228]. Commerce and the arts flourished in independent wealthy **Burgundy** (eastern France), **Alsace-Lorraine** (southeast) and **Flanders** (north) [60, pp 90-99].
-He died 1477 when the French attacked, assisted by **Swiss foot-soldiers** armed with **halberds** (a sharp axe mounted on the end of an eight-foot pole). Standing shoulder-to-shoulder soldiers formed "a barrier of jagged steel that cavalry could not break through" [8, pp 51, 42-51].
-The **French** monarchy **absorbed Burgundy** and ruled all of France [48, pp 20-21].
-1483-85 **Richard** III brother of Edward IV, usurped the throne from his young nephew Edward V who with his little brother, in the tower of London apparently were murdered. Richard III died in the War of Roses.
-1485-1509 **Henry** VII **first Tudor king** was also a **Lancaster** (of Welsh-English-French blood) [16, p 331, 775] had wisely married Elizabeth of **York** in 1486, ending the War of Roses. Daughter Margaret married James IV of **Scotland** promoting unity. Professional civil servants were trained; trade with the **Netherlands** encouraged.
-1477 and 1485 **Christopher** (**Cristoforo**) **Columbus** from **Genoa**, **Italy** visited England twice, France and Portugal, seeking funding to sail west **in search of Cathay** (**China**), believing the world is round [95, pp 230-1].
-1486 **John Cabot** settled in **England** (born in **Genoa**, a citizen of **Venice**, had been to **Mecca** for the spice trade; was familiar with **Marco Polo's book**). He met **Bristol** merchants who financed Atlantic fisheries and traded with **Iceland**. They had previously commissioned ships to find "Brasil" [112,,p 42-3] [see next page].
-1490 Henry VII took control of wool trade from bankers in Florence, Italy; promoted English bankers.

The Inquisition was Intensified in Spain [Continued from p 27]

-1208 the Inquisition begun by Pope Innocent III so as to eliminate people who were considered heretics, continued for 500 years,.
-It took 100 years to stamp out **Albigenses** in southern France, Spain, Germany and Italy.
-The **Waldenses** were destroyed, yet today are the leading Protestant body in **Italy** [45, pp 776-790; 48, pp 66-67].
-1478 **Isabella** of **Castile** began inquisition against Christian **Jews** who secretly practiced their original faith.
-1479 **Ferdinand** of **Aragon** married **Isabella** of **Castile** uniting their kingdoms and 3 other Spanish houses.
-1483 Ferdinand and Isabella appointed Dominican monk **Torquemada** as Inquisitor.
-1487 Pope Innocent Vlll gave Torquemada the title **Grand Inquisitor** [95, pp 233, 235, 237; 16, p 363]. 10,200 people were burned, 97,000 imprisoned/tortured. **Lutherans** and **Calvinists** were kept out of Spain [See pp 62-63]
- 1492 Ferdinand and Isabella took over **Muslim Granada**; intensified the Inquisition; ordered 150,000 **Jews** to convert or leave; had thousands tortured for heresy [139, p 228]; personally controlled the religious police; forbade study in foreign universities [48, pp 23, 66-70; 45, p 790]. Importing of books was punishable by death.

Renaissance Popes, Bankers and Artists

[Continued from pp 39, 41]

-1377-1417 there were **two popes**, in Rome and Avignon, France. There was luxurious living and much immorality [139, p 185]. When both popes died, papal courts in both Avignon and Rome again elected rival popes.
-1409 a joint council overturned the Avignon election; elected Alexander V, a third pope [21 b, p 41].
-1414-7 the lengthy 16th Ecumenical **Council** held at **Constance** ended this rivalry with the election of **Martin V** as Pope (1417-31). The Council of Constance also **martyred Jon Hus** [See pp 47, 52].
-1420 Pope Martin V proclaimed a crusade against Hussites [21f, p 105].
-Throughout Europe cities became independent and wealthy from mining, crafts and commerce [111, pp 180-1].
-Italian city-states (**Milan**, **Venice**, **Genoa** and **Florence**) and the papacy were in a power struggle, yet travel, banking, diplomacy and international trade expanded [48, pp 27-42; 49, pp 123-127] [See below p 52].
-Merchants of **Genoa** and **Venice** had dominated trade by land with the far east, for 500 years [21 f, p 11]. **Ships** of **Venice** were mass-produced for speed and maneuverability on the Mediterranean [111, p 183] not the Atlantic.
-**Medici bankers** in Florence [21 f., p 47-] held political power over popes and governments [60, pp 40-7] and were patrons of artists, sculptors and architects [139, pp 185-7].
-1452-1519 artist **Leonardo da Vinci** had genius in all branches of learning [12 Vol 9, p 1020-1] [See p 63].
-1450-1626 **St. Peter's Church, Rome** was built over a period of 176 years [Continued p 63].
-1447-55 **Pope Nicholas** V born 1397 son of a physician, studied at University of Bologna, tutored wealthy families in Florence, and graduated with an MA. He was a renowned **Humanist scholar**. At this time this meant studying the classical literature of Greece and Rome and cultivating classical style in literature and art.
-1450 he founded the **Vatican library** containing a copy of every known Greek and Roman work. The number of books grew from 340 to 1500, all artistically ornamented. Pope Nicholas V authorized the king of **Portugal** to attack people along the west coast of Africa, seize their property & capture their people as slaves [45, p779].
-1458-1503 corrupt popes bought their way to power; had many illegitimate children [45, pp 778-9].
-1492-1503 Pope Alexander VI (Rodrigo **Borgia**) ignored the Bible, created Cardinals for wealth; appointed his ruthless son **Cesare** a Cardinal [60, p 136; 49, p 127; 21f, pp 59-64]; granted his daughters divorces and noble marriages.
-1498 he executed Dominican reformer **Savonarola** who had cleansed Florence of luxury and frivolity [16, p 663].

Search for Ocean Trade Routes to Cathay

-1394-1460 **Henry the Navigator** aided the infant science of navigation, made ships maneuverable and raised money for many voyages of exploration [16, p 330; 139, pp 194-5]. His father was King John I of Portugal, and his mother daughter of **John of Gaunt** (Duke of Lancaster, son of King Edward III of England)[16]. He built an observatory. His brother **Pedro** visited courts of Europe, learned current navigation lore, received a copy of **Marco Polo's *Travels*** [see p 26] and **Ptolemy's *Geography*** and 1406 had it translated into **Latin** [21f, pp 8-42]. Portuguese traded ever farther south along west Africa and began slave trade [60, p 53].
-Meanwhile **Chinese explorers and traders** were familiar with the East China Sea, Indian Ocean and East African coast. They had diplomatic and commercial relations with more than 30 countries [116, pp 5-6; 139, pp 210-223].
-1419-1444 Venetian **Niccolo de Conti** returned overland by caravan, after exploring **India, Java** and **Sumatra**. His reports stimulated many to travel, but the Indian Ocean was controlled by Arab ships [95].
-1453 **Constantinople fell to Turkish Muslims**. High tariffs were charged on caravans of spices, silks, cotton, dyes, perfumes, drugs, porcelain and precious stones [21f, p 11]. Europeans craved new routes to China. The **Portuguese** were the first Europeans to seek trade routes by sea only, to eastern Asia.
-1484 **King John** II **of Portugal** decided [21f, p 23] to search for the southern tip of Africa, after **astronomer Abraham Zacuto** discovered how to measure latitude by measuring the angle of the noonday sun.
-1487 **Bartholomeu Dias** sent by John II, rounded the southern tip of Africa, explored the eastern shore and returned home by the same route in 1488 [110, pp 86-9; 95, p 235]. **Cape of Good Hope** was named by King John II.
-1490 sugar cane was planted on Portuguese St. Thomas near Africa, and slaves placed there for work [95, p 235].
-1492 **Ferdinand** and **Isabella of Spain** conquered **Granada**, the last **Moorish** (Muslim) section of **Spain**. They outfitted **Columbus** with three ships to sail **west** to **China** [21e, p 60-61; 139, pp 194-5]. He discovered the islands later called **West Indies** [139, pp 194-9].
-1493 needing land for restless soldiers blocked from Africa by the Portuguese, they sent Columbus back to the West Indies as G**overnor**, **with colonists** on 17 ships.
-1496 **John Cabot**'s voyage across the Atlantic (according to an old Paris map) and/or in 1497 with Sebastian, his son, was funded by merchants in Bristol, England, with 20 men on one ship. Cabot named the first land sighted, **St. John's** on the feast day of St. John the Baptist [112, p 42-53] later named **New Founde Lande**.

Map: Voyages of Discovery to America 1492 to1611 [9b, p189]

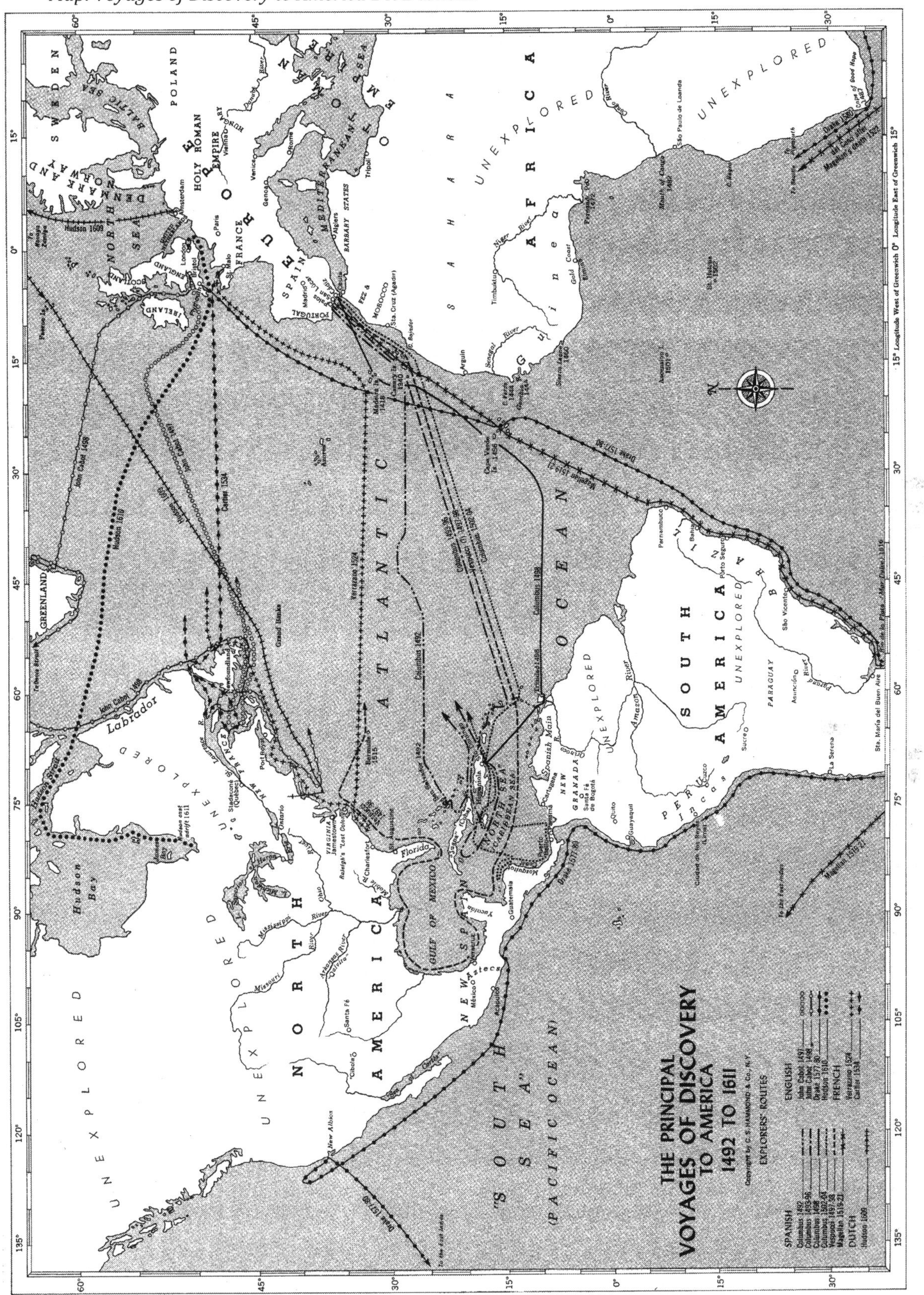

-Bristol England was home port for fishing on the Grand Banks. **Vikings** had sailed to Iceland and Greenland.
-1497 **John** and **Sebastian Cabot** returned to **Bristol**, England August 6th and publicized bountiful fishing grounds near Newfoundland [119b, p 298]. King **Henry** VII, who earlier was unable to fund **Christopher Columbus**, now gladly provided Cabot with 5 ships, 300 men, a generous agreement & letters of patent to sail again.
-1498 Cabot **explored** and claimed for England the **east coast of North America** [95, p 240; 112, p 53-4; 119b, p 155]. He was impressed with the area he named **Acadia** (later named **Nova Scotia**) [9 Vol 1, pp 96-7]. He died 1498.
-1497-9 and 1502-03 **Vasco da Gama** was sent by **King Manual** of **Portugal** (as Admiral) and again in
-1524 (as Viceroy) on three voyages around **Cape of Good Hope**, East Africa (**Mozambique** and **Kenya**) to **Calicut**, south India. Near **Goa**, India he destroyed an Arab colonists' ship and established spice trading. Thus Muslim monopoly of overland spice trade ended between **Venice** and **India** [95, p 240].
- He also tried to find **Syrian Christians** living in south India because the Byzantine Church had lost contact.
-1499 **Pedro Alvares Cabral** sailed with 13 ships to discover the rumored continent of **Atlantis**. Driven off course by winds, they discovered **Brazil** and claimed it for Portugal. Then he turned and sailed eastward and:
-1501 reached **India**. Muslim traders were routed and **Hindu** rulers played one against the other with treaties. **Portuguese colonists** stayed to run permanent depots and garrisons to collect spices, and speed up loading the many ships that followed [21e, pp 104-5]. Trade also began 2500 miles farther east at **Malacca** [21f, p 30].
-The **Portuguese** set up a central exchange in **Antwerp**, **Netherlands** because of its convenient position, for spices, copper and silver. **German** and **Italian bankers** [21e, p 106] gave liberal credit to the Portuguese to finance sailings to the far east. By controlling the spice trade, **Portugal** became the primary naval world power.

Onset of The Protestant Reformation in England and Bohemia [from pp 39-41]

- In England and Scotland, **Lollards** propagated the beliefs of **John Wycliffe**, such as simple living and reading the Bible in their own language. English King **Richard** II's **wife**, Queen **Anne**, daughter of **Wenceslas** IV, and **Bohemian students in Oxford University** spread Wycliffe's writings to Bohemia [p 16].
-1383 Holy Roman Emperor Charles IV died. The powerful kingdom of **Bohemia-Hungary was divided** between two sons: **Wenceslas** IV of Bohemia (1378-1419) and **Sigismund** king of Hungary through his wife.
-1410 Sigismund was **crowned Holy Roman Emperor** by the pope. (He died 1437).
-1371-1415 **Jan Hus**, born in the village of Husinec south Bohemia, studied at the local school and Charles University, Prague; graduated 1396 with a Master of Liberal Arts Degree. He studied Wycliffe's writings.
-1398 Hus was appointed professor and in 1400 was ordained priest. He developed Wycliffe's beliefs further, teaching Christ, not Peter was the foundation of the church; poverty for clergy; the Bible as the only creed and allegiance only to Christ. He was against power held by one man, the Pope.
-1402 Hus had so large a following that he was invited to preach outside the university in **Bethlehem Chapel** [21f, pp 93-112], which could seat 3000 people [10, pp 31-33]. He rejected purgatory, sale of indulgences and prayers to saints. He preached in Czech, not Latin or German, and composed hymns into Czech for congregational singing. His beautiful chorales with instrumental accompaniment were popular, and still are.
-1409 Jan Hus was elected Rector of Charles University in Prague, Bohemia [10, p 33]
-1409 the **University of Leipzig, Saxony** was founded by some scholars from Charles University who preferred the German language [77, p 667-; 70, p 275; 21f, pp 93-100]. Leipzig also became a major centre of learning [16].
-1411 **King Wenceslaus** IV withdrew support of Hus since he benefited from the sale of **indulgences** [10, p 31-33]. Priests and some of the nobility feared their privileged lifestyle would disappear, so persecution broke out.
-1412 Hus was excommunicated by the Archbishop, but continued preaching in Bethlehem Chapel [55, p 197].The majority of the population of Bohemia, Moravia (just to the east) and Silesia (to the north) followed Jan Hus.
-1413 he compiled his doctrines in depth under the title ***De Ecclesia***.
-1414-15 Emperor Sigismund challenged Hus to declare his position at the **Council at Constance**. Although promised safe conduct, Hus was seized, condemned as a heretic; burned at the stake [55, pp 138-9; 10, p 33; 21f, pp 93-100].
-After his martyrdom a "storm of indignation" arose from both working classes and aristocrats. A petition was signed by 450 noblemen [10, p 31].
-1419-1436 the **Hussite Wars**[10, pp 31-37; 9 Vol 4, pp 188-9] crusades waged by the Holy Roman Emperor against the followers of Jan Hus, killed most of them and annexed the province of Moravia [21f, pp 100-112]. The movement persisted underground. Many escaped NW to **Saxony,** other German states and north to **Silesia** and **Poland**.
-Poland became known as "a paradise for heretics" [pp 55, 64-65, 66].
-Silesia helped Emperor Sigismund crush the Hussites, but later, nearly all became protestants[12 Vol 10, p 803]. Emperor Sigismund kept on eliminating followers of Hus as heretics, until he died in 1437.

-1421-71 Protestant **Hussites ruled Bohemia, Moravia and Slovakia**. Several Hussite groups/sects evolved. **Ultraquists** (moderate aristocrats) won the leadership. Meanwhile some followers of Hus turned away from use of force and became **pacifists:**
-1457 the **Unitas Fratrum** (Unity of Brethren, later called **Moravian Church**) was founded at **Lititz**, 100 miles east of Prague. Articles of faith included refusal to carry arms or take oaths. The early years were marked by growth/prosperity, but persecution became severe, so the faith was cherished underground.
-1467 wishing to maintain an unbroken line of apostolic succession, they sought out a **Waldensean** bishop in north Italy, to ordain their first bishop [p 27]. This apostolic line has continued until the present.
-1501 the Unity **printed the first Protestant Hymn Book** [12 Vol 12, p 136]. Singing was very important to them.
-1471 **Ladislaus Jagiellon** eldest son of Casimir Jagiellon IV of Poland [10, pp 31-37] was elected king of Bohemia.
-1490 he also succeed to the throne of **Hungary**, claimed through both his mother and wife.
-1471-1526 Jagiellon Hungarian kings were elected to rule Bohemia [9 Vol 4, p 188]. The last to rule was young King **Ludwig** who died fighting the **Turks**, without a son or heir to succeed him. [Continued below p 55]

Expanding Power of Austrian Habsburg Emperors

[Continued from pp 29-30; 40-41]

-1378 Holy Roman Emperor Charles IV died and the powerful kingdom of Bohemia-Hungary was divided between two sons, **Wenceslas** IV **of Bohemia** (until 1419) and **half-brother Sigismund**, **king of Hungary** through his Hungarian wife. 1410 Sigismund was crowned Holy Roman Emperor (until he died in1437).
-1438-1806 (368 years) Austrian **Habsburg** rulers, with one exception held the title Holy Roman Emperor.
-1438 **Albert** II Habsburg, Duke of Austria since 1397, was King and Emperor with capital in **Vienna** (**Wien**).
-1440-93 Frederick III Habsburg became Austrian King; 1452 Holy Roman Emperor [16, p 318].
-1493-1519 **Maximillan** of Habsburg Holy Roman Emperor. Born 1459, son of Frederick III, married the daughter of the Duke of Burgundy. He pushed back the Turks on the Danube River. 1496 gained **Habsburg control of Spain** by his son Philip's marriage to Juana, daughter of **Ferdinand** and **Isabella** of Spain [48, pp 47-50].

The Spread of Reformation in Europe

-1438 **movable type printing press** invented by Johannes **Gütenberg**, mass-produced old literary works.
-1450 Gütenburg printed the Mass on his press in Mainz; 1450-55 he printed the **Latin Vulgate Bible** [3]; [16].
-1466 a Bible was printed in **German** at a press in **Strasburg, Alsace** by Johannes Mentel [21f, pp 112-121].
-1470 a **French Bible** was printed at the Sorbonne, Paris. Soon 110 presses flourished across Europe [111, p 181].
-1466-1536 **Erasmus a great Dutch scholar**, helped the reformation but did not join it. He chose to free men from false ideas about religion. He did this in two ways: by promoting scripture reading and by writing witty satires about priests and monks, referring to them as "unholy men in holy orders" [45, p 786]; [48, pp 12, 52].
-1483-1546 **Martin Luther** born poor, studied law, was sociable, musical and enjoyed debating; in 1505 he became an Augustinian monk, fasting/scourging himself severely for two years, zealously seeking salvation.
-1508 he became a professor at Wittenburg University [continued pp 58-59].
-1511 while in Rome, he was appalled at the corruption and vice he saw. Reading in Romans "The just shall live by faith" he suddenly experienced peace by realizing salvation is by trust in Christ, not from penance, rituals or sacraments. **Luther** became a reformer, a century later than **Jan Hus**. [Continued p 58]
-1484-1531 **Ulich Zwingli** in **Zurich** was convinced that the church could be purified through study of the Bible. Many accepted his teachings opposing Mass, celibacy, indulgences, images, et cetera [48, pp 58-65]; [52, pp 47-80].

Native Prus→ Ducal East Prussia→ Kingdom of Prussia

[See pp 28-29 and 41-42]

-1308 the **Teutonic Knights** annexed much of **Pomerania**, including the city of **Danzig** (Gdansk),
-1362 Danzig joined the **Hanseatic league** which was formed for mutual protection of ports and trade.
-Cut off from access to the Baltic Sea, Poland felt threatened by these increasingly powerful knights, only nominally under the suzerainty of Rome and the Holy Roman Emperor [98, p 63].
-After conquering the lands along the Baltic Sea the **Teutonic Knights** turned SE under papal authority, ordered to conquer heathen Russia and to extend the boundaries of Christendom.
-The Knights drove the **Turks** from most of the province of **Volhynia** (**Wolinsk**), the homeland of the **Wollin** a Slavic people, west of Kiev [65] (now the north half of the Ukraine).
-To keep the Turks out of **Volhynia**, the knights invited farmer families to occupy old estates and also to develop new land. They spoke a variety of Germanic dialects and brought German culture to NE Europe.

-1386 the **Lithuanians** accepted Christianity and were **united with Poland** [maps pp 38, 55, 56, 61 and 68]. Though Germanic, some knights, assimilating Polish culture became noblemen, with serfs, of feudal estates.
-1408-10 the **Teutonic Knights** were defeated at Grunwald south of Gdansk [28, p 488] by Poland-Lithuania, assisted by Ruthenians and Tatars, their military might broken. Their Grand Master was killed. They gave up much land which was soon called **West Prussia** and became **a Polish fief** [27, p 10].
-Although they had brutally wiped out the native Prus and Kashubs [p 15], ironically the Knights were called Prussians (Preussen in German; Prusy in Polish).
-1427 10,000 knights/peasants/burghers died of **Bubonic Plague** [60,pp26-9,75] military capability weakened.
-1447-92 **Casimir** IV in thirteen years' war 1454-66, crushed the Knights [continued pp 64-65, 66]. Because of high taxes many of the Knights who were of noble families, took the side of the Poles [60, p 75].
-1466 in the **Treaty of Thorn (Torun)** the Knights gave up lands on both sides of the Vistula River, including **Marienburg**, and moved east on the Baltic Sea to **Königsberg (Kaliningrad)**, in Russia/Lithuania [28, p 480]. Here the Knights began to develop **East Prussia**. Teutonic Knights' Grand Master, Louis d'Erlichshausen became a Polish vassal, was forced to accept Polish members, but allowed to keep parts of East Prussia.
-**Danzig** on the Baltic Sea, since it was a Hanseatic League member, became a free city [60, p 75] [pp 55, 64-66].

Muslim Advances and Defeats in Eastern Europe

[Continued from p 43]

-1396 **Ottoman Turks defeated Hungary** and parts of **Poland**; were **repulsed from Vienna** and **Germany**.
-Poland and the Balkan nations (**Serbia** and **Bulgaria**) were at that time, in a golden era of expansion, wealth and power [12 Vol 9, p 6] [See p 42.] They were defeated by the Ottomans.
-1380s -1390s **Tamerlane** (Timur) of Samarkand, Asia with fleet-footed cavalry **destroyed the Golden Horde** sacking their city **Sarai**, in southern Russia.
-Then **Muscovy** (Moscow) gained power [20, pp 99, 174; 53, p 96].
-1402 Tamerlane attacked and defeated the **Ottomans**, **Mamluks of Egypt** and **Syria**, and **Persians**. Although he and his forces left to invade India and other nations, the Ottomans were so seriously crushed that they gave up invading Europe until 1453, 50 years.
-1453 Orthodox Christian Constantinople fell to the Ottoman Turks, ending the Eastern (Byzantine) Roman Empire. Gunpowder was used for the first time. **Scholars fled** to universities of Europe and stimulated the **Renaissance** [12 Vol 9, pp 1019-1021; 167 p 70-75].
-**The Roman Empire for eleven centuries** had ruled the whole of Europe, North Africa and the Middle East, but now was little more than one city, Constantinople.
- Syrian and Thomas **Christians in India** lost contact with the Eastern Orthodox church, Constantinople [117].
- The **Patriarchate of Moscow** gradually became respected as leader of the Orthodox Church.
-1453 the immense, fabulously beautiful **Cathedral Hagia Sophia** in Constantinople, became a **Muslim mosque**. All icons (holy pictures) and mosaics of saints and Bible scenes, inlaid with gold and precious gems and colored marble, were plastered over because they were considered idolatrous by Islam.
- Ottoman Turkish conquests spread into Greece, the Balkans, eastern Europe and Russia [14, pp 22-23; p 32].
-1447-92 **Casimir** IV king of **Poland**, **Lithuania** and **Kiev**, 1456 pushed back Turkish tribes south of Kiev and kept access to the Black Sea open [12, Macropedia Vol 25 pp 930-6].
-1456 Hungarian **János Hunyadi** defeated Turks; died of Plague [55, p 278]. 1458-90 **Matthias** his son ruled.
-1480 **Ivan** III declaring himself **Tsar** (Caesar) of Russia, refused to pay further tribute to the Mongols, [14, p 54]. The Golden Horde had kept the Russians subjected since 1241. Their capital was at **Sarai** on the Volga River, north of the Caspian Sea [167, pp 66-67] [maps p 56]. Tamerlane had sacked Sarai in 1395, but the **Mongols** (called **Tartars** or **Tatars** by the Russians) continued to exact tribute for some decades.
-1498-99 **Tatars** from central Asia **invaded Krakow,** southern Poland causing much damage. For 140 years Muslims threatened the southern boundaries of Poland.
-All eastern European nations struggled to keep back Muslims invaders.
-1500 at last 250 years of **Mongol domination ended in Russia** (since 1241). Now all Russia came under the rule of **Moscow** [Continued p 65].
-1475 and 1484 Ottoman attacks **cut off overland trade** with the Orient and Arab ships controlled Indian Ocean ports [117]. Portugese explorers began to challenge them. [See pp 49-50, 52].
-1497-1524 Portugese shipping by establishing trading posts in **India** and **Malacca**, controlled spice trade by sea and became wealthy.
-**Portugal** became the primary naval power of the world [see p 52].

Expansion of the Jagiellon Dynasty 1386-1572 - **Nearly** 200 **Years** [from pp 41-42]
-1370-84 **Louis of Anjou (**elected king) united **Poland** and **Hungary** [20, p 148].
-1384-6 his daughter **Queen Jadwiga** succeeded. She married Lithuanian Grand Prince Wladyslaw [p 53]. Holy Roman Emperor Sigismund, son of Charles IV of Bohemia, ruled Hungary through this Hungarian wife,
-1386-1434 **Wladyslaw** II (**Vladislav** or **Ladislaus**) founded the **Jagellonian Dynasty** [60, pp 28-29], uniting **Poland, Lithuania** and **Kiev**, a huge kingdom including much of Russia and part of the Black Sea coast. The Muslim Mongol Golden Horde had occupied most land north of the Black Sea since 1240 [maps pp 56, 68].
-1410 the **Teutonic Knights** defeated by Poles and Lithuanians [27, p 10] at Tannenberg, became a Polish fief.
-1419-1436 the **Hussite War** led by the Holy Roman Empire (under Sigismund) killed thousands of followers of martyred Moravian Reformer **Jan Hus**. Some pacifist Moravian Brethren escaped to Saxony and Poland.
-1434-44 King **Ladislaus** III of Poland and Hungary was killed in the **battle of Varna** against the **Turks** [27, p 11].
-1447-71 King **Casimir** IV ruled, but with power centered in the **Sejm (parliament)** democracy was by the gentry, with no vote for the middle class & poor. Trades & crafts flourished. Towns and cities prospered [27, p 11].
-Mongols were pushed back south of Kiev so access to the Black Sea then opened up [12, Macropedia Vol 25 pp 930-6].
-1466 in the **Treaty of Thorn** (Torun), the **Teutonic Knights**, decisively defeated by Polish and Lithuanian armies, became a vassal of the Polish state. [See above p 54]. They gave up the huge fortress of Marienberg and fled east to **Konigsberg** (**Kaliningrad**), where they began to develop **East Prussia**.
-The entire aristocracy of Poland before 1500 originated from Germanic states. The first kings of Poland were married to German princesses who brought artisans, priests, farmers and educators into Poland.
-Dating back to 1355 with the Golden Bull, **Germany** was composed of over 100 small principalities ruled by a Duke, Marquis or Knight, not a united country. Each was heavily guarded, so escape unaided was almost impossible. Escape was provided by noblemen when they had purposes of their own.
-1471-92 **Wladyslaw** (**Ladislas**), eldest son of Casimir IV of Poland, was elected king of **Bohemia,** and he claimed **Hungary** [60, p 128] through his mother in 1490 and also by marriage in 1491.
-1475 and 1484 **Ottoman** attacks in eastern Europe cut off trade with the Orient.
-1492-1501 **John Albert** I second son of Casimir IV was elected king of Poland by the Sejm (parliament).
-1492 Ivan III **of Moscow** invaded Lithuania, but King John Albert I of Poland was able to repulse him.
-1480 Ivan III ended 250 years' Mongol domination in Russia (since 1237), gained power and ruled all Russia.
-1498-99 **Teutonic Knights** rebelled in north Poland. **Tartars** from central Asia invaded Krakow, Galicia province, south Poland. **Ottomans** for 140 years threatened the southern borders of Poland [pp 64-66, 68]
-Until 1526 Jagiellons ruled Hungary & Bohemia [maps pp 55,56, 68].

Maps: ***Poland United (a) under Mieszko l about A.D. 1000; United (b) with Lithuania*** **1492**

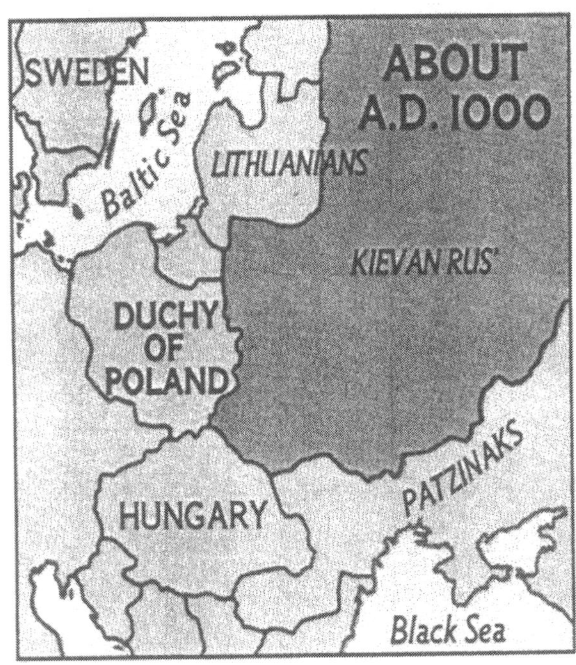

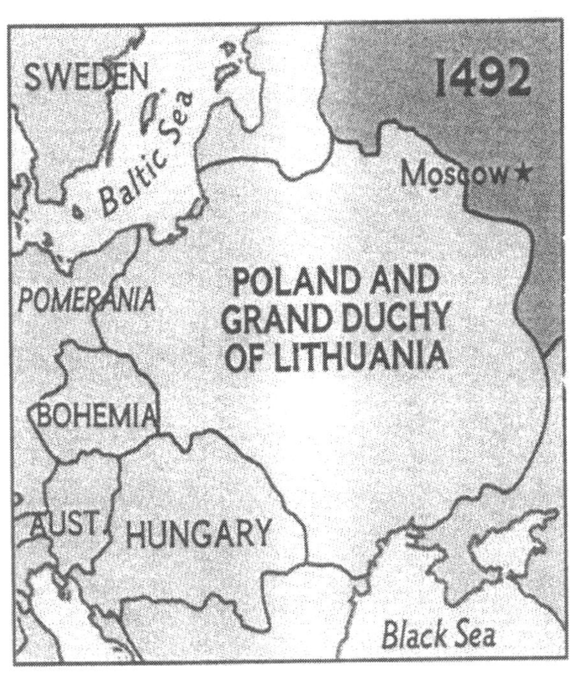

Russia: Rise of Moscow by the Fifteenth Century [Continued from pp 16 and 30-31]

-1263 **Daniel** of the **Rurik Dynasty**, son of **Alexander Nevski**, founded the **House of Moscow**. The princes were obliged "to seek a patent" from the **Mongol Khan** in order to rule as Grand Prince.

-1264-71 **Nevski's brother Yaroslav**, Grand Prince of **Vladimir**, to the east, founded the **House of Tver**. The houses of Tver and Moscow struggled for leadership [12, p 244]. Muscovy (Moscow) by absorbing the House of **Vladimir-Suzdal** and other Slavic states, gained strength. Gradually the princes of Moscow became dominant, forming the **Grand Principality of Moscow**, which they ruled until the male line died in 1598. Moscow was built at an ancient fortress, at the heart of **a network of rivers**, between dense forests & treeless steppes [map 94]. It is situated on **Moskva River**, a branch of **Oka River**, which joins the **Don River** that runs into the **Black Sea**. The **Volga River** [139, p 245] runs into the **Caspian Sea**. Trade in furs to the south [53, pp 95-115], brought great profits. 1380 **Dmitry** Prince of Moscovy led an army against the Tartars, reducing the tribute [136, p 88].

-1453 **Ottomans** conquered the last strongholds of the Byzantine Empire so people looked to the **Patriarchy of Moscow** to lead the Orthodox church, throughout eastern Europe, replacing Constantinople.

-1462-1505 **Ivan** III, **the Great**, Grand Duke of **Moscow**, adopted the title **Tsar** (Czar; Caesar)[14, p 54]. He chose the Roman eagle as Russian emblem [16] [p 65]. He expanded his empire northwest into **Novgorod** and **Lithuania** and east to the **Ural Mountains** [20, p 201-4, 227-9]. His **Tsarina Zoe**, was a **Byzantine Greek princess**.

-1480 Tzar Ivan III issued laws, made treaties with western European rulers, and felt strong enough to stop paying tribute to the Tartars, whose capital was at **Sarai** on the **Volga River**. Pressure from these Tartars relaxed. **All of Russia was under the rule of Moscovy** [20, p 246; 60, pp 103-7]. However three other **Mongol Khanates** (**Kazan**, **Sibir** and **Astrakhan**) continued threatening southern Russia [map 1300-1598 below].

-1484-89 the walls of Moscow & the Cathedral of the Annunciation were built, reusing earlier foundations. Ivan began to rebuild/build other churches in the fortress, employing **Italian architects** and sculptors.

Maps: ***Russia during the Tartar Invasions 1237; Growth of Russia*** from 1300 to 1598 [9b, p 187]

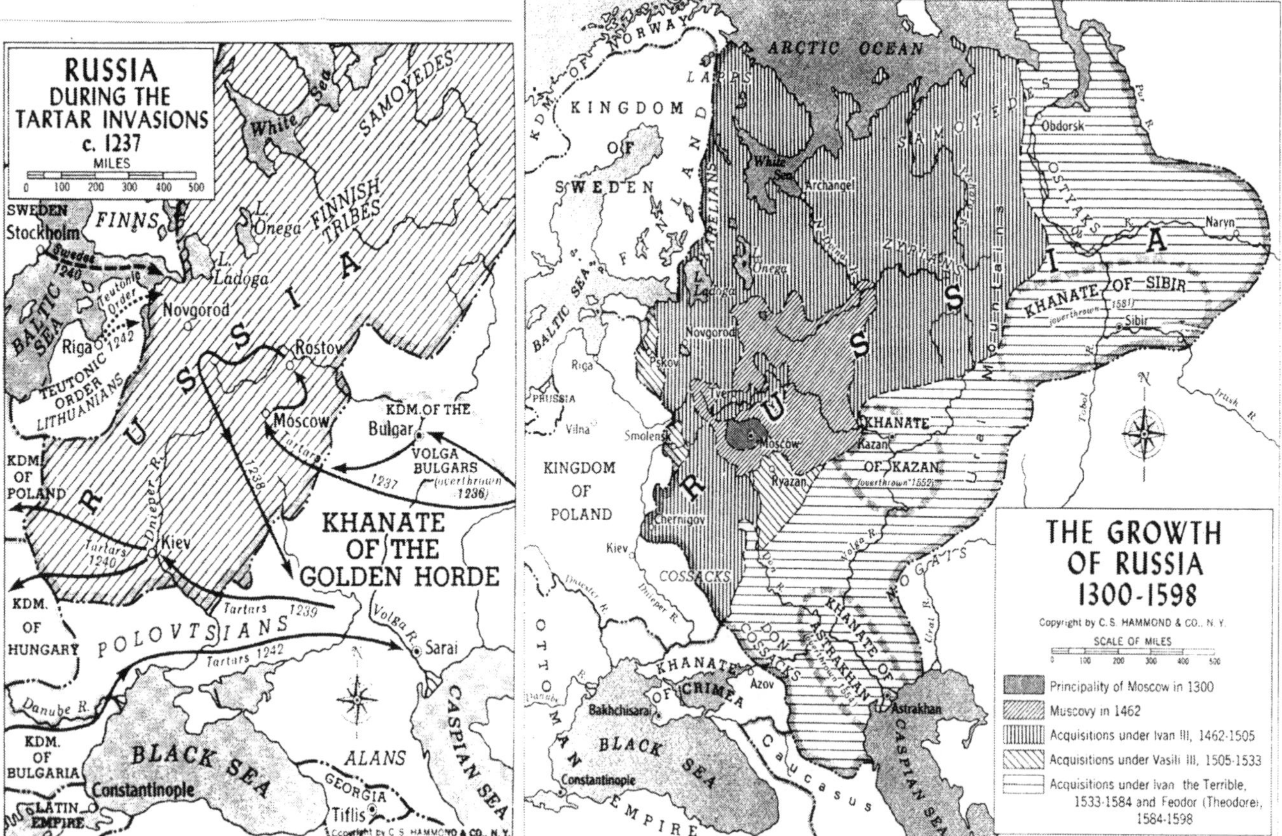

Chapter Ten - 1500 to 1599

Reformation, Counter-Reformation and Emerging World Powers

Portuguese & Spanish Found a Sea Route for Spice Trade [See pp 49-52, 54 and map p 51]

-1497-9 & 1502-03 **Vasco da Gama** sent by King Manual I of Portugal (as Admiral) and 1524 (as Viceroy) on three voyages around the **Cape of Good Hope**, along the east coast of Africa, Mozambique to Kenya and across the Indian Ocean. They destroyed an Arab colonists' ship; at **Calicut**, SW **India** established trading. They tried to find Syrian Christians there. Overland Venetian-Muslim spice monopoly ended [95, p 240].

-1499 **Pedro Alvares Cabral** sailed with 113 ships, driven off course by winds, discovered **Brazil** and claimed it for Portugal. 1501 they sailed back south of Africa to **India**. Muslim traders were routed; Hindu rulers played one against the other with treaties. Portuguese men stayed to run depots/garrisons to collect spices so that little time was lost loading the many ships that followed [21e, pp 104-5].

-The Portuguese set up **an Exchange** at **Antwerp** on the North Sea because of its central location, to sell spices and buy copper & silver. German & Italian bankers flocked there to offer liberal credit to finance frequent sailings to the far east. Trade also started farther east at **Malacca** [21f, p 30].

- Portugal controlled the spice trade and soon was the primary naval world power [21e, p 106].

-1499-1502 Italian **Amerigo Vespuscci** made two voyages along the coast of what he called a ***New World***.

-1507 a German geographer called it **America** [116, p 10].

-1500 **Vincente Yanez Pinzon** a **Spaniard** who commanded the Nina on Columbus' first voyage, explored the mouth of the **Amazon River**, South America. Other explorers and colonizers followed.

-1502-05 **Francisco de Almeido** the **first Portuguese Viceroy to India** [21e, pp 106-118], on his way to India set up forts on the **east coast of Africa** and cleared the **Indian Ocean** of Muslim ships.

-1505 he built forts at Calicut, Cannanore and Cochin along Malabar Coast, SW India, and discovered **Ceylon**.

-1510 **Alfonso de Albuquerque** the next Viceroy, seized **Goa**, a Muslim ship-building port, west coast of India, made it the capital, settled 450 **Portuguese colonists** and built a cathedral, convent and hospital.

-1511 Albuquerque sailed 2000 miles east and took **Malacca (Molucca)**, at the entrance to the **China Sea**.

-1515 Albuquerque seized Hormuz at the mouth of the **Persian Gulf**. Thus Portugal controlled far east trade.

-1524 **Vasco da Gama** returned to India as Viceroy; corrected abuses that had crept in under administrators; died in Cochin December 1524 while looking for legendary **Prester John** (presbyter).

-1519-20 Portuguese **Ferdinand Magellan** was in India under Almeido [21e, p 121], in service of Spain. In harsh storms he **rounded south America**. Three months crossing the Pacific they sighted only two islands, uninhabited. 1521 March, Magellan reached **Guam** starving, but regained health. In the **Philippines** he made friends and converts, but was killed by enemies. His ships *Trinidad* and *Victoria* reached the Moluccas.

-1522 September, the *Victoria* led by **Juan Sebastian del Cano** and 18 emaciated survivors from a crew of 270, and a small cargo of cloves, reached Spain, completing a **first voyage around the world** [16, p 456]. Other survivors from the *Trinidad* returned as Portuguese prisoners[21e, p 121-162; 12 Vol 7, p 669].

-1542 **Jesuit Francis Xavier** was sent by the king of Spain to control the faith in Goa, India and far east [117].

-1564 Spanish Miguel Lopez **de Legazpe** landed in the **Philippines** and in 1571 founded **Manila** as a Spanish colony. Chinese junks and Portuguese ships were trading there. The **Ming Dynasty** traded porcelain, silks, jewelry and drugs for **silver from America**, further enriching Spain [60, pp 122-126].

-1580 **Habsburg** King of Spain **Phillip** II became **Phillip** I of Portugal so acquired the Portuguese Empire, the large fleet & inherited the **Netherlands** [pp 62-3]; second wife: **Mary Tudor**, **Queen of England** [pp 59-60].

Spanish Occupation of America

-1513 Spanish Vasco Nunez **de Balboa** walked across the **Panama** and saw the Pacific Ocean [116, p 10].

-1518-21 Hernando **Cortez** conquered the capital of the **Aztec** nation in what is now Mexico city, and ruled as governor until 1540 [16, pp 65, 168]. **Mexico** became a base for Spaniards to explore and colonize Central America and the present southern and central United States [167, pp 82-87]. He built a ship at Acalpulca.

-Colonies with Roman Catholic priests, churches and Spanish culture were established [116, p 11-12; 139, pp 196-201]. Millions of indigenous people died in epidemics of small pox, measles and influenza, brought by colonists. Many native survivors married Spaniards. Spain lost interest in far east spice trade [16, p 477, 488], having vast wealth in gold from **Aztecs** in Mexico and **Mayans** in Central America.

-1520 to Puerto Rica, Cuba & Mexico, Spain brought slave laborers, sugar cane, wheat, horses, cattle & sheep; took to Europe squash, pumpkins, tobacco, potatoes, corn, coffee, chocolate & much gold.

-1526 Francisco **Pizarro** began the conquest of **Peru** and the **Inca Empire** in south America [16, p 358 and 580].
-1535 he established the capital **Lima** [139, pp 196-201]. 1532 Afonso **de Souza** founded sugar plantations in Brazil.
-1513 Juan Ponce **de Leon** explored the **Florida** coast around the southern tip from east to west [116, p 12].
-1539 Hernando **de Soto** (1496-1543) received licence to conquer Florida. With 600 troops, he landed on the east coast, marched across what was later **Georgia**, **Alabama**, **Mississippi**, south **Louisiana** and **Arkansas**, and south to the mouth of the **Mississippi River** [16, p 192; 116, p 12-13; 125 Vol 14, p 472]; 1540 **North Carolina**.
- Settlements were started with sugar **Plantations** farmed by **slaves from Africa** [9 Vol 2, pp 45-6].
-1534 **French** explorers were colonizing **Canada** [p 69-70]; 1555 French colony in Rio de Janiero, S America.
-1539 Spanish Explorer-Franciscan Missionary Marcos **de Niza** was the first European known to have visited the area of present-day **Arizona**, in an expedition from Mexico city. It was the home of culturally-advanced **Navaho** Indian tribes who built irrigation canals, aqueducts, fortifications and cities scattered throughout the valleys/canyons of the region [9 Vol 2, p 348]. This impressed **Spanish conquistador** (conqueror) Francisco Vasquez **de Coronado**, Governor in Mexico. He heard from explorer **Cabeza de Vaca** tales about Seven Cities of **Cibola** being fabulously rich. 1540-42 **de Coronado,** with 300 Spanish soldiers and many Indian troops, was sent on an overland expedition to explore and claim the cities for Spain [9 Vol 7, p 224]. They went north to the present border of Arizona, turned NE to Cibola, but found only poor villages. He sent a small group, led by Garcia Lòpez **de Càrdenas** westward. They discovered the **Grand Canyon**, returned and the whole group wintered near the present **Santa Fe**, New Mexico [Maps 128 and 130].
-In the spring they crossed the upper **Rio Grande** and the Great Plains of **Texas** and wrote descriptions of the bison (**buffalo**) [139, pp 202-3]. They went north crossing the Arkansas and Canadian Rivers [not near Canada], looked for, but did not find a wealthy city in the present **Kansas** and **Nebraska** [16, p 520].
-1544 on their return to New Spain, disappointed authorities demoted Coronado. He wrote unique reports (now in a memorial near **Bisbee, Arizona**).
-1539 Spanish explorer Francisco **de Ulloa**, and in 1540 navigator Hernando **de Alarcón** sailed the Gulf of California. 1540-41 **de Alarcón** twice went up **Colorado river** as far as the present **Yuma, Arizona** [9 Vol 1, p 313].
-1542 Portuguese Juan Rodriguez **Cabrillo**, employed by Spain, explored San Diego Bay and died.
-1543 survivors probably went as far as **Oregon** [125 Vol 3, pp 38-60]. Others ascended rivers to **Utah** and **Colorado**.
-1592 **Juan de Fuca** a Greek, visited **Vancouver Island** for Spain [16, p 789]. Earlier 1579 by Francis Drake (p 60)
-1598 the New Mexico-Arizona region became part of New Spain. **Jesuit missions** were opened [9 Vol 2, p 348].
-Spanish colonists settled **New Mexico** [125 Vol 4, pp 848-9]. [Spanish rule continued pp 70, 71, 75, 95, 98, 106-107, 126-130 and maps pp 97, 128 and 130]. For **French** explorers see p 69; for **English** p 60].
-By 1600 there were 900,000 slaves in Latin America; by 1700 there were 27,000 slaves in English America.

Lutheran Reformation Spread Throughout Europe [Continued pp 52-53]

-1466-1536 **Erasmus** a great **Dutch** scholar, decided to free men from false ideas about religion. He did this in two ways: by promoting scripture reading, and by writing witty satires about priests and monks, referring to them as "unholy men in holy orders". He helped the reformation but did not join it [45, p 786; 48, pp 12, 52].
-1483-1546 **Martin Luther** was born poor, studied law, was sociable, enjoyed debating and was musical.
-1505 Luther became an Augustinian monk, fasting and scourging himself severely for two years, zealously seeking salvation. When he read in Romans "The just shall live by faith," suddenly he experienced peace, and realized salvation is from trust in Christ and not from penance, rituals or sacraments.
-1508 he became a professor for life at the University of Wittenburg.
-1511 during a visit to Rome, appalled by corruption and vice he saw, he became a reformer. This was a century later than Jan Hus who was martyred in 1415.
-1517 Luther was horrified that itinerant Friar **John Tetzel** sold ***Indulgences*** signed by the Pope. These certificates granted pardon for sins of those who bought them, their friends or deceased relatives, without confession or repentance. This was a main source of revenue to build the new St. Peter's in Rome [more p 63].
-In protest against their sale Luther posted 95 theses on the door of a church in **Wittenberg**. Printed copies were sent all over Europe [48, p 52]. Across Europe 110 presses flourished [111, p 181].
-Learned men were sent to argue with him to get him to recant, but he only found more faults with church beliefs and practice. By 1522 Luther had translated the New Testament in German.
-1521 **Emperor Charles** V held a **Diet** (Council of Princes) at **Worms** in Hesse, to consider ways to stop the reformation, and Luther was summoned. He endured much questioning but refused to recant. He was banned from the Holy Roman Empire. Abducted by friends, kept safe in Wartburg castle, Luther wrote sermons.

-1525 Luther married a nun, had 6 children. To correct ignorance of believers, Luther prepared **catechisms** to ground children early in the faith [53, p 29]. He composed hymns including *A Mighty Fortress is our God*.
-1534 Luther completed translating the Old Testament. Wittenburg **printer Hans Lufft** during the next forty years produced 100,000 copies. Literacy spread rapidly from reading printed hymns and the Bible.
-1546 Martin Luther died apparently of a heart attack, at 63 years. During the next 200 years, widespread Bible reading resulted in **standardization of the many German dialects**. Ability to read was a Lutheran requirement for confirmation so our **maternal ancestors became literate**, though not all could write. [The author's maternal grandmother's relatives were Low German, from NW Poland, of Brüder Gemine (Moravian) faith. Her paternal relatives as well as her maternal grandfather's relatives were Swabish from SW Germany and later central Poland. All lived later in Volhynia, Russia, and came to Canada 1894 and 1896.] [See pp 148-150; 168-171]. Ability to speak in **High German** was a status symbol across Europe. Anything printed was in High German, but many spoken dialects persisted. Even today Low German is spoken and High German read.

Other Reform Theologians [48, pp 58-65; 52, pp 47-80]

-1484-1531 **Ulrich Zwingli** in **Zurich** became convinced the church could be purified through study of the Bible. Many churches accepted his teachings to reform the mass, celibacy, indulgences, images, etc.
-1509-1564 **John Calvin** was born **in France**. He studied the classics. From German classmates he learned to like Lutheran ideas, but with his scholarly mind he thought deeply and taught and wrote very carefully.
-1536 Calvin had to flee from France when the university authorities discovered he no longer believed as a Roman Catholic. In **Geneva**, **Switzerland** Calvin met with followers of the late Zwingli and was invited to share his ideas with preachers, which he did by writing a book ***The Institutes of the Christian Religion***. Though he was but 26 years old, Calvin's book became highly influential in many lands. The basic ideas are that all people are naturally wicked (original sin) and deserve to go to hell. God is not only just but also merciful. God chooses (elects) some to be saved. Those who believe must lead Godly lives with no half-heartedness. His teachings seemed stern and thorough [48, pp 58-65]. In two years he was **told to leave** Geneva.
-1541 the leading citizens felt they needed his firmness to strengthen the city, so they invited him back. Calvin's church had no bishops. Ministers had to be well educated and able to preach. Elders were carefully selected. They made sure all members of the congregation behaved correctly. The elders and members kept each other to strict standards. The Calvinists were called **Puritans**. Ornaments and statues were removed.
-In Geneva the **Consistory** was formed to be the spiritual court for the whole city, but when a problem could not be settled, they would ask the city council to help. The city was largely cleansed of rowdiness and immorality. The people worked hard and studied diligently.
-Calvin's Academy attracted scholars from many lands. Calvinism spread to **France, Scotland,** the **Netherlands**, **Hungary, Poland, Berlin** and **Bohemia**.
-400 AD the first Christian church was founded in **Scotland** by **St. Ninian**. About 562 **St. Columba** and other Irish missionaries settled in **Iona**. In 1192 the Scottish church became subject to the pope.
-1440 the third university in Britain began, at **St. Andrews,** 1472 archbishopric; 1492 **Glasgow** [12, Vol 10, p 563].
-1540 **in Scotland** Roman Catholic priest **John Knox** (1515-1572) began teaching reformation ideas.
-1553 **Knox studied Calvinism** in Geneva. In 1559 he was called back to Scotland to lead a reform movement of both church and state [45, pp 791-2; 12 Vol 10, p 562]. **Mary Stuart, Queen of Scots** was also **Queen of France**, by marrying Francis II. She plotted to assassinate Protestant **Queen Elizabeth**. After Elizabeth became Queen also of Scotland, Romanism was defeated [continued p 60].
-The Church of Scotland was established and called **Presbyterian** because the ministers and elders of several churches formed a Presbytery, the governing body of a district, similar to the Consistory in Geneva. Several Presbyteries formed a Synod and several Synods the General Assembly, the final court of appeal.
-1525-34 **William Tyndale** translated the Bible from Hebrew and Greek into English.

English Tudor Monarchy Broke with Rome; Spain Became their Major Enemy

-1509-1547 King **Henry** VIII was educated, creative and a composer of choir music. For his book refuting Luther's views he was honored a ***Renaissance Man*** and ***Defender of the Faith***.
-1529 he broke with Rome for a **divorce**. England's economy suffered because of a slump in wool exports. England was dependent on Spain for dyes. Spain had increased her own wool production [112, pp 74-5; 48, pp 5-19]. North Atlantic **fisheries** were growing. The English & French, like Spain wanted to gain wealth from America, so **explorers**/adventurers multiplied. 1527 African slaves were growing sugar cane in Jamaica.

-Before 1509 Portugese, Basque and English fishermen had **whaling stations** around Newfoundland and Labrador [112, p 93-112]. Whale oil was used to produce soap, leather, wool, lamp fuel and bones for lady's corsets.
-1539-40 **William Hawkins** in four voyages from Plymouth exported cloth and tin to Africa and **Brazil**.
-1534 **Jacques Cartier**, a **Huguenot** (French Protestant) urged by the Huguenot Governor of **Burgundy**, was commissioned by **King Francis** I **of France** to discover islands for gold and valuables [119, Vol 5, p 193].
-1535 his second voyage circumnavigated Newfoundland, explored the St. Lawrence River as far as present-day Montreal, which he named **Mount Royal** [112, p 58-73], and **wintered** there. They called the aboriginals **Indians** thinking they were in India. When his men suffered scurvy, pine needles were recommended. Antioxidants cured the scurvy. Pine needles lack vitamin C. **Chief Donnaconna** was taken to France.
-1540 Cartier made a third voyage up the St. Lawrence and wintered again. **Sieur de Roberval**, a **Huguenot**, joined him with more ships and colonists. Stones thought valuable minerals taken to France, were found to be worthless. Disappointed and distracted by internal strife, France lost interest in Canada for 60 years.

King Henry VIII's Three Children of Different Mothers, ruled England in Succession:

-1547-1553 **Edward** VI; 1553-1558 **Mary Tudor**; and 1558-1603 **Elizabeth** I.
-1553 a company of merchant-adventurers sent ships NE **to find a passage north of Russia to China**. Named **Muscovy Company**, they set up trade with Ivan the Terrible of Moscow [112, p 76].
- **Mary Tudor** had in 1554 **married Hapsburg Philip** II, **King of Spain**, but had no children.
-1553-1558 **Mary Tudor** as Queen of England, known as *Bloody Mary,* restored Roman Catholicism and persecuted Protestants. After she died her husband continued to fight and persecute English Protestants, aiming to restore Roman Catholic supremacy. He assisted a different Mary: **Mary Stuart Queen of Scots** , in her lifelong plots to supplant Queen Elizabeth I [16]. She was a staunch Roman Catholic, heir to the throne of England, next of kin and rival of Queen Elizabeth. 1558 married to **King Francis** II became **Queen of France**. He died 1560 and she returned to Scotland. She married twice more, but due to plots to become queen of England she was imprisoned 1568-87 by Elizabeth I.
-1558-1603 **Elizabeth** I fluent in Latin, Greek, Italian and possibly French; in 1559 established the Church of England; kept Jesuits out of England; in 1570 was excommunicated by Pope Pius V, who funded plots to dethrone her. She promoted prestige and education of country gentlemen [53, pp 59-93]. She toured England much. With growing prosperity, wooden houses were replaced by brick homes with proper chimneys, and were furnished elegantly. Queen for 45 years, single though courted by many explorers & even Czar Ivan IV [p 66].
-Sir Walter Raleigh emphasized shipbuilding, exploration and world trade, aiming to break Spanish and Portuguese commercial monopolies. **Atlantic fisheries employed** 10,000 **men**.
-John Hawkins son of William Hawkins, an explorer and trader in slaves, ivory, gems, hides, tobacco and potatoes [16, p 323], was elected to parliament. 1588 he was knighted for service in Spanish Armada.
-1576 **Martin Frobisher** explored Canada's northern coasts in search of a NW passage to Asia. Failing to find a route, English leaders instead began to put their energy into planning to colonize America.
-1577-80 **Francis Drake** sailed around **Cape Horn** south tip of **S America**, up the coast to present **Vancouver** & Queen Charlotte Is., across the Pacific to East Indies & Indian Ocean, east coast of Africa [16, p 204], around **Cape of Good Hope,** along west Africa back to England, the first to circumnavigate the world [12 Vol 4].
-English seamen including Sir Francis Drake [12 Vol 4] plundered Spanish galleons returning from America.
-1583 **Humphrey Gilbert** claimed **Newfoundland** for England and **started a colony** there.
-1585-87 **John Davis** discovered/explored Cumberland Sound, Baffin Is. and Davis Strait named after him.
-1584 **Sir Walter Raleigh** claimed the present **North Carolina** for England. 1540 **Hernando de Soto** had claimed it for Spain [125 Vol 14, p 472]. Because of overpopulation/unemployment in England, emigration began.
-1587 **Raleigh** settled 150 people in land he called **Virginia**, named for the virgin Queen Elizabeth.
-1588 the **Spanish fleet of** 130 **ships** was sent to attack England. Small maneuverable English ships were quick to intercept them with long-range guns and unmanned fire ships packed with explosives. Astonished and crippled [16, p 49, 571], the **Spanish Armada** was further battered in a gale. Spain's naval power was broken.
-1564-1616 **William Shakespeare:** popular poetic historic drama/wit added colorful words/national pride.
-1587 Mary Stuart after being in prison 19 years was reluctantly executed for treason. Elizabeth aging/ill.
-1594-97 Dutch Navigator **William Barents** with English funding, searched for a NE passage to Asia [p 72].
-1603-25 **James** I (since 1583 **King James** VI **of Scotland**) became **King of England,** selected by Queen Elizabeth I, his cousin. Unlike his mother, Mary Stuart, he was a Protestant. [Continued p 70-71].

Hapsburg Kings Were Crowned Holy Roman Emperors [from pp 26, 30 and 53]

-1438-1806 **Austrian Hapsburg** (Habsburg) kings, with one exception were titled Holy Roman Emperor.

-1493-1519 **Maximilian of Habsburg** [48, pp 47-50]; became Emperor. 1477 by marriage to Mary, daughter of Charles the Bold [p 49] he inherited Burgundy (east France) which included Flanders (west Netherlands), Alsace-Lorraine and parts of Switzerland [95, pp 228-231]. By the marriage of **his son Philip** of the Netherlands to **Juana**, daughter of Ferdinand and Isabella of Spain, Hapsburgs ruled all Spanish possessions.

-1500 **Charles** Maximilian's grandson, born in Flanders inherited rule of Netherlands, Naples, Sicily, Aragon (south Italy), Germany and Austria; fluent in German, Spanish, French and Dutch,

-1516 he was King Charles l of **Spain** and Spanish territories in **America**; 1519-1556 **Charles** V Holy Roman Emperor, crowned by the pope [10, p 296]. 1543 he approved trade of African slaves for American colonies.

-1521 **Ferdinand** young brother of **Emperor Charles** V, married Anna [16, p 476-7], heir of the Polish-Lithuanian **Jagiellon** dynasty. 1471-1526 Bohemia was ruled by elected Jagiellon Hungarian kings [9, Vol 4, p 188] [p 64].

-1526 Hapsburg King **Ferdinand** I **of Austria**, became also king of **Hungary** and **Bohemia** ending 70 years of protestant rule in Bohemia. The capital transferred from Vienna, Austria to architecturally superior Prague, Bohemia [10, pp 29-37]. See tourist books Bajcar, *Poland* [27] and Dydynski, *Poland: Lonely Planet* [28]. Ferdinand I made German the official language of Bohemia and suppressed Czech, considered a peasant language.

-1531-1548 **John Augusta, an Ultraquist aristocrat** (moderate Hussite Protestant, see pp 52-53) had learned to hate the *Unity of Brethren*, but unsatisfied, decided to see for himself, was converted, found rest with the Brethren; 1532 consecrated a bishop of the *Unitas Fratrum (Unity of Brethren)*. Aiming to unite Protestants he revised the Confession; sent copies to Luther and Calvin, who approved. He visited Luther. He had a rich Baron take a copy of the Confession to King Ferdinand I who reacted with rage. Three days later he had 12 nobles and 33 knights took it back to the king, who now was convinced & promised to allow them to worship as they pleased, if they were loyal subjects [134, bk 1, chaps 8 & 9]. 1546 war broke out against Saxony. Ferdinand called the Protestants to arms. Ultraquists obeyed but the Unitas Fratrum refused, being **pacifists**.

-1548 the Brethren were told to leave Bohemia-Moravia within 6 weeks and their property was seized. Nearly 2000 fled to Poland in two groups via Breslau or Frankenstein [Continued p 65 below]. Other exiles spread NW to Saxony and Silesia. Already forty Brethren students were studying in foreign universities.

-Charles V as Emperor, fought defensively against threats from the French, Turkish **Ottomans** and German Protestant Dukes [48, pp 43-45]. He tried often to gain theological compromise with the Protestants yet actively persecuted them in the **Inquisition** [48, pp 56] [See below p 62]. Because of constant wars, despite vast gold revenues from **America**, he faced **bankruptcy** in all his domains.

Map: *Europe in 1560: Emergence of Modern Nations* [4] [Compare with map on p 68]

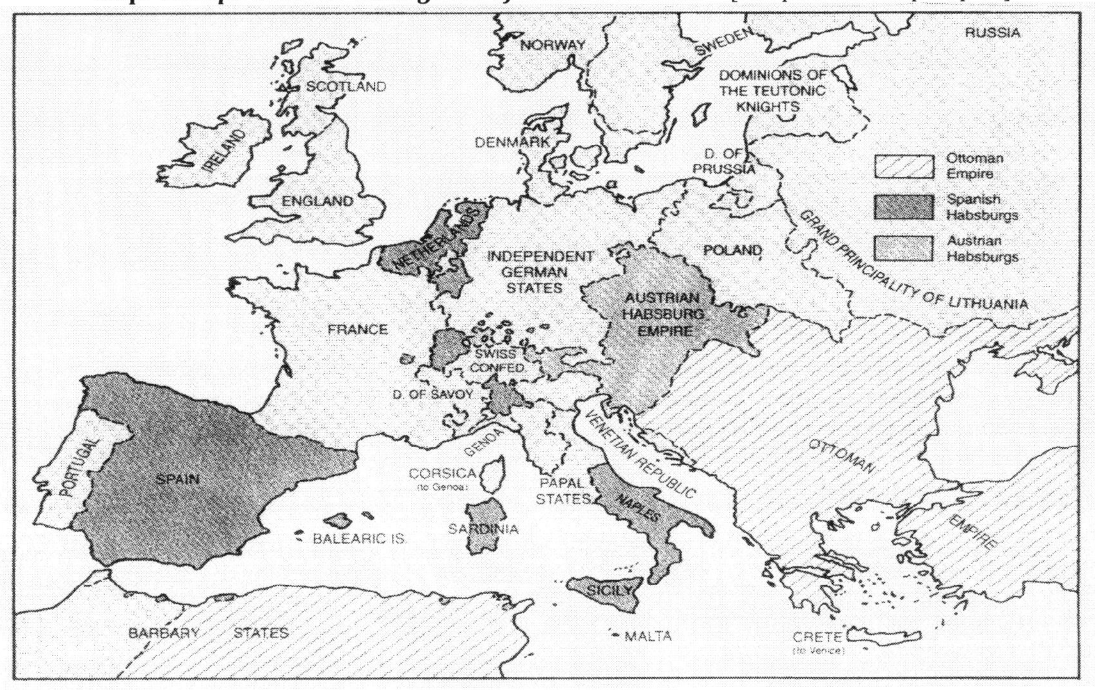

-1532 **Menno Simons** a Catholic priest became an itinerate **Anabaptist** preacher along the Baltic Sea with a large following. He was expelled [77, p 185]. 1535 death by fire of Anabaptists, was decreed by Emperor Charles V.
-1546-55 Pope Paul III provided an army to Charles V for a crusade to exterminate Protestants[45, p 780, 788-9].
-1555 Charles V became physically ill and depressed. He divided the Hapsburg dynasty into **Spanish** and **Austrian branches,** and retired. He transferred**Spain** to his son **Philip** II, who also ruled Portugal [p 57] and was married to Mary Tudor [p 60]. He transferred **Austria** to brother **Ferdinand** I.
-1558 Charles V died of malaria [53, pp 32-35] [See below under Inquisition]. Successive Hapsburg kings were crowned Emperor, had little authority over the loose collection of rival German states.
-1558-1564 **Ferdinand** I **of Habsburg**, crowned Holy Roman Emperor, like his brother Charles V tried to balance Protestant and Catholic rulers, but actively supporting the **Counter-Reformation**, summoned the **Jesuits** to Bohemia and founded a new university in Prague which soon outstripped that of Charles IV [p 40].
- 1523-1571 Unitas Fratrum Bishop **Jan Blahoslav** was a poet and writer of musical and poetic theory. Hymns and chorales (a total of 743) were published. He wrote a scholarly Czech grammar and translated the New Testament into Czech. The Gospel and Epistles were printed in 4 languages, 6 columns: 1. Grammatical notes, 2. Greek, 3. Czech, 4. German, 5. Latin and 6. Exposition. He contributed to the **Czech Kralice Bible**.
-Brethren who remained in Bohemia-Moravia cherished their faith underground and passed it on quietly.
-1564-76 Emperor **Maxmilian** II succeeded his father Ferdinand I and persecution of Protestants lessened.
-1576-1612 Emperor **Rudolf** II born 1552, moved his official residence from Vienna to Prague in 1583; economic prosperity returned to Bohemia [10, pp 37-38].
-1579-93 the **Czech Kralice Bible** was a scholarly translation directly from Hebrew and Greek, not from the Latin Vulgate. Much beloved for centuries, it became a literary model of classical Czech.

The Inquisition was Intensified by the Jesuits

[Continued from pp 27 and 49]

-The Inquisition, called *The Holy Office*, begun in 1229 by Pope Innocent III, & 1249 by Innocent IV, continued for 500 years to eliminate people who were considered heretics. Intolerance was especially high in Spain.
-1522 the Inquisition in the **Netherlands** was ordered by Charles V, Holy Roman Emperor (1519-56) of Spain, Bohemia, Netherlands, Naples, Sicily, Aragon (S. Italy), Austria, parts of Germany and Spanish territories in **America.** He ordered all Lutheran writings to be burned and prohibited Bible reading in meetings.
-1534 the **Society of Jesus (Jesuits)** was founded in **Spain** by **Ignatius Loyola**. Intelligent young men were highly educated under exacting, harsh conditions to suppress their feelings, become zealously obedient to the pope and their superior, self-disciplined [45, pp 780-781, 788-793; 48, pp 68-69; 52, pp109-111] and skilled at writing and arguing.
- The **three major assignments** of the **Jesuits:**
  1). To compel Protestants to return to the Roman Catholic Church,
  2). To recover territory from followers of Mohammed,
  3). To convert the heathen all over the world.
-1540 Pope Paul III recognized the Jesuit order. Though *Vicar of Christ* he had many illegitimate children.
-1542 he ordered great effort in the Inquistion, aided by Cardinal Caraffa (Pope Paul IV - 1555-59) [52, pp 105-110].
-1540-70 supported by Popes Paul III, Julius II, Paul IV and Pius IV and V, the Jesuits tortured and put to death more than 900,000 **Waldenses, Anabaptists** and other Protestants [45, pp 776-7, 785].
-Lutheranism became **the state religion** in **Denmark** 1536, **Sweden** 1539 and **Norway** 1540.
-1546-55 Charles V's crusade against Protestants, ended with the **Peace of Augsburg**. Lutherans agreed to permit Catholic teaching in Lutheran states, but Catholics still forbad Lutheran teaching in theirs [45, p 788; 3, p 244].
-1556-1598 Holy Roman Emperor **Phillip** ll reissued the orders of his father, Charles V.
-1522 until 1598, mainly in the Netherlands, 100,000 protestants were killed [45, p 789].
-1576-1612 Holy Roman Emperor **Rudolf** ll intensified persecution especially of Moravian Brethren in Bohemia and Anabaptists in the Netherlands. Half of the Dutch population migrated to America [pp 71-72].

The Counter-Reformation

-The Reformation was spreading rapidly throughout Europe. Roman Catholic leaders became alarmed, when they realized that their whole church seriously needed reform, so they sought ways to revitalize it [52, pp 105-113].
-1545-63 the **Council of Trent**, between Italy and Austria, was in session 18 years, with church leaders from all of Europe involved. Led by Jesuits, for the first time clerical dignitaries sorted, clarified and codified their beliefs. The doctrines ***Justification by Faith Alone*** and ***Primacy of Scripture Over Tradition*** were opposed.

-**Council of Trent** reaffirmed allegiance to the ***Authority of the Pope*** and the ***Veneration of Mary and Saints***. Some faults of the church were condemned: simony, traffic in indulgences and laxity in monasteries. Men for the priesthood were to be carefully selected and seminaries were set up to educate priests. Bishops were given power to correct priests, under the authority of the pope. A ***Forbidden Books List*** was drawn up. A **Catechism** similar to Luther's was prepared [9 Vol 7, pp 275-6; 48, p 70].
-The Roman Church turned increasingly to **pomp** and **ceremony** to display their power. Protestants emphasized simplicity, the Roman Church began the elaborate **baroque** architectural style, with gilded pictorial representations of Bible characters and miracles by saints [52, pp 109-112; 45, p 792; 48, p 70] [See p 85].
-**Singing**, popular with John Hus' followers, began to appeal to Catholics; Oratorios were composed. Biblical street dramas drew crowds; Protestant peasants were tempted to attend this "fun way" to learn Bible stories.
-German priests trained in Rome returned home educated and eager to win back the Lutherans.
-The church became confident and aggressively spread their dogma. The **Inquisition was intensified** [p 62].
-Jesuit political power to carry out severe persecution continued for over 200 years [70, p 393].
-1564 the **Counter-Reformation spread to Poland** considered a *haven for heretics*. The majority of Poles were Protestant. 50 Jesuit houses were built in Poland, which gradually stamped out Protestant influence.
-1596 **Union of Brest** (**Brzesc**) now in **Byelorus** (**White Russia**, between Lithuania and Kiev) created the **Uniate Church** (**Greek Catholic**)[12, Macropedia Vol 25, p 946]. Six of ten Orthodox synods came under the Pope. Orthodox Bishops of **Lvov** and **Przemzsl** in the southeast refused to join [12 Vol 2, p 503].
-In **France** because of religious wars, the Counter-Reformation was delayed until the seventeenth century.
-1529-1559 in France 500,000 people were **Huguenots** (Reformed Protestants), including **King Henry** IV.
-1572 one night **St. Batholomew's Day**, urged by the pope, 70,000 Huguenots were killed, [45, pp 789-790]. 500,000 fled to England, Prussia, S. Africa, West Indies, etc [45, p 790].
-1598 when the **Edict of Nantes** granted freedom of conscience some respite came, but the pope urged Jesuit persecution of Protestants to be continued undercover. He called the edict "a cursed thing".

Dutch Independence from Hapsburg Spain and Supremacy in The Far East

-1556-1603 **Philip** II king of the **Spanish branch of the Hapbsburg Dynasty**, had inherited the **Netherlands** (Dutch speaking Holland) and persecuted Protestants there. His second wife was **Mary Tudor**.
-1553-1558 **Mary Tudor** was **Queen of England**. She was succeeded by her **half-sister Elizabeth** I, a Protestant. During Phillip II's long reign his main goal was to restore the supremacy of the Roman Catholic church; he supported many plots by **Mary Stuart Queen of Scots** and **France** to supplant Elizabeth I [p 60].
-**Philip** II helped persecute and crush **Huguenots** (Reformed Protestants) in France [12 Vol 6, pp 127-8].
-1568-84 Dutch **William** I **of Orange** led a rebellion of northern Netherlands provinces against Phillip II;
- 1579 The northern Dutch provinces united as a Calvinist republic.
-1609 they **won independence** for Protestant Calvinist Holland, but SW Netherlands (**Belgium**, including Dutch **Flanders**) remained Roman Catholic and under Habsburg rule [48, pp 63, 72-73; 16, p 817].
-By the 17th century the **Dutch** were the **foremost European merchants and sailors**, with an **Empire in the Far East Indies** (Java, Malaysia, Borneo, Sumatra, Molucca, etc)
-Holland was the first nation to support public schools by taxation, and to legalize freedom of the press and religious tolerance.

Some Late Renaissance Artists, Philosophers and Scientists

-The **Renaissance ended**, but renaissance spirit continued in southern Italy and north Europe [12 Vol 9, p 1020-1].
-Dutch artists painted impressive scenes and portraits. There were efficient clocks all over Europe [20, p 246].
-**Copernicus** taught at University of Rome; influenced **Johannes Kepler**, **Galileo** and **Isaac Newton** [p 83].
-1490s-1527 about 35 years, High Renaissance art flourished in Europe [12 Vol 9, p 1020; 139, pp 184-7]. [pp 71-72]
-1452-1519 **Leonardo da Vinci** excelled as artist (***Mona Lisa, Last Supper***), anatomist, musician, architect, writer, scientist, engineer, inventor: ***Renaissance Man*** (knowledgeable in every branch of learning) [12 Vol 9, p 10].
-1475-1564 **Michelangelo**, 1483-1500 **Raphael** and others were outstanding Renaissance artists [12 Vol 9, p 1020].
-1450-1626 St. Peter's Church was built over a period of 176 years. 1546-64 Michelangelo built the dome, which was completed in 1590 by his successors [16, p 652] using his plans.
-1527 Rome was sacked by Spanish and German mercenaries of Holy Roman Emperor Charles V [95, p 255].
-1540 **Polish astronomer** Nicholas **Copernicus** (1473-1543) studied at Universities of Bologna and Padua. He demonstrated rotation of the earth and planets around the sun, opposed by the church [See more p 64].

-1561-1626 **Francis Bacon**, English philosopher/statesman influenced European scientific research [16, p 67].
-1571-1630 German astronomer **Kepler** discovered that planets move in ellipses, not circles.
-1564-1642 Italian mathematician-astronomer **Galileo** emphasized careful observation using a **telescope**. He developed theories of mechanics, such as inertia [see below pp 64, 75, 83-84]. He was tried for heresy.

Revival of Learning in Poland, Jagiellon Dynasty and Ottoman Invasions 1386-1572

-1386-1572 Jagiellons ruled **Poland, Hungary**, **Bohemia** and **Kiev** until 1548. [from p 55]
-1492 **Ivan** III **of Russia** invaded Lithuania, but King **John Albert** I of **Poland** was able to repulse him.
-1498-99 **Teutonic Knights rebelled** in northern Poland. **Tartars** from central Asia invaded Krakow, south Poland (**Galicia** Province). For 140 years Muslims threatened the southern boundaries of Poland. (250 years of Mongol domination in Russia ended in 1500 (since 1241). **Moscovy** rule of all Russia began.
-1492-1501 **John Albert** I second son of Casimir IV was elected king of Poland by the **Sejm** (**parliament**).
-1501-6 **Alexander Jagiellon**, brother of John Albert succeeded to the Polish throne. He lost much land on the east bank of the Dnieper River, near **Kiev**, to Russian **Ivan** III [60, p 128].
-1500 the Polish priests and king ordered the German population to become Polanized, meaning change their names, use the Polish language and become adherents of the Roman Catholic Church, or lose everything. Protestant Poles were outlawed, had property seized, and were stripped of their titles. The majority of the aristocracy, merchants and artisans complied, even though most were ethnic German and Protestant.
-Many Poles studied under Renaissance influence in Paris at the Sorbonne and in **Italy** at Padua and Bologne universities. "Ideal government" was their aspiration. Printing presses spread Polish literary works.
-1505 Polish nobles created a **republic** headed by **elected kings** through the **Seijm** (parliament) and limiting royal power, a step towards **democracy**, but **serfs** were bound to the land and had no voice.
-1506-48 **Sigismund** I **Jagiellon** was elected king. He promoted public education and religious tolerance.
-1524 Muslim **Ottomans** conquered most of **Hungary** killing the Hungarian **Jagiellon king**, cousin of the Polish king. They advanced toward **Vienna** 1529. Muslims threatened south Poland another century [p 80].
-1523-26 the Protestant Reformation spread throughout Poland through many Polish nobles who had studied in Protestant universities Wittenburg, Leipzig, Königsberg, Tübingen and Basel, Switzerland.
-Polish nobles also brought humanist ideology from the Sorbonne, Paris and Padua and Bologne, Italy.
-1473-1543 **Nicolaus Copernicus** (**Mikolaj Kopernik**) was born at Torun (Thorn) Poland, studied at the university of Krakow, and then in University of Bologna in canon law and astronomy. He lectured in **Rome**; discovered that the earth revolves around the sun, not the sun around the earth, as was held by **Ptolemy**. The University of Krakow became renowned through him [12 Macropedia Vol 25, p 945-6]. He studied medicine at Padua; received a doctorate in canon law; but was banished to do administration in his uncle's bishopric in Poland.
-Copernicus published several books and articles which influenced **Johannes Kepler**, **Galileo** and **Isaac Newton**. Galileo was tried for heresy so the theories were suppressed, but a few Jesuits believed these scientific findings secretly [9 Vol 7, pp 197-198; 54]. [See above]
-1525 the **Teutonic Knights** converted to Lutheranism, as did burghers in the towns of Poland [97, p 295].
-1506-48 King **Sigismund** I "the Old", added the **Mazovian Plain** to Poland. He advocated religious tolerance, Italian humanism, printing of literature in Polish rather than Latin [28, p 13], and a peaceful foreign policy.
-Refugees such as **Jews** and Protestants were welcomed. Poland became known as *paradise for heretics* [91; 45].
-1515 by allying with the Habsburgs, he inadvertently brought Roman Catholic influence into Poland. This alliance ended the right of Jagiellon rule in **Bohemia** and **Hungary** [27, p 12]. The nobles forced him to establish serfdom [60, p 128].
-1526 his only son died **fighting the Ottoman Turks** [10, pp 31-32].
-1548-72 **Sigismund II Augustus** (**Zygmunt**), the last king of the Jagiellon dynasty, 1569 **reunited Poland** and **Lithuania** and wrote a moving testament [97, p 322] regarding love, harmony and unity in multiethnic Poland. Norman Davies describes multiculturalism during Sigismund II's reign [97, p 317; 55, p 278] as follows:

> "People prided themselves in their descent real or imagined from Sarmatians or Chazars [prehistoric Asians] or from Dutch, Swedish, Italian or Scots immigrants. The Roman Catholic majority was surrounded by a colorful array of sects and faiths - by Calvinists, Lutherans, Arians, Unitarians, Orthodox, Uniates, and Old Believers; by orthodox Jews, Karaim, Chassidim. Frankists, Armenian monophysites and Tartar Muslims... Vernacular speech was conducted in anything from the four main regional dialects plus Kashub, Ruthenian [Byelorussian and Ukranian forms], Lithuanian, Latvian and to 1600 Prussian, Platdeutsch, Yiddish, Tartar

"or Armenian. The Royal Court of King Sigismund II was Italianate. Liturgical languages were Church Latin, Old Church Slavonic, High German, Hebrew, and Arabic. Documents were written in a variety of alphabets including Roman, Cyrillic, Hebrew, and Arabic. Even the calendar showed marked variations." [Davies continues], "The attitudes encouraged were practical toleration... cultural cross-fertilization where open-minded people could learn from their neighbors, and it encouraged a strong tradition of education, which each community had to emulate by excellence in their schools and academies."

-1547 Calvinist Polish landlord Raphael **Leszczyniski** founded the town of **Lezno** (Lissa in German) located 78 km south of Poznan, 97 km north of Wroclaw, Silesia, for Low German and Czech Protestants persecuted in the Inquisition by **Jesuits** and Emperor **Ferdinand** I [62, pp 12-13]. For two centuries Moravians (Unitas Fratrum = Unity of Brethren = Brüder Gemine) [12 Vol 12, p 138; Vol 4, p 613] thrived in Poland [77, p 761] [pp 76-80].
-1548 May, nearly 2000 Brethren from Bohemia-Moravia expelled from their homeland, traveled north in two parties, via either Frankenstein or Breslau. Sympathetic Polish villagers donated meat, eggs and milk. It took two months to reach Posen. A nobleman welcomed a large group, but his bishop ordered them away. They found refuge in Königsberg, Lutheran East Prussia. Other refugee groups were well received.
-1550 **Calvinism** attracted large numbers of Polish and Lithuanian nobility [97, p 295]. Lutherans and Calvinists established churches. In 1552 Sejm suspended ecclesiastic sentences (religious imprisonments). For 130 years Poland was the only country without religious persecution [12 Macropedia Vol 25, p 945]. Some Calvinists formed the **Polish Brethren** [p 80]. 1563 the Calvinist Brest (Brzesc) Bible was published, and in 1601 a **catechism**.
-A haven from religious persecution was offered also to Jews, Anabaptists and Mennonites from the Netherlands, as well as sects from Germany [97, p 295]. **Menno Simons** had a large following along the Baltic [77, p 185].
- 1530-84 **Jan Kochanowski** a graduate of the universities of Krakow and Padua, Italy, was leader and founder of the use of vernacular Polish in literature. "His **Psalter** did for Polish what Luther's Bible did for German." [97, p 295]. Polish dialects became uniform, linguistic standards rose and national pride increased.

Ottoman Turks Conquered the Byzantine Empire and the Balkans [from pp 43, 54-55]

-1347 Turks ruled Albania, 1389 Serbia, 1396 Bulgaria, 1453 Constantinople, 1463 Bosnia for 4 centuries.
-1481-1512 Sultan **Bayzid** (Bajazet) II; 1492 invaded Hungary and other nations along the Danube [16; 3].
-1512-1520 **Selim** I took Anatolia, Khurdistan, attacked Persia and Egypt; annexed Syria. [maps 38, 61, 68]
-1520-66 **Suleiman** I the Magnificent took Belgrade, Rhodes; 1526-9 took Buda, killed Louis II of Hungary;
-1541 began to rule Hungary; built baths and mosques. 1551 Suleiman took Tripoli; killed nephews & his son.
-1566-1574 Sultan **Selim** II made peace with Hapbsburg Maximillan II; attacked Cyprus and Venice [16; 55; 95];
-1574-95 **Murad** III strangled brothers; attacked Austro-Hungarian border [maps 38; 68].
-1595-1603 **Mohammed** III had 19 brothers murdered. 1596 attacking Hungary lost 30,000 troops. A small portion of Hungary remained free [map 68]. 1603-17 **Ahmed** I invade Hungary; 1618-22 **Osman** II strangled.
-1620 defeated Polish. 1623-1640 **Murad** IV won Baghdad from Persia. 1640-49 **Ibrahim** fought Venetians &
-1669 took Crete. 1649-87 **Mohammed** IV; 1687-91 **Suleiman** III; 1671-3 Turks attacked Poland;
- 1683 Ottoman Turks were defeated in Vienna by Polish **Jan Sobieski** ending Turkish expansion in central Europe, but taking away thousands as slaves. 1690 Turks drove Austrians from Bulgaria, Transylvania & Serbia & retook Belgrade, [99, pp 226-7]; were in control the remainder of four centuries [maps 68, 184].

Rurik Dynasty in Russia until 1598 [Continued from p 56 and Map: p 56]

-1462-1505 **Ivan** III **the Great**, Grand Duke of Moscow, adopted the title **Tsar** (Caesar) and expanded NW into **Novgorod** and **Lithuania** and east to the **Ural mountains** [20, p 201-4, 227-9]. The domains of Russia in the north were expanded by annexing **Smolensk** from **Lithuania**, and **Pskov** an independent city-state in the NE.
-His **Tsarina** was **Zoe,** a Byzantine Greek princess. He issued laws, made treaties with western European rulers, and chose the Roman Eagle as the Russian Emblem [16]. All parts of Russia came under the rule of **Moscovy** [20, p 246; 60, pp 103-7]. By 1480 Ivan III felt strong enough to stop payments of tribute to the Tartars (Tatars, Mongols or Golden Horde) but three other Mongol Khanates continued active [map p 56].
-1484-89 the walls of Moscow and the Cathedral of the Annunciation were built, on earlier foundations. Ivan began to rebuild/build other churches in Moscovy, employing **Italian architects** and sculptors. His son:
-1505-33 **Tzar Vasily** continued to transform Moscow as a showplace of renaissance architecture. The Red Square and **Kremlin** and were built [136, p 91]. The population included German craftsmen, merchants & scholars. He expanded Russia by annexing **Lithuanian Smolensk** and **Pskov**, an independent city-state in the NW.

It took constant military resistance to keep back the **Mongol Khanates** of Kazan and Crimea in the south. He had no children with his wife of 25 years.

-Second **wife Lithuanian Elena Glinskaya**, bore **Ivan** three years before he died, and **Yuri**, was born deaf.

-About thirty boyars (noblemen) plus regional princes jostled for the throne, but **Csarina Elena** ruled as Regent five years, assisted by **Prince Obolensky**. She died in agony, probably of poison. **Boyars** (noblemen) seized control, got rid of Prince Obolensky, but continued having power struggles.

-Young **Ivan** gathered like-minded adolescents around him, rode recklessly about the city streets, but loved books and worship, guided by Orthodox **Metropolitan Macarius** (equivalent to Archbishop).

-1547-84 **Ivan** IV was crowned Czar at age 16, in an extravagant ceremony by Macarius, with boyars and archbishops. The jeweled crown was fur trimmed. In his teens he married **Anastasia**, a devout, wise and loyal wife. Due to complaints of corruption, injustice and fires in Moscow, he exiled incompetent boyars and redistributed land to military men who served well. Each landlord, soldier or boyar, according to the amount of his arable land, was required to provide armed mounted soldiers and horses for distant campaigns. He defeated Khanates **Kazan** and **Astrakhan** and gaining control of the **Volga River** [map p 56].

-1558-83 he attacked **Livonia** in the north sporadically, determined to gain access to the **Baltic Sea**.

-1560 after Czarina Anastasia died, restraining influence was lacking [102, pp 31-60]. He banished wise advisers, was widowed and remarried seven times; became known as **Ivan the Terrible** carrying out cruel justice and massacres. 1566 he proposed to England's Queen Elizabeth I and was refused; 16 years later in 1582 he proposed to English heiress Mary Hastings [53, p 113]. 1571 a huge **Tartar** army from **Crimea** overran southern Russia, invaded Moscow and burned down wooden houses. The next year the Tartars (Tatars or Mongols) attacked again, but were defeated. Russian colonists in the far east, unaided by Czar Ivan, defeated Tartar tribes and invaded **Siberia**. 1584 he died. Lands in north were recaptured by Poland, Lithuania and Sweden.

-1576 the **German** residents built St. Michael's Evangelical Church in Moscow [92, pp 6-7].

-1584-98 **Fyodor** Ivan's simple-minded son, **last of the Rurik Dynasty**, ruled gently, with **Boris Godunov** his brother-in-law administrator. Fyodor liked retreats in monasteries; died childless; Boris took the throne.

-1598-1605 **Czar Boris Godunov** ruled until he died suddenly, after slander that he had killed **prince Dmitry**, a pretender [102, pp 60- 80]. Eight years of anarchy followed. The Poles invaded, but the Orthodox church inspired a volunteer army to assemble, and in 1612 forced the Poles to withdraw. [Continued p 79]

Polish Republic: Elected Kings After the Jagiellon Dynasty 1569 to 1795 [maps 56, 86, 94]

-1569-1795 **Sejm** (parliament) ruled as a republic with elected kings, in administrative and military roles.

-1548-1572 **Sigismund** II **Augustus**, the last king of the Jagiellon dynasty, in 1569 reunited Poland and Lithuania, and developed a thriving multicultural society, which was largely Protestant [See above pp 64-65].

-1564 the **Counter-Reformation** began in Poland with an influx of **Jesuits** who built 50 houses which gradually stamped out Protestant influence [See p 65]. 1573 the **first free election** was held by the Polish parliament. Nobles mistrusted strong central authority. Majority vote was Protestant. Religious toleration was guaranteed for Lutherans, Calvinists, Brethren, Orthodox and Roman Catholics. The king's authority was weakened: he was not crowned until he swore to guarantee toleration, free elections, regular sessions of Sejm (parliament), surveillance by 16 resident senators, and the right of nobles to approve taxes, declaration of war, foreign treaties, and the right of resistence.

-The **Polish Republic** lasted 223 years, ruled by eleven elected kings in turn, for an average of 20 years. Seven of them were foreigners. The population consisted of 8 to 12 % nobility. Serfs were tied to the land. The clergy, city burghers and Jews were protected by separate charters and had no representatives in Sejm.

-1576-86 King **Stephen Bathory** of **Transylvania** was elected Polish King. He defeated Tzar Ivan IV of **Muscovy** and recovered Livonia (eastern **Latvia**, including the city of Riga), and southern **Estonia** [27, p12].

-1587-1632 **Sigismund** III, Swedish **Vasa Dynasty** was elected King of **Poland**, and 1592 also King of **Sweden**. Poland the ***Granary of Europe*** exported grain from Baltic Seas Ports.

-1596 the capital of Poland was transferred from Krakow to **Warsaw** [27, p 39]. Warsaw became a city comparatively late in Polish history, but its central position and location, on the **Vistula**, the major river, favored rapid development [27, p 39-57] as major city.

-1596 Union of Brest (Brzesc) in Byelorus (White Russia), between Lithuania & Kiev created the **Uniate Church** (**Greek Catholic**), an effort to unite the Greek Orthodox and Roman Catholic Churches. Six of ten Orthodox synods came under the Pope [12, Macropedia Vol 25, p 946]. Orthodox Bishops of **Lvov** and **Przemzsl** in the SE refused to join [12 Vol 2, p 503]. [Continued p 80]

Chapter Eleven - 1400 to 1599

Architecture During the Renaissance

Architecture In the Eastern Roman Empire During Muslim Supremacy [from pp 30-32, 54]

-1453 the eastern Roman Empire at Constantinople fell to the Ottoman Turks.
-The great domed cathedral of St. Sophia became a mosque. Biblical murals and icons (mosaic pictures of saints) were covered with texts from the Qur'an (Koran). Islam forbad art of persons or animals, but allowed ornamentation with decorative lattices and geometrical or floral mosaic designs, inlaid with colored stones.
-Tall slender minarets with a spiral staircase were added. Five times a day the Muezzin climbed to the top to call people to prayer.
-The Eastern Orthodox churches were persecuted but survived.
- In individual countries Orthodox churches were governed by Patriarchs (Metropolitans) and autocephalous (independent) synods, without an international head. [See p 32].
-All levels of clergy were encouraged to marry.
-A new wave of Muslim invasion into Europe began.

Spanish Alterations to Moorish Muslim Architecture [continued from pp 36 and 48]

-1402-1507 at **Seville** an inland port the third largest cathedral in Europe was built, seating 12,000 people.
The first: St. Peter's, Vatican in Rome, built 1450-1526,
The second: St Paul's, London, England, burned down 1666, rebuilt 1675-1710 [16, p 652].
- The Seville cathedral is in Gothic style. Gold, silver and gems were applied lavishly to the altar and images. It is built on the site of a twelfth century mosque that was destroyed. However:
- 1511 the central dome collapsed. It was rebuilt in Renaissance style [42b, p 71]. The **Giralda**, the original minaret, was preserved with its original Moorish artistry and turned into a bell tower, completed 1568. Many elaborate chapels inside the cathedral.[28b, 42, pp 984-6; 42b, pp 70, 716-717, 722-723; 139, p 229], were dedicated to saints.
- Spanish kings employed Moorish architects to build palaces, churches and public buildings. Gothic and Moorish crafts were combined in a style known as Mudéjar. "Richly decorated stonework and tiling covered walls, arches and door frames with a maze of abstract and geometrical designs [139, p 229; 42b, pp 67-68]."

Renaissance Style Neo-Classical Architecture

-Greek scholars escaped to universities in Italy bringing with them their devotion to Greek and Roman classical manuscripts, art, sculpture and architecture, which stimulated search for old manuscripts and hunger for learning. Renaissance means rebirth. The knowledge, skills and styles of ancient Greece and Rome were revived, reinterpreted and expanded [9 Vol 2, pp 280-2; 42b, pp 71-72].
-1438 the development of printing by **Gutenberg** in Mainz was quickly followed by setting up of printing presses all over Europe, and the publishing of many kinds of books and **newspapers** in many languages.
-In the 15th Century in Italy wealthy merchants sponsored artists, sculptors and scientific architects.
-1420-1436 a **large dome** designed by **Brunelleschi**, was built in **Florence** at the cathedral of Piers. It resembled Roman construction but incorporated some Gothic features [9 Vol 2, pp 280-1].
-The **palazzo**, a new style of opulent urban residence several stories high built around an inner court, became popular in Italy. The author recommends modern high rises be built around inner courts/playgrounds.
-1485 a book on architectural theory published by **Vitruvius**, became influential in promoting classicism.
-1503-1612 the new basilica of **St. Peter in Vatican city** by **Michelangelo** evolved from Brunelleschi's in Florence. It was the prototype for later churches and the state capitol in **Washington** DC [see p 143].
-1579 four ***Books of Architecture*** by **Palladio** were published. They included the classical proportions and dimensions which enabled the application of **Palladian principles** later in **England** and **America**.
-Italian architects built many major cathedrals in France and some in Spain and England [9, Vol 2, pp 282-4] and later in **Russia**. The round arch was reintroduced. Domes were used instead of Gothic towers and spires. The Gothic arch was thought ugly and barbarian.
-For decorative purposes **Greek** style columns were added to Gothic style buildings [24, Edward Norman, pp 176 -195].
-A trend to classical Greek style columns spread all over Europe in the 16-18th centuries. An example is Lazienki Palace, pictured in Bajcar [27, after p 240, described in p 47]. It was the summer palace of King Stanislaus Augustas in Warsaw, Poland.
-Dydynski describes architecture in every town in a remarkable little travel guidebook. He says "Renaissance fashion flooded Poland [28, pp 234, 238, 249-1, 245, etc]."

Bells and Carillons

[Continued from p 48]

-The **chiming bell** evolved in **England**. A clapper was inserted and a rope used to swing the bell. Bell-ringing became a skill, called *change ringing*. Bells were cast of better and better amalgams of bronze and tin, in shapes that, with experience improved the tone. Flaring and thickening of the lip also improved the tone. A lathe was used to fine-tune bells[12 Vol 3, pp 441-5; 9 Vol 3, pp 412-3]; sets of bells with different pitch produced a tune.
-The **carillon** evolved in **Flemish Belgium and Holland**, consisting of fixed, cup-shaped bells struck by a mallet or hammer. Originally four bells in a row were used. They had a keyboard and range of 4 octaves. Gradually precise tones and pitch were achieved.
-By 1554 as many as 24 bells were assembled to produce carillon music.
-The word **belfry** originally referred to a wooden tower for fortification, without a bell [12 Macropedia Vol 5, p 933].

Clocks and Clock Towers

[Continued from p 48]

- 1410 in **Prague** in the **Old Town Hall tower** an amazing **astronomical clock** was built based on the **glockenspiel mechanism**. It still draws crowds hourly today. It strikes the hour and marks the phases of the moon, equinoxes, season, date and many Christian holidays. In the 19th century a procession of Apostles, and several medieval style caricatures of evil, were added [10, pp 140-141, 169; 55, p 812].
- Mechanical clocks were extremely large and lacked a cover to protect them from dust [12 Vol 3, pp 392-3].
- 1500 German **Peter Henlin**, a locksmith, made portable time pieces, with the hour hand only [12 Vol 3, pp 392-3].
- 1582 **Galileo** discovered the time-keeping property of the **pendulum**. [Continued p 86]

Map: *Political Divisons of Europe in the 16th Century* [41, p18]. [Compare with maps pp 38 & 61]
Spanish Hapsburgs included Spain, Aragon, Burgundy, the Netherlands, Milan and other parts of Italy.
Austrian Hapsburgs included Bohemia, Moravia, part of Hungary and some German States.
Poland and Lithuanian held much of Russia and were threatened by the Ottomans who ruled the Balkans.

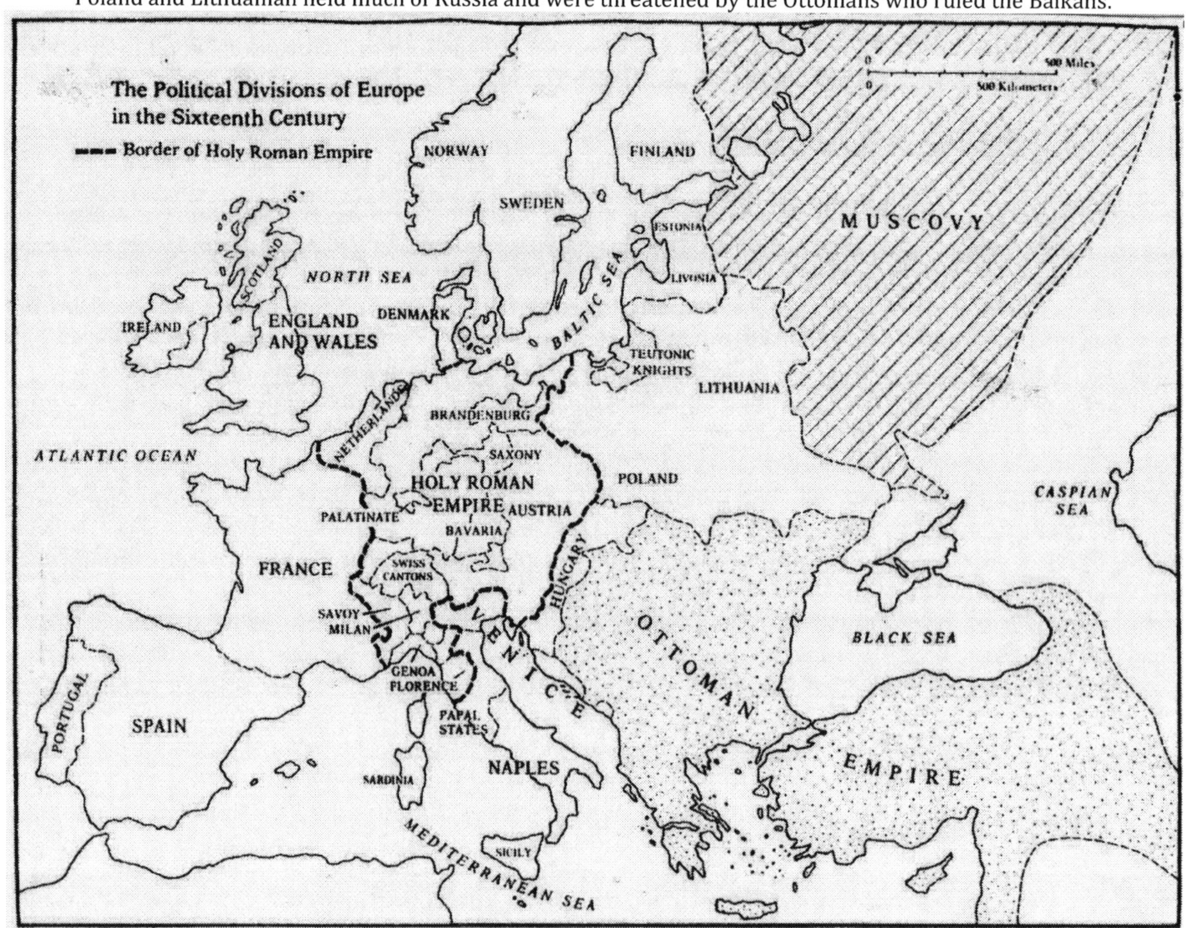

Chapter Twelve - 1600 to 1699

Rival World Powers and Explorers

French Protestants Prominent in the Discovery and Colonization of the New World

-1523 persecution of Protestants became severe. **Jean Vaillière** was burned at the stake in Paris [12 Vol 6, p 127].

-1529-1559 over a quarter of the population of France influenced by Humanism, Luther and Calvin were **Huguenots** (Protestants)[12 Vol 6, pp 127-8]. Derivation and meaning of the name are unknown. Many were skilled artisans, noblemen, merchants & shipbuilders in Newfoundland fisheries & later in Canadian fur trade [120, p 1113].

-1534 Protestant refugees fled to **Martin Bucer**'s Reformed church in Strassburg (**Strasbourg**) a free city.

-1534 and 1535 a **Huguenot**, **Jacques Cartier** (1494-1557) commissioned by King Francis I, circumnavigated Newfoundland, claimed Gaspé for France [119 Vol 9, p 58], explored the St. Lawrence River as far as present-day Montreal, named it Mount Royal, and wintered there [112, pp 58-73] [p 60]. **Sieur de Roberval** (Jean Francois de la Roche) also Huguenot, joined Cartier, and stayed on to explore the St. Lawrence River further [112, pp 71-3].

>1534 **John (Jean) Calvin** a young French priest/scholar was exiled to Basel Switzerland;1538 to Strasbourg.

-1541-42 **Huguenots** began colonizing **Canada**, 1555 **Brazil** and 1562-64 the **Carolinas** [120, p 1113].

-1559 Protestants from every province of France sent 72 deputies from 15 churches, to a synod in Paris; drew up a confession of faith, influenced by **John Calvin** [12 Vol 6, p 127]; by 1561 there were 2,150 congregations.

-1562 **Jean Ribault** a Protestant colonizer brought 150 Huguenots in three ships to **Florida** and claimed it for France. He built a fort and settlement of soldiers in **South Carolina** named Port Royal [16, p 590; 630]. While he returned to France the soldiers deserted the Fort. Ribault was exiled to England for his faith.

-1565 Jean Ribault was sent back to Florida with seven ships of colonists [12 Vol 10, pp 35-6; 125 Vol 16, p 321], but **Spaniards** executed them as heretics; he died. More than 1450 Huguenots settled in **Quebec** and **Louisburg** (Cape Breton, Atlantic Canada).

-1572 **St. Bartholomew's Day** during the night, urged by the pope, 70,000 Huguenots were killed in Paris, and thousands more were massacred all over France [12 Vol 6 p 127; 45, pp 789-790]. Many fled to other countries.

-1591-1660 in France **Vincent de Paul** & **Louise de Marillac** began the Sisters of Charity to serve the poor.

-Due to wars, the Counter-Reformation did not gain momentum until the 17th century. **Mysticism** spread.

-1598 some respite came to the Huguenots when the **Edict of Nantes** granted limited freedom of conscience. The pope calling the edict "a cursed thing" approved continuing **undercover Jesuit persecution**. Many escaped to England, Prussia, English America, South Africa, etc. Some were forcibly converted to Roman Catholicism. Others lived as Catholics while secretly keeping their Reformed convictions and marrying into families sharing their views [120p 1113; 12 Vol 6, pp127-8]. Reformed pastors served fishermen and sailors but were not allowed to solemnize marriages or baptisms. All of the major early explorers and colonizers of New France were Huguenots; "**Huguenots may be said to have been the real discoverers of Canada**" [119 Vol 5, p 193].

-1603 Pontgravé, François Gravé **Du Pont** a Protestant, made a reconnaissance trip up the St. Lawrence as far as the Lachine Rapids, above Montreal, with **Samuel de Champlain**, the Royal geographer/cartographer, who wrote a detailed description. Champlain also was a Protestant. He had been a billeting officer 1594-8 in the French army and had made a voyage to the **West Indies** for the King of Spain 1599-1601.

-1604-5 Pierre Du Gua, **Sieur de Monts**, a Protestant born in **Saintonge** (Saint Onge) France, a personal friend of king **Henry** IV [119 Vol 5, p 193], acquired Royal Patents for colonization, **fur commerce** and government. He started settlements in **St.Croix** and **Port Royal** in **Acadia** (**Nova Scotia**). Henry IV was a protestant.

-1605-56 **Samuel de Champlain**, also born in Saintonge, mapped/explored the coast twice, from Cape Breton south to Martha's Vineyard, now Massachusetts, in search of an ideal location for settlement. 1604-6 he spent three winters in Acadia but retreated. **Sieur de Monts** never visited north America again, but backed Champlain and pursued commercial ventures, until retiring in 1617.

-1608 Champlain commissioned by Sieur de Monts, established the settlement called **Quebec** on the **St. Lawrence River**. He built up a vast fur trading network, providing kettles, knives, etc. to establish friendly relations [125 Vol 7, p 564]. More settlers arrived [12 Vol 3, p 74; 121 Vol 1, pp 192-4]. He joined with **Algonquins** to fight **Iroquois** marauders. This enhanced French prestige but the Iroquois allied with the English [p 103].

-1609 Champlain explored **Lake Champlain**, named for him. It is 107 miles long, now bordered by Vermont, New York State and Quebec. Soon it was used for travel and invasion from New England to Quebec.

-1610 Champlain married Hélène Boulle, daughter of the protestant Secretary of the King's Chamber. He urged appointment of a Viceroy. 1611 Champlain was named **Commandant of New France**.

- 1615 Because missionary and parish work was restricted to Roman Catholics, Champlain brought four humble **Recollet priests** (Franciscan) vowed to poverty [120, p 1113]. to Quebec [119 Vol 9, p 65, 58].

- 1615 Champlain explored Lake Huron and formed a Huron-Algonquin alliance. With a band of Hurons he penetrated Iroquois territory in New York, south of Lake Ontario and was wounded. He wintered in Huronia. One **Recollet priest** was with him and one ministered on the Saguenay River, while two remained in Quebec.
- 1620 French king Henry IV gave Champlain administrative authority over Quebec and his wife joined him. Agriculture began. A great demand for beaver, fox, marten, mink and otter furs grew in Europe [125 Vol 7, p 564]. Felt hats were made from beaver fur. A group of French merchants, the ***Company of New France*** received a charter from the King to trade in the interior. They promoted liquor and lowered moral standards. Champlain protested vehemently, so they were replaced by the ***Company of One Hundred Associates***.
-They brought 300 Roman Catholic settlers annually from France. Trading posts were established along the St. Lawrence River, around the Great Lakes and in 1621 at Port Royal, Acadia. More than half of the fur merchants were **Huguenots**. They loved to sing Psalms in French.

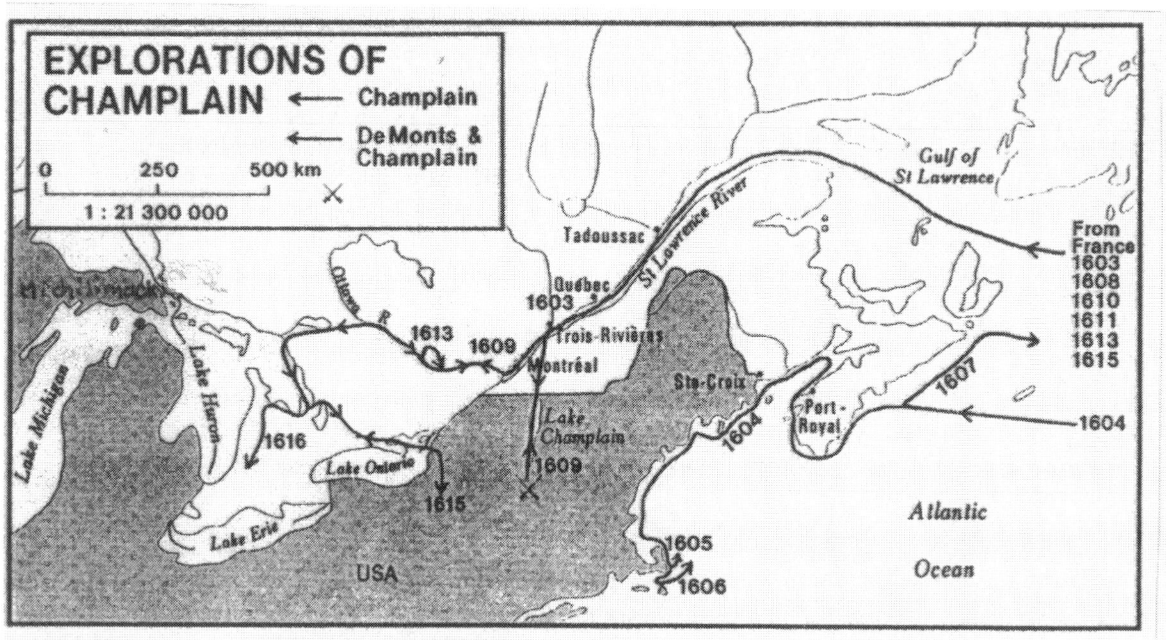

Map: ***Explorations of Champlain***[121 Vol 1, p 316].

Fur Traders in Waterways Around the Great Lakes [from pp 58; 59-60]

-1539-42 Florida and the Gulf area at the mouth of the Mississippi River (Georgia, Louisiana, Alabama and Arkansas) had first been explored and settled by **Spaniards** under **De Soto** [16, p 192, 445, 526], looking for gold.
-1540-2 Spaniard **de Coronado** with 300 Spanish and many Indian troops, went overland from Mexico, where Coronado was a Governor; explored north of the Rio Grande River (present Texas, New Mexico, Kansas, Colorado and Nebraska) looking for gold and wintered near present Santa Fe [See pp 57-58].
-1629 Frenchman Jean **Nicolet** (1598-1642) was **sent by Champlain** to Lake Nippissing to trade furs, and
-1634 **Nicolet** explored Lakes Huron and Michigan and built Fort Michilimackinac [120, p 898]. French forts with Indian wives [9 Vol 2, p 47] were set up on the Illinois and Fox Rivers [125 Vol 14, p 405] and present Wisconsin.
-1658-59 Pierre-Esprit **Radisson** [95, p 323], born in France 1636 [121, p 1540], and his brother-in-law Medard Chouart des **Groseilliers** of Trois Rivière, and some Iroquois, explored and traded fur [16, p 494] around Lakes Superior and Michigan. There they heard about and planned trading in the "Bay of the North" [Continued p 73].

Non-Conformists Fled to America during Tudor/Stuart Dynasties/Cromwell Republic

-1547-53 **Edward VI** was King of England; 1553-58 **Mary Tudor** ruled, and their half sister followed [p 60]:
-1558-1603 **Elizabeth** I ruled England 45 years, the Elizabethan Age, regarded as one of the greatest periods of English history [167, pp 88-99]. She established the Church of England, taking over abbeys and churches. She promoted world exploration and defeated invasion by Spain [53, pp 59-93]. She had gallant courtiers and international suitors of high rank, but remained single. Roman Catholic **Mary Stuart**, **Queen of Scots** and **France** (not Mary Tudor) repeatedly tried to depose her, but was imprisoned 19 years and executed 1587.

-1600 privately owned **East India Company** was incorporated by royal charter for spice trade [12 Vol 4, p 329] with India and south-east Asia. 1612 the power of the **Portuguese** in **India** was pushed back into **Goa**.
-Trade expanded into silk cloth, raw cotton, saltpetre (to cure meat), spices and indigo (excellent blue dye).
-1564-1616 **William Shakespeare** was/still is the poet-dramatist par excellence of pathos, satire and wit. The sonnet was designed. He broadened/enriched English vocabulary; enhanced confidence of poor and rich.
-1603-25 **James** I **Stuart** a Protestant, son of Mary Stuart, Queen of Scots, became king of England, after 20 years as James VI, King of **Scotland**. Though not devout he had the ***Authorized Version*** of the Bible translated
-1604-11 by 54 Hebrew & Greek Anglican and Puritan scholars, revising many other translations [16, p 825-8].
-1600 Roman Catholic Douai translation of the Bible from Latin to English was published [16, p 203].
-Reformed (Calvinist) theology spread to Scotland, Hungary, Bohemia, Moravia, Poland and Austria. With severe persecution in Austria, some protestants escaped to Poland and Romania [pp 59, 64-65]. The Church of England assimilated some Calvinist ideas but retained bishops and persecuted Puritan dissenters.
-1607 **John Smith** founded **Jamestown**, **Virginia** the first permanent English settlement [116, p 15] in America. He was captured by Indians; rescued by a girl, **Pocohantas**. 1614 he mapped the coast calling it **New England**.
-1587 the area was renamed **Virginia** for virgin Queen Elizabeth by **Sir Walter Raleigh.** His settlement did not survive. A daring explorer, he prayed courageously "Disturb us, oh Lord if we stay too close to the shore."
-1619 the first Representative Assembly in the British colonies met at Jamestown [16, p 798].
-1620 seeking freedom of worship 100 young **Pilgrim Fathers** (**Puritans**) migrated to North America, with a stop-over in Holland, led by **Miles Standish**; founded a colony called **New Plymouth**, now **Massachusetts**.
-1621 **James** I granted **Acadia** (later **Nova Scotia)** to Scotch poet Sir William Alexander [9, Vol 1] his tutor.
-1625 **Charles** I son of James I, became King of England. He ruled 11 years (1629-40) with no parliament.
-1619 his nephew **Prince Rupert** born 1619 in Prague, son of Protestant king Frederick I of Bohemia and Elizabeth Stuart, daughter of James l; in Thirty Years' War (1618-48) [p 76]. he grew up in court of Charles l.
-1626 a Puritan colony was founded at **Salem**, **Massachusetts** by **Roger Conant**. 1629 first Congregational Church had **Roger Williams** as pastor [12 Vol 10, p 350]. 1630 **Boston** was founded by **John Winthrop** [9 Vol 4, p 251].
-1629 Scots settled in **Nova Scotia** (**Acadia** in French) [121 Vol 1, p 5-6]. 1632 the French drove out many. 1630-70 colonists from Loire, France settled Acadia. 1671 the population was 400; by 1701 it was 1400.
- 1639 **Harvard** College, later University, and a library were founded. In 1701**Yale** University was founded.
- 1643-1684 four Puritan Colonies formed a confederation for trade and protection from raids by French, Dutch and Indian foes, and to settle religious disputes, and by 1670 there were 12 English settlements. **Boston** became the major seaport. English settlers developed **fur trade** in New England and Virginia; formed an alliance with the **Iroquois** Indians; extended trading from Maine in the north to Georgia in the south, on the Atlantic coast[125 Vol 7, p 564]; pushed Indian tribes into the mountains and began to settle east of the Appalachian mountain ranges (Allegheny, Catskill, Great Smoky, Blue Ridge, etc) [9 Vol 2, p 214].
-1638 **Prince Rupert** fought in Europe against the Hapsburgs, and was taken prisoner for three years. When freed, **Charles** I gave him command of an English fleet on the Atlantic and West Indies [12 Vol 10, p 242].
-1642 **Civil war** in England. Prince Rupert commanding Royalist cavalry, won at first [110, p 96]. A Puritan member of Parliament, **Oliver Cromwell** Commander of Ironsides Cavalry, was the revolutionary leader.
-1649 **Charles** I was beheaded. His son **Charles** II was in exile [p 73].
-1653-9 Cromwell was **Lord Protector**, virtual dictator of England. Scots and Irish were crushed. A measure of religious toleration was provided. **Jews** excluded from England since 1290, were allowed to return.
-Cromwell won foreign prestige by his stable government & vigorous army/navy. Allied with France, he captured **Dunkirk** from **Spain** [9, pp 340-2]. He disliked the **Society of Friends** (**Quakers**) begun by **George Fox**.
-**Thomas Carlyle** improved Cromwell's image/reputation in *On Heroes* and *Cromwell's Letters Today* 1841.
-1608-74 **John Milton** wrote *Parasdise Lost;* favored Cromwell; freedom of speech; wrote sonnets.

The Netherlands Overcame the Counter-Reformation and Prospered [pp 62-63]

-1583 with Emperor Charles V's grandson **Rudolf** II living in Prague, Bohemia, economic prosperity returned to Bohemia [10, pp 37-38]. **Hapsburg dynasty divided into Spanish and Austrian branches**. Their kings were crowned Emperor, but had little authority over the loose collection of hundreds of rival German states.
-1556-98 **Phillip** II of Habsburg, king of **Spain** succeeded his father Charles V as Holy Roman Emperor. Mary Tudor, Queen of England 1553-58, was his second wife. 1558-1603 half-sister **Elizabeth** I English Queen.
-Hapsburg **Phillip** II who inherited the **Netherlands** from his father, intensified persecution of Protestants in the **Dutch Netherlands** (Holland), although the wealth and power of Spain were waning.

-1568-84 **William** I of **Orange** (royal house of the Netherlands) rebelled against Habsburg Phillip II.
-1609 **Dutch Netherlands** won independence from Phillip II [48, pp 63, 72-73] but **Flanders**, Roman Catholic western Netherlands, remained under Habsburg rule.
-1594, 1595 & 1596-7 Dutch navigator **Willem Barents** made 3 voyages to seek a northeast passage to Asia. On the third voyage Barents' ships were frozen in for the winter and in the spring he died. Survivors reached **Lapland**. Three times he had crossed **Barents Sea** (named for him) [9 Vol 3, pp 278-9], ice-free in the south.
-1602 the **Dutch East India Company** was founded to protect Dutch trade in the Indian Ocean and to assist their war of independence from Spain [12 Vol 4, p 299]. The company prospered as a seafaring commercial power.
-1607 and 1608 **Henry Hudson** financed by the **English Muscovy Company** tried to find the **NE passage**.
-1609 the **Dutch East India Company** lured **Hudson** to try a third time to find a NE passage. Head winds and storms forced him back. He sailed in search of a **NW passage** instead. 150 miles up the broad river later named for him, but decided it did not lead to Asia [118]. The Hudson River and **Lake Champlain** became **a** gateway to and from New England to the Great Lakes [118]. He sent his log and reports to Holland.
-1610-11 **Henry Hudson** financed by the **British East India Company**, the **Muscovy Company** and private sponsors sailed directly to the huge bay, later named **Hudson Bay** for him. He explored it and **James Bay** and wintered there. He and his son and the two instigators of mutiny, were lost in a mutiny. After his ship was sailed back to England, the discoveries formed the basis for English claims to much of Canada [12 Vol 6, pp 117-8].
-1624-52 Dutch **Nieuw Amstersdam** was founded on the Hudson River [12 Vol 6, pp 117-8] with stone mansions.
-1626 the Island of **Manhattan** was purchased by the Dutch Governor for the equivalent of $24.
-1664 the English seized the Dutch colony and renamed it **New York** in honor of the Duke of York, brother of Charles II, but the Dutch Reformed Church was allowed freedom from English control [12 Vol 9, p 996].
-1619 **Batavia (Jakarta)** became the capital of the **Dutch East India Company** and a base to conquer **Java**.
-1621 the **Dutch West India Company** was constituted for the purpose of economic warfare against Portugal and Spain, by striking at their **West Indies** colonies and transporting **slaves** from west Africa [12 Vol 4, p 301].
-1634-48 **Dutch colonies** were established in the **West Indies** at Aruba, Curacao and Saint Martin and in
-1667 Dutch colony **Guyana (Surinam)** between French & British **Guiana,** South America [12 Vol 4, p 301; Vol 5, p 547].
-1636-45 the **Dutch East India Company** defeated the British fleet in the East Indies, displaced Portuguese and built **a huge Dutch Empire** in Malaysia, Java, Sumatra, Celebes, the Moluccas, Timor, Bali, etc.[12 Vol 4, p 299].
-1642-3 Abel Janszoon **Tasman** reached the **Australian** island, named **Tasmania** for him, and sighted **New Zealand**. 1644 he explored the north and west coasts of Australia [116, p 17].
-The international centre of finance and culture was in Holland; the **foremost sailors were Dutch** [12 Vol 4, p 301].
-1652 Jan van Riebeeck established a colony named **Capetown** at **Cape of Good Hope** for refueling of coal, for trading vessels of the Dutch East India Co. **Dutch Calvinists** and **French Huguenots** settled there.
-Dutch settlers, **Boers** meaning farmers, developed their own dialect, strict Calvinism and insisted on keeping slaves[12 Vol 11, p 33; Vol 2, p 319].

Jesuit Missions, Fur-Trading, and Settlements in New France [Continued from pp 70-71]

-1622 Armand Jean du Plessis, **Duc de Richelieu** (1585-1642) was ordained **Cardinal** in France, and in
-1624 he became the **Chief Minister** of France. His aims were:

1. to suppress the political power of the Huguenots,
2. to vindicate royal authority,
3. to secure France from the threat of Hapsburg domination [16, p 631].

-1625 **Jesuits came to Canada** [120 Vol 3, p 306], including Father Jean de **Brébeuf** who is renowned for work among **Hurons** on Georgian Bay, Lake Huron. Iroquois imprisoned, tortured and killed him in 1649 [9 Vol 4, p 333].
-1627 in Canada and 1659 in Acadia, the **Jesuits** and **Cardinal Richelieu** proclaimed all Protestant worship and teaching illegal. 1633 Richelieu forbade admission of Huguenots to Canada [119 Vol 5, p 193].
-1627-8 in a siege under Richelieu, **Rochelle** a Huguenot centre in western France, was crushed [16, p 635].
-1628 **Acadia** fell to the English, and **Quebec** fell temporarily 1629-1632 [119 Vol 6, p 6] under **David Kirke**.
-1632 **Louis** XIII appointed **Champlain Intendant (Governor) of Quebec**. Ile St. Hélène in Montreal is named for his wife. 1632 Champlain appointed **Capuchin priests (Franciscans)** to worked in Acadia [119 Vol 9, p 65].
-1634 **Trois Rivières** was founded between Quebec and Montreal. **Jesuits** worked here and in Gaspé, Acadia and Cape Breton [120, p 58]. **Recollect priests** (Franciscans) favored by Champlain, returned to Gaspé [see p 70].
-1639 at Quebec the **Ursuline Sisters** established education for girls [119 Vol 9, p 58] and nurses' training at **Hôtel Dieu** (hospital), some of them orphans or of mixed blood. Madam Champlain also taught native girls.

-1635 **Champlain died** and became known as Father of New France. He was an author of note. A series of books describing his explorations was published [121 Vol 3, p 305-7]. His widow entered a convent in France.
-1641 Paul de **Chomedey de Maisonneuve** brought 200-300 settlers to **Montreal**, including **Jeanne Mance**.
-1645 she founded **Montreal Hôtel Dieu** hospital.
-1653 again de Maisonneuve brought 100 colonists and militia to Montreal [168,pp 47-50].
-1657 **Sulpician priests** came to Montreal and 1663 became owners of Montreal Island. As **seigniors** (feudal lords) they granted land to settlers, built schools, mills and massive stone buildings and laid out the main streets of Montreal and a canal to Lachine. **Maisonneuve** was governor of Montreal until 1665 [121, p 1073].
-1653 **Marguerite Bourgeoys** chaperoned **brides** for settlers from France [121 Vol 1, p 261] and recruited teachers from France and Canada; 1658 founded the **Congregation of Notre Dame School** for French and native girls.
-1659 the first bishop of Quebec, **Jesuit Francois de Laval** (1523-1708) arrived. All religious were subject to him, and as Pope's Vicar General he refused to submit to civil authorities. He founded a theological seminary. He opposed sail of liquor to Indians and immigration of non-Roman Catholics.
-1663 the colony became a royal province governed by the bishop and five appointed councilors.
-1665 **Radisson** and **Groseilliers** were reprimanded by the Governor of Quebec for **fur-trading** 1658-65 without a licence in lakes Superior and Michigan [p 70] so they went to **Boston** and took passage to England.
-In England they met **Prince Rupert** ([p 71] ho with other noblemen agreed to finance fur trade around the Hudson Bay. **Radisson** married an English woman. [continued below]

English Colonial Expansion by Charles II and William of Orange

[Continued from p 71]

-1658-59 **Richard Cromwell** succeeded his father as **Lord Protector**, but resigned due to power struggles.
-1660-1685 **Charles** II was hailed king of England and called back from exile in France and the Netherlands. His cousin **Prince Rupert** was appointed Privy Councillor and Naval Commander.
-1663 the **Carolinas** were granted to the Duke of Albemarle and seven other British noblemen [map 51, 97].
-1540 the Carolinas were explored by **Spanish de Soto** [12 Vol 12, p 152]; and later by **the French** [16, pp 533,701-2], so the naming of **Fort Carolina** was either for **Charles** IX of France or for **Charles** I of England [125, Vol 18, pp 640-66].
-1583-1650 settlers moved from Virginia [125 Vol 14, p 472] to the Carolinas.
-1664 **Nieuw Amsterdam** was seized from the Dutch and renamed **New York** for Charles II's brother **York**.
-1665 in London 8000 died of **Black Death** [95, p 325]. 1666 the **Great Fire of London** destroyed the city centre.
-1670 the **Hudson Bay Company** (HBCo) was granted a **monopoly** by Charles II for trade & commerce in the entire territory draining into Hudson Bay (present Manitoba, Saskatchewan, Alberta, Minnesota, the Dakotas, Quebec, Ontario & NW Territories) named **Rupert's Land** for **Prince Rupert** first Governor [map 117].
-**Raddison** was appointed guide, translator and adviser [119, Vol 5, pp 182-92]. He established the Nelson River post north of Lake Winnipeg [121, pp 1229, 1540], but became dissatisfied with the HBCo [map 121].
-1674 **Radisson** and **Groseilliers** defected to France, who never trusted them fully, so they did other work.
-1681 **William Penn** (1644-1718) founded **Pennsylvania** on land granted by Charles II to rid England of nonconformists, dissenters from the Church of England [95, p 334] (Presbyterians, Quakers, Puritans, Baptists, etc.)
-French **Louis** XIV invaded east of the Rhine twice. He persecuted Protestants so Penn visited Europe to invite them to migrate [12 Vol 9, p 74]. 1682 the city of **Philadelphia** (brotherly love) was founded [16, p 571] [maps 104, 157].
-1682 **Raddison** and **Groseilliers** were hired by **French Compagnie du Nord** to challenge the HBCo fur trade using inland rivers via the Great Lakes [19 Vol 5, p 183-6]. When their furs were taxed and a ship taken, Raddison went to France for restitution, but failed. He returned to his wife in England.
-1684-7 Radisson was HBCo Director of Trade at Ft. Nelson, with French price on his head; retired in England.
-1685-88 **James** II second son of Charles I, became Roman Catholic; tried to convert England, so was exiled.
-1688 his daughter **Mary** and her husband **William** of Orange, a German-Dutch Reformed Protestant were invited from Holland to become King and Queen as joint Sovereigns: **William** III **and Mary** II. This event is still resented in **Ireland**. In Scotland and Ireland **Jacobites** tried to reinstate James II. Emotions still run high in the annual Belfast Orangemen parade. William's mother was Mary, daughter of Charles I of England [16].
-Many Germans emigrated with William and Mary to settle in England. The use of stocks for punishment was introduced to England from Holland. Jailers were called stockmen. Some of the Stockman family migrated to England, and others remained along the Baltic Sea in domains of the Teutonic Knights. Julius Stockman married Adeline Schneider, the author's aunt [40, Part 2 Chap 8]. His German dialect included Turkish words from combat with Turks.
-Mary II reigned during William III's many absences [16]. She died 1694. He was sovereign until he died in 1702.

Jean Talon Two-Term Intendant (Governor) of New France - 1665-68 and 1669-72

-1665-68 **Jean Talon**, Intendant (Governor) achieved remarkable improvements in a short time in **Canada, Acadia** and **Newfoundland** [121, p 1783]. He started mining of iron ore and silver, weaving of textiles, a clothing industry, flour milling, fisheries, tanning, lumbering and many fine ship building yards [119 Vol 10, pp 9-10; Vol 5, p 231].
-Splendid ships were manufactured in New France and exported for the navy of France [119b Vol 4, pp 266-76, 287-8]. Fish and flour were exported to **French West Indies**.
-Because of a shortage of women Talon brought filles du roi (daughters of the king) from France to provide brides. He subsidized large families and promoted immigration. The population of 2500 rose to 10,000.
-1668-80 French Roman Catholic Sulpicians established missions on the north shore of **Lake Ontario** on the **Bay of Quinte** (now Belleville, Trenton and Deseronto) [119 Vol 8, p 387].
-1669-72 in Talon's second term to offset activities of the HBCo he sent fur traders/explorers via the Ottawa River & Lake Huron to **Sault Ste Marie** to claim the entire Great Lakes, the north-west and **Mississippi River** for Louis XIV [168, p 50-51]. Hundreds of forts were built. Radisson and Groseilliers were with HBCo at this time.

Governor Frontenac and Intendant Duchesneau [see more p 96 and map 97]

-1672-82 Comte de Louis de Buade **Frontenac** was Governor of New France upon advice of **La Salle** [16, p 270], in
-1673 he established **Cataraqui** (later **Kingston**) 175 miles SW of Montreal on the St Lawrence River.
-1675-1682 Frontenac's authority was split with Intendant Jacques Duchesneau [121, p 529]. When Duchesneau demoted local fur traders, harmony and prosperity began to decline [147 Vol 4 # 48; 168, p 59-69]. He outlawed beggars. There were many single men without families.

Map: *Fur Trade until 1790* [121 Vol 2, p707] [see also maps pp 97 &108]

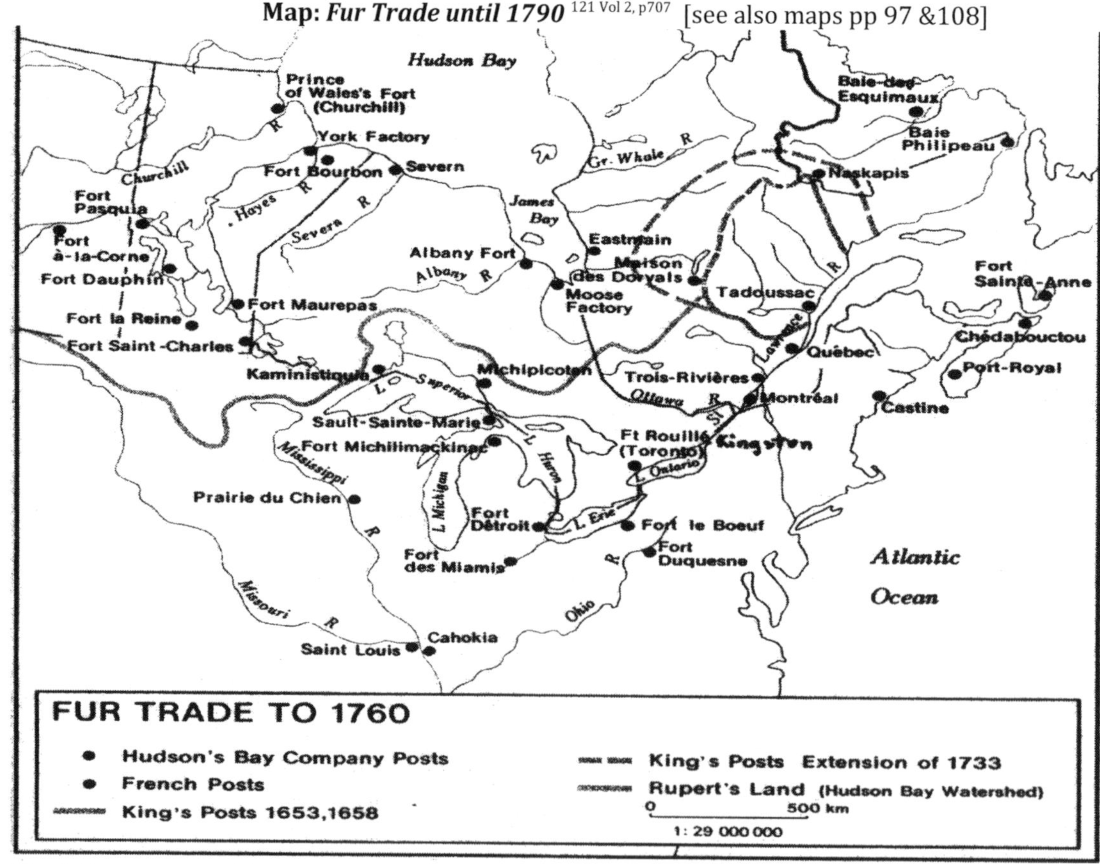

-1682 both Frontenac and Duchesneau were recalled to France [119b Vol 3, p 309; Vol 4, p 288].
-1672 there were 25 parishes in New France. Tax on the faithful was a 13th of their crops [119, Vol 9, p 59].
-The **population of New France** was about 15,000, while **that of New England** was 400,000 and growing rapidly, because religious minorities were welcome [120, p 1943]. There were serious food shortages.
-1670-1683 the Sulpicians erected magnificent Bonsecours Church (Notre Dame) [119, Vol 9, p 66; 261] in Montreal.
-1677-8 René-Robert Cavelier, Sieur de **La Salle** (1643-87) had a **ship-building industry** on Lake Ontario.

-1682 French **Campagne du Nord** hired **Raddison** to challenge English fur trade. He establishing forts but left for England. 1684 HBCo rehired him! 1687 retired in England, to escape French price on his head [p 73].
-1685 the **Nantes Edict** was revoked so persecution intensified. 500,000 Huguenots fled. They were skilled craftsmen, merchants and seamen [95, p 337; 12 Vol 6, p 127] their exodus severely damaged the economy of France.
-1689-98 **Frontenac** had a second term as Governor. Iroquois wars escalated [see New France, pp 96-98].
-1692 In **Quebec** City Hôtel Dieu Sisters founded a hospital for the elderly/crippled and mentally ill and fed vagrant beggars. 1694 in **Montreal** a General Hospital was opened for orphans and cripples.

Quebec French Fur Traders Explored the Mississippi and Saskatchewan [from pp 57-58]

-1665 French **Jesuit** missions and fur trading posts were set up in **Wisconsin** [16, p 820; 9 Vol 2, pp 361-2].
-1668 and 1671 **Jesuits Dablon** and **Jacques Marquette** began settlements and missions on Lake Michigan.
-1672 Fur-trader **Louis Joliet** (1645-1700)[16, p 356, 386] was commissioned by **Governor Frontenac** to determine the route and mouth of the Mississippi [maps 74 & 97]. 1673-75 Joliet joined by **Marquette** [16, p 469] and five traders, sailed down the Mississippi & portaged to other rivers. 1686 they explored the Prairie du Chien, Wisconsin, canoed south past the Missouri, Ohio and Arkansas River entries, into the Mississippi [116, p 14].
-1673-1739 more Frenchmen explored **Nebraska**. The French were respectful of Indians.
-New Englanders friendly at first, copied Indian farming of corn (maise) and vegetables [9 Vol 2, p 47], but the Indians were pushed west into the Appalachian mountains for refuge from disease epidemics and settlers.
-1670-82 René-Robert **Cavelier** Sieur de **La Salle** (1643-87) explored [16, p 539] the **Ohio**, **Mississippi** and **Illinois** Rivers. 1677-8 La Salle had a ship-building industry on **Lake Ontario**. 1678 **Fort Niagara** was founded [120, p 898]. 1682 **La Salle** sailed down the **Illinois** and **Mississippi** Rivers to the **Gulf of Mexico**; claimed the entire region drained by the Mississippi River, for **France**; named it **Louisiana** for King Louis XlV [116, p 14].
-1684-6 **La Salle** explored **Texas** to find a connection to the Mississippi River [16, p 415-6, 496; 121, p 954] [map 97].
-1686 **Henri de Tonty** built a trading station where the **Arkansas River** enters the Mississippi [9 Vol 2, pp 361-2].
-1690-92 in the north **Henry Kelsey**, a **HBCo** trader, explored from Hudson Bay to **Lake Winnipeg**, and up the **North Saskatchewan River** where he saw the great plains and **buffalo herds** [119 Vol 5, p 189] [map p 108].
-1688, 90 and 94 Pierre **Le Moyne d'Iberville et d'Ardillières** raided English posts on **James Bay** and **Hudson Bay**, sank two ships, seized furs; **raided** from **New England** and down the **Mississippi in Louisiana**.
-1698 he and his brothers built a settlement near the present **Biloxi**, the first in the area [p 98; map p 97].

Sixteenth Century Philosophers, Scientists and Artists [Continued from pp 63-64]

-1561-1626 in England, lawyer **Francis Bacon**, member of parliament, orator, thinker and author was appointed Solicitor General in 1607 and Attorney General in 1613. His ***Essays*** were among the most significant written since Greek philosophy. He anticipated the telephone and wrote the ***Advancement of Learning*** and a biography of King Henry II [16, p 67]. His scientific research methodology was influential.
-1571-1630 German astronomer **Kepler** discovered that planets move in ellipses, not circles.
-1564-1642 Italian mathematician-astronomer **Galileo** emphasized careful observation using a **telescope**; developed theories of mechanics, such as ***inertia***. The Roman church tried him for heresy.
-1606-69 **Rembrandt**; 1632-75 **Vermeer**; about 1582-1666 **Frans Hals** and other Dutch artists painted many highly skilled life-like landscapes and portraits [12 Vol 12, p 320-1].
-1665 **Robert Hooke** (1635-1703) a physician, made a telescope combining three lenses, able to magnify up to 100 times; wrote a best-seller ***Micrographia*** describing fungi, protozoa, algae and microorganisms [3, p 303]; did underwater explorations in a glass barrel; invented the balance spring for watches.
-1629-95 **Christian Huygens** a scientist/mathematician, applied the pendulum to the clock; devised a new method to grind clearer telescopic lenses; investigated polarization and wave theory of light; discovered rings surrounding Saturn; and published both popular and scientific books of his discoveries [16, p 351].
-1642-1727 mathematician-astronomer Sir **Isaac Newton** studied gravity, spectrum, optics, etc [16, p 527].
-1687 his ***Mathematical Principles of Philosophy*** was published and quickly became popular in Europe. He built a small but powerful telescope with reflecting mirrors. Newton developed the scientific method.
-1596-1650 French **René Descartes** made contributions to optics, physiology, physics, logic and psychology. He used mathematics to express scientific and religious ideas to build a logical view of God and the world.
-1618-48 saw **a revival of mysticism** with renewed interest in **Thomas à Kempis** (1380-1471), **Kaspar Schwenkfeld** (1489-1561) a Silesian nobleman, **Jacob Bohme** (1575-1624) and others [12 Macropedia Vol 26, p 218].

Origin of the Kingdom of Prussia [Continued from pp 53-55]

-1614 **Elector Sigismund** ordered "Confession of Brandenburg" to reconcile Calvinism and Lutheranism. Rulers of large German States were Electors, meaning they had a vote to chose Holy Roman Emperors.
-1618 Albert, son of Teutonic Knights' Grand Master Albert **Hohenzollern** died without a son. His eldest daughter married **John Sigidmund Hohenzollern**, Elector of **Brandenburg**. Thus **Ducal Prussia** (east) combined with **Brandenburg Mark** (west), **to found Prussia**, the largest German state [12 Vol 9, pp 751-3].
-1618-48 **Berlin** the capital of Prussia, was neutral during the **Thirty Years' War** but had to provide quarters for several Swedish armies, which exacted heavy contributions. Berlin was a town of only 12,000 after the **Bubonic Plague.** It was a member of the **Hanseatic League** since 1359 [9 Vol 4, p 9].
-1640-88 **Elector Frederick William** of Brandenburg acquired **Pomerania** [12 Vol 9, p 588] when their duke died without an heir. He adorned **Berlin** with new public buildings [9 Vol 4, p 9] and **assumed the title of king**, although still under **suzerainty of Poland** [53b, p 51].
-1660 he ended Poland's suzerainty over Ducal Prussia (East Prussia) [12 Vol 9, pp 759-60] [see pp 90, 92].
-1688-1713 **Elector Frederick** III of Brandenburg succeeded his father still under the Holy Roman Emperor.

Bohemia and Central Europe Before The Thirty Years' War 1618-1648 [from pp 61-63, 65]

-1591 the **Calvinist Reformed church** entered **Bohemia**, made rapid advances and greatly influenced religious development of the kingdom [109;12 Vol 4, p 613]. Habsburg Holy Roman **Emperor Rudolf** II (1552-1612) tolerated Calvinists, Lutherans, and Hussite Ultraquists but not the Unitas Fratrum (Unity of Brethren= Brüder Gemine in German) because they were pacifist. By 1602 with 90% of the population of Bohemia protestant, Emperor Rudolf II suppressed the Unity of Brethren and began to persecute all protestants.
-1592-1670 **Jan Komensky (Comenius** in Latin) was born to Unity of Brethern parents 1592 [10, pp 38-39] in Moravia. Comenius' parents and sisters died in an epidemic before he was 12. His school days were boring and unhappy, but in Latin school in Moravia, the rector was so impressed by the boy's thirst for learning that he gave him the middle name **Amos** (love of knowledge). While studying at Calvinist **University of Heidelberg** Comenius began writing a Latin/Czech dictionary, a grammar and an encyclopedia.
-1614-16 he taught high school, was Pastor of Unity Church and School Master in **Fulnek, Moravia**. He married. In 1609 he wrote ***Ratio Discipline*** which taught tolerance/harmonious relations/unselfish life style.
-1603-9 **Baron Wenzel von Budowa** traveled in German states, Holland, England, France & Italy; translated the **Qu'ran** into Czech; critiqued Islamic creed [134, bk1, chap 13]; was **Ambassador** in **Ottoman** Constantinople.
-1612-37 **Habsburg Ferdinand** II was king of Hungary and Bohemia, and 1619 Holy Roman Emperor [16, p 246].
-1618 the **Thirty Years' War** (1618-1648) broke out after **Ultraquist Hussites** appointed a Protestant King and threw two jurors out of a window, 1620 at the ***Battle of the White Mountain*** near Prague [10, pp 38-39]. Hussites were defeated, ending 70 years' Protestant rule in **Bohemia** [9 Vol 7, p 188].
-1621 on June 21 the **Day of Blood** 32 Protestants were beheaded, even those loyal, or elderly, and scholarly Baron Wenzel **von Budowa** [134, bk 1, chap 15]. Both Reformed and Unity of Brethren clergy were ordered to leave Prague in 3 days and all Bohemia in 8 days. Influenced by the Elector of Saxony, Lutherans were permitted to stay [109], but 1627 were expelled also. All Protestants in Bohemia-Moravia were outlawed [12 Vol 12, p 138] and fighting spread into Saxony to destroy German Protestants [50; 48, pp 74-75], but Roman Catholic French joined the anti-Habsburg Protestants.
On one side in the 30 years' war was the House of Habsburg (**German Roman Catholic states** and **Spain**).
On the other side were **Sweden, German Protestant states** and **France**.
-1618-48 the German population shrank from 17 to 8 million from famine, plague, war and persecution.
-The Unitas Fratrum refused to take up arms. After **Fulnek** was invaded, **Comenius** with his wife and children hid in the woods. His church, school books and manuscripts were burned, neighbors were killed or fled into exile. His wife and a daughter died while escaping to the estate of Baron Charles von **Zerotin**. While hiding seven years, he was consecrated Bishop of the Unitas Fratrum. He wrote ***Labyrinth of the World***; ***Paradise of the Heart*** and books on **primary school reform**, in several languages and the following motto:
* ***In essentials unity, in non-essentials liberty and in all things charity.***
In 1628 forty clergy taking refuge in Zerotin were expelled. Before they fled to Poland, Comenius prayed:
* ***Preserve there a hidden seed to glorify Thy name.*** They found asylum in **Leszno** Poland (**Lissa** in German) 78 km south of Poznan, 97 km north of Wroclaw, Silesia [27, pp 182, 190-1; 12 Vol 7, p 301], where the grammar school was already famous, and had added a gymnasium (higher school).
-Later, after teaching 13 years [134, bk 1, chap 16] he was appointed director [see p 65].

-1648 when the 30 Years' War ended; the **Treaty of Westphalia** [12, Vol 10, p 803] granted religious freedom to anti-Habsburg Silesia. Comenius hoped the Unity of Brethren would be allowed to return to their homeland. Instead their right to exist in Bohemia-Moravia was denied. The church stayed underground; informers reported them. Churches, Bibles and hymn books were destroyed. Some were hidden in loaves of bread.
-As 200 years earlier, many Bohemian/Moravian Brethern died or fled. The population of Bohemia dropped by more than three-quarters [45, p 790]. 36,000 Unity families fled to Silesia, Poland, Dresden, Berlin, other parts of Europe, and some, like the **Cennick** family, to **England** [134, bk 1, chap 15; bk 2, chap 11]. Two million followers of Jon Hus were eliminated, yet today two denominations trace their origin to the Unitas Fratrum: both the **Evangelical Czech Brethren Church** and the **Moravian Church** (Unity of Brethren=Brüder Gemine).

Moravian Bishop Comenius Reformed Education in Many Countries

-1641-42 Comenius was in **England**, invited by **Samuel Hartlib**, to consult on education, but civil war began. His primary school reform book was printed in English. **Cardinal Richelieu** invited him to **France** [12 Vol 3, p 482].
-1650-4 Comenius, at Sarospatak, **Hungary** near the present Slovakia border in the northeast, taught and revised the teaching system at **Calvin College**, founded 1531. Closed during the Counter-Reformation, it had continued teaching in exile, and was reopened 1703. Here Comenius wrote ***Orbis Pictus (The Visible World in Pictures***) the first ever picture book for children. It taught Latin in sentences, instead of as grammar.
-1654 ***Orbis Pictus***, published in Nurnberg became most widely used/reprinted textbook in German [100, pp 381-3].
-Often **Comenius** used a double column system with Latin on one side and the vernacular language on the other. He wanted ordinary Latin learned in the early grades so that people of all countries could communicate in one language [12 Vol 3, p 482]. Comenius wrote 154 books.
-Comenius' educational methods and philosophies were much ahead of his time, and even similar to the best of today. He wanted education to be a joy, not a terror, as in his childhood. Teaching he said should proceed from the simple to the complex, "and from the concrete to the abstract, girls should be educated as well as boys, and the poor as well as the rich. He urged governments to spend 100 times as much on education as they did to prepare for war," quoted from the Winston-Salem Journal, 1992 [50].
-He was offered several prestigious positions, even to be Principal of **Harvard** College (later University) in America. Harvard was founded 1636 [12 Vol 5, p 732] by a Puritan minister from Cambridge, England. Comenius chose instead an invitation from the government of **Sweden** [12 Vol 3, p 482]. He wrote a series of textbooks for school reform. Also in **Romania** Comenius revamped the school system.
-1655 **Charles X Augustas Vasa**, Protestant king of **Sweden** invaded Prussia and Poland, took **Warsaw** and **Kracow** and occupied **Lissa**. In 1656 the Poles' counter-attack burnt down the Moravian grammar school and the town. The Brethren scattered in Europe. A considerable number settled in **England** [134, bk 1, chap 16].
-1657 Comenius moved to **Amsterdam** and published ***Didactica Opera Omnia*** and a collection of his books.
-1657 brothers **Paul** and **Adam Hartmann** and **Paul Cyrill**, ordained Moravian ministers from Lissa, went to England to raise support for exiled Moravians, carrying a treatise to the **Archbishop of Canterbury**. They studied at Oxford. 1660 Comenius dedicated his ***Ratio Disciplinae*** to the Church of England.
-News of the destruction of Lissa reached **Oliver Cromwell**. He invited them to find refuge in Ireland, but instead, rebuilding of Lissa (Lesno) began.
-Both **Prince Rupert** (later of the Hudson Bay Co) and the Church of England sent money to rebuild Lissa.
-1660 **Paul Hartmann** was ordained a Presbyter by the Church of England; 1671 Chaplain & 1676 Rector. Comenius' daughter married Pastor **Peter Jablonski**. Their son **Daniel Ernest** was born 1660 in Danzig.
-1670 at 78 years of age **Jan Amos Comenius** died. His last great philosophy of education ***Consultation,*** was lost but rediscovered in **Halle**, Germany in 1935. He is highly regarded today in the Czech Republic, his native land.[10, pp 39, 85-86, 96-98, 263]. Evangelical Czech Brethren also trace their origin to the Unitas Fratrum [12, Vol 12, p 138].

More Moravians Fled to Prussia and Poland

-1650 in Dresden so **many Hussite** and **Unitas Fratrum exiles** were arriving from **Bohemia** and **Moravia** that they were granted the use of Johannis-Kirche Lutheran Church. Others settled at Wesgau, near **Barby**, and in **Zittau**. About 1670 another congregation organized near **Messersdorf**, and later one near **Görlitz**.
-1673 Adam Hartmann was consecrated a Bishop in Lissa, at the request of Moravians in England.
-More Hussite exiles kept coming so for lack of space, 500 moved to Berlin in 1732 [57, pp 6-7].
- 1680 Adam Hartmann received the degree DD at **Oxford** and he was referred to as a Bishop [134, bk 1, chap 16].

-1683 King **Charles** II of England issued a cabinet order stating the Moravian Brethren deserved assistance because of their stand against the papacy, but also for having preserved the succession of Episcopal Orders.
-1660-1741 **Daniel E. Jablonski**, Comenius' grandson [57, pp 9, 28, 68] born in **Danzig** [12 Vol 6, pp 461-2], studied in Frankfort an der Oder and three years at **Oxford**, England where he received the DD degree.
-1683 Jablonski had a preaching position at Magdeburg.
-1686-91 Jablonski headed the Moravian College at **Lissa** (**Lezno**) **Poland**.
-1691 he was appointed court preacher at **Königsberg**, East Prussia (NE Poland) last headquarters of the Teutonic Knights' Grand Master. 1618 through marriage, East Prussia and Brandenburg in the west had amalgammated to found **Prussia** [see p 76].
-1693 Jablonski was appointed court preacher at **Berlin**, West Prussia, under Elector **Frederick** III (1688-1713) of Brandenburg, who 1701 became Frederick I of Prussia. [See above pp 75-76 and continued p 111].
-**Jablonski** and **Elector Frederick** I tried to amalgamate the **Lutheran** and **Calvinist Churches**, and also to reform the Lutheran church by introducing the episcopate and liturgy of the Church of England [12 Vol 6, pp 461-2].
-1699 Jablonski was consecrated Bishop of the Unity of Brethren (Moravian Church). He was able to call several synods (some in Warsaw, Poland). He aided Moravian Brethern refugees in Poland, Lithuania, Russia and Hungary.
-1700 Gottfried Wilhelm **Leibnitz**, renowned mathemetician and scientist from Hanover, urged **Fredrick** I to found the **Berlin Academy of Sciences**. Bishop Jablonski was co-founder with Leibnitz [see pp 88, 90].

The Pietist Movement

-1648 after the Thirty Years' War some Lutherans felt ashamed of the secularism and lax piety of Lutheran elite clergy. Preoccupied with debating details of theology, they had lost interest in prayer and pastoral care.
-1606 **Johann Arndt**, Father of Pietism wrote the widely read four volume: *True Christianity* [12 Macropedia Vol 26, p 219].
-1635-1705 Philip Jacob **Spener** born near Colmar, **Alsace**; educated at **Strasburg** University, became a pastor in Strasburg, and 1666 pastor at **Frankfurt on Main**, emphasizing personal faith in Christ. He revitalized confirmation classes, which most pastors left to indifferent school teachers. He retaught his sermons in midweek groups; and published a book *Resusitation of Personal Piety in the Lutheran Church*.
-1685 **Spener** was called to **Dresden**, **Saxony**, as **chief court chaplain**. His influence spread in the **Universities** of **Leipsic** and **Wittenburg** and throughout **Saxony**. He corresponded with many people and was known as "spiritual counselor of all Germany" [12 Macropedia Vol 26, p 219].
-Spener's graduate students Augustus Herman **Francke**, Paul **Anton** and John Caspar **Schade** preached in German, not Latin, not learned expositions but the awakening of genuine piety [12 Vol 9, p 435]. Some of the faculty, who preferred a life of amusement, stigmatized them ***Pietists*** [57, pp 1-6].
-1691 the Elector of Saxony expressed his displeasure with Pietism, so **Spener** was glad to accept a call to **Berlin**, where he taught until his death 1705 [57, pp 1-6]. Spener developed a friendship with **Daniel Jablonski** who succeeded him as chief court chaplain in Berlin. Large numbers of persecuted Bohemian and Moravian Brethren**,** Huguenots (French Reformed) and Calvinists found refuge in Berlin.
-1692 **Augustus Herman Francke** (1663-1727) dismissed for his *Pietism* from the **University of Leipsic**, was invited to the newly founded **University of Halle** as Professor of Oriental Languages, and later of Theology, assisted by **Paul Anton** and other *Pietists*.
-1698 at **Halle** many visionary institutions began to be established: a charity school, orphanage, home for poor, Teacher Training School, Divinity College, Infirmary and Apothecary, Medical Faculty and Missionary Training, Linguistics Courses, Book-Store, Print Shop and Foreign Missionary Society. [12 Macropedia Vol 26, p 219].
-1706 **missionaries** from Halle were sent to **Tranquebar**, **South Africa** [57, pp 5, 180, 274-5].
-Graduates of Spener at Leipsic spread Pietism in the Universities of **Halle**, **Jena** and **Tübingen**.
-In later years graduates from these universities entered the ministry of the Unity of Brethern (Moravian Church) and served throughout Europe, the West Indies, America, Greenland, borders of Tibet and south and east Africa.
-At **Jena** Pietist **Buddaeus** republished ***Ratio Discipline*** and a number of other books by **Comenius**, and recommended the practices of the **Unitas Fratrum** to the Lutheran Church.
-1700 **Nicholas Ludwig** was born to Count George Louis **Zinzendorf** and wife Charlotte Justina **Gersdorf**. Her family of **Dresden**, **Saxony** were devout *Pietists* and personal friends of Spener.
-Count George Louis Zinzendorf and his brother held high positions under the Electors of Saxony. Their grandfather left his castle in Austria during the Reformation for conscience sake.

-Three sisters were married to Franconian Counts. Gersdorf castle in upper Lusatia had been the hunting lodge of former Bohemian kings. The Count selected Spener as godparent for their baby son, but died when the baby, the **future Count Nikolaus Ludwig von Zinzendorf** was six weeks old. His mother remarried. His grandmother Lady Gersdorf and aunt Henrietta cared for him with carefully selected tutors. Spener, Augustus Herman Franke, Paul Anton and other leading Pietists were frequent guests in their home [pp 99-100].

Russian Romanov Dynasty 1613 **to** 1917 [Continued from pp 65-66]

-1584-98 **Fyodor**, **last of the Rurik Dynasty**, the gentle, simple-minded son of Czar Ivan IV, liked retreats in monasteries; delegated administration to brother-in-law Boris Godunov. He died childless; Boris succeeded.

-1598-1605 **Czar Boris Godunov** ruled until he died suddenly, after slander that he had killed Prince Dmitry, a pretender [102, pp 60-80]. Eight years of anarchy followed. The Poles invaded, but the Orthodox church motivated a volunteer army to mobilize, and in 1612 it forced the Poles to withdraw.

-1613 a national assembly met to elect a Czar. Of the original 35 noble families only 9 had survived being dispossessed and banished by **Ivan the Terrible**, so the choice was easier than in the past [53, pp 113-114]. They elected Michael a 16 year old boy, great-grandson of the father of Czarina Anastasia, Ivan IV's first wife.

-1613-45 **Tzar Michael founded the Romanov Dynasty** which ruled until 1917.

-1626 "New Church" a second German church was built in **Moscow** to accommodate the growing German population; called *German Evangelical Officers Church,* since ethnic German army officers attended [92, pp 6-7].

-1645-76 **Tzar Alexis** I, father of **Fyodor**, **Ivan** and **Peter** [12 Vol 10, pp 159-60] placed a ban on smoking [95].

-1648-9 Ukranian serfs were oppressed by Polish feudal lords. Seeking independence, there were **uprisings** by **Cossacks** (escaped serfs, traders, clergy and bandits) from around the **Don** and **Dnieper** Rivers; led by **Bogdan Chmielnicki** (Khmelniysky). Tzar Alexis suppressed revolt [95, p 329]; promised autonomy [see p 80].

-1676-1682 at 15 years of age Tzar **Fyodor** III succeeded. In 1682, his two young brothers succeeded:

-1682-1689 mentally defective **Ivan** V, 15 years, and half-brother **Peter**, 9 years, ruled jointly [12 Vol 10, pp 159-60]. Ivan's older **sister**, **Sophia ruled as Regent** until 1689. Peter largely self-directed his education. He became a practical carpenter, blacksmith and printer. His tutor Zotov was liberal-minded and non-traditional. When 13 years old Peter created a regiment of boy-soldiers, commanded by foreign officers. He deployed them in war games with real weapons. 1689 he banished Sophia to a convent. Brother Ivan was sickly and died so:

-1689-1725 **Tzar** (Czar) **Peter** 1, later **the Great**, was 6 feet 6 inches tall. As a boy he had often been in the German suburb, keenly interested in German technical skill, orderliness and culture [92, pp 6-7]. He surrounded himself with The Jolly Company of boistrous young men later called Synod of Fools and Jesters. To settle him, his mother arranged marriage with **Eudoxia Lopukhina**, daughter of a Moscow nobleman.

-Tzar Peter tried to capture **Azov**, south Russia, to gain a naval base but failed as he lacked a navy. He therefore mobilized an army of carpenters and worked with them all winter to build a squadron of galleys and hundreds of barges. In the spring they attacked the Turks and lost. He sent 3000 high-born colonists to Azov; and ordered each monastery, boyar and merchant to build a ship there [53b, pp 18-22], with 20,000 Ukranian craftsmen. He soon realized they lacked technological skill so**:**

-1696 Tzar Peter sent 50 young Russians to **England, Holland** and **Venice** to study shipbuilding, seamanship, navigation and fortifications, at their own family's expense. They were not to return until they had a certificate of proficiency from their foreign employers. Tzar Peter joined them in disguise as a shipwright apprentice. He also studied printing methods, and participated in surgical operations, dentistry, etc.

Tzar Peter was fascinated with microscopes, barometers, wind gauges and all practical equipment.

-In Holland living with a blacksmith, he worked as a carpenter in shipyards until he qualified as a shipwright.

-In England he worked in the dockyards and roamed the streets at will. He studied European ways 1½ years in **Prussia, Holland, England** and **Vienna**.

-He **recruited 600 men** mainly from **Holland**: shipwrights, hydraulic engineers, mathematicians, naval officers, and barbers. He ordered Russians to be clean-shaven.

-He was called home to settle a rebellion. Finding it already settled, he nevertheless tortured many, to root out any high-level plots by boyars. He disbanded the military [53b, pp 18-22], organized a new standing army on western lines, and restored Sophia's Regency. [The rest of Czar Peter I's reign continued in p 93].

-Between 1600 and 1700 **Scottish Presbyterian missionaries** went to the **Ukraine**, **Romania**, **Hungary** and **Italy**. By the Dniester River they were beaten and strung up on willow branches, but congregations that they started survived, per a Ukranian-Canadian Presbyterian friend, a descendant of these early Presbyterians.

Poland A Republic With Elected Kings - 1569-1795 [Continued from pp 64, 66]
-1587-1632 **Sigismund** III, Swedish **Vasa Dynasty** was elected King of Poland. 1592 he also ruled Sweden.
-1596 he transferred the capital of Poland from Krakow to Warsaw [27, p 39] comparatively late in Polish history. This central position and location on the major river the Vistula, favored rapid development, so Warsaw soon became the major city of Poland [27, p 39-57]. [See Maps pp 38, 68 and 94 - Russia 1598-1801].
-1596 Union of Brest (Brzesc) now Byelorus (White Russia) created the **Uniate Church** (**Greek Catholic**) an effort to unite the Orthodox and Roman Catholic Churches [12, Macropedia Vol 25, p 946]. Thus six of ten Orthodox synods came under the Pope. Orthodox Bishops of **Lvov** and **Przemzsl** [map p 31] in the SE refused to join [12 Vol 2, p 503].
-1600 Poland invited German Protestant farmers to develop their lands, which were still largely wilderness [61]. A wave of German colonists came from the NW [6;62, pp 12-13]. Their towns had self-government based either on the Schultz system with **hereditary mayors**, or on Hollandry democracy with **elected mayors** [62, pp 14-20].
-About 1600-60 [pp 71, 92] 30,000 **Calvinist Scots** settled in **Posen** villages as shopkeepers and middlemen.
-1600 as **Sigismund** III **Vasa** was Roman Catholic, the Protestant Swedes dethroned him [28, p 14] but crowned Gustavus II Adolphus and made war between Poland and Sweden until 1629. The Poles lost part of **Livonia, Latvia** & south **Estonia** [maps 38, 68].
-1610 Polish nobles expanded into Russia and took **Moscow** [91] [maps 61, 68, 86, 94]. Polish nobles saw no need for either taxes or standing army, but when foreign armies became aggressive they assembled troops and won in several campaigns. They lost in 1622 to **Sultan Othman** II [p 65].
-1618-48 The Thirty Years War in Europe had **Hapsburgs** on one side and **France**, **Protestant Germans** and **Swedish kings** when Protestant, on the other [p 76]. Many Polish nobles studied in France [p 64] and had Humanist leanings. The French though largely Roman Catholic, did not like the Hapsburgs.
-1631-32 Gustavus II known as "First Soldier of Europe" from victories in the 30 Years War, died in battle.
-1632-48 King **Ladislaus** IV Protestant son of Sigismund III, elected king, built up the Polish Baltic Sea fleet. He granted five landlords the right for each to establish one Protestant city: Rawitsch, Obersitzko, Kahme, Schwerwnz and Bojanowo [62, pp 12-13]. Lissa (Lezno) was established earlier for many Moravian refugees.
-1644 hundreds of families of German cloth makers from **Silesia** began to migrate north into adjoining parts of Poland as far as **Posen**.
-1648-68 **John** II **Casimir Vasa** was elected king of Poland. He granted trademarks [62, p 13] making it illegal to sell other cloth under its name. Charters were granted to protect the Protestant religion, education and German language. 1652 noblemen in the **Sejm** (**parliament**) began to use the veto. Bills required a unanimous vote**.** One negative vote was enough for a bill to be dropped/reconsidered. This paralyzed government and led to anarchy. His reign consisted of bloody wars and disasters;
-1654 **Moscovy** used **Ukranian Cossacks** to push back eastern and southern Polish borders to occupy territories long held by Poland [91;95, p 318, 321; 12 Vol 3, p 663], but promises of Ukrainian independence were broken.
- Protestants and Orthodox were persecuted. People in western Poland got help from Prussia, but Lithuanian Orthodox & Protestants from Russia, causing disunity from ethnic/religious/humanist/national differences.
-1655-56 a Swedish invasion devastated Poland [27, p 12]. Cities were plundered and burned, and the economy destroyed. Out of a population of 10 million, 4 million died [28, pp 14-15]. Towns declined. Protestant parishes almost totally disappeared [12, Macropedia Vol 25, p 946]. Swedish armies burnt surrounding villages but saved **Lissa** (**Lezno**) where **Comenius** the Unitas Fratrum Bishop/Education Reformer, was in exile. Poles burned Lezno and again Comenius lost everything [see pp 65 and 76].
-1669-73 **Michael** (**Korybut**) **Wisnioiecki**, a Lithuanian, succeeded John II Casimir Vasa. His reign was one of internal fighting between **Poles** who had French leanings and the **Habsburgs**. 1671 **Turks** attack Poland.
-1674-96 **Jan** (**John**) III **Sobieski** was the elected king. He, as an Army General in 1670 had suppressed **Ukranian Cossacks** who rose against the Poles [95, p 328]. 1676 when Cossacks joined with the **Turks**, Poland lost two-thirds of the **Ukraine**. 1676-1696 **Sobieski** regained much of the Ukraine from the **Turks** [16], but Kiev remained in Russia. He tried but failed to regain control over Prussia [12, Macropedia Vol 25, p 946].
-1679 the black death killed 70,000 in Vienna.
-1683 **Sobieski** defeated Muslim **Turks** at **Vienna**, ending Turkish expansion into central/northern Europe. He won back much of **Hungary** [99, pp 226-7] but Muslims remaining firmly in control in SE Europe.
(1688 William of Orange, a Dutch-German Protestant, & English wife Mary became King & Queen of England.)
-1697-1717 **Augustus Frederick** II, Elector of **Saxony** a Roman Catholic was elected Polish King. He was also Frederick **Augustus** I of the Wettin house. 1700-2 Charles II of **Sweden** attacked Poland and took Warsaw and Krakow. Saxon Wettin Dynasty elected kings ruled Poland until partition in 1763 [more pp 92, 111].

Chapter Thirteen

Revival of the Classics: The Renaissance and Reformation - *A Review*

The Classics of Ancient Greece and Rome

-**Greek Classics** written by renowned scholars included works on philosophy, mathematics, medicine, logic, astronomy, politics, democracy, ethics, religion and myths. Among the most significant scholars are Homer (about 800 BC), Plato (427-450 BC), Socrates (about 469-399 BC), Aeschylus (525-456 BC), Aristophanes (450-387 BC), Euclid (about 350-290 BC), Sophocles (496-406 BC) [3], and Aristotle (384-322 BC) [110, pp 22-40].

-**Roman Classics** include writings by Livy, Tacitus, Virgil, Seneca, Cicero and others [16, p 152]. Rome admired, preserved, adapted and augmented Greek ideas of philosophy, law, science and architecture [12 Vol 4, p 504]. They enslaved Greek intellectuals.

-**Jewish scholars** in **Alexandria** had accumulated great libraries of scripture, traditions and theology.

-**Jews** and **early Christians** though greatly influenced by Hellenic (Greek) culture, were reluctant to study Greek philosophy because of their many gods and goddesses. It was difficult to separate out the good.

-Most Catholic clergy were barely literate and lacked access to the moral and spiritual teachings of scripture.

-The Early Church had some fine scholars such as **Jerome** (about 340-420) with Paula and another woman who translated the Old Testament from Greek and Hebrew into Latin [25, pp 266-7]; **Augustine** (354-430) whose theological writings were/still are highly valued by Roman Catholics, Lutherans and Calvinists [9 Vol 3, pp 58-9].

-Various powerful Germanic tribes pushed southwest from lands around the Baltic Sea (the present Denmark and Sweden). They kept pushing other tribes out and in turn, were pushed farther southwest themselves.

-Aggressive tribes sacked Rome. Roman culture became intellectually, morally and politically weak [pp 1-4].

-Later, Slavic tribes also moved in from the east.

The Middle Ages 476 to 1453 - 1000 Years [For details see pp 1-56]

(Medieval is the adjective meaning Middle Ages)

-476 the last Emperor of Rome was deposed. Anarchy, wars, floods, plagues and famine followed. In west, south and SE Europe and England, Roman colonies and culture crumbled. The early part of the medieval era is referred to as the **Dark Ages** because of political anarchy and little literacy. Roman families had difficulty surviving from many invasions of Goths and Asian tribes [see pp xiv, 4-6]. Migrating tribes staked out domains and slowly became civilized, as did central Europe later, aided by the acceptance of Christianity.

-590-604 **Pope Gregory** generally regarded as **the first pope**, was a **Benedictine** Monk. He restored civil order. With resources from his family inheritance and papal estates, he provided relief for great numbers of starving people in Europe.

-By 600 he had commissioned missionaries to set up 200 monasteries in Europe [maps: pp 6,10]. Monasteries became oases of refuge, stopovers for travelers and centres of healing.

-Each monastery had several books, usually classics. Monks made copies of them and began schools.

-In the **western Roman Empire** ability to read the Greek Classics declined, but in the **Eastern Roman Empire (Byzantine)** at **Constantinople** where the common language was Greek, scholars were familiar with the Classics [pp 1, 2-3]. Secular and church Byzantine leaders were in contact with people in the Balkans, Kiev (Russia), Georgia, Armenia, Syria and south **India**, with both Thomas and Syrian Christians [117, pp 16-28].

-"Events at the end of the Middle Ages beginning in the 12th century, set in motion a series of social, political and intellectual transformations that culminated in the Renaissance." [12 Vol 9, p1019]. Among these trends were weakening of the Roman Church, and rise of city-states, national monarchies and the Holy Roman Empire.

-1182-1226 **Francis of Assisi** rejected the accepted customs of the church, to work instead among the poor and to praise the beauty and spiritual qualities of nature [pp 25-26]. His example inspired Italian poets and artists to enjoy the world around them. This included:

-1266-1337 artist **Giotto** and 1265-1321 poet **Dante** author of *the Divine Comedy,* and others.

-**Arabs had an advanced civilization** with vast philosophical, literary, medical and scientific knowledge. They had translations of the Greek Classics and were familiar with them, and they had scholars who added to the accumulated knowledge [pp 16-18, 36].

-Most **Crusaders were illiterate**. They became curious about Arab, Greek and Hebrew knowledge and returned to Europe eager to encourage education and gracious living [See pp 25-26].

-**Universities** were founded in Italy, Paris, England and around Europe in the 12th-15th centuries [98, pp 157-166]. Early Renaissance (revival of learning) curriculums emphasized **theology** and the **Classics** of both Greece & Rome. The study of Greek was required so that **Aristotle** (384-322 BC) could be understood.

-Aristotle's book ***Politics*** became the basis of modern political philosophy [16, p 48].
-**Humanism** was an intellectual movement, including **Rationalism,** initiated by secular men of letters, first in Italy. It was a study of human nature that emphasized dignity of man without need of penance, and the unity and compatibility of truth from any source.
-Humanists began to develop an integrated new body of knowledge. Many scholars felt freed from old dogma. Confidence in human creative and intellectual ability was the impetus that began the Renaissance [12 Vol 9, p 1020].
-1225-74 **Thomas Aquinas** in Paris and Italy organized the knowledge of his time to reconcile faith with intellect, by synthesizing the teachings of: **Aristotle** and other Greek sages; **Augustine** and other early Christian theologians; **Averroes, Avicenna** (Ibn Sina) and other Islamic scholars; and **Maimonidies** (Solomon ben Yehuda ibn Gabirol) and other Jewish thinkers [9 Vol 2, pp 223-4].
-**John Wycliffe** (1320-84) a scholar at **Oxford** University, translated the Bible into English from ancient manuscripts [16, p 89; 825-6]. The **Lollards** preaching his views, using the English Bible, brought about profound changes in England. Bohemian students at Oxford and Richard II's wife Anne, sister of King Wenceslas IV, spread Wycliffe's teachings to **Czech-Moravian Bohemia**.
- Many Englishmen considered Wycliffe a heretic, but influential **John of Gaunt** supported him [16, pp 825-6].
-1347-51 **Bubonic plague** took the lives of 33 million people, a third of the population of Italy, France, England, German states and northwest Poland, but did not affect Bohemia, east Germany, northern Italy or part of Aquitaine, southern France.
-Large numbers of serfs escaped from their feudal bonds. Unemployment and overpopulation were eased [See pp 39-40]. Civil wars followed.
-Humanist scholars became interested in **Individualism** and **Naturalism** but it took the Renaissance a century more to resurface [12 Vol 9, p 1020] after millions of deaths.
-**Jon Hus** (1371-1415) rector of Charles University in Prague, **Bohemia** brought Protestant faith to most of the population, and wrote hymns and chorales in the Czech language. Thousands came to hear him preach in Bethlehem chapel that sat 3000.
-His **martyrdom** stimulated a storm of protest and Hussite wars, and 70 years of protestant government [See pp 52-53; 61-62].
-1457 the **Unitas Fratrum** (later called **Moravian Brethern** or **Brüder Gemine**) was founded by believers who refused to carry arms. Bishops were ordained at first by a Waldenses Bishop, in Apostolic succession. He and others composed beautiful chorales and hymns. They sang lustily from their hymn books and read the Bible translated into the common language. Persecuted Protestants carried the love of scripture, music and learning far and wide. [Continued p 83]
-1415-1775 waves of exiles continued to flee from Moravia-Bohemia, persecuted by the Habsburg Holy Roman Emperor. They scattered into Saxony, Silesia, Hanover, Prussia, Poland, Lithuania, Volga River and England [57], bringing renewal to Lutherans in mid-week fellowships (Brüder Gemine) [See pp 76-79, 98-103].

The Renaissance 1453 to 1527 [from pp 52-53; 57-59, 63-65 and 75-79]

- 1453 after the fall of Constantinople, Greek Orthodox scholars fled to Europe [12 Vol 9, pp 1019-21], settled at the universities and greatly stimulated the Renaissance (revival of learning).
-1438 movable type printing presses mass-produced translations of the Bible in common languages, sermons and catechisms on Christian doctrine for the masses [See p 53].
-A translation of the works of **Aristotle** from Greek into Latin by philosopher **Boethius** (450-524) was rediscovered, printed and became popular.
-1447-55 **Pope Nicholas** V born 1397, studied at University of Bologna, Italy, received an MA, and became a **humanist scholar**. He founded the **Vatican library** of 1500 books, of all known Greek and Roman works.
-1455-8 his successor Pope Calixus lll, lived a blameless life.
-They were preceded and followed by poorly educated, immoral popes [45, p 778-81] [see pp 50, 53].
-1452-1519 **Leonardo da Vinci** excelled as engineer, architect, human anatomist, artist (*Mona Lisa, Last Supper*), writer, musician, scientist and inventor. He was the ultimate ***Renaissance Man*** (a genius knowledge-able in every branch of learning) [12 Vol 9, p 1020-1]. [See p 63]
-1475-1564 **Michelangelo**, 1483-1500 **Raphael** and others were outstanding Renaissance artists [12 Vol 9, p 1020].
-1490's to 1527 High Renaissance art flourished for about 35 years [12 Vol 9, p 1020].
-1450-1626 **St. Peter's Church** in **Rome**, was built over a period of 176 years [16, p 652]. 1546-64 **Michelangelo** built the dome of St. Peter's and it was completed in 1590, according to his plans [pp 67 and 85].

-1466-1536 **Erasmus** a great Dutch scholar, decided to free men from false ideas about religion. He did this in two ways: by promoting scripture reading, and by writing witty satires about priests and monks, speaking of them as "unholy men in holy orders", he helped the reformation; but he did not join it [45, p 786;48, pp 12, 52].
-1478-1533 **Sir Thomas More**, a ***Renaissance Man,*** a scholar with wide influence, was elected to the House of Commons in England and became Treasurer of the Exchequer and also Speaker of the House, and was sent to Germany on public business. 1529 More became Lord Chancellor. He was a member of a circle of scholars. He was author of the influential book ***Utopia***, describing an ideal state.
-1532 he resigned, not accepting the divorce and remarriage of King Henry VIII, and refusing to recognize him as head of the church. In 1535 the king had him beheaded for treason.
-1527 Rome was sacked by Spanish and German mercenaries of Holy Roman Emperor **Charles** V [95, p 255], thus bringing an end to the Renaissance [12 Vol 9, p 1020-1]. 4000 inhabitants of Rome were killed, art treasures were looted and Pope Clement Vll was imprisoned. **The Western Roman Empire came to an end**.
- However Renaissance spirit continued in northern Italy, northern Europe and England [See pp 85-86].

The Reformation, Scholarship and Rise of European Nationalism

-1329-84 **John Wycliffe** and 1371-1415 **Jon Hus** were pioneers of the Reformation [See p 82].
-1483-1546 **Martin Luther**, horrified by the sale of indulgences (to pay for forgiveness of personal sin or sins of dead relatives) reacted by posting 95 theses (a list of doctrinal errors) on the Wittenburg church door. This money was being raised by authority of the pope for the building of St. Peter's Cathedral in Rome.
-For the story of Luther's trial, and the establishment of the Lutheran church throughout German and Scandinavian Europe see pp 58-59.
-He translated the Bible into High German, which gradually standardized many German language and dialects.
-He wrote hymns and catechisms. Ability to read was required for confirmation, so literacy of men and women became the norm.
-1509-64 French **John Calvin** promoted scholarly theology; developed Geneva city administration that eliminated crime and inspired hard work and diligence. Students from other countries spread his teachings.
-1515-72 his student **John Knox**, founded the Presbyterian church in **Scotland** and influenced **England**.
-1567-1611 King James VI of Scotland became **James** I **of England** 1604-11. Protestant but not a devout Christian, he commissioned careful translation from Hebrew and Aramaic, by 54 men from a broad spectrum of theological views. He authorized what became known as the **King James Version** (or Authorized Version).
-1535 in Spain the Society of Jesus (**Jesuits**) was founded as a scholarly, zealous, obedient order, to compel protestants back into the Roman Catholic Church [See pp 49 and 62-63].
-The **Inquisition** removed protestantism from Spain and parts of Italy. The Holy Roman Emperor persecuted protestants and sent **Jesuits** into France, Bohemia and Poland and other countries to persuade and force the protestant populace to return to Roman Catholicism.
-Unitas Fratrum (Moravian Brethern) Bishop **Comenius** (1592-1670) was the **outstanding educational reformer** for many countries [pp 76-77]. During the Thirty Years' War (1618-48) he continued to write and teach in Hungary and Poland. Next he reformed the curriculum in Romania, Sweden and Holland, and visited England and France. His books translated into many languages, had a profound lasting affect. They used two columns, in the local language and in Latin, and featured pictures to make reading a pleasure for girls & boys.
-The **Counter-Reformation** codified Roman Catholic beliefs (1545-63), reformed much laxity in the church, and began to create an educated priesthood. A **catechism** similar to Luther's was prepared. Friars touring with street dramas of Bible stories attracted many peasants back to the Roman Church [see pp 62-63].
- Universities expanded their curriculums adding Law, Astronomy, Medicine and Politics, etc.
-1572 in one night 70,000 French protestant **Huguenots** were massacred. To escape ethnic cleansing 500,000 fled to Protestant areas: England, the Netherlands, Prussia, south Africa and America. Huguenots were ship-builders and craftsmen. In many countries they pioneered factories, industries, plantations, and vineyards [127]. In Holland Huguenots cast bells and carillons with beautiful resonance. 50,000 settled in England where some manufactured silk [3;45, pp 789-790;16, p 337] [See pp 98-99].
-1598-1685 persecution of Huguenots moderated by the Edict of Nantes, but was intensified in 1685 [48, pp 62-63].
-1543 Polish astronomer Nicholas **Copernicus** demonstrated rotation of the earth and planets around the sun rather than around the earth, **Ptolemy**'s view [See pp 63-64].
-Copernicus influenced **Johannes Kepler**, **Galileo** and **Isaac Newton** and a few Jesuits. This new knowledge was considered heresy by the Roman Catholic Church.

-1561-1626 **Francis Bacon**, English philosopher/statesman influenced European scientific research [16, p 67].
-1571-1630 German astronomer **Kepler** discovered that planets move in ellipses, not circles.
-1564-1642 Italian **Galileo** is notable for developing observation using a **telescope** and for theories of mechanics, such as inertia.
-1582 Pope Gregory VII set the Gregorian Calendar 13 days ahead of the Julian Calendar [46 BC Julius Caesar].
-1676 Greenwich Observatory settled Standard Time [16, p 119, 304, 390], adopted in Europe.
-1564-1616 **William Shakespeare**, English poet-dramatist par excellence, had knowledge of Italian culture; dared to hint that royalty/leaders identified with villains, yet in a subtle way had likeable or amusing qualities. He added many words and metaphors to the English language.
-1596-1650 Frenchman **René Descartes** made notable contributions to optics, physiology, physics, logic and psychology. He tried to build a logical view of the world and of God that all **rational** men could accept, using mathematics to express scientific and religious ideas.
-1622-1673 Jean Baptiste **Molière**, French dramatist dedicated to the theatre and writing, excelled in comedy, from farce to subtle satire, reflecting the people and their customs [16, p 499].
-1628-88 **John Bunyan** on the side of Parliament and **Oliver Cromwell** in civil war against **Charles** I, was jailed 1660-72 for Puritan preaching [16, p 113, 150; 174]. He wrote influential books, notably ***Pilgrim's Progress***.
-1631-1700 **John Dryden**, English poet and dramatist, became a political satirist and poet Laureate. He translated **Virgil** [16, p 206].
-1658-95 **Henry Purcell** sang in Westminster Abbey as a boy and went on to compose sacred and secular music, still admired. 1689 he became organist of Westminster Abbey [16, p 604] [For musicians see pp 85-86, 91].
-1629-95 Dutch **Christian Hughens** ground and polished lenses used for telescopes and spectacles. He also applied the pendulum to the clock.
-1679 the Black Death killed 75,000 in **Vienna.** In 1681 83,000 died in **Prague**, spared in earlier plagues.
-1642-1727 English mathematician-astronomer Sir **Isaac Newton** studied gravity, spectrum & optics [16, p 527]. Newton's ***Mathematical Principles of Philosophy*** was published 1687 and quickly became popular in Europe. He built a small but powerful telescope with reflecting mirrors. He captured in a few mathematical equations the laws governing motions of the planets [12 Vol 4, p 504]. He developed the scientific method: exploring properties, establishing them by experiments, and formulating hypotheses that explained them.
-The idea of Isaac Newton that the universe is governed by a few simple natural laws, was debated by other thinkers who formulated ideas of **Skepticism, Atheism** and other new concepts about God [12 Vol 4, p 504]:

1. **Deists** believed a very few religious truths sufficed, and that God is detached. Their views spread in England, Germany and France (**Voltaire**, **Rousseau** and **Diderot**) [See *The Enlightenment* pp 87-93].
2. **Theists** believed in a God who is in touch with His creation [16, p 188-9].
3. **Rationalism** affecting Lutheran clergy, led to preoccupation with intellectual theological debate, neglect of their flock, and moral laxity. Some who were spiritually devout, began **a spiritual resusitation** [57] dubbed:
4. **Pietism** in 1648 after the **Thirty Years' War,** feeling ashamed of the secularism of Lutheran clergy, Pietists emphasized holy living and personal relationship with God [see Chap 12, p 78]. Their movement spread into several universities in German speaking Europe.

Summary

"The intellectual and political edifice of [Roman Catholic] Christianity, seemingly impregnable in the European Middle Ages, fell in turn to the assaults made on it by Humanism, the Renaissance and the Protestant Reformation. Humanism bred the experimental science of Francis Bacon, Nicolaus Copernicus and Galileo and the mathematical rigour of René Descartes, G.W. Leibniz, and Sir Isaac Newton. The Renaissance rediscovered much of classical culture and revived the notion of man as a creative being, while the Reformation, more directly but in the long run no less effectively, challenged the monolithic authority of the Roman Catholic Church. For Luther as for Bacon or Descartes, the way to truth lay in the application of human reason. Received authority, whether of Ptolemy in the sciences or of the church in matters of the spirit, was to be submitted to the probings of unfettered minds" [12 Vol 4, p 504].

Efforts to systematize natural laws by scholars like Leibnitz 1647-1711, led into *the Age of Enlightenment*, the intellectual movement of the 17th and 18th centuries [See *The Enlightenment*, pp 87-93].

Chapter Fourteen - 1500 to 1699

Baroque Architecture and Music

Baroque Architecture [continued from pp 47, 52-53 and 68]

Out of the Counter-Reformation of Roman Catholic revival, after the Thirty Years' War 1618-1648, baroque music, art and architecture, characterized by elaborate ornamentation, was pioneered in Italy. Groupings of images in dramatic action were arranged as tableaus and multidimensional murals. Lifelike emotional scenes from the Bible and of suffering martyrs, filled domed ceilings and arched alcoves, embellished with delicate railings. Furnishings also in homes and public squares had gilded moldings, elegant statues and fountains.

-1565 in **Bohemia** at Hutna Hora salt mine town, the Gothic Church of St. Barbara, begun in 1380 by **Peter Parler** 1330-1399, was updated in Baroque style with pinnacles, gargoyles and spectacular spires [55, 1330-pp 215-6] rivaling **St. Vitus** cathedral [See p 47]. 1694 a 27 bell carillon was built in Prague [10, pp 153-4].

-1626-1750 to attract Hussites in Bohemia back to the Roman Catholic fold, the Hapsburgs built more than 50 shines to the Virgin Mary modeled on the **Loreto**, Italy shrine.

-1694 the spectacular ***Sun of Prague*** shrine was set with 6,222 diamonds donated by pilgrims [42, p 177; 55, p 193].

-1675-1735 in Prague the elaborate Baroque **St. Nicholas Church** (Chram svateho Mikulase) was built with lavish sculptures, frescoes and gargoyles [55, p 177; 10, pp 141, 157, 152, 157].

-Baroque spread to Spain, France, Flanders, Holland, England, Bavaria and Dresden, Saxony [9 Vol 3, pp 282-298].

-1676-1706 in **Paris** one of the greatest baroque churches, **Les Invalides** was built. Many palaces of Louis XIV, including the rebuilding of **Versailles** (1669-1710) [9 Vol 3, pp 296-7], and the **Louvre** (1667-79) absorbed the talents of Baroque architects. Baroque style was individualized by the ethnic and artistic talents of architects.

-1665 in London, England one-third of the population died from plague. 1666 the great fire of London burned three days destroying 300 homes, leaving 100,000 homeless [11, 232], melting the bells of old St Paul's Cathedral..

- 1675-1710 **Sir Christopher Wren** rebuilt **St. Paul's Cathedral** [16, pp 652, 825] in baroque style and mathematical genius. The width is 100 feet and the dome reaches 365 feet. He built the first square belfry topped by a tall spire [9 Vol 2, pp 282-3; 9 Vol 3, pp 295-6]. He built or influenced the planning of many other English churches. His plans for the new city of London were often frustrated because of private ownership of land. A more open city was built, largely of stone instead of wood [11, 232]. 1702-14 dainty furniture was named for Queen Anne.

-1681 in Prague, spared earlier from Black Death, 83,000 died.

-In **Portuguese** and **Spanish America** Baroque style cathedrals were built [9 Vol 3, pp 282-298].

-In **Vienna**, Austria recovery was delayed 1618-48 by Thirty Years' War; 1678 the black death took 75,000 lives; Turk invaders were pushed back. 1716-37 the awesome masterpiece **Karlskirche** was built [9 Vol 3, pp 287-8]. Lutheran architecture and music being protestant was less elaborate.

-By 1770 the Baroque style embraced Switzerland, Austria, Roman Catholic German Dutchies, Poland and St. Petersburg (Russia) [29, Stierlin, p 47-54; 7, Zierer, p 68].

Music in the Church

-The **art of organ building** began in Alexandria about 240BC when Greek Ctesibius built the first hydraulis (water organ). Air was forced through a rank (row) of pipes by the weight of water[172]. Nero and the Arabs used hydraulis music. The 14th-15th centuries saw great advances in the use of mechanical devices. Various stops release pressurized air from a wind chest below a rank and control volume. One inch to 32 foot pipes produce high to low pitch. Different materials (wood or metal) alter tone. Different shapes alter timbre. National schools of organ building were established, notably French, Dutch, German and English[12 Vol 8, pp 993-4].

-1680 **Henry Purcell** 1659-1695 became organist in Westminster Abbey [3, pp 301, 311, 313]; court composer 1683.

-Great **Baroque musicians** included **Corelli** 1653-1713, **Vivaldi** 1675-1741 and **Scarlatti** 1685-1757.

-1685-1750 High Baroque organs reached greatest popularity through Johann Sebastian **Bach**, a devout musician who composed anthems every week for his choir, hundreds of cantatas for choir and organ or orchestra, and some for clavier and violin. Bach was not impressed by the excesses of the Baroque, but was familiar with and drew on French, German and Italian musical styles of the era, to created his own dignified melodic counterpoint. His music is still considered great because of both technical facility and expressiveness, especially vocally. "He could convey the complex texture of a multi-voiced fugue" [9 Vol 3, pp 179-181; 12 Vol 8, pp 993-4].

- 1665-1759 Georg Friedrich **Handel** was more elaborate in his style. Both he and Bach developed outstanding **choirs** including women singers. Earlier, counter tenors sang the high notes. Handel led a choir and wrote an opera in Hamburg. Then he gained experience in Italy for three years.

-1710 Handel became chapel master for George, Elector of Hanover, and 1712 settled in England two years before the crowning of **George** I as King of **England**. Handel produced popular operas and sacred oratorios.
-1742 the ***Messiah*** was first performed in Dublin, Ireland [16, p 317]. Handel hardly ate or slept while composing this inspired charismatic work.

Development of Efficient Clocks

-1600 German locksmith **Peter Henlein** made the first portable time pieces, but only with hour hands.
-1670 the first clocks with minute hands were made [12 Vol 3, p 392-3] with a glass or brass cover to keep out dust.
-1656 Dutch astronomer **Christian Huygens** (1629-95) applied the pendulum [12 Vol 3, p 392-3] to control time. Because temperature changes expand and contract the pendulum making clocks inaccurate, much research was carried out to produce amalgams that expanded less.
-1674-75 Huygens developed use of springs in watches [12 Vol 12 Macropedia, p 514].
-1670 in England **William Clement** introduced the tall Grandfather Clock, which soon became popular.

Maps: *Europe in* 1648 *and in* 1763 [9b, p 194]

Chapter Fifteen - 1690 to 1795

The Enlightenment Led to Both Reforms and Violent Revolutions

An intellectual movement called T***he Enlightenment*** which had its roots in both **Greek philosophy** and **Italian humanism**, introduced new views about religion, reason, nature and man. Quickly these beliefs became a new world view that became widely accepted and resulted in a scientific and theological revolution.
-Scholars now felt free to probe and question all received authority whether from Greek philosopher **Aristotle** (384-322 BC), **Egyptian geographer Ptolemy** (127-51 AD) or renowned early Christian theologian **Augustine** (353-430 AD), as well as Roman Catholic scholars, Protestant reformers or free church thinkers.
-It became popular to question all dogma and authoritarianism.
-Ideas that the universe was governed by a few natural, simple, discoverable laws stimulated rational efforts to identify and organize them clearly, just as in mathematics [12 Vol 4, p 504].
-Discoveries in the previous century already greatly altered beliefs about science and religion [pp 81-84].
-Professors began to think freely and agitate against ignorance and corruption. Rich, poor and middle class people joined the protest movement; millions of people of all classes began to think for themselves.
-Many people especially in England, France and Poland became energized with new discoveries and attitudes in science, philosophy, politics and culture [38, all chapters].
-This evolving world view stimulated radical developments in philosophy, politics and art.
-The study of anatomy and the human form was pursued for both art and the advance of medical knowledge.

Broad and Overlapping Concepts in *The Enlightenment* [as follows - **a** to **f**]:

a. In Psychology and Philosophy

-The *Enlightenment* produced **secular** theories of **Psychology** (science of mind, emotions and behavior [123]).
-**Thomas Hobbes** (1588-1679) saw humans as motivated mainly by survival and maximization of pleasure.
-**John Locke** (1632-1704) a physician and civil servant in England and Europe, emphasized progress in history. He described the mind as being at birth a **tabula rasa** (like a blank slate) on which experience creates the individual's character. He disagreed with original sin or innate qualities [12 Vol 4, p 504; 16, p 438]. but:
-**George Berkeley** (1685-1753) an Irish clergyman-philosopher founded the philosophy of **Idealism**. He held that "matter cannot exist independent of the mind" and sense can be explained by "a deity continually evoking perception in the human mind" [9 Vol 3, pp 447-8].
-Berkeley traveled widely in Europe and America; assisting in the development of Yale, Columbia and a number of other Universities, and wrote books that are still influential.
-**David Hume** (1711-1776) a Scottish lawyer, thinker and writer wrote regarding human nature, morals, politics and history, and was librarian of the *Advocates Library* in Edinburgh [16, p 349].
-**Immanuel Kant** (1724-1804) excelled in theology, mathematics and physics. He remained in East Prussia but wrote many books that were influential throughout Europe, such as: *Critique of Practical Reason; Critique of Judgement* and *Critique of Pure Reason* [12 Vol 6, p 726].
-**Jeremy Bentham** (1748-1832) worked to bring about reform of the legal system and wrote *Introduction to the Principles of Morals and Legislation*, which made him world famous. He worked out a formula to assess pleasure [9 Vol 3, p 438]. He claimed that actions were right if they tended to produce the greatest happiness and pleasure to the greatest number of people, which he called **Utilitarianism**.
-George William Frederick **Hegel** (1770-1831) was professor of philosophy in Jenna, Nuremberg, Heidelberg and 1818-31 in Berlin. He was a foremost exponent of **Idealism**.

b. In Science and Technology

[Continued from p 75]

-There were revolutionary scientific discoveries in the previous century [pp 82-84]. Many new discoveries continued to be made.
-**Astronomers** realized that the Milky Way is not a cloud of cosmic gas but rather a galaxy of stars to which our sun belongs.
-1686-1736 Gabriel Daniel **Fahrenheit** from Gdansk (Dansig), **Poland**, invented the mercury thermometer.
-1743-94 **fire** was understood by **Lavoisier** to result from the element of **oxygen** uniting with matter. Oxygen was found to be vital for respiration, and that **water** consists of oxygen and hydrogen.
- **Chemists** began systematically to weigh, measure and test substances.
- Scientists/scholars actively engaged in **research** especially **in Polish** and **Italian universities**.

-1645-1711 Gottfried Wilhelm **Leibnitz** born at the end of the 30 Years' War, a philosopher-mathematician in Hanover, invented differential and integral **calculus.** He said substance consists of **atoms**, individual, self-contained and in harmony with the Creator. He applied his knowledge in **engineering** and **geology**.
-Leibnitz corresponded with hundreds of leading European scholars [12 Vol 7, pp 250-1].
-He persuaded Frederick I, king of Prussia to found the **Academy of Sciences** in **Berlin** [16, p 424].
-1660-1741 **Daniel Ernest Jablonski,** born in Danzig, Poland, was educated in **Frankfurt** an der Oder and earned a DD in three years' study at **Oxford**, England. He was **Cofounder** and **Director of the Academy of Sciences in Berlin**. 1747 his correspondence with Leibnitz was published, six years after his death and with additions in 1799. He became a bishop of the Unitas Fratrum (Moravian Brethren) [See below **c.** Religion].
-1708 **two** privately owned **English East India Companies** dating from 1600, amalgamated; became active politically as **Agent** of British government in India [12 Vol 4, p 329]. Shareholders elected 24 directors annually.
-Not until 1858 was the East India company transferred to the British Crown.
-With steam power, machinery and factories, **Industrialization** grew first in Britain, later in France [53b, p 161-7].
-1733 the flying shuttle revolutionized speed of textiles manufacture.
-1740 the crucible method of manufacturing **Sheffield steel** began.
-1749 Thomas **Chippendale** mass-produced graceful furniture [95, pp 363, 366, 371].
-1754 high quality china clay was discovered in Cornwall; a **fine china industry** began in Plymouth [95, p 374].
-**Travel around Europe** became common for both the poor and the wealthy [64] (curiosity and pilgrimage).
-**World trade** and **European colonization of other continents**, begun before 1600 by Portugal [p 57-8], escalated with the Netherlands, England, Spain and France.
-1602-1798 the **Dutch East India Company** became foremost sailors and merchants of Europe, displacing the Portuguese in south-east Asia. [See Chap 12, pp 71-72]
-Explorers were curious about other cultures, spices, silks & gold in America, Africa and the far east [53b, pp 71-95].
-1759 **James Cook** mapped Quebec coast [pp 105, 109]; 1768-79 Pacific coastlines, **flora & fauna** [9.Vol 7, pp 182-3].
-1772-5 his second and 1776-9 third scientific exploration and mapping of the whole Pacific Ocean.
-1761-1834 **William Carey** Baptist Missionary; eminent botanist; philologist of many Indian languages [156]; Serampore Ecumenical clergy education; Bible translation from ancient manuscripts in many languages.

c. In Religion

-**Individual access** to God, without the need of priest or ritual, promoted a sense of independence, but
-**Skepticism toward Religion** increased. People began to believe that the only way they could arrive at truth was through rational science. Revelation and mysticism were out of fashion. Many new attitudes about faith arose. Protestant theology was developed.
-**Deists** believed a few religious truths sufficed: the view that God is detached spread in England, Germany and France (Voltaire, Rousseau and Diderot). **Theists** believed God is in touch with His creation [16, p 188-9].
-1762 **Jesuits** were condemned/suppressed in France. Previously they were the persecutors of dissenters.
-1645-1711 Gottfried Wilhelm **Leibnitz** born the end of the 30 Years' War, to a pious Lutheran family in Leipsig, became a philosopher-mathemetician. [See above **b.** Science]. He said substance consists of atoms, individual - self-contained - in harmony with the Creator. His **religious philosophies** were both rational and devoutly Christian. He corresponded with hundreds of leading European scholars [12 Vol 7, pp 250-1].
-1660-1741 **Daniel Ernest Jablonski** born in Danzig, Poland, educated in **Frankfurt** an der Oder and in **Oxford**, England; 1685-91 was head of **Moravian College Lissa (Leszno) Poland**; 1691 was appointed court preacher in **Königsburg**, East Prussia and 1693 in **Berlin**, West Prussia. [See pp 77-78, **b.** above & p 90]
-1699 he was consecrated Bishop of Unitas Fratrum (Brüder Gemine=Unity of Brethren=Moravian Church). He called frequent Synods in Poland, several in Warsaw; aided Moravian Brethren in Poland, Russia and Hungary. 1700 in Lissa 30,000 people attended a Union Synod (of Brethren and Reformed/Calvinist) [57, p 9].
-1722-60 **Pietist Count Zinzendorf** (1799-1760) provided refuge near Dresden for 300 Moravian Brethren who were escaping severe persecution by Roman Catholic Habsburgs and Jesuits in Bohemia. [See pp 52-53, 61-65, 76-78]. They grew in faith and self-support and joined with other Moravians earlier settled in **Berlin**, Poland, Russia and other parts of Europe and England [57].
-1732 Moravians began their world-wide missionary movement [See pp 98-104].
-1703-1791 **John Wesley** and brother **Charles Wesley** (1707-1788) graduated from Oxford; were ordained to the Anglican priesthood. 1735 admired Moravian fellow-passengers while sailing to Georgia, east America.

-John and Charles **Wesley** returned from Georgia to England frustrated and doubting their faith. They attended **Moravian** services, heard Luther's commentary on Romans read, and began to grasp faith by the grace of Christ. **Charles** wrote about this experience, "By degrees the Spirit of God chased away the darkness of my unbelief. I found myself convinced . . . I saw that by faith I stood." Three days later **John** felt "strangely warmed" and assured of forgiveness and justification by faith. "Gone were their preoccupations with trying to put themselves right with God through moral achievement and mysticism [124, pp 34-9 and 31-3]."
-The brothers as horseback circuit riders, preached to many groups, lacking approval by the Anglican Church.
-They established Methodism. Both brothers composed inspiring hymns. [See **f.** p 91]
-1716 **Gilbert Tennent** an Irish Presbyterian in **New Brunswick** built a log college to train ministers. Irish and Scotch graduates spread revival in **Pennsylvania** and built more log colleges to educate ministers, who went out to preach the urgency of conversion; the **Great Awakening** spread in the 13 colonies [77, p 956].
-1734-5 the **Great Awakening** flourished. It was led by Presbyterians in Virginia, Baptists in North Carolina and **Johnathan Edwards** among Congregationalists in New England, [77, p 956;16, p 300].
-1714-1770 **George Whitefield** was ordained an Anglican priest. In 1738 while preaching in a crowded church he began to care deeply for more than a thousand people standing outside, and began to plan outdoor preaching, illegal except at a public hanging. Soon there was an execution in Bristol. Whitefield walked unafraid among the depraved, violent, unwashed men, preaching "Blessed are the poor in spirit, for theirs is the kingdom of heaven" and "Jesus was a friend of publicans and sinners". Tears washing white gutters in the coal dust down their cheeks. Anglican pulpits closed to Whitefield. Next Sunday he preached with his big voice to 10,000 coal miners. Lives changed. Though poor they collected money to build a school for their children. Starting in 1750 Whitefield sailed seven times to America. He preaching in Georgia, New York, Boston, Philadelphia and Harvard University, adding to the **Great Awakening** (revival) [124, pp 40-2]. Many times **Benjamin Franklin** heard him preach and said he had a voice like an organ [16, p 815]. Whitefield built an orphanage in Savannah, Georgia. Because pacifist **Moravians** refused to fight the Spanish in Georgia, Whitefield invited them to Pennsylvania.

d. In Education and General Knowledge

-Reform of Elementary Education by Jan Amos **Comenius**, Moravian Brethren Bishop, after Thirty Years' War (1618-48) deeply influenced Hungary, Romania, Poland, Sweden, England and Holland [See pp 76-78].
-1751-84 **Denis Diderot** (1713-84) published in installments the 17 volume French **encyclopedia**. He included concepts from 500 year old books by **Roger Bacon** (1214-94) [9 Vol 3, pp 184-5]. Educated in Oxford and Paris, Bacon believed that men should use their new scientific knowledge to achieve power over nature to have happier, healthier, longer lives, and also set up a utopian academy of scientists. Long suppressed, these ideas at last took root [38, all chapters].
-Philosophers broadened their education in mathematics, science, theology, astronomy, etc.
-1747-55 **Samuel Johnson** (1709-84) labored patiently writing ***Dictionary of the English Language*** [97, p 375].
-Jean Jacques **Rousseau** (1712-78) wrote modern theories of education and child rearing, stressing experience rather than books. French Revolution leaders based their ideas and policies on his theories [16, p 643].
-Polish elite studying in Paris since the 16th century; were on the side of the French against the Habsburgs and planned **ideal government**. **Democracy** was practiced in the Polish **Sejm (parliament)**; a new **constitution** was drawn up.
-From 1569 to 1795 (236 years) the Polish republic elected kings as administrators [pp 66 and 80].
-1769-1821 **Napoleon Bonaparte** educated from 9 years of age in France, was influenced by philosophers of the *Enlightenment*, especially Voltaire and Rousseau, and became committed to change in France and Europe.
-1789 the **French Revolution** guillotined many [53b, pp 135-160], observed by 20 year old Napoleon Bonaparte.
-1792 the French **Republic** was declared. Idealized government turned into a reign of terror.
-In the aftermath, seeing much amiss, Napoleon's commitment to change intensified [53b, p 135-159] [pp 131-135].

e. In Politics and Government

-Rather than aiming to build a Christian kingdom of God, philosophers now looked at life as a social contract aiming to protect both natural rights and self-interest. This was in sharp contrast to actual trends in society, so **the *Enlightenment*** became **critical and reforming**, and **eventually revolutionary**.
-To counteract this tendency toward revolution the thinkers of *the Enlightenment* discussed concepts of a higher form of social organization, functioning as a **political democracy** based on natural rights.

-Politically there was a ferment of new ideas, such as:

* freedom of speech and the press
* personal liberty
* democracy
* taxes on the nobility
* humanitarianism

-1688 Roman Catholic **James** II **of England** was replaced by Protestant **William** III **and Mary** II making England the ***Home of the Enlightenment***. Mary was James II's daughter. **Jacobites** plotted to reinstate James.
-1643-1715 **Louis XIV of France** reigned 72 years; built **Versailles** palace a glittering court [See p 85]. Manners, fashions, furnishings, theatre, literature and the arts became elegant and extravagant. Conversation of men and women became intellectual and brilliant. He was the most influential figure in Europe [16, p 444].
-Louis X1V's queen was a **Habsburg** from Austria. He fought to force Habsburg rule on the Dutch, but lost to William of Orange. He invaded the Palatinate, sacking Heidelburg twice 1688 and 1693. He paid 500,000 crowns to Charles I of England to adjourn parliament for 15 months; fought to have James III, Old Pretender, a Roman Catholic, succeed Queen Anne of England[3]: Queen Anne's War (War of Spanish Succession)[p 95].
-1685 Louis XlV revoked the Edict of Nantes; persecution intensified; 500,000 Huguenots fled to Protestant countries. Exodus of these skilled craftsmen, merchants & seamen severely damaged French economy [95, p 337].
-Montesquieu (1689-1755) satirized the decadence and insincerity of French society and admired the English constitution. He had great influence on the early part of the Revolution [16, p 503].
-Leibnitz (1645-1711) German philosopher-mathematician applied his knowledge into **engineering** and **geology**. [See under both **b**. Science and **c**. Religion above]. He corresponded with hundreds of scholars and was appointed **political adviser** in many princely states. He persuaded Frederick I, king of Prussia to found the **Academy of Sciences, Berlin** [16]; met with **Peter the Great of Russia** in 1711 and 1716.
-Daniel Ernest Jablonski (1660-1741) born in Danzig, Poland, educated in **Frankfurt** an der Oder and **Oxford**, England, was head of Unitas Fratrum **Moravian College** in **Lissa** (**Leszno**) **Poland** 1685-91.
-1691 Jablonski was appointed court preacher in Konigsburg East Prussia and 1693 in **Berlin**, West Prussia. He was Cofounder and Director of the Academy of Sciences in Berlin. In
-1699 Jablonski was consecrated Bishop of the Unity of Brethern. He called Synods in Poland frequently; several in Warsaw; and aided Moravian Brethern in Poland, Russia and Hungary. 1700 in Lissa 30,000 people attended a Union Synod (Unity of Brethern and Reformed) athough Jesuits and Hapbsburg opposed [57, p 9].
-Voltaire (1694-1778) a French **playwright** and **philosopher**, educated by Jesuits 1704-10, imprisoned in the Bastille 1718, banished to England 1726-9, introduced the ideas of **Isaac Newton** to France [3]. In **Berlin** he was a close friend/counselor of Frederick II of Prussia. He later settled by Lake Geneva.
-Voltaire was not democratic but **believed in enlightened despotism**. He promoted many kinds of social reform, **spreading ideas of liberty and equality** [16, p 800].
-He wrote of the Holy Roman Empire "It is neither holy, nor Roman, nor an empire." About a disagreement he said "I do not agree with a word you say, but I will defend to death your right to say it." [110, pp105-6].
-1618 Brandenburg acquired Ducal Prussia (NE Poland) the old domain of the Teutonic Knights. Berlin was the capital. 1695 **Berlin University** was founded [See pp 53-55; 75-76, 110 & 113].
-1701 **Prussia was founded**. Frederick III of Brandenburg was named **Frederick** I, **King of Prussia**, by the Holy Roman Emperor.
-1715-1774 **Louis** XV, grandson of Louis XIV of France was weak and sensual. He reigned 60 years [16].
-1750 there was famine in France [95, p 372].
-Jean-Jacques **Rousseau** (1712-1778) wrote modern theories of education/upbringing of children, stressing experience rather than books. French Revolution leaders based ideas and policies on his theories [16, p 643].
-1702-1714 English **Queen Anne** daughter of James II was last of the Stuart Dynasty; her only child had died.
-1714 **George**, Elector of Hanover, great-grandson of James I, was crowned **King George** I of Great Britain.
-Benjamin Franklin (1706-90) born in Boston apprenticed as a printer, 1723 moved to Philadelphia, was a printer in London, England; returned home; bought the Philadelphia Gazette;
-1735 Franklin was postmaster; 1751-64 Pennsylvania State Assembly member;
-1757-62 and 64-75 Agent in London. He researched electricity, invented bifocal spectacles, lightning rods, and the Franklin stove, to save heat [16, p 264];
-Thomas Jefferson (1743-1826) wrote the first draft of the **Declaration of Independence**, with help of **Benjamin Franklin.** 1776 the **Declaration of Independence** was proclaimed.

-1776-83 **Benjamin Franklin** was envoy in Paris; solicited funds in France for the **War of Independence**.
-Powerful ideas of French philosopher/politicians found expression in **reform** in England and Poland but in France and America **revolution** [12 Vol 4, p 504]. Benjamin Franklin & Thomas Jefferson served again in Paris.
-1777-83 the **American Revolutionary War (War of Independence)** was fought [more on pp 113-4, 118].
-**Thomas Jefferson** with many roles, believed in free speech and education, and the ability of the common man to prosper under representative government, but not believe in highly centralized government.
-1785-8 Franklin president of the Pennsylvania Executive Council, helped write the Constitution.
-1785-9 **Jefferson** negotiated commercial treaties in **France**.
-Next Jefferson became Secretary of State, but because of controversies in Congress he retired 1793.
-1800 Thomas Jefferson was called back from France to become **President** [pp 110, 113-4, 117].

f. In the Arts and Architecture

-The study of **anatomy** and the human form was pursued for both art and to increase medical knowledge.
-**Arts, Music, Poetry** and **Artisan skills** reached new pinnacles of excellence [See p 135; pp 143-4].
>1685-1750 **Johann Sebastian Bach** born in Saxony to a Lutheran family, descended from seven generations of musicians; was violinist, organist and composer with positions in many places. He produced, in great variety, thousands of compositions of **sacred** cantatas, oratorios and hymns and **secular** music. He developed complex counterpoint in Italian style; created polyphony, the octave and major/minor scales. His solo music sounded like more than one instrument. His clavier playing influenced development of the piano. "Modern music owes a vast debt to Bach" [16, p 66 and 512; 9 Vol 3, pp 179-181]. [Compare pp 85-86]
-**Sophia of Hanover**, granddaughter of James I, was heir to the throne of England. Her court was a cultural centre where **George Frideric Handel** was chapel master.
-1712 Handel settled in England; composed many operas and Oratorios died 1759. Sophia died so her son:
-1714-27 **George** I became the first of five Kings of both Hanover and England.
-1714-1787 Christoph Willibald **Glück** born in Bavaria, produced successful operas in Italy and Vienna, but "he failed to compete successfully with Handel in London." [16] His operas related words to music in a new way.
-1703-1791 **John Wesley** and his brother 1707-1788 **Charles Wesley**, both graduates of Oxford University were ordained to the Anglican priesthood. They were rejected by the Anglican Church when they establish the Methodist movement. Traveling on horseback they often preached outdoors [See above **c.** p 89] Both became prolific **hymn-writers**, especially Charles. Their hymns are still honored in churches today.
-Charles' nine years at Oxford, studying Classics, especially Greek and Latin poets, lent dignity and elegance, without hint of doggerel, to the poetry and hymns he wrote. Examples are "Love divine, all loves excelling" and "Jesus lover of my soul." Many thousands of poor illiterate people were transformed by words and music.
-1725-1807 **John Newton** in the Royal Navy was a wicked trouble-maker. He was flogged and put on a crowded slave-trading ship, where sailors raped the slave women. Newton became the ruthless captain of such a ship. Eventually he repented and was overawed at "God's power to redeem a depraved blasphemer like myself." He preached and wrote hymns including: "Amazing Grace" and "How Sweet the Name of Jesus Sounds [124, 43-4]."
-1732-1809 **Franz Joseph Haydn,** Austrian performer/composer, produced many string quartets, 104 symphonies and some oratorios[16, p 324]. [Dec 2000 the author's daughter sang in the première of a rediscovered Haydn Mass].
-1756-1791 **Wolfgang Amadeus Mozart** a highly gifted and prolific performer and composer "combined the richness and melody of the Italian school with a knowledge of harmony and instrumentation gained by his training in the German school [16, p 509]." His youthful delights, charm and musical genius impress listeners today.
-1770-1827 **Ludwig von Beethoven** as a child in Prussia, showed extraordinary genius at the piano. He studied under Mozart in Vienna where he remained, troubled much by deafness, but he composed nine symphonies, several concertos, two masses, an oratorio, an opera and much chamber music [16, p 83].
-**Neoclassical Architecture:** In the 17th and 18th centuries people began to turn away from the elaborate life-like tableaus/murals/delicate gilded excesses of the Baroque; returned to Roman ideas for sobre dignity.
-**Rococo Architecture:** became more elaborate than Baroque in the reigns of Louis XIV and XV [p 143].
-**Romantic Architecture:** "Romanticism was a reaction against reason, artificiality and display, and was marked by a love of the unusual and the highly emotional [32, Gibson pp 46 - 53]." [See p 143].
-**Neogothic Architecture:** The Gothic style of architecture was revived, adding hidden steel braces, and reaching new excellence in the building of churches, law courts and houses of parliament. [See p 144]

Grand Tours by Young Englishmen

-Thousands of English youth from noble families, aged 15 to 21, toured the continent by stage coach with a tutor, spending two or three years learning languages, culture, art and science of Brussels, Paris, Versailles, Marseilles, Switzerland, Pisa, Florence, Venice, Rome & Naples. They learned Greek and Roman classics.
-A four-volume guide book by **Nugent** helped them avoid being deceived by art dealers or brothels.
-They traveled back via Germany in December to see candle-lit Christmas trees for the first time [139, pp 242-3].

Polish *Enlightenment* and Scottish Settlers

[Continued from pp 64-65 and 76-80]

-1618-1648 during the Thirty Years' War, neither the Roman Catholic French, nor the Protestant Polish sided with the Hapsburg Holy Roman Empire, which ruled Austria, Bohemia, Hungary and Spain. Neither did the Poles like Orthodox Christians, Ruthenian Boyars (nobles), Cossacks and Russians. They favored Parisians.
-1650 there were 30,000 Scots merchants, craftsmen, soldiers and refugees settled in Poland attracted by religious tolerance [pp 64-65]. 1560 Scotland became a protestant country; some Scot missionaries in Poland: "by the Dniester River beaten and strung up on willow branches" per a Ukrainian-Canadian Presbyterian descendant. 1640-58 in British civil war, republic of Oliver Cromwell [p 71] Catholics fled. Some Stuart Dynasty Catholic kings and queens ruled; some exiled Pretenders (Jacobites) [pp 90, 95].
-1569-1795 the **Polish Republic elected kings** as administrators for over 200 years [p 80]; several of the Swedish Vasa dynasty, some Roman Catholic and others protestants. 1600-29 & 1655-60 opposing Swedish Vasa kings invaded Poland destroying over half of the population. Eight to 12% of Polish population were nobility; learned in Paris philosophy, architecture and ideal government of T*he Enlightenment*. Democracy was practiced in **Sejm (parliament)**; a new **constitution** was drawn up. The culture of Paris affected music and literature. Construction of theatres and palaces in Poland flourished [27]; [28].
- Though protestant and humanist for a century, slowly Poles found their identity as devout Roman Catholics.
-1704-9 Stanislas I was made king of Poland by Swedish Charles II. 1713-4 Charles II: imprisoned by Turks.
-The **Wettin Dynasty** of **Saxony** ruled **Poland** until Partition in 1763. [Continued pp 92, 111, 113]
-1686-1736 Gabriel Daniel **Fahrenheit** invented the mercury thermometer to measure temperature. He was born in Gdansk, Poland. Polish scientists and scholars engaged in research in Polish and Italian universities.
-1745-6 half-Polish Jacobite Bonny Prince Charlie **Stuart**, grandson of **Sobieski**, invaded Britain: George II.

The Growing Power of Prussia

-1525 the Teutonic Knights secularized and disbanded to form a duchy. Grand Master **Albert Hohenzollern** become the Duke of East Prussia. Lacking a male heir, the eldest daughter in 1618 married the Elector of **Brandenburg** (West Prussia), so east and west merged to found powerful Prussia [see pp 53-4, 64, 75-78]. Ironically the name Prussia came from ancient Slavic Prus whom the Knights had crushed and destroyed.
-1640-88 **Frederick William** the "Great Elector" of Brandenburg in 1660 ended Polish rule. [See maps p 86]
-1684 he offered refuge to **French Huguenots**. In 1574 and again in 1695 Berlin University was founded [3].
-1688-1713 his son **Elector Frederick** III in 1701 crowned himself **Frederick** I **of Prussia** [9 Vol 4, p 303] at the city of Königsburg. Holy Roman Emperor **Leopold** I established the Kingdom of Prussia in exchange for a promise of military aid [95, p 345]. 1713-40 his son **Frederick William** I built up his army by conscripting tall peasants and nobles for two years and enforcing strict discipline. His **queen Sophia Dorothea** was from the **house of Hanover**, a sister of **George** II, **King of England**. Her court enjoyed *Enlightenment* culture.
-1732 **Frederick William** I settled 12,000 Protestants from Salzburg, Austria in East Prussia [3].
-1740-86 his son **Frederick** II, **the Great** born 1712, succeeded. In 1742 Prussia annexed **Silesia**, the SW Polish province, founded in 966 by the Piast Dynasty, who had encouraged Germans to immigrate to increase productivity of farms, coal mines and textiles. 1526 Silesia was taken by Catholic Austrian Hapsburgs;
-1424-35 **Silesia** had helped **Sigismund**, Holy Roman Emperor crush the Protestant Hussites, but during the Reformation almost all Silesia had become Protestant. Now Silesians welcomed their take-over since Prussia was Protestant and had good economic development practices and efficient administration [12 Vol 10, p 803].
-Frederick II induced **Moravians** from Herrnhut, Saxony, to settle in Silesia [See p 102].
-**Voltaire** lived as Frederick II's guest in Berlin for a time and called him "the great philosopher king".
-Thrifty, hardworking honest bureaucracy developed; arts & sciences were promoted; judicial & educational systems improved. Lutheran state religion allowed freedom of conscience for other protestants and a large Roman Catholic minority. Leather, paper, pottery and textile industries and breweries thrived.
-**Berlin**'s population 12,000 after the 1361 Bubonic Plague; was 150,000 by 1786 [9 Vol 4, p 9]; 800,000 by 1870.

Russian *Enlightenment* [Continued from pp 56; 65-66 and 79]

-1689-1725 **Tzar Peter** 1 was 6 feet 6 inches tall. As a boy he played with comrades in the German suburb. He became keenly interested in German technical skill, orderliness, culture [92, pp 6-7] and their Evangelical Lutheran church. However he surrounded himself with boisterous young men called the *Jolly Company*, later called the *Synod of Fools and Jesters*. To try to settle him, his mother arranged a marriage with **Eudoxia Lopukhina**, daughter of a Moscow nobleman.

-Young (Czar)Tzar Peter tried to capture Azov, southern Russia, to gain a naval base, but failed, as he lacked a navy. He therefore mobilized an army of carpenters and worked with them all winter to build a squadron of galleys and hundreds of barges. In the spring they defeated the **Turks**. He sent 3000 high born people to **colonize Azov** and ordered each monastery, boyar (nobleman) and merchant to build a ship [53b, pp 18-22], assisted by 20,000 Ukrainian craftsmen.

-1696 Peter I sent 50 **young Russians to England**, **Holland** and **Venice** to study shipbuilding, seamanship, navigation and fortifications, each at his family's expense. They were not to return until they had a certificate of proficiency from their foreign employers. In disguise, the Tzar himself joined them as an apprentice of ship-wright skills. He studied printing methods and participated in surgical operations and dentistry, etc.

-Czar Peter was fascinated with microscopes, barometers, wind gauges and all kinds of practical equipment.

-In **Holland** Czar Peter I lived with a blacksmith and worked as a carpenter in shipyards until he qualified as a shipwright. In **England** he worked in the dockyards and roamed the streets at will. He spent 1 1/2 years of study in **Prussia, Holland, England** and **Vienna** to learn European ways [53b, p 15-29]. He recruited, mainly from Holland, 600 expert naval officers, shipwrights, hydraulic engineers, mathematicians and barbers.

-Czar Peter was called home to settle a rebellion. Finding it already settled, he nevertheless tortured many to root out any high-level plot by boyars. He disbanded the military [53b, pp 18-22] and organized a new standing army on western lines [136, pp 151-161]. He promoted modern methods and life styles.

-He restored his older sister **Sophia's Regency**. He ordered men to be clean-shaven.

-The German Evangelical Church in **Moscow** was later renamed St. Peter and Paul to honor Peter I who was the sponsor [92, pp 6-7]. Funds also came from two German firms, Knoop and Wogau. A Gymnasium (high school) and girls' secondary school with 1200 students, belonged to the church. The German population was 20,000.

-1700 **Peter** I declared war on Sweden to gain access to the Baltic Sea, but failed, so vigorously built up the navy and military; 1703 he conquered part of the Baltic; began to build the **new capital, St. Petersburg**. The laborers suffered from meager provisions & primitive construction methods, on swampy land [139, p 244-251].
He loathed the Asiatic look of the wooden buildings of Moscow, so built with stone in Baroque style.

-1719 the German houses and Evangelical Church of wood, were enlarged [92, pp 6-7].

-1716-7 his **second visit to Europe** included **Paris**. Next he set up colonies and built a **navy** in the Black Sea.

-1721 Peter I was declared **Peter the Great**, **Emperor of Russia** after he conquered most **Baltic** countries. Before he died in 1725 he crowned his successor:

-1725-27 **Empress Catharine** I his capable **Lithuanian** second wife [see p 112].

-1727 **Peter** II, her eleven year old son, died of smallpox [53b, p 28-9].

-1728 two more German Evangelical Churches and a Reformed Church were built in St. Petersburg for a German population larger than in Moscow. Each had schools attended by German and Russian children.

-1730-40 **Empress Anna**, **Peter I's niece** was dominated by **Ernst Biron,** her German lover and secretary. She had an elaborate ice palace built as a practical joke; court life was crude with an elegant veneer.

-1741-61 **Empress Elizabeth, Peter I's daughter**, seized power, assisted by the Imperial Guard.

-1743 Empress Elizabeth gained a military and diplomatic victory against Sweden.

-1755 she **established Moscow University**. [Continued pp 111-112]

The Age of Enlightenment Abruptly Expired

"The Enlightenment expired as the victim of its own excesses [12 Vol 4, p 504]." [above pp 87-90]. Some reasons:

* The deists could not bring solace or salvation.

* Abstract reason provoked a contrary reaction, an exploring of sensation and emotion which came to be called **Romanticism** [See p 143].

* After the French Revolution people began to doubt that man was capable of self-government.

-However "An enduring legacy of *the Enlightenment* was the belief that human history is a record of general progress." [12 Vol 4, p 504]. (This concept has endured but is being questioned at present).

RUSSIA
1598-1801
Copyright by C. S. HAMMOND & CO., N. Y.
SCALE OF MILES
Russia in 1598
Acquisitions 1598-1689
Acquisitions under Peter the Great, 1689-1725
Acquisitions 1725-1762
Acquisitions under Catherine the Great, 1762-1796, to the accesssion of Alexander I, 1801
ARCTIC OCEAN
KINGDOM OF SWEDEN
RUSSIA
PRUSSIA
POLAND
AUSTRIA
HUNGARY
OTTOMAN EMPIRE
PERSIA
BLACK SEA
CASPIAN SEA
Kirghiz Steppe
KAZAKHS
TURKMEN
KALMUCKS
CIRCASSIANS
LITHUANIA
LIVONIA
ESTONIA
BESSARABIA
GEORGIA
Stockholm
St. Petersburg
Novgorod
Riga
Vilna
Warsaw
Smolensk
Chernigov
Kiev
Poltava
Moscow
Vologda
Archangel
Kola
Nizhni Novgorod
Kazan
Perm
Ufa
Samara
Voronezh
Saratov
Uralsk
Astrakhan
Azov
Sevastopol
Constantinople
Tiflis
THE RUSSIAN ADVANCE INTO SIBERIA
1598-1801
Copyright by C. S. HAMMOND & CO., N. Y.
MILES
Russia in 1598
Acquisitions 1598-1689
Acquisitions 1689-1725
Acquisitions 1725-1762
Acquisitions 1762-1801
NORWAY
SWEDEN
SIBERIA
Sea of Okhotsk
Bering Sea
KAZAKHS
MONGOLIA
MANCHURIA
JAPAN

Chapter Sixteen – 1690 to 1755

Explorers and Freedom Seekers in Europe and America

The War of Spanish Succession and Queen Anne's War 1701-1714

-1620 the French **Company of New France** [p 70] received a charter to go west via the Great Lakes and fan out beyond. Other companies based in Montreal followed. 1665 **Bubonic Plague** killed 68,596 in London.

-1670 the English **Hudson Bay Company** claimed the whole watershed of Hudson Bay. English-French rivalry for interior N America persisted more than a century.

-1700 Charles II Habsburg king of **Spain**, died without an heir. The 4 claimants were: his son, a grandson Philip of Anjou, his cousin Louis XlV of France, and a prince of Bavaria. The War of Spanish Succession broke out for balance of power: England, Austria, Netherlands and Prussia against France and Spain.

>1688 **William of Orange** and wife **Mary** II daughter of James II, both ruled Britain; she died 1694; he 1702.

-1702 **Anne** (1665-1714) became **Queen of Great Britain and Ireland, the last Stuart** monarch. She was the sister of Mary II, a Protestant, though their father James II converted to Roman Catholicism.

-1702 Queen Anne appointed **John Churchill (Duke of Marlborough)** the Commander-in-Chief. He had served under James II and William and Mary. King William had disgraced and demoted him. Marlborough and his wife **Sarah,** Queen Anne's friend, favored the **Whigs political party,** as Anne did for a time.

-1704 he captured **Gibraltar** and foiled French invasions of Austria and of Holland in 1706, 08 and 09 [16, p 469].

-1707 England and Scotland became the **Kingdom of Great Britain**, with Anne Queen of both.

-1708 the **two English East India Companies** amalgamated and became politically active as **Agent** of the British government in India [12 Vol 4, p 329]. Shareholders elected the 24 directors annually.

-1711 due to popular dissatisfaction with the Whigs, Queen Anne cooled toward the Marlboroughs, dismissed him and others from office [9 Vol 2, pp 162-3] and became a **Tory** (Conservative).

-1712-13 the **War of Spanish Succession** was ended by the **Treaty of Utrecht** [16, 787], as follows:

1. The Spanish throne went to **Philip of Anjou**, grandson of French king Louis XlV. He agreed not to unite France and Spain under one crown.
2. The unsuccessful claimant, Emperor Charles VI, was compensated with the Netherlands and part of Italy.
3. Louis XlV was forced to recognize Protestant succession in England and to stop giving aid to Roman Catholic **Stuart pretenders** to the throne of England [16, p 141, 376]; including Jacobite **Bonny Prince Charlie**.
4. England received **Gibraltar**, **Port Royal**, **Acadia**, **Gaspé**, **Maine**, **Newfoundland**, **Hudson Bay** and commercial privileges in Spanish America[12 Vol 2, p 789] with **Grand Banks** fishing schooners built in Massachusetts.
5. France kept **Ile Royal (Cape Breton)**[119 Vol 1, p 5-7] and **Ile St Jean** (later called **Prince Edward Island**). French settlers in **Placentia**, Newfoundland, were deported [119 Vol 5, pp 232] to **Ile Royal** (**Louisberg**) [pp 96; 109].

-1714 the war in Europe had ended but French/English hostilities continued. **France** extended fur trade and settlements into **Ohio** and **Mississippi** [12 Vol 2, p 786; 168, pp 86] [Continued pp 105-6].

Great Britain during the Reigns of Kings George I and II of Hanover [from p 73]

-1702-14 **Queen Anne** daughter of James II, sister of Mary II, was last of the **Stuart** Dynasty.

-**Sophia of Hanover, granddaughter of James** I was heir to the throne of England. If Queen Anne had no issue, the throne was to go to her descendants, passing over any Roman Catholics [12 Vol 5, pp 685-6].

- Sophia's court was a cultural centre, where **George Frideric Handel** was chapel master.
- 1712 Handel settled in England and composed many operas and Oratorios (died 1759).
- Sophia predeceased Queen Anne, so:

-1714-27 **George** I, **Elector of Hanover**, **Sophia's son** was the first of five monarchs of both **England** and **Hanover.** He reinstated the Duke of Marlborough, who had done much to secure his accession, and died 1722. George I spent little time in England; ministers ruled [16, pp 282, 469], and in this way began the modern pattern of government by ministers with the king as a figure-head. Hanover had access to the sea at **Bremen**.

-1727-60 **George** II born 1683, settled in England in 1714; did not interfere with politics. Whig party **Sir Robert Walpole** was Prime Minister until 1742 [16, p 282]. Slave trade from Africa increased.

-1745 forces of George II defeated the **Jacobites** who tried to take the British throne for Roman Catholic **Stuart heir Bonny Prince Charlie** who led an unsuccessful rebellion in Scotland [16, p 141].

-George II participated effectively in the **Seven Years' War** [167, p 100-105] [See p 105].

-1760-1820 grandson **George** III succeeded, as the son/heir of George II [pp 110-111; 117-118].

Early Settlement in Atlantic Canada and French/English Strife [from pp 69-73]

The English claimed the area by right of being discovered and explored by **John Cabot** 1497-8 [9 Vol 1, pp 96-7].
-1604 the first successful colony was of French people at **Port Royal** (later named **Annapolis Royal**). They named the area **Acadia** which means "garden of the gods" in Greek mythology. Ship building began [120, p 2153].
-1621 the area was granted by **James** I of England to Scottish poet-statesman **Sir William Alexander**, and was then named **Nova Scotia** [168, pp 56-58; 83-].
-The area changed hands from French to English at least six times [119b Vol 1, pp 40-44].
-1713 Acadia (Nova Scotia) was ceded permanently to the British by the **Treaty of Utrecht** [16] which ended the War of the Spanish Succession and Queen Anne's War [9 Vol 1, pp 96-7; 168, pp 89-90] [See above p 95].
-"The British conquest brought freedom of worship and the term ***French Protestant*** came into use [120, p 1113]."
-1749 a military post with 2576 colonists and flourishing city with 3 law courts was established at **Halifax**, Nova Scotia, by **Governor Edward Cornwallis**, twin brother of the Archbishop of Canterbury [119 Vol 3, p 119].
-1750 Canada's first Anglican Church was built in Halifax. Soon the population grew to 6000 [119 Vol 5, pp 232-3].
-1751 the French built **Fort Beauséjour**, near present **Sackville NB**, at the **Chignecto Isthmus**, to defend their claim to the part of Acadia north of the **Bay of Fundy**. The struggle continued until:
-1755 they capitulated to British regulars and Massachusetts volunteers, under the command of **Robert Monckton**, Lieut Governor of **Annapolis Royal** [9 Vol 7, p 126; 119 Vol 7, p 126] which the British renamed **Fort Cumberland** [120, pp 895-6].
-1750-3 **Charles** II of England and Hanover sponsored persecuted refugees**: German** & **Swiss** protestants and French **Huguenots** to settle in **Nova Scotia** [119b Vol 6, pp 225-6] at **Lunenberg** named for a city in Hanover.
-1753 St. John's Church near Lunenburg was built in wooden Gothic style, the second oldest church in North America, with services in English, French & German. [Damaged by arson in 2001. Was restored by donations]
-1755 when the **Seven Years' War** began, though the **Acadians** attempted to remain neutral [9 Vol 1, pp 96-7], the English, doubting their loyalty, deported them to Ohio, Quebec, Magdalene Islands and Louisiana, now known as **Cajuns** (Canadians)[12 Vol 1, p 51]. Their ordeal was described by Henry Wadsworth **Longfellow** in the epic poem *Evangeline*. 14,000 Acadians fled; a few hundred hid in forests[119b Vol 1, pp 40-44; 9 Vol 7, pp 289-190] [pp 103, 110].

New France (Quebec, Great Lakes, Mississippi and the Midwest) [pp 69-75; Maps: pp 74, 104]

-1672 the population had risen to 10,000 when Intendant (Governor) **Jean Talon** retired to France [p 74]. Mining iron ore and silver, textile weaving, a clothing industry, tanning, lumbering and ship building thrived.
-Talon sent explorers/fur traders to **Sault Ste Marie** to offset the activities of the Hudson Bay Co, and claim the entire Great Lakes, the far West and the Mississippi River for **Louis** XlV. Hundreds of forts were active.
-1672-82 and 1689-98 Comte de Louis de Buade **Frontenac** was Governor of New France, in
-1673 he established **Cataraqui**, renamed **Fort Frontenac** (later **Kingston**) up the Saint Lawrence River.
-1689 wars with the **Iroquois** became troublesome, but by 1701 they were pacified [119b Vol 4, pp 287-8].
-1690 an English attack on Quebec was repulsed.
-1713 though the French population was only 18,000 [119b Vol 4, p 267-8] after losing Acadia and Newfoundland to the British, New France strengthened holdings and built a chain of new forts on the Great lakes, Ohio and Mississippi valleys, blocking expansion west from heavily populated New England.
-1732 in the Quebec shipyard 10 great ships were built that year, in a growing industry.
-1734 a road was built from Quebec to Montreal. Until then travel was only by river.
-1737 an iron foundry was established at Trois Rivières. Iron pots, utensils and cannon were produced.
-1737 widow **Marguerite d'Youville** (educated in Ursuline Convent, Quebec) sister of explorer Sieur de La **Verendrye**, with three widows, cared for abandoned children and indigents [119b Vol 10, p 400]. Canonized 1955.
-1747 she was in charge of Montreal General Hospital; 1753 she founded Sisters of Charity (**Grey Nuns**).

Fur-Trading and Exploration of the Great Lakes and Louisiana [Continued from pp 70-74]

-From the sixteenth to the nineteenth centuries, European demand for furs stimulated expansion of fur trade in North America and the development of Canada and the United States.
-French fur-traders took a shortcut from the **St. Lawrence River** up the **Ottawa River**, and a series of rivers and **Lake Nipissing** to **Lake Huron** [map p 70] and the Great Lakes in the heart of the continent.
-1694 the fur-trading centre was **Fort Michilimackinac** at the north end of **Lake Michigan**, near the east end of Lake Superior [16, p 487; 120, p 898].

Maps: *European Claims in North America* 982-1750 [151]
Route of La Salle [119b, Vol 6, p 75]

-1684-6 **La Salle** explored **Texas**. Since Indians were familiar with hundreds of rivers and lakes by canoe, French fur-traders hired them as guides to penetrated Ohio, Illinois and Mississippi Rivers **to Gulf of Mexico**. The Mississippi watershed was named **Louisiana** for King Louis XIV [116, p 14]. Forts were established for settlers.
-1690-92 **Henry Kelsey** a Hudson Bay Co (HBCo) trader, explored from the Hudson Bay to **Lake Winnipeg**, up the **North Saskatchewan River** to present Alberta; saw the great plains and buffalo herds [119 Vol 5, p 189].
-1688, 1690 and 1694 Frenchman Pierre **Le Moyne d'Iberville** et d'Ardillières raided English posts on James Bay and Hudson Bay, sank two ships and seized furs.
-1690 his men massacred some 60 English colonists at Corlaer, **New England**.
-1696-7 d'Iberville looted across **Newfoundland**, killing 200 English.
-1698-1702 he made **annual visits** to **Louisiana, Mississippi** and **St. Louis**, establishing **forts** for fur trade.
-Though ruthless, 1699 he was the first Canadian-born recipient of the French **Croix de Saint Louis** [120, p 1129].
-1699 three brothers Jean Baptiste Le Moyne **Sieur de Bienville** and François **Sieur de Sauvole**, and the above harsh Pierre **Sieur d'Iberville**, founded the town called **Biloxi** [9 Vol 4, p 68], still active today [125 Vol 2, p 308].
-1694-7 Sieur Antoine de Lamothe **Cadillac** commanded **Fort Michilemackinac**, northern **Michigan**, the most important French trading post [125 Vol 3, p 308]. 1683 Cadillac did fur-trading in **Acadia** (later **Nova Scotia**).
-1701 he founded Pontchartrain (**Detroit**); was Commandant 1701-10; was Governor of Louisiana 1711-17.
-1702 Sieur **de Bienville** and brothers founded **Mobile, Alabama** [16, p 20].
-1706 Sieur d'Iberville plundered the English colony of **Nevis** in the **West Indies**. He died of yellow fever.
-1718 Sieur de Bienville became **Governor of Louisiana,** and laid out the capital, **New Orleans**.
-1726 Pierre Gaultier de Varennes **Sieur de la Vérendrye** (1685-1749) traded fur on **Lake Nipigon** 35 miles north of **Lake Superior**. Born in Trois Rivière, Quebec; fought in France in War of Spanish Succession [95].
-1731-38 **Vérendrye** and three sons and a nephew **built a string of forts west of Lake Superior,** from Fort St Pierre & Fort Francis on **Rainy Lake**, via the **lake of the Woods** and numerous rivers to the **Red River**.
-1738 **Vérendrye** built Fort Rouge at the junction of the **Assiniboine** and **Red Rivers**, which later was named **Fort Douglas**, and later renamed **Fort Garry** and **Winnipeg**. Here thousands of nomadic first nations people had camped seasonally many years [12 Vol 7, p 77].
-1738 Vérendrye also established Fort la Reine (**Portage la Prairie**) and forts up the Assiniboine River west to the present **Saskatchewan**, and the same year, south to the **Missouri River**, now North **Dakota**.
-1743 he looked over territory west of the Missouri Territory, later set aside in the present **North Dakota** as a national historic preserve [16, p 792] and set up a lead tablet at **Pierre**, **South Dakota**, claiming the Dakota area for France. The Sioux Indians called themselves Dakota, meaning "allies" [16, p 181]. Vérendrye sent 30,000 beaver pelts to Quebec annually [12 Vol 7, p 77], self-employed. For details see [119b, pp 95-97] [Maps pp 108, 121].
-1743 sons of Vérendrye traded in present-day **Nebraska**, **Wyoming** and **Montana** [16, p 792; 502; 826].

Spanish Explorers and Colonies in North America

[from pp 57-58 and 74-75]

-1682 although French **La Salle** claimed the Mississippi watershed for France and named it **Louisiana**, Spain possessed large parts of the area, particularly southern parts of the present Louisiana and Mississippi.
-1697 Spanish settlements and missions began in **Lower California** and the **Mexican Peninsula**.
-About 1730 **horses** were introduced to the plains. Native people became mobile. Postal delivery improved.
-1732 **Louisiana** was yielded formally by Spain to **France**, by right of settlement. [See maps: p 97]
-1733 British King **George** II settled 114 poor people from England in **Savannah Georgia** [16, p 283].
-1735 and 1738 **Moravian missionaries** sailed to Georgia to minister to settlers and slaves. In the second group, Anglican **John** and Charles **Wesley** were impressed with calm Moravian faith. When ordered to take up arms against Spanish invaders, being pacifists Moravians migrated to **Pennsylvania**. [See p 101 below]
-**Spain** controlled more than the west half of the future **United States**: California, New Mexico, Nevada, the Colorado River and Grand Canyon, Arizona, Texas and the area around the Gulf of Mexico [pp 106-7].

European Protestant Dissidents Fled

[Continued from pp 69-73]

-1562 and 1565 Huguenots in Florida and South Carolina were defeated, expelled and killed by the Spanish. Many more came on ships along the Atlantic shores.
- 1685 after the **Edict of Nantes** was revoked, more than 1,450 French Protestants, keeping their faith secret, forced to live as "good Catholics" [120, p 1113], migrated to **Quebec** and **Louisburg** (**Cape Breton**) [map p 97]; also "merchants, artisans, soldiers, fishermen, indentured servants and *filles du roi* (orphans as brides)".

-1688 & 1693 **Louis** XIV's armies twice sacked Protestants in **Palatinate** (German Rhine) and Heidelburg.
-1671 **William Penn** toured German states inviting persecuted protestants to migrate to Pennsylvania for religious liberty. From 1683 to 1775 many of various denominations migrated: Lutherans, Reformed, Moravians, Quakers, Mennonites, Amish & Dunkards, the majority expecting immunity from military service.
-1740's-50's French protestant (Huguenot) commercial activity was significant with New France. Both government and Catholic religious communities imported goods from **Huguenot** and **Jewish** firms.
-1709 some German refugees went to Rotterdam and from there, on ships provided by **Queen Anne** of England, went as settlers to county Limerick, **Ireland**. Their farming methods were so superior that the Irish grew envious and resentful. Rents were raised 600%. **John Wesley** noticing their growing poverty and backsliding faith, from lack of pastoral care, returned to Ireland often to help. Being fluent in German, revival came with his preaching. [See Palatinate area on map p 68.]
-1760 some Palatinate Germans led by Irish-born **Barbara Heck** (1734-1804), with her German Bible, assisted by **Captain Thomas Webb**, migrated from Ireland to New York [p 115]. In New York they planted the first Methodist Church in the New World. Webb was Commander of British forces in **Albany NY**.
-1759 Captain Webb had been blinded in one eye on the Plains of Abraham, Quebec [pp 104-105].

Moravian Brethren Found Refuge with Count Zinzendorf

[Continued from pp 76-79, 88]

-1690 **Christian David**, born in Moravia, apprenticed as a carpenter with secret Brethren who taught him not to pray to saints or go on pilgrimages. He was impressed by persecuted Brethren in jail; received a **scholarly Kalice Bible** (in the Czech language); studied it so much that it permanently influenced his speech.
-Christian David joined the Prussian army, felt shocked by morals of soldiers and nominal Christians and was received as a member of a Lutheran church in **Berlin**.
-1715 he left the army, went to **Silesia**, was seriously ill and saw persecution by Jesuits. He found fellowship with **Pietists**, joy in Christ and married. David went several times into Moravia to bring revival to secret Brethren. In **Kunwald** and **Fulneck** 100 year old "dead bones" came to life. [See Ezekiel 37 in the Bible]
-1722 David went to Saxony, met **Pietist Count Nicholas Ludwig von Zinzendorf** and told him that oppressed Moravian Brethren were yearning for a place of refuge so that they could practice "the heart religion of the primitive Christians." The count showed interest in settling a few families. In a dangerous escape May 27- June 8 with 10 families David returned to the Count's estate at **Berthelsdorf**, 70 miles from **Dresden, Saxony**. The Count was not at home but his surprised grandmother and steward provided for them graciously. They named the place **Herrnhut** "under the care of God" and built houses and industries.
-1724 en route to Lissa, Poland, 5 persecuted Brethren leaders with families from Moravia, stopped over at the Count's estate and decided to stay. They zealously used **Comenius' Catechism** and **sang Brethren hymns**, but had no knowledge of Moravian church customs or discipline, having worshiped for generations underground. They were Melchior **Zeisberger**, **John Toeltschig** and 3 men named **David Nitschmann:** the elder, carpenter and weaver (later Syndic, meaning legal representative or agent).
-Other people of diverse backgrounds found refuge at Herrnhut. A Lutheran clergyman ministered the sacraments. Zinzendorf wanted to bring the Moravians into the Lutheran church but they resisted. Choirs (Schools and industries) were built. Christian David went secretly into Moravia 10 times to bring out refugees.
-1726 an old book by **Comenius**, *Ratio Disciplinae* was found in a local library. Count Zinzendorf was impressed/surprised at how similar the traditions and beliefs were to those of the refugees [57, p 38] [pp 76-78].
-By 1727 about 300 German and Czech-speaking refugees had settled on Count Zinzendorf's estate. Besides the Moravian Brethren from 20 places in Bohemia and 18 in Moravia, there were Ultraquists, Schwenkfelders (Anabaptist mystics), Calvinists and one critical outspoken Lutheran. To try to settle serious dissension the Count, only 26 years old, took leave of absence from his post in Dresden as King's Councilor. He conferred individually with the leaders and joined their nightly Bible study and worship. He lectured them for three hours on the sin of schism [134, bk 2, chaps 1, 2 and 3] stressing that living on his estate meant that he was their feudal lord. He read the Manorial Statutes to them. The refugees suddenly stopped quarreling and shook hands. They agreed to comprehensive new rules of conduct regarding handling of disagreements, adherence to scripture, avoidance of frivolous pleasures and alcohol, discipline of loafers, education of children, care of the aged and ill, the role of Elder, etc. They chose 12 Elders and **Christian David** was appointed Chief Elder.
-24 men and 24 women covenanted to meet in turn for prayer around the clock.
-Revival began. Taking turns round the clock, Prayer Watch was held non-stop for 100 years.

-1728 ***Daily Texts*** were prepared, at first passed from house to house verbally, later a printed page for each day and annually a book, consisting of Old and New Testament verses (to be read from the Bible), a few hymn stanzas and short comments, carefully selected to stimulate and influence thoughts for the day. These were read by each family morning and/or evening before food. This practice spread to other denominations.
-1731 a group of 74 refugees arrived in Herrnhut, bringing the population to 600, mainly born in Moravia.
-1732 the **first Easter Sunrise Service** was held at Herrnhut cemetery, with trumpets, horns and violins and old glorious Brethren hymns, chorales and liturgy. More were composed, including some by Zinzendorf [57, p 66].

The Modern Missionary Movement Began

-1727 Zinzendorf was decorated at the coronation of the King of Denmark. There he saw **Eskimos** from Greenland and a black man from St. Thomas, West Indies.
-In Herrnhut in Saturday meetings to awaken caring, he provided news and geography [134, bk 2, chap 3& 4] of other cultures. He sent Brethren in 2's to all **German** and **Baltic States**, **Silesia**, **Hungary**, **England**, **Switzerland** and **Austria** to start **diaspora** fellowships, but within state churches.
-1728 at a day of prayer, 26 single men volunteered to serve overseas [57, p 51].
-Zinzendorf started a live-in *Choir Settlement* for single men for their education, industrial skills, Bible study and service of the poor. *Choirs* provided **higher education** for elders and missionaries.
-1730 **Anna Nitschmann** started a *Choir* for single women.
-1729 Christian David visited **Bishop Daniel Ernest Jablonski** in **Berlin**. He and **Christian Sitkovius** in Thorn (Turin), **Poland** were the only remaining bishops of **Unitas Fratrum** (Unity of Brethren) [57, pp 45-46, 69-71].
-1729 for circulation in high places, Zinzendorf wrote a statement interpreting the high standards, pacifism and apostolic (episcopal) origin of the Moravian Brethren, plus their loyalty to the Lutheran Augsburg Confession. At the University of Jenna he set up a student fellowship with Augustus Gottlieb **Spangenberg**, a lecturer in theology. Student societies were founded in several other universities.
-1732 at high risk Christian David and others made evangelistic tours in Bohemia-Moravia.
-In Bohemia **David Nitschman** was **martyred**. His father also **David Nitschman**, migrated to Herrnhut.
-Bohemian **Jesuits** placed **Jan Gilek** in a dungeon, chaining his left hand to his right foot. 1735 Gilek escaped via Silesia to **Berlin**, started a congregation of Bohemian Brethren at nearby Rixdorf; brought more groups from Bohemia-Moravia
-1732 the Moravian missionary movement began in St. Thomas, **Danish West Indies** [57, pp 48-58]. A Danish pastor ministered to **Huguenot refugees** with **Leonard Dober** and **carpenter David Nitschmann** ministered to **black slaves** living in deplorable conditions, teaching them to live orderly lives, work hard and be content.
-1733 Theologians **Spangenberg** from **Jena** and Oettinger from Tübingen taught theology to Zinzendorf.
-1733 Matthew & Christian **Stach** began a mission in **Greenland** with David Christian as carpenter [57, pp 58-62].
-1734-6 Moravian missionaries went to **Lapland**, to **Surinam**, south America and **Guinea**, west Africa.
-1735 **David Nitschmann** a refugee who arrived 1724, descended from old Brethren roots, was consecrated the **first Bishop** of the ***Resusitated Moravian Church***. Aging **Bishop Jablonski** came to Herrnhut to officiate.
-1734 en route to America **Spangenberg** and 9 other Moravians ministered in **England**, applied for and received a land grant in **Georgia**. There they cleared land, grew crops, adjusted to hot climate and started a school for Indian children. Spangenberg became a **British citizen**; wrote to Zinzendorf urging the same.
-1736 February **Bishop Nitschman**, 23 Moravians, **John** & **Charles Wesley** & the **Governor** reached Georgia. Spangenberg led a group to **Pennsylvania**, with the Governor's commendation letter to **William Penn**.

Zinzendorf During His Exile From Saxony

-1733-6 **Zinzendorf** studied theology; was ordained a Lutheran clergyman. Noblemen disapproved.
-1736 **Zinzendorf** was **exiled as a heretic** by the **Saxony government**, who preferred Lutheran intellect-ualism to his Pietism and zeal.
-At **Wetteravia** at Frankfort-on-Main, he leased run-down Ronneberg Castle to build up an educational and theological centre, named **Herrnhaag**. 56 Jewish and Gypsy squatter families and 30 or 40 old brethren families from Moravia settled there [134, bk 2, chap 7]. It became Unity of Brethren headquarters.
-1736 July he went to universities Magdelburg and Jena, then east to Königsberg (Livonia) to start a Bible Society to print the Livonian Bible, and to encourage Unity of Brethren who were leading **Diaspora** fellowships. Zinzendorf's purpose was to revive the Lutheran church as a "church within a church".
-He wrote urging **Prussian King Frederick William** I to help poor **Austrian refugees** on his Baltic lands.

-In reply Zinzendorf was invited as a guest for three days at the Prussian king's hunting lodge, where king **Frederick William** I asked Bishop Jablonski to consecrate Zinzendorf as a Bishop. Zinzendorf refused, hoping for union of Lutherans and Moravians (Unity of Brethern=Unitas Fratrum).
-1736 December, the first Synod of the ***Resusitated* Unity of Brethren** (Unitas Fratrum) was held near Ronneburg at Marienborn Castle. The value of the episcopate was reaffirmed.
-1735 January, Zinzendorf visited authorities in **Holland** and arranged for a *Choir Settlement* (boarding school) to influence the Dutch and to train missionaries [57, pp 75-77, 84-85].
-1737 January to March in **England**, Zinzendorf encouraged Moravian missionaries already in London, and he evangelized German businessmen settled there. He conferred with the **Archbishop of Canterbury** for recognition of the Unity of Brethern (Moravians). The Archbishop was impressed and wrote open letters for Moravian colonists in Georgia. He urged Zinzendorf to be consecrated Bishop, by Bishop Jablonski [57, pp 71-77].
-1737 May, **Zinzendorf** was consecrated Bishop by Bishops Jablonski and Nitschman. Letters of congratulation came from the King of Prussia, Bishop Sitkovius and the Archbishop of Canterbury.
-1738 Bishop Zinzendorf conducted his first ordination: **Peter Böhler**, from the University of Jena.
-1739 January, Bishop Zinzendorf sailed to St. Thomas, **West Indies**, where he found two Moravian missionaries in prison. He gained their release [pp 100]. Missions began in **Dutch Guiana**, S. America and **Ceylon**.
-1739 February to May in London**,** England **Peter Böhler** ministered to **John Wesley** after his discouraging mission in Georgia. Böhler and Wesley went to Oxford where Böhler preached and conversed in Latin. With **Charles** Wesley as teacher he began to preach in English [134, bk 2, chap 9].
-1739 May 1, Böhler founded the first English Moravian society, in the home of book publisher **James Hutton**. For space they moved to *Great Meeting House* **Fetter Lane.**
-1739 a convert in **Greenland** was baptized; teachings of Christ's death & resurrection had impressed them.
-1739 June 12-20 a Synod met at **Gotha**. Three major decisions were made as follows**:**

1. To lay emphasis on the Unity of Brethren as an apostolic ecclesiastical organization;
2. To adopt the term **Diaspora** for the Unity of Brethren's special calling as a leaven amongst other bodies in Brüder Gemine (midweek fellowships).
3. To publish the first catechism of the *resusitated* Unity of Brethern [57, pp 96-7], and Zinzendorf's sermons.

-Throughout **Poland** many Moravian Diaspora congregations were meeting [51]. Workers went to **Dutch Jews**, the **Baltic**, **Sweden** & **Norway**. There were new Diaspora *Settlements* in **Germany** and French **Switzerland.**
-1738-40 the **Wesleys** worked with the Moravians for two years, and then launched out on their own becoming the great **Methodist** mass movement. Moravians in a quiet way built *Settlements* and Diasporas in **Yorkshire**, **Wales** and **Ireland**, as a loosely-knit group of 40 congregations and 5000 participants [12 Vol 7, p 310].
-1740 schools in Herrnhaag had 600 boys/girls & a theological seminary with graduates from all universities.
-1739-55 Anglican **John Cennick**, a preacher all over Wiltshire, was drawn to the Moravians' discipline/ openness/tolerance. 1746 he studied in Herrnhaag, heard hymns in 22 languages and missionaries' letters. Then in Ireland he preached to thousands. He discovered he was a descendant of a Kunik (Cennick) who escaped from Bohemia to England 100 years earlier [p 76] after the "Day of Blood" [134, bk 2, chap 11; 57, p 128].
-London Publisher **James Hutton** published the very first hymn book in English [134, bk 2, chap 9], a Manual of Doctrine, and Zinzendorf's sermons in English.

Ministry of Bohler, Zinzendorf and Others in London and Pennsylvania [from pp 98-99]

-For 50 years diverse groups of persecuted refugees and dissenters took up homesteads in Pennsylvania. They disagreed with each other and lacked pastoral care. Their moral standards were low.
-1738 Moravians in Georgia were expected to take up arms against **Spanish invaders** [57, pp 96-97]. Being **pacifists** they migrated to Pennsylvania, led by **Spangenberg**, invited by evangelist **George Whitefield** [57, p 81]. Letters were sent to Bishop Zinzendorf in Europe, asking for workers and colonists.
-1740 **Peter Böhler** in South **Carolina** ministered weekdays to **slaves** and Sundays to Moravians. Evangelist George **Whitefield** gave Böhler ship passage to Pennsylvania where he was hired to build the *settlement (*residence/industrial school) named **Nazareth** [57, pp 80-83]. Whitefield argued predestination versus Böhler's faith in free grace.. December, Bishop **David Nitschman, Anna Nitschman, her father David** (uncle of the bishop), **Christian Frolich** (as missionary to Indians) & others, reached Pennsylvania, bought land and began building the site later named **Bethlehem.** 1741 Böhler en route to Europe started a group in **New York.**
-1741 September Zinzendorf in **London** en route to America, tried but failed to find unity with **John Wesley.**
-Leonard Dober, Chief Elder for 6 years, resigned since the role gave too much authority to one person, so:

-1741 **Synod in London** abolished the Chief Elder role, designating *Christ alone Head of the Church* [57, pp 96-101].
-1741 December **Zinzendorf** and his daughter, using his untitled name **Louis von Thürnstein**, which he felt more appropriate, ministered throughout **Pennsylvania** to colonists who lacked clergy. He organized a union of several denominations; found pastors & teachers; started schools; pastored a Lutheran congregation.
-With the Governor's approval Zinzendorf named the two Moravian *Settlements* **Bethlehem** and **Nazareth**.
-1741 in June **Böhler** returned from Herrnhut with fifty-seven colonists. Their industries thrived so were able to support 15 *Itinerants* (*Heralds*) sent out on foot to bring unchurched colonists in New England to personal faith in Christ. They avoided promotion of the Moravian Church and religious controversy [57, pp 102-110].
-Bishop Zinzendorf ordained a pastor; organized English and German churches and a **native congregation** of **10 converts**. Then in other parts of New England he organizing union congregations and appointing clergy.
-Alarmed by news from Silesia of actions by the Prussian king he left America.
-1743 Jan 9, he sailed to Europe, visited thriving Moravian congregations/*Settlements* in **Yorkshire**, England for a month & tried again to unite with Wesley. He stopped over in **Holland** and then returned to Herrnhaag.

Zinzendorf Coping with Policies of Prussian and Russian Monarchs

-1740-1786 atheist King **Frederick** II of Prussia succeed his father, a Christian. 1742 he annexed **Silesia**, a Polish province, claimed by Roman Catholic Austrian Habsburgs since 1526. Fredrick II had induced Moravians from Herrnhut to migrate to Silesia because he was impressed by their industry and thrift. Moravian congregations were established and were flourishing. He granted them liberty of Conscience. 4000 Silesians had joined them and many more did later. Zinzendorf wrote letters disavowing the arrangements made in Silesia, reiterating that Moravian Brethren were to associate with Augsburg Lutherans already there.
-1743 July, Moravian Synod agreed regarding Silesia, that evangelism among the heathen was essential but growth at the expense of other churches was wrong. They decided to centralized work in *Settlements*. The old Brethren orders of Presbyter, Deacon and Alcoluth were revived; the Board of 12 Elders was dissolved.
-Reports of the Unity (Moravian Brethren): Membership in 50 congregations around the world [57, p 115], was 20,974, plus several times as many **adherents**. There were 500 evangelists.
-The ***Tropus* concept:** each denomination was not a church but only a ***tropus***. Together the various ***trope*** combined are the church. The role of Moravians would be to help combine *trope* to establish the wide church.
-After Synod, Zinzendorf went to Prussia to try to persuade King Frederick to reverse his policies, but the king refused Augsburg Lutheran oversight and overruled the decisions of Synod [57, pp 112-117].
-Then Zinzendorf went to **Silesia** to build up four *Settlements* to stop formation of Moravian congregations.
-Zinzendorf and son visited Diaspora and churches in **Livonia** (part of Lithuania). There were 70 students in the Brethrens' College. Evangelists were fluent in the Lettish language. He sought release for three Moravian leaders in **Russian** prisons. **Czarina Elizabeth** (who ruled 1741-61) ordered the Zinzendorfs to leave.
-After another visit to Silesia they settled at Marienborn and Herrnhaag. His wife joined them. Their *Society of Little Fools* was zealous for missions and education, but spent lavishly for seven years for many programs, unaware of debts. They composed and sang sentimental hymns like "entering the wounds of Christ", gave childish names to individuals and Christ, e.g. Little Lambkin.

More Moravian Colonists and Missions in America

-1744 Joseph **Spangenberg**, consecrated Bishop, sailed with his wife and colonists to America. He also had oversight of congregations in the West Indies. Peter **Böhler** returned to Europe, via England to minister there.
-1742-48 opening of 15 schools in Pennsylvania, including higher level studies and schools for girls.
-1745-1808 **David Zeisberger** began 63 years' highly effective work [134, bk 2, chap 14], among **Iroquois Six Nations** and **Delawares**, starting when they were "still savages, cruel with other tribes and whites." He was a linguist who understood their idioms and won their trust. They built schools, industries and orchards.
-1748 there were 500 Iroquois Christians [See p 104].
-1746 the *Irene*, a Moravian owned ship was built to transport colonists and bishops for pastoral visits overseas and export products made in *Settlements* for sale in Europe, crossing the Atlantic often, for a decade.
-1746 Christian David took a prefabricated church to Greenland. 300 locals attended its dedication.
-By 1747 there were 32 thriving industries in **Bethlehem** & **Nazareth**, 40 & 50 miles north of Philadelphia, and in **Lititz**, 60 miles west of Philadelphia [57, p 144]. Called *the Economy*, the industries supported *Itinerants* in 32 locations, each with several preaching points, missions in the West Indies, plus sending funds to pay off debts in Herrnhaag Europe, where there had been too much spent of a variety of programs.

-Immigration of Moravians from Europe to Pennsylvania increased. Bishop Spangenberg advised all to become citizens (naturalized British Subjects). He held nondenominational Synods two to four times a year to foster fellowship among Christians of many origins, yet Synods gradually were more Moravian in practice.
-1748 First Moravian Church, **New York City** and fellowships in **New Jersey** and **Maryland** were organized.
-1749 the British House of Commons passed an Act recognizing "the somber and industrious Moravians in Pennsylvania." A grant was made of 100,000 acres in **North Carolina** to develop similar *Settlements*.
-1752-3 Bishop Spangenberg & five elders went on horseback [57, p 170] to North Carolina and began **Bethabara**. Colonists came from Pennsylvania and Europe with Peter Böhler and others. By 1756 there were 65 settlers.

Zinzendorf in Favor in Europe Again had Headquarters in England

-1747 Zinzendorf's banishment from Saxony was revoked, so he transferred the Herrnhaag theological school and his residence to better quarters at **Barby** near Herrnhut. He was even invited to develop industries as at Herrnhut. The king of Saxony, after examining their doctrine and practice, issued a decree granting religious liberty. Their objection to taking oaths was resolved by granting *Permission to Affirm*.
-At last Zinzendorf had insight to deal with his Herrnhaag *Society of Little Fools*. He called a Synod where he with deep sorrow confessed guilt for the sentimental language and fantasies of the past seven years [57, pp 124-7].
-Bishop Spangenberg came from America for a year to write letters of apology to rebuild the Brethrens' good name. Debts from overspending at Herrnhaag emerged. Careful accounting and selfless donations followed.
-1749 the new Count of Ronneberg and Marienborn castles broke Zinzendorf's leases. Herrnhaag closed so residents scattered to French Switzerland, German States, Russia and America. To encourage everyone Zinzendorf wrote a circular letter honoring the ancient Moravian Brethren discipline and apostolic faith.
-1749-55 Moravian headquarters for five years were in Chelsea, England, near London, to be at the hub of world travel to enable movement of missionaries and colonists. Zinzendorf toured Moravian centres which were growing fast in Britain in Yorkshire, Derbyshire, Bedfordshire, Cheshire, Wiltshire and Ireland.
-Zinzendorf worked hard to keep the English congregations within the Anglican Church.
-There was criticism of the sentimental phase of Moravians, but Zinzendorf and other leaders avoided theological disputes [134, bk 2, c haps 13 & 14].
-1754 a Moravian hymn book in English was printed, the first in England. Anglicans sang only psalms.
-The reprinted King James Authorized Version (of 1611) of the Bible became widespread popular reading.
-Zinzendorf's ***Handy Guide for Daily Conduct***, in English, was effective as leaven for evangelical revival.
-In **Yorkshire** there were 4000 members and in **Ireland** 500 [57, pp 164,144]. A count of Diaspora adherents in all countries was 17,000. They enjoyed fellowship, singing, orchestral music and Bible study, but remaining members of other denominations, as a deliberate policy [57, pp 192-199].
-**Self-support** was established, without leaning on Count Zinzendorf, by developing thriving **handicraft industries** in some 20 *Settlements* in Europe, Britain and America [12, Vol 7, p 310].

Onset of The French and Indian War in 1754 before the Seven Years' War 1756-63

-1713 after losing Acadia & Newfoundland to the British, the French built a chain of forts along the Great Lakes & Ohio to Mississippi Rivers [12 Vol 2, p 786] blocked westward expansion of overpopulated New England. Competition for trading rights between French and English fur traders, from the **Allegheny Mountains** to **Mississippi River**, led to conflict [125 Vol 7, p 564]. As well, Indians were angered by loss of land to settlers.
-1727-60 King **George** II Hanover born 1683 settled in England 1714, supported by the **Whig Party** (liberal).
-1754 the **Albany Congress** convened to strengthen ties, was attended by representatives of New York, Maryland, New England, Pennsylvania and the Iroquois Confederacy.
-A plan by **Benjamin Franklin** of Pennsylvania for colonial **union** with elected representatives of colonial legislatures, was delayed [119 Vol 1, p 337].
-1754 the British built **Fort Cumberland** in the Allegheny Mountains for defense. At the same time New England forces under **George Washington** were building **Fort Duquesne** on the **Ohio River** [map p 104]. One of his soldiers was **Daniel Boone** [9 Vol 1, p 337].
-The French attacked and burned Fort Duquesne, starting war. Most Indians were on the French side, but
-The **Six Nations** (**Iroquois**) were on the English side. Iroquois land was located in Pennsylvania and New York; **Delaware** land was in Delaware and adjoining New England.
-Moravian *Settlements* Bethlehem and Nazareth, on the west bank of the Delaware River, were surrounded by both tribes, many at both were Christians. [See p 113].

-1755 **Gnadenhutten** was a neat attractive Christian Indian village, a model *Settlement*, with exemplary industries and school. One night an angry mob of Indian strangers broke into a house. **Bishop John Nitschman** who was visiting, was shot dead. Five more people were killed, one scalped and the house burned.
-Moravians were **pacifists** but Bishop Spangenberg offered the land of the ruined village for military purposes; advised the British about where to construct a line of forts; appointed unarmed patrols to do sentry duty, and built barricades and block houses to protect Bethlehem (40 miles north of Philadelphia) where 600 fugitives were protected [134, bk 2, chap 14]. Industrial production continued; friendly Indians protected the harvest.
-**Benjamin Franklin** [pp 90-91] visited and was impressed by the defense measures. Their industrial production continued, especially in Nazareth (10 miles farther north).
-1755 Nazareth Hall, an attractive spacious stone building was under construction:
-At Bethabara, **North Carolina** a stockade had to be built around the *Settlement*. Neighboring refugees arrived so a second *Settlement*, **Bethania** was built. [Europe/Russia in the Seven Years' War pp 105,110-113]
-During the Seven Years' War the *Settlement* at **Lititz** (60 miles west of Philadelphia) continued active industrial production. A fine residence built there for Moravian Bishop Hehl: used by army 1777-83 [p 113]
-1755 **General Braddock** arrived from England as Commander-in-Chief and directed the commanders in New England in a four-pronged attack, with many casualties [95, p 375]. [Seven Years' War continued, p 105]. Afraid they would be disloyal, he deported the Acadian French population from Nova Scotia [p 96].
-1742-1807 Iroquois **Joseph Brant** (Thavendanega in Mohawk) grew up in Mohawk territory south of Lake Ontario, was educated in Lebanon, Conn, sponsored by **Sir William Johnson**, a British colonial official, and joined the Church of England; translated the Book of Common Prayer and parts of the New Testament into **Mohawk**; aided the British in the French & Indian War [for Johnson & Brant see pp 114-115].

Map: *The Seven Years' War 1756-63* [119b Vol 9, p 281]

This war was worldwide. The French and Indian War had begun 1754. Fort Pitt later became Pittsburg.

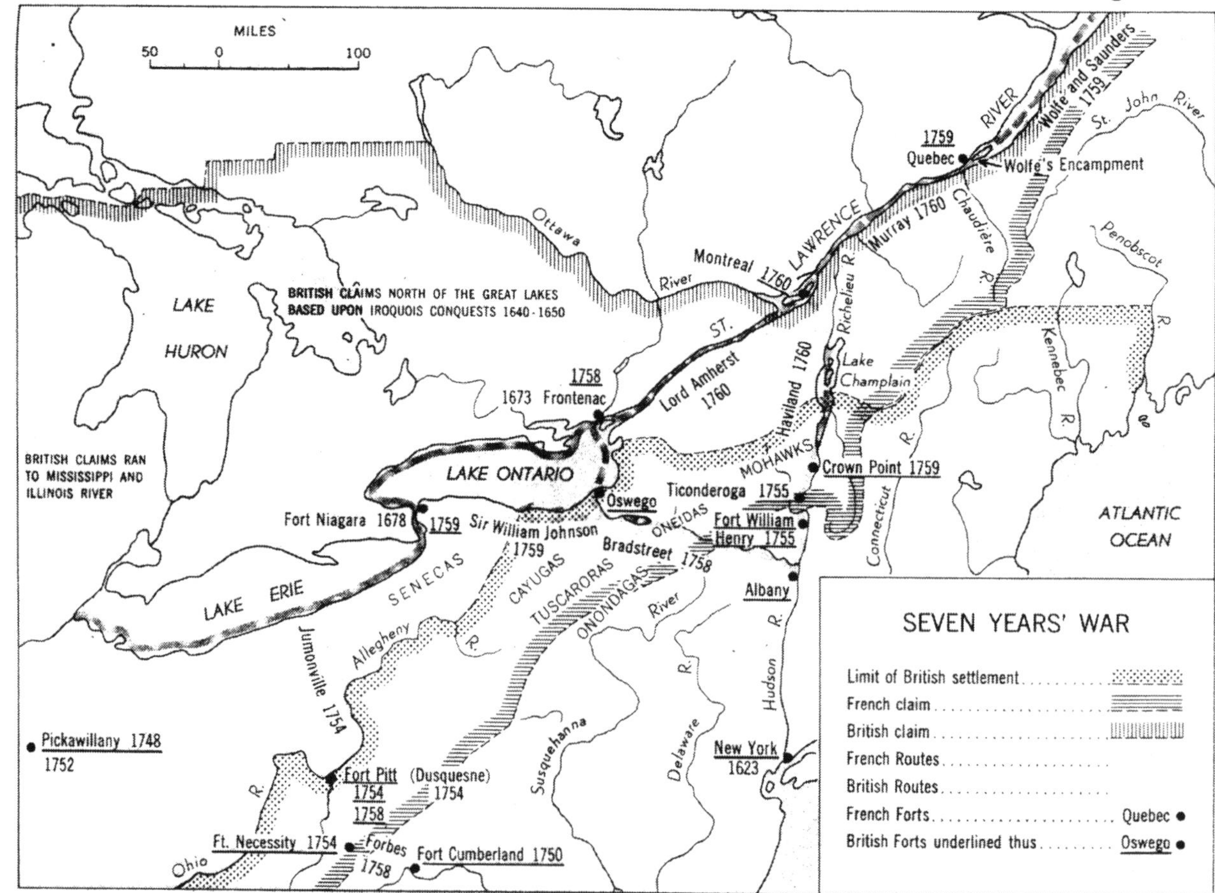

Chapter Seventeen - 1756 to 1795

Seven Years' War and Revolutions in America and France

The Seven Years' War 1756-1763 [Continued from pp 103-104]

-1754-63 **French and Indian War** began two years before the Seven Years' war. It was fought by England **and** her American Colonies against the French and Indians, as part of the **Seven Years' War**. Fighting took place in **New York, Pennsylvania, Ohio** and **Canada** [167, pp 112-114] [maps 104, 157].

-There were many battles at the Great Lakes, Lake Champlain, and Atlantic Canada [119 Vol 9, pp 279-282].

-The **English** were aided by **Iroquois**; the **French allies** were from other tribes, such as **Pontiac** or **Ottawa**.

-The **French** built ships in **Quebec**. The British built both barges and sailing ships for the war at **Oswego**, southeast shore of Lake Ontario. Barges were sturdy & carried heavy cargoes: flat-bottomed, propelled by sails, oars or poling when winds failed [119b Vol 9, pp 126-36]. The world's largest, most impressive sailing ships were built [120 pp 933-6, 2153] on **Lake Ontario** and **Nova Scotia** south coast of and **Bay of Fundy**.

-1756-63 the **Seven Years' War** was fought by **Austria**, **Sweden**, **Saxony**, **France** and **Russia** on one side, and on the other side **Prussia** and **Great Britain** [53b, p 29, 60-66] [pp 110-112].

1. **French** and **English** fought to keep their colonies and trade in **India** and **America**.
2. **Austria** fought but failed to take **Silesia** back from **Prussia** [53b, p 60, 68], often demanding food, fodder, camp sites and medical care for up to 2000 troops at a time, from Moravian Brethren in Saxony. One day 2000 lbs. bread were supplied to Austrian troops. Another time in Herrnhut, near Dresden the men's *Settlement* was pillaged. **Russian** troops plundered Moravian Brethren who were neutral, in **Poland** and on the **Baltic**.

-1756 Bishop Zinzendorf's wife and only son died with the stress of conflict around them. She had nobly managed their property for 23 years. 24 clergymen were pallbearers. [Continued p 111]

-1757 when a new church was dedicated near Herrnhut, over 1300 communicants partook of communion. Invading army officers were present and impressed; prejudice lifted [57, pp 158-9].

-1756-60 the French invaded Hanover. **King George** II defeated them with British troops [12 Vol 10, pp 666-7].

-1756-61 and 66-68 energetic **Prime Minister William Pitt** the elder, motivated English strength [16, pp 579, 676].

-1758 in western **Pennsylvania** the British won back **Fort Duquesne** from the French, and renamed it **Fort Pitt** for Prime Minister Pitt [16, p 267;119 Vol 7, p 121] in 1764; later renamed **Pittsburg** [map: pp 70, 104].

-The British controlled Lake Ontario [16, p 258] capturing strategic **Fort Frontenac** (Cataraqui, later **Kingston**).

-1759 the British captured the fort that was later named **Fort York (Toronto)** [119 Vol 8, pp 23].

-1757-62 **Benjamin Franklin** (1706-90) was **Agent** in London, England, for Pennsylvania [pp 90-91; 110].

- 1759 **James Cook** (1728-79) joined navy in 1755; now given command of a sloop surveyed and charted the St. Lawrence estuary and coasts of **Newfoundland** and **Labrador** [119b Vol 3, p 99] to prepare for **Wolfe's invasion**. [see p 109 re the Pacific 1768-79] [167, pp 106-111; 168, pp 90-93].

-1759 **Fort Niagara** was captured by the British (founded by French fur traders in 1678) [120, p 898].

-1759 **General Wolfe** invaded Quebec from the south via **Lake Champlain** [map pp 70, 104]. On the Plains of Abraham he defeated French Commander **Montcalm.** Both died from wounds. When winter followed both sides suffered from severe cold and hunger [126, Episodes 3 and 4].

-1760 **Montreal** fell to the British. **Nova Scotia** was also ceded to them.

-1760 King **George** II died. **George** III succeeded until 1820. Through **James Murray**, **Governor of Quebec**, the British granted freedom of religion, French language rights and jury membership [126, Episodes 3 and 4]. Fifteen **Scottish/English/American** merchants in Quebec were furious, and struggled for years to discredit Murray.

-1763 the **Treaty of Paris** ending the Seven Years' War, **gave all French territories to the English**. France was expelled from **India** & N America. **French Quebec** with a population of 70,000 **became a British colony**.

-In Quebec **British form of land tenure** applied in new areas, but the **French Seigniorial system** begun in New France in 1623, was not changed by the British. It had evolved from feudalism and included paying taxes and various dues to the Seignior (Seigneur). Every habitant (peasant) was allotted a long narrow strip of land fronting on the river. This gave them the advantages of neighbors nearby and a transportation route.

-Each Seignior was obliged to see that roads, a grist mill and communal bake oven were built, and habitants (residents) provided military service. Seigniors were judicial, administrative and religious leaders, with provincial civic privileges and duties, but few were wealthy.

- Some aspects of British *Common Law* were added [121, p 984]. Eight million acres were granted under seigniorial tenure, a quarter of which was held by the Roman Catholic Church for religious, educational and hospital purposes. Construction of villages was not allowed.

- Before 1763 the only urban centres were **Quebec**, **Montreal** and **Trois Rivières** [119, pp 267-8]

-The British assigned the Ohio River valley to French Quebec [104 Vol CXXV, No 7, 2001, pp 27-29] angering New England.
-The **Mississippi River** became the border between British and **Spanish** Territory. Spain ceded **Florida** to Britain but kept **Cuba** [95;9 Vol 7, p 381]. [British history continues pp 107, 109-111, 114 -119].
-1764 "British conquest brought freedom of worship and the term *French Protestant* came into use. The Protestant religion gained official status and soon some **Huguenots** were appointed to important offices in the Governor's Executive Council, the courts and bureaucracy [120, p 1113]." The Church of England was favored.
-World-wide British naval supremacy and the **British Empire** in **India** were established, but in **Indonesia** the **Netherlands** remained strong. The **Dutch East India Co.** went under government control [See p 72].

Migration West Across the Appalachian Mountains from New England

-South of Lake Ontario **David Zeisberger** continued to orientate new Moravian missionaries for **Iroquois** and **Delaware** work. A linguist, he wrote grammars/dictionaries. He understood their idiom and wrote useful books: children's sermons, child care, lexicon, hymns, etc. [24, pp 175-7] [pp 102-104; maps pp 74, 97, 104 & 128].
-In 11 locations Indian *Settlements* had schools, industries, orchards, orderly streets, remarkable cleanliness, daily worship and their own governing boards.
-1764 **Fort Pitt** (later **Pittsburgh**) expanded by the English on the site of **Fort Duquesne** [16, p 258, 580] [p 104]
-1767-71 **Daniel Boone** (1734-1820) explored the wilderness around the **Kentucky** River [maps p 128, 157]
-1769 he led a party of explorers from North Carolina to Kentucky [16, p 397], known as "the dark and bloody ground" from wars between **Cherokees** & **Iroquois**. Indians were hostile when settlers occupied their land.
-1775 hired by a Carolina company, Boone built the **Wilderness Road** for pioneers to reach Kentucky.
-1778 Boone was captured by Indian raiders, but escaped and the settlement survived. More settlers, following river valleys through Pennsylvania to **Pittsburg**, floated on barges down the **Ohio** River [125, p 477-8].
-By 1784 there were 30,000 settlers in the area; 1790 **Kentucky Territory** was formed; 1792 Kentucky State.
-1771-1800 **St. Louis** was under **Spanish** rule. 1788-98 Boone lived in **West Virginia;** until 1820 in **St. Louis**, Missouri, founded 1763 by **French** traders [map p 97] named for **King Louis XV** [16, p 496; 652] [map 157].
-At the close of the century land companies brought a stream of land-hungry settlers across the **Allegheny** and **Blue Ridge** Mountains to occupy land in the **Ohio** valley and **Kentucky**.
- Many were squatters on land the Indians claimed and fought for.
-The pioneers seeing land that was not cultivated, pushed the Indians west farther and farther and began homesteads [9 Vol 2, pp 47-8], not understanding that uncultivated land was in use.
-1794 a treaty to establish boundaries was forced on the Indians by settlers and eastern philanthropists who tried to be fair to the Indians, but from far away.
-1763 major fur trading **Fort Michelimackinac** at the north end of **Lake Michigan** was ceded to the British,
-1796 it was returned to the US [16, p 489] (later Mackinaw City) [founded 1634 by **Jean Nicolet**; map p 70, 74].
-1800 **St. Louis** was restored to France in a secret deal with **Napoleon.**
-1803 it was sold to the USA.

Early Spanish and French Rule in Mississippi and California [See pp 57-58, 70, 73 and 97-98]

-1539-42 **Spaniards under De Soto** were the first white men to explore and settle what is now Louisiana.
-Since 1634 the Mississippi and all its tributaries were explored/settled by **a** succession of French fur traders and missionary priests, via the Great Lakes, through the western plains to the Gulf of Mexico [map 97].
-Meanwhile the western half and southern portions of the future United States were in Spanish control **California, New Mexico, Nevada, Arizona,** areas **along the Colorado River, Texas** & **Louisiana** [Map p 97].
-1682 French **La Salle** had claimed the entire Mississippi watershed, naming it Louisiana for French King Louis XV, and today many of the population of Louisiana are of mixed French descent, and speak Creole.
-1718 **New Orleans** was founded on the delta of the Mississippi River.
-1732-62 Louisiana was under France by right of settlement [16, p 445].
-1759-1823 Spanish **Francisan Friars** were the first colonists in **California**; they developed a chain of twenty-one missions, spaced one day's walk apart for convenience of communication [16, p 120; 488]. They converted Indians and taught them weaving and farming.
-1769-70 Spanish military forts were built at **San Diego** and **Monterey** (later called **San Francisco**).
-1776 settlers from Spain established pueblos (villages) along the coast.
-1776 **San Francisco** was settled by Spaniards [16, pp 120, 658]. Trappers and traders reached California by ship.

Early Settlement and Sovereignty of Louisiana [from pp 70, 73 and 96-98 and maps pp 97, 157]

-1763 In the Treaty of Paris ending the Seven Years' War Spain kept the Mississippi south of the 31st parallel but [125 Vol 20, p 167] Britain received Florida from Spain, all of Canada and all French territory east of the Mississippi, from France [125 Vol 20, p 167] [p 105].
However French-Canadians continued to have language and legal rights in their fur trading settlements along the Mississippi. This angered Americans.
-1781 **Spain** again took control of southern portions of **Florida**, **Alabama** and **Mississippi** [16, p 495] [map p 157].
-A new dialect called **Creole** was spoken by people born there [16, p 172, 445, 495], a combination of Spanish, French, English and African languages. The town of **New Orleans**, founded in 1718 thrived.
-1783 Independence from Britain after the American Revolution, more than doubled United States territory. Boundaries moved north to the Great Lakes, west to Mississippi River and south to the 31st parallel.
-1783 the **Northwest Territory** was formed, including the present **Ohio**, **Indiana**, **Illinois**, **Michigan**, **Wisconsin** and part of **Minnesota** [16, p 534]. 1798 the **Territory of Mississippi** was named [maps 128, 130].
-1795 the sugar cane industry began [125 Vol 12, p 497].
-**Plantations** growing sugar, cotton and tobacco prospered through the labor of slaves [Continued p 126].
-1800 In a secret treaty Spain ceded Louisiana to **Napoleon** (France)
-1803 the ***Louisiana Purchase*** from France again doubled the size of the USA [16, pp 445; 653; 95, pp 409-410].
[Continued pp 126-130]

Rival Hudson Bay and North-West Company Fur-Trader/Explorers [pp 70-75, 95-98]

-1670 **HBCo** with a charter from English King Charles II, hired **Radisson** as guide/translator/adviser [p 73].
-1674 after building Fort Nelson **Radisson** and **Groseilliers** defected to the French, but not trusted, soon left.
-1682 French **Campagne du Nord** rehired Radisson to challenge English fur trade at Hudson Bay by using inland rivers via the Great Lakes [119 Vol 5, p 183-6]. After establishing forts he returned to England to his wife.
-1684-87 Radisson with Groseilliers was reinstated by the HBCo until retirement in England [pp 70, 73, 74].
-1691 **Henry Kelsey** for the HBCo explored from the Hudson Bay up the Nelson River to **Lake Winnipeg**, up the **Saskatchewan River**, across the great plains and as far as the present **Alberta** [119 Vol 5, pp 189-190; Vol 1, p 98, 116].
-1713 after the **Treaty of Utrecht** [p 95], the French stopped sending ships into the Hudson Bay [119b, Vol 4, p 306] and instead used the inland canoe route pioneered 1629 by Jean **Nicolet** to the Great Lakes [Map p 70].
-1726-38 Pierre **de la Vérendrye** (1685-1749) traded fur on **Lake Nipigon** and **Lake Superior**. With three sons and a nephew he built a string of forts on the **Lake of the Woods** and **Rainy River** and numerous rivers west to the **Red River** [See maps pp 97, 108, 121 and 125]. 1738 at the junction of the Assiniboine and Red Rivers la Vérendrye built **Fort Rouge**, later named Fort Douglas, Fort Garry and **Winnipeg**. Here thousands of nomadic first nations people had camped seasonally for centuries. Continuing westward Vérendrye built forts up the **Assiniboine River** into the present **Saskatchewan** and south to the **Missouri River**, now North **Dakota**, the Sioux name for *allies*, claiming the Dakota area for France [16, p 181; 168, p 80; 137].
-Self-employed, he sent 30,000 beaver pelts to Montreal annually [12 Vol 7, p 77] [See details [119b, pp 95-97]].
-1743 two sons of Vérendrye traded as far as present-day **Nebraska**, **Wyoming** and **Montana** [16, p 792; 502; 826].
-**Fort Garry**, a large **Métis** settlement, grew up at the junction of the Assiniboine and Red Rivers [119 Vol 7, pp 53-56].. Catholic missionaries came to minister, **Grey Nuns** to educate them French language/culture [map 125].
-The **Métis** way of life was intermediate between Indian and European. Métis means *to mix*. [Continued pp 124-126 and 154-155, 160-162]. Spring and autumn they gathered for buffalo jumps from steep cliffs.
-Branches of the **Red River** rise in **Minnesota** and flow north 355 miles through **North Dakota** to Lake Winnipeg. Land along the Red River surveyed in narrow strips as in Quebec [16, p 620] is visible from satellites.
-Forts also in **North** & **South Dakota**, **Minnesota**, **Montana** and **Wyoming** were settled by retired French & Métis **Voyageurs** (guides employed by NWCo explorer-fur traders) plus wives, children & Catholic missions.
-The **North-West Company** (**NorWesters** or **NWCo**) [119 Vol 5, p 190; Vol 4, p 63], was loosely organized partnerships of fur trader/merchants from **England** & **Scotland** with headquarters in Montreal with hired **Voyageurs**.
-The **HBCo forbad intermarriage of fur traders with Indians**. There were some private alliances but the children were brought up either as Indians or as British [119 Vol 7, pp 53-56], but not as Métis (or half-breeds in USA).
-1754-5 **Anthony Henday** was sent by the **HBCo** to the southern part of the present province of Alberta, to establish a fur-trading relationship with the **Blackfoot Indians** [119 Vol 1, pp 98, 116]. They were expert horseback riders, buffalo hunters and fierce warriors [9 Vol 2, p 27; Vol 4, p 113], much feared by other tribes [maps 108, 117, 121].
-1754 Henday was the first white man to enter the present **Alberta**, and sight the Rocky Mountains.

-1763 **New England** fur traders, because of local decline in fur-bearing animals, when the **Seven Years' War** ended, went north **via Oswego** on Lake Ontario to **Montreal to join the NorWesters** to access their Great Lakes fur trade route. It was explored by **Jean Nicolet** in 1629 [see pp 70, 74] and much used since by the French. By canoe and portage via the Ottawa River, Lake Nippissing and Lake Huron, they crossed huge Lake Superior to **Grand Portage**, south of the present **Fort William**. They went farther west using a chain of forts built by French explorers, chiefly **la Vérendrye** and sons [see p 107].
-1764 **Simon McTavish** migrated from **Scotland** to **Albany** NY. He visited **Detroit** in 1772.
-1768 **Joseph Frobisher** and brothers Benjamin and Thomas sailed the Hudson Bay and went inland for fur.
-1773 Frobisher went up the **Churchill River** from Hudson Bay and traded fur on the **Saskatchewan River**.
-1774 Simon McTavish settled in Montreal, joined the **NorWesters**; made many summer trips by canoe, barge and sail to **Grand Portage** centre to do business & socialize with partners who wintered in the west [p 108].
-1779 Frobisher was a NWCo partner. By 1787 he and Simon McTavish [119b, p 303] had controlling interest.
-1798 McTavish retired in Montreal mansion *Beaver Hall,* gathering place for fur-traders. 1804 died wealthy.
-1770-2 **Samuel Hearne** of the **HBCo** explored what is now **northern Manitoba** and the **Coppermine** River, and reached the **Arctic Ocean**, an amazing accomplishment [119b Vol 4, p 72]. [map 121]
-1774 Samuel Hearne built **HBCo Cumberland House** on the Saskatchewan River [119 Vol 3, p 169] west of the present Manitoba border [See maps p 117 and 121]. In 1780 **Nor-Westers** built **another Cumberland House nearby**. The HBCo and NWCo were in hostile competition. HBCo staff had remained in their factories (forts) and waited for furs to be brought to them, but now there was a decline in furs, so to survive, HBCo began outreach wilderness work like NorWesters. On canoes and barges both went up and down all the major rivers in the northwest [119b Vol 2, pp 177-9, 226-8].
-The mighty **South** & **North Saskatchewan Rivers** rise in the Rocky Mountains [See maps p 117, 164]. Both have very high cliffs in some areas. One first flows south via Calgary, and the other east through Edmonton, 200-300 miles apart as they cross Alberta. In Saskatchewan the South Saskatchewan turns north and joins the North Saskatchewan before draining into Lake Winnipeg.
-The **Athabasca** and **Peace Rivers** rise in the Rockies, traverse northern Alberta and flow into Lake Athabasca. From there the **Mackenzie River** flows to the **Arctic Ocean**.

Map: *Early Explorations of the Western Plains and Wintering at Grand Portage* [119b, Vol 4, p 71] [see map 164]

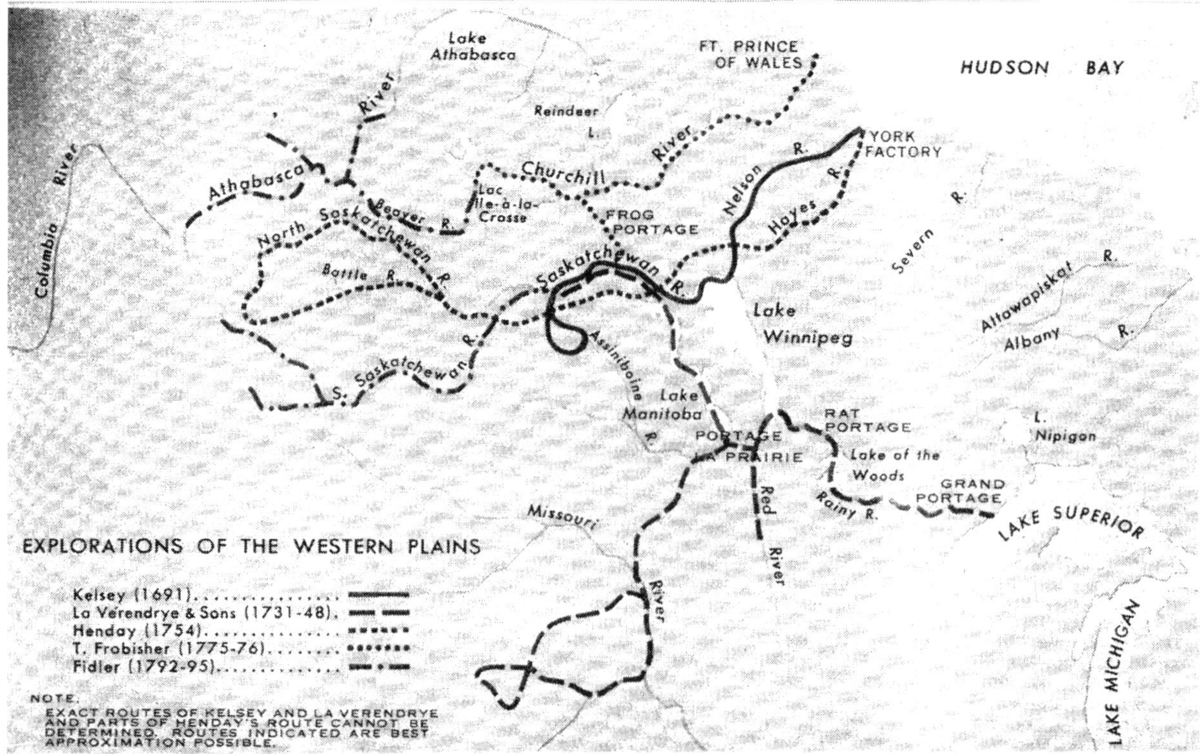

-1777-78 **Peter Pond** for the HBCo, established the first trading post on **Lake Athabasca**, now northern Saskatchewan & Alberta) canoeing a long route via portage **la Loche** [119 Vol 6, p 55; Vol 1, p 98, 116; Vol 9, p 206-14] [map 121].
-1778 Peter Pond started **Fort Chipewyan** [119 Vol 1, p 98; 12 Vol 6, p 119]. 1788 it became the NorWesters' **field headquarters**. Many forts/trading posts and Roman Catholic missions were built throughout north USA & Canadian *prairies* (1875 constituted Canadian NWT [119b Vol 1, p 116]; 1905 Saskatchewan and Alberta).
-1787-88 English **David Thompson**, with HBCo since 1784, wintered at the site of **Calgary** [119b Vol 10, p 71].
-1788 **Fort Vermilion** in the present **north**west Alberta, was built [map 117].
-1789-90 **Philip Tunor** a qualified English **surveyor** and **map-maker** was stationed at HBCo Cumberland House, where he taught his skills to **Peter Fidler** and **David Thompson** [119b Vol 10, p 161; 71].
-1789 **Alexander Mackenzie** a NWCo partner, from **Chipewyan**, descended the **Mackenzie River** to the Arctic Ocean [168, p 138-140]. He built forts to the **Arctic Ocean** [maps pp 117 and 121] and surprisingly:
-1792-3 went to the **Pacific Ocean** [see below]. It is amazing his travels included both the far north and the far west in an age of travel by canoes and barges [119 Vol 9, p 206-] [map 121].
-1790 **Fort Saskatchewan** was built east of the steep banks at Fort **Edmonton** on N. Saskatchewan River.
-1792-4 **Peter Fidler** for the HBCo, explored/mapped the Athabasca & North & South Saskatchewan Rivers.
-1792 Fort George and Buckingham House were built by the NWCo and HBCo (now Elk Point Alberta, near the present Saskatchewan border) [120, p 897]. Here the rival NWCo and HBCo cooperated at times.
-1794 Fort Augustus (**Edmonton**) 45 miles SW of Fort Saskatchewan, was built in the "flats" below the high banks of the North Saskatchewan River [Continued pp 166-168].
-1796 **David Thompson** surveyed a new route via Wollaston Lakes to Lake Athabasca. The next year he left the HBCo and entered the service of the NWCo, to combine his surveying skills with fur-trading.
-1797-98 **David Thompson** explored the **headwaters** of the **Mississippi River**, a journey of 4000 miles. Rocky Mountain House, north of Calgary was Thompson's main headquarters. [Continued pp 125-126]

Exploring and Mapping the Pacific Ocean [from pp 57-58, 60 and p 72]

-1579 **Sir Francis Drake** claimed the west coast of North America for English Queen Elizabeth l. A few **Spanish** explorers sailed by, but paid scant attention to the future Oregon and British Columbia.
-1592 **Juan de Fuca** discovered the large island that was later named for Captain Vancouver.
-1741 Danish **Vitus Bering** sailing for Russia, visited the coast of the present British Columbia [116, p 16]. His Lieutenant Alexksei Chirikov claimed **Alaska**; 1784 **Russia** started a colony on Kodiak Island [map p 97].
-1768-71 English Captain **James Cook** [p 105]commanded a **scientific expedition** in the islands of the South Seas. He circumnavigated/surveyed New Zealand and Botany Bay, east Australia [16, p 165; 9 Vol 7, pp 182-3].
-1772-75 James Cook was promoted to Commander. 1772-5 he returned to the Pacific, crossed the Antarctic Circle, mapped the southern hemisphere; on return was decorated Fellow of the Royal Society.
-1774 the Pacific coast of North America was entered on charts by **Spanish** explorer **Juan Pérez**.
-1775 Spanish **Bodego Quadra** reached Sitka, Alaska but did not land [119 Vol 2, p 84; 168, pp 136-140].
-1776-9 Captain **James Cook's** third scientific expedition, explored the **Antarctic**, and sailing northward:
- discovered Sandwich Islands (**Hawaii**); pioneered/proved chronometer to determine accurate longtitude.
- searched for a NW passage from Pacific to Atlantic, surveying/mapping from **Oregon** to **Bering Strait**,
- collected/catalogued flora and fauna from New Zealand, Australia, Hawaii, Bering Strait and Pacific Canada,
- traded otter skins with the Indians, which his crew sold the next year in China [119 Vol 2, p 84].

-1779 Due to ice in these Arctic waters, Cook turned back [9 Vol 7, pp 182-3]. Sadly, he was killed in **Hawaii**.
-1789-95 there was a **Spanish settlement** at **Nootka** started by **Martinez** [120, p 1789-95].
-1792 American **Robert Gray** discovered the mouth of the **Columbia River**; named it for his ship [9 Vol 7, p 24].
-1793 Sir **Alexander Mackenzie** a NWCo partner [see above 1789-93], starting from Lake Athabasca (in the present northern Alberta and Saskatchewan) took a very long and complicated route to the **Pacific Ocean:** He ascended the **Peace** and **Parsnip Rivers**, stopped to build **Fort St. John** in northeast British Columbia; crossed the divide to the **Fraser River**; went west up the **West Road River**, found a pass through the **Coast Mountains,** reached the **Pacific Ocean** near the present **Bella Coola** [9 Vol 4, p 372; 119 Vol 2, p 84]; narrowly missed seeing Captain Vancouver [maps pp 117, 121].
-1792-3 two separate expeditions, **George Vancouver** and a **Spanish** party mapped the coast [map p 117], met in Georgia Strait and cooperated;
-1795 **Spain withdrew claims** to the area, the future British Columbia [9 Vol 4, pp 371-3].
-1789-1795 the **French Revolution** was taking place [See p 116 below].

The Maritime Provinces (Atlantic Canada) Under British Rule [from p 96]

-1749 a military post opened at **Halifax**, Nova Scotia by **Governor Edward Cornwallis** with 2576 colonists.
-1750 Canada's first Anglican Church was built in Halifax. The population [119 Vol 5, pp 232-3] reached 6000.
-1752 the **Halifax Gazette**, the first newspaper in Canada began publishing [119b Vol 7, p 390].
-1752-4 each year for three years, 2500 **Hanover Germans**, **French Huguenots** and **Swiss** settled SW of Halifax at **Lunenburg**, sponsored by George II, king of both Britain and Hanover [120, pp 1668-9, 1672]. Worship was held in a tent in three languages, French, English and German. In 1752 they organized the first Lutheran Church in Canada. In 1755 their beautiful wooden Gothic style St George Church was built. Their minister was later re-ordained Anglican [119b Vol 6, pp 225-7]. The church was seriously damaged by arson Oct 31, 2001 and rebuilt.
- 1755 when the **Seven Years' War** began, though French **Acadians** attempted to remain neutral, the English, doubting their loyalty, deported them [9 Vol 1, pp 96-7; 12 Vol 1, p 51] to French Louisiana and colonies in the south. Their ordeal was described by Henry Wadsworth Longfellow in ***Evangeline***, an epic poem. Descendants are known as Cajuns (Canadians). Acadia their home was renamed **Nova Scotia** resettled by Loyalists from New England. 1754 **Robert Monkton** was Governor of Annapolis Royal [p 96] and 1756-61of Nova Scotia.
-1759 he was Brigadier-General under Wolfe in the capture of Quebec; 1761-3 was Governor of **New York.**
-1760-68 before the Loyalist influx, already 8000 **New Englanders** [120, pp 1668-9, 1672] had settled in what was later **New Brunswick**, between Maine and Nova Scotia. Rhode Island merchants built a trading post at the mouth of the St. John River. Baptists from Massachusetts established Maugerville.
-1761 Rev. Ebenezer **Moulton**, Baptist minister from Massachusetts visited Nova Scotia at **Horton**, now **Wolfville**. As a follow-up, Cornwallis Baptist Church was organized 1763 [119 Vol 1, pp 150-1].
-1763 a Baptist congregation from Massachusetts settled in Sackville. Yorkshire Methodists settled in Chignecto, Cumberland County (the neck of land between **Amherst**, New Brunswick, and nearby **Sackville**).
-1764 Acadian French were allowed to return in large numbers, not to their original land but north along the Restigouche River and Estuary [119 Vol 7, p 289]. They set up a fishery, stimulated by English merchants.
-1761 & 1762 on land grants obtained by Alexander McNutt, 500 **Irish** settlers from Donegal [119b Vol 10, p 151], came to **Truro** on the peninsula that became **Nova Scotia**. They grew flax and started a linen industry.
-1763 settlers from Massachusetts organized a Baptist church at Horton, now Wolfville [119b Vol 1, pp 315-9].
-1763 the Province of **Nova Scotia** was incorporated. It included the future **New Brunswick** [maps 121,180].
-1765 there were 80 families at Sackville. They were granted representation in the Assembly in **Halifax**.
-1767 settlers began to arrive in **Pictou County**, eastern Nova Scotia.
-1772-74 one thousand **Scots**, including 189 in highland kilts, settled Pictou.
-1776 Scots from Dumfries settled **Prince Edward Island** [119 Vol 5, pp 232-3].
-1774 English Yorkshire farmers came to **Chignecto** between Nova Scotia & New Brunswick [to p 116].

British Rule of North America after the Seven Years' War- 1763 [from pp 105-106]

-1760-1820 **George** III at 22 years of age succeeded his grandfather George II. Born in England, he never visited Hanover. When Parliament ministers were weak, he took the lead in selecting Prime Ministers. George was troubled by wars with France, American states and around the world. Because coffers were drained by war tariffs/taxes were placed on sugar, stamps, tea, etc., to boost British economy. Direct trade by colonies with other countries was not allowed [53b, pp 97-121].
-Dutch ships would have charged less. Americans resented having to channel trade through Britain [See below and pp 113-114 and 117].
-1762-4 **Benjamin Franklin** (1706-90) returned from his post as Agent in London 1757-62, wrote articles in the Philadelphia Gazette urging that both British and French rule in America be driven out.
-Franklin considered the French population of 65,000 small [126, Episodes 3 and 4], compared to nearly a million in the 14 colonies, which was more than the whole population of England.
-He counted Canada as the 14th colony and expected French colonists "to blend with our people in both language and manners." [Compare pp 90-91]
-1766-68 **William Pitt** (1708-78) was Prime Minister of England, a 2nd term [16, pp 579, 676] [see below re his son].
-1764-75 Benjamin Franklin a second time was Agent in London for Pennsylvania.
-1773 the **Boston Tea Party** was a protest against British taxation without representation. 342 chests of tea from the British East India Co. were thrown into Boston harbor [12 Vol 2, p 405; 9 Vol 4, p 252-3; 95, p 372].
- William Pitt in retirement, spoke in the House of Lords on behalf of American colonists who felt coerced and denied a voice [167, pp 112-115].

-1774 the **Quebec Act** confirmed French rights of religion, law, land and office [121, p 984], but Americans called it "an intolerable act [126, Episodes 3 and 4]." Quebec ruled **Wisconsin** and the **Ohio Valley** [125 Vol 21, p 366].
-1781 **William Pitt** the Younger was elected Member of Parliament**;** 1782 **Chancellor** of the **Exchequer**.
-1784 to 1806 **Pitt** was **Prime Minister** several terms, in very difficult times (American Revolution 1775-83 and French Revolution 1789-95) [see pp 113-116, 117]. Pitt was born 1759, died 1806.
-1788 and 1811-20 **George** IV, Prince of Wales, was appointed **Regent** during mental illnesses of **George** III.

Prussia, Russia and Austria Divided up Poland 1756 to 1772 [Continued from pp 75-80; 92-94]

-1740-86 Prussia became a great military power under **Frederick** II **the Great** [16, p 600]. He built elegant Potsdam. As absolute monarch, he had good administration and financial recovery, which *Enlightenment* Philosopher **Voltaire**, also not a democrat, admired[16, p 265] [p 90].
-Since 1742, **Silesia** was willingly under Prussian rule, but 1526-1742 had been under Austria. Austria had fought years but failed to take Silesia back
-1756-63 during the **Seven Years' War**, aided only by Britain, **Prussia** suffered the great loss of 853,000 troops [95, p 380], but in 1763 gained back Silesia in the Treaty of Paris.
-1772 **First Partition of Poland: Prussia** and **Russia** invaded and occupied much of Poland [53b, p 50].
-The western part of **Silesia** remained with Prussia, **Galicia** in the south went to **Austria**, and
-The eastern province of **Volhynia** (now northern Ukraine) went to **Russia**, but was permitted a fair amount of self-government under Empress **Catherine** II **the Great** 1762-96.
-Many Polish political, cultural and military **leaders fled to Paris**. Polish planning of a new constitution took place in Paris. Their ideas and literature drew from the *Enlightenment.* French became the polite language of Polish aristocrats. Soon the economy of Poland recovered; industry developed [28, p 15] [p 113].

Moravian Brethren Influence in Saxony, Silesia and Worldwide [from pp 99-103]

-1756-63 the **Seven Years' War** exhausted Moravian congregations in Silesia and Saxony. Troops from both sides several times came through and camped at Herrnhut, requiring vast amounts of food, fodder and caring ministry for up to 2000 troops at a time [57, pp 158-9]. [See p 105]. From the stress of conflict:
-1756 Zinzendorf's wife and son died. Advised by his colleagues, Zinzendorf married **Anna Nitschman**, an early refugee from Moravia [p 99]. She had served in Herrnhut, Georgia and Pennsylvania [pp 100 & 101].
-1760 Zinzendorf, 60 years old, died May 9 and his 2nd wife May 21. 4000 people came to the funeral. The church was thriving everywhere even without his influence in court circles. Experienced Bishops like Spangenberg, Leonard Dober, Peter Böhler, John de Watteville (Zinzendorf's son-in-law) and others were recalled to Europe and replaced by other capable bishops.
-The **"resusitated" Unitas Fratrum** was referred to as **The Unity**, but in England and overseas usually called the **Moravian Church**, while in Swiss, German, Polish and Baltic congregations and *Diasporas* (fellowships) were called **Brüder Gemine**, as now. There were 17,000 German diaspora adherents. These fellowships helped overcome ***Rationalism*** spreading among **Lutherans**.
-It was Moravian policy to a serve as "church within a church" refraining from "sheep stealing".
-1761 in **Rixdof near Berlin** a new Unity of Brethren church was built, mainly of refugees from Bohemia.
-1762 ***Settlements*** (**choirs** meaning **industrial residences**) thrived in Britain, Europe and overseas. But at their height of success Bishop Spangenberg closed them in America and sold the equipment to individual members, because they were no longer needed for protection of pioneers, as **frontier life was ending**.
-1764 at General Synod in **Marienborn** near the Rhine, 90 leaders were present, including seven from Britain. Four boards were appointed**:** 1). to write a Constitution, 2). Executive Board to function between general synods, 3). Board of Syndics to deal with government relations 4). Wardens' Board to handle finances.
-1769 at General Synod a permanent constitution was accepted. The governing board of the Unity was to exercise advisory rather than mandatory power over congregations. Individual congregations would cover their own expenses and the salary of their pastor. Teaching of the Catechism was to have priority.
-1769 General Synod decided to revise the Liturgy and *Daily Notes;* theological studies and missions would continue under the Missions Board; the Bible remained the only rule of faith and practice; both Apostles' and Nicene Creeds [12 Vol 7, p 310] were approved; the **role of Bishop** was not executive but to select and ordain ministers, and visit congregations periodically to guide and encourage them; appointed by General Synod.
-1772 the Jubilee of the founding of Herrnhut was celebrated.

-1762-1773 tired of living in a war zone, and hearing that **Catherine the Great** was inviting immigration to Russia [see p 112], some Moravian Brethren from Herrnhut, Saxony migrated via the **Volga River** in SE Russia and started a colony **near Saratov** which they named **Sarepta** [57, p 208] because the prophet Elijah resided with a widow during a famine in a place by that name (1 Kings 17:9 and Luke 4:26). This colony thrived for a hundred years [90, p 3]. Their mission was to evangelize people in Central Asia, but there were few contacts with Asian people [57, p 285]. [Continued pp 112, 136-138]
-1773 in Wetteravia, **Rhine River area**, some congregations still prospered, but the lease for Marienborn expired, and the new Count sold Herrnhaag land and buildings. Moravians scattered to America, Saxony, England and Russia.
-By 1792, 65 years after continuous prayer began [pp 99-100], 300 missionaries had been sent worldwide.
-The **Easter Sunrise Service litany** summarizes the main beliefs.
-Moravian ***Daily Notes*** begun 1723, for morning/evening family worship, still translated in many languages.
-Moravian *Chorale* singing and instrumental music influenced the public, up to the present day.
-*Love Feasts* with sweet buns and coffee became a tradition.

Russia During and After the Seven Years' War

[from pp 93 and 111; maps p 94]

-1741-61 **Empress Elizabeth**, Peter I's daughter, seized power from her cousin **Empress Anna**, assisted by the Imperial Guard. 1743 she gained a military and diplomatic victory against **Sweden**.
-1755 Elizabeth **established Moscow University** and in 1758 the **Academy of Fine Arts** at **St. Petersburg**.
-1756-63 in the **Seven Years' War** she maintained an alliance with **Austria** and **France** against **Prussia** and **Britain**. She groomed her nephew, grandson of Peter III, Duke of **Holstein**, as heir. In 1744 at 17 he married a 16 year old German cousin (French mother tongue [107]) second lady-in-waiting to Empress Elizabeth[102, pp 185-213], and was renamed Grand Duchess Catherine Alekseyevna. She endeared herself to the people becoming fluent in their language, adopting their culture, joining the Orthodox Church; friend of *Enlightenment* leaders.
-1761-62 **Czar Peter** III, chosen heir of the Russian throne, was immature, near alcoholic, and spoke no Russian, but admired Prussia the enemy. He freed the gentry from compulsory state service, nationalized monastery lands, and made peace with Prussia, ending the Seven Years' War (1756-63). He was murdered.
-1762-96 **Empress Catherine** II **the Great,** his widow, reduced huge foreign debt of the Seven Years' War. "Intellectually a child of the *Enlightenment*" she corresponded with **Voltaire**[77, pp 1012-5]; introduced small pox vaccination [53 b, p 34]; 1764 built the fabulous **Hermitage** and filled it with priceless art treasures.
-1763 she invited ethnic German farmers from the border of France and Germany to settle along the **Volga River** and north of the Black Sea, so as to keep out Turks, as well as to introduce diligent farming methods into Russia. They were granted the right to purchase land, have freedom of worship, and other incentives. Some founded 13 German villages around St. Petersburg; Hundreds of villages were established in SE Russia, the majority near the lower Volga[92; 93]. Though merely a village, **Saratov** soon became a large town. Roman Catholics and Lutherans gradually became the majority.
-This invitation by Catherine the Great was made 100 years before the mass migration of ethnic Germans to **Volhynia** (now northern Ukraine) not until 1863 [map 140].
-1763-68 a large number of people emigrated from **Hessen** and the **Rhinelands** to the Volga River territory. The Hessian village of Herrnhag emigrated *en bloc* [92, p 12] probably mainly Unity of Brethern (Brüder Gemine) people [57, pp 92, 93, 94, 119, 123, 125-127, 206, 389]. Many migrated through Lübeck to St. Petersburg where some remained, but most chose to travel by land, or by a water route down the **Volga River** to Saratov, or on the **Danube** in the south [maps 94, 137].
-Six **Unity of Brethren** men with wagons and 17 horses, dismantled the wagons to travel south by boat.
-1765-1773 they founded **Sarepta** on 8000 acres beside the **Saratov River**, and 1000 acres [57, pp 211-2] on the nearby island. They found watermills and irrigation were not possible, as river banks were treeless and steep. More families arrived and settlements were established on both sides of the mighty river [92, p 12] [See p 111].
-1730-83 Russia fought a series of wars winning control of **Ottoman** fortresses;
-1774 Russia acquired the treeless steppes along the **Black Sea**, and 1783 the **Crimea** [92;93;95, pp 387, 395].
-1774 **Cossacks from the Don River**, rebelled against authority, looting villages in SE Russia, including **Sarepta**. They were unorganized poor **Ukrainians** who for over a hundred years had refused serfdom and Polish and Russian domination [136, p 124] [See pp 79, 80 and maps pp 38 and 137].
-Amazingly, a Moravian Brethren Bishop and his wife traveled thousands of miles by horse-drawn carriage from **Herrnhut**, Saxony to **Sarepta** to bring relief and spiritual aid [57, pp 230-1].

Conditions Before the Second and Third Partitions of Poland

[Continued from p 111]

-1787 **Poles** and the **Teutonic Knights** joined to declare war on the **Ottoman Empire** which controlled Turkey, Constantinople, the Middle East, the **Balkans** in SE Europe, the **Baltic Sea port of Gdansk** (Danzig) and **North Sea port of Hamburg**. The Turks were driven out but with terrible slaughter. For the story of Julius Stockman's roots see *Roots and Branches* [40, Part 2, 8]. His German dialect contained Turkish words [69] and his ancestors may have fought the Turks; he married Adeline Schneider, the author's aunt.
-Large areas of land were left untenanted. The knights invited German Lutheran farmers to cultivate vacant land, granting the right to use their own language, customs and religion. Many Teutonic Knights and ethnic German noblemen were given titles to these lands, and had serfs.
-1783 a Lutheran church was founded at **Nowograd-Wolynsk (Volhynia** or **Wolinien)** [WV Vol 89, No 3, p 11].
-1791 a new liberal constitution had invigorated the Polish Sejm, so **Russia** invaded [See pp 132-140].
-1786-97 in Prussia **Frederick William** II succeeded his uncle Frederick the Great.
-1793 the **Second Partition of Poland** confirmed that Prussia would continue to rule **Silesia**, and gave eastern Poland to **Russia** and part of **Galicia** in the south to **Austria** [map 140].
-1795 the **Third Partition of Poland** Posen (**Poznan** in Polish) in NW Poland and Silesia in the SW were awarded to **Prussia**. Central Poland (Mittel Polska) went to **Russia,** while **Austria** received a larger portion of the south. **Poland ceased to exist as a nation.** However Russia allowed self-government [pp 132, 136-138].
-1797-1840 **Frederick William** III ruled Prussia [pp 132-134 and 136-140].

American Revolutionary War (War of Independence) 1775-1783

[from pp 91, 110-111]

- 1774 Sept-Oct after **Boston** port was closed [16, p 100], the **First Continental Congress** [16, p 165; 627-8] was held in **Philadelphia**. Representatives of 13 colonies, lacking representatives in the British Parliament, struggled for independence from a king and Parliament 3000 miles across the ocean. Apr 1775 war broke out.
-1775 May-Dec the **Second Continental Congress** appointed **George Washington** as the **Commander-in-Chief** (born 1732-died 1799). He was 11 when his father a Virginia Plantation owner died. He had 20,000 troops, all inexperienced. Congress controlled the interests/activities of the 13 colonies during the war.
-1776 June, **Thomas Jefferson** (1743-1826) was elected chairman of the committee to draw up the Declaration of Independence. He wrote the first draft [16, p 378] emphasizing free speech and education, and the ability of the common man to prosper under a representative, not highly centralized government [167, pp 114-117].
On the committee were **John Adams**, Harvard law graduate, **Benjamin Franklin** and **John Hancock**.
-For respite from war, top level military headquarters were located 40 miles north of Philadelphia in Moravian school/industrial buildings at **Bethlehem**. The British took New York.
-1776 July 4 th, the **Second Continental Congress** with representatives of 13 colonies in ongoing meetings, drew up and proclaimed the **Declaration of Independence**. It took until **August 9th** for all 13 independent states to win the approval of their state and sign individually [16, pp 182-3].
-1776-83 **Franklin** was in Europe as Envoy, actively seeking support and maintaining an intelligence service, to keep Commander-in-Chief Washington informed of political movements in Europe and Britain. Increased military and naval assistance from France gradually arrived.
-1776 Dec, the **Third Continental Congress** as the sovereign governing power, was held in **Baltimore**.
-A large minority of Americans remained loyal to Britain. In New York alone 15,000 volunteered for the British army and 8000 formed a Loyalist Militia. British loyalties were deeply felt. A line was drawn to separate Loyalists and Patriots. The choice was to fight or flee. Some who joined the British were **Jessup's Corps** and **the King's Royal Regiment of New York**. In the Niagara area **Butler's Rangers** were organized.
-The Army Hospital for wounded American soldiers was set up in the Moravian *Settlement* House in Bethlehem (now called the **Old Colonial Hall**). General John Sutter was buried in Bethlehem cemetery. Prisoners of the British were quartered there [167, pp 114-117]. 1776-8 fighting took place in nearby New Jersey.
-1777 September, the British took Philadelphia. The Continental Congress fled 60 miles west of Philadelphia to **York**. The Moravian *Settlement* at **Lititz** near York, was the Army Hospital. 10,000 US troops wintered near Philadelphia at **Valley Forge**, suffering food shortage, small pox and typhoid. Many died and many deserted.
-Many Indians were becoming corrupted by whites supplying alcohol and guns.
-Since Christian Indians were hospitable, their Moravian missionaries, **Zeisberger** and others, were suspected by both sides of being on the opposite side [pp 102; 104]. An atrocity, a massacre followed:
-1782 Colonel Williamson & US troops attacked Indian industrial **Gnadenhutten** [p 104] leaving 90 corpses.
-1769-1815 every Moravian Indian *Settlement* was abandoned as residents were killed & fled west [57, pp 318-323].

-1775-80 **Benedict Arnold** was a general in the Revolutionary Army in command of West point, NY.
-1775-83 about 80,000 **Loyalists** left the separating American colonies, including 3000 blacks fleeing slavery. The route taken by 66,000 migrants was the **Mohawk Trail** (from the Hudson River along the south shores of the Great Lakes). Some crossed to the north shore of the St. Lawrence River. Others went across to Canada at **Niagara**, and some farther west at Pontchartrain (**Detroit**).
-These Loyalists began the first English-speaking communities in **Upper Canada** (later called **Ontario**).
-Many settled in the **Eastern Townships**, **Quebec**, north of Vermont and New York State [12 Vol 2, p 786].
-Another 15,000 went to **Nova Scotia**, 12,000 of them on the northern side of the **Bay of Fundy**, and in:
-1784 succeeded in dividing from Nova Scotia to form **New Brunswick** province [Continued p 116].
-1778 **John Adams** went to **Holland** as **American envoy**, and in 1785-8 to **Britain** [9 Vol 1, pp 124-5; 16, p 10].
-1778 Britain offered full self-governance to the colonies. Benedict Arnold went to New Brunswick/London.
-1778 twelve modern **French ships** and munitions, and a **Prussian General** and troops, reinforced the American side. 8000 **German mercenaries from Hesse** were among the 30,000 British troops. Many difficult battles were fought throughout the colonies, including in the south [125 Vol 16, pp 274-8; 9 Vol 2, pp 74-64].
-1778-84 **Tadeusz Kościuszko** (1746-1817), a **Polish nobleman**, who believed in independence for Poland and for the US, was a volunteer soldier in the US, as an engineer with Colonel rank, at Saratoga and West Point. At the end of the American Revolution he was honored by Congress with the rank of Brigadier General. He returned to Poland 1784 where he planned and led the 1794 Polish Insurrection [See p 132].
-1779 **Spain** joined the war. Spain had long controlled the south and more than the west half of America.
-1780 while 6000 **French troops** were arriving in the US, **Britain** was kept distracted from supplying more troops for America by French military action at **Gibraltar** and other European ports, plus renewed action under Washington. Thus the English colonies in America were strong enough to win independence.
-1783 the **Treaty of Paris** negotiated by **Franklin**, **Adams** and **Jay**, officially ended the war. Britain gave up territory **east of the Mississippi** and **south of the Great Lakes** (now Michigan, Wisconsin and Illinois).
-Acting together, the 13 English colonies became the **United States of America** [125 Vol 21, p 366].
-It took 5 more years for 13 state assemblies to agree and sign the *Articles of Confederation* & the *Constitution*.
-1785-9 **Thomas Jefferson** was envoy in Paris negotiating commercial treaties, one of his many roles.
-1788 Federal Union was established. 1797 Federal Union elected **George Washington first President** and Jefferson Secretary of State [16, p 806, 627-8]. 1793 Jefferson retired due to his dislike of controversies in Congress.
- 1797-1801 **John Adams**, a Harvard trained lawyer, became President. [Continued pp 117-119, 126-130]

Early Settlement of Upper Canada by Loyalists and Pacifists [from pp 105-6 and 113-114]

-Since before the time of Champlain there were French fur-trading ports on the Great Lakes [See map p 70].
-1668-80 there were missions on the north shore of Lake Ontario established by Sulpician priests.
-1755 the British began to build large sailing ships [119b Vol 9, p 128] at **Oswego**, south shore of Lake Ontario, now New York State. Large ships were also built on Lakes Superior, Huron and Michigan.
-1754-63 during the **French and Indian War** (Seven Years' War) the British built forts [map p 104].
-1759 Fort Niagara, built 1678, was taken for the British by **William Johnson**[120, p 898]. He was the British Superintendent of Indian Affairs in New York region. He was knighted and made a Baron. His estate was in Mohawk Valley, south of Lake Ontario and the Saint Lawrence River.
-Baron William Johnson had two wives, **Catherine Weisenberg** and **Mohawk Molly Brant**.
-1774 Catherine's son **John Johnson** inherited the estate/title [119 Vol 5, pp 356-7]; was knighted 1765.
-1764 **Fort Erie** was founded at the entrance of the Niagara River [120, p 896].
-1775-83 the American Revolution (War of Independence) stimulated further building of forts.
-1774 Mohawk **Joseph Brant** (1742-1807) [see p 104] was secretary to **Guy Johnson**;
-1775 he was presented in the Court of King George III (1760-1820) [9 Vol 4, p 305]. Brant had the rank of Captain on the British side in the American Revolutionary War.
-His older sister **Mary** (**Molly**), wife of Sir William Johnson, influenced the Six Nations to maintain loyalty to the British [119b Vol 2, pp 51-52].
-1776 Second **Baron John Johnson**, a Loyalist, fled north to Canada with many of his tenants and **Scottish** neighbors and two battalions he commanded, of the **King's Royal Regiment of New York**, active in forays to defend Canada, near the end of the Revolutionary War (American Revolution)[119 Vol 5, pp 356-7; 414].
-1776 Many **Pennsylvania Dutch** (**Deutsch**, in German) **to avoid military service**, migrated to the **Niagara** area. Lacking government or surveyors, they squatted near walnut trees, indicating soil fertility [119 Vol 8, pp 143-4].

-1778 **Loyalists** settled at the western tip of Lake Ontario, later named **Dundas** and **Hamilton**;
-**Jessup's Corps** from around Albany, New York [119 Vol 1, p 96], settled on the **Bay of Quinte**, north shore of Lake Ontario (now Kingston to Trenton, Belleville, Deseronto and Picton) [119 Vol 1, p 96] [See pp 118-123]
-1780 settlement of the **Niagara Peninsula** by Loyalists began. The **Glengarry Highlander Regiment** had settled in the Mohawk Valley, New York. 1783 after the American Independence War [119 Vol 5, p 234] they moved north to develop **Glengary County**, Upper Canada.
-**Butler's Rangers** settled at **St. Catherines** in the Niagara peninsula[120, p 2063], named for Catharine, Robert Hamilton's first wife [119 Vol 9, p 144].
-1780 **Loyalists** and **apolitical Americans** began to settle around Pontchartrain (**Detroit**), the western tip of **Lake Erie**. La Salle had traded in the area in 1679, on St. Clare's Day arriving at the lake bordering on present Detroit, so named it St. Clair Lake [map p 74]. It is three feet higher than Lake Erie [119 Vol 9, p 144].
-1760 some **Palatinate Germans,** led by Irish-born **Barbara Heck** (1734-1804), with her German Bible, migrated from Ireland to New York, and planted the first Methodist Church in the new world, in New York. assisted by Captain Thomas Webb, Commander of British forces in Albany, NY (blinded in one eye on the Plains of Abraham, Quebec in 1750). Due to the War of Independence Barbara Heck and her family first moved to **Camden**, near **Lake Champlain**, but when burned out by revolutionary neighbors, fled to Montreal.
-About 1778 Barbara Heck and family went up the St. Lawrence River to the future **Elizabethtown**, still in the wilderness [124, pp 46-8], and began a Methodist church 1791, without even a circuit-riding preacher for another five years [119 Vol 7, p 51-3]. She was buried 1804 beside the ***Little Blue Church***, at nearby **Prescott,** named for General Robert Prescott [119 Vol 8, p 298-9]. [1810-12 Jessup's Corps settled here [pp 118-119; maps p 157, 180].
-1783 **Kingston** (formerly Fort Frontenac or Cataraqui 1673) up the St. Lawrence River, was re-founded by a first wave of **Loyalists** [119 Vol 8, p 23]. It was renamed in honor of King George III [119 Vol 5, p 414].
-Five boatloads of **Pennsylvania Dutch**, **Quakers** and French **Huguenots** [119 Vol 8, p 143-4] sailed up the Saint Lawrence to **Cornwall** [168, pp 109-111].
-1784 a **Lutheran** congregation was organized and 1788 the church built, at Morrisburg [119b Vol 6, p 227].
-1783 the **King's Royal Regiment of New York** disbanded: the First Battalion settled above **Lake St Francis** on the St. Lawrence River; the Second Battalion around **Kingston** and the **Bay of Quinte** [119 Vol 9, p 247; Vol 5, p 414].
-1783 **Sir John Johnson** was appointed Superintendent of Indian Affairs in British North America.
-1784 on the St. Lawrence River east of Lake Ontario, Loyalists founded **Elizabethtown** [1812 **Brockville**].
-1754-63 Mohawk **Joseph Brant** aided the British in the French and Indian War.
-1784 the **Six Nations** led by Chief Joseph Brant, loyal to the British, migrated from New York area and received land along the **Grand River** west of Lake Ontario, north of Lake Erie [119 Vol 8, p 48; 210c; 119b Vol 2, pp 51-52].
-1785 **Joseph Brant**, in England a second time [first in 1775, see above] collected funds to build the first Anglican church in Upper Canada, the Mohawk Chapel at the Six Nations Indian Reserve, on the Grand River, completed the same year. He joined the Church of England and translated *Book of Common Prayer* and parts of the New Testament into Mohawk.
-1775-83 he fought in American War of Independence. **Brantford,** founded in 1830 was named in his honor.
-1786 a young priest Father Alexander **Macdonnell**, brought in 500 Roman Catholic Scottish Highlanders.
-1789 Post Offices were opened: Cornwall, Augusta, Kingston, Niagara [119 Vol 8, pp 273] and by 1800 eight more.
-***United Empire Loyalists*** genealogical societies still meet across Canada. Many Loyalists later went far west.
-1791 the **Canada Act** divided Quebec into **Upper** and **Lower Canada**, later Ontario and Quebec, roughly dividing by the Ottawa River. Both had elected Assemblies [119 Vol 8, p 48; 119 Vol 5, pp 414-6].
-Upper Canada Legislature first met at **Newark** (later called **Niagara-on-the-Lake**) [168, p 116].
-**Lower Canada** included: New France colonists, Eastern Townships Loyalists and powerful English and Scottish fur merchants. Some had migrated from New England to Montreal [see p 108].
-1792-96 **Col. John Graves Simcoe** (1752-1806), had commanded the **Queen's Rangers** in the American Revolution, and became the first Lieut Governor of Upper Canada [119b Vol 8, p 312; 168, pp 124-125].
- Simcoe set up counties with **Municipal Councils,** rather than **Town Meetings** as in New England.
-In response to Simcoe's advertisements in the Philadelphia newspaper well-to-do Pennsylvania Dutch migrated to Canada with livestock and equipment [119 Vol 8, p 144].
-Simcoe set up English civil law, trial by jury; 1793 declared slavery illegal; granted land to loyalists hoping for rapid economic growth; started university prep schools (high schools); endowed the Church of England.
-1793 **Jacob Mountain** was consecrated Anglican Bishop of Quebec, including Upper Canada [119b Vol 1, p 162].
-1793 a part of the Six Nations (Mohawks) settled on the **Bay of Quinte** [119b Vol 9, p 320]. [See above].

-1793 Lieut Gov. Simcoe established **naval base** Penetanguishene, Georgian Bay, Lake Huron [119 Vol 8, pp 141-2].
-1796 Simcoe moved the Upper Canada legislature to **York** (later renamed **Toronto**). He started a road system for military reasons, notably Dundas Street from London to Toronto, and Yonge Street (named for Sir George Yonge) 33 miles from Toronto to Lake Simcoe (named for his father) [119b Vol 10, p 392, 395; Vol 9, p 38; 120, p 2166].

Atlantic Canada and American Revolution (War of Independence) 1775-83 [p 110;113]

-During the American Revolution politicians in **Maine** tried repeatedly to take over the **St. John River Valley** for the US, but were resisted by inhabitants [119 Vol 7, p 289; Vol 1, pp 150-1] and,
-1760-63 British sea power defeated Americans in the **Bay of Fundy**. At that time 4500 New Englanders came to live in Atlantic Canada. Cornwallis Baptist Church was built [119 Vol 1, pp 150-1; Vol 7, p 407-9].
-1778 a Baptist Church was built at Horton, the future Wolfville, NS, by Loyalists [see p 120].
-1781 **William Black** traveled the Maritimes (Atlantic provinces) organizing Methodist churches [119 Vol 7, pp 51-2].
-**Thomas Carleton** arranged emigration of people loyal to the British, in New York and New England.
-1783 **Charles Inglis** (1734-1815) loyalist rector of Trinity Church New York city, came to Halifax.
-1783 **Loyalists**, including many **black** escaped slaves, settled near Halifax, some with white Loyalists, and others on their own by ***Underground Railway*** [120, p 1672]. This migration increased in the US Civil War 1861-65.
-1783 returned from exile, 2000 **Francophone Acadians** returned from exile in southern states and settled in northern New Brunswick where earlier 2000 had found refuge [pp 104 and 110].
-1783 about 12,000 **Loyalists** [119 Vol 7, p 289] arrived in the Bay of Fundy, and moved north up the St. John River and its tributaries and east to Petitcodiac Valley [168, p 111]. Some Loyalists came as refugees because they were pacifists who refused to bear arms. Others had been soldiers who fought on the British side.
-1783 & 1784 disbanded soldiers from the **Hamilton** and **Royal Highland regiments** came to Nova Scotia.
-1784 the Province of **New Brunswick** (NB) was established because the Loyalists newcomers living along the St. John River felt Halifax, the capital of Nova Scotia was too far away for effective government [53b, pp 104-5]. Thomas Carleton was the **first Lieut Governor**, and **Fredericton** capital of New Brunswick. The British government gave compensation for property losses in the US. Commerce with New England fell off [119 Vol 7, p 291]; earlier inhabitants of St. John felt pushed out of their privileged trading rights. To try to create harmony:
-1785 a Royal Charter united the two communities of Loyalists as **St. John**, NB, Canada's first city [145, p 11].
-1785-7 the University of New Brunswick had its origin in an Academy of Arts established at **Fredericton**.
-Ship-building, lumbering and fishing industries developed rapidly [119 Vol 5, pp 232-3]. Fish were traded for sugar, rum and molasses from the **West Indies**.
-1787 **Charles Inglis** became Anglican Bishop of Nova Scotia, the first bishop consecrated to work outside the British Isles. Twenty churches were built during his term of service [12 Vol 2, p 787].
-1788 the Anglican **King's College**, was founded at Windsor, Nova Scotia [119 Vol 1, p 163]. Students and faculty were forbidden to worship in Roman Catholic, Presbyterian, Baptist or Methodist meetings [119 Vol 10, pp 195-7].

[Continued p 120]

The French Revolution 1789-1795 [167,p118-222]

-1789 in Paris a National Assembly was called for the first time since 1614. The tricolor flag was adopted and talk of a republic began. Assembly abolished all class privileges and began to prepare a new **constitution**.
-1789 July 14, a mob destroyed the **Bastille Prison** Fortress [16, pp 78, 268]. There were uprisings all over France. Noblemen began to flee to England and other countries. 1791 **King Louis** XV1 escaped but was captured.
-1792 March, **France** declared war on **Austria** and **Prussia** and intervened to help **Austria**, but was defeated.
-1793 Jan 21 a **Republic** was established led by extremist lawyers **Danton** and **Robespiere** and physician-philosopher **Marat**. Emperor **Louis** XV1 **was guillotined** (beheaded). His Austrian born wife **Marie Antoinette**, daughter of the Holy Roman Emperor and Empress, also was guillotined [16, p 467].
-Men and women were addressed as Citizen rather than as Monsieur or Madame. God was given the new name of Supreme Being. Fashion in clothing was simplified. Roman Catholicism was banned in France.
-All treaties with foreign countries were repudiated, and the intention of France to overthrow all hereditary rulers in Europe was declared and begun. **Holland** was invaded and **Britain** threatened.
-1793 the **reign of terror** began, dominated by Robespiere. About 17,000 aristocrats and politicians were imprisoned and guillotined. Then the leaders guillotined each other [16, pp 268, 635; 111, p 258].
-1794 July 28 Robespiere was the last guillotined. The reign of terror ended. Food shortages were severe.
-1795 in October, stability was established, and the Revolution ended [16, p 268]. [See more details p 131]

Chapter Eighteen - 1795 to 1849

Pushing Back Frontiers in the USA and Canada

Overview of the United States, Canada, Great Britain and France

-There were two Canadian routes to the western prairies. The shorter less expensive route via the Hudson Bay was used by the English **Hudson Bay Company** (HBCo.) They waited at **factories** (large forts or trading posts) <u>for Indians to bring furs to them</u>.

-<u>The much longer route</u> of the **North West Co** (NWCo or NorWesters) was up the **Ottawa** and **Mattawa** Rivers, **Lake Nippissing** and a series of rivers/portages to **Lakes Huron** and **Superior** [119b Vol 6, pp 411-2], and via the **Rainy River** and **Lake of the Woods** to the **Red River** [map pp 70, 121].

-Swift **war canoes** [119b Vol 2, pp 210-1; 226-7] were used and, for heavy loads the **voyageurs** (French or Métis guides) built 30 foot long, <u>narrow flat-bottomed</u> **batteau** with sails [119b Vol 1, p 338] and larger **Durham boats** [119b Vol 3, pp 324-5].

-NWCo explorer-traders eagerly surveyed every part of the west, opening forts. Both NWCo fur-trader partners who wintered in the west, & Montreal merchants/suppliers became wealthy.

-The **HBCo began to open factories inland** <u>to be able to compete with the</u> **NWCo**. At York Factory on Hudson Bay [119b Vol 10, p 393] the HBCo built **York boats:** <u>flat-bottomed</u>, <u>pointed at both ends</u>, with sails, 4 or more pairs of huge oars and crews of 8 to 15. Boats were rolled or dragged on logs on portages. Via Lake Winnipeg (larger than Lake Ontario) they carried <u>supplies and household goods for settlers</u>, and for new factories up **North** and **South Saskatchewan Rivers** to the **Rocky Mountains** and on the **Athabasca** and **Mackenzie Rivers** to the **Arctic Ocean**. HBCo opened trading posts on the **Columbia river** west of the Rockies.

-1754-1763 <u>American exploration/migration in the west slowed due to</u> the French and Indian War, Seven Years' War (1756-1763) [pp 103-5], War of Independence (1775-83) and War of 1812 (to 1815) [p 119].

-1762-1800 **Spain** controlled land west of the Mississippi River [16, p 444] [See pp 118 and 126; map 128].

-1783 after the **American Revolution** (War of Independence) **French voyageurs** no longer had access to the Mississippi and Ohio Rivers, so spread NW for furs [125 Vol 3, pp 144-5].

- 1791 in British North America, <u>two provinces</u> were established**: Upper** and **Lower Canada**, later called **Ontario** and **Quebec**, roughly divided by the Ottawa river. Lower Canada, formerly called New France, had a powerful **Scottish/English minority** of <u>merchants</u> in **Montreal** and <u>Loyalists</u> in the Eastern Townships.

Map: ***Fur Trade After 1760*** [121 Vol 2, p 707] with provinces as today. See old borders: maps pp 174 and 163.

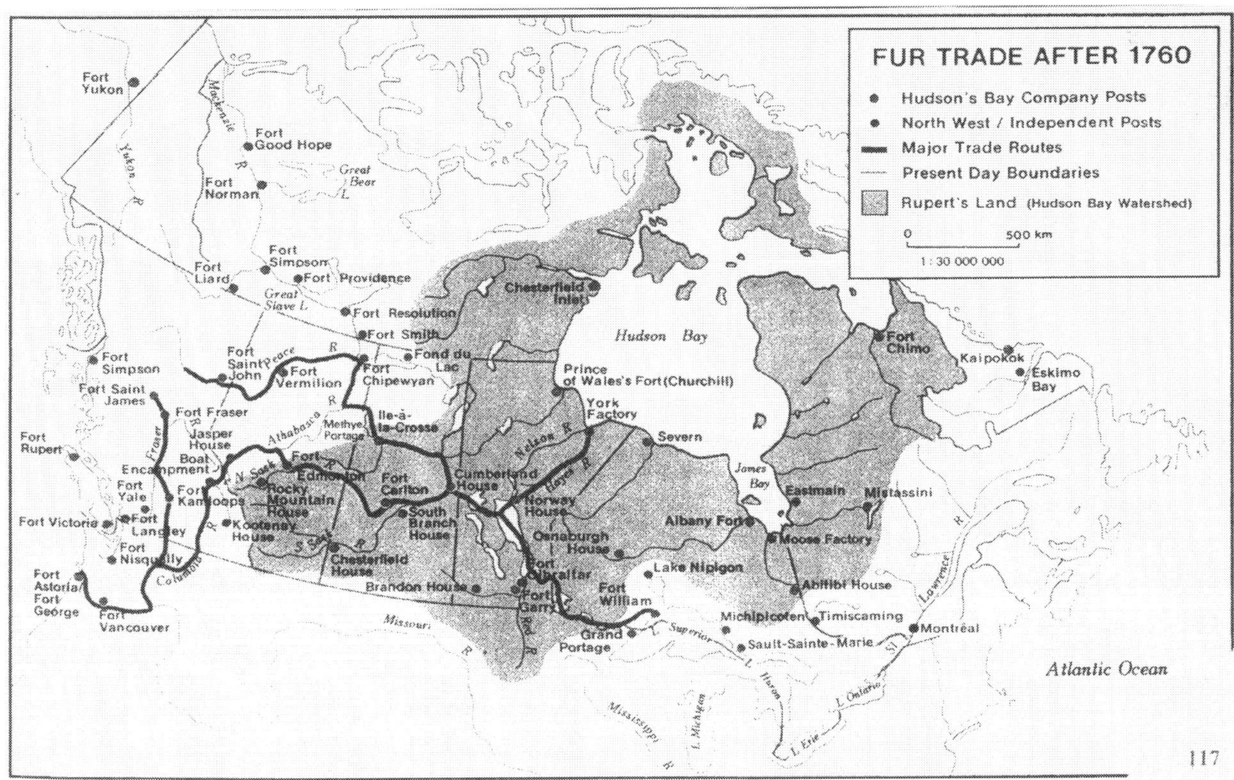

Turmoil in Britain, America, France and Europe

[continued from p 116]

-1781 **William Pitt the Younger** (1759-1806) was elected member of Parliament in London;
-1784-1806 he was **Prime Minister** for several terms **during the French Revolution** 1789-95 and the **Napoleonic Wars** 1799-1814. When the English feared a possible invasion by Napoleon, Pitt stimulated English strength[16, p 579]. Pitt's government reorganized the **East India Company** and improved Customs laws.
-1801 Great Britain and Ireland became the **United Kingdom**, and **Hanover** a separate self-governed nation.
-1776 July 4 representatives of 13 states proclaimed the Declaration of Independence; Aug 9 th each signed.
-1760-1820 **George** III's reign was burdened with balance of power struggles, alliances, blockades, banking crises, and diplomacy to maintain supremacy at sea, during the American Revolution (1775-83), French Revolution and wars of Napoleon [pp 131-135].
-1788 and 1811-20 **George** IV, Prince of Wales, was appointed **Regent** during mental illnesses of George III.
-1788-1868 about 162,000 convicts of political and petty crimes were exiled to **Australia**.
-1788-97 **George Washington** was elected first President of the USA, in a Federal Congress in Philadelphia. It took until1788-90 for the first 13 states to sign the constitution. The 14 th, Vermont signed in 1791.
-1789 the **French Revolution** guillotined many[53b, pp 135-160]. Napoleon Bonaparte was a 20 year old student.
-1792 the **French Republic** was declared. Idealized government turned into terror.
-1794-96 **James Monroe** was American Minister in France, London and Madrid[16, p 502].
-1796-97 **Napoleon Bonaparte** commanded the **Italian Campaign** and 1798-99 the **Egyptian Campaign**.
-1799 in a coup **Napoleon declared himself First Consul** (Master) of France, under his **new constitution** which gave him autocratic power. [Continued p 132].
-1762-1800 **Louisiana** was under **Spain**, but in 1800 was recovered by **Napoleon** in a secret deal[16, p 445].
-1797-1801 **John Adams** a Harvard trained lawyer was President; 1801-9 **Thomas Jefferson** was President.
-1803 **James Monroe** in Paris arranged the **purchase of Louisiana**, which included the entire watershed of the Mississippi River plus the vast region west to the Rockies[16, p 445]. 1809-17 **James Madison** was President.
-In the 1790's **Methodists** and **Quakers** pressured Parliament in England to abolish **slave trade**[110, p 119].
-1804-6 **US Army Officers Lewis and Clark** [pp 127-8] crossed the Dakotas, Rocky Mountains and reached the Pacific Ocean via the **Columbia** River. Meanwhile NorWesters traded furs/explored all over the NW.
-1807 **Britain abolished slavery** and began to use the British Navy to shut down slave trade. In 1808 import of slaves into the US was shut off, but not internal slavery; and
-1815 **Slavery** was banned in most of Europe.
-1807 British imports of ships and lumber from Quebec and Nova Scotia rose dramatically as lumber from the Baltic (Scandinavian) was cut off by Napoleon and later by Russia[120, p 2153; 119b Vol 9, p 298; Vol 7, p 291].
- **Canadian** manufacturing of ships for local needs and export prospered[125 Vol 14, p 539].
-1818-1844 Charles XIV (Jean Baptiste Jules Bernadotte, French Marshall married to a relative of Napoleon) was chosen **King of Sweden** and **Norway**[16, pp 87, 141, 534, 665, 735], founding the present **Swedish royal family**.
-1817-25 **James Monroe** was USA President[16, p 502]. 1823 the **Monroe Doctrine** asserted that the US would regard as an unfriendly act any effort of a European government to extend influence in the western hemisphere, or any other country recognized as independent: a lasting principle of US foreign policy.
-1820-1830 **George** IV who had been Regent 1788 and 1811-20, became the **King of Great Britain**, **Ireland** and **Dominions Beyond the Seas** and **Emperor of India**. Next 1830-37 **William** IV [continued p 135].
-1837 Hanover separated from Great Britain with Ernest Augustus, Duke of Cumberland as King.
-1837-1901 **Queen Victoria** [pp 141-142, 164 and 174]. Canada was the foremost ship-building nation:
-1843 Liverpool registered 136 Canadian ships. Many people emigrated from **Sweden**[119b Vol 9, p 442] and by
-1900 over 600,000 **Norwegians** emigrated due to economic recession[125 Vol 14, p 539; 119b Vol 7, pp 384-6].

Migration to Upper Canada Due to the American Revolution

[from pp 114-116]

-1780-1814 Loyalists and refugees from Pennsylvania and New York wanting to escape war began to settle mainly in five areas: the **Niagara** peninsula, the **Detroit** region, Bay of Quinte (north shore of the St. Lawrence River and Lake Ontario), the **Eastern Townships** of Quebec and **Atlantic provinces** near Maine.
-1784 veterans of American Revolution (War of Independence) migrated in large numbers; 1792 to **Dundas.**
-1787 Britain bought 1/3 of present York County from three Mississauga Chiefs, Iroquois allies[119b Vol 10, p 96-]
-1786 a young priest Father Alexander Macdonnell, brought 500 Roman Catholic **Scottish Highlanders**.
-1794 to fight the French he organized the Glengarry Fencible Regiment, the first Roman Catholic force.
-1802 they disbanded; Macdonnell became Bishop of **Kingston**. 1803 another 1000 Highlanders arrived.

-1796 the **Jay Treaty** clarified **US and British borders**. Detroit and a large area between Lakes Huron and Michigan went to the US [16, p 378 and 489]. Then the British built **Fort Malden** (**Amherstburg**) across from Detroit.
-**Fort Michilimackinac** [120, p 898] the north end of **Lake Michigan** was ceded to the US [pp 70, 96; map p 121].
-1799 the elegant yacht *Toronto* was built for Lieut Governor Simcoe for use on Lake Ontario [119b Vol 9, p 132b].
-1800 **Philemon Wright** a Massachusetts farmer began a thriving lumber business on the Ottawa River.
-1800 Waterloo county was settled by **Swiss Mennonites from Pennsylvania**. Their farming skill and vocal and instrumental music were admired [119 Vol 10, p 271]. They were pacifists escaping participation in war.
-1800 at Newmarket 40 **Quaker** families settled [119b Vol 7, p 324].
-1803 **Thomas Talbot** received 5000 acres on **Lake Erie** for settlements. Settlers had to help build roads and community facilities prior to receiving land titles.
-1804 **Lord Selkirk** settled 111 **Highlanders** at **Lake St. Clair** between Lakes Erie and Huron [119 Vol 5, p 234].

The Indian Confederacy, War of 1812 and Growing Canadian Defense

-1794-1805 to keep white men from advancing west **Chief Tecumseh**, (born 1768 and died 1813) organized and mobilized an **Indian Confederacy**, from the Great Lakes to Mexico to resist invasion of the midwest.
-1808 he and his brother established an Indian village in **Indiana**. He was greatly respected.
-1811 the village was seized by the US; 1812 he went to Canada and joined Brock for recapture of **Detroit**.
-1812 the US declared war against Great Britain and Upper Canada, choosing a time when Britain was distracted in danger of invasion by Napoleon.
- 575,000 US troops engaged in the war [16, p 804-5]. The total population of Upper Canada was 77,000 [119 Vol 8, pp 48-49].

The Purposes of Invasion of Canada:

1. to gain rights on the high seas for trade and commerce.
2. to take over Canada hoping it would become the 14 th state.
3. to take over west Florida.

-1812 on July 12 US forces commanded by General **William Hull** crossed into Canada from **Detroit**, west end of Lake Erie, mistakenly assuming that settlers from the US would welcome and support them. Within a few days though greatly outnumbered, they were driven back by Major General Sir **Isaac Brock**, in command of the British garrison in Upper Canada, assisted by Loyalist settlers and **Chief Tecumseh** [168, p 130-131].
-Aug 16 in a bloodless recapture of **Detroit**, Hull was compelled to surrender [9 Vol 4, p 390; 119 Vol 10, pp 263-257].
-1812 July 17, US invaders were repulsed from Fort **Michelimackinac** (at north Lakes Michigan and Huron).
-1812 Oct 13 at the battle for **Queenston Heights** and **Lundy's Lane** [16, p 447] on the **Niagara River** east of Lake Erie [map p 121] almost 1000 Americans were killed, but only 28 Canadians & 77 wounded. **Brock** was mortally wounded. His second and third in-command defeated the US army [168, pp 132-3].
-Brock was knighted by King George III; Elizabethtown was renamed **Brockville**. Canadian sense of national unity and courage rose to resist their large southern neighbor [120, pp 1958, 2475-8].
-1812 at **Kingston** (Ft. Frontenac) chief naval base for Upper Canada [119 Vol 5, pp 414-6], large ships were built for use on either the Great lakes or the Atlantic..
-Four-horse stage coaches traveled on a 6 days per week schedule, Quebec to Toronto [119b Vol 9, p 36].
-There were some US raids at **Lake St. Clair**, between Lakes Huron and Erie, and also in the Niagara area between Lakes Ontario and Erie. [For maps and details see [119b Vol 7, p 70-72]]
-1813 **Chief Tecumseh** lost his life in the **Thames River battle**, at Fort Meigs on St. Clair Lake, across the river from **Detroit**, near the present **Windsor** [16, p 745; 119 Vol 10, p 30]. A suburb is named for him [168, p 130-131].
-1813 January, US General Harrison invaded **Detroit**, 70 wounded British soldiers were hospitalized near London in the **Moravian Church** at nearby Fairfield (founded 1792).
-**President Jefferson** had boasted that "to take Canada was a mere matter of marching." Two US armies were destroyed; a third army from Kentucky, was defeated Jan 1813.
-1813 October, in the **Battle of the Thames** the US burnt down the Moravian industrial S*ettlement*. Two heart-broken missionaries found their way back to Bethlehem, Pennsylvania. Another hid in the woods with scattered believers until 1815, not knowing the war was over. Then 120 Christian Indians built houses on the opposite bank of the Thames River [57, pp 321-2; 119b Vol 7, pp 158-9].
-Meanwhile in **Labrador** under English Moravian leadership, a mission was established and all became literate in their own language. Several clusters of believers continue today [147 Vol 4 # 48, pp 1142-7].
-The US burned **Newark** (**Niagara-on-the-Lake**). The Canadians retaliated against **Buffalo** [120, pp 2475-8], where the Niagara River exits Lake Erie. US overland forays failed. Kentucky Troops rushed home to harvest crops.

1813 the US planned to take Kingston, but diverted to **York** (later **Toronto**), burned down public buildings. Canadians burned a large new ship so it would not be used against them [168, p 134-136].
-1813-4 7000 US troops set out to attack **Montreal** but divided at **Long Sault Rapids** and at **Crysler's farm** were driven back [119 Vol 2, p 321; Vol 3, p 167]. Reinforcements were repulsed at **Chateauguay** by **Col de Salaberry**.
-1814 US naval forces and privateers defeated British ships: **Commodore Perry** in the **Battle of Lake Erie**.
-1814 US naval force defeated the British on **Lake Champlain** in the **Battle of Plattsburgh**[map pp 70, 104]
-1814 May, Canadians took back **Oswego**, south shore of Lake Ontario [119b Vol 10, p 263-7]. Since York was burned:
-1814 Canadian troops burned the **Library of Congress, Washington** [125 Vol 20, pp 164-5; 168, p 134] were halted at **Baltimore**. There, imprisoned on a British ship, **Francis Scott Key** wrote the ***Star Spangled Banner*** [16, p 716].
-1814 HMS St. Lawrence was built at Kingston, with a displacement of 2304 tons, 112 guns and 1000 men. British control of Lake Ontario was established [119b Vol 9, p 132c]. Many medium-sized ships also were built.
-1814 Sept in **Nova Scotia** Lieut. Governor Sir John **Sherbrooke** led a force from Halifax and took **Maine**.
-American finances were strained. Being against continuing the war, **New England** was threatening to secede from the United States [16, pp 321; 805] and join Canada. Both sides felt the war was getting nowhere.
-1814 Dec 14 the **Treaty of Ghent** officially ended the war. **Maine** and **Oswego**, the south shore of Lake Ontario, were returned to the US. It took time to notify British forces in the **Gulf of Mexico** [map p 128]. Not knowing the war was over, in 1815 the **Battle of New Orleans** the British lost 700 men, and withdrew.
June 15 **Napoleon** defeated at the Battle of Waterloo, British reinforcements available too late in America.

Atlantic Canada (Maritime Provinces) 1795-1849 [Continued from pp 96-97 and 110, 116]

-1788 **King's College** was founded by Church of England in Windsor Nova Scotia. Faculty & students were forbidden to worship in RC, Presbyterian, Baptist or Methodist churches [119b Vol 10, p 195-7]. 1818 moved to Halifax.
-1818 **Dalhousie College**, later University, was founded based on the University of Edinburgh's principles of religious toleration, in Halifax by Lord Dalhousie Lieut Governor of NS 1816-19, Governor of Canada 1820-28. Controversies over government support delayed opening until 1838; closed 1845-9, reopened with Presbyterian assistance and later endowed by New York philanthropists [119b Vol 3, p 195-6].
-1800 nine **Baptist** congregations in New Brunswick NB and Nova Scotia NS [119b Vol 1, p 315-9] formed the NS Baptist Association. Weekly journals were published. Dissenters from Britain and Baptist Loyalists from New England, had differing theology, but 1846 joined in the **United Baptist Convention** of NS, NB and PEI.
-1828 **Horton Academy** at Wolfville NS with 50 students, was founded mainly by Baptists, without restrict-ions of creed. **Dalhousie** & **King's** forbad hiring of Baptist professors or granting degrees to Baptist students.
-1839 **Acadia University** was establish by highly qualified Baptist Scholars with approval of the NS legisla-ture. In 1843 graduates received degrees [119b Vol 1, p 41-42; Vol 10, p 195-7].
-There was an **intellectual awakening:** literature/libraries/newspapers/periodicals flourished [119b Vol 7, p 408].
-1840 in Saint John NB, 30,000 **Irish** arrived due to the potato famine in Ireland.
-The **Salvation Army** began three Corps.
-1848 responsible government began in Nova Scotia, the first in the British colonies [119b Vol 9, p 390] [p 155]

Establishing Canadian Nationhood After the War of 1812 (Actually 1812-1815)

-1815 **morale in Upper Canada rose**. The settlers gave their civilian soldiers credit for driving back the US and holding their own. 2000 **US army veterans** settled in Upper Canada [119 Vol 8, p 164-5]. There was a new sense of community and nationhood. Statues of **Sir Isaac Brock** were sculpted, and a university named for him.
-Morale in the US also rose because independence had been affirmed for the second time. At last people felt free both to expand west to the **Great Plains** and **Rocky Mountains,** and to emphasize industrial growth.
-The War of 1812 made it urgent for Canada to have a larger population. Policies to encourage immigration were adopted; government and British philanthropists sponsored groups of emigrants. Proactive surveying and preparing of selected townships, roads, towns, school and church sites prior to emigration, helped make pioneer life less hazardous and lonely than on the American frontier [119 Vol 8, p 210d-g]. Settlers themselves helped build roads and amenities. Additional assistance was provided for distressed people, such as weavers from Scotland and northern England; schools, grist mills and markets were provided.
- Great Lakes Forts doubled as supply centres for both **fur-traders** and **farmers.** Tools, seeds, initial necessities and food were provided free where required. After the heavy forests were cleared, crops and orchards were abundant.
-1807 there was a grammar school in 8 districts. In 1816 common schools were established [125 Vol 14, p 769].

Map: *Routes of the Explorers* [150, pp 24-25] – Provincial Boundaries as today [compare maps pp 128, 163, 174]

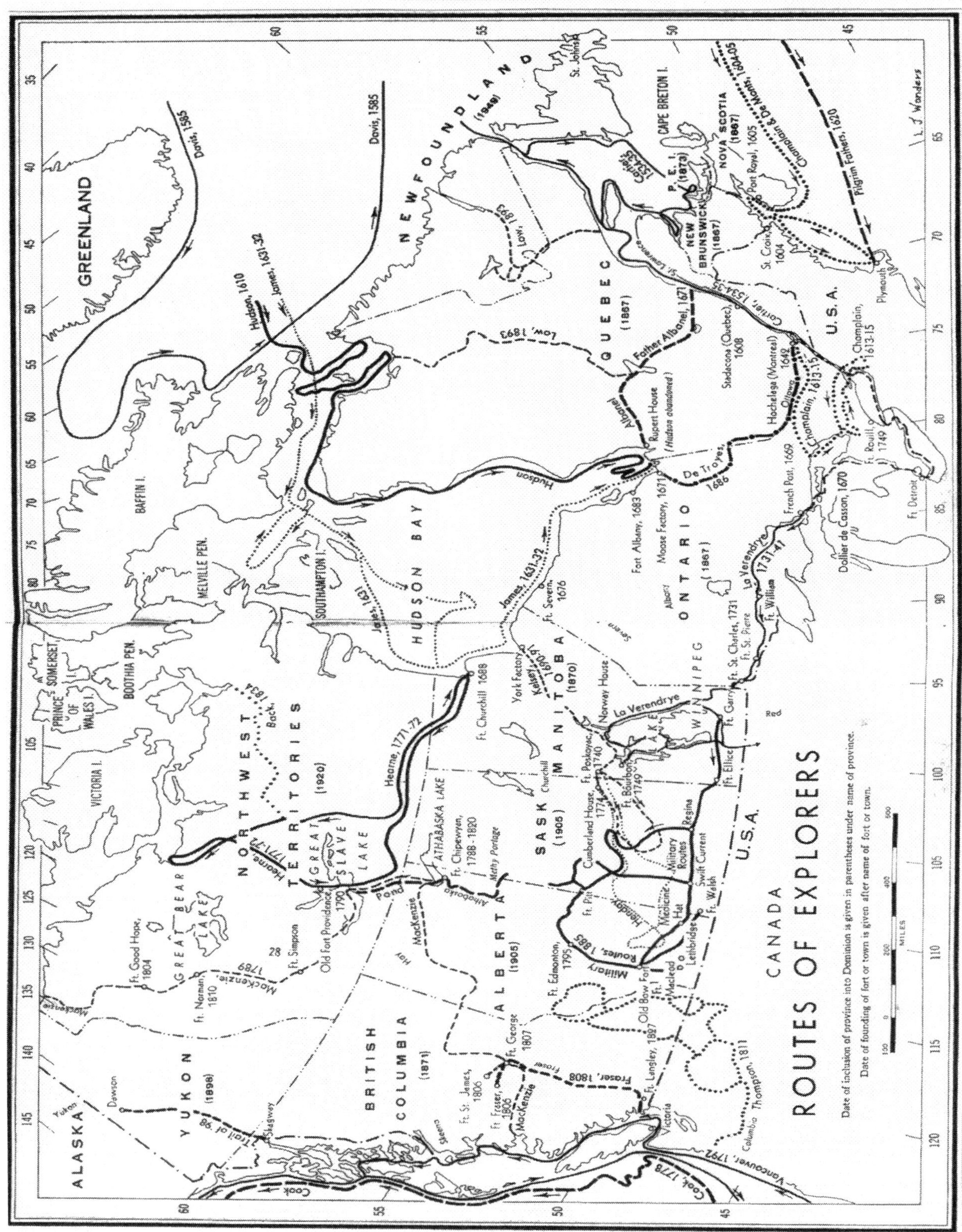

-1813 **George Hamilton** bought property at the western tip of Lake Ontario. 1816 the village of **Hamilton** was incorporated. 1824 Burlington canal was built. Hamilton became a town in 1833 and city in 1846.
-St. Catherines was named for the wife of **Robert Hamilton**, member of the first Upper Canada legislature.
-1815 to 1840 the Upper Canada population grew from 77,000 to 430,000, mainly from the British Isles.
-1816 Scottish Highlanders settled at **Kingston, Perth** and **Bytown** named for **Lieut Col. John By**, and later renamed **Ottawa** [119 Vol 9, p 247-251], where **lumbering** and **papermaking** industries mushroomed.
-1817 Fashionable passengers going to Bytown from Montreal went by stage-coach and, at **Long Sault rapids** transferred to elegant passenger boats. Stage coaches connected **Montreal**, **Kingston** and York (**Toronto**).
-1819 the **Bank** of Kingston began, but 1821 merged with the government Bank of Upper Canada [119 Vol 1, p 293].
-1820 Scottish lowlanders were settled at **Lanark**. 1824 **McNab township** was settled [119 Vol 9, p 247-251].
-1817-1824 south of the Great lakes the **Erie Canal** linked the Hudson river to Lake Erie from Albany to Buffalo, greatly stimulating migration and commerce [i6, p 230] in the USA.
-1821-5 in the St. Lawrence **Lachine Canal** was built for ships around Long Sault rapids to **Ottawa River**.
-1823 Irish settlers came to **Bathurst**. Peter Robinson brought 2000 Irish Catholics to **Peterborough**.
-1824-9 **Welland Canal** built with 40 wooden locks, raised ships 100 metres from Lake Ontario to Lake Erie.
-1826-32 **Rideau Canal** was built by **Lieut Col John By**, as an alternate military route from Montreal, via Bytown to Kingston, if the St. Lawrence River route, bordering the US was invaded [120, p 390; 125 Vol 14, p 874]. No longer needed for defense, it was used for commerce. The **Trent Canal** begun in 1833 linked numerous rivers/lakes 224 miles from Trenton, Lake Ontario, north to Georgian Bay on **Lake Huron** [119 Vol 8, p 52; Vol 2, p 219].
-1827 Sir John **Galt,** Scottish novelist, with the Canada Company [147 Vol 5 # 55] planned and founded **Guelph**.
Waterloo Township was settled by **Mennonites** and **Pennsylvania "Dutch"**(**Deutsch** in German). They had skill as grist-mill and sawmill operators, craftsmen, farmers and in instrumental and vocal music [119 Vol 5, pp 234-5].
-1828 **Goderich** salt mines, 1831 **Stratford** and 1834 the **Eastern Townships** in Lower Canada were settled.
-1829 Church of England **King's College** (later University of **Toronto**) was founded but due to exclusive rules for professors, Methodists started **Victoria College** nearby; Presbyterians opened **Queen's** at Kingston.
-1830 **Brantford** was founded in honor of **Mohawk Chief Joseph Brant** (1742-1807) [see p 114].
-Before 1796 Baptists among the Loyalists built Beamsville church, Niagara area. By 1851 Baptists built about 150 churches in Upper and Lower Canada. 1819 the Western Association of Baptist Churches began and other Associations followed. 1838 Canadian Baptist College opened in Montreal [119b Vol 1, pp 315-9; 168, p 159-163].
-1830 the town of Sandwich (renamed **Windsor** in 1836) was founded across the river from **Detroit**, where there was an old French settlement and ferry across the river [119b Vol 10, pp 335-6]. The Detroit River between Lakes Erie and St. Clair is 29 miles long and up to one mile wide [119b Vol 3, pp 260]. Both became industrialized cities.
-1831 34,000 **Irish immigrants** landed in the port of Quebec. By 1833 with 66,339 arriving from the British Isles, immigration reached its height. For a time Canada was more attractive than the US, to immigrants.
-1825-46 over 626,628 **immigrants** landed at **Canadian ports**, the majority for Upper Canada. In 1834 York was incorporated as the city of **Toronto** with 9000 inhabitants, and grew to 21,000 [119 Vol 5, pp 234-5; Vol 10, p 97].
-1815-40 the population of Upper Canada rose from 77,000 **to** 430,000, mainly from the British Isles.

Authors and Pioneers in Upper Canada: Three English sisters were noteworthy authors:

1. **Agnes Strickland** 1796-1874 remained single, was the author of biographies of famous people, including Queen Victoria. Her sisters married, emigrated to Toronto-Coburg area, among the first homesteaders. Adjusting to life without comforts/social contacts was extremely hard, living too far apart to visit each other.
2. **Catherine Parr Traill** 1802-99 had 9 children. She pressed specimens of wild flowers and herbs and wrote out-standing botanical books. She also wrote *The Backwoods of Canada and Tips for Settlers.*
3. **Suzanna Moodie** 1803-85 had 7 children. 1852 she published her two volume *Roughing it in the Bush*, about the difficulties they faced as pioneers, 2000 copies sold; reprinted three times. Wrote 7 more books; died in 1885 at 82 [148]. Other Authors [168, pp 272-274];

-1831 first newspaper in Upper Canada published at Windsor.
-1837 **William Lyon Mackenzie:** newspaper publisher, member of legislature; 1835 first Toronto mayor.
-Louis Joseph Papineau, Lower Canada Speaker of the House, **led a rebellion** because government was dominated by Britain, clergy lands were untaxed [119 Vol 8, p 50; 119b Vol 6, pp 277-8] and churches were dependent on both Britain and the US. In 1841 to end this revolt, Upper and Lower Canada were joined.
-1837 Angus MacDonald a poor man from the Isle of **Skye**, Scotland and his wife Catherine Ann MacDonnell who had been raised in the castle of the chief of the clan, where she had received a good education, and they

came to Canada to escape restrictions the British government imposed on Roman Catholics. They settled on 1000 acres, 12 miles from Bytown; had cattle and sheep, wove woolen cloth, made men's suits that did not wear out, grew vegetables, hay and grain, and raised a large family of tall boys and girls. Their mother educated the MacDonald boys, as the school was four miles away. When grown enough, they went with their father to cut timber for ship spars and masts, and for lumber, while the younger boys cut cord-wood and hauled it to Bytown to sell for fuel. At fifteen **Archie "Rory"** joined older brothers. (Archie's son Ervin wrote a remarkable biography of him[129].) Archie became a highly skilled agile lumberjack, able to clear log jams. With great courage he led a multicultural group of aggressive men, settling disputes and fights. For years they floated logs 700 miles down the river over rapids and falls, often in sudden storms. In 1868, 29 years old, he adventured south west via St.Louis, Missouri and later to Colorado and Oregon, [more pp 158; 160; 175-6].

-1845 **Welland Canal**, between Lakes Ontario and Erie concrete blocks replaced wooden locks [119, p 215].

-1850 the nine-foot wide Welland Canal channel was open for ships from the Atlantic Ocean [119 Vol 8, p 48-0] to sail into the Great Lakes. It was rebuilt with fewer, longer, wider locks in 1887 and again in 1913.

-1841 a network of 6000 miles of post roads had been finished, some with McAdamized paving that was invented by Canadian John Loudon McAdam [119b Vol 9, pp 35-42].

-1842 **Queen's University**, Kingston was founded [125 Vol 8, pp 21-51]. 1842 a daily schedule of stagecoaches crossed Upper Canada and 1852 was extended from **Detroit** to **Quebec**, with branch routes [168, pp 162-3].

-1846 fleeing potato famine in Ireland 32,753 came to Quebec and Montreal; in 1847 84,445 [119 Vol 5, p 235].

- 1847 a **telegraph line** from **Quebec** to **Toronto** was opened and 1849 connected with **Atlantic Canada.**

-1851 there were 150 Baptist churches in Upper and Lower Canada with about 10,000 adults [119b, Vol 1, p 315-9].

-1850 new farming lands in Upper Canada were running out so new-comers and youth from large families resettled **north** around **Lake Huron** and some went west to **Winnipeg** [119 Vol 8, pp 210f -h] [pp 155-156].

Lower Canada (Renamed Quebec in 1867)

-1791 the united province was divided in two again, Upper and Lower Canada with legislatures [119b Vol 6, p 208].

-1785 for social and business dining, the ***Beaver Club*** was formed in **Montreal** by associates of the **NorthWest Co** [See p 108] a loosely organized group with up to 50 members. At first only those who had wintered once in the far west were eligible for membership. Fur-traders became wealthy and partnerships kept changing. **Ogilvy** and **Morgan** thrived as merchants of imported fashionable goods [119 Vol 7, p 161].

-1789 Nor'Wester **Alexander Mackenzie** reached the **Arctic Ocean.**

-1793 he reached the **Pacific Ocean** overland. After disagreements with **Simon McTavish** a powerful NWCo leader, he withdrew and went to England, where his journals were published, and he was knighted 1802.

-1798 the "New NorthWest Co" was formed. Their freight was marked **XY** while "Old NorthWest Co" cases were marked **NW**. There was rivalry and confusion [119 Vol 7, pp 358-360]. 1803 **Sir Alexander Mackenzie** gave his name to the new company; 1804 it was absorbed into the NWCo, but with Sir Alexander excluded [119b Vol 10, p 387].

-1800 the population of **Montreal** was 9000; in 1832 it was 40,000 and incorporated as a city [119 Vol 7, p 138-150].

-1804-8 Sir Alexander Mackenzie sat on the Lower Canada Assembly; retired in Scotland [119b Vol 6, pp 274-5].

-1813 **McGill University** was founded by a bequest from Scottish **James McGill**, since 1744 a fur trader with partner **Isaac Todd** [168, p 162]. In 1766 he wintered in Indian country; was a charter member of the ***Beaver Club*** but not a member of the NWCo. James McGill represented Montreal in Lower Canada Legislature [119 Vol 6, pp 264-6].

-1852 **Laval University** was established in **Quebec** city by the Seminaire de Quebec, a college of arts and theology founded by Bishop Laval in 1663. The four faculties were theology, civil law, medicine and arts.

-1824-9 magnificent **Notre Dame Church**, one of the largest on the continent, was built to resemble Notre Dame in Paris [119b Vol 7, p 146]. Montreal was built with many gray limestone mansions and institutions.

-1792 a **bank** was established in Montreal for private use. See history of banking in Canada [119b Vol 1, pp 292-314].

-1817 **Bank of Montreal** began to circulate the first domestic currency since the French regime; branches opened in York (Toronto), Kingston & Quebec city, and more after the 1841 union of Upper & Lower Canada.

-1820 **George Simpson** came to the HBCo appointed **Governor of Rupert's Land** [119 Vol 7, pp 358-360].

-1821 **HBCo absorbed** the **NorthWest Co**. Simpson ruled the company for nearly 40 years, traveling rapidly on inspection trips all over western North America with a Highland piper. He was a Director of the Bank of Montreal and of the Bank of British North America [119b Vol 9, p 317].

-1860 he was knighted Sir George Simpson after making his third trip to the Pacific. It was a round the world trip via Siberia. He lived in **Lachine** (named for China) Montreal; entertained Prince of Wales (Edward VII).

-1841 Upper and Lower Canada were again united.

Stern Wheelers and Steam Ships Evolved for River, Lake and Ocean Transport

-By 1732 the shipyard in Quebec was building naval and merchant ships for France and the West Indies.
-By 1800 the shipbuilding industry in Quebec and Nova Scotia become the primary supplier of vessels of all kinds to the United Kingdom. 1808 **David Munn** built twenty 350 ton ships.
-1809 at Trois Rivières **John Molson** built the first Canadian steamship named *Accommodation*, which was also the first wooden paddle steamer in Canada, and probably in North America. It was 85 feet long. It plied between **Montreal** and **Quebec** in 36 hours, on a regular schedule.
-Ship-building on the Great Lakes was impressive. 1816-7 the 700 ton *Frontenac*, a wooden sidewheeler steamer, with auxiliary sails, began regular voyages between Kingston and Niagara. The SS *Ontario* was the first steamer launched on Lake Ontario, a few days earlier. It was only 237 tons [119b Vol 4, p 288].
-1811 a steamboat the *New Orleans*, built at **Pittsburg**, reached the mouth of the Mississippi. 1814 there were 20 arrivals at **New Orleans**. 1816 regular service upstream, attracted cotton and sugar plantation passengers with ornate state rooms, famous chefs & orchestras. 1834 there were 1200 arrivals.
-1853 the steamboat run shortened from 25 days to 4.5 days [12 Vol 11, p 229-30]. By 1870 railways were preferred.
-1819 meanwhile **up the Ottawa River** steam-powered vessels went from Grenville, Hull and beyond, to carry passengers to logging/sawmill industries. Because of Long Sault & Lachine Rapids near Montreal, stage coaches met steam vessels to provide continuous comfortable service. Canals were built [119 Vol 8, p 80] [p 122].
-1820 Alexander Allan began the **Allan Line** that brought European immigrants up the St. Lawrence River.
-1833 the first steam-powered ship crossed **the Atlantic** with **Samuel Cunard**, Halifax-born son of a Loyalist, on board. It was a 1370 ton paddle-steamer, in 1831 built in Quebec. A contract to carry mail began.
-1835 the first steamer on **the Pacific coast**, the ***Beaver***, a fast 108 ton side-wheeler with auxiliary sails, was built in England for the **Hudson Bay Co**mpany [119b Vol 9, p 128; 119b Vol 1, p 348]. For 20 years she carried supplies, freight and passengers from **Vancouver**, **Oregon** on the **Columbia River** to northern trading posts.
-1839 the Canadian **Cunard Line** was foremost [119b Vol 13, pp 169-170; Vol 9, p 298]. In 1840 one of their steam ships crossed the Atlantic in 15 days. 1841 Cunard began to carry **mail** and passengers by **steamer** from Halifax to Liverpool, Quebec & Boston. Cunard owned 40 excellent sailing ships but ship-building changed to steam.
-1843 of the 156 ships over 500 tons, registered at Liverpool, 136 had been built in Canada.
-1849 the golden age of Canadian ship-building began with the **California gold rush** [119b Vol 9, p 128]. Again orders increased with the Australian gold rush 1851, the Crimean War 1854 and the Indian Mutiny 1857.
-1853 in one year 80 ships over 1000 tons were built in eastern Canada; in 1875 **the peak year**, 500 ships.
-Passenger Ship Ports-of-Call: the **Allan** (Quebec) and **Cunard** (Halifax) were based in Canada.
-1869 the American **Collins Line** was competitive, so Cunard transferred their Port-of-call to New York.
-1878 the Canadian merchant marine numbered 7196 vessels (lake and coastline). Building of **steel hulls** began so **wooden ship building in Canada declined**. The major ship builder became **Scotland** on the Clyde.
-1889 **Scotland** launched 97% of steel hull tonnage in the world, but only 10% a decade before.

The Métis and Selkirk Settlements along the Red River

[from pp 107-109; maps 108, 125]

-1734 La Vérendrye built many French trading posts. Fort Rouge was at the junction of the Assiniboine and Red Rivers. Here thousands of nomadic peoples had camped seasonally for many years. Retired Voyageurs and their Métis descendants settled along the Red River. They were mobile by canoe and horseback all over the western plains (later named Minnesota, the Dakotas, Montana, Saskatchewan and Alberta). They had settlements at NorWester posts. Roman Catholic missions accompanied them, favoring the French language.
-Huge annual and semi-annual buffalo hunts were an exciting part of their life style. They traded in buffalo hides, meat and pemmican (a sausage made of dried meat and berries).
-The Métis thinking of themselves as a new nation, neither European nor Indian, resented European settlers.
-1774 the Hudson Bay Co (English) began to build posts inland, because they were losing out to the NorWesters (Scottish, French and Métis). There were many clashes but both prospered. The HBCo had centralized administration. The NWCo consisted of independent partnerships.
-As it was sanctioned, only a few HBCo staff formed alliances with Indian women, but these women and children had better income, schools, and tended to assimilate into English culture, unlike the French Métis.
-The NWCo wintered at **Grande Portage,** Great Lakes in fur trade to Montreal and Europe [119b Vol 7, pp 358-360].
-1805 their headquarters were moved to **Fort William**, a bit north on Lake Superior, to shorten the distance. Some 3000 **fur-traders** came to ship furs, buy supplies and enjoy **social activities** [119b Vol 4, p 232].

-1811-15 **Earl of Selkirk**, a shareholder of the HBCo, brought several ship-loads of impoverished Scottish crofters into the Hudson Bay, and then 500 miles up the Nelson River [see map p 121] to Norway House on Lake Winnipeg plus 250 miles to the forks of the **Assiniboine** and **Red Rivers**. Farms were in narrow strips along the river banks, similar to those of French *Habitants* in Quebec, for irrigation, transport and nearness of neighbors [121Vol 3, p 1836-7; p 1673-4].
-Strip-farms extend from present Winnipeg to **South Dakota** and **Minnesota** [seen now by satellite].
-1816 conflict between the HBCo and NorWesters came to a head: **Seven Oaks Massacre**, led by Métis **Cuthbert Grant**. Assiniboine river forts were destroyed, but raiders were stopped before reaching Fort Douglas (Winnipeg).
-Selkirk Settlement Governor Robert Semple and 19 officers died [119b Vol 9, p 270]. Selkirk leading more settlers to Red River received news of the battle, and seized NWCo Ft William.

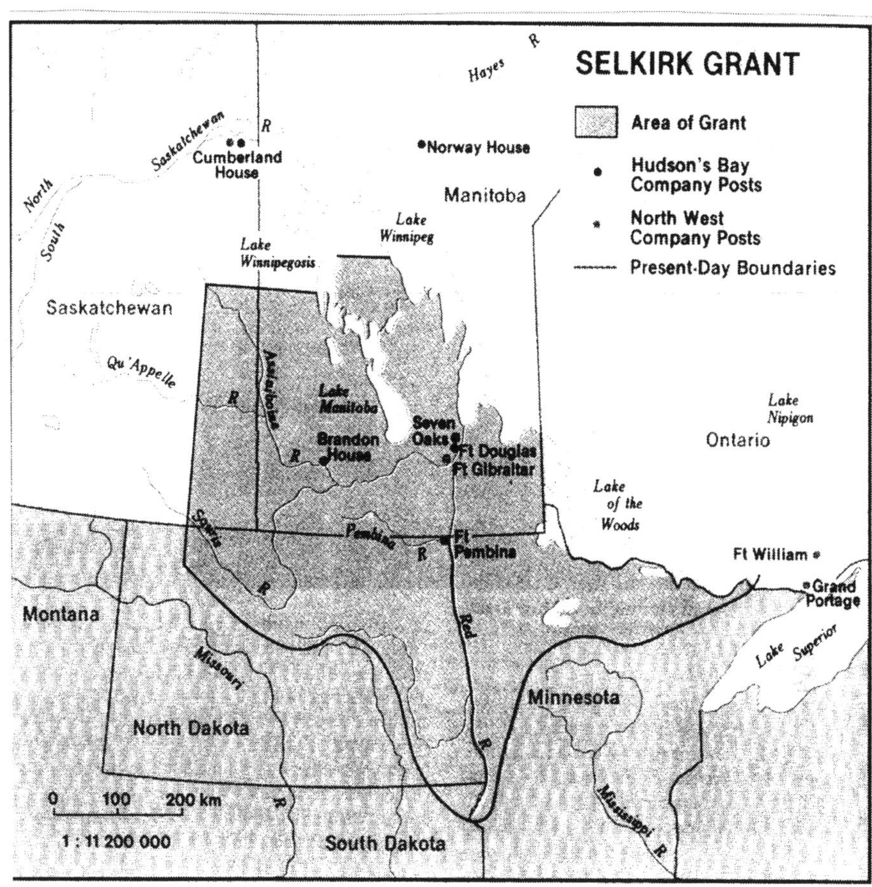

Map: Selkirk Settlement [121b Vol 3, p 1553]

Next year he returned to the Red River, reinstated the evicted colonists and restored order.
- He accused **Simon Fraser**, great NWCo explorer of the Fraser River from Rocky mountains to the Pacific Ocean, of complicity [p 129]. 1818 Lord Selkirk lost to the NWCo in a court battle aimed at ruining their fur trade. He retired in England.
-1819 Simon Fraser retired on his Loyalist homestead in Upper Canada [168, p 142-144].
-1817 **St. Boniface** was founded on the east bank of the Red River across from Fort Garry, by German Swiss disbanded mercenaries, sponsored by **Lord Selkirk**, named for the patron saint of Germany.
-French Fathers **Provencher** and **Dumoulin** and some French colonists from Quebec joined them. A basilica was built, and the Métis who had lived there for generations were included in the community [119 Vol 9, p 143].
-1818 the **Red River Cession** ruled that the 49th parallel was the boundary between British and US territory, from Lake of the Woods (west of Lake Superior) across the Prairies and Rocky Mountains, based on **David Thompson's survey** [95, p 421] [p 127]. Settlements in Dakota/Minnesota went to the US, but trading back and forth continued, with French Canadian voyageurs active at US forts, and American fur-traders in Canada.
-1821 the Hudson Bay Co took over North West Co, granting shares to North West Co partners. Fur trade was diverted from Montreal to the Hudson Bay. The HBCo now had exclusive rights [119 Vol 5, p 191; Vol 7, p 360] to trade in furs and supplies for 21 years in the **Northwest Territories** (later Manitoba, Saskatchewan and Alberta), the **Pacific slope** (British Columbia) and what is now **Oregon**, **Washington**, **Idaho**, **Montana** and **Wyoming**.
-HBCo settlements and forts, called **factories**, were established. White wives and children, and in a few cases Indian wives and children, lived in elegant comfort with imported fine furnishings.
-1846 US border agreements forced the Hudson Bay Co to withdraw north of the 49th parallel [12 Vol 6, p 119]
-1830 Lac la Pluie on the Rainy River near lake of the Woods, was renamed Fort Frances, in honor of Frances Simpson, who had traveled with her husband Sir George Simpson, [119b Vol 4, p 216; Vol 9, p 317].
-By 1831 enough wheat was produced in Red River Settlement by Scottish settlers to begin retail sales.

- Métis were semi-nomadic and found farming dull. They preferred massive buffalo hunts spring and autumn.
-Some Métis moved NW in search of buffalo, establishing several settlements [maps p 117. 163] : **Batoche** (at junction of North and South Saskatchewan Rivers), **Cypress Hills, Lac Ste. Anne** and **St. Albert** near **Fort Edmonton**. Employment for Métis was boat brigades and wagon trains to **St. Paul, Minnesota** [119b Vol 7, pp 53-56].
- Resenting white settlers arriving, they began to demand a separate Métis nation.
-1840 **Grey Nuns** from Montreal brought education, Christian faith and French culture to the Métis [120, p 921].
-By 1850 groups of **Red River carts** made regular round trips from Fort Gary south to **St. Paul, Minnesota**, and northwest to **Fort Battleford** and **Fort Edmonton,** to carry supplies for settlers.
-**Red River carts** originated in both Scottish and French tradition. Constructed of wood, they had very noisy wheels tied together with leather. They were easily repaired, carried heavy loads [121 Vol 3, p 1836] and floated across streams. [Continued pp 161-162].

The First Great Migration of Settlers West of the Appalachian Mountains [from p 106]

-The 13 original colonies extended all along the Atlantic seacoast from Maine to Georgia. The Appalachian Mountains (the Allegheny, Blue Ridge Mountains and other ranges) were a natural western boundary. In time there was a feeling of being hemmed in and overpopulated. **Trappers** made a good living for some years in these nearby mountains, but fur-bearing animals were becoming scarce.
-1783 **US Northwest Territory** was established [map p 157] including the present states of Ohio, Indiana, Illinois, Michigan, Wisconsin and part of Minnesota [16, p 534]. It was a rich fur-trading region [125 Vol 13, pp 508-9].
-1796 the **Jay Treaty** clarified some **US/British borders**. The large area between Lakes Michigan and Huron, including **Detroit**, went to the US [16, p 378 and 489]. French Fort Michilimackinac [120, p 898] at the north end of Lake Michigan was ceded to the US [maps pp 74, 152, 157] so was no longer a voyageur fur-trading hub.
-Late 1700's to early 1800's the first migration of pioneer settlers crossed the Appalachians, pushed back Indian tribes, and occupied land mainly in the **Ohio** Valley, **Kentucky** and **Arkansas** [9 Vol 2, pp 360-1].
-1800 Congress created **Indiana Territory**. 1803 Michigan Territory became part of Indiana [map p 128].
-1800 **in a deal with Spain** **Napoleon** acquired Louisiana for **France** (under Spanish control since 1762).
-1805 **Michigan Territory** was established. 1809-18 Wisconsin was part of Michigan.
-In the 1820s lead mining prospered with manufacture of shot and paint [125 Vol 21, pp 365-8].
-1812 steam boats from **Pittsburgh** provided service on the **Ohio** and **Mississippi** Rivers [p 124, map p 130].

Spanish Possessions on the Gulf of Mexico and in Louisiana [from pp 96- 98 and 106-107]

-1539-42 the French and British had colonies in the Spanish area on the Gulf of Mexico [125, Vol 20, p 167]. They spoke **Creole**, a combination of Spanish, French, African dialects and English [16, p 172, 445]. **Plantations** growing sugar, cotton and tobacco prospered through the labor of **slaves. New Orleans** became wealthy. Roman Catholic Dominican, Ursuline and Normal Colleges to train teachers, and Loyola and Xavier Universities, were founded.
-1803 in the **Louisiana Purchase** [16, p 445] the US bought from France the vast region known as Louisiana, from the 31st parallel near the Gulf of Mexico and west of the Mississippi to the Rocky Mountains.
-In 1815 after the end of the War of 1812 the British had many casualties in the Battle of New Orleans.
-1819 in the **Florida Cession** the US acquired Spanish territory around the Gulf of Mexico. [See below]

Spanish Territory Ceded to Mexico and the United States [Continued from pp 106-107]

-1776 trappers and traders arriving by ship **via Cape Horn**, settled in California around the missions.
-1812 **Fort Ross**, a **Russian** fur-trading post, was built in California. 1824-40 Russia withdrew to Alaska.
-1821 **Mexico** became independent of **Spain**, and inherited many Spanish settlements on the Gulf of Mexico, Arizona, New Mexico, Texas and California, ruling more than the western half of the present US.
-1822 **California** became **a province of the Republic of Mexico**, with its own legislature and army.
-1826 only **Cuba** and **Puerto Rica** in the New World remained Spanish colonies [16, p 627].
-1841 settlers came to California by land. A trapper, **Jedediah Strong Smith** (1798-31) opened up the west via the **Missouri River** and **Santa Fe Trail** [16, p 693] [maps 128, 130]. By 1846 Franciscan mission property in California was all sold, some of it to ranchers, who became wealthy from sale of hides and tallow for candles.
-1836 **Texas** won independence from **Mexico**. The first settlements were Spanish missions. Many Americans settled in Texas and began self-government, with their own famous police force **Texas Rangers** [16, p 752]-1845 **Texas** was annexed by the US. The Mexicans fought back. 1846-8 the **USA** annexed **California** [16, p 120].

-1839 meanwhile emigration from New England on the **Oregon Trail** began [p 130].
-1846 **New Mexico**, settled by Spanish colonists in the 17th century, became part of the US [16, pp 525-6].
-1847 **Utah** was settled by **Mormons** led by **Brigham Young** [maps pp 130, 157].
-1848 Mexico ceded **Nevada** and **Utah** to the USA.
-1848 **San Francisco** (a mere hamlet settled by Spaniards in 1776) annexed by the USA. A **gold rush** began.
-1849 The population of San Francisco's expanded 20-fold [16, p 658]. Known as **the 49ers**, 6000 prospectors traveled west across America on the **Oregon Trail** and **California Trail** [pp 157; 159-160; map p 130].

Expansion West of the Mississippi River

- 1784-97 **David Thompson** with the HBCo, in 1798 went into NWCo service to be free to combine mapping/ surveying skills with fur-trading [p 109]. He made a 4000 mile journey surveying/mapping the head-waters of the **Mississippi River**. Based at Rocky Mountain House north of **Calgary**, in 1799 he married the half-breed daughter of an Irish fur-trader [119b Vol 10, p 71]. The term Métis is preferred in Canada. For more about his explorations/surveys see pp 109, 125 and 129]. His survey of 1809-18 was the basis for establishing the 49th parallel as the boundary between the USA and Canada [see below] [168, p 139; 121 Vol I pp 504-5; Vol III p 1775].
-The **NWCo** held sway over the entire northwest. Loosely organized partners had head offices in Montreal. The wilderness headquarters were first at **Grand Portage** on Lake Superior; 1805 they were moved to **Fort William**, a town of several thousand [119b Vol 7, pp 358-60][map 117]. At that time British territory included the watershed of the **Red River** that rises in **Minnesota** and flows north 355 miles through North Dakota into **Lake Winnipeg**, [16, pp 444-5, 620] (map 125).
-1800 large **Indiana Territory** was organized, including present **Illinois**, **Wisconsin** and parts of **Michigan** and **Minnesota**; 1816 Indiana became a state [map p 128].
-1803 by the ***Louisiana Purchase*** from France, the United States acquired the **vast region west of** the entire Mississippi River to the **Rocky Mountains**.
-1803 **Ohio** had received statehood.
-1804 May, US Army Officers, **Meriwether Lewis** and **William Clark**, authorized by Congress and sent out by President Jefferson, began ascending the **Missouri River** at Independence; wintered near the present Bismarck, **North Dakota** [map p 128]; crossed Rocky Mountains; descended the Snake & **Columbia Rivers**.
-1805 the huge Territory of **Michigan** was formed, including North and South Dakota [16, p 486; 533].
-1805 Nov, Lewis and Clark wintered in **Oregon** at the mouth of the **Columbia River**, Pacific Ocean [16, p 428].
-1806 Sept, back in St. Louis, Missouri, they described the terrain, plants, animals and people along the 2000 mile route, which soon was named the **Oregon Trail** [116, p 16].
-1807 Lewis was appointed Governor of Louisiana.
-The **Mississippi River** is up to a mile wide [16, pp 495-6]. **Four major branches** of the Mississippi River are:

1. The **Minnesota River** begins in South Dakota, flows through Minnesota and south into the Mississippi.
2. The **Missouri River** flows from the Rocky Mountains, through North Dakota and joins the Mississippi.
3. The **Ohio River** descends southwest from the Appalachian Mountains to the Mississippi.
4. The **Arkansas River** rises in central Colorado in the Rocky Mountains and drains into the Mississippi in Arkansas. Principal tributaries: the **Cimarron** and **Canadian Rivers** rising in the Rockies in New Mexico, flow one through Texas and the other through Kansas, and enter the Arkansas River in Oklahoma [map p 157].

-1807 **Britain** abolished slavery and used the British Navy to stop slave trade;
-by 1815 slavery was banned in Europe.
-1790 US census showed a slave population of 700,000, in 1830: 2 million, and in 1865: 4½ million [16, pp 691-2].
-1808 US Congress made import of slaves illegal, but internal slavery continued [125 Vol 10, p 82].
-1811 building of the **National Road** (**Cumberland Road**) began. It extended from Cumberland, Md through the Allegheny Mountains to **Vandalia**, Ill., 80 miles east of **St. Louis** [125 Vol 15, p 478].
-1812 the large **Territory of Missouri**, including Arkansas was formed; 1820 statehood [16, p 496; 9 Vol 2, pp 360-1].
-Veterans of the War of 1812 settled in Arkansas;
-1819 **Arkansas Territory** was inaugurated; 1836 statehood [16, p 48].
-1817 **Mississippi** became the 20th state. **Ohio** Indians sadly surrendered their last 4 million acres [95, p 420].
-1818 **Red River Cession:** the 49th parallel became the boundary between US & British territory, from Lake of the Woods, across Prairies and Rocky mountains, based on **David Thompson's Survey** 1809-18 [95, pp 413-421].
-1819 **Florida Cession:** the US acquired Spanish territory south of 31st parallel around Gulf of Mexico, Florida, part of **Louisiana, Mississippi** and **Alabama** [125 Vol 20, pp 158-9]; 1845 Florida became a State [16, p 254].

Map: *Explorations West of the Mississippi by 1821* [151].

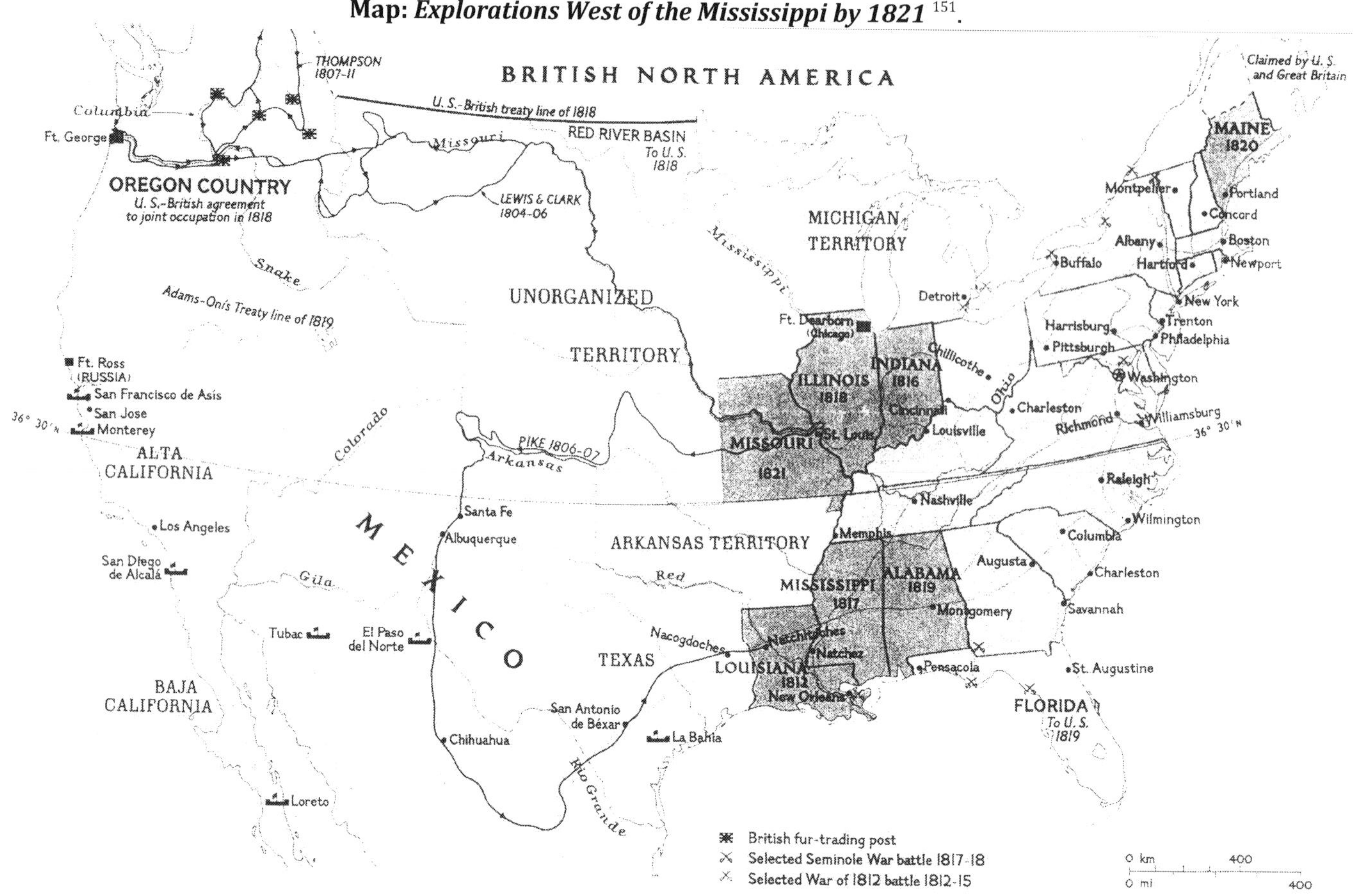

-1821 Hudson Bay Company absorbed North West Co [119 Vol 7, pp 358-60], ending clashes and trading difficulties.
-HBCo gained control of all fur-trading forts even those west of the **Rocky Mountains** and on the Pacific Ocean, as far south as **Vancouver on the Columbia River in Oregon territory** [maps pp 128, 130].
-1820 lead miners poured into **Wisconsin** (Indian for badger) and lived in dug-outs like badgers [125 Vol 21, p 366].
-1823 **Champlain Canal** via the Hudson River provided a water route to **New York City** [125 Vol 20, p 334].
-1825 the 363 mile **Erie Canal**, Albany to Buffalo, connected the Hudson River and Lake Erie [9 Vol 1, p 336] facilitating travel from New York and New England to the Great Lakes. Using this route settlers poured into the present **Indiana, Ohio and Michigan**.
-1825 in the far west, the **Ashley Fur Company** began to hold **an annual trappers' rendezvous on the Oregon Trail** in the Rocky Mountains [map p 130]. Indians and white men came from far and wide to sell furs and buy supplies to last for a year.
-Many rugged white men were trappers because few Indians were interested [125 Vol 7, p 565].
-1830 the **Church of the Latter Day Saints** was founded in New York by **Joseph Smith** and the Book of Mormon published. The church spread rapidly in Ohio, Missouri and Illinois.
-1843 a revelation of prophet Smith allowed polygamy. He was shot during indignant protests. **Brigham Young** was his successor [16, p 505]. See Salt Lake City on map p 130.
-1847 the Mormons trekked to Utah. A Reorganized Mormon group settled in **Missouri**.
-1837 **Michigan**, a Territory since 1805, received statehood. Mining and forestry prospered [125 Vol 13, pp 508-9].
-1838 **Iowa Territory** was created; received statehood in 1846 [See maps pp 130 and 157].
-1846 the **Territory of Wisconsin** was formed. Farmers from **Scandinavia** settled in large numbers [16, pp 820].
-1834 Cyrus McCormick patented the harvest reaper. Farm machinery came into wide use [125 Vol 20, p 167].
-1834 Louis **Braille** invented a system of raised point writing that enabled the blind to "read" [95, p 433].

Exploration & Early Settlement of the Pacific Watershed [pp 57-60, 72,109; maps pp 121,128]
-1784 **Simon Fraser** (1776-1862) born in Bennington, Vermont, son of Captain Simon Fraser, who died in a US prison for loyalty to Britain, fled to Cornwall, Upper Canada with his mother/siblings [119 Vol 4, pp 254-5, 274].
-1792 Simon Fraser entered the service of the North West Co.
-1801 he became a partner and 1805-8 was appointed Superintendent west of the Rocky Mountains;
-1809 extended to **Athabasca** (now northern Alberta) and back to the **Red River** [maps pp 108,117, 121].
-1788-89 two ships from **Boston**, the ***Washington*** and ***Columbia,*** traded along the NW coast of North America and returned via China. ***Columbia*** was the first ship flying the Stars and Stripes to circle the world.
-1792 **Robert Gray** as Captain of the *Columbia,* sailed into the **Columbia River**, named by him for his vessel. He returned to Boston via China [119 Vol 5, p 29].
-1793 Sir **Alexander Mackenzie** a NWCo partner, starting from Lake Athabasca (now northern Alberta) ascended the **Peace** and **Parsnip Rivers**, through the Rocky Mountains, in search of a route to the Pacific Ocean. He stopped to build **Fort St. John** in NE British Columbia, climbed over a divide to the **Fraser River**, went west up the **West Road River**, found a pass through the **Coast Mountains**, and reached the **Pacific Ocean** at **Bella Coola** [119 Vol 5, p 190; 143 inside cover; pp18-20, 40], a complicated, arduous, long route [maps 121, 166].
-1805 the NWCo established **Fort Nelson** in NE British Columbia [120, p 898], named for Admiral Horatio Nelson. The same year Simon Fraser built **Fort McLeod**, north of present Prince George, BC [compare p 166].
-1804 May, US Army Officers, Meriwether **Lewis** and William **Clark** began ascending the **Missouri River**. They wintered near the present Bismarck, **North Dakota**; crossed the Rocky Mountains; descended the **Snake** and **Columbia Rivers**. 1805 Nov, they reached the mouth of the **Columbia River** [16, p 428] [pp 127-128].
-1806 **Fort St. James** was established by **Simon Fraser** on the Fraser River north of present Vanderhoof, the oldest continuously inhabited community in **New Caledonia** (later called **British Columbia**) [120, p 899]. He also founded **Fort Fraser** 1806 and another fort 1807 [119b Vol 4, pp 217-8]. He did not allow sale of intoxicants.
-1808 **Simon Fraser** explored the entire **Fraser River** from its source to the ocean, an outstanding achievement. Greatly disappointed it was not the Columbia River [119 Vol 4, p 274] he went east to **Red River** NWT where in
-1816 Lord Selkirk accused him of complicity in the **Seven Oaks Massacre** [above p 125; map p 125].
-1807 **David Thompson**, a NWCo partner since 1804 [pp 109, 127] crossed the Rocky Mountains at Howse Pass, with his wife and children [119b Vol 10, p 71; Vol 2, p 84]; built **Kootenae House** the first trading post on the Columbia River, in the present Washington State [168, p 139]. He roughed mountains and canyons by canoe.
-1808 he mapped the **Kootenay region** (SE British Columbia). 1807-8 he explored large parts of the present **Montana, Idaho** and **Washington;** built many trading posts, including **Spokane House** [map p 166 shows mountains & forts but not rivers. See maps pp 117, 121, 177 for forts & routes.]
-1809 Experienced Thompson began his **survey/mapping from Lake Superior to the Pacific**, a million square miles [95, p 413]. Findings were used 1818-19 to determine the border between the US & Canada [p 153].
-1808 **John Jacob Astor** a German-American financier from New York organized the **American Fur Co**, dealing directly with Indians on the Missouri and Columbia Rivers[168, p 139].
-1811 he founded **Astoria** (renamed **Fort George** by the British). 1818-1846 Britain and the US had an agreement for joint occupation of Oregon [Map p 128]. 1815-1834 Astor shipped fur on his own ships to China and many other countries, but sold his fur-trading business; devoted himself to financial affairs [9 Vol 3, p 7].
-1811-2 **David Thompson** ascended the **Columbia River to its source**, turned around and went down all the way to Astoria, Pacific Ocean, and back to its source again, 1150 miles each way [119b Vol 10, p 71] [map 177]. It rises south of Jasper from the Columbia Ice fields, flows turbulently around the Big Bend, and:
- In 1935 the author with her parents, traveled the entire Big Bend, by a U-shaped gravel road 100 miles north and 100 miles south around the Selkirk Mountains. Forest on the arid east side consisted of slender lodgepole pine, and on the west side of huge rain-forest cedar, then followed the Columbia River south-east through the **Kootenays** in Canada [pp 153; map 177] through several spectacular canyons. At **Trail** the river was placid turquoise.
-We then crossed the border into the US **Kootenai** area, along a branch river to **Spokane,** and later saw the mighty Columbia at **Bonneville Dam**, between Oregon and the present Washington State. Then after a visit with relatives near **Tacoma** and **Puget Sound**, we went south through Redwood forest via **Vancouver**, Washington to **Portland**, Oregon, viewing **volcanic Mount Hood** and the mighty Columbia River again. The river continued wide to its mouth at the present **Vancouver, Oregon** [9 Vol 4, pp 371-3].
-1825 **Fort Vancouver** was established at the **mouth of the Columbia River**, the end of the **Oregon Trail**, by the Hudson Bay Co [16, p 260], near the 46th parallel. Supplies for the fort were brought by sea [map p 121].

-1827 the HBCo founded **Fort Langley**, near the Fraser River mouth [9 Vol 4, p 372; 120, p 899] [p 153; map p 121].
-1832-35 Benjamin **de Bonneville** born in **Paris** 1796; emigrated as a boy with his parents; joined the US army. When on leave, with private funding, he went on a trading/exploring expedition across the Great Basin desert of **Utah** and **Nevada** to **California**. He explored the Rockies and Columbia River in the present Washington State. He failed at fur-trading, publicized his discoveries & gave negative information to the US army of British activities in Oregon. The great Bonneville Dam, built 1933-7, was named for him [125 Vol 20, p 462].

The Second Great Wave of Migration Across the US 1834-44 [12 Vol 6, p 119; 125 Vol 20, pp 166-8].

-1837 telegraph and postal service began. **Jedediah Strong Smith** (1798-31) a trapper, opened up the west via the **Missouri River** and **Santa Fe Trail** [16, p 693] [See pp 126-128 above]. Settlers began to demand that the US take control of **Oregon** from the **British** [See p 129] and of southern territories from **Mexico**.
-1839 migration began from **New England** along the **Oregon Trail**, a journey of 4 to 6 months.
-1840 the **Oregon Trail** "was thick with wagon trains" of pioneers trekking west [119 Vol 8, pp 990-1]. The main stopping place was trading post **Fort Laramie**, **Wyoming**, founded 1843 [16, p 258].
-1842-3 British interests moved north from 46th parallel to 49th [9 Vol 4, pp 369-72]. The HBCo built **Fort Victoria** to stop the US from claiming **Vancouver Island** [120, p 899]. The first Governor was **Richard Blanshard**.
-1843 **Portland**, **Oregon** was founded where the **Williamette River** enters the Columbia [119 Vol 8, p 62; pp 990-1], and grew rapidly as more and more pioneers arrived from eastern US [16, p 590].
-1845 the **Texas Cession** from **Mexican rule**, was a huge addition to the U S [See pp 126-129 and map 157].
-1846 the **Oregon Treaty** determined the boundaries of Oregon, from the watershed in the Rocky Mountains and between 42°- 49° south to north. British territory was pushed back to the 49th parallel.
-1849 the **Territory of Oregon** joined the United States, including the present Washington & part of Idaho.
-1849 Great Britain proclaimed **Vancouver Island** a Crown Colony, and named **Victoria** the capital.
-1840-60 over 300,000 people crossed the Rockies into Oregon and California, 30 to 200 covered wagons at a time. 2000 cattle and 10,000 sheep accompanied them. They traveled 12 to 20 miles per day. 10,000 trekkers died en route from shortage of food, small pox, cholera and firearms accidents [125 Vol 15, pp 486-7].

Map: *The United States From Atlantic to Pacific in 1850* [151]

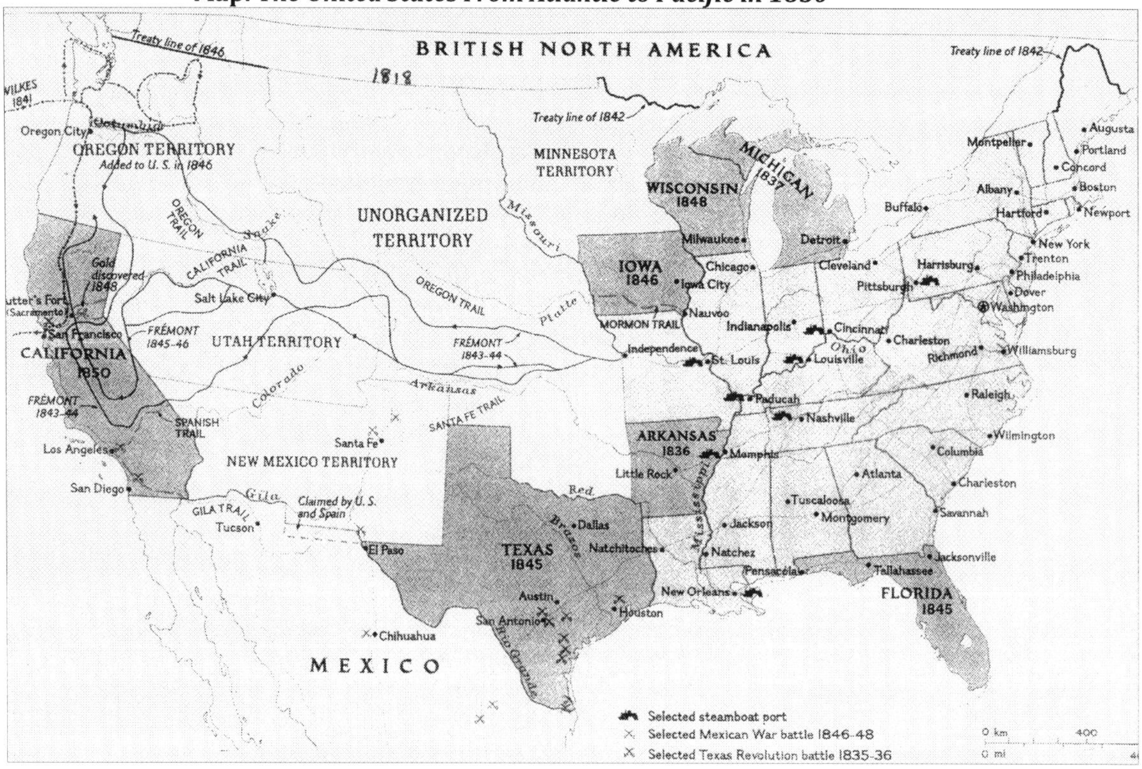

Chapter Nineteen

European Wars and Power Struggles 1795-1901

The French Revolution: 1789 to 1795 [Continued from p 116]

-1789 the **Estates-General** of nobles, clergy and commoners, called together for the first time since 1614, began writing a constitution. Charles Maurice de **Talleyrand**, a bishop with revolutionary ideas, was elected to represent clergy [110, p 107]. He suggested the government take over the church. He wrote a new **Civil Constitution for Clergy**, allowing them to marry. When some priests refused to serve under the government he ordained new priests. Excommunicated by the Pope, he took up a career in politics and diplomacy.

-1789 July, a mob destroyed the Bastille (prison); there were uprisings all over France. King **Louis** XVI was forced to move from secluded Versailles to Tuileries Palace, Paris [111, p 258]. Crowds filled the surrounding park.

-1791 by plebiscite a new Constitution was introduced and another in 1793. A new calendar with three 10 day weeks per month, replaced the Gregorian calendar until 1806 [110, pp 107-8]. Saint days were abolished. The metric system for weights and measures began. People were called **citoyen** (citizen) instead of monsieur or madame. The honorific *vous* (thou) was replaced by *tu* (you). Clothing was simplified, jewelry disapproved.

-1792 **Francis** II succeeded his father Leopold II, as **Emperor of Austria**. His **sister Marie Antoinette**, **Queen of France**, was in prison. This led in March to war between Austria and France [16, p 268]. In April **Prussia** rushed to support Austria and in August took **Verdun**. In August, urged by **Danton**, the people of Paris stormed Tuileries Palace. King Louis XVI ordered the Swiss Guard to fire on them. 600 Guardsmen died.

-1792 November **the French National Convention** offered to help all nations who wanted to overthrow their kings. Treaties with foreign countries were broken. This provoked the opposition of all monarchies [95, p 1793].

-1792 Charles de Talleyrand became ambassador to **England**.

-1792 September the **French Republic** was declared by extremists: **Danton, Robespierre** and **Marat**.

-1793 January, King Louis XVI was executed. February **France declared war on Britain, Holland and Spain**.

-1794 back in Paris, Talleyrand was under suspicion and banished. 1794-96 he lived in **America** [95, p 404].

-1794 April, **Robespierre** executed **Danton** and suspended the constitution. Juries convicted with no defense. Idealized government turned into terror [95, p 1794; 53b, pp135-160] and over 300 people were guillotined (beheaded) every month, up to a total of 17,000 [111, p 259; 167, p 112-3].

- 1794 June Robespierre declared himself high priest of a festival to the Supreme Being [110, p 109]. In July he and Marat was killed. In October Queen **Marie Antoinette** was guillotined;
Then the reign of terror ended [30, p 7]. The armies of neighbors were massing on French borders.

-1794-5 winter, the French army overran Holland, compelling Prussian & Spanish armies to withdraw [16, p 268].

-1795 Oct the Revolution ended when a third new constitution created a new **Directory of five officials** and **two chambers**: the *Council of Elders* (**Senate**) and the ***Council of 500*** [30, pp 18, 20; 16, p 197]. They ruled until 1799, aiming to end rule by royal families throughout Europe.

-1795 **Napoleon** only 26 years old, was commissioned to conduct campaigns in Italy, Egypt, and German States [See the details next page]. His influence on Italy & Switzerland grew; he enforced a treaty with **Austria** [16, p 197]; 1796 subdued Austria [16, p 268].

-1797 **Talleyrand** became French Foreign Minister, until 1807. [Continued pp 133-135]

The Education and Rise of Napoleon Bonaparte

-Napoleon (1769-1821) born in Corsica to a noble but not wealthy family, from 9 years of age studied at Brienne Military College, northern France. He knew more Italian than French; was a loner, but eager to learn.

-1784 at 15 he won a scholarship to an elite military academy in Paris. It was a finishing school for gentlemen. The young officers were popular in the salons of the upper classes. He was much influenced by philosophers of *The Enlightenment*, especially **Voltaire** and **Rousseau**. Among his friends were **many Polish refugees** who were planning ideal government for Poland. Napoleon became committed to change in France/Europe.

-At military college he chose the artillery so as to learn mathematics [110, p 109]. He also liked history, law and some science. The best military posts went to French nobility; he was sent to **Venice** as a second lieutenant.

-1789 when the Revolution began, 20 year old Napoleon was on leave in Paris, but was not a revolutionary.

-1792 when the Republic was declared, he took leave from the French army in Venice.

-1792 in October he returned to his homeland **Corsica,** where he became a lieutenant in the National Guard, but he was not trusted, being too French, too young and too ambitious. His family home was sacked and he was declared a traitor.

-1793 June, he fled to chaotic France with his widowed mother, three bothers and three sisters.

-Napoleon was reinstated in the army as an artillery Captain and sent to **Toulon** on the **Mediterranean** Ocean to fight the British [16, p 766]. Because of success December 1793 in the siege of Toulon [30, p 7] he was promoted to **Brigadier General** at age 24 [110, p 109]. Napoleon wrote a history of Corsica and a novel.
-1795 Oct, in command of artillery guarding a meeting in Paris, there was an attack that he ended with grape-sized canon balls. This impressed superiors.
-1796 March, he married widow **Josephine** and was sent two days later to Italy [30, p 8] as Commander of the Armée d'Intérieur (Commander-in-Chief). The French goal was to challenge Austria and all her allies. Daily he wrote love letters to Josephine.
-1796 Oct, the French National Convention dissolved.
-1796-98 during numerous battles in the **Italian Campaign** he revitalized the demoralized army [30, pp 8-15]. Greatly outnumbered by the enemy, he divided his troops and made surprise attacks from several directions. He demanded gold and silver from the defeated enemies, and used it to pay his troops and provide uniforms. He then relentlessly attacked **Austrians at Millesimo**, non-stop, taking great personal risks [167, p 126-131].
-1797 January after defeating the Austrian army **at Rivoli**, Napoleon dictated his own peace terms.
He set up other Italian republics and 1797 December Napoleon returned to Paris in triumph.
-1798 February he occupied **Rome**, proclaimed a Roman republic and took the pope into custody.
-1798 May he led his army into **Milan** and set up the **Lombard Republic**. 1798-99 July Napoleon in the **Egyptian Campaign**, though successful on land, was defeated at sea by the British under **Horatio Nelson**.
-1799 February the **Syrian Campaign** began, but plague broke out among the French troops. They were defeated in July by **Turkish-British troops**. In August Napoleon secretly returned to France, leaving another general in charge. Despite losses he had gained experience and skill [110, p 109].
-1799 November, Napoleon at age 30, **ousted the French regime** naming himself **First Consul** under a new constitution that gave him autocratic power [16, p 516; 53b, p 135-159].
-He revitalized the French army [111, p 261]. Fleet-footed and well dressed, they were taught "A village should feed a battalion for a week, a division for a day."

Three Partitions of Poland and an Insurrection [p 111 First Partition; p 113 Second and Third]

-**Napoleon's** interest in Poland was broad and long term. Polish noblemen fled to Paris after the **First Partition** of 1772. **French** became the polite language of Polish aristocrats. Polish ideas for ideal government drew from *The Enlightenment* [See p 92]. Under Russia the semi-autonomous government of **Central Poland** had much freedom.
-1791 a new liberal constitution invigorated the **Polish Sejm** (parliament). **Russia** was alarmed so invaded.
-1793 the **Second Partition** further divided Poland among **Prussia, Russia and Austria**. The Polish refugees in Paris continued to plan **Insurrections** to overthrow Russia and Prussia.
-1794 an **Insurrection** was planned and led by **Tadeusz Kościuszko** (1746-1817). He had serving as an engineer in the American Revolution with **Colonel rank** at Saratoga & **West Point**, USA [125 Vol 9, p 384];
-1786 USA Congress promoted him to **Brigadier General** [16, p 405]. In Polish history he is great [54] [See p 114]
-1795 in the **Third Partition** Poland ceased to exist as an independent country [12 Vol 5, p 84]. Prussia kept **Silesia** in the SW, and annexed **Poznan** (Posen in German) in NW Poland [12 Vol 9, pp 658-9]. Russia acquired **Lithuania** and **Volhynia** (Polish Ukraine) [53b, p 35]. **Lubin**, south Poland [WV Mar 92, p 9, 13] went to **Austria**.
-France welcomed Polish exiles, loudly endorsing their efforts to restore independence [WV 89, No 3, p 8 map].
-1797 **Napoleon** set up the **Polish Legion** in **Italy**, to fight for Poland's independence [27, p 14]. Napoleon's crack personal troops were all Poles. He was very mobile with his spirited light weight **Polish Lancers**. For ten years they spearheaded the battles of Napoleon throughout Europe, and became famous.

Conflicts in Russia, Poland, Prussia and Austria 1795-1804 [Continued from pp 112-3]

-1763 **Catherine** II **the Great** invited ethnic German farmers from Alsace and Germany to settle in the Volga area and keep out the Moguls and Turks. Thousands came, but many only got as far as Poland or north Russia.
-1797-1840 Prussian **Frederick William** III succeeded his father Frederick William II (1785-97). Early in his reign he invited people from **Alsace** and **Württemberg**, SW Germany, to settle in **Prussia** [105, p 51-2; 92].
-1798-9 Thus many **Swabians (Schwabs)** migrated to **Poland** settling in **Lodz, Warsaw** and **Plock** areas. They were craftsmen, proud of their long cultural history. Local Germanic people found it hard to understand their High German dialect and accent, mixed with French, and felt put down by their superior airs. The author's Schwab grandfather Adolph Klammer, was an apprenticed carpenter in the Russian Polish army.

-1796-1801 Russian **Czar Paul** I succeeded his mother Catherine the Great [32, pp 214-8]. He was unpopular due to a violent temper. He sided with England but quarreled, joined Napoleon; was killed in a scuffle with nobles.
-1801-25 **Czar Alexander** I, oldest grandson of Catherine the Great, like her 50 years earlier [92], invited farmers from **Alsace, Baden** and **Württemberg** to settle in Russia [See pp 111-112 and below pp 136-140].
-1801-1815 there was mass migration to Poland and Russia from Alsace-Lorraine, Württemberg and other SW German states due to overpopulation, conscription and occupation by both French and German troops. During this period most migrants settled either in Poland or the treeless steppes near the **Black Sea**.

Napoleon's Focus on Law, Infrastructure and Vital Statistics [from pp 116 and 131]

-1800 June, Napoleon's army entered Austria via Switzerland and won major battles, living off the villagers.
-1801 foreign minister **Talleyrand** skillfully negotiated with the Pope to permit priests who married, to continue as priests. After this agreement the Pope became a supporter of Napoleon [110, p 110].
-1802 after another successful **Italian campaign** Napoleon declared himself **Consul for Life** [16, p 516]. He created the elegant cavalry, **Legion of Honor**, drawing on ideas from ancient Rome [30, p 43]. Members were honored with money, five ranks and titles for meritorious service of the Empire, not just of France.
-1804 **Haiti, French West Indies** became a republic; Napoleon's army could not suppress rebel slaves [95, p 410].
-1804 March, the **Code of Napoleon** became law in France, Belgium, Luxemburg and the Palatinate (on the Rhine River). This efficient system of laws was based upon reason and common sense, rather than vested interests or class privilege. Adopted in many countries, it influenced nations for centuries [12 Vol 8, p 511].
-1804 after another successful campaign in **Italy** the French Senate proclaimed Napoleon **Emperor** Dec 1804 in Notre Dame Cathedral, Paris when Napoleon crowned himself Emperor [30, pp 30-1]. The Pope was present.
-Napoleon became zealous for every phase of the nation's development [30, p 43]. All over France he had a network of canals and roads built and ports enlarged. He encouraged industrialization in textiles and steel and had great steel bridges and towers built. New agricultural products such as potatoes, beet sugar, chicory for coffee and cattle breeding were spurred by fairs, exhibitions and state subsidies. Talent, science and art were rewarded, but under government control. At the same time Napoleon maintained control of Europe with mobile troops capable of 30 miles per day, rather than the usual 6 or 7 miles per day of enemy armies.
-1792-1835 **Francis** II **of Hapsburg-Lorraine/Austria** was Holy Roman Emperor. In 1804 he took the title of **Emperor** of Austria/Bohemia/Hungary/& Italy. 1797-1809 he was frequently at war with Napoleon.
-The industrial, educational and agricultural *Settlements* of Moravian Brethren (Brüder Gemine or Unity) in Saxony, Prussia, Poland and Silesia, were repeatedly trampled and forced to provide provisions to both sides.
-1804 to 1814 Napoleon made **Warsaw, Poland** his headquarters and had a Polish mistress and son.
-1805 October, at **Trafalgar**, near **Spain** the British fleet under Admiral **Horatio Nelson**, defeated the French and Spanish fleets, sinking 20 enemy ships and losing none, ending Napoleon's plans to invade England, but Nelson died [110, p 111; 30, p 34-5].
-1805-9 Napoleon's varied interests included completing Milan Cathedral [6, p 101; 91, pp 108-9]. He also appointed the author's ancestors Johann Schneider and son, sculptors/stone masons from Alsace-Lorraine, to repair the Cathedral of the Decapitation of St. John the Baptist, **Warsaw**, Poland [40, Part 1; WV 69, pp 10-11] [See pp 144-146].
-1805 Nov, Napoleon took **Vienna**; Dec he defeated Austrian & Russian armies [95, p 411] at **Austerlitz** in Moravia. He ousted Austria from Italy and Germany [30, pp 36-41]; fought Prussia in **Saxony** where Brethren *Settlements* had to care for 20,000 wounded soldiers of both sides, and give fodder for horses/cattle on maneuvers [57, pp 306-311].
-1806 he confederated over 300 **German states:** combined them to form only 83 [30, p 36] and distributed some Hapsburg (Austrian) lands among them. 1806 he occupied **Hamburg** [under George III of England [pp 134-5].
-1806 Oct 14, the Prussians were defeated at **Jena** in **Saxony,** and lost **Posen** (Poznan). Oct 27 he occupied **Berlin**, capital of Prussia, which suffered little [30, pp 40-1]. It was a lively cultural centre with a famous university founded in 1574 and refounded 1695 [9 Vol 4, p 9; 3] [See pp 90, 88, 92 and 111, 113].
-1806 Napoleon founded the **Grand Dutchy of Varsovie (Warsaw)**, a new puppet state within his empire, added **Posen** and implemented the **Napoleonic Code** for administration of legal matters, collection of taxes, military conscription and vital statistics [WV Mar 96, p 9] [The author found some records of ancestors in archives].
-1806 Napoleon **dissolved the Holy Roman Empire** [16, p 341, 319]. Francis II remained Emperor of Austria only.
-1807 Feb Napoleon defeated an Austrian-Russian army at Eylau Poland; June defeated Prussian-Russians at Friedland [95, pp 410-12]. Troops on both sides requisitioned food/stole horses/plundered farms/schools/churches.
-1807 July Napoleon negotiated the **Tilsit Treaty of Peace** and Alliance between Russia and France, and
-1808 September-October, tried/failed to reconcile with Russia. Napoleon was impatient for unity and order.

-1807 Charles **de Talleyrand**, foreign minister 1797-1807, tried unsuccessfully to modify aggression [16, p 740] but Napoleon continued to force his goal to unite and modernize small feudal regimes.

-1808 March, troops of Napoleon invaded **Spain** so as to depose the Bourbon king and install **Napoleon's brother Joseph** as King. May-July Spaniards rebelled, not wanting new rulers who looted gold from their churches. In August **English Duke of Wellington** arrived with troops, and assisted by locals (**guerrillas** in Spanish) with small attacks, began to drive the French out of Spain [30, pp 46-7; 110, p 111]; accomplished in 1814.

-1809 Napoleon divorced Josephine [16, p 387, 467] because they had no children, and April 1810 married **Marie Louise,** daughter of Emperor Francis II of **Austria**; 1811 March a son born, was named King of Rome [30, pp 51-3].

-1809-1812 there was relative peace. Napoleon continued to promote orderly, centralized administration.

-1810 **Prussia abolished serfdom** giving serfs lands they cultivated for their feudal lords [95, p 414]. 1812 **Napoleon Boneparte massed** 453,000 (600,000 ?) soldiers in Poland with 22 French Generals & 200 officers quartered in Moravian Brethren *Settlements* [57, pp 306-311] in **Saxony** and a division of Württemberger troops [12 Macropedia Vol 24, pp 748-55] in tents around their *Settlements* in **Silesia**. In June advance began into Russia with 90,000 **live cattle for food** [110, p 111].

Map: *Confederation of the Rhine and Grand Duchy of Warsaw* [44, p 128]

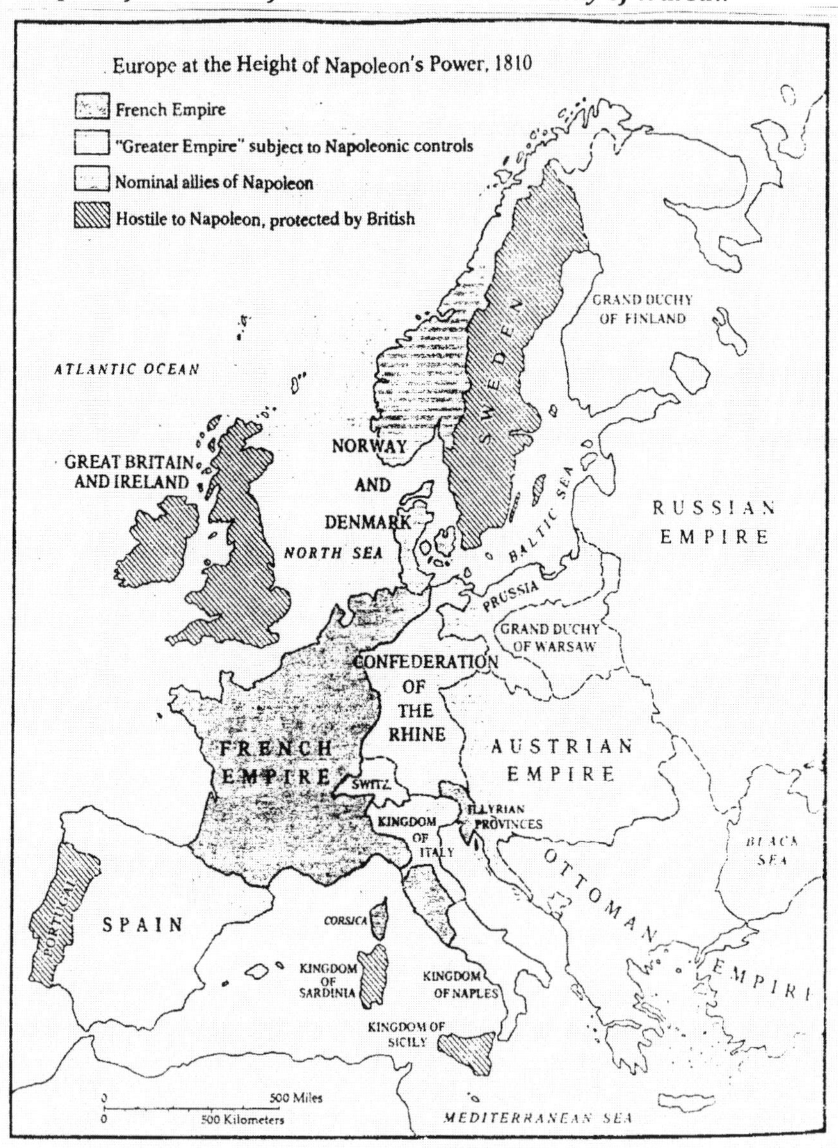

-Like their **Scythian** ancestors [58, pp 16-25] the Russians had deserted and burned their own villages. Fires/heavy fighting surrounded them. In September, deceived by success in battle, Napoleon occupied Moscow, also empty. It was a trap. The Russians attacked.

-Supply lines were cut off by sub-zero weather with much snow. By November fewer than 10,000 (100,000?) soldiers survived; December Napoleon escaped to Paris [30, pp 54-6] and his troops scattering. **For insight into life in Poland** [33 WV, pp 13-31] see a remarkable travelogue by an Englishman in 1814, who went by stage-coach from St. Petersburg, 1900 miles across Poland to **Berlin**, describing villages, farms, orchards, forest and inns en route. This English traveler visited St John's church cathedral in Warsaw [see pp 144-146]. He also viewed the city from the dome [cover photo WV Jun 93] of the Lutheran church. Acoustics in the church were excellent [30]. West of Warsaw via Posen, they had interesting stops at inns. There were dangers from robbers, wolves and river crossings on floating bridges.

-Napoleon's troops were still roaming about in Poland after defeat in Russia [167, pp 124-131].

-1813 May, Napoleon still had some success against Prussians in Saxony, and truces.

-1813-4 Wars of liberation erupted all over Europe [95, pp 416-7]. Prussia broke away from Varsovie.
-Russian and Prussian troops occupied Dresden, Saxony. Napoleon's troops won victories at Hamburg & Dresden, had losses at Leipsig & Danzig and several other areas.
-1814 April, forced to abdicate, Napoleon was imprisoned on the **Island of Elba**, near Italy, but
-1815 March escaped to Paris. 1815 June, at **Waterloo** in Belgium, he was defeated by **British Duke of Wellington** and **Prussian** allies. Napoleon abdicated a second time.
-He was imprisoned by the British at **St. Helena**, off the west African coast. He died May 1821.

Literature and Music

[Continued from p 91]

-Ludvig von **Beethoven** (1770-1827) was born in Prussia, studied in Vienna, composed 9 symphonies, 32 piano sonatas, two masses and an opera, during this time of war [16, p 83; 95, pp 404-426].
-1818 Beethoven became completely deaf, but continued writing outstanding compositions.
-During this period other musicians excelled: Joseph **Haydn** (1732-1809), Gioacchino **Rossini** (1792-1868), Carl Maria von **Weber** (1789-1826), Franz **Grüber** (Silent Night) and Franz **Schubert** (1797-1828) [95, pp 416-7].
-Some famous **authors** were: **Goethe** (1749-1832), **Robert Burns** (1759-96), Samuel Taylor **Coleridge** (1772-1834), William **Wordsworth** (1770-1850), William **Blake** (1757-1827), Walter **Scott** (1771-1832), Francisco **de Goya** (1746-1828), **Jane Austen** (1775-1817), Lord **Byron** (1788-1824), Jacob and Wilhelm **Grimm** - Fairy Tales (1785-1863), John **Keats** (1795-1821) and later Charles **Dickens** (1812-70).

Great Britain During the reigns of George IV and William IV

-1760-1820 **George** III was King of England and Hanover, but **never visited Hanover**. When mentally ill,
-1788 and 1811-20 his son George IV was Regent. The coffers were drained by wars [see pp 117-120].
-1820-30 **George** IV became monarch of both Hanover and Great Britain. He visited Hanover only once.
-1830-37 **William** IV, third son of George III, in 1827 had become Lord High Admiral and Duke of Clarence.
-1833 a charter extended power to the middle class, and the beginning of **rights for peasants** [12 Vol 5, pp 685-6].
-1837 William IV died without an heir so connection ended with **Hanover**.
-Ernest Augustus, the Duke of Cumberland, became King of Hanover.
-1837-1901 **Queen Victoria** began her long reign [continued p 141].

Impact of Napoleon on British Interests and Overseas Missions

-Taxation in England and colonies rose to make up for loss of trade in Europe by blockades by Napoleon.
-British ship builders unable to import lumber from the Baltic began a huge lumbering industry in **Canada**.
-Steam power in factories with machine-run looms started the ***industrial revolution***.
-**England** was the first nation to build vast mechanized factories. As the machine age began many laborers were no longer needed so unemployment became serious [57, p 312].
-Moravian Brethren Bishops sailing to America and the **West Indies** to reinforce and encourage missions in many places, made stopovers in England and Denmark, strengthening the church there also.
-Communications with Moravians headquarters at Berthelsdorf, near Herrnhut in Saxony were precarious during the war. As a result the work went ahead with less supervision.
-In Fulnek, England & Ireland Moravian schools for boys & girls were built of stone in simple gracious design. Self-supporting *Settlements* produced many crafts [57, p 313], some established by single men, others by women.
-**Britain became the foremost sea power**, trading and setting up colonies around the world.
-1804 the **British and Foreign Bible Society** was founded and a growing interest in foreign missions.
-1806 the south African **Cape Colony** became a British possession. Freeing of slaves was opposed by the descendants of Dutch colonists of 1652 (**Afrikaners** or **Boers**, meaning farmers) [12 Vol 2, p 319] [pp 72, 136].
-1808 two **Moravian Brethren Bishops** returning after two years in America, approved the building of a theological seminary in Fulnek, England, because of a shortage of ministers [57, p 314].
-1811 in England the future **George** IV, 49 years, became **Regent** because of **King George** III's mental illness.
-1812 & 1816 **Luddites** (for Ned Ludd) rioted in England blaming machines for unemployment/poverty.
-1815 English Moravian Brethren **La Trobe** and **Schmidt** restarted a mission in **Cape Colony**, S. Africa.
-1817 the *London Association in Aid of Moravian Missions* founded in response to news of much war damage of churches and *Settlements* in Europe. They raised $3350 the first year, tactfully, without publicity [57, pp 312-4].
-1817 in Lititz, **Pennsylvania** the first Synod of the Moravian American Province was held. 12 ministers, and 13 deputies, participated for the first time; sent proposals to Unity Synod in Herrnhut, Saxony.

Redistribution of Land and Recovery After the Napoleonic Wars

-1797-1840 **Prussian Frederick William** III participated in **the Congress of Vienna.**
-1814-24 France recalled king **Louis** XVIII **Bourbon** from exile in England, to become their monarch [16, p 444].
-1814-15 the **Congress of Vienna** redistributed Europe. Representatives of all European States participated, including Britain. **Talleyrand** secured fairly favorable terms for France; Russia kept Central Poland Province (Mittelpolen) and also acquired Poznan and the east part of the Baltic Sea were together called *Congress Kingdom of Poland* [12, Vol 5, p 84]. Austria kept east and west **Galicia** which they had ruled[WV, March 92, p 9] since the partition of 1772; and Lubin [WV, Mar 90, pp 10-13] since 1795. Prussia kept **Silesia,** part of the Baltic and, in place of Poznan received the **Saxon kingdom**[16; 106, pp 38-41.] *Congress Poland,* was semi-autonomous until 1914, and active in Industrial development and construction., The Roman Catholic leaders preserved Polish culture, language and identity [27, p 14]. Map: *Europe in 1815 After the Congress of Vienna*[46c]

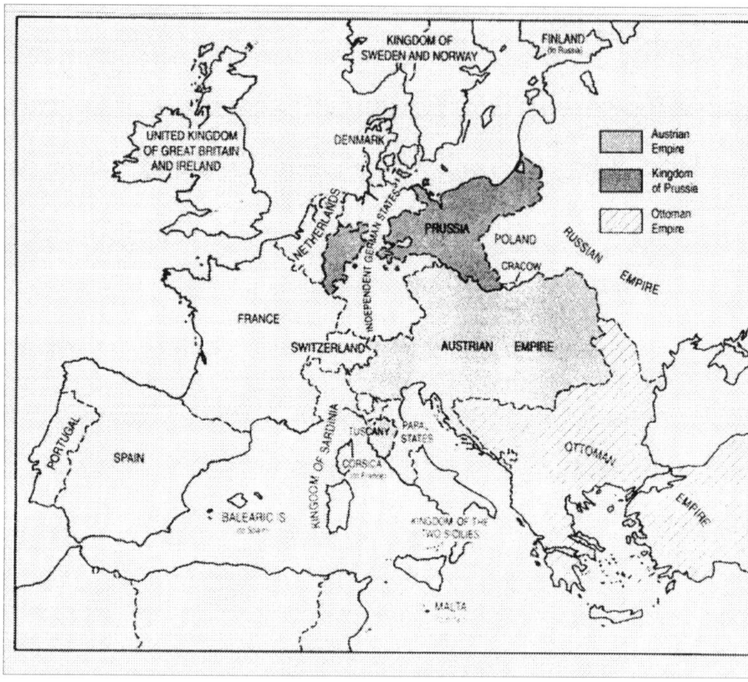

-1818 the General Synod of Unity (Moravian) met in Herrnhut, Saxony and agreed to some of the American province proposals. The Theological Seminary & Archives in Herrnhut were transferred to Gnadenfeld on the Polish border.-1822 Centenary of *Resusitation* of the Unity of Brethren celebrated in Herrnhut [57, p 345] for three days by thousands, including some English representatives. The name *Unity* was used more often than *Moravian.* The Centenary of the *Hourly Intercession* (continuous prayer watcb)[pp 99-100] begun in 1723, was a time of renewal. The *Daily Texts* printed in many languages ages are still widely distributed
-1815-24 Louis XVIII Bourbon, brother of guillotined Louis XVI, ruled France.
-1824-30 **Charles** X Bourbon ruled, but not equal to the task, abdicated and died in Italy [16, p 140].
-1830-48 Louis Philippe **Bourbon** king of **France** was deposed and the **Second Republic** established [16, p 445].
-1807 **Britain** abolished slave trade; 1833 abolished in colonies[3]. 1802 **Danish** slave trade ended;
-1847 emancipated[110, p 119]. Moravian missions thrived in **British** & **Danish West Indies.**
-1835 to escape British anti-slavery law 12,000 S African **Boers** trekked inland [12Vol 2, pp 319-20; Vol 11, p 33; 139 pp 314-7] with their **slaves.**
-1836 the Unity (Moravian Brethren) General Synod in Herrnhut, Saxony, was chaired by Bishop Currie who had served 20 years in **Surinam,** South America. There were reports from 39 schools in various countries.
-1838 a two-story Normal School for Hottentot teachers was founded by Moravians in **South Africa** [57, p 42]

Russian Czars Invited Ethnic Germans to Settle Vacant Land

[from p 112; see map p 137]

-1762-96 **Catherine** II **the Great** ruled Russia. 1763 she began to promote development of farming in southern Russia, attracting settlers from **Alsace-Lorraine**, **Baden**, **Württemberg**, **Hesse** and other SW German duchies to migrate to Russia. The large treeless plain by the Black Sea, had for centuries been held by nomadic **Mugols**, followed by **Turks**. Settling of farmers in the south would help prevent re-invasion.
-Thirteen **Lutheran villages** were founded at St. Petersburg [WV, Mar 93, p 8], but the majority settled near the lower **Volga** River. **Saratov**, a village with Moravian Brethren beginnings, became a populous Roman Catholic and Evangelical Lutheran centre.
- **Mennonites,** from the north coast of Europe, settled in many large colonies in south-eastern Russia [p 138; maps 94, 137].
-1798-9 Franconian (Rhine River) immigrants went to south Russia due to promises of concessions: freedom of religion, purchase of land at nominal cost, freedom from military service, and their own schools.

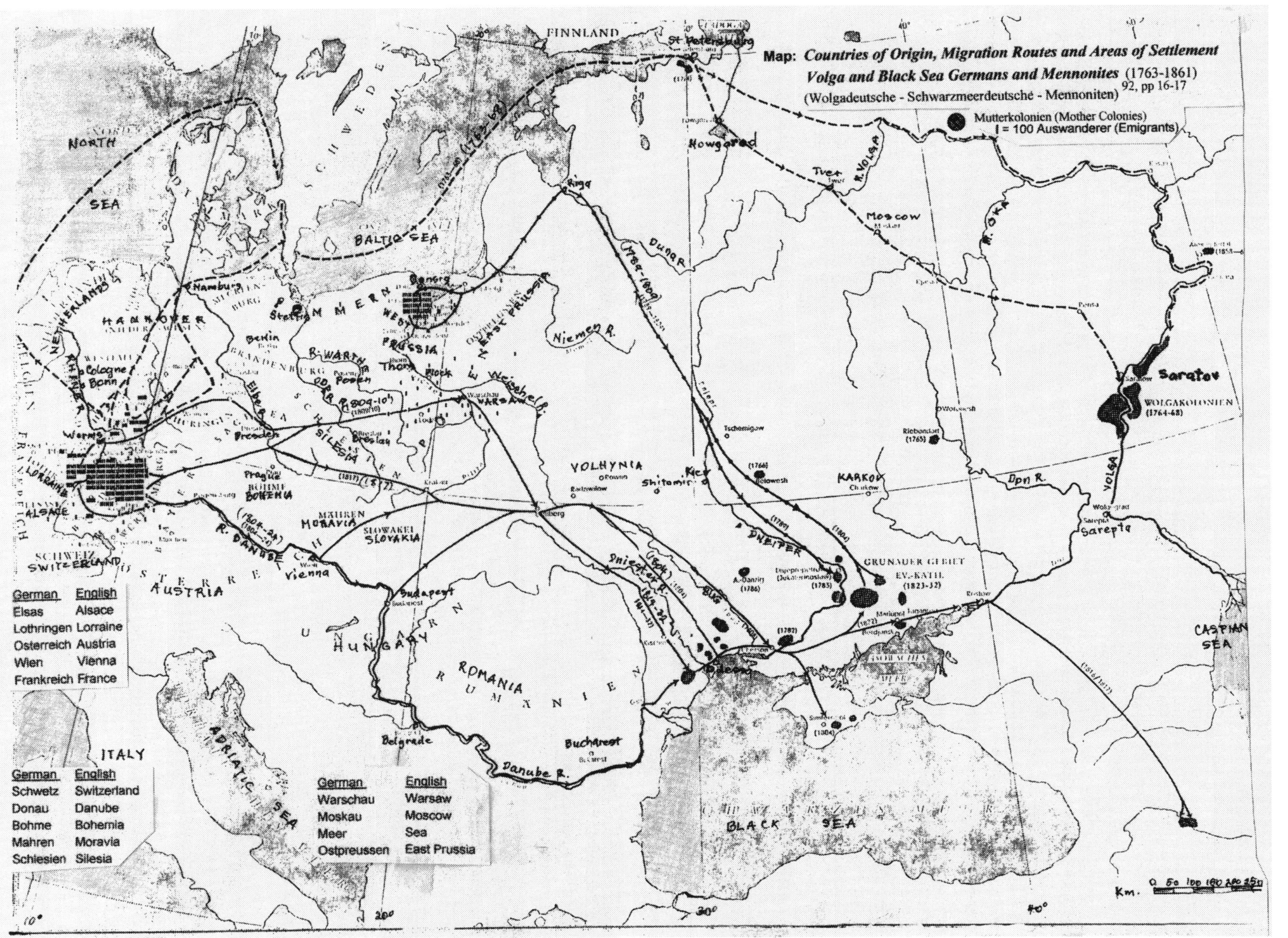
Map: Countries of Origin, Migration Routes and Areas of Settlement
Volga and Black Sea Germans and Mennonites (1763-1861)
(Wolgadeutsche - Schwarzmeerdeutsche - Mennoniten) 92, pp 16-17
Mutterkolonien (Mother Colonies)
I = 100 Auswanderer (Emigrants)
German English
Elsas Alsace
Lothringen Lorraine
Osterreich Austria
Wien Vienna
Frankreich France
German English
Schwetz Switzerland
Donau Danube
Bohme Bohemia
Mahren Moravia
Schlesien Silesia
German English
Warschau Warsaw
Moskau Moscow
Meer Sea
Ostpreussen East Prussia
FINNLAND
NORTH SEA
BALTIC SEA
BLACK SEA
ADRIATIC SEA
CASPIAN SEA
ITALY
St. Petersburg
Tver
R. VOLGA
Moscow
R. OKA
Saratov
WOLGAKOLONIEN (1764-68)
VOLGA
Sarepta
Riga
Niemen R.
EAST PRUSSIA
PRUSSIA
Danzig
Stettin
Berlin
Hamburg
HANNOVER
NETHERLANDS
Cologne
Bonn
Worms
LORRAINE
ALSACE
SWITZERLAND
Posen
Breslau
SILESIA
Dresden
Prague
BOHEMIA
MORAVIA
SLOVAKIA
Vienna
R. DANUBE
AUSTRIA
HUNGARY
Budapest
ROMANIA
Belgrade
Bucharest
Danube R.
VOLHYNIA
Shitomir
Kiev
KARKOV
Dpn R.
DNEIPER
Dniester R.
GRUNAUER GEBIET
EV.-KATH.
(1823-32)
Km.

-1796-1801 **Czar Paul** I succeeded his mother Catherine the Great [102, pp 214-8]; was unpopular. Czar Paul I sided with England but quarreled and joined Napoleon; was killed in a scuffle with nobles.
-1801-25 **Czar Alexander** I, oldest grandson of Catherine II [102, pp 219-39], like her invited settlers from south-west Germany [92, pp 6-21] and promised the same concessions.

-1804-14 settlers arrived in large numbers. Some traveled via Poland and others by the Baltic Sea to St. Petersburg. They continued down the Dnieper River to **Odessa**, the treeless steppes north of the Black Sea, now **south Ukraine**. Czar Alexander's appointee, **French** expatriate **Governor Duc de Richelieu**, saw to it that they settled in and were treated fairly. Settlers found the early years extremely difficult in the **Steppes** due to lack of building materials, water, rain and experience. Richelieu provided acacia, willows and aspens the only trees that survived. Peas, beans and potatoes did well. Orchards and art of grafting developed.

-1814 **Czar Alexander** I defeated **Napoleon** [See above p 134].
-1815 the Moravian settlement at **Sarepta** since 1765, still had the goal of outreach to central Asia. Efforts were renewed when there were two converts from **Lake Baikal**, and the gospels were printed in a **Tatar** dialect. Czar Alexander l approved [57, p 432]. 1822 an imperial edict forbad further evangelism of Moguls [57, p 432].
-1823 fire swept through the town of **Sarepta**, and burned for a week. Donations flowed in from the **Moravian** churches and Diaspora in Germany, England and America, notably $1000 from the congregation in New York[57, p 443]. Attractive homes were again built of wood [92, p 50 (see photograph)] [see p 112].
-1817 Czar Alexander l initiated generous privileges for Brethren in **Livonia** and **Esthonia** [57, p 311], the Baltic.
-1817 at last 1360 **Swabian** people from **Württemberg** reached Odessa, after traveling 3 years by the 1700 mile route via the Danube River [93, pp xi and 233]. En route 1300 people died in conflicts, food shortages & exposure [Map p 137 by Karl Stumpp, *The German* Russians [92] and Joseph S. Height, *Homesteaders on the Steppe* [93]]
-1825-55 **Czar Nicholas** l (1796-1855) succeeded his brother Czar Alexander l; waged war against **Persia** increasing his dominions [maps 94]. 1848 he helped put down a **Hungarian** revolt against **Austria**.
-Gradually wheat fields, orchards, vegetable gardens, and vineyards in southern Russia became very productive. Sheep, cattle and horses thrived/multiplied. Germanic settlers were able to build fine village and district schools and churches, both **Lutheran** and **Roman Catholic**. In 1803 **Odessa** on the Black Sea was a fishing village, but by 1850, 50 years later, the population of Odessa had swelled with German craftsmen, farm equipment manufacturers, two doctors, an Evangelical hospital, secondary schools, great churches (Catholic, Evangelical Lutheran, Reformed and Baptist) and many **Jews** [92, pp 8-21].
- 50 **Russian cities** had a population of 500 to 5000 **ethnic Germans** [92, p 9]. The Roman Catholic seminary at **Saratov** benefited all Russian communities [92, pp 6-21].

Polish Attempts to Gain Independence from Russia

[Continued from p 132]

-1830 **Czar Nicholas** l reformed **Russian** law with Napoleonic Code influence.
-1830-31 he suppressed a Polish Insurrection (Uprising) trying to extinguish their nationalism [16, p 528]. About 6000 Polish leaders forced into exile, mainly fled to **France** [12 Macropedia Vol 25, p 949].
-Polish composer pianist **Frederic Chopin** (1810-1849) toured many cities of Europe[54]. 1831 Chopin settled in Paris, went to **England** to give a concert for Polish refugees the year before he died, of tuberculosis [12 Vol 3].
-1830, 1846 and 1848 there were **three major Insurrections** (Uprisings, Rebellions) by Polish nobility to overthrow Russian rule of Poland. The insurrections failed, but the Poles did have internal independence.
-The Polish Roman Catholic church preserved and defended Polish culture, language and identity.

Germanic People In Poland

[Continued from pp 55, 64-66, 80, 88, 92, 111 and 113]

- For many centuries ethnic Germans had moved into Poland from the west, south and north, in successive waves. Their spoke various forms of Plautdietsch (Low German) and other dialects and several versions of High German, Through Luther's Bible a common language was emerging. See examples of settlers as follows:
-1798-9 on invitation from Prussian king **Frederick William** III many **Swabians** (Schwabs) migrated to Poland and settled in **Lodz**, **Warsaw** and **Plock** areas. They were craftsmen, proud of their long cultural history. Local Germanic people found it hard to understand their High German dialect and accent, mixed with French, and felt put down by their superior airs.
-They practiced **Schultz** type village government, with a privileged hereditary Schultz (mayor) [62],[66].
-**Hollandry** village democracy, with elected officials [66; 67] was enjoyed by Mennonites and other Germanics who had lived in Poland for centuries.

-1801-25 **Czar Alexander** I, oldest grandson of Catherine the Great, like her 100 years earlier [92], invited **Alsace**, **Baden** and **Württemberg** farmers to settle in Russia [pp 112, 132-133 136]. Many stayed in **Poland**.
-About 1805 Johann Schneider I and son Johann II, migrated from Alsace to Warsaw where they lived 60 years. They were **Roman Catholic** in **Alsace-Lorraine** but became **Lutheran** in Poland [See pp 144-148].
-Uncles and cousins of the author reported that a brother of Johann Schneider l or ll was a Bach Choir conductor in Berlin. Another relative Eugene Schneider, manufactured munitions in France.
Johann Schneider III, Baroque builder of inns/palaces even inserted an elegant fish pond in a palace ceiling.
-1842 the author's grandfather Johann Schneider IV, was born at Pomoschno 20 miles NW of **Warsaw**, near Neo-Gothic Lutheran church built 1782 at **Neuhof** (**Nowy Dwor**). His father Johann III died when he was 9.
- Johann IV worked for strangers and an uncle and learned to grow and graft grapes which suggests living in the south, perhaps in Bessarabia or Odessa [WV 89 no 3, pp 7-8; WV Mar 90, pp 10-11]. His great grandfather and grandfather, Johann I & II were from Alsace where viniculture was common; Johann III was born in Poland, a climate too cold for grapes. He learned many languages; returned to Poland; 1863 migrated to Volhynia with relatives.

Some Ethnic Germans Were Settling in Volhynia (Northern Ukraine) 1800-1860

-Since the era of **Teutonic Knights** some Polish and Germanic nobility were owners of estates in Volhynia.
-1801 a Lutheran parish was established in **Shitomir** (**Zhytomir**), the capital city of the province of Volhynia, 90 km west of **Kiev**. It served a large area: the counties (kreis) **Shitomir**, **Nowograd-Wolynsk**, **Saslaw**, **Staro-Konstantinow** and, **Owrursch**.
-At **Annette** and **Josephine** [map 149] 80 km NW of Shitomir, in the county of **Nowograd-Wolynsk** (Volhynia=Wolinien) [WV, Vol 89, No 3, p 11-13], a landlord founded Lutheran settlements, with colonists from Prussia.
- 1825-55 **Czar Nicholas** l, born 1796, succeeding brother Czar Alexander l, ruled Russia & Congress Poland. The German speaking population of Volhynia was small during this period.
-1831 after a Polish Insurrection (Uprising) **urban Lutherans** who were loyal to the Russian Czar felt threatened by the Poles, so they began to migrate east into western Volhynia [WV, No 3, 89, p 11; WV, Dec 95, pp 8-10].
Five Groups of Ethnic Germans Settled in Volhynia, now northern Ukraine [WV, Mar 95, pp 16-18]:

1. **Mennonites** who were farmers skilled with haying, purebred dairy cattle, windmills and water wheels;
2. **Silesians** who made quality oak furniture;
3. **Kaschubian** farmers from Pomerania and Poznan, Prussia, who migrated 1833 [see pp 15-16];
4. **Bughollanders** who had lost their German language but were Protestants, who in 1836 bought land around the village of **Josephine**, vacated by Mennonites who moved to south Russia; and
5. **Low German** wool and linen **cloth-makers** who came 1833; considered higher class Burgers (citizens).

Modest Reforms by Russian Czars and Turks

-1851 Russia's first **railway** line, from St. Petersburg to Moscow was completed [39, p 144].
-1853 War between Russia and Turkey (Russo-Turkish) and 1854-56 the **Crimean War,** were attempts by Russia to conquer Turkey and secure dominance in south east Europe [see p 147].
-The **British** and **French** invaded Russia for balance of power.
-Thousands on both sides died, half of them from Typhus and Cholera.
-Neither side gained, but peace was signed in Paris [16, pp 173, 646; 777].
-Britain was shocked into making military reforms[74, pp 13-19], especially by **Florence Nightingale** in health care and sanitation [39, p 145] [See p 142]. Other good results were that:
-The Allies forced the Muslim Ottoman Sultan to reform prisons, abolish torture and grant civil rights to Christians. The Black Sea was made neutral.
-1855-81 **Czar Alexander** II succeeding his father Nicholas I, was autocratic, but made some good changes. He accomplished judicial reform: trial by jury, judges independent of administration, proceedings in public, fewer and less severe corporal punishments (floggings) and an independent bar.
-He started elected rural and town government, liberalized the educational system, and reduced military service from twenty-five down to six years. However: "The final decision was always his, so that he was called his own prime minister" [102, pp 259-287]. 1856 Czar Alexander II spoke out against slavery & planned release of serfs. By negotiating with unwilling noblemen for six years, **he prevented civil war**.
-He annexed large parts of southern and eastern Asia [102, pp 273-4].[Map p 94]
-1861 **Russian** serfs were freed by Czar Alexander II.
-The same year civil war in the **USA** began and lasted four years, mainly over the issue of slavery.

Map: *Central Europe 1850* [63,WVSep 93,p12].German (English): Kgr (Congress of Vienna 1815, p136), Mahren(Moravia), Galizien (Galicia), Osterreich (Austria), Wein (Vienna), Ungarn (Hungary), Schweiz (Switzerland).[See maps p 136, 137].

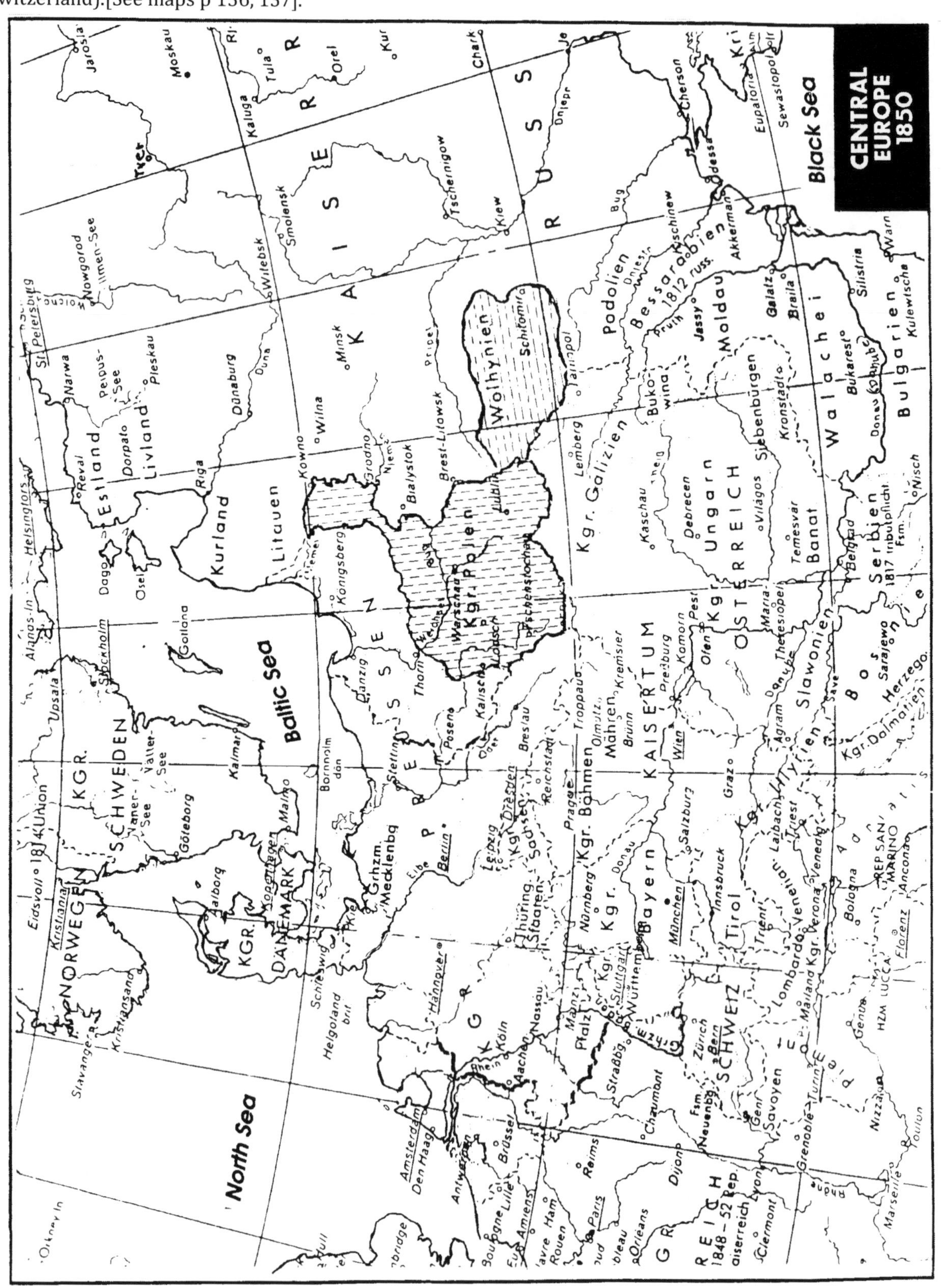

Famine and Civil Unrest in Europe

-1833 sketches of English life by author **Charles Dickens** (1812-70) were published in newspapers. His serialized *The Pickwick Papers* and books *Oliver Twist, Nicholas Nickleby, Old Curiosity Shop* and other books stimulated the upper and middle classes to respect the poor and appreciate their struggles.
-1842 Charles Dickens was in America.
-1843 he returned to England and wrote *Martin Chuzzlewit* and *The Christmas Carol* and for 17 years, many other books that have become classics, such as *David Copperfield* and *A Tale of Two Cities*. He created fascinating characters who seem alive.
-1845-6 Potato crops failed throughout Europe, from **Ireland** to **Russia**.
-1847 English Moravians donated corn (wheat) to **Ireland.** 1¼ million Irish fled mostly to America [95, pp 442-3].
-1848 **Karl Marx** along with coauthor **Friedrich Engels**, published *The Communist Manifesto*. Marx was run out of **Belgium**, was in **Germany** a few months and after an uprising there, in **England** until his death 1883.
-1848 **Switzerland** with a new constitution became a federal union [3, p 414].
-1848 **Kirchentag** (Church Diet - Evangelical Alliance) in Wittenberg had wide representation [57, p 388].
-1848-9 the civil unrest in **Denmark**, **Prussia**, **Saxony**, **Austria**, the **Palatinate** (Rhine) and **Baden** caused many villagers and burghers to flee. **Milan** threw off Austrian rule.
-1848-9 Czar Nicholas assisted in putting down the **Hungarian revolt** against Austria.
-Some **Moravian Brethren** from **Saxony** went to **Australia, Illinois**, USA, and **Nicaragua** [57, p 387].
-1851 a Moravian Normal School was founded in **Surinam**, S. America, to prepare former slaves as teachers.
-1855 a Moravian mission began in Leh, **Ladak**, north India. [Rev. Dr. Sam Marx, born to missionaries there married the author's university classmate. He took his medical degree at McGill. They served in Nicaraugua.]
-1862 **Wilhelm** I of **Prussia** and his chief minister **Bismarck**, together planned to crush Austria [16, pp 91, 600].
-1866 Prussia in the **Seven Weeks' War** first took over **Schleswig-Holstein** and Moravian Brethren were forced to billet 1000 soldiers; a church was used as a hospital. Prussia moved south into Saxony to attack **Austria** "to unify the fatherland." The railway passed through transporting troops and supplies. Members of three Moravian Brethren *Settlements* dressed wounds of friends and foes even at the front [57, pp 439-440; 16, pp 675-6].
-1867 after 45 years of experience in leprosy care in South Africa [57, p 506], Moravian Brethren were able to open an asylum for **lepers** at **Jerusalem**, continuing until the present.
-1869 After 400 years underground or in exile, Moravian Brethren with permission of the Austrian government, established four congregations in **Bohemia** and **Moravia**, motherland of their persecuted ancestors.
-1870-71 in the **Franco Prussian War**, France lost Alsace-Lorraine, and paid high indemnity [139, pp 286-287].
-1871 the **German Empire** was founded when (William I) of Prussia was proclaimed **Kaiser Wilhelm** (Emperor) and **Bismarck** was Chancellor, uniting hundreds of German states and kingdoms [16, p 284], except Austria.
-1888-1918 Kaiser **Wilhelm** II dismissed **Bismarck** and expanded Germany's power [16, p 818; 110, pp 145-150].

The British Empire Under Queen Victoria

-1837-1901 **Queen Victoria**, granddaughter of George III.
-1840 Queen Victoria married her cousin **Albert,** Prince of Saxe-Coburg-Gotha. He died 1861.
-Her reign of 64 years saw vast colonial expansion and industrial, social and scientific change.
-She honored **constitutional monarchy** policies determined by Parliament, yet was able to be an influence.
-Prime Ministers were outstanding, notably: Melbourne, Peel, Palmerston, Disraeli, Gladstone, Salisbury and
-**Benjamin Disraeli**, a Jew, 1837 member of Parliament, 1852 Chancellor of the Exchequer, Prime Minister twice 1867-8 and 1874-80. British diplomacy impacted the **Near East** [74, pp 128-133], so in:
-1875 Disraeli purchased controlling interest in the **Suez Canal.**
-1877 Disraeli named Queen Victoria **Empress of India** [16, pp 198, 359, 596, 729]. 1878 Disraeli was made an Earl.
-Wars in which the British were involved were as follows:

China	1839-42 First Opium War between Britain and China. 1842 Hong Kong was British.
Afghanistan	1838-42, 1878-9 [16] for defense of the Indian frontier.
India	By 1800 most French, Dutch and Portuguese territories in India ceded to Britain.
Indian Mutiny	1858 transfer of the East India Company from private control to the crown. Hindus rebelled against reforms in favor of caste equality [74, pp 32-7]. The British began to realize that conflicts are not won by the sword, but that social reform must be sensitive and wait for readiness.

Two Sikh wars	1846 the Treaty of Lahore ended the first Sikh War with the East India Company. 1849 Britain annexed the Punjab.
Two Burmese wars	1852 Lower Burma went under the British crown; 1886 Upper Burma also.
Crimean War	1854-6 between Russia and allies (Turkey, England, France and Sardinia) Neither side gained [74, pp 13-20]. **Florence Nightingale** with 38 nurses made the hospitals efficient and in four months reduced the death rate from 42% to 2%; made rounds with a lamp, to touch each soldier personally. She went on to found an exemplary school of nursing in London, with nursing supervised by nurses (not doctors). On request she wrote plans that reformed both nursing and standards of sanitation in many countries.
Zulu wars	1870 the British lost, but 1879 annexed Zululand [74, pp 97-103]; 1897 added to Natal. 1899-1902 Boers (Dutch farmers) resisted inclusion in a South African unified government. Britain won. More than 7000 Canadians volunteered for military service.

-1796 English physician **Edward Jenner** developed smallpox vaccination [95, p 404].
-Advances were made in medicine, surgery, anaesthesia and public health [111, pp 288-9; 296-7; 139, pp 296-7].
-A Prussian historian wrote "The English think **soap** is civilization." In Victorian England "Cleanliness was next to godliness," but not till late in the century was a proper **water supply** & **drainage system** built [74, pp 38-9].
-Machinery evolved for use in factories, homes and farms [139, pp 264-283]. Iron kitchen ranges with ovens began to replace wood fireplaces for cooking [139, p 268]. The large new **middle class** [111, pp 272-283; 139, pp 278-285] enjoyed a comfortable life style, but conditions of the poor were desperate [110, pp 122-124; 139, pp 269-271].
-The polluted air was referred to as *London fog* or *pea soup* [110, p 124].
-1770-1870 coal production multiplied 30-fold [111, pp 264-271]; 500,000 British adults and children worked in coal mines. Around the world "coaling stations" were built to supply steam ships with coal [110, p 135].
-1800s frozen meat began to arrive in England from Australia and New Zealand [111, p 267; 139, pp 332-3].
-1845-7 famine struck **Ireland** when the potato crop failed. Two million died. 1¼ million emigrated.
-1848 streets of **Paris** were redesigned and widened. Elegant new sewers became a **tourist** attraction [110, p 132].
-1851 **London** was the largest city in the world, with a population of 2.4 million [95, p 447].
-May to October the **Great Exhibition** and **Crystal Palace** drew 6 million awestruck visitors [139, pp 276-7].
-1839-59 German **Baedeker** published **guidebooks** [74, pp 38-9; 16 p 68] popular with English and European travelers. Railway building proliferated [139, pp 272-3]. 1855-73 **Thomas Cook**, after arranging successful tours in England by railway, organized popular **Cook's Tours** to Paris, Switzerland, Italy and the world.
-Steamships, telegraph and photography enjoyed exciting new advances [111, pp 272-7; 292-5; 139, pp 274-5, 293].
-1852 New York mechanic Elisha **Otis** invented the lift (elevator), which soon stimulated the construction of multistory buildings [95, p 448], first in the USA but soon in Britain, France and other countries.
-1889 the **Eiffel Tower** was completed in Paris, 984 feet high and fitted with elevators.

The American Civil War 1861-1866

[continued from pp 138 and 155]

-As early as 1780 pacifists & conscientious objectors migrated west and north from Pennsylvania and New York, to escape the War of Independence (American Revolution) and the conscription of sons into the army [pp 118-9;158]. A new wave of migrations into Canada took place before, during and after the War of 1812-15. People loyal to Britain migrated into Upper Canada (Ontario), the Eastern Townships of Lower Canada (Quebec) and New Brunswick. Those who had slaves took them with them, but they were freed in 1793 [p 115]. Many thousands of black people on their own went to Canada in the *Underground Railway*.
-1861 **Czar Alexander** II freed Russian serfs; prevented civil war by negotiating with unwilling noblemen for six years. 1863 onwards many thousands of Germanic Farmers migrated into **Volhynia**, Russia from Poland.
-1854 the Republican Party was formed to prevent extension of slave ownership. **Abraham Lincoln** soon became its leader. 1860 he was elected President [16, pp 433; 150-1]. In 1861 the 11 southern states seceded from the **Union** and formed **Confederate States of America**. The Union had forts in the south. Attempts to take them over resulted in cutting off of supplies and firing of guns. The north fought back to prevent break up of union.
-1861-65 the US **Civil War** with many harsh battles lasted four years, mainly because of fear of economic collapse from freeing of slaves. There were 4 million slaves in the US [9, pp 100-102], only half a million in the north.
-1862 Lincoln proclaimed Emancipation of slaves; 1864 he was assassinated [p 158; map 157].

Chapter Twenty - 1690 to 1890

Rococo, Neoclassical, Romantic and Neogothic Architecture

Late Baroque Art and Architecture

[Continued from pp 85-86 and p 91]

-Varied characteristics of Baroque style evolved in all countries of Europe and their colonies [9, Vol 3, pp 288-298].
-1618-48 because of the Thirty Years' War and struggles to push back the Turks, Baroque architecture did not flourish in Austria until the 18th century; 1716-37 in **Vienna** the elaborate Baroque masterpiece Karlskirche was built. Skilled use of lacquers, inlay and gilt achieved murals of exquisite elegance.
-1764 Russian Catherine the Great, built the fabulous **Hermitage**; filled with priceless art treasures [p 112].

Rococo Architecture

-1715 **Italians** brought exuberant Rococo style to **France**, **Bavaria** and **Austria** [9 Vol 2, p 283]. It caught the fancy of the aristocracy and bourgeoisie and spread to south-western **German** churches [12 Macropedia Vol 19, p 429].
-1730-1770 in **Württemberg** and **Bavaria** the Rococo abstraction movement flourished. This made great demands on sculpture. Various materials combined with clay and resins were developed to be pliable and durable. Saints and cherubs were made with lifelike expressions and gestures as if in awe and in mid-flight. There were dazzling lifelike scenes such as of the transfiguration, with rays of glory, angels and the Trinity conversing and moving in dynamic triumph [29, Stierlin, p 136]. Ancestors of the author were sculptors and masons from this area both sides of the Rhine, who migrated to Poland were they built and repaired cathedrals, churches and palaces [pp 33-35; 144].
-Dydynski refers to Baroque and also Rococo style in churches in **Poland** [28, p 261] [See p 144].

Neoclassical Architecture

-In the 17th and 18th centuries people began to turn away from both elaborate life-like Rococo tableau's, and the delicate gilded excesses of the Baroque. Wanting sombre dignity they returned to Roman and Greek styles. Some churches and public buildings were built to resemble Greek temples. Columns were added.
-**La Madeleine** church in Paris first completed in 1763, looks like a Greek temple [24, Edward Norman pp 232, 242, 249-251].
-In Italy and France pamphlets and books about architecture were published. Drafts of comparative designs were presented with pictures, so clients could select their building styles preferences [31, Mignot, pp 13-22, 48].
-Apartment blocks, schools and homes were built in neoclassical style during this period [31, Mignot, p 38-41].
-In **England**, houses built in a curved row, in stately neoclassical style [9 Vol 2, pp 283-4], were known as **Georgian**.
-In **America** after independence, this style was called **Federal** [9 Vol 2, p 284].
-**Moravian Brethren** with stone and fine carpentry, built many gracious permanent *Settlements* for adult education, worship and industries. They were commandeered in wartime as hospitals in Europe and Pennsylvania. Because they were sturdily built to last, many are still in use in Europe, England, Georgia, Pennsylvania, West Indies, North Carolina, south and east Africa and Jerusalem.
-Benjamin Henry **Latrobe** (1764-1820) born at Fulneck, Yorkshire, England to a Moravian minister and third generation Moravian mother, educated at Fulneck and Nieski, Silesia, traveled to Italy, studied **Greek Revival** style architecture and apprenticed with England's foremost architects.
-1795 **Latrobe** inherited land from his mother in Pennsylvania and emigrated to America where he introduced comprehensive professionalism into architecture. 1804 Latrobe built **Baltimore Cathedral**.
-1806 **President Jefferson** appointed him Surveyor of Public Buildings.
-1815 Latrobe rebuilt the **US capital** in Washington [burned in the war of 1812, see p 120].
-See a long list of Latrobe's engineering and architectural accomplishments in England and the USA, north to south: www.mistral.co.uk/hammerwood/latrobe.htm

Romanticism-"Until the middle of the eighteenth century, most artists, architects, writers and composers based their work on sets of formal rules, many of them arising from the study of Greek and Roman art" [32, Gibson pp 46 - 53]. These ideas of the Classical Movement were questioned, and the Romantic movement arose. Romanticism was a reaction against reason, artificiality and display, and was marked by a love of the unusual and the highly emotional." Romanticism was a flight from the Realism of *Enlightenment* [16, p 638]. It enjoyed nature, simple life, common things and value of individuals. Musicians were **Wagner** and **Schubert** [16, p 638].
-Medieval and Chinese themes became fashionable [24, Edward Norman, pp 252-279, 9, p 283; 12 Vol 5, pp 382-4; 16, p 638].
-Authors of Romantic works were **Wordsworth**, **Keats**, **Emerson**, **Goethe**, **Chateaubriand** and **Rousseau.**
-In the mid 19th century Romanticism declined with the advance of science and industrialism [16, p 638].

Revival of Gothic Architecture

-Many Gothic churches were completed with Neoclassical features such as a facade with Corinthian columns.
-1805-9 **Napoleon** completed **Milan Cathedral** in Italy [6, p 101] with Greek columns [see pictures [91, pp 108-9]].
-Such authors as **Horace Wampole** and **Sir Walter Scott** generated nostalgia for medieval times. Architectural theorists such as Frenchman **Viollet-le-Duc** were interested in liturgical significance of Gothic architecture. **John Ruskin**'s books spread an urge to return to morally superior medieval ways of life.
-The Gothic style of architecture was revived and reached new excellence in the building of churches, law courts and parliaments [9 Vol 2, pp 284-5].
-1795-1860 the **Houses of Parliament in London** were built in a "conscientious adaptation of medieval English Gothic mode" [12 Vol 5, p 384; Vol 10 Macropedia, pp 606-606J]. 1859 the accurate **Big Ben Clock** was installed.
-**Greenwich**, London was chosen to reckon **Standard Time** around the world [16, pp 304, 713].
-Later in the 19th century modern building materials and supporting beams used in Neogothic buildings, made buttresses and thick walls unnecessary.

Architectural Heritage of Poland

-The various architectural styles of Europe were all adopted or adapted in Poland, as in France and German states. [See Chapters 2, 4, 6, 8, 11 and 14 and Chap 15, pp 91 and 92]. There are fine churches, civic buildings and palaces of all architectural styles in Poland.
-968 the **first capital** and bishopric were located at **Gniezno**, in the north-west.
-There were three earlier bishoprics, **Krakow** (Galicia) **Wroclaw** (Silesia) and **Kolobrzeq** (on the Baltic Sea)
-1000 they came under the leadership of Griezno, the first archbishopric.
-1058 the capital was transferred to **Krakow** in the south.
-1596 five centuries later, **Warsaw** became the capital because of its central location. Although other cities have a longer history, architecture in Warsaw is impressive. Damaged in wars and insurrections was repaired and updated. For further reading, refer to tourist guides by Fodor [42] and Frommer [55, pp 428-430].
-See an outstanding history of architecture in Poland in *A Travel Survival Kit* by Krzytof Dydynski [28, pp 35-38]. This book devotes many pages to geography, customs, practical suggestions and Polish vocabulary. The cities and towns are described individually. Roads and districts fan out like a pie or spider's web from centrally located Warsaw [28, pp 35-38, 108-144, 225-6].
-The rest of the book by Dydynski is divided into geographical regions, as shown in the map on page 26. The regional map introduces a section about each region. Within each region each significant city and town is described in detail regarding historic sites, architecture, places to eat and stay, etc. Alternate place names in English, German and Polish are given on p 518. Maps listed on p 51 help clarify details.
-Architectural styles of many buildings throughout Poland are identified by Bajcar [27] and Dydynski [28]. They span more than 1000 years: **Romanesque**, **Gothic**, Bohemian **Przemysl** (Premsyl) [pp 29, 35], **Byzantine**, **Renaissance**, **Rococo**, **Italian**, **Lithuanian**, **Russian Orthodox**, **Neogothic** and more.
-Magnificent underground **salt mine cathedrals**, with floor tiles, sculptures and chandeliers made of salt were beautifully crafted. A unique hospital in the salt mines, was used as a sanitarium for lung diseases [54].

Geographic Circumstances of Johann Schneider I and II - Stone Masons and Sculptors

-Johann Schneider and son Johann (referred to as I and II) from **Alsace-Lorraine**, were sent by Napoleon to Warsaw, Poland to repair the ***Cathedral of the Decapitation of St. John the Baptist*** [69 WV, Vol 3, No 3, pp 10-11, 86], according to cousins of the author: Adolph, Earl [86] and Cecil [69].
-They moved to Warsaw likely between 1805 and 1810. The family and community histories of these cousins record more details [40, Part 2, Chapters 2, 6 and 8] which suggest skill in Gothic and Baroque [p 143].
-Also Johann IV's youngest child, Augusta nee Schneider Klapstein wrote [40, Part 2, Chapter 9] that these forefathers migrated to Poland from **Württemberg**, a district in south-west Germany just across the Rhine river from Alsace. It is bordered by Switzerland in the south, **Bavaria** in the east & **Baden** in the north.
-**Alsace** and **Lorraine** are districts located along the west side of the Rhine River.
-925 AD Alsace west of the Rhine, became part of the German **Dutchy of Swabia** or **Alemannia**, within the Holy Roman Empire. The building of **Strasbourg cathedral** began in 1015 [pp 33-35, 48. 144].
-Major cities in Alsace are **Strasbourg**, **Colmar** and **Mulhouse**, on the west side of the Rhine.
-1225 in this area, a bridge was built across the Rhine River. **Freiberg** is nearby on the east side of the river. The Schneiders who were sculptors and masons, could have worked on churches on both sides of the river.

-1648-1871 Alsace was ruled by **France** [9 Vol 1, pp 311-2, 417]. 1871 Alsace became a **German possession**.
-The author's cousin Reinhart, son of August Schneider married Eugenie Reppert, whose grandmother also was a Schneider. He wrote that her Schneider family was probably related to Johann, since they lived on the France/German border at **Mulhouse (Muhlhausen)** 50 miles south of Strasbourg, near **Freiberg** [40, Part 2, Chap 4]. Eugenie said that her Schneider and Reppert families fled to Poland because of war. Local residents had to provide food for troops.
-1806 **Napoleon** amalgamated numerous German dutchies into the **Confederation of the Rhine** [30, p 36] [p 133, maps 134, 140]. **Prussia** acquired Polish territory [pp 132-33];1788-9 invited settlers from Alsace [138].

Library Search - Evidence of the Appointment of Johann Schneider I and II to Warsaw

Is it feasible that these stone mason/sculptors were commissioned to repair St. John's Cathedral, Warsaw? The reliability of the information from these cousins is confirmed by the following:

1. *First confirmation:* Napoleon took a special interest in the southern German Dutchies: Württemberg, Baden and Bavaria, and nearby German-speaking French Alsace.
-1806 July, Napoleon founded the Confederation of the Rhine so as to bring **all** south-western German speaking dutchies into a union under French protection.
- It was his policy to unite independent states and duchies into confederacies, on a regional basis.
-Napoleon had military and administrative ability to carry on campaigns in several places simultaneously.

2. *Second confirmation:* There are many beautiful churches and cathedrals in both Württemberg and Alsace Districts. By completing, repairing and updating them, stone masons and sculptors would have gained professional skill. *Architectural styles from Roman Basilica, Romanesque, Gothic, Renaissance, Baroque, Rococo and Neoclassical are all included.* Father and son probably had knowledge and skill in all these architectural styles. Rococo artistry was highly developed in this geographic area. Johann V's son Adolph insisted that their ancestors built elaborate palaces. He added that in a palace they placed a large aquarium with gold fish in the ceiling [40, Part 2, Chap 2].
-Being Roman Catholic Johann Schneider I and II were employed in Catholic church updating and repairs. They became Lutherans some years after they migrated to Poland. Johann III and IV were born near Warsaw.

3. *Third confirmation:* There is a St. John's Cathedral in Warsaw, formerly called the *Cathedral of the Decapitation of St. John the Baptist.*
- Present-day tourist books about **Poland** have maps showing the location of St. John Cathedral in Warsaw's old town, near the Vistula River. Fodor [42, p 843] calls it "**a Basilica,** the oldest church in Warsaw, dating back to the 14th century." Adam Bajcar [27, p 41, 48-49] says the Cathedral of St. John and the Old Town were destroyed by fire January 17, 1945. He states that the Cathedral was rebuilt after the war, in Gothic style, and lists the famous people who were buried earlier in the cathedral crypts.
- Bajcar wrote a clear parallel two-column "History of the Government" & "History of the Culture" [27, pp 9 to 18].

4. *Fourth confirmation:* Napoleon was much interested in completing, repairing and updating unfinished and damaged cathedrals, throughout Europe.
-Between 1805 and 1809 Napoleon actually had a fine facade built on the cathedral at **Milan**, Italy. See a picture of this outstanding building [6, p101; 91, pp 108-9]. Greek style columns are included in the Neogothic design.
-In many parts of Poland in palaces, town halls and churches, Gothic and Classical design are combined.
-Dydynski's *Travel Survival Kit* [28] describes ancient buildings of all eras and styles of architectural genius, town by town throughout Poland. St. John's Cathedral (**Katedra Sw Jana**) is described [28, pp 119 and 122-123].

5. *Fifth confirmation:* A letter by Robert Johnson, an Englishman describes in detail his journey in 1814 by stagecoach from St. Petersburg, Russia, via Warsaw to Germany. He spent several days in Warsaw; saw disrepair of the city and cathedral, from neglect under Russian rule [Partitions 1772 pp 93, 95, 111, 113]. He says he made this visit "about a year after Napoleon had retreated from Russia," but saw French troops still camping and roving about in several locations in Poland [33]. He remarks, "The **cathedral** stands in the centre of the city. It consists of a lofty body, without either spire or dome. Its interior is neatly decorated with private altars and the seat of the late king." He admired the acoustics and architecture [for a photo see WV, Vol 6, June 1993, p 1].

.

-The Schneider families would have traveled to Warsaw by stagecoach, or in their own horse-drawn carriages. There were regular stagecoach routes.

6. *Sixth confirmation:* Descendants often talked about the spiritual crisis Johann I and II faced when they discovered how the famous statue of the Weeping Virgin was made to weep "live" tears [69 WV, Vol 3, No 3, pp 10-11]. They saw a fish bowl in her head, filled to the brim with water. At the moment chosen for the Holy Virgin to weep, the priest fed the fish so that they jumped vigorously, causing water to splash through the openings for her eyes. Father and son were appalled and responded by becoming Lutherans.
-Dydynski refers to a weeping virgin statue in a church [28, p 252-3].

Building Skills In Volhynia

-1862 when serfs were set free in Russia, ethnic Germans were invited to migrate to Volhynia (the present northern Ukraine) to buy or rent land and introduce improved farming methods. Schneider descendants were among the thousands who did so [40].
-1842-1921 Johann IV, like his ancestors was a skilled builder. He was a leader of men, able to mobilize neighbors to accomplish work together. Sons of the three oldest sons Fred, John and August often spoke to the author about their grandfather's accomplishments as a builder for noblemen and estate-holders. Grandson Reinhart Schneider wrote "Grandfather made a wager that he would put up a hotel in one day." He wrote the following [40, Part 2, p 2]:

"Our ancestors had built elaborate mansions from stone or bricks, but as there were plenty of logs in Volhynia, that became the building material of choice. In the woods, ahead of time the logs were measured, planed and notched at the ends to be ready for mitered corners. Plenty of wooden pegs were made and holes drilled in the logs for the pegs.

"On the appointed day many horse-drawn wagons hauled in the logs, and a big crew erected the building, driving pegs into the logs to lock the corners together.

"A two-storied building was neatly built." Reinhart added "The gaps between the logs were probably filled and plastered with the traditional mortar made of clay, straw and cow manure. Then the walls were coated inside and out with lime whitewash. By evening the hotel was complete and looked attractive.

"A verandah with fretwork would have been added. There were skilled sawyers, carpenters and cabinet-makers who were able to work together to finish the hotel inside the same day, with smooth wooden floors, stairs and moldings." Author's comment: Probably the logs were hidden smoothly with plaster, as was customary when relatives settled in Canada in 1894-96, and improved their homes.
-1894-96 a large beautiful Lutheran church was built of stone in Neogothic style at Shitomir (Zytomyr), the capital of Volhynia. It is now a Baptist Church. A photograph is shown in [WV, Vol 7, March 1994, p 1 and note p 24].
-Many other churches in Poland and Volhynia were pictured in other issues of this quarterly journal.
-The railway station in Zhitomir was elegant [WV, Vol 6, Dec 1993, p 1]. The station at Strathcona, S. Edmonton, Canada, where they arrived in 1896, was similar but much less impressive. It is now a heritage site. Also an apartment block with a former corner grocery store, built by Johann in 1905 when he retired, is now a heritage site. He had success grafting apples, and his wife with roses in the cold climate of Edmonton.

Building and Musical Skills of Pioneers in Canada

-John Schneider, Johann's second son was an adult and already married when they came to Canada in 1896. Near Fort Saskatchewan, 45 miles east of Edmonton he built a large attractive home in the same manner described above. The author visited John's widow and his son Adolph about 1954. At that time, because of the neat plaster and lacey fretwork, she did not suspect their home was made of logs. Adolph and his mother told her the identical story told by a cousin, about Johann building an inn in a day.
-Adolph also told her about the fish aquarium his grandfather built into a palace ceiling.
-Adoph named one of his sons **Eugene** after French munitions manufacturer Eugene Schneider.
-Another son made his own **violin**. All were musicians who were active in community bands, and took pride in having an ancestor who had led a **Bach choir** in **Berlin**. Another son studied at the Moravian University at **Bethlehem**, Pennsylvania but returned to the University of Alberta where he earned a Masters degree. He taught high school, became principal in Peace River, Alberta and developed a fine high school band and choir.

Pioneering First in Russia and Later in America

Reforms and Oppression Under Tzar Alexander II [Continued from p 139]

-1730-1878 the Russo-Turkish wars helped get some autonomy for Bulgaria, Romania & Serbia[16, pp 73;646; 777].

-1855-81 **Czar Alexander** II was autocratic, but made some good changes. He accomplished judicial reform: trial by jury, judges independent of the administration, proceedings in public, fewer and less severe corporal punishments (floggings) and an independent bar. He started elected rural and town government, liberalized the educational system, and shortened military service from twenty-five down to six years. "The final decision was always his, so that he was called *his own prime minister*" [102, pp 259-287]. Russian occupation of Poland continued.

-He was able to avoid civil war by negotiating for six years with noblemen over his plan to free serfs. Yet because he delegated rule to harsh ministers [102, pp 275-8] **nihilism** (violent socialism) spread [106, pp 115-6].

Mass Migration of Ethnic Germans from Occupied Poland to Volhynia 1863-1875

-1861 many millions of **Russian serfs were freed**. (The same year **civil war in the USA over the issue of slavery** began and lasted four years.) Russian peasants no longer provided free labor for titled landlords. Neither nobles nor serfs were skilled farmers, so the land was largely uncultivated. Willingly in **Volhynia (Wolinsk, Wolinien)** landlords leased or sold their land to German farmers from Central Poland and Austria.

-1863 January, **the last major *Polish Insurrection*** seeking independence from Russia, was crushed. Leaders were tortured, executed or deported to **Siberia** and had their estates confiscated. Use of the Polish language was suppressed, and the Roman Catholic church was persecuted. Unsettling conditions increased the flow of migration [WV, Sep 89, No 3, p 11-13; WV, Dec 95, p 9]. The *Polish Insurrections* failed because the leaders (Polish noblemen) were landowners and basically **rural**. They had not won the support of **urban** artisans and businessmen, who were multicultural, the majority ethnic German. "As it came clear that armed protest could not succeed, Polish patriots reconsidered their strategy and advocated *organic work*, a pacifist endeavor to recover from the Russians, the economy, education and culture. This change was reflected in literature and arts, which moved from the visionary political poetry of **Romantics** to more realistic prose of the **Positivists**" [28, p 16].

-1863-75 ethnic German immigration to Russia was mainly into swampy and heavily forested **Volhynia**, the northern half of the present **Ukraine**. The capital was **Zhytomyr (Shitomir)** [map p 140].

-Land-hungry because of large families, the settlers cleared and drained dense forests and turned it into fertile farmland, often moving to start all over again in new locations to better themselves [WV, Dec 92, pp 17-20].

-These **Polish-German settlers in Volhynia** dug wells, built windmills, built tight-fitting, neatly planed log houses with expertly dove-tailed corners and **chimneys**, and taught Slav neighbors to do the same.

-Their Russian neighbors were surprised to see crop-rotation, dairies, orchards, horse-drawn iron plows and four-wheel buggies (carriages) for travel to town, etc [WV, Dec 92, p 20].

-Many hard-working innovative farmers multi-tasked as carpenters, blacksmiths and linen and wool weavers.

-Polish-Germans were of many different origins, already blended into a somewhat homogeneous culture, through living for centuries in Poland. Familiarity with Luther's Bible had standardized the German language and dialects. Migrants were from Congress Poland (central), Posen (Posnan) NW Poland, and some from east **Galicia** (south Poland, occupied by **Austria** since 1772) [WV, Mar 90, pp 10-13]. The "melting-pot" continued.

-Western Russia was referred to as **White Russia**, because **Ukranians** and other Slavs were fair-haired (descended from Vikings pp 16; 31 and map 31], while most Russians had black hair.

The Author's Family Exemplifies Experiences of Life in Volhynia

-1863 a mass migration from Congress Poland to all parts of Volhynia began.

-**Johann Schneider** 21 years old, migrated from Pomoschno, **Neuhof** parish (**Nowy Dwor** in Polish), 20 miles NW of Warsaw, with his married sister Anna Kossman, 18, and extended family, friends and neighbors, including **Christian Mielke** and daughter Justine and relatives.

-They settled at **Glückstahl** [WV Sep 93, p 11] near Mirapol, 80 km west of **Zhytomyr** (Shitomir) [see map p 149]. [**Note**: The author wants a list of families who settled there. There was a Glückstahl in Odessa, south Russia. Are they the same ?].

-1866 **Johann** and **Justine** married, cleared and improved land at Glückstahl, sold it and bought new land to clear, as many families did, thus increasing their assets and acquiring skill.

-They moved six times [40, Part 2, Chap 5] to locations, all identified [map p 149] [WV, Sep 90, pp 12-13].

-1870 As migration from Congress Poland to Russia continued, Johann Schneider's mother and brother Carl and bride, Juliana Barz migrated to Glückstahl, to evade being drafted into the Russian army.
-1882-96 Johann and Justine lived 14 years at **Justinowka** [see underlined in map p 149]. He was magistrate and passed as Russian, being fluent in that language. She was a nurse-midwife. Both spoke 7 to 9 languages. They had their own dam in the river, did fish farming and had their own wind/water mill for grinding grain and oil seeds commercially for multiethnic customers. Pears, apples & berries were cultivated but the climate was too far north for grapes. They were the author's grandparents. They had 12 children; 9 survived [40, Part 2].
-The Schneiders, Roman Catholic in **Alsace-Lorraine**, had became Lutheran in **Poland**. In Volhynia they became interested in the Moravian Diaspora. 1896 in Canada Johann and five youngest children joined the Moravian church, as some Lutherans did. [Personal examples are used to illustrate conditions in Russia.]

Only Orthodox and Evangelical Lutheran Churches were Recognized in Russia [p 139]

-1801 a Lutheran parish was established in Shitomir (**Zhitomir**), the capital city of the county. It served the east Volhynian counties (kreis) of Shitomir, Nowograd-Wolynsk, Saslaw, Staro-Konstantinow and Owrursch.
-With Lutheran colonists from Prussia [p 139] a landlord founded **Annette** and **Josephine** near **Nowograd-Wolynsk** (=Volhynia or Wolinien) [WV Vol 89, No 3, p 11-13], 80 km NW of Shitomir [map p 149].
-1831 after a **Polish Uprising**, urban Lutherans feeling threatened by the Poles, migrated to west Volhynia.
-1832 **Czar Nicholas** I granted a constitution to the **Evangelical Lutheran Church** to oversee congregations all over Russia. For a time thousands of Moravian Brethren fellowships (Brüder Gemine) in northern Russia, on the Baltic Sea [57, p 347] were self-run, but Russian authorities closed their thriving college at Hennersdorf.
-1840 more than 250 prayer halls of the Moravian Brethren in Baltic Russia were placed under Lutheran guidance, by the government. Itineration (touring) by Moravian Brethren pastors was forbidden. [See p 102].
-1800-1860 Germans of five ethnic origins settled in the province of **Volhynia** (west of Kiev) [WV, Mar 95, pp 16-18] [See p 139]. At that time in history the population of German speaking people in Volhynia was small.

Low Germans Migrated from NW Poland to Volhynia

-1866 among thousands from NW Poland who migrated to Volhynia, was **Ludwig Henkelmann**, born at Lizawy, Kalish, **Poznan** (Posen), west Poland, and his brothers Gottlieb and Martin, relatives and friends. They trekked 500 miles by wagon to Zhitomir.
-Recently **Zhitomir Archives** found a document stating Ludwig bought 200 acres (twice as much as most) near the village of Starchanka (10 miles NW of Zhitomir), and the village was renamed **Ludwigowka** in his honor [in map p 149 see oval outlines of villages where their extended family lived].
-Their ancestors, of early Moravian Brethern roots [pp 64-65, 76-78, 90, etc] sang hundreds of their hymns lustily. For hundreds of years they had lived in NW Poland.

Population Growth in Zhitomir County and Parish

-1859 the population of Shitomir parish was 5825, but by 1888 it was 75,000 [WV, no. 3, 1989, p 11-13]. There was far too much responsibility for the one pastor, **Peter Stelz** 1842-1866 and **Heinrich Wasem** 1869-1907.
-1866 the **Lutheran German Teachers Institute** in **Warsaw** educated Versammlugshalter, also called Cantors or Sacristan Teachers. They taught school in German and Polish and later also in Russian.
-These lay pastors led Sunday and midweek worship, read sermons, baptized and registered infants, taught catechism, ministered to the sick and dying, had secretarial roles and wrote wills [103, pp 31-3, WV, Mar 92, pp 20-1].
-Pastors came spring and fall, to confirm young believers, conduct holy communion, and preach.
-Families took young couples to the three city churches to solemnize marriages.
-1896-9 Shitomir parish was divided into three [WV Sep 89, pp 11-12]: **Rozyszcze** (West Volhynia)[WV Mar 90, pp 14-17], **Heimthal** [WV, Sep 90, pp 14-17] and **Shitomir** [WV no 3, 89, pp 11-13; WV, no 4, 1989, pp 5-7; WV Mar 95, pp 16-18].
-By 1880 the total population of the three parishes was 75,000, with 37,938 in Shitomir parish.
-By 1890 in **Rozyszcze** (Roshischtsche) the population had grown to 40,000, with 100 preaching places.
-1888 Shitomir parish was subdivided into six adjunct parishes [WV Dec 89, pp 5-7; Sep 90, pp 16-17].
-1894-6 a Neo-Gothic stone church was built. See photograph [WV Mar 94, cover] minus the steeple.
-1904 the population in Shitomir parish had dropped to 17,074 due to mass migration to the Americas.
-1905 Rozyszcze parish was divided into three: **Rozyszcze**, **Wladimir-Wolynsk** (Volhynia) and **Lusk**.
-1907 The population grew to 20,000 because of the high birth rate, good health and low mortality rate.

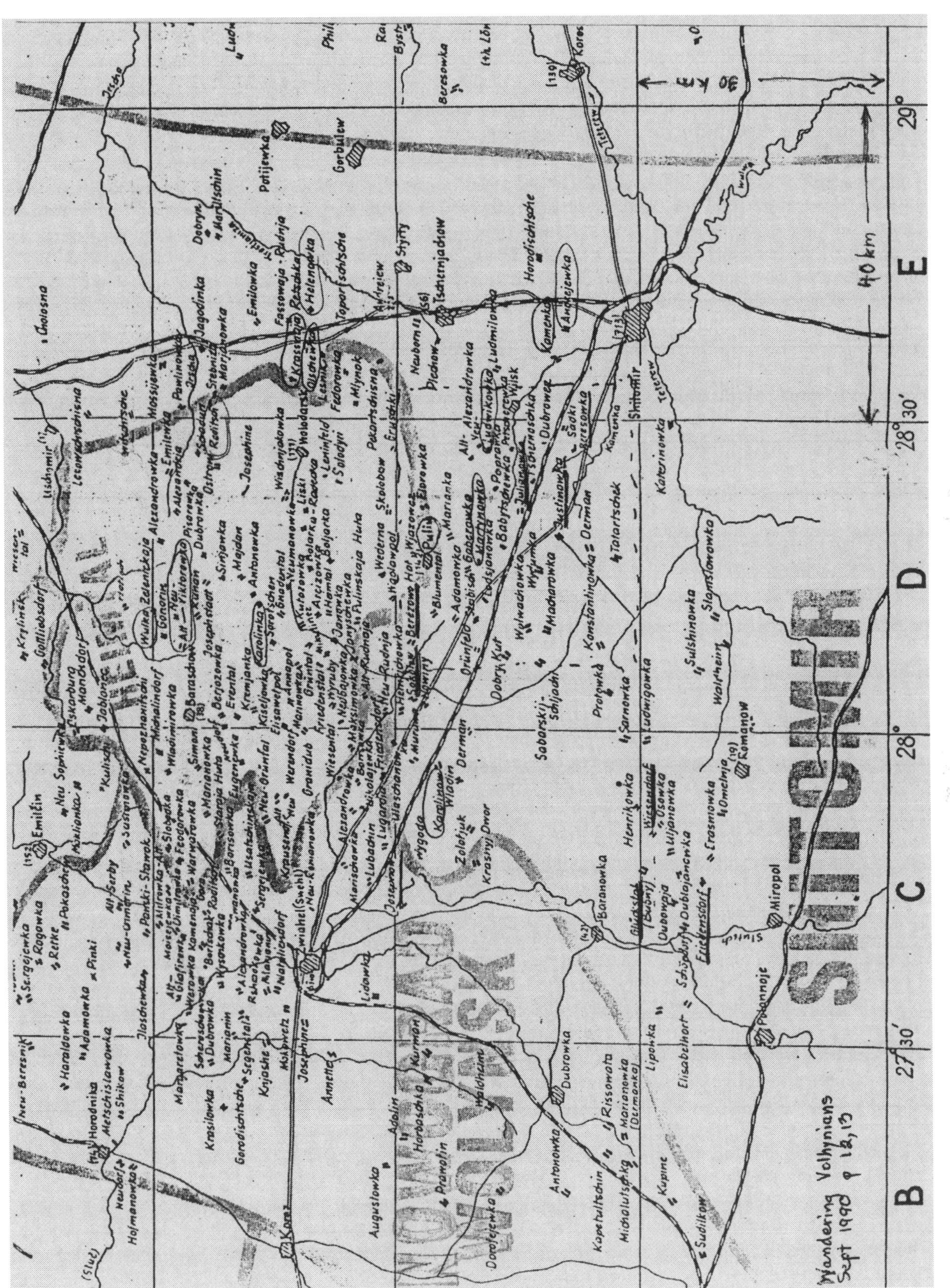
B
C
D
E
27°30'
28°
28°30'
29°
40 km
Shitomir
Wandering Volhynians
Sept 1990 p 12,13

Village Schools in Volhynia

-After 1866 graduates of **German Teachers Institute (Lutheran) Warsaw**, Poland were employed as Cantor-Teachers all over Congress Poland and Volhynia [WV Dec 91, p 17; 71, p 16, 20] and were required to be members of the Lutheran church [See p 148]. This level of education was uncommon in Russia, so teachers were needed also in clerical and leadership roles. Artisans also found they were much needed/respected.

-1890 there were 400 **Cantorial schools** (Lutheran church schools) with chapels for worship. See a list of Cantor-Teachers, with dates and villages where they taught/served 1878 to 1912 [WV Mar 92, pp 20-21].

-However, standards were falling because Kantor-Teachers from Congress Poland had died or retired. To fill this need, the pastors tried to establish a Teachers College in Volhynia, but government refused approval.

-1865 **Adolf Schmidt** was born in Heimthal. He studied there at the Lutheran academy (high school boarding). 1860 his father had migrated from Kalish, near Posen, Poland; his grandfather from Mahrburg, **Hessen-Nassau**. The family moved to a fine estate in **Sokolov** near Shitomir [see Sokolov in map p 149].

-1891 Adolf married Luise Schneider, the author's aunt [44, Part 2,Chap 3]. In the winter they skated on their own lake. Instrumental and choral music filled their home. Luise sang soprano and Adolf tenor. He played a fine cornet (a brass trumpet with valves).

-1902 they migrated to Canada, grieving for many friends and relatives and the beautiful home left behind.

Personal family examples are given because they illustrate actual conditions/life style in Russia.

-1904 instead of a college, an academy for Sexton-Teachers was opened in Heimtal, with government approval. [See Heimtal County on map p 149]. The congregations took up a collection to cover building and maintenance expenses. Fifteen students attended the first year and 13 the second. There were 40 rooms, including boarding facilities for students from other parts of Volhynia [WV Sep 90, p 15]. [Continued pp 176-7].

Moravian Colonies and Lay Minister-Teachers

-1823 Moravian Brethren who had thrived for 100 years at **Sarepta**, lower Volga [pp 111-112,138; map p 137] had a disastrous fire, were being pressured to join the established Lutheran church, so migrated [90, p 5], some to the USA and many to rented land in Volhynia, but still facing poverty planned to migrate again.

-1863-75 groups of Moravian Brethren from Poland settled in 20 to 30 villages in Volhynia [71, p 23], but since ordination of their clergy was illegal, they accepted sacraments from Lutheran clergy.

-1872 **Ludwig Klapstein** a Moravian-minded pietistic Versammlugshalter (Cantor-teacher) had a teaching post in **Lubin**, Poland (occupied by Austria 1795). About 1879-88 he taught in **Heimtal**, Volhynia. He was also a violinist. Because of spiritual convictions he and his wife and children migrated to Canada 1888 [p 164].

-1869-71 **Andreas Lilge** and his older brother **Ludwig** studied in Warsaw Teachers' Institute to become Sacristan Teachers (Cantor-Teachers). Born 1851 at **Augustowok,** a little north of Warsaw; Andreas apprenticed as a Cabinet Maker 1865. Both taught and ministered in several villages in Poland [71, pp 12-18, 132-3].

-1876 **Ludwig Lilge** with his family migrated to take up a Lutheran teaching post in Volhynia.

-1878 **Andreas Lilge** with wife and four children followed, to teach in Volhynia at Karolinchen, 80 km NW of Zhitomir[map p 149]. He was an active Moravian lay minister and zealous to become an ordained minister, so

-1880 applied to **Herrnhut, Saxony** for theological education, but being married with children was refused,

-1881-82 **Andreas Lilge**, 30 years old, went alone to **Lutheran Concordia Seminary**, **Springfield** Ill, USA. After completing one year of a three year course, he still preferred the Moravian Church [71, p 19].

-He visited Moravian headquarters in Bethlehem, Pennsylvania and was in the home of **Clement Hoyler**, still a child (later pioneer pastor for Moravian parishes around Edmonton, Alberta) [84; 86; 88; 89; 71; 73] [pp 169-172].

-1882 returning to Volhynia Andreas taught school and preached at **New-Victorowka** [map p 149].

-1884 **Pastor Herman R. Steinberg** was sent as missionary to Volhynia by the Moravian Synod in Herrnhut, to be assisted by lay ministers like the Lilge brothers. Russian authorities did not allow him to perform the sacraments, so he was recalled to Poland after a year [71, p 74].

-Andreas Lilge lost his teaching position when he was openly Moravian Brethren [71, p 15-22]. The Lutheran Church, but not the Moravian, had Russian approval.

-1886 Moravians in **Schadur** [page 149] had a prayer hall that could seat 400, the largest Moravian congregation in Volhynia. They were originally Roman Catholic from Moravia, Bohemia. They migrated to southern **Brazil** with their Hernnhut appointed teacher/pastor Wilhelm Lange and set up a colony called **Bruederthal**, generously funded by Moravians around the world [71, pp 21-7, 137-9]. Unfortunately the land was not suitable for farming. Farmers migrated to Canada and the US. Craftsmen and tradesmen doing better, stayed.

-1885-91 **Andreas Lilge** with approval of Herrnhut headquarters [71, pp 21-4], served as a lay minister in Moravian colonies: Olgenburg, Goroschke & Victorowka [86, pp 2-16;71] but a Lutheran pastor came for marriages.
-1890 Anna Blank Lilge **Klammer**, Andreas Lilge's mother, widowed twice, emigrated to Novogrod, Volhynia (Wolinsk, Wolinien) with her son **Adolf Klammer**, born at Tarscheminer Kempe, **Neuhof (Nowy Dwor)** parish, north of Warsaw. Adolf was educated in Polish and German but did not learn Russian.
-Adolf had served in the **Tsar's army three years** and completed apprenticeship in cabinet-making/ carpentry. He met the Henkelmann family [See p 148] and married the second daughter, Julianna at Shitomir (the author's maternal grandparents). The author's mother, Rennetta said that when her parents argued he would call her a **Kashub** (Low-German/tribal from Pomerania, NW Poland) and she called him a **Schwab** (from Alsace/Baden pp 1, 26, 132, 138) which was typical of mixed marriages of different German ethnic groups [WV Sept 93, p 20-21; Dec 95, pp 9-10]. Schwabs (Suevi= Schwebish) were newcomers to Poland, and felt superior.

Emigration Due to Restrictions on Land Purchase and Language of Instruction [p 148]

-1855-81 **Czar Alexander** II delegated rule to harsh ministers [102, pp 275-8] so ***Nihilism*** (violent socialism) spread [106, pp 115-6]. 1871 the right of ethnic Germans to exemption from military service ended [WV, Mar 93, p 8]. All young men were drafted to serve a minimum of three years in the Czar's army, some in the Russo-Turkish wars of 1730-1878. To avoid the draft many hid or migrated to adjoining countries or overseas.
-A railway was built from Moscow to Saratov. The town grew rapidly [12 Vol 19, pp 1061-2].
-In the 1870's 7000 German **Mennonites** from southern Russia settled in **Manitoba** and 10,000 in the US.
-1880 the purchase of land in Russia became difficult for Lutherans and Baptists, as earlier by Moravians. Even leasing was restricted. Conversion to the Orthodox Church was demanded by authorities.
-A tide of migration of ethnic Germans began from **Volhynia** to the **Caucasus** near the Black Sea. from **Courland** near the Baltic Sea some migrated to **Brazil**, **Siberia** and **America** [WV Sep 93, p 11].
- For a list of **Baptists** who migrated to Brazil see [WV Dec 93, p 11]. For Lutherans in South America see [WV Dec 94, pp 9-12].
-1881 Czar Alexander II was **assassinated** by *Nihilists* (terrorists) who had stalked him.
-1881-1894 **Tzar Alexander** III (1845-94) at age 36 succeeded his father. He governed autocratically, introducing repressive measures to bring about **Russification**.
-He controlled appointment of local officials and was **anti-German** and **anti-Semitic**.
-Entry to secondary schools was restricted to the upper classes. Newspapers were suppressed.
-Count Dmitry **Tolstoy** was his Minister of the Interior [102, pp 288-292].
-1890 **Russian** was proclaimed the language of instruction. Since many teachers were bilingual ethnic Germans, secretly they continued to teach German when they had time.
-The author's father Chris Schneider and his brother Alexander had such a teacher and became fluent in both languages [40, Part 2, Chap 5 & 6].
-1894 Tzar Alexander III died of nephritis. **Tzar Nicholas** II succeeded. [continued p 178].

Migration from Russia to the US and Canadian North West Territories

-1860-69 the transcontinental railway was completed across the USA [p 158]. Branch railways opened the country to miners and farmers. Frontier land was quickly filled by Americans and Europeans. Hundreds of thousands of German-Russians (Roman Catholic, Lutheran, Baptist and Mennonite) settled in Connecticut, New York, Chicago, Wisconsin, Oklahoma, North Dakota, Minnesota, Oregon and California [WV, Sep 92, p 5-6].
-1878 a railway linked **St. Paul, Minn & Winnipeg**. Surveying [p 161] & telegraph lines opened west Canada.
-1881 the **Canadian Pacific Railroad** reached **Winnipeg** and
-1883 it reached **Calgary**. [Continued pp 156, 157-8, 161-163; see map p 164]
-1890 all land in the USA was occupied and the frontier ended. Americans began to migrate north to settle all over western Canada. Ranchers from **Texas** trekked north to Canada with large herds of cattle.
-1888-92 various ethnic German families from **Odessa**, **south Russia** (Black Sea) & **Volhynia** (north Ukraine) settled for one to three years in southern Alberta but, because of drought, trekked north.
-1891 the railway reached **Strathcona** (South **Edmonton**). Various groups of Lutheran and Reformed colonists took homesteads around Edmonton, mingling with neighbors who had migrated from **Ontario, Quebec, Britain** and **the US**. Various **Slavic people** from **Poland** and **Austria** began to arrive also. Schools and communities were multicultural from the beginning.
-1892 **Andreas Lilge** and his wife Wihelmine and ten children migrated to the USA to prepare the way for oppressed Moravians to take homesteads. In **Wisconsin** in a Moravian parish he taught German.

- 1893 May 24-June 6 Andreas Lilge attended Moravian Synod in Bethlehem PA and received encouragement but not financial help, because of failure of Volhynian emigrants to succeed as farmers in Brazil [pp 149-150]. Hired to teach Moravian summer school in **Minnesota**, he found people suffering severe **drought** [71, pp 27-32]
-1893 June, in response to his invitation, two families from Volhynia joined them, the **Ludwig Grams** and **Franz Heffners**. Others indicated interest in coming. He did not find land in the US, so at his own expense:
-1893 July he went by train to **Winnipeg**, Manitoba. Unable to find land there he went by rail to **Edmonton**. There he met with Minister of the Interior T. Mayne Daly, who arranged for a whole township of land to be reserved for Moravians, 40-50 miles NE of Edmonton [71, pp 133, 33-59]. The **Grams** family moved to Edmonton.
-1893 September in Winnipeg Lilge applied to government and railway officials for concessions. The Methodist Minister, **Rev. G.R.Turk** and the **Manitoba Free Press** helped much to obtain rail passes, steamship subsidies, and financial aid from the government for 100 Moravian families to immigrate to Canada.
-1893 in October his family joined him. He gave all of his time in arrangements, but had no income. Two of his daughters had work as domestics. November he telegraphed families in Volhynia to prepare to emigrate.
-1894 January he was in **Ottawa** to finalize government assistance. He became an **Immigration Agent** [71, p 37].
-1894 March the first few Moravian families arrived from Volhynia. They went to Edmonton and visited the land chosen, but complained that it was heavily forested and far away from urban centres.
-1894 May the second group arrived. Some who could afford it, chose to buy **Papaschase Indian Reserve** land near Edmonton. Lilge donated the $1500 he had earned as Immigration Agent, to buy doors, windows, stoves and supplies[71, p 73] for destitute families. Much help came from **Mennonite** settlers in Manitoba [pp 168-169]. Telegrams & letters went back & forth to four shipping companies and families trying to emigrate.
-1894 June-July more families came on three ships. A picture of some of the newcomers in Edmonton is on page one of the July 6th **Edmonton Bulletin**. There were agonizing delays and misunderstandings [71;73;84;85].
It was extremely difficult for families as follows:

- To find buyers in Russia for their possessions so as to have some cash;
- To travel 300 miles by wagon (or train if they could afford tickets) north to Libau (the Baltic seaport);
- To wait for ship passage while food supplies and money were dwindling. Some ran out of food and money;
- To have families feel torn apart. Unexpectedly only a few of the 100 families were accepted on each ship.
- To avoid Russian government attention, which could stop mass emigration [71, pp 43-44];
- To screen out unsuitable families with divisive sectarian beliefs [71, pp 50-52];
- To keep the loyalty of some Moravians, becoming relatively satisfied by Lutheran services[71, pp 56-57].

Map: *British North America and the United States 1846-1890* [86, p 1].

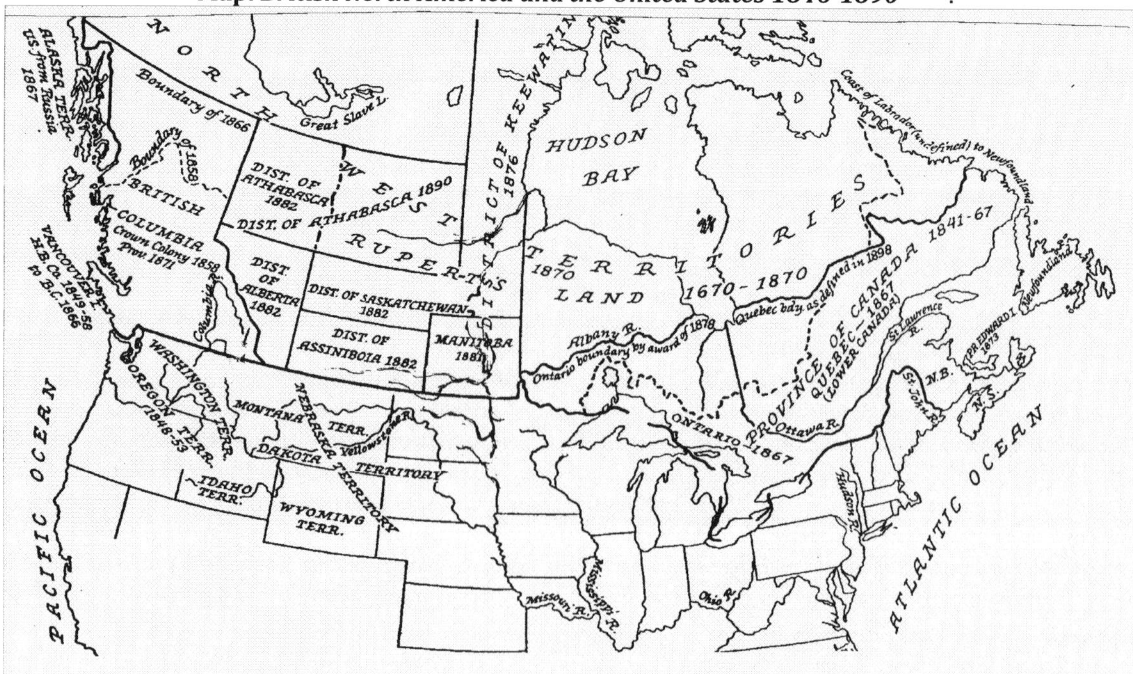

Chapter Twenty-Two

Nation-Building of the United States and Canada - 1849 to 1892

Early Settlement of the Fraser River Delta and Vancouver Island [from p 129; map p 121]

-1827 **Fort Langley** founded on the Fraser River [9 Vol 4, p 372] for fur trading, also established a farm, boat and barrel building and a fish packing industries [120, p 897]. The Factor's wife and other ladies enjoyed a comfortable life style [now a Heritage Site]. Many first nations tribes fished and traded crafts with them and each other.
-1831 **Fort Simpson** and 1833 **Fort McLoughlin**, were built up the coast near the present **Bella Bella**, to waylay American fur traders, prospectors and settlers sailing up the coast [119b Vol 4, p 222].
-1843 to bolster British claims to Vancouver Island **Fort Victoria** and the **HBCo headquarters** was erected and transferred there, replacing **Fort Vancouver** (near the **Columbia River** mouth in Oregon).
-1843 Oregon Trail trekkers founded **Portland** up the Columbia River [16, p 590] [See pp 129-130; map p 130].
-**Oregon Territory** included the present **Washington State** and **BC**.
-1846 the **Oregon Treaty** established the **49th parallel** as the boundary between **British** and **US territory**, from the Rocky Mountains to the Pacific Ocean, mid-channel in the Strait of Juan de Fuca.
-1849 **Oregon Territory** joined the **Union** (United States).
-1848 **Yale** was established in the Fraser River Canyon, at the head of Fraser River navigation. By 1858 in a 14 mile stretch **Hope** to **Yale**, 30,000 miners came from California [128 Vol 1, pp 85,148-153] and found much gold. Unlike those settled in Chilliwack and Hope, some miners rashly made war against peaceful tribes, killing many.
-1849 Great Britain proclaimed **Vancouver Island a Crown Colony**, naming **Victoria the capital**. The first Governor was **Richard Blanshard**. 1851 the Chief Factor of the HBCo, **James Douglas**, doubled as Governor of Vancouver Island colony and the **Queen Charlotte Islands** [9 Vol 4, p 372]. 1852 **coal mining** began at Nanaimo.
-1856 a **Legislative Assembly** met with elected representatives [119b Vol 2, pp 84-5].
-1858 **British Columbia Crown Colony** (formerly New Caledonia) was created; **capital** at **Fort Langley**.
-1858 **Walter Moberly** came to BC to find a suitable route for a **transcontinental railway**, and was given many other assignments [pp 154, 156, 162] as first professional engineer in BC. In 1834 he had come from England to Barrie, Upper Canada, studied engineering and worked on the Ontario, Simcoe and Huron railway.
-1859 the **capital** was **moved to** Queensborough (**New Westminster**) to guard entrance to the Fraser River.
-Under Royal Engineer **Col R.C. Moody**, **Walter Moberly** planned the capital and site for **Vancouver**.
-1859 **Edgar Dewdney**, civil engineer/surveyor, laid out New Westminster; did road building on the north shore of the Fraser River from **Hope** to **Yale** & east to the Columbia River along the US border [pp 160, 163].
-1860-61 **Jesuit Father Fouquet** began work among **Sto'lo nations** at **Mission** on Fraser River north shore.
-1866 **British Columbia** was founded merging the two **Crown Colonies**; 1868 **Victoria** became the **capital**.
-No treaties were made with the many *First Nations* (indigenous tribes, called Indians) in BC [more p 156].

Early Settlements in the Kootenay and Columbia River Region [from pp 129-130]

-1807 **Kootenay House** opened by **David Thompson** was a HBCo trading post until 1856 [pp 109; 125-126].
-1810 Fort Spokane (**Spokane House**) built by the NWCo, was a principle trading post.
-1821 the NWCo became part of the HBCo. 1825-26 **Fort Colvile** [map p 177], named for a HBCo official (misspelled Colville [119b, Vol 4 p 213]) was built on the Colombia River to replace Fort Spokane [p 158].
-1846 the **Oregon Treaty** establishing the 49th parallel as the boundary between British and US territory, from Manitoba to the Pacific Ocean divided the Kootenay region in half, **Kutenai** in the USA. 276 of 407 miles of the Kootenay River are in Canada. It loops into the US, reenters Canada, forms Kootenay Lakes and flows into Columbia River at the present Castlegar. **Spokane** and **Fort Colvile** are in the US, but until 1871 HBCo trading continued in Fort Colvile [119b Vol 4, p 213] [Maps pp 121, 177].
-1858 **Crow's Nest Pass** was described by Capt Blakiston, of the **Palliser expedition**, as used by native travel. **Kutenai Indians** had the annual buffalo hunt on the prairies (now Saskatchewan) [119b Vol 6, pp 20-21, 23].
-1859-65 **Edgar Dewdney**, civil engineer/surveyor, built a 450 mile **road** on the north shore of the Fraser River to **Hope** & overland to southeast BC, near the US border [128 Vol 4, pp 44-55], to protect Canadian sovereignty.
-1864 Gold was discovered at **Cranbrook**, east Kootenay Valley, and miners began to arrive [119b Vol 3, p 142], and
-1867 Gold in west Kootenay at Forty-Nine Creek; 1886 several major mines were begun.
In the **Crownest Pass**, coal was mined by men from south-eastern **Europe**, **Britain** and **Nova Scotia**.
-1868-69 Dewdney was MLA (provincial); 1872-79 MP (Member of Parliament Ottawa) [119b Vol 3, p 262; 142].
-1866 **Thomas Ellis** traveled Dewdney Trail to **Judge JC Haynes' ranch at Osoyoos**; filed for a 320 acre homestead [128 Vol 2, p 136-9; Vol 4, p 47-8]; began ranching with oxen and horses imported from the US [p 160].

Settlers Via the Great Lakes and Canadian Prairies (NorthWest Territories - NWT's)

-1846 a **Roman Catholic mission** was established at **Ile-a-la Crosse** in the present NW **Saskatchewan**, and had wide influence. Later an **Anglican mission** began at **Lac La Ronge** farther north [125 Vol 17, p 146].

-1840-48 **Methodist Rev. Robert Rundle,** a missionary in HBCo settlements in the future Alberta: Fort Pitt, Ft Edmonton, Lesser Slave Lake, Rocky Mountain House ; Bow River. Mt Rundle, **Banff** named for him [119b, p 113].

-1851 **Methodist Rev. George Millward McDougall** (1820-1876) educated at Victoria College, Coburg ON, with his wife **Elizabeth** nee **Chantler,** went to Garden City Sault Ste Marie area; their three sons; went to mission schools and Victoria College. 1860 they went to Rossville HBCo settlement in the NWT's.

-1865 their son **John Chantler McDougall** (1842-1917) married Abigail Steinhauer in 1865 [119b Vol 6, p 258], and Elizabeth Boyd 1872. He served with his father as a teacher; 1869-70 interpreter in **Red River Rebellion** and -1885 in the **NW Rebellion** [pp 155; 162-3]. 1874 ordained a Methodist missionary

-1873 John Chantler McDougall with his wife **Elizabeth** nee **Boyd** McDougall (1853-1941) drove a wagon to Morley, on the Stoney Reserve, Rocky Mountains foot-hills near **Calgary** and lived there 25 years. She often went by canoe or bobsled with her husband to encourage settlers and churches in Alberta, though they had six children. 1898 she moved to Calgary [121 Vol 2, p 1053]. She was president of *Southern Alberta Pioneer Women & Old Timer's Association. She* said "Many bachelors left the west when unsupported by a wife". 1906 he retired in Calgary and authored *Forest, Lake and Prairie,* some other books, and a biography of his father who died near Calgary in a snow storm. On the North Saskatchewan river bank, a church and hill are named for him.

-1854 **French Oblates** opened a mission at **Lac La Biche**, a NWCo post in the present north east Alberta.

-1853-1903 Oblate **Father Valentin Vegreville** served Edmonton-Battleford 50 yrs [130, p 2] [pp 155, 162, 169].

-1852 **Father Albert Lacombe** started the first school west of the Red River settlement, at St. Albert, north of Edmonton. He worked with **Cree** and **Blackfoot** Indians who both liked him [119b Vol 6, p 42] though they were enemies. His roving ministry established schools, churches and social services for Indians, Métis and settlers, from the Bow River in the south to the Peace in the north. He wrote a Cree dictionary and grammar.

-By 1850 **Red River carts** carried supplies in regular round trips **Fort Garry** (later **Winnipeg**) to **St. Paul, Minn**, and NW to **Fort Edmonton** via **Fort Carlton**, a large stopover centre for transfer of supplies and freight. Red River carts originated in both French and Scottish tradition; drawn by one ox or horse, made of wood tied with leather, and easily repaired could carry heavy loads and float across streams [121 Vol 3, p 1836].

-1857-60 Captain **John Palliser** leading a British exploration party, found large areas of fertile land from the Great Lakes, across the present **central** Saskatchewan and Alberta [119 Vol 5, pp 192, 235-6; 125 Vol 17, pp 146-7] to the Rocky Mountains. He assessed six passes in the Rocky Mountains for suitability for a railway.

-1857-58 **Geologist Henry Y. Hind**, Canadian Government Surveys, favored the **central** prairies [119 Vol 5, p 128].

-1858 the **Hudson Bay Co** changed focus from furs to retail trade [12 Vol 6, p 119].

-1858 at the age of 14, **Louis Riel** a Métis (born in St. Boniface, grandson of a voyageur and the first white woman in the west, Marie Anne Gaboury) was sent by **Bishop Taché** to Sulpician College in Montreal, but after several years, was unsuited to a religious vocation [168 pp 281-282]. 1865-8 he **studied law** in the US [120 p 2019].

-1866 a **Presbyterian mission** was named **Prince Albert** for Queen Victoria's consort [120, p 1895]. It was established by **James Nisbet** for Scottish Métis descendants of fur-traders. Settlers also came from **Ontario**.

Confederation Founded Canada 1867 and the Province of Manitoba Inaugurated 1870

-1867 **Canada was founded by Confederation** of the provinces of Ontario, Quebec, Nova Scotia and New Brunswick. The first Prime Minister Minister **John A. Macdonald** 1867-73 and 1878-91 struggled to get the CP rail built across Canada. Was knighted by Queen Victoria. The **British North America Act** [9 Vol 4, p 575] delineated federal and provincial authority/autonomy.

-1868 there were 3638 post offices in Canada; tripled by 1900 [119b, Vol 8, p 275]. A growing number of **loyalist** settlers migrated from the USA. **Icelanders** came to Lake Winnipeg area [119b Vol 5].

-1866 **Walter Moberly** [p 153] left BC for railway construction in the US; was recalled 1870 to survey mountain passes for the CPR. He recommended the pass later named for Major A.J. **Rogers** [119 Vol 7, pp 119-20].

-1868 a road was built from **Lake of the Woods** to **Assiniboia** (Red River Settlement) to open a route to the west and to provide work for Métis and Selkirk settlers suffering from failure of buffalo and crops.

-1869 the **HBCo** sold land to the Canadian government but kept enough property to open thriving urban retail department stores and mail order service [119 Vol 5, pp 192, 235-6; Vol 7, pp 361-4]. Steam boats and barges came into use on the Saskatchewan Rivers, so a smaller **Ft. Carlton** was built upstream [168 p 284] and large Carlton House was no longer needed for stopovers of wagon trains carrying freight to **Battleford** and **Edmonton** [119b Vol 2, p 248].

-1869-1870 **The Red River Rebellion** arose because the 12,000 Métis of **Assiniboia** (the Red River Settlement) objected that they had not been consulted regarding land surveys [p 160]. Many American and Canadian settlers were moving in, so the Métis feared loss of land, nation status and culture.
-*The National Committee of the Métis* with **Louis Riel**, Secretary, stopped the surveyors and took Fort Garry and seized **William McDougall**, the first Lieut Governor of the North West Territories [119b Vol 6, p 259] (not related to Rev George and son John McDougall, Cree interpreter). Riel as President of *Métis Provisional Government* demanded Métis Province [119b Vol 9, pp 27-28] with full partnership in Canada [119b Vol 7, pp 361-4; Vol 6, pp 354-5; 147 Vol 5 # 57, pp1345-51].
-1870 so the **Province of Manitoba** was formed out of Assiniboia (Red River Settlement) and admitted into Confederation. They received 1,400,000 acres, much less than Métis expected [125 Vol 3, pp 147-8] [map 152]. Over half of the population was **French** speaking **Métis**. A prisoner held by Riel was shot, which angered settlers.
-Riel and many Métis fled from Fort Garry (later named Winnipeg) to the **junction of the North and South Saskatchewan Rivers** and settled at **Duck Lake** and **Batoche**, 35 miles south of Prince Albert [continued pp 161; maps 163 and 164].
-**Gabriel Dumont**, prominent head of the colony, organized **huge buffalo hunts** [119b Vol 3, p 314]. One such jump, a present Heritage Site, is the 300 foot high river bank on **South Saskatchewan River** near Leader at the Alberta border. Buffalo (bison) were forced to jump over the high cliff to their death.
-1868 William T. Smith from **Kentucky** established a huge cattle ranch and modern barns near this location.
-**North** & **South Saskatchewan Rivers** both rise in **Columbia Icefields** in the Rocky Mountains [map p 164].
-The **North Saskatchewan** cuts deep valleys across Alberta via **Edmonton**, reaching **North Battleford** where the **Battle River** [map 164] enters from central Alberta, and flows via **Prince Albert** into the north end of Lake Winnipeg.
-The **Bow River** flows through **Calgary** SE into the **South Saskatchewan River**, which crosses one third of Saskatchewan, then turns north, curving east near Prince Albert and joins the **North Saskatchewan.** They flow as one into the north end of Lake Winnipeg [maps pp 125; 163; 164].
-The **Assiniboine River** rising in central Saskatchewan, flows southward, joins with the **Souris** and **Qu'Appelle Rivers**, then turns east, and empties into the **Red River**, which runs into **Lake Winnipeg**.

Upper & Lower Canada and the Maritimes (Atlantic Canada) were Thriving [pp 118-120]

-1825-1846 a total of 626,628 British and European immigrants landed at eastern Canadian ports [119 Vol 5, p 235].
-Meanwhile in Ontario cheese, agricultural fairs and scientific farming became popular. Networks of Railways were built; 1853 Grand Trunk railway from Montreal via the Eastern Townships to Portland, **Maine** [120, p 711].
-1856 with the opening of a railway from Montreal to Toronto, public funds diverted from roads to railways.
-1854 there were 1618 saw mills in Upper Canada, most run by water; but use of steam began [119 Vol 10, p 273].
-1858 **Ottawa** (formerly **Bytown**), incorporated as a city in 1854 [147 Vol 3 # 33, p 776-781], was chosen by Queen Victoria as Canadian **Capital**, ending rivalry of five cities [119 Vol 8, p 80]. In1859 construction of **Parliament** began.
-1850 new land for farming had run out in Upper Canada, so many adult sons of large families and new immigrants began to migrate north to **Parry Sound**, Nippissing and Algoma. There fertile top soil was thin, the climate severe, insects troublesome and roads muddy. Eyes turned west of the Great Lakes [119 Vol 8, p 210g-h].
-1850 to 1900 a half million **French Quebecers** [119 Vol 8, p 365, 125 Vol 10, p 82] moved to **New England**, **Michigan** and **Kansas**. Some migrated on foot again to the Canadian NWT still looking for homestead land, as follows:
-1894 French settlers founded **Vegreville** [the author's home, p 169] 70 miles east of Ft Edmonton [130, pp 1-6].
-1861-65 because of the **American Civil War** [p 142] and lack of transcontinental railroads, migration from Europe to the US slowed. Australia, New Zealand and Canada became attractive to the British [168 p 212-216].
-1867 **Canada was inaugurated by Confederation** of **Nova Scotia**, **New Brunswick**, **Quebec** and **Ontario**. Provincial and federal powers was determined by the **British North America Act** [119b Vol 8, p 366]. 1870 Manitoba was added. 1873 **Prince Edward Island** (PEI) joined [147 Vol 5, # 55, pp 1297-1303], delayed by landlord and businessman struggles [168 p 243, 259].
-1869 the **Timothy Eaton** Company founded in Toronto opened the largest *Department Store* in America.
-1884 T Eaton Co. launched its mail order business, selling a wide range of manufactured items including clothing, sewing machines, fashions, furniture, musical instruments, bicycles, saddles and farm machinery.
-In Chicago, **Sears Co** began by selling watches by mail order. 1893 they amalgamated with **Roebuck Co.** but sold out to a clothing manufacturer.
-1894 their 500 page **Sears-Roebuck** catalogues were used by mid-western rural customers. They had broad interests, even ownership of **Encyclopedia Britannica** [12 Vol 10, p 587].

-1876 the Inter-Colonial **Railway** from **Halifax to Quebec** [119 Vol 7, pp 390, 409] and many short lines were built.
-1876 the first long distance **telephone** call, Brantford to Paris, Ontario, was pioneered by Scottish born Canadian **Alexander Graham Bell**. 1877 Bell Telephone Co was founded.
-1878 the first telephone exchange in the British Empire was installed in **Hamilton**, Ontario [119 Vol 8, p 51].
-1879 **telegraph** lines, railway and postal connections multiplied.
-1875-96 a period of financial depression led to a variety of schemes to assist emigration to western Canada[119 Vol 5, p 236]. Titled **English families** sent their landless youngest sons to the west [119 Vol 8, p 210j] who, since they received money periodically from family in Britain, became known as ***remittance*** *men* [p 177].
-1881 **Canadian Pacific Railway** reached **Winnipeg**, starting a demand for Ontario manufactured goods.
-The whistle of trains lured many to leave rocky **Parry Sound**, Ontario. Parents of many were originally from Pennsylvania. Landless sons of large families migrated to western Canada from Ontario and the USA. Among them were **French** formerly from Quebec.
-1883 nickel and copper were discovered at **Sudbury,** Lake Superior and the mining industry began.

The Upper Fraser Valley, Cariboo and Okanagan 1848-1867 [from pp 153-154]

-1848 **Yale** at the Fraser River Canyon, was established as the head of steamboat navigation up the river.
-1858 A rush of over 3000 prospectors panned for gold between **Hope** and **Yale** [128 Vol 1, pp 85, 148-153]. Indians withdrew or were driven out. About 70,000 dwindled to 28,000 from small pox, tuberculosis & alcohol.
-1862-66 the second gold rush was in the **Cariboo** about 400 miles up the deep gorges of the Fraser Canyon, attracting 25,000 multiethnic miners, largely from San Francisco, including 2000 Chinese. Alarmed at lawlessness, BC **Governor Douglas** sent Judge Matthew Baillie **Begbie** and Royal Engineers. They maintained firm control of law and order. Some prospectors stayed in the Fraser Valley to become farmers.
-Walter **Moberly** [pp 153-4, 161] laid out/supervised construction of 400 mile engineering marvel: **Cariboo wagon road** from **Hope** to **Barkerville**, through Fraser and Thompson River canyons [119 Vol 2, p 239]. Mules and even camels carried supplies [128, pp 60-69]. **Barnard's Express** stage coaches took 5 or 6 days to Barkerville.
-Ranching, lumbering and fishing settlements and hotels sprang up. Social life was both rugged and elegant.
- A self-taught Chinese man became an outstanding photographer [119b Vol 8, p 210; Vol 1, p 323; 128 Vol 2, pp 128-135; 80-89; 48-53].
-When gold declined, miners bought property and settled down or moved south east to the **Kootenays**.
-1860-2 **Oblate missionaries Fathers Charles Pandosy** and **Pierre Richard** settled south of **Kelowna**, planted an orchard, wheat and potatoes; began an itinerant ministry with native peoples on **Flanagan Lake**, fostering farming & orchards [128, p 161]. An Oblate missionary and **Luc Girouard** settled the present **Vernon**.
-1862 200 ***Overlanders*** came from Ontario by a northern route to Kamloops & Barkerville [See below]
-1862 **Forbes** and **Charles Vernon** began the Coldstream Ranch and cattle industry in northern Okanagan.
-1864 **Moberly** was elected to the Legislative Council representing **Cariboo** West, but resigned 1865 to become assistant Surveyor General. He discovered **Eagle Pass** through which the CPRailway was later routed.
-1867 **Cornelius O'Keefe** and **Thomas Greenbow** drove cattle from Oregon to the north end of Okanagan Lake. O'Keefe took a homestead of 160 acres. [Continued pp 159-160]

Overland by the Yellowhead Route to Interior British Columbia

-Rugged *Yellowhead route* from Edmonton and **Jasper** was used by various pioneers before there were roads.
-1862 June, about 200 brave Ontario pioneers, called ***Overlanders*** sailed on the Great Lakes [140] and took a US railway to Winnipeg. On Red River Carts pulled by oxen they made the long trek to Edmonton via Battleford. They traded their oxen and carts for pack horses to go via **Jasper** to the **Cariboo** (central BC), another long precarious trek. Six men drowned on rafts on the **Fraser** & **Thompson Rivers**. A woman with three children kept up with the hardy men. She gave birth to a fourth in October [120, p 1742], hours after reaching **Kamloops**.
-A gold rush had begun on the upper Fraser River in 1860. Most of the *Overlanders* went to the new mining settlement, named **Barkerville** for a pioneer miner. Few struck it rich in the gold rush, but pioneers **Robert** and **Daniel McMicking** [131, p 440] and others had successful careers in BC. **John Bowron** started a lending library and a dramatic association at Barkerville [128 Vol 3, pp 87-9; 134] [p 159]. 1868 Barkerville destroyed by fire; rebuilt.
-1863 early June to late August, **Dr. Walter B. Cheadle** and **Viscount Milton** with an Irishman and native guides, traveled in dangerous conditions from Edmonton to Kamloops and Victoria [128 Vol 3, p 86-91; 119b Vol 2, p 324], looking for adventure and an overland *North West Passage*. They reached Kamloops starving.
- Cattle were brought northwest on the Cariboo Road to the **Chilcotin Plateau**, west of the Thompson River; ranching began [pp 159 and 177-178.

Map: Growth of the United States from 1776 to 1867 [9b, p 199].

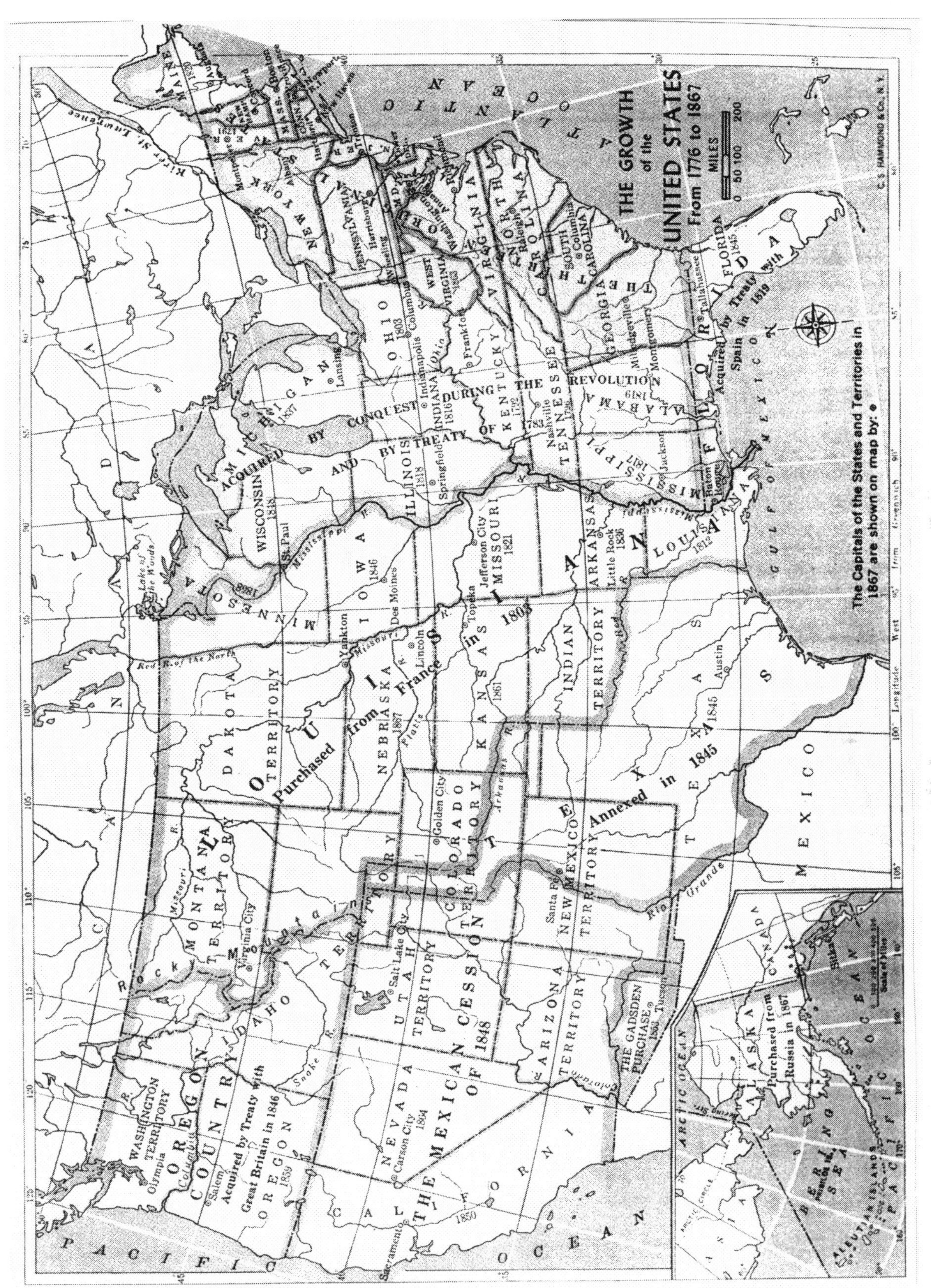

Migrations West Before and During the 1861-65 **American Civil War** [pp 117-8, 126-130, 142]

-1842-5 **John Fremont** explored several routes over the Rocky Mountains [16, p 267]. His guide for three long journeys was **Kit Carson** (beaver trapper in Arizona, California, Idaho and Wyoming). **Fremont** explored the **Oregon Trail** from Mississippi to Wyoming, Great Salt Lake region, and Colorado to California [map p 130]
-1845 iron ore was mined in upper **Michigan**, and 1855 carried via the **Soo canal** to Great Lakes smelters.
-1846-8 Kit Carson participated in the **Mexican War**; was Indian agent in **New Mexico**, and 1861-65 served in the **American Civil War** [125 Vol 3, pp 16, 38-;250;130]. 1848 **Nevada** and **Utah** were ceded to the US by Mexico.
-1846-8 the US took **California** in the Mexican War. **John Fremont**, active in the conquest of California was appointed the first Governor of California; 1850 became US Senator.
-1847 **Utah** was settled by **Mormons** led by **Brigham Young** [pp 128 and 159; maps pp 130 and 157].
-1848 **Wisconsin** with a population of 305,391 received statehood; 1850 **California** also [maps p 130, 157]
-1853 **Washington Territory** was founded with Olympia as Capital. The north part of present **Idaho** and western **Montana** were included. **Cattle industry** in Montana was begun, with a herd driven from Oregon.
-The coastal **Indians signed treaties** with the US government to live on reservations, which freed up land for settlers coming either via the Pacific Ocean or cross-country by covered wagons [maps pp 128, 130]
-The inland tribes resisted reserves and made war until 1858, but gave in; signed a treaty 1859 [125 Vol 21, pp 67-8].
-1840-60 over 300,000 people trekked by covered wagon from the east to Oregon & California [map p 130] Many conscientious objectors migrated west to **Ohio**, **Indiana**, **Illinois**, **the Dakotas**, **Pacific NW**, **California** and **Canada** to escape military conscription [12 Vol 2, p 503] and religious ostracism [map 157].
-1859 **Oregon** became a State; **Washington Territory** expanded to include parts of present **Wyoming**.
-1860-61 the **Pony Express** mail delivery was inaugurated. Relays of ponies took 10 days from **Missouri** to Sacramento **California**. One of the riders was **Buffalo Bill** [16, p 588]. 1861 coast to coast telegraph line installed.
-1861 **Dakota Territory** was set up, including much of **Montana** and **Wyoming**. 1863 **Idaho Territory** was established. Homesteading began slowly due to travel and fear of Indians [125, Vol 14, p 496].
-1861 the **American Civil War** began. July 3, 1863 defeat at **Gettysburg**, west of Philadelphia.
-1865, April 9 **General Lee surrendered.** President **Abraham Lincoln** freed slaves throughout the USA in the Emancipation Proclamation, but was assassinated. A decade of troubled *Reconstruction* followed.
-1865 the **US census** showed a slave population of 4½ million. In 1830: 2 million; 1790: 700,000 [16, pp 691-2].
-1865 the ***Ku Klux Klan*** engaged in terrorism [16, p 407, 619]; in 1876 was brought under control.

Migration While Building the US Transcontinental Railway 1860-69 [from pp 127-130]

-1860-69 building of a transcontinental railway began from the east by the Union Pacific, with **Irish** laborers and, from the west by the Central Pacific, with **Chinese** workmen [125 Vol 21, p 234]. Settlers and prospectors came in large numbers. Gold in Idaho, Montana and BC stimulated the economy and population of Washington.
-Mining camps had no effective law enforcement so local residents formed **vigilante** committees [125 Vol 13, p 758].
-1866, 1000 longhorn cattle were brought from **Texas**. Herds expanded rapidly on lush prairie grassland.
-The rail moved west bringing an influx of miners from **England** and **Wales** and settlers from **New England**, **French Canada, Germany** and other countries,
-Many remained in the mid-west (**Kansas, Nebraska** and the **Dakotas**) as far as the railway was built.
-There was a rush to occupy homesteads en route [168, p 301-313]. [125 Vol 3, p 485].
-Homesteading on the great plains was discouraging at first. Sod houses and dugouts were built because of lack of wood. There was little water or rain and lack of fencing materials. Raids by Indians were frequent.
-Agriculturists developed dry-farming skills. Wagon trains of settlers went farther west to greener pastures.
-1869 after the **Civil War** many more settlers were going west.
-1867 **Alaska** was purchased from **Russia**.
-1869 the transcontinental railway was completed, crossing the **Sierra Nevada**, a 400 mile mountain range along the east side of California[16, p 685].
-1906 Earthquake and fire in San Francisco took 500 lives.

Promise of Railway From Sea to Sea Convinced British Columbia to Join Confederation

-Construction from the east across the Canadian prairies (North West Territories) went ahead rapidly.
-1870-71 **Hugh Nelson** a member of the BC Legislative Council for New Westminster [119b Vol 7, p 263] strongly urged the colony to enter Confederation. He had been a lumberman in BC since 1858.
-1871 **British Columbia** joined Confederation on condition that Canada build a transcontinental **railway.**

Pioneer Settlers in Fraser Valley and Interior BC 1872-1885 [Continued from pp 153, 156]

-1857-62 a gold rush brought 30.000 prospectors up the **Fraser River** from **Hope** to **Yale;** and 1862-66 up deep canyons 400 miles to **Barkerville**. 1858 the Crown Colony of BC was formed to counter lawlessness.
-1862 Some took up farming in the Fraser Valley. AC Wells a harness maker from Napanee, Ontario, joined the gold rush. In 1867 he founded Edenbank farm on Luckakuck stream, with cattle driven from Oregon.
-1872 there was a heavy flood of several streams, that tore away rich land, so farmers united to use fallen logs, horses and dynamite to build dikes. Friendly indigenous people spoke of rivers in the past changing their course, **Chilliwack** means "flowing back up stream". Tribes had adapted, moving freely without boundaries.
-1870 without treaties, land was surveyed and divide into 24 Sto'lo reserves **Mission** to **Hope** [170].
-1873 **Chilliwack** (first named Centreville) in the **upper Fraser Valley**, was the 3rd township incorporated, after only **New Westminster** and **Victoria**. Chilliwack Agricultural Society and plowing matches began.
-Some settlers came across the Panama isthmus, some bringing Holstein cattle and Clydesdale horses north to Langley BC [132] and shallow draft Fraser River stern wheelers. Regularly 30 stops were made for passengers, apples, baled hay, barley, oats, potatoes, chickens, dairy products, horses, cattle & household furniture.
-1871-79 **Hugh Nelson** represented New Westminster as an MP (Member of Parliament) Ottawa; 1879 was called to the Senate; 1887 was appointed Lieutenant Governor of BC [119b Vol 7, pp 263-4] [continued p 160].
-1872 **Okanagan** post office and a general store were opened on **O'Keefe's ranch**. He built a mansion. Within 40 years he had cattle grazing on over 15,000 acres [128 Vol 2, p 1].
-1883-6 **Thomas Shorts** carried passengers & freight on a 22 foot row boat on 69 mile long **Okanagan Lake**.
-1886 he launched the first of his paddle-wheel steam boats. For years Captain Shorts kept building a better boat reusing the engine, and he launched other boats. 1893 CPR railway began steamer service [128 Vol 1, pp 46-51].
-1875-82 and 1886-94 **Forbes Vernon** was MLA for the Vernon area; 1894-8 BC Agent in London [131, pp 743-4].
-1883 **Charles Vernon** sold his share of Coldstream Ranch to Forbes and moved to Victoria. 1885 the town then called Centreville was incorporated and in 1892 renamed **Vernon**.
-1883 T**ranscontinental Canadian Pacific Railway** construction neared **Revelstoke** from east and west,
-1883 Archibald "Archie" Rory MacDonald trekked large herds of Shorthorn and Hereford cattle more than 200 miles, from Washington State to Revelstoke BC, to supply beef to feed men building the railroad. He was paid handsomely and made three trips with cattle from the US, bought cheaply because of depression.
-Archie in 1839 had been born to Scottish parents near Bytown (**Ottawa**) where he was a highly skilled log roller and supervisor. 1868 he went to St. Louis, Missouri, and moved westward, gaining experience in mining and cattle breeding. [see pp 122-3]. On the third trip, nearing Revelstoke, a wild steer he was towing behind his boat, dragged him over a sandbar. Both legs and some ribs were broken, his bowels showed through abdominal wounds and he was unconscious. Three assistants placed him on a makeshift stretcher, took him to a nearby abandoned shack and made a fire to keep him warm.
-They took the cattle to Revelstoke, got paid, but were told that the nearest doctor was in **Fort Colvile**, Washington State, a former major Hudson Bay Co trading post [119b Vol 4, p 213]. While they went for bandages/disinfectant/tobacco/rum for Archie's pain, although he never drank or smoked, the cabin caught fire. Archie still semi-conscious, dragged himself, in his blankets to the shore & put out the fire.
-The men returned, dressed his wounds, built a raft and added a tent and sails. They hunted for game and Archie ate the heart of the offending steer. More rum delayed their journey.
-4th day they reached **Arrow Lakes** [129]. 6th day they rested at a settlement. 7th day in rain the three assistants passed the bottle/fished/dined on trout. Archie drifted in and out of consciousness/singing Gaelic songs.
-10th day they bought eggs and milk at a homestead. 16th day they passed the location of the present **Castlegar** and entered the Columbia River at the **Dewdney Trail**.
-The 18th day they navigated very difficult rapids, entered USA, and near **Fort Colville** renting horses and wagon, took Archie 12 bumpy miles to the hospital. The doctor recommended amputation but Archie refused.
- Resetting of his bones was extremely painful. He was nursed by Mary the young daughter of **Colonel Prouty** who was in charge of troops at the fort. In four months Archie left hospital on crutches [129] [continued p 161].

Events After Completing the Transcontinental Canadian Pacific Railway

- 1885 the transcontinental CP Railway was completed, last spike driven at Craigellachie near Revelstoke.
- 1884 settlers from Ontario, US and England started ranching **Chilcotin** meadows, a 200 mile wide, 150 mile long plateau, north of Lillooet, between the Fraser River and Coast Mountains [128 Vol 3, pp 6-17; Vol 1, pp 80-84].
- 1891 Coldstream Ranch, Vernon sold to **Lord Aberdeen**; 1893 appointed **Governor General** of Canada.

-1887 **Canadian Pacific Steamship Lines** operated between **Vancouver and the Orient** [119b Vol 2, p 207].
-1891 the population of BC reached 98,173 by settlers from Ontario, US, Europe & British Isles [128 Vol 3, pp 6-17].
-1892 the Shuswap and Okanagan Railway began service [131, pp 378, 744]. Shareholders included Forbes Vernon and WC Heaton-Armstrong, British settlers who began dairying, cheese-making, fruit growing & vegetable processing. The town was named **Armstrong** and is still the location of well-known Armstrong Cheese Co.
-**Orchards** of apples, pears, cherries, peaches and apricots were developed commercially. An **irrigation** system with **high wooden trestles** was built on the hills around arid Kelowna and Penticton.
-1889 **BC Fruit Growers Association** was founded to exchange information and give the growers a voice.

Developments in South-Eastern British Columbia

[Continued from pp 153-154]

-1872 Thomas **Ellis** returned to Ireland, married and brought his bride on the narrow **Dewdney Trail**. Together they became largely self-sufficient with their own cattle, wheat, fruit, poultry and fish. His pack train of 20 to 30 horses went to Vancouver twice a year. He built steamships to trade produce and supplies on Okanagan Lakes. He bought up abandoned homesteads in southern Okanagan and provided a place to rest for miners trekking to the Kootenays. He sold land to establish **Penticton** town site in 1892.
-1872-79 Edgar **Dewdney** was Kootenay Member of Parliament in Ottawa (MP); 1879 Indian Commissioner.
-1874 **North West Mounted Police** started policing the Kootenay area from **Fort Macleod**, NWT (now Alberta) via **Crow's Nest Pass** [pp 153, 162]. With this protection English settlers began lumbering/ranching.
-1880 orchards did well around **Creston** on reclaimed **Kootenay** flood lands [131 p 716; 119b Vol 3, p 148].
-1884-93 mineral and coal discoveries led to numerous **mining** enterprises on east and west **Kootenay** River and Lake, **Arrow Lakes** and the great **Columbia River** [9 Vol 4, p 372; 119b Vol 7, pp 94-5, 98]. Mines in the east Kootenay were served by pack-horse trains, branch railroads and stern wheelers. Horses learned to walk with snow shoes up to the mountainside mines [128 Vol 1, pp 140-7].
-Thriving communities sprang up, some temporary, but **Kimberley**, **Slocan**, **Nelson**, **Trail** and **Rossland** have survived with fine heritage homes [119b Vol 2, pp 85-6; Vol 9, p 89]. Editors, doctors [128 Vol 3, pp 17-21; 70-75; 42-47]; and hotel-keepers were colorful [Vol 1, pp 14-21, 70-77, 112-121. Vol 4, pp 114-9; 32-7, 68-73].
-1888 **Nelson**, near Forty-nine Creek mine on the west arm of Kootenay Lake, was named for **Hugh Nelson**, Lieut. Governor of BC 1887-1892 [p 158-9]. Major mines were opened nearby in 1867 & 1886 [119b Vol 7, pp 263-4].
-1887 **North West Mounted Police** built **Fort Steele** (12 miles NE of Cranbrook) [119b Vol 4, p 229].
-1881-88 **Edgar Dewdney** transferred east to the prairies as **Lieut. Governor** of **Northwest Territories**.

Settlement Enabled by the US Transcontinental Railway and Branch Lines

[from p 158]

-1861-66 the Civil War; 1869 the transcontinental railway was completed, linking **Sacramento**, California to eastern USA. Soon branch railway lines crisscrossed the continent. 1870 immigrants began to arrive from **Denmark**, **Norway**, **Sweden** and **Germans from Russia** and **Austria**, receiving homesteads all over the US midwest, NW territories and states. The rail through **Utah** brought outside influence [16, pp 786-7]; by 1890 some **Mormons** were less in favor of polygamy [16, pp 786-7] [pp 128, 130,158].
-1873 barbed wire for fences and windmills to pump water from deep wells became available [125 Vol 21, p 235-8].
-Circuit rider preachers held camp meetings, visited for weddings and baptisms, sang **Wesleys'** hymns.
-Lumber and furniture from Michigan were sent west for buildings of treeless towns and farms [125 Vol 13, p 509].
- Frontier towns such as **Butte**, **Montana** and **Wichita**, **Kansas** thrived;
-1876 **Virginia City** [map p 157] had a population of 27,000 with 20 laundries, 50 dry goods stores, 150 saloons, 6 churches, an opera house and theatres for Vaudeville and Shakespeare plays.
-Young **Mark Twain** was a reporter on the newspaper [125 Vol 21, p 237].
-1870 **Thomas Edison** was able to send four messages simultaneously on one **telegraph** wire [125 Vol 21, p 241].
-1871 forest fire in northeast **Wisconsin** killing 1200 people, did not shock the nation as much as: the night of the **fire in Chicago**, the largest grain and meat packing centre in the US. 300 people died and much property was destroyed [125 Vol 21, p 365-8; Vol 10, pp 74-5].
-1870 a **railway** passed through **Dakota Territory**. The population of 2405 rose rapidly.
-1874-83 10,000 **Mennonites** plus many **Lutherans** from **Odessa**, southern Russia on the Black Sea, settled in the Dakotas [93, p 29].
-1878 telephone calls were made across the country, and began to be preferred above telegraph.
-1883 railways to Washington Territory brought miners & supplies; exported beef and metals [125 Vol 13, p 758].
-1900-1930 touring **Chautauqua** brought culture in a tent to towns in both USA and Canada, mainly midwest.

-1884 **Montana** was granted statehood. 1880-90 the population rose from 39,000 to 143,000. Immigrants from Ireland, England and Europe mined gold, silver and copper at **Butte**; smelters were opened [125 Vol 13, p 760].

-1882-83 **Archibald "Archie" Rory MacDonald** [continued from p 159] trekked cattle three times from Washington State to Revelstoke BC, more than 200 miles, to supply beef to men building the Canadian Pacific transcontinental railroad. Starting the last return journey he was seriously injured; it took his drinking friends 18 days to get him to the hospital at **Fort Colvile**, Washington, still a **Hudson Bay Co Trading Post** and **US army barracks**, but Archie refused amputation. Mary, the young girl who nursed him, was daughter of Colonel Prouty in charge of the fort. After four months Archie left the hospital on crutches.

-Archie lived in the hotel and went for longer and longer walks each day. He chatted with everyone. In Fort Colvile he met a young man from **Ontario,** who with two **Canadian partners**, had a stake on a mine four miles away. They were hauling ore by wagon and mules to **Spokane** [See map p 177]. From there ore went by train to the **smelter at Butte**, **Montana**. Archie advised them to hire an experienced man to sort it and ship only high grade ore. They hired him. Archie could mount his horse, but the mine was four miles away.

-Mary Prouty told her parents. They invited him to live at their home near the mine. Her two brothers worked at the mine. With Archie's advice and hard work for two years, the mine did well.

-Archie feeling stronger, said he planned to go to South Africa to prospect for gold. The family, especially Mary did not want him to leave. Mary proposed marriage to him, a surprise since he was 30 years older, and there were eligible young cavalrymen at the fort, but he agreed. They took a homestead with a large hayfield and built a house and garden. In 1887 their first child, a girl was born.

-1888 the railway reached Colville, named for Andrew Covile [119b Vol 4, p 213] a HBCo governor. Archie's mining job came to an end. It was no longer necessary to sort ore since rail transport was inexpensive.

-1893 Ervin Austin was born. (He is the author of an exceptionally fine biography of his father [129].) Archie bought, fattened and sold horses and beef cattle. In a dispute with a **French Canadian** he won a fight, after which he walked away without his crutches, and never used them again. He and Mary had more children.

-1896 Mary died. The children studied in local and **Spokane** boardings/orphanages; had summers with dad.

-1886 there were riots in **Chicago** over the high price of equipment and shipping, and the low prices for crops so farmers and city workers united and elected a more understanding Illinois state governor in 1892.

-1889 the Dakota Territory with a population of 190,983 was divided into two states, North & South Dakota.

-1890 all land in the US was occupied; the frontier ended. Due to overpopulation many went north to Canada to find homesteads. Some went into mining.

-1905 Widower Archie Macdonald and three adolescent sons migrated to **Alberta** [continued pp 177-8].

Surveying of the Canadian North West Territories for Settlers

-1872 the Dominion Lands Act was passed to provide grants of homesteads [119 Vol 5, p 236] to encourage settlement of the west. Well ahead of their arrival systematic surveying of land was completed. The land was divided into ***Townships*** measuring 6 miles on each side, containing 36 ***Sections*** one mile square. Road allowances were one mile apart, east to west and two miles apart north to south. Every 24th mile the east-west road is a ***Correction Line***; to adjust for the curvature of the earth, so north-south roads take a short jog. In the centre of each township a Principal ***Meridian*** runs north-south. The first Principal *Meridian* is at 97º longtitude (north-south), the second 102º, third 106º and so on. ***Ranges*** are numbered to the west & east from the Principal *Meridian*, numbers increasing to the east [119b Vol 6, pp 63-5]. Starting at the US border (49th parallel) ***Townships*** are numbered from one northward. ***Homesteads*** consisted of *a* ***Quarter Section*** (160 acres) An iron stake, engraved with a Roman numeral (hard to read), was driven into the corner of each *quarter* [89, p 8]. Early trapper and Indian trails crossed the square q*uarters* anywhere.

-Newcomers went to a Land Office for a list of ***quarters*** available; went on foot or by wagon to choose one. After a difficult search in the wilderness they returned to the Land Office to file a claim and paid the $10 fee. In three years they received full title to the ***quarter*** if they lived on it at least six months each year, cultivated crops on at least 30 acres and built a house worth at least $300 [93, p 29].

-Often it took only three years to earn Canadian citizenship, as with the author's grandparents.

-**Treaties were made** with 13 aboriginal nations, granting rights, protection and reserves of land, on the basis of one square mile per family of 5. This amount of land thought generous did not satisfy their traditional nomadic way of life. The Atlantic Provinces, Quebec and British Columbia did not arrange treaties [119b Vol 10, p 136].

North West Mounted Police (NWMP) Kept Order From Winnipeg to the Rockies

-1873 the North West Mounted Police were organized/recruited in Eastern Canada. They trekked west to their headquarters at **Emerson**, near the US border south of Winnipeg.

-1874 they set up **Fort Macleod** near the US border, now southern **Alberta**, and put a stop to illegal whisky imports from the US [120, p 897].

-1875 the NWMP built **Fort Brisebois** (later named **Calgary**) and established law and order, which made ranching safer. The **Blackfoot** Indians who had acquired horses from Mexico in the 16th century, were fierce fighters **to outwit**, not to kill. **Crowfoot** their **head Chief**, was a noted warrior and wise leader.

-1875 a NWMP post was built at **Fort Saskatchewan**, 30 miles downstream from Fort Edmonton.

-1866 Chief Crowfoot rescued **Father Albert Lacombe** from a band of hostile **Cree**.

-1877 the Blackfoot treaty was signed agreeing to lands near **Calgary** [119b Vol 1, pp 403-4; Vol 3, pp 162-3] and in the foothills as far south as the US. The tribe had no permanent villages, but roamed with the buffalo until they were almost extinct about 1889. Then needing new sources of food, they became farmers, coal miners, and cattle-keepers, but they felt it was demeaning to be "servants to cows". 1882 **Scots** had settled at **Red Deer**.

-1875 the NWMP built **Fort Walsh** in SW Saskatchewan and rebuilt **Fort Carlton** [p 155, map p 163] near the junction of North and South Saskatchewan Rivers [119b Vol 9, pp 100-1]. The Indian tribes soon respected these sturdy police in red tunics, for their horsemanship, bravery, fairness, honesty and justice.

-1876 the NWMP established headquarters at **Fort Battleford** on the North Saskatchewan River, which became the **capital** of the **North West Territories** [121 Vol 2, p 675]. Telegraph lines were installed as far west as Edmonton. Because the railway was expected settlers began to take up homesteads farther north.

-1873 in a by-election [121, pp 1584-5] and again in 1874 **Louis Riel** was elected a Member of Parliament, Ottawa, but in 1876-78 was in Quebec mental asylums [119b Vol 9, pp 27-28]; was expelled from Canada for 5 years [p 155].

-1878 Riel settled in Montana, married, taught school in a Jesuit mission, and became an American citizen.

-1874-79 about 18,000 **Mennonites** arrived from Russia [121 Vol 3, p 1836-7]. They were the first to engage in farming inland from the Red River, south of Winnipeg.

-1874-83 in **the Dakotas** 10,000 **Mennonites** and **many Lutherans** from **Odessa**, southern Russia [93, p 29], settled. Thousands of Roman Catholics and Lutherans from **Odessa** homesteaded in the present Saskatchewan. **Ranchers** from **Texas** and **Kansas** drove cattle north into the Canadian prairies.

-1876 **wheat** was taken by oxcart from Winnipeg to ships on Lake Superior for export [119 Vol 5, p 235].

-1883 a grain elevator was built at **Port Arthur** but in a tax dispute, the CPR transferred to **Fort William**.

-1871-86 increased immigration to the prairies came via Lake Superior, Rainy River and Lake of the Woods.

-1876- 81 over 40,000 settlers came from the north Ontario [120, p 1425] where all homestead land was occupied.

-1873 **Prince Edward Island** (PEI) joined Confederation [147 Vol 5, # 55, pp 1297-1303] after land owners agreed.

-1875 **Walter Moberly**, formerly in BC [pp 153 and 156] was employed in Manitoba in railway engineering and built the first sewer system in **Winnipeg** [119 Vol 7, p 120].

-1875 a large number of **Icelanders** settled along Lake Winnipeg.

-1875-96 during **a** financial depression, numerous schemes by the nobility funded migration from the British Isles to Manitoba and central NWT (the present Saskatchewan) [119 Vol 5, p 236] [maps 152, 164].

-1876 **Keewatin District**, Manitoba to the **Arctic** was formed, and in 1912 part was transferred to Manitoba.

-1877 the **University of Manitoba** was opened and merged with **St Boniface College** that had begun 1818. **Anglican** and **Presbyterian colleges** also came under the university [119b Vol 10, p 196].

-1878 the *Saskatchewan Herald*, first newspaper west of Winnipeg [119b Vol 9, p 223] was published at Battleford.

-1878 a **railway St Paul, Minnesota to Winnipeg** [125 Vol 21, pp 340-2] stimulated manufacturing and outfitting.

-1881 the boundaries of Manitoba were extended west and east as at present, but north only to 53°.

-1883 **St. Boniface**, near Winnipeg was incorporated as a town; 1908 as a city. A large flour mill and two large meat packing plants were built [119b Vol 9, p 142].

Development of the Canadian North West Territories but Métis Resistance

-1881 the **Canadian Pacific railroad** reached Winnipeg, and by 1883 was completed up to **Calgary**, unexpectedly on a **southern route**. Grain elevators and small villages were built about every ten miles to cater to the needs of settlers. Immigrants from Great Britain, Ontario, Europe and the US moved west as fast as the railway, settling at the end of the line as it was constructed [119 Vol 5, p 236]. In 1882 **Scots** had settled at **Red Deer**.

-Some settlers trekked north to **Battleford** by oxcart. Others stayed on the train until **Southern Alberta**.

-Settlers already homesteading farther north were greatly disappointed that the **railway** unexpectedly was built in the south. **Telegraph lines** had been built on the **Battleford Trail** to **Edmonton** [119b Vol 1, p 338]. The southern route was chosen to keep the US from control of Canadian territory. Now more telegraph lines and communities were added along the railway in the south [147 Vol 5, 52, pp 1232-6].
-1881-88 Edgar **Dewdney** was transferred from BC as **Lieut Governor** of the **North West Territories.**
-1882 the **NWTs** were organized for federal administrative and postal purposes, and divided into **four districts::** **Athabaska**, **Alberta**, **Saskatchewan and Assiniboia** [map 164]. The **capital** was moved from Battleford south to **Regina**, on the **railway**. Pioneers from Ontario, Britain, the USA and eastern Europe settled along the line as it was being built. Many German-speaking people who had never lived in Germany, came from **Poland**, **Russia**, **Romania** and **Austria**. Most communities were multicultural rather than culturally homogenous [119b Vol 4, pp 353-8].

Map: *North-West Rebellion* [128, p 128]

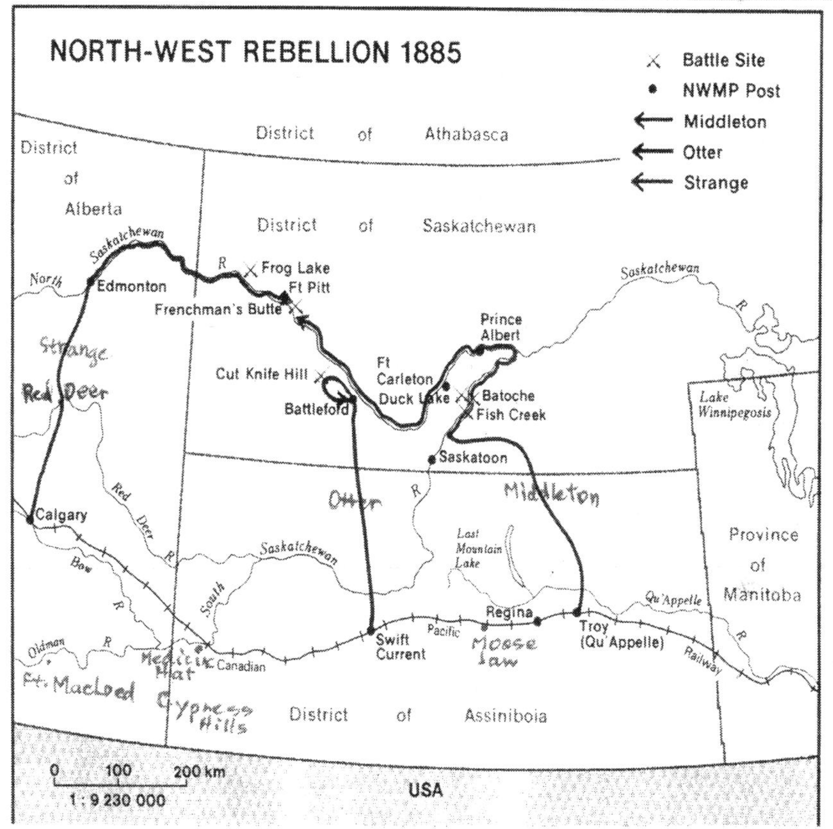

-1883 settlers came **by train** from Ontario to Moose Jaw and **by ox cart overland** north, to begin the settlement of Nutana (1901 renamed **Saskatoon**). .
-Settlers built a saw mill, ferry, store, school, hospital and church. It was kept as a **Temperance Colony** until the population swelled. **Steam-boats** plied the South Saskat-chewan River to **Medicine Hat**. **Stage coaches** took passengers to **Battleford** [119b Vol 9, p 231-2].
-John McDougall interpreted and taught Indians during the **Red River Rebellion** 1869-70.
-1872 in Ontario he remarried and [p 154] in 1873 trekked with his wife and father, to serve with him the **Stoney tribe** in Alberta. 1874 was ordained a Methodist missionary and 1885 was **NW Rebellion** interpreter.
-1884 the **Métis** so as to claim nationhood and effectively **to protest invasion** by surveyors, settlers and trains, sent four men to Montana to ask **Louis Riel** to lead the **North West Rebellion** [121 Vol 3, p 1837-8] .They set up their headquar-ters at **Batoche**, 35 miles SW of Prince Albert. Riel appealed for support to Cree Indians led by **Poundmaker**. Conflict was intense and nine HBCo settlers were killed at **Frog lake**, west of Battleford.
-Oblate **Father Vegreville** an itinerate missionary in Battleford area [pp 154, 169] was taken prisoner [130 p 2].
-Chief Big Bear [119b Vol 4, p 287; Vol 1, p 387] restrained the Crees from further fighting. There were few **NWM**ounted Police. At **Duck Lake**, between Prince Albert and Saskatoon, the Métis rose up and destroyed nearby **Fort Carlton**. 4000 militia under General **Middleton** came by train. One third rode to **Batoche**, one third led by **Sergeant Otter** to Battleford & the rest under **Sergeant Strange**, went via Calgary, constructed a fort at **Red Deer** 70 miles north, [120, p 1983]; and rode on north to protect **Edmonton**. The Métis failed to win wide support of the Indians. **Father Lacombe** influenced Alberta Indians not to join in the rebellion [119b Vol 6, p 42; Vol 3, p 145]. The Blackfoot **Chief Crowfoot**, though pressured by **Poundmaker**, his Cree son, forbad both nations to rebel.
- Edgar **Dewdney,** Lieut Governor of NWT [pp 153, 159 and 163 above] helped prevent an Indian uprising.
-1885 in May the rebels were defeated at Batoche. Riel was tried for treason and executed at Regina in Nov. Eight Indians were hanged, Big Bear and Poundmaker were freed. 100 years later Riel was exonerated.

-1889-1892 **Dewdney** was MP for E **Assiniboia**, Manitoba; returned to BC as **Lieut Governor** [119b Vol 3, pp 262; 142].
-1885 November 7 near **Revelstoke** BC at Craigellachie **the last spike was driven** to complete the transcontinental **Canadian Pacific Railway to Vancouver BC**, greatly stimulating the flow of immigrants, political leaders, communications, produce and forest products.
-1887 a group of 41 **Mormons** from Utah and Idaho began a colony in **Alberta** 14 miles north of the US border, named **Cardston** for their leader, **Ora Card**. His wife was a daughter of **Brigham Young**. They ranched and built a cheese factory, flour mill, saw mill and a canal system to irrigate the semi-arid land and grew sugar beets. 1903 they built a sugar factory; started towns Raymond, Sterling and McGrath.
-1882-88 many European immigrants settled at **Dunmore** (now **Medicine Hat**, Alberta), but due to drought for three years, when a branch RR line was built north of Calgary as far as **Red Deer,** many moved that far.
-1891 the railway reached **Strathcona (South Edmonton)**. A flood of immigrants arrived by train.

Map: *Four Districts of the NWTs from* 1882 to 1905 [155].

After 1905 the Sask/AB border ran through Lloydminster. Athabasca was added.

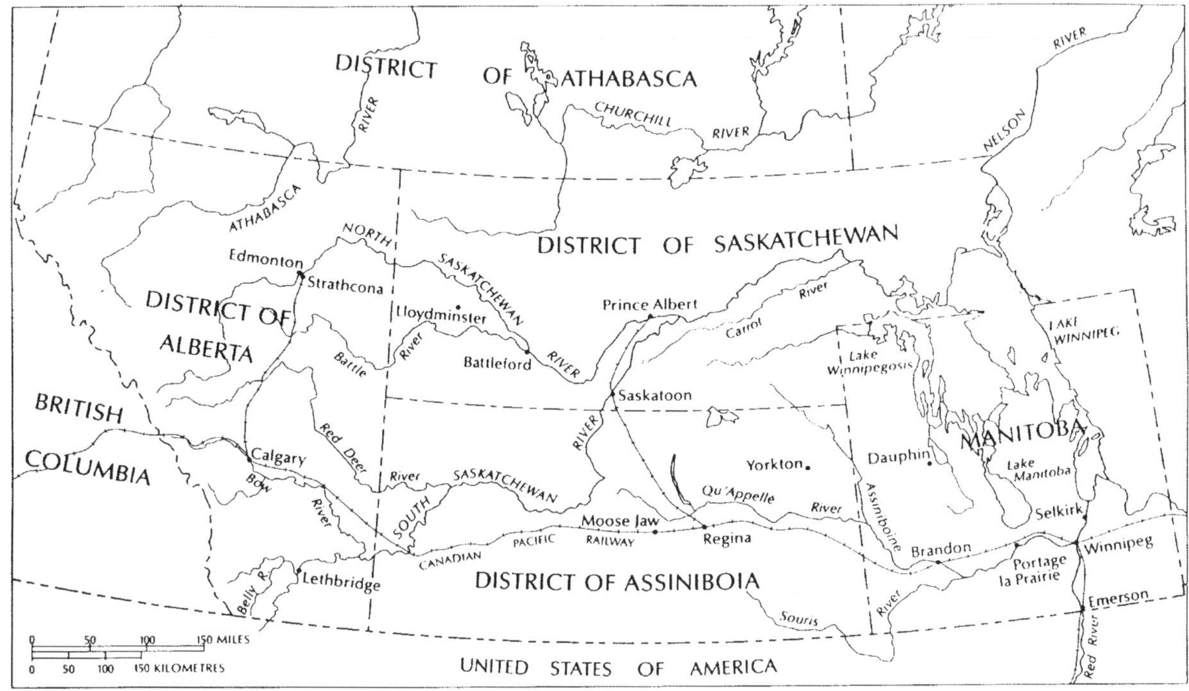

Immigrants from Galicia (in Austria) and Volhynia (in Russia)

-1880 much migration of ethnic Germans from **Odessa** (now **south Ukraine**) and **Volhynia** (**north Ukraine**) went to **Brazil**, **Siberia**, the **Caucasus**, **Courland** (Baltic Sea), to the **USA:** Connecticut, New York, Chicago, Wisconsin, Oklahoma, N Dakota, Minnesota, Oregon & California [Sep 92, p 5-6] and to **Winnipeg, Canada.**
Russian Baptists migrated to N. America and **Brazil** [WV, Sep 93, p 11]; some Lutherans to **S. America** [WV Dec 94, pp 9-12].
-Large numbers of **Ukrainians** and **Poles** from **Galicia** and **Bukovina** migrated NE of Edmonton [166].
-Many Germans from **Galicia**, **Bukovina** and **Bessarabia** [142, Part 2, Henry G. Meyer, pp 22-30] migrated to **S. America**.
-1888-91 forty or fifty **Reformed (Calvinist)** German families from Austrian **Galicia** (annexed in 1772 from Poland) went by CPRail to southern North West Territories (NWT- later Saskatchewan and Alberta could trace **Swabian ancestry** in southwest Germany and Alsace, prior to migrating to **Galicia** in 1782-5.
-In Austria they lived 15 miles north of Stryj (Stryy) which was 30-40 miles south of **Lemberg (Lvov=Lwow)** in villages named **Josefsberg** (Korosnica), Kryywula, Brigidau and Dersow. They left Austria because of Roman Catholic government religious intolerance, army draft, and some because of loss of investments in a failed oil drilling scheme in the Carpathian mountains. They spoke Schwabisch German(Swabish or Alsacian), plus Polish and Ukranian. Their settlement at **Dunmore**, NWT near **Medicine Hat**, was named **Josephburg** for their home-town in **Austria** [87, pp 6-12, 20-1; 130, p 127-9, 483-9, 546-50].

-1888-92 various ethnic German families from **Odessa** (south Ukraine near the Black Sea) and **Volhynia** (north Ukraine) settled for a year or two in southern Alberta, but because of drought, trekked north by oxen.
-1890 the railway went north to **Red Deer**. **Germans** from eastern Europe plus **Lutheran** and **Baptist Scandinavians** fanned out east of **Wetaskiwin**, and **Camrose**, central Alberta.
-After three years of drought and crop failures near Medicine Hat, two more Austrian Reformed communities named **Josephburg** were created, one in SE Saskatchewan and another in **Beaver Hills**, 40 miles east of Edmonton, south of Fort Saskatchewan. They thrived on the fertile land. In 1900 as homesteads were all claimed, some Reformed Austrians went 30 miles east to Brush Hill, near **Vegreville** [See p 169].

Settlements Around Edmonton

-1891 the branch railway reached **Strathcona** (**South Edmonton**). Groups of Lutheran colonists went NW and took homesteads in **Spruce Grove** and **Stony Plain**, mingling with neighbors who had migrated from Ontario, Britain and the US. Others went east to settle in Beaver Hills south and east of **Fort Saskatchewan**.
-1892 the CPR ***Edmonton Special*** brought many settlers from rocky, overpopulated **Parry Sound**, **Ontario**, where the transcontinental train whistle lured them daily to the west. They settled around Edmonton and Fort Saskatchewan (a NWMP post) [87, pp 12-20].
-Methodists and Presbyterians from Parry Sound, some of them of German origin from Pennsylvania 90 years earlier, settled among multiethnic neighbors, described vividly by descendants in community histories, such as: [86; 87; 88; 89; 90 86; 87; 88; 89; 90, 130; 166]. Most no longer spoke German.
-1888 **Ludwig Klapstein** a Versammlugshalter (teacher/lay pastor) from **Lubin**, Poland [WV, Mar 92, pp 9-19] (occupied by Austria 1795) after teaching in Heimthal, Volhynia for 8 years, migrated to Canada with wife and 6 children. Son Emil was born in Dunmore, NWT now Medicine Hat, Alberta. Due to drought they trekked to south Edmonton [pp 168, 171]. The settlement was later named **Heimtal**, now **Leduc**.

Great Britain During the Reigns of William IV and Queen Victoria [from pp 135; 141-2]

-Familiarity with British history is valuable because of many settlers from Britain, but also since immigrants of Germanic ancestry from Poland, Austria and Russia became **British Subjects** quickly, often in three years.
-1837 William IV died without an heir so the connection with Hanover came to an end**.** Hanover was separated from Great Britain. Ernest Augustus, Duke of Cumberland, became King of Hanover.
-Germany was still a collection of many separate nations and duchies.
-1837-1901 **Queen Victoria**, granddaughter of George III, in 1840 married Albert, Prince of Saxe-Coburg-Gotha, her cousin. He died 1861. Her reign of 64 years saw vast colonial expansion and industrial, social and scientific change. Queen Victoria honored the constitutional monarchy policies determined by Parliament, yet was able to make her influence felt.
-Canadian indigenous peoples refer to her as ***The Great White Mother***.
-The British **Prime Ministers** were outstanding, notably: **Melbourne**, **Peel**, **Palmerston, Disraeli, Gladstone** and **Salisbury**. British diplomacy impacted the near and far East [74, pp128-133].
-1837 Benjamin **Disraeli** a Jew, became a member of Parliament, 1852 Chancellor of the Exchequer, and
-1867-8 and 1874-80 Disraeli was Prime Minister.
-1875 Disraeli arranged purchase of controlling interest in the **Suez Canal** and,
-1877 he had Queen Victoria named **Empress of India** [16, pp 198, 359, 596, 729]. In 1878 he became an Earl.
-1845-7 famine struck **Ireland** as the potato crop failed. Two million died. Irish immigration to the Canada and the US totaled 1¼ million.
-1846 exactly 32,753 Irish landed in Quebec and Montreal. In 1847 there were 84,445 [119 Vol 5, p 235; 95, p 442].
-Railway and steamship building and industrialization greatly multiplied.
-1883-5 **Gilbert Elliott** was Chief of Staff under **General Middleton** [see p 162 above] in the Northwest Rebellion in Canada.
-1877 he had served in the **Russo-Turkish war** and in
-1879 he served in the **Afghan** Campaign and in **Egypt**.
-1891 **Gilbert Elliott** became an Earl and received the title **Lord Minto** [119b Vol 7, p 112].
-1893-98 **Lord Aberdeen** was **Governor General** of Canada. He had a ranch in interior BC [pp 158-9].
-**Lady Aberdeen** founded the *National Council of Women* and the *Victorian Order of Nurses* (with a Public Health Nursing emphasis) [119b Vol 1, p 34]. She promoted BC peaches [see p 167].
-1898-1904 **Lord Minto** was Governor General of Canada. 1905-10 he was Viceroy of India [119b Vol 7, p 112].

Map: ***Alberta and Saskatchewan Inaugurated*** 1905 [160, p 40]. Notice that settlement of the provinces was largely in the southern half. After World Wars I & II new settlers wanting homesteads went a little north to Peace River. See the **Alaskan Panhandle** that reaches south along the west, almost as far south as Edmonton. Compare maps pages 175 and 177.

Chapter Twenty Three – 1894 to1914

Escape from Russian Anarchy, Homesteading and Farming Excellence

Continued Development of British Columbia

[Continued from pp 153-4, 156-160]

-1885 The railway from sea to sea was completed greatly stimulating the economy and cultural exchange.

-1887 heavily-forested **Stanley Park**, now in the centre of Vancouver, named for Governor General Stanley, is surrounded by a 8.5 km sea wall walk. Aboriginal rights to the land were ignored. Saw mills were set up to harvest awesome, ancient Douglas fir in the temperate rain forests of Vancouver Island and the Fraser Valley.

-1889 a contract for trans-Pacific mail service was awarded to the Canadian Pacific Railway (CPR) by the British government. Three ships, the *Empress of India*, *China* and *Japan* carried the mail until World War II.

-1890 the **University of BC** charter was approved by the legislature of BC, but it was not until 1915 that it opened [119b Vol 2, p 88]. 1899 Vancouver High School affiliated with **McGill University**, Montreal.

-1872 and 1894 floods around **Chilliwack** carried away fertile land. Farmers uniting built dikes using fallen logs, dynamite and horses. 1920 **Sumas Lake** west of Chilliwack was drained by BC government. 59 square miles of fertile lake-bottom were subdivided/sold mainly to Dutch Reformed farmers [119b Vol 9, pp 434-5].

-Salmon fishing, dairying, orchards, vegetable and hops industries [143, pp 96- 103, 117-127] were developed.

-1891 the population of **Vancouver** was 13,709 and grew to 163,220 by 1921. Many different Salish and Sto'lo Indian tribes, skilled in fisheries, crafts and weaving living in Vancouver, the Fraser Valley and interior BC, lost their land to settlers[169]. Potlash celebrations were discouraged. Boarding schools were built. Methodists built a school for native children at Chilliwack, which later was a tuberculosis hospital.

-1891 the population of BC reached 98,173 [128 Vol 3, pp 6-17] with settlers from Ontario, USA, Europe and Britain.

-1900-1950 the **BC Electric Railway** (**Interurban**) from **Chilliwack** around the south shore of Sumas Lake, to Langley & **New Westminste**r made 4 round trips daily, carrying milk, fruit, pork and passengers.

-1893 Lord Stanley donated the **Stanley Cup** that still encourages excellence in ice hockey [138, pp 619, 675].

-1896-1901 the gold rush on **Klondike Creek** attracted 27,000 people to the **Yukon** [16, p 402; 830]. In 1901 only 4000 were left. Vancouver prospered. 1903 the disputed **Alaska/Canadian** border was settled by an international tribunal, leaving the ***Panhandle*** fiords south to Queen Charlotte Islands, under USA [map 166].

-Trade flourished across the **Panama Isthmus. Vancouver** port grew rapidly, especially after the **Panama Canal** was completed 1915, opening up direct trade with Europe and the West Indies [119b Vol 10, pp 210-11].

-1907-09 about 4700 **Sikh** laborers immigrated from India and worked in BC sawmills. Though often called Hindus they have a monotheistic religion [119b Vol 3, p 331] and are a minority in India.

-1909-10 at the mouth of the **Fraser River** at **New Westminister** the largest saw mill in the British Empire and a local railway, hired 200 **Francophone** families from **Quebec**. They have sustained French culture.

Central and Southern British Columbia

[Continued from pp 159-161]

-1892 the **Shuswap and Okanagan Railway** began service [131, pp 378, 744]. Shareholders included Forbes Vernon and WC Heaton-Armstrong. British settlers began dairying, cheese-making, fruit growing and vegetable processing, and named the town **Armstrong**, still the location of well-known **cheese-makers**.

-1886-94 **Forbes Vernon** had a second term as Member of the Legislative Assembly (MLA) for Vernon area.

-1892 Penticton town site was purchased.

-1893 CPR steamer service on Okanagan Lake began [128 Vol 1, pp 46-51].

-1893-8 **Lord Aberdeen, Governor General of Canada** in 1891 bought the Coldstream Ranch at Vernon. **Lady Aberdeen** was influential in Vernon and Ottawa, promoting BC **peaches** and founding the ***National Council of Women*** and the ***Victorian Order of Nurses*** (public health and home nursing) [pp 159, 165].

-1894-8 Forbes Vernon was BC Agent General in **London**, England [131, pp 743-4].

-1892 rich deposits of lead, silver, zinc and other minerals were mined at **Kimberley**, SE BC.

-Coal mines were developed on Vancouver Island and the **Crowsnest Pass**, BC border with southern Alberta.

-1895-6 a smelter was built at **Trail** by Fritz A. Heinze of Butte, Montana. In 1898 it was sold [119b Vol 10, p 119] to the CPR. Mines and smelters were opened at **Greenwood** and **Grandforks** [119b Vol 7, pp 94-108; 143, pp 107-116; 152-5].

-1898 a CPRailway linking Lethbridge, NWT (now Alberta) to **Fort Steele**, **Cranbrook** and **Nelson**, carried forest products east and coal and coke to smelters at **Trail/Rossland**. 1915 this southern CPR reached **Hope**.

-The Kettle Valley Railway tunnels near Hope, were named for **Shakespearean** plays [119b Vol 2, p 206].

-1899 over 7427 **Doukhobors** came from the Crimea, Russia to SE **Saskatchewan**, and lived communally.

-1908 a large group of this sect settled at **Nelson** to evade schooling for their children [119b Vol 3, pp 299-301].

-1907 **Nelson** started hydroelectric generation on Kootenay River [119b Vol 7, p 264], the first in a BC town.

Development of the Canadian North West Territories [from pp 154-5, 161-4; map p 164]

-1882 building of the CPRailway across Saskatchewan went quickly on the flat prairie southern route [see pp 161-162]. It was expected the transcontinental railway would go through Saskatoon and Battleford. Instead it was built along the south, so the capital of Saskatchewan was moved from **Battleford** south to **Regina**.
-1882 the NWTs were reorganized for federal administrative & postal purposes as four districts: Athabaska/ Alberta/Saskatchewan/Assiniboia [Map p 164]. Telegraph lines were on **Battleford Trail** to **Ft Edmonton**.
-1882 NWMPolice headquarters was moved [119b Vol 9, pp 206, 101] to **Regina** from Emerson, Manitoba [map 164].
-Thousands of settlers filled Saskatchewan, coming from Ontario, Britain, the USA and eastern Europe. Both German-speaking & **Slavic** people from Poland, Russia, Austria and Romania. Communities were multi-cultural rather than culturally homogenous, as were the one-room schools, soon erected every 6 miles.
-1890 a railway from Regina to Saskatoon was completed [121 Vol 3, p 1643]. Saskatoon later was a railway hub.
-1890 all land in the US was settled so many land-hungry people migrated north into western Canada.

Rapid Settlement of Alberta [See details pp 154-5, 161-165]

-1861 **St. Albert**, a Métis settlement at a mission station just north of Edmonton, was named for **Father Albert Lacombe**. Settlers of other origins settled there also. His mission field was the whole of the west.
-1893 **Lacombe** village between Calgary and Edmonton, was named for him by Anglophones[119b Vol 6, p 42].
-1882-88 many immigrants settled at **Dunmore** (now **Medicine Hat**, Alberta). They came from Ontario, the USA and eastern Europe. A variety of ethnic German families from **Poland**, **Austria**, **Volhynia** (north Ukraine) and **Odessa**, S Ukraine (Black Sea) settled first in south Alberta, but suffered drought three years.
-1888-96 **Clifford Sifton**, Ontario-born lawyer, was MLA (member of Legislature) for Manitoba and owner of the influential **Winnipeg Free Press** for 30 years. More below.
-1890 when an RR line was built north of Calgary as far as **Red Deer**, many moved that far, filling up central Alberta. **Scandinavian** (Swedish, Danish and Norwegian) and east European German Lutheran, Reformed and Baptist families fanned east from Wetaskiwin. A few trekked by oxcart to Strathcona (South Edmonton).
-1888 **Ludwig Klapstein** a Versammlugshalter (teacher and lay pastor with Moravian leanings) from **Lubin Poland**, settled in Dunmore for three years, but 1890 due to drought moved to S Edmonton. Ludwig taught school and violin and had Moravian worship services in his home. (1910 son Emil married the author's aunt Augusta Schneider. Some years later Emil was the first to sell gasoline and vulcanize tires, in **Rosetown** SK.)
-1891 the railway reached **Strathcona** (South Edmonton). Settlers came from Ontario, the US and England.
-1892 Edmonton was incorporated as a town after the CPR "Edmonton Special" brought many settlers from **Parry Sound, Ontario**, some of German origin in Pennsylvania 90 years before. After the transcontinental railway passed through, train whistles attracted people to adventure in the west [86;87;88]. They pioneered all around Edmonton [see p 165, maps pp 164, 173].
-German Lutherans from varied places in Europe settled among the Methodists and Presbyterians from Ontario. One-room schools, six miles apart, were all multicultural.
-1894 **Ukranians**, some educated like Peter Svarich, and many illiterate, began settling NE of Edmonton. Orthodox, Roman Catholic, Anglican, Methodist and Presbyterian churches, hospitals and missions sprang up.
-1894 led by **Andreas Lilge**, the author's maternal great uncle, 100 ethnic Germans families from Volhynia (N Ukraine), arrived and claimed homesteads 40-50 miles east of Edmonton north of Beaver Hills. They could not afford to hire horses or oxen, so had to walk. They suffered severely the first two winters developing the community of **Bruderheim** [See circumstances p 169-171].
-About half of the families chose to use the last of their money to buy land on the Papaschase Indian Reserve in Edmonton and developed **Bruderfeld** there (now Millwoods a suburb of Edmonton).
-1896 many Lutherans arrived from Volhynia, including the author's father, aged 13 [below & pp 171-172].
-1896-1911 **Sir Wilfrid Laurier** was Prime Minister, reelected 1900, 1904 and 1908 [119 Vol 8, p 232, 236].
-1896-1911 **Sir Clifford Sifton** MP (Member of Parliament) inaugurated a vigorous immigration policy for settlers, first from the British Isles and later also from eastern Europe [119 Vol 9, p 307].
-1899-1903 his brother **Arthur Lewis Sifton** served in the NWT legislature, representing Banff. 1903 he was Chief Justice; 1910 became **Premier of Alberta** [continued p 174].
-1898 Rev **John** & **Elizabeth McDougall** moved to Calgary, after living on Morley Stoney Reserve 25 years.
-She became president of **Southern Alberta Pioneer Women** and **The Old Timers' Association**. "She voiced the conviction that frontier women had made possible their husbands' activities, citing that a large number of bachelors leave the prairies when unsupported by the labor and sympathy of women" [121 Vol 2, p 1053].

Direct Migration on the Battleford Trail Overland from the East

-1894 **French** families from the US [formerly from Quebec] trekked to start a community named **Vegreville** 70 miles east of Edmonton on the **Battleford Trail** [pp 154-5;162-3], with an inn for travelers and a French post-master. Baptist, Presbyterian, Anglican & Roman Catholic families from US & Ontario joined them. A hotel, livery barn, blacksmith/machine shops, 2 banks, police, stores, butcher shop & cafés kept busy [130, pp 1-6].

-1900 at **Vermilion**, 50 miles east of Vegreville [map p 173] settlers arrived from Ontario, Britain and the US by ox or horse-drawn covered wagons on the Battleford Trail, some driving herds of cattle [119b Vol 10, p 223].

-1903 Greek Orthodox (Ukranian) monastery in Mundare, 55 miles east of Edmonton, educated young men.

-1903-5 the CN Railway was built along this more northern route [119b Vol 2, p 201] via Saskatoon, Battleford, Lloydminster, Vermilion and Vegreville to Edmonton. A flood of immigrants of many ethnic backgrounds quickly homesteaded all the land, but suffered much from black flies, frost and hunger.

-1903 before the CNR arrived, 2000 **Barr Colonists** came from England led by Anglican **Rev. Isaac M. Barr** and later by **Rev. George E. Lloyd**, who began **Lloydminster**, 188 miles NW of Saskatoon, 165 miles east of Edmonton.

-1904 new **Marquis wheat** with high yield, ripened early [119 Vol 1, pp 98, 118] and was rust-resistant. Prosperity began.

-1905 the Saskatchewan/Alberta border was moved east to mid Lloydminster.

-1905 the whole village of **Vegreville** was moved 5 miles north when the railway came from the east. The land near the Vermilion River was wet so dams had to be built to control floods.

Map: ***Barr Colony*** [155, p 128] [See new provincial border map p 173]

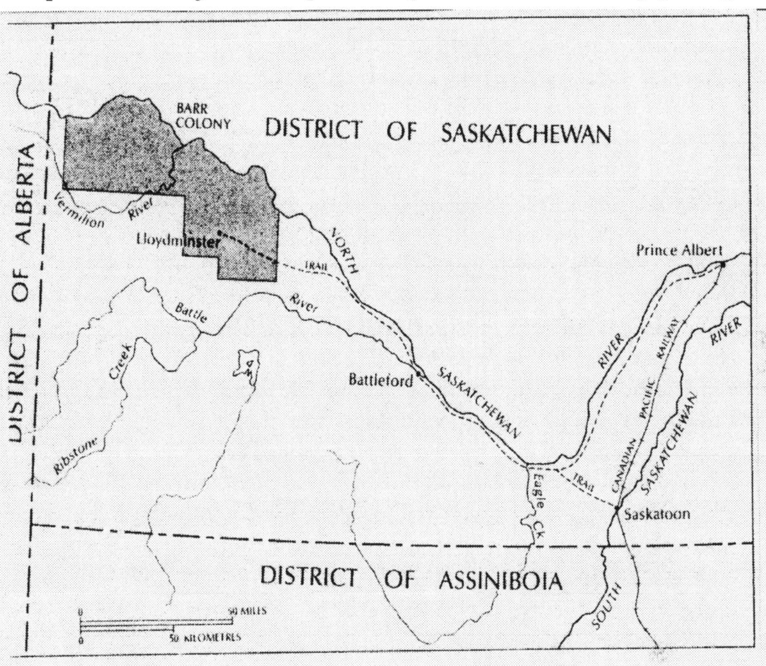

-At the new **Vegreville**, two hospitals, Catholic and Presbyterian, a large town school, high school and many rural one-room schools (six miles apart) were built. A Separate School with boarding was opened [130] for Roman Catholic French, Irish, American and Slavic students. Many branches of Ruthenian (Ukranian), Romanian, and Polish peoples settled a 200 mile ribbon of land north of the railway, northeast from Edmonton as far as **St Paul de Métis** [map p 173]. Vegreville, founded by French and American pioneer families still is a multicultural community. Reformed families came from Austria; Lutherans from Russia. The Americans were Baptists or had German ancestors who in the USA were Methodists (became United Church in 1925). The **Presbyterians** built **four boarding homes** in Vegreville for Ukranian students, one of them for girls, to enable high school education. A **synagogue** was built by over 10 **Jewish** families. A.L. Horton founded an influential weekly newspaper. Major Frank JW **Fane**, veteran NWMP of the 1885 NW Rebellion [130, p 457-8], were police magistrate & post-master at Beaver Lake, He & his wife moved to Vegreville, were social leaders. **Agriculturists** and **Home Economists** were busy. Agricultural fairs, school drama and music festivals, had enthusiastic competitors, including the author. She studied at a one-room school and Vegreville High school. Her parents Chris Schneider & Rennetta nee Klammer [p 170] were active in ethnically mixed social groups.

Circumstances of Volhynian Moravians & Lutherans Settling Near Edmonton [p 150-153]

- 1892 **Andreas Lilge** and his wife Wihelmine and ten children and two other families migrated to the USA to prepare the way for persecuted Moravians to migrate to America. In Wisconsin he studied Lutheran theology, taught German school in a Moravian community, did not find land in the US, so went to Winnipeg.

-1893 Lilge, counseled by a Methodist Minister, Rev. G.R.Turk, the Manitoba Free Press and **Mennonites**, in Dec. received an agreement for homestead land, CPR Railway clergy pass, steamship concessions, plus loans from the Canadian government, for 100 Moravian families to migrate to Canada.

- Endless misunderstandings and delays were suffered by all involved: Lilge, the government, RR authorities and Moravian immigrants [71;73; 84; 85]. It was hard to find buyers for possessions in Russia, travel overland to Libau (Baltic seaport) and to wait for ships willing to accept assisted passengers, unexpectedly only a few at a time. The ships took them across the North Sea, by train to **Liverpool** and by ship to **Halifax** or **Quebec**.

-1894 March to July, sponsored families (225 people [90, p 18]) arrived in **Strathcona** by train via Calgary:

March - first group - Riemer, Vogel and Fenske and families [71, pp 48, 52-]

May - second group - arrived Winnipeg May 6 with 8 families - Michau, Busenius, Stoltz, Paul and Andreas' brother Ludwig Lilge in charge [71, p 57] walked 50 miles NE to the designated township, **Spring Creek** in **Beaver Hills**, later renamed **Bruderheim;** did not like what they saw: heavily wooded, far from town. By telegram they notified Andreas. He advised them to inspect it and nearby townships and if necessary choose a better whole township that met government obligations [71, p 57], which they did.

June 10 - ***MS Lake Winnipeg*** - Julius and Samuel Prochnau and families [71, pp 58-9, 133].

June 15 - ***MS Sarnia***, July 6 reached Strathcona - Adolf Klammer, Wilhelm Lilge, L Lippert and families. Strathcona (south Edmonton) railway station was similar to the station they left in Zhitomir, but not as grand. Compare the cover photographs [WV Dec 93] with [84, cover] Edmonton Bulletin July 6, 1894. Please try to identify the young men in this photo, from passenger lists. They were wearing their best Sunday suits.

June 21 - ***MS Buenos Aires***, July 9 arrived Strathcona - Anna Blank Klammer, Eva Kruger, Charlotte Werner, Adolf Schultz, Sam Kitlitz, Ludwig Henkelmann, Gustav Frederking, Wm Diebert - about 25 families.

-Those who could not walk or buy a horse to travel 50 miles into the wilderness, decided to use up the last of their money, or borrow enough, to make a down-payment for land on **Papaschase Indian Reserve** (now Millwoods, a suburb of Edmonton). **Adolf Klammer** gave up his last $100 to let his father-in-law **Ludwig Henkelmann** and teenage sons buy land.

-The defection of half of Andreas Lilge's Moravians to remain near Edmonton, made it very difficult for him to collect the subsidies the government had promised for 100 families. He filled up the shortfall with **Lutherans**, some of whom later joined the Moravian church. Assistance from Moravian authorities in Bethlehem, Pennsylvania was not available because of donations they had made to rebuild burnt-out **Sarepta** on the **Volga River** [p 138], and for many Volhynian Moravians to migrate to **Brazil** [71, 30] [pp 150, 174].

-All who lacked money had to choose their homestead in the townships designated for them, 45 to 55 miles east in the bush, gather logs and build a house for their individual families, clear land and grow vegetables and wheat to survive the winter. **Adolph Klammer** was one of these, for he had given money to his father-in-law, **Ludwig Henkelmann** to help purchase ship passage during their 13 day layover in Libau on the Baltic Sea. Adolph was in grief and fear that his aged mother (also Andreas Lilge's mother) Anna Blank Lilge Klammer, would come to harm, because she was not allowed on the same ship.

-Before she arrived safely on the next ship, he had to make a long hike in the wilderness to stake out his claim for a homestead. He returned to find his two infants had died of measles in Strathcona immigration shed. Their mother, Julianna had only flour soup to feed them. He was comforted by his mother's safe arrival. (Their daughter Rennetta, born in Canada 1899, was the author's mother; she married Chris Schneider in 1915. He arrived in Strathcona in 1896 as a boy of 13) [40, Part 2, Chap 5] [pp 171 and 169].

-1894 July 12 Andreas Lilge arrived in Edmonton with 90 new arrivals and half a freight car of food and equipment from Manitoba Mennonites [71, p 60-1]. In August he was back in Manitoba appealing again to government and churches. His son Wilhelm, born March 24 in Winnipeg, was baptized by Rev. Turk.

-He brought his family to their homestead, made a rough log and sod house and left his 15 year old son Ludwig responsible for the family. Lilge was a skilled cabinet-maker, but had no time or money to make improvements for his own family. He was intent on providing the settlers' basic physical and spiritual needs.

-The only money he earned, $1500 as Canadian Government Immigration Agent, he used to outfit settlers with a cow and tools [71, p 73]. He made repeated appeals to Ottawa, supported by the Winnipeg Free Press and Methodist minister Rev. Turk.

-1894 November, Lilge again toured Manitoba Mennonite congregations to receive loans and gifts in kind: plows, stoves, flour, equipment, clothes and livestock.

-12 babies died of hunger, exposure and respiratory infections, including Adolph Klammer's two.

-1894 **Ludwig Henkelmann** was elected lay pastor of Bruderfeld congregation on **Papaschase Reserve**, near Edmonton [90, p 239]. He borrowed $64 for his first payment for 160 acres (total cost $600); found carpenter work; bought oxen and built a log house with expertly fitted corners.

-His teenaged sons had casual jobs. That was their only income.

Three Moravian Churches Were Established

-The people who settled in **Beaverhills** suffered severe hunger for two winters. Lilge persisted repeatedly in finding relief for them from Winnipeg [71, pp 44- 85]. He organized Moravian churches in both Bruderheim and Bruderfelt, receiving formal recognition from Moravian authorities in Bethlehem, Pennsylvania [71, pp 87-101]:

-1895 May 6 - two Elders, three Trustees were elected for Bruderheim Moravian Church and 44 communicant and 16 non-communicant members received; Sunday School Superintendent and teachers named.

-1895 June 27 - Elders **Ludwig Henkelman** and **K Vogel** were elected for Bruderfeld Moravian Church, and 3 Trustees. 43 communicants were received, a total of 99 souls, but no Sunday School. The report of the founding of this church was in Lilge's handwriting, but signed by the elders. They made an urgent plea for an ordained pastor. Elders preached twice each Sunday, and an Edmonton Lutheran pastor administered the Sacraments, hoping to take over the congregation [71, pp 88-90]. Henkelman and three neighbors each donated five acres of their land at a crossroads, and built Bruderfeld Moravian Church and parsonage.

-Andreas Lilge's mother Anna Blank Lilge Klammer, though staunchly Lutheran, his two brothers and his half-brother Adolf Klammer and wife Julianna (daughter of Ludwig Henkelmann), were among Bruderheim Moravian charter members. Andreas Lilge was licenced to preach but not paid. Hail ruined crops two years.

-1895 Lilge applied for a Post Office in Bruderheim; was appointed Postmaster, a part-time position.

-1895 Nov 4 to Dec 3 **Rev. Morris Leibert** from Moravian headquarters in Pennsylvania, approved both new congregations, served communion, visited homes with Lilge and promised to recruit a minister for them.

-1896 **Rev. Clement Hoyler** was installed minister of Bruderheim and Bruderfeld and resided at the latter. As they were 40 miles apart, Andreas Lilge was installed as assistant and licensed to preach for a year; he also conducted the choir and played violin.

-1896 Rev. Hoyler inaugurated Heimtal Moravian Church (near Leduc, see map p 173), started in **Ludwig Klapstein's home** [See p 165]. He then had a three-point charge, traveling by horse and buggy half a day, on deeply-rutted muddy trails, for worship services [84]. Often shafts were broken. Horses sank deep in the mud. Wearing waist-high rubber boots Rev. Hoyler made repairs, yet upon arrival looked dignified in a clerical suit.

-1897 April, at the congregational meeting, Hoyler read a letter from Moravian headquarters renewing Lilge's position as assistant with license to preach. In a stormy scene the congregation refused. With stamina and humility Lilge stepped down and remained in the congregation until after the new church building was dedicated in May [71, pp 107-110]. Historian Rev. Kurt H. Vitt, pastor of the Bruderheim Moravian church 1976-82, thoroughly researched circumstances surrounding the life story of Andreas Lilge. He quotes many letters and sources that reveal Andreas Lilge's truly unselfish and dedicated service, and how he was misunderstood [71].

-1897 **Gottfried Henkelmann**, nephew of Ludwig, a sacristan-teacher who had served as a Moravian lay minister in Volhynia, arrived in Edmonton. He was willing, capable and suitable to take Andreas Lilge's place as assistant pastor. However the Bruderheim congregation rejected him as they had rejected Lilge [71, p 110] saying he was not educated enough. Like Lilge he was fluent in Russian, Ruthenian, Polish, German and soon in English. 1903 Henkelmann was ordained as a minister. His first resident pastorate was **Heimthal** 1905-8 [84, p 430]. Later he was pastor of the Moravian church in Calgary.

Homesteaders Filled All Available Land - Two Lutheran Churches were Established

-1896 people from Ontario and the US, Ukrainians and other Slavic people and ethnic Germans from various parts of eastern Europe filled in the remaining land. By then living conditions in Canada had improved.

-1896 **Johann Schneider** [pp 146, 147-8] a magistrate in **Justinowka** (pronounced Justinofska) 10 miles NW of Zhitomir, Volhynia, who spoke Russian so flawlessly that he was accepted as one of them; heard conversations which made him realize German people were no longer welcome in Russia [40, Part 2]. Two sons after finishing their required service in the Russian army, had gone ahead to Bruderheim. One of them, August, was a skilled carpenter who helped build the Moravian church building. (He remained Lutheran).

-Johann sold his property and migrated to Canada with Chris 13 (the author's father); 4 younger siblings &.

-son John, still in the army, smuggled out, joined the group and his bride before they boarded the ship.

-1902 older sister Luise Schmidt & family (of **Sokolov**) [pp 176-7] farmed at Bruderheim and Vegreville.

-As in 6 locations which they cleared and improved in Volhynia, they again had heavily forested land and muskeg (peat bog) to clear near Bruderheim, but with better equipment. They cleared, tilled and harvested land with multiple teams of horses as well as a steam engine, and quickly prospered selling wheat. He planted fruit trees and grafted them with superior frost resistant varieties. The Schneiders were Lutherans, but in Canada Johann, wife Justine and several of their children joined the Bruderheim Moravian church.

-1906 Johann retired in Edmonton, opened a corner store [now a heritage site] & donated land for Norwood Moravian Church. The author's father Chris and younger brother Alex, farmed his homestead and their's.
-1910 his youngest daughter **Augusta Schneider** [40, Part 2, Chapter 9] the author's aunt, married Emil **Klapstein**, Ludwig's son [above pp 165, 169]. He became a street car driver. She was a skilled dressmaker.
-1898 Lilge wanting to be ordained as a Moravian minister to serve somewhere else, but slandered by people he had worked extremely hard to help, having lost credibility, and urged by his staunchly Lutheran mother Anna Blank Lilge Klammer, left Bruderheim Moravian church and held worship services in his home.
-His brother Ludwig and half-brother Adolph Klammer joined him, but he did **not** split the church. As a true shepherd, Andreas cared deeply that many non-Moravian newcomers had no church or pastor, so he gathered together Lutherans who lacked pastoral care, and had worship services with them. He was familiar with their form of worship, having studied in Lutheran Seminary in Springfield, Ill. Also in Manitoba he had been acquainted with the Lutheran church. He organized *Bethlehem* Lutheran church, the first in the area.
-1900 he was recognized as a pastor in Lutheran ministry by the Manitoba Synod [86, pp 38-9, 49; 71, pp 113-6].
-1900 a few miles south he obtained 40 acres of land near **Beaver Hills** from government, and he founded a second Manitoba Synod Lutheran Church, later named *Bethany* [71, p 117] for people from Ontario, Galicia and Volhynia. They had occasional visits from a Lutheran pastor from **Ponoka**, 100 miles south [see map p 173].
-1901 Lilge was able at last to build a modest two-story house and move his family out of their sod dwelling.
-1902 he resigned as the first Bruderheim Postmaster, a part time responsibility since 1895.
-1904 Lilge built ***Mud Lake School*** near Bruderheim, the first school in the area. The same year he started construction of the *Bethlehem* Lutheran Church. The congregation were worshiping in his home [71, pp 118-122].
-He suffered from Bright's disease, a chronic kidney infection (probably tubercular) with no cure.
-His oldest son Ludwig was convicted as an accomplice in the murder of F. W. Leslie and jailed until 1910.
-1905 the **CNRailway** arrived from eastern Canada. It made pastoral visits from Edmonton easy.
- A Missouri Synod pastor was appointed in Edmonton. Lilge was sad that the Manitoba Synod was displaced.
-1906 daughter Hulda died (tuberculosis?). Then Andreas and wife Wilhelmine adopted the two youngest of her three children. His brother Ludwig died of tuberculosis (Tuberculosis was called Consumption.)
-1907-9 Andreas Lilge was Lutheran pastor in Wetaskiwin [71, p 122-6] and was very well liked. Son Ernest came to live with them and died of tuberculosis. Two other sons working the Bruderheim farm, somehow acquired the deeds and sold it, leaving their grieving parents without a retirement home.
-In Bruderheim, Bethlehem Lutheran church (Manitoba Synod) gave in to offers from Missouri Synod for pastoral care. This Synod did not recognize his qualifications, so Andreas had neither a family home nor a church home to return to, in his declining health and old age. A source of comfort was playing his violin.
-1909-12 Andreas was pastor of a bilingual Polish-German Lutheran church at Russell, Manitoba [71, pp 124-6] but as the parsonage in Russell was not yet completed his family remained in Bruderheim. Not far from Russell there was a Missouri Synod pastor who was more accomplished in Polish than he was, so he felt unneeded.
-1912 as he left for the USA he walked slowly and a friend carried his trunk to Bruderheim railway station, as remembered by neighbor children [71, p 128]. He was feeble from Bright's disease, a chronic kidney infection, probably tubercular. In 1914 the last letter from him was written from Detroit dated in January. Efforts later to locate him failed. This was a sad unknown end for a visionary, selfless, dedicated man.
-He led the way for hundreds of oppressed Moravian and Lutheran families from Russia to homestead in the North West Territories and become successful farmers and loyal Canadians.
-Andreas Lilge founded four churches (2 Moravian and 2 Lutheran) that were vital to the well-being of the newcomers. All these churches have thrived since.
-His widow lived with a daughter in Portland, Oregon in another community of Germans from Russia.

Settlers in Acquired Land in Five Ways 1890-1905

1. By applying for a homestead with a registration fee of $10.
2. By purchasing land, such as from from Papaschase Indian Reserve.
3. By purchase of Canadian Pacific Railway land. The Canadian Government had paid for the building of the railway with land, rather than money, with the understanding that the CPR could sell the land to farmers to regain their investment. They held title to some land in every township. Younger sons bought this land.
4. By purchase of Hudson Bay Company land, similarly.
5. By requesting wet or unfertile land to be surveyed, draining and developing it [see below p 173].

Some who found no land became miners in Nordegg, Alberta or Sudbury, Ontario. Others became policemen.

Ethnic Germans from Eastern Europe and Russia Became Naturalized Canadians

-Before the year 1900 most of these east European German pioneers became naturalized citizens three years after emigrating from Europe. This meant they were proud **British Subjects**. Most learned English quickly. Johann Schneider hired a live-in tutor to teach English to his family until a school was built nearby.

-Most Moravians were conscientious objectors to war. They were devoted to supplying food for the nation. They bought shares to build grain elevators. They built towns, roads & telephone lines. Though pacifists, many served in the two World Wars on the allied side [86, pp 194-200; 87, pp 247-254]. Though of German origin, they had no loyalty to Germany. Their ancestors were from Alsace (France), Poland, Austria or Russia.

-These immigrants were pioneers in setting up school boards & establishing schools, spaced six miles apart, all of which had multi-ethnic students from Ontario, the US, Britain, and eastern Europe [86, pp 57-97; 87, pp 157-214].

-With their carpentry skills they built many one and two-room schools. Some of their children went to high school in Fort Saskatchewan & Edmonton and became school teachers, secretaries, nurses and entrepreneurs.

-The author's grandfather, **Johann Schneider** toured with **Sir Wilfred Laurier, Prime Minister** 1896-1911, during his third election campaign, to translate his speeches into several Slavic and Germanic languages.

-Johann Schneider was an interpreter for court cases also. 1906 he left his homestead to Chris and Alex, his two youngest sons, and settled comfortably in Edmonton, running a confectionery-grocery store, growing roses and grafting fruit trees. A daughter married a police-man, one became a milliner and another a dressmaker. A son-in-law was an Edmonton streetcar conductor. Chris married Rennetta Klammer parents of the author. Rennetta's maternal grandfather was **Ludwig Henkelman**.

Map: *Villages and Settlements near Edmonton*[9b, adapted from p 58]. Ovals show Bruderheim, Papaschase (Bruderfelt) and Hay Lakes/New Sarepta districts. See old 1882 border and the new 1905 that splits Lloydminster.

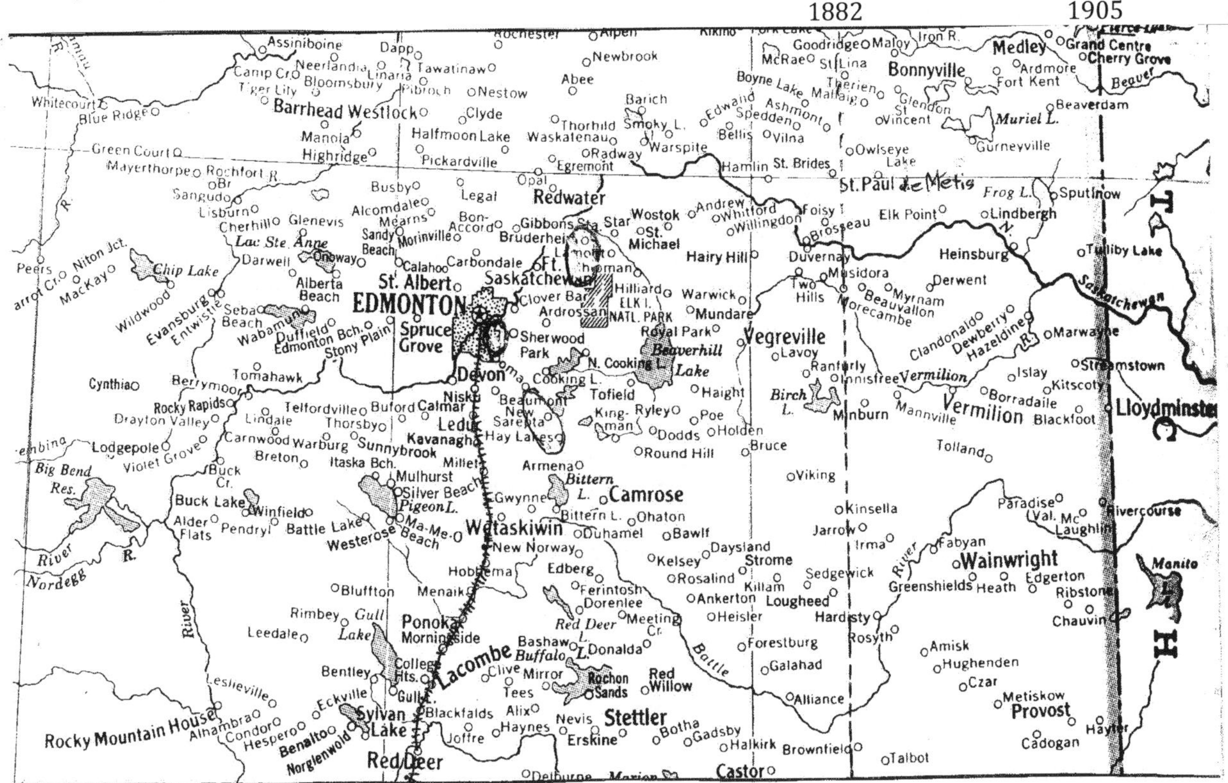

Landless Settlers Searched South-East of Edmonton For Homesteads

-1902 since homestead land around Edmonton was totally filled with settlers, Rev. Clement Hoyler and **Ludwig Henkelmann** in a party of 9 men, made a thorough search for undeveloped land. Not wanting to be far from railroads and Edmonton, they chose two townships 50 miles SE of Edmonton. This land had not attracted other settlers because of many lakes and wetlands.

- Henkelmann asked that it be surveyed, remembering skills he had learned as a youth, farming lowlands in northern Poland, before migrating to Volhynia in 1863.

-1903 April, the survey was complete [90, pp 18-24, 55]. Thirty Moravian families filed for homesteads of 160 acres on township 49-22-W4. **Ludwig Henkelman** and five sons [90, pp 235-241] filed for six quarters. Other Moravians, Lutherans and Evangelical (Reformed) families filed for homesteads in three townships. Some came from **Portland, Oregon**. A Moravian family who had tried living in **Brazil** resettled here.
-A few had ancestors who had lived 100 years at **Sarepta** on the **Volga River**, SE Russia [pp 111-112; 137]. Due to religious restrictions they had escaped to rented land in Volhynia, but suffered oppression again, so came to Canada. Thus the new locations were named **New Sarepta** [90, p 3] and **Hay Lakes** [89, pp 7-8] [map p 174].
-Other settlers came from **Scandinavia**, **Great Britain**, **Ontario**, the **USA.** Others with Germanic roots came from various countries in eastern Europe. **Slavic people** settled to the east, near Vegreville.
-1904 October **New Sarepta** Moravian Church was organized in Ludwig Henkelman's residence, with a congregation of 35 and 18 charter members. Ludwig was elected Elder, and Gustav Henkelman and Emil Diewert trustees. A chapel was completed December 1905. Rev. Hoyler led worship. In 1909 the Heimtal pastor filled in. A resident pastor was appointed 1912 and in 1918 a new church was built [90, pp 55-57]. He and his wife were both born to Moravian missionary parents, he in **South Africa** and she in **Labrador** [84, p 431].
-1905 **Strathcona** Moravian Church was inaugurated since the population of Edmonton had grown and it was not convenient to travel to Bruderfeld (the present **Millwoods**) for worship.
-1907 North Edmonton Moravian Church was inaugurated, and 1913 **Norwood** Edmonton Moravian Church, first in the home of **Johann Schneider**. Later these three churches united with Strathcona Moravian Church.
-1906 New Sarepta School District #1548 was organized in Fred Henkelman's residence. Why was there such a long delay? It took until 1909 to acquire land to build a school since homesteaders could not donate land until they had title. CPR % Hudson Bay Co land was not available for purchase near enough for small children
-1909 Fred gained title to his homestead and sold a small portion for a school [90, p 622].
-Other schools [90, pp 586-647; 89, map pp 240, 272-3, 495, etc] and an English Moravian Mission [pp 36-7] were opened.
-Ludwig's son Martin Henkelman for his growing family bought 6 more quarters of wet land, drained it and sold hay in Saskatchewan and to dairies in Edmonton [89, pp 768-770]. This was labor-intensive work.
-1906 the **Hay Lakes** Lutheran Church was organized in Robert Stebner's home and named *Friedenstal*, later renamed *St. Stephens* [89, pp18-19]. German Lutherans from New Sarepta worshiped with them when possible.
- Several other Lutheran churches, some of them **Scandinavian**, were organized 89, pp 12, 19-34.
-1908 the Lutheran pastor from **Wetaskiwin** (Wisconsin and Manitoba Synods) came on horseback to these congregations. Besides Hay Lakes and New Sarepta, he also cared for: **Stettler**, **Bashaw** (near Lacombe), **Lacombe**, **Ferintosh**, **New Norway**, **Duhamel**, **Waldheim** and **Beaver Creek** [90, pp 51-54] [map p 173].
-The Moravian churches in Haylakes and in New Sarepta continued to thrive.

Wide Influence of Bishop Clement Hoyler 1896 to 1925 [Continued from pp 171, 173]

-1902 **Calgary** Central Moravian Church (later renamed Good Shepherd) was inaugurated.
-1908 **Rev. Clement Hoyler** was consecrated Bishop of the Canadian District of the Moravian Church.
-1909 Rev Hoyler with his family moved to **Saskatchewan** to lead Moravians settled there.
-1909-1910 three Moravian Churches were inaugurated in **Saskatchewan** by Bishop Clement Hoyler, at **Pleasant Point**, **Dundurn** and **Watrous**, in 1925 absorbed into the United Church [84, pp 439-40, 449].
-Under the leadership of Bishop Hoyler, a Moravian church was inaugurated at **Rosedale**, near Chilliwack BC to minister to Moravians from the **West Indies**, who had come to Canada for the education of their children. They were joined by Moravians from the US and Alberta. They later transferred to other denominations.
-1914-25 Hoyler returned to serve Edmonton Moravian church.
-Since 1896 he had made **scholarly observations** and kept records about flora, fauna and meteorology. He was active in academic, professional and ecumenical circles and Canadian Bible Society in Edmonton. When he was a young seminary student at Bethlehem PA, he had founded the college journal, the Comenian, named after Bishop Comenius 1592-1670, of the Unitas Fratrum (Unity of Brethern) who, exiled from Moravia, wrote many influential books and accomplished educational reforms in several countries [pp 76-77]. In his youth Hoyler chose a worthy model for his life in Comenius.
-Hoyler in turn was the academic and spiritual role model for descendants of ethnic German migrants from Russia who settled in Canada [84, pp 1-7, 440-44].
-In his tenure 57 ministers and missionaries came out of the Canadian District of the Moravian Church:
25 of them ordained ministers. Some were nurses and doctors. Hundreds more became teachers and musicians. Most excelled as farmers and community leaders.

Map: A Network of Railways in Alberta and Saskatchewan [150, part of p 33]. See the rivers also.

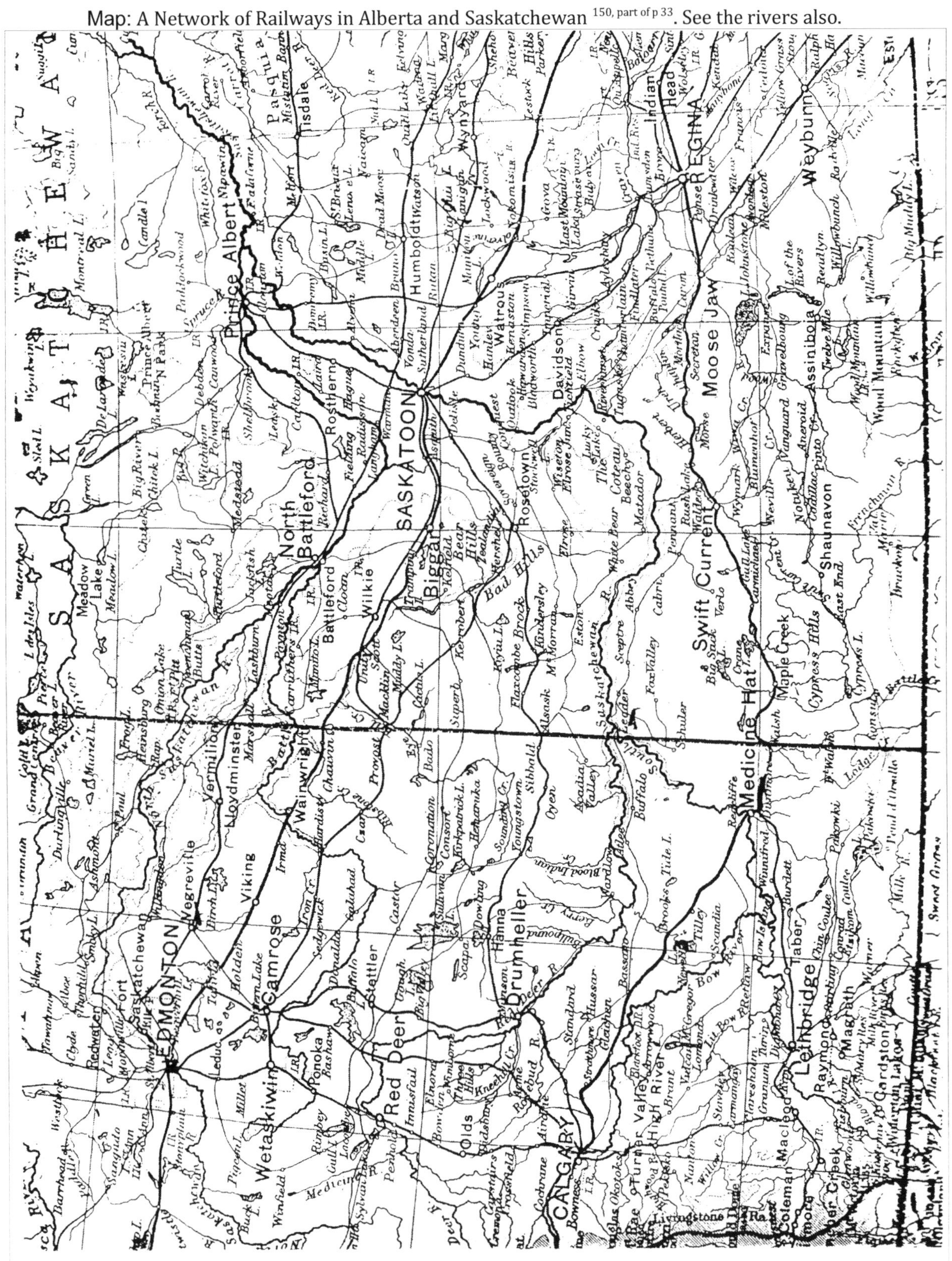

The Prairie Provinces (Former North West Territories) Began to Thrive 1905 to 1914

-1895 the population of **Edmonton** (north side) was 1,165 and of **Strathcona** (South Edmonton) only 505.
-1895 the population of **Calgary** 3,207, was less than 700 in 1891. By 1901 Edmonton grew to 2,626 [144, p 118].
-1901 Queen Victoria added Royal to the NWMP (RNWMP). In 1920 the name was changed to Royal Canadian Mounted Police (RCMP), after amalgamation with the federal Dominion Police, based in Ottawa.
-1902 the Low Level Bridge was completed in Edmonton. There were several coal mines underneath the city.
-1904 Edmonton became a city, with a population of 8,350. A funicular railway served the steep river bank named McDougall Hill for Methodist Superintendent Rev John McDougall [See pp 154 and 163, 165].
-1873 his wife Elizabeth, the first white wife to live in Alberta, had 6 children, yet visited churches with him.
-1901-11 the population of Saskatchewan rose from 91,279 to 492,432 [125 Vol 17, p 147],
and of Alberta grew from 73,022 to 374,295.
-1900 and onwards, great grain elevators were built at **Fort William** and **Port Arthur** on **Lake Superior**.
-1901 **Oldsmobile** automobiles and in 1903 **Fords** were mass-produced in Detroit, Mich, boosting road building. 1905 in Ontario 117 Fords were produced [119b Vol 1, pp 254-9]. Ordinary folk bought cars.
-1904 **King Edward** VII succeeded Queen Victoria.
-1905 the Provinces of Alberta and **Saskatchewan** were established, with changes in borders [compare maps pp 164 and 173 with 176].
-1905 **Regina** capital of Saskatchewan, had an influx of Ontario businessmen [119b Vol 1, p 230 & map p 239]. The *Leader* newspaper began publishing weekly. Soon networks of railways filled the prairies [map p 175] [119b Vol 2, pp 201-202]. All land was taken up by homesteaders. Every ten miles a village and grain elevators were built. Farmers bought shares in grain elevators & telephone lines.
-1905 **Edmonton** became the capital of **Alberta** [144, p 118] with A.C. **Rutherford** as Premier.
-1905 **Ocean-going ships** via the **Welland Canal** and St. Lawrence River took 3,966,000 bushels wheat [119 Vol 5, p 117] to **Europe,** and during WW 1 doubled. In 1934, 116,500,000 bushels [125, p 147]

Map: District and Provincial Borders Compared [85, p 91].

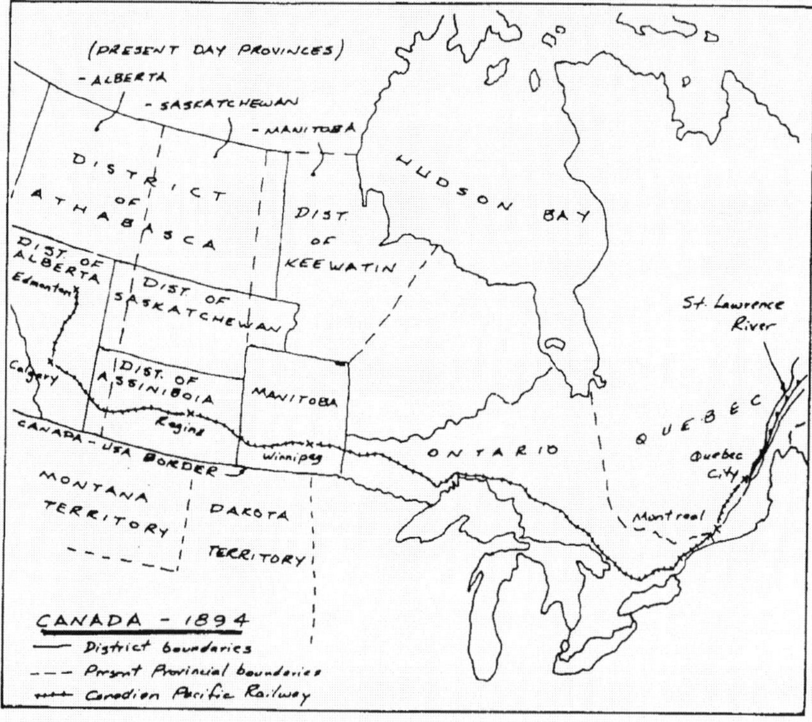

-1908 both the University of Saskatchewan (at Saskatoon) and University of Alberta (at Edmonton) began to hold classes. A **faculty of Medicine** was located at U of A; a strong **faculty of Agriculture** at U Sask.
-1910 **Arthur Lewis Sifton** was elected Premier and Chief Justice (Sir Clifford Sifton's brother) [119b Vol 9, pp 306-7].
-1912 **Strathcona** joined Edmonton; 1913 the High Level Bridge was built, double-decked for trains/cars.
-1911 *St. John's* Lutheran Church, New Sarepta was organized with resident pastor and bride [90, pp 48-54].
-1910-16 some of the homesteaders of Evangelical Church (Reformed background), began a church in New Sarepta, served by ministers responsible for several congregations [90, pp 44-48].
-1911-14 Canadian National Railway from Calgary to Edmonton, was constructed parallel to the CPR, through **Camrose** and **Hay Lakes** [map 175]. The dairy industry already doing well, began to thrive because fresh milk taken by train to Edmonton [89, pp 1-54] a city enjoyed for commerce, family connections and education.
-1910 two intended transcontinental railroads via Edmonton, reached the Rocky Mountains [119b Vol 2, p 201], opening up much land for settlers.
-Mail was carried north from **Edson** to the **Peace River**. Settlers trekked the same route. Landless pioneers finding little fertile land west of Edmonton were soon lured northward.

-1911 Grand Trunk Railway reached Jasper [p 166]. Railway construction in **Yellowhead Pass** began.
-1914 January, the first train on the new railroad reached **Prince George**, BC [p 166], a new town at the confluence of the Fraser & Nechako Rivers, near Fort George, built in 1807 by **Simon Fraser** [119b Vol 4, p 218].
-1915 the railroad reached **Prince Rupert** [p 166], with passengers from **Quebec** [119b Vol 2, p 201]. This was Canada's second transcontinental to the **Pacific Ocean**, but much more northerly.
-Later a third transcontinental went in a southerly route through **Lethbridge** AB, the **Crowsnest Pass**, **Nelson**, **Trail**, **Hope** and **Chilliwack** [pp 153, 160, 166 and 167].

Adventurous Pioneers in Interior British Columbia [Continued from pp 159 and 167]

-The pattern of settlement of BC resembled that of Alberta."Government and railway propaganda attracted experienced farmers, ambitious business men, and scions of wealthy British families to the prospect of stock [cattle] and fruit ranching, particularly in the **Okanagan**" [119 Vol 8, pp 210 k-l]. Noble British families did not have enough land or commerce to establish more than one or two sons in England, so younger sons were sent to Canada and nicknamed ***remittance men*** because of funds sent periodically from family in England. They were educated, but not in business or farming. In Canada they added color and a touch of style to frontier life. With support from England, they were able to try out ingenious ventures. In **Calgary**, other prairie towns, **BC mining centres** and the **Okanagan** they established lively social/drama clubs, tennis, polo and hunting. Some started newspapers,
- British style Canadian law, order & bureaucracy early preceded miners and settlers into interior BC.
-**Yellowhead route** through Jasper was used by hardy pioneers long before the railway went through.
-1862 about 200 ***Overlanders*** went from Ontario via the Great Lakes to the US, by railway to Winnipeg, Red River carts to Edmonton, pack horses to Jasper & an arduous trek to Cariboo (central BC) [p 156].
-1905-7 widower **Archie Rory MacDonald** [pp 122-123, 159 and 161] transferring from Fort Coville with three teenage sons, took the train to Strome, Alberta, east of Wetaskiwin [map p 173]. Two winters they suffered extreme cold in shacks made of thin lumber, and not insulated [Continued p 178]

Map: *MacDonald Homesteads* [129, p 34] [In Fort Colville WA, Stome AB and the Chilcotin BC]

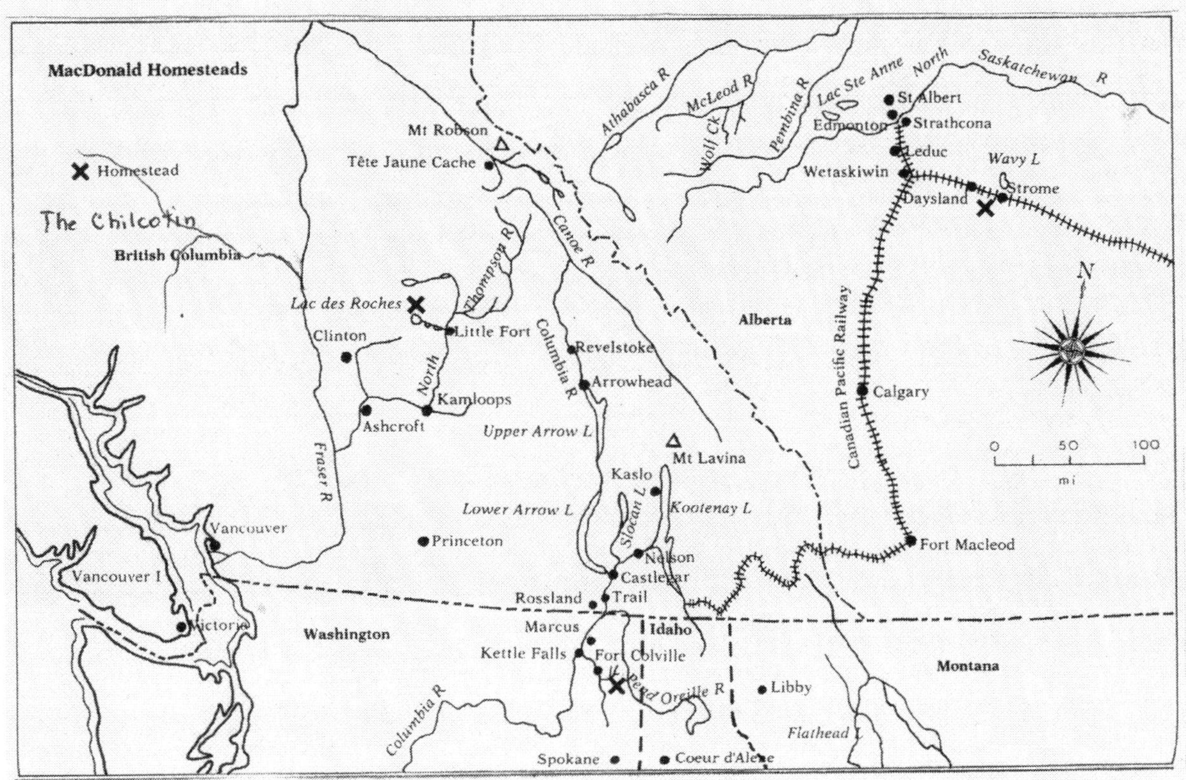

-1907 although Archie and sons improved their home in Alberta, harvested good crops, and survived a prairie fire, they decided to sell out and buy several pack horses and return to their beloved BC, in search of good meadows for ranching. Archie 68, and his sons Angus 17, Dan 16 and Ervin Austin 14 (the biographer [129]) traveled in severe conditions on the **Yellowhead route** through muskegs and river gorges. Roads west of Edmonton were hardly even trails. Dense forests were filled with fallen logs, moss and mud. Yet in BC Archie and sons found the occasional homestead, received vegetables, camping supplies and encouragement to continue.

-They followed the **North Thompson** and **Clearwater Rivers**, and at last, after traveling nearly four months, found a location for their dream ranch, in the Chilcotin northwest of Clinton and 100 Mile House. All had learned resourcefulness and many skills, and they were good cooks.

-They had extreme difficulties, but built fine herds of horses and cattle, a trap line, and a large home [129].

-Other settlers came; there was social life for the boys and a few roads and schools were built.

British Leadership in Canada After Queen Victoria

[Continued from pp 141-2 and 165]

-1901 Queen Victoria's reign of 64 years ended. To Canadian "Indians" she is ***The Great White Mother***.

-1901-1910 **King Edward** VII Saxe-Coburg-Gotha, eldest son, 60 years of age succeeded her. He had visited India in 1875. He was keenly interested in foreign affairs, and in promoting peace.

-1898-1904 while **Lord Minto** was **Governor General** of Canada, Canadian autonomy advanced. 1877 he had served in the Turkish war; 1879 Afghan Campaign and Egypt; 1883-5 Chief of Staff under General Middleton in NW Rebellion in Canada [p 163]. In 1891 had become an Earl, and 1905-10 was Viceroy of India [119b Vol 7, p 112].

-1899-1902 the Boers (descendants of Dutch colonists) invaded Natal, South Africa. Over 7000 Canadians volunteered for military service. Railway and steamship building had greatly multiplied.

-1904-1911 **Earl Grey**, Lady Minto's brother, succeeded Lord Minto as Governor General of Canada.

-1910-36 **George** V respected for diligent Empire service, changed his surname to Windsor in WWI.

Refugees From Russian Anarchy and Revolution 1905 to 1928

[from pp 148, 150-152]

-1881-94 **Tzar Alexander** III (1845-94) governed autocratically & harshly. He was anti-German and anti-semetic. Hundreds of thousands of Russian-Germans, Poles and Ukranians migrated to North America.

-1890-91 crown prince **Nicholas** II toured Egypt, India, China and Japan. At Vladivostok, as railroad chairman, he inaugurated the Trans-Siberian Railroad and before its completion in 1891, he returned home along the projected route. The journey took nearly 3 months, and he was fêted all the way.

-1894-1917 **Tzar Nicholas** II opposed democracy, but 1905 allowed **Duma** (parliament) to function.

-1902 **Adolph Schmidt**, Johann Schneider's son-in-law, reluctantly left his well-to-do family and comfortable estate at Sokolov, Volhynia; with pregnant wife and several small children migrated to Canada; rented near Bruderheim; found only 160 acres to buy near Vegreville; boarded a school teacher to earn a little cash; sent daughters to Edmonton relatives for high school.

-In 1905 Revolution came **in Russia** and **Poland** and war with **Japan**.

-1910-1928 there were repeated violent raids by both the revolutionary *Reds* and the *White* rebels. Livestock and crops were taken. Village schools closed. Years of anarchy greatly distressed the farmers, for example:

Karl Schneider Johann's younger brother had a fine farm in Volhynia, 50 km. west of Kiev. Karl had secondary education but there were no schools for his large family. Several children died of small pox. He and his family were sent to **Kar'kov,** SE Russia. They existed on dried bread on the two week journey, locked in a freight car. They had foresight to take buckets with them to use as toilets. After two years working in a coal mine, they returned to Volhynia to find their farm was occupied by strangers.

-1912 Karl and wife Julianna (Barz or Bartz) and 5 youngest daughters, two sons-in-law and grandchildren came to Canada. They booked on **the Titanic**, but two children had "pink eye"(conjunctivitis) so their passage was providentially delayed two weeks.

-1914-18 over 200,000 **Volhynian** Germans, including Karl Schneider's older married daughters and several grandchildren were expelled to **Siberia**. In Canada he received a letter from **Tomsk,** Siberia and sent a care parcel. The thank you letter was on a scrap of brown paper. He grieved for the rest of his life [40 Part 8, Chap 2].

-1917 **Lenin** (1870-1924) returning from years in Paris, London and Switzerland, became President, and with Trotsky, set up a **Council of Commissars** and a government system known as **Bolshevism**.

-**Joseph Stalin** was General Secretary. Opposition was ruthlessly crushed. The capital was transferred to Moscow and the **Kremlin** was built. **Lenin was Dictator** until his death in 1924.

-1915 **Emil Roleder** graduated from the Lutheran Academy for Sexton-Teachers in Heimtal, Volhynia and taught in several places. He had often bicycled to the comfortable Schmidt estate at Sokolov, to visit a classmate [see p 150]. He like many, was banished to Siberia.
Unsettled conditions continued. Many people who were exiled after some time found their way back.
-1918 exiles returned from Kar'kov to Volhynia found their homes were occupied by others [40, Part 8, Chap 2].
-1921 **Emil Roleder** returned from exile in Siberia and taught school again. He went to Sokolov; married Adolf Schmidt's niece; came to Canada in 1928. His moving autobiography is ***Faith under Four Flags*** [103].
-1925 **Germany** raided **Volhynia** as far east as **Kiev**, followed by Polish forces. Russian communists burned churches, destroyed Bibles & hymn books; harassed people for their beliefs. Those who admitted faith in God were imprisoned/starved. Many ethnic Germans were sent to Siberia. Later a few came back from exile in Siberia to rejoin wives and children who had remained in Volhynia, but they were soon shot [40, Part 8, Chap 1].
The identity and fate are unknown of the siblings of Justine nee **Mielke** (Mrs. Johann Schneider), and relatives of Emilie nee Mielke (Mrs. Alexander Schneider).
-The fate of two brothers of Johann Schneider, Anna (Kossman) & Karl, is emerging.
-There is a list of village name changes. There also are lists by village of people exiled to Siberia. A search can be made [See p 183 for genealogy].
-1928 some people, including some of Karl Schneider's grandchildren. were able to escape from Russia to Germany and later settle in north Alberta, Others remained in Siberia. Some later escaped to **Shanghai**, China.
-1929 there still was a "teachers' training seminary in Heimtal" [WV Sep 93, p 11]. Churches were desecrated.
-1929 Dictator **Joseph Stalin** closed all escape routes for emigration, intensified oppression of people of **German** and **Ukrainian** ancestry, seized their land for collective farms, had millions killed[105, p 52].

After American Civil War and Confederation: Atlantic Canada [pp 120,123-24; 155-56]

-1861-65 the **American Civil War** came to an end [pp 157, 159-160].
-1863 **President Abraham Lincoln** proclaimed emancipation of slaves. 1864 he was assassinated. A difficult ***decade of reconstruction*** affected travel, trade, social and cultural relations with Canadian and **New England neighbors**. In 1898-99 **Hawaii, Philippines**, **Guam** & **Puerto Rico** came under US rule.
-1865 **Ku Klux Klan** founded by white supremacists, in disguise violently terrorized those who favored better conditions for former slaves [16, p 407, 619]. Illegal since 1876 still erupts in the US and Canada [121, p 951].
-Duties and tariffs levied by both the US and Canada drained income away from Canadian Atlantic Provinces.
-Large corporations in Montreal and Bay Street, Toronto, bought up many local industries.
-1867 **The Dominion of Canada** was inaugurated by the **confederation** of **Nova Scotia**, **New Brunswick** and Upper and Lower Canada, renamed **Ontario** & **Quebec**. Long undecided, misgivings continued. They had many ties with Boston and other parts of New England, renewed periodically.
-Ship-building in Atlantic Canada (the Maritimes), based on wind & wood was replaced by the iron steamship industry in **Scotland** [119b Vol 7, pp 289-293, 404-410], resulting in economic recession in the Maritimes.
-1872 **British Columbia** joined **Confederation**. 1873 **Prince Edward Island** joined after the Dominion of Canada absorbed their debt, incurred from building a railway the length of the Island [121 Vol 3, pp 1479-81].
-1876 after the Intercolonial Railway **linked Montreal** and **Halifax** the antagonism over joining Canada moderated. It was routed across the State of **Maine** [see map p 180].
-To get employment there was a brain drain to Toronto, Montreal and New England, especially to Boston. Some expatriates longing for home, returned later.
-Overcrowded people of **Ontario** and **Quebec** began to look toward the vast lands of the Canadian West.
-Much revenue went into building the transcontinental railway to the Pacific Ocean, completed 1885.
-After that a network of railways crisscrossed the prairies and Ontario, map p 175. Immigrants from Europe disembarked either at Quebec or Halifax, Nova Scotia, most on their way to western Canada, Quebec and Ontario. Few remained in Atlantic Canada.
-Atlantic Canada's economic progress has been modest. Fruit growing, fisheries, mining and maritime trade, plus higher education & culture, enriched the life style of these friendly, hospitable provinces.
-Several excellent universities, a lively press & authors/artists associations [121 Vol 2, pp 1236-8,1287-1291],kept standards high. Their faculties of law, medicine, education & theology have been renowned through the years.
-Famous authors are **Bliss Carman:** The *Pipes of Pan*, **LM Montgomery:** *Anne of Green Gables* and **Thomas Chandler Haliburton:** *Sayings and Doings of Samuel Slick,* and *The Clothmaker*.

Map: Overview of New England, the Atlantic Provinces, Quebec and Ontario Nelson World Atlas 1974, p 55. The transcontinental Canadian Pacific Railway crosses Maine; the CNR goes around the north of Maine.

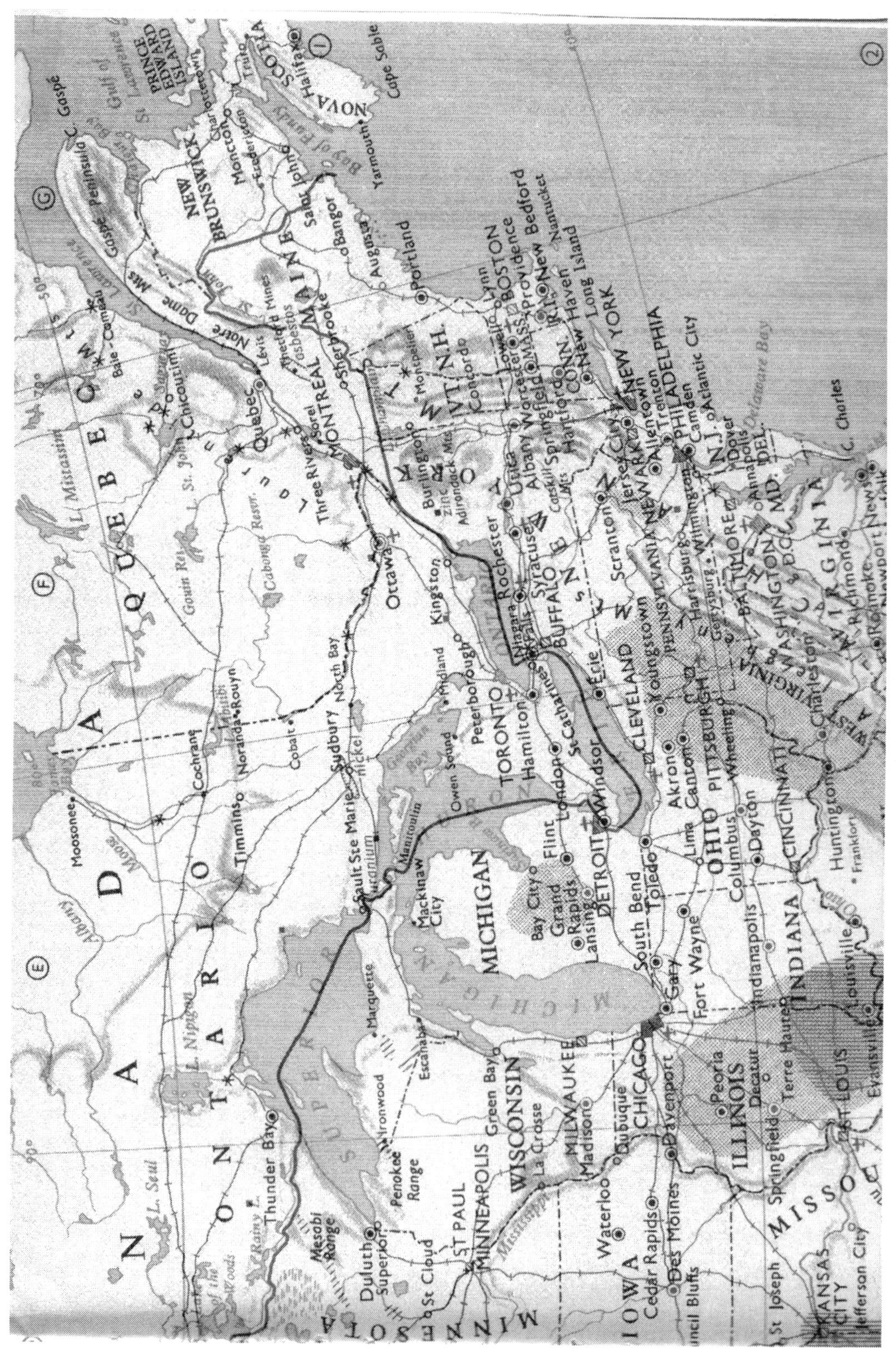

Migrating Into Frontiers of the Past and Future

This book starts in the last millennium BC with people groups migrating in Europe, either east to west or north to south. It describes circumstances surrounding 3000 years of migration. Germanic, Gothic and Slavic tribes from NE Europe & nomads (Mongols, Huns, Turks, Magyars & others) from Asia, pushed westward displacing other tribes to the west. They stopped for a time in places that seemed to have potential for a brighter future. Norsemen/Vikings crossed the Baltic & North Seas and went up all rivers in Europe, Britain & Russia [maps pp 31, 38], and around west and south Europe to Italy, Greece & the Middle East [pp 21, 23, 25]. They settled, built communities and churches and stayed for shorter or longer periods, depending on how well they could provide for the needs of their children.

However more than a thousand years ago some groups were migrating from west to east into Poland. Again, many trekked eastward 1796-1814 during the Napoleonic wars,

The struggle of nations for supremacy for trade with the Orient on land and sea, led to growing knowledge of navigation, mapping and shipbuilding. This book integrates and correlates the drive of European peoples to find freedom from oppression and poverty. Fishermen early sailed northwest on the Atlantic.

Persecuted French Huguenots were foremost in exploring North America, but had to keep their faith secret [pp 69,73]. When shipping improved, English nonconformists and dissidents fled overseas to escape discrimination and war. German protestants found refuge in Pennsylvania. Pioneers overcame great hardships.

For Millenniums Our Ancestors Migrated Again & Again If in Need of the Following:

1. **Stable living conditions**. Some families went on a long trek to escape from war and/or famine. Others migrated to protect their sons from conscription into military service. They went in groups and set up villages with their own form of self-government. In Poland and Russia these were either the **Hollandry** or **Schultz** systems, different forms of democratic self-government [67] [p 138]. Their own craftsmen went with them.

2. **Fertile land and a good livelihood for their sons**. For hundreds of years groups of farmers moved from other parts of Europe into Poland. Most spoke Low German. Before 1800, people from near France who spoke High German or Swabish, were invited to settle on the grassy land north of the Black Sea, to protect it from invasion by Mongols and Turks. Many only got as far as Poland, Austria or along the Danube and settled there.

   After Russian serfs were freed in 1862, thousands of Germanic people moved en masse from Poland into **Volhynia** (now north Ukraine). They cleared forests and drained swamps to start new farms. Some bought land from other groups who were moving on, e.g. a few Mennonite farmers who between 1790 and 1830 in Volhynia had built up excellent farms and mills run by water and wind. Gradually they sold out to Lutherans, and moved to southern Russia, to be near "the Mennonite hub" [65]. Others migrated to South or North America.

   Overpopulation made it necessary for young men with little or no inheritance to search either for land or urban employment. For this reason the English nobility sent their younger sons to Canada. The inheritance was not enough to split among several sons. They became known as *Remittance Men* [p 177] because money was sent by their family to augment what they could earn in Canada. Academically educated and not accustomed to hard labor on the land, they worked in publishing, law, the military, politics, teaching and the arts. In towns and mining communities they started debating/drama clubs, libraries and newspapers.

3. **Satisfactory education of their children and accreditation of their teachers**. In eastern Europe teachers went into frontier areas to accept teaching positions, and when established, families followed. They accepted supervision of school inspectors and the regulations for teaching in the language and customs of their adopted country. The Russian government accepted Lutheran teachers. After 1891 when a teacher said he was Moravian or Baptist, he lost his job [71]. Only Orthodox & Lutheran churches were state religions.

4. **Freedom of religion**. Moravians left Volhynia before most Lutherans did, because their clergy were not permitted to perform sacraments and their teachers lost their jobs because their faith was not recognized, even though they were qualified in the Lutheran Teachers' College in Warsaw. After 1900 persecution of Lutherans began also. The Russians became jealous of their skill and prosperity, and afraid of their population growth.

5. **Creative adventure into uncharted frontiers**. In the inner spirit of human beings there is a longing to try something new or to venture into the unknown. Our ancestors were hardy pioneers, researchers and adventurers. *Necessity is the mother of invention*. They had to be innovative. Though they had blacksmiths, carpenters and cabinet-makers, etc. all farmers out of necessity acquired a variety of these other skills.

Homesteaders had many challenges to solve. They found efficient ways to pull stumps out of fields, to store food to last all winter, to cope with drought, frost and hail, to breed better and better purebred cattle, to graft large tasty, frost-resistant apples and plums in the colder climate of Alberta, and so on.

Here is an example of the innate drive to invent better equipment and tools: In the late 1930s prairie farmers had a machine to separate weed seeds out of grain, but no one was satisfied with equipment various machinery companies had manufactured. The author's father "tinkered away" until he had invented/ perfected a special flap that improved the efficiency of the machine. Because his spelling was poor, her father had her in her teens write his letters to acquire patents and try to persuade farm machinery companies to buy his patent and manufacture his better mill. None did. Meanwhile neighbors had him install this special feature on their faulty machines. It was disappointing not to market it far and wide, but his idea spread. Its principle was incorporated later into the community grain cleaning mills set up centrally, the patent probably pirated.

What Can be Learned from the Experience and Skills of Ancestors?

There is much benefit from exploring the circumstances surrounding the migrations of ancestors. Pioneers were able to adapt to greatly changed surroundings. Diverse survival skills developed. There is much to admire in these innovative people. Techniques and recycling wisdom they acquired, which later became dormant, likely will be needed in the future. Some inactive skills are ready to be applied when the need arises. For example, in 1902 when no more land was available around Edmonton, a party of nine including Ludwig Henkleman and Rev. Hoyler, found waste wet land 30 miles SE, and asked to have it surveyed [p 173]. Ludwig had left Poland in 1865 at 18 years of age, to farm in Volhynia. 1894 he migrated to Edmonton. With skills he had not used since youth on swampy land in Poland, he and his sons and neighbors drained wet fields, sold hay and built up fertile farms & dairies. The community was named Hay Lakes [90, pp 7-8; 89, pp 7-8, 766-771].

If a real interest is shown in elders, they open their hearts and talk about their experiences. Some who are forgetful about recent events remember the past in accurate detail. It can be fulfilling and enriching for them to be given the opportunity to share what they have experienced. Their reminiscences are highly valuable and should be recorded for posterity. Otherwise valuable insights are lost. For example, in the 1940's there were bubbling ***Neon Lights*** adorning businesses and theatres. Now no one knows how to manufacture them.

Frontiers of the Future More Exciting Than Space Travel and Illicit Drugs

Risk-taking is an innate drive in youth and adults. Some youths experiment with dangerous drugs. Exciting computer technology swallows up the time of others, whether for entertainment, creativity or to earn a living. Youths fascinated with non-polluting energy could invent practical low-cost technology, an urgent vital need.

The underemployed and unemployed today could explore old ways to become productive. Skills of the past can be rediscovered. For example, they can reclaim unused bits of land. In China every square inch of land in and around urban areas is used to grow vegetables and greens. Valleys between mountains are not left rugged and randomly cluttered with boulders. Rocks are quarried to build a cascade of small terraces. In SE Asia tiny fields are arranged and sloped to catch water efficiently from mountain streams.

In Canada and the USA river banks and rough valleys could/should be terraced, irrigated & developed to produce vegetables, or landscaped to create fine parks. There is much serious soil erosion. When top soil on river banks slides into the water, as on the Peace River, Alberta fertile land is wasted and water is polluted for fish swimming upstream to spawn. Experience past and recent can overcome food shortages of grain, fruit, vegetables and fish. Though they may not realize it, many immigrants from Asia grew up involved in or at least observing basic skills required for terracing. However to undertake reclamation of eroded land in America they would need on-going support; subsidies/trains/schools/health care. Many immigrants are better suited to rural rather than urban life, where unemployment and gangs bring them disappointment..

In several countries reforestation has been so effective that arid places are receiving dew, rain and wild life again. Planting of hedges & trees is urgently needed to prevent soil erosion/loss of topsoil/drought/famine.

These are frontiers of the future as exciting as space travel. Why do youth try out illicit drugs? Because their natural drive to take risks is thwarted. **Our ancestors ventured into the unknown far from home**.

Life Styles and Human Interest

This book brings to life the interrelatedness of events of over three thousand years. References superscripted throughout the text give credit to sources, offering further reading and colorful illustrations, e.g. [155; 158-9].
You are invited to augment, correct or clarify information in this book, to help revise a second edition.

Genealogical Research and Family Histories

There are many resources to assist with developing a family tree and genealogy of ancestors. Through the internet geographic information, ship passenger lists, old maps and ongoing research findings are available.

- *The **American Historical Society of Germans from Russia*** (AHSGR) has broad application.
- *The **Society for German Genealogy in Eastern Europe*** (SGGEE) focuses on a smaller geographic area.
- The ***Wandering Volhynians Journal*** unfortunately is no longer published, but four issues per year for ten years are still available, and are invaluable.
- Other ethnic journals are helpful [WV June 98, p 21; March 97, pp 17-18]. Great strides have been made in the past few years in cataloging birth, marriage, death and information about cemeteries.

One of the weakest links in family histories is the frequent omission of the maiden surname and family of maternal ancestors. These can sometimes be found in old vital records. In birth records the mother's village and her parents' names are sometimes given. Sponsors at weddings and Godparents at baptisms, are often given. These can provide clues to identify maternal ancestors. Usually female sponsors were close relatives.

There are Latter Day Saints (LDS) Genealogy Libraries where original birth, death and marriage records are available for viewing on microfilms, without obligation and at very little expense [WV Dec 97, pp 8-9].

For understanding of vital statistics on microfilms in a foreign language, such as Polish, it is possible to get vocabulary lists to help read key details. The names of people involved and their roles can be picked out. Those records that look significant can be photocopied and later given to an expert for translation. A Polish person may not be familiar with the archaic Polish used, but may be keen to learn and help.

There are lists available of village names in two or three languages, from the past and present. German and new Slavic names of villages are listed [WV, Vol 3, Dec 1990, p17; WV March 98, pp 15-18]. Some progress has been made in locating relatives who were exiled, for example from Volhynia to Siberia and Kazakhstan [WV March 98, pp 11-14].

There are several versions of some place names, such as for Volhynia, sometimes Wolynsk, Volynien or Wolyn. Zhytomyr is also spelled Zhitomir, Shitomir or Gitomir. Often the new names bear no resemblance to those used a hundred years ago. Spelling of surnames varied with the whims of registrars & customs officials. Low German, High German [WV March 98, p 7] and dialects of Alsace and Bavaria [92; 93] are compared.

Web Sources For Genealogy

LDS Family Search site <http://www.familysearch.org/>

American Historical Society of Germans From Russia <http://www.ahsgr.org/>

The Society for German Genealogy in Eastern Europe <http://www.sggee.org/> membership $30

Passenger List Index <http://www.ahsgr.org/surname/>

National Library and Archives - Canada <http://www.collectionscanada.ca/index-e.html>

Canadian Genealogy and History Links <http://www.islandnet.com/~jveinot/cghl/cghl.html>

Our Roots - Digital library of published Canadian family history books <http://www.ourroots.ca/e/>

The oldest and largest free genealogy site on the Internet; <http://www.rootsweb.com/>

Ancestor search - a free site with many records and genealogy *tools*
<http://www.searchforancestors.com/utility/index.html>

The large site hosted by Family Tree Maker (a popular genealogy program)
<http://www.genealogy.com/community.html; <http://www.genealogy.com/index_a.html>

Genealogy Learning Center <http://www.genealogy.com/genehelp.html>

Genealogy Surname Forums <http://genforum.genealogy.com/surnames/>

Cyndi's List of genealogy sites on the Internet <http://www.cyndislist.com/>

Alberta Genealogy Society <http://www.compusmart.ab.ca/abgensoc/>

Alberta Genealogy Society Links page <http://www.compusmart.ab.ca/abgensoc/links.html>

Map: ***Europe in*** 1995 [46c]

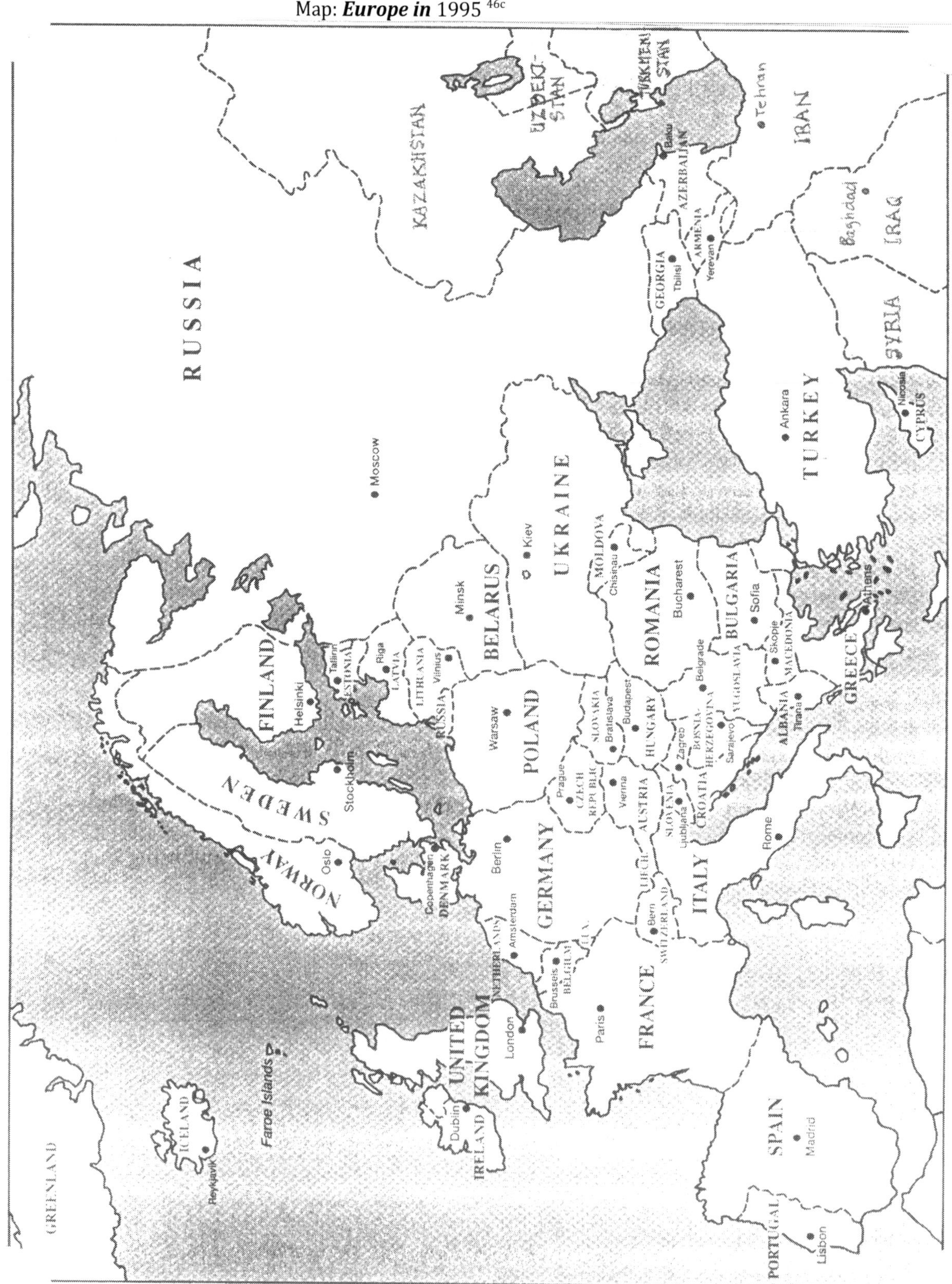

People Migrations in Europe and America: Nation-Building From Prehistory to 1913
Resources for College History Courses and Family Genealogies

Chapter Twenty-Five
BIBLIOGRAPHY

It has been rewarding to be able to fill in large gaps in European and American history, as well as fit together overlapping bits and pieces, yet do so succinctly in one volume. Surprising interconnections were found.

These details, plus super-scripted references are of value for further research by academics and students, at any level. These books are available in public libraries, or may be located by librarians after a short or long wait. A few of them are in the children's section. Much interesting, significant history is left out of elementary, high school and university curriculum's. Other relevant books can be spotted next to these on library shelves.

Page numbers of material cited in this review of history, are for the most part, given in the text along with the reference number. Only in the early months of writing were page numbers sometimes omitted. The author's reliance on the Journal ***Wandering Volhynians*** (WV) kept growing. It became laborious to number the references individually, so the details may be in the super-scripted notes [WV, month, year and pages], for the sake of easy access and accuracy. The author's gratitude to Ewald Wuschke, WV Editor, is profound.

Readers who are researching the ancestral roots of their family tree probably want to locate the village(s), region(s) and province(s) they came from [p 183]. Typically ancestors migrated long distances several times.

The direction of population flow, and reasons for migration are indicated throughout this book. For more information about any particular aspect, area or era of interest or concern, the following reference materials offer rich resources to help bring to life events and culture of bygone years.

---

1. Edward James. ***The Franks: The Peoples of Europe***. New York: Basil Blackwell Inc. 1988.

2. Jerry Frank. ***Readers Write***. Vancouver, BC: Wandering Volhynians, Vol 6, No. 2, June 1993, p 3. (An article regarding Frank and Gothic roots).

3. Bernard Grun. ***The Timetables of History: A Horizontal Linkage of People and Events***. A Touchstone Book. New York: Simon and Shuster. 1982.

4. Albert Breyer, ***The German Settlements in Central Poland: Vistula River Valley.*** Vancouver, BC Wandering Volhynians. Vol 4, No 3, Sep 91, pp 11-22; Dobrin District - pp 13-17; Warthe River Villages - pp 17-18; Kalish District - pp 18-20; Gostynin District - pp 20-22.

5. Albert Breyer, ***The German Settlements in Central Poland: The Industrial Centre of Lodz***. Vancouver, BC: Wandering Volhynians. Vol 4, No 4, Dec 91, pp 13-18; ***Schwabian Settlements Near Warsaw***, pp 18-20.

6. Robin S. Oggins. ***Cathedrals***. New York: Michael Friedman/Fairfax Publishers.1996. See pp. 69, 81, 93, 98-101; opposite page 116 for a neo-gothic **gargoyle**; and p 104 for helpful maps.

7. Otto Zierer, Editor. ***Germany: Concise History of Great Nations.*** G. Irvins, translator. New York: Leon Amiel Publisher. 1977.

8. Monica Dambrosio and Roberto Barbieri. ***The Late Middle Ages.*** English translation by Star Language Centre. Accuracy review by Dr. Imre Bard. Austin, Texas: Raintree and Steck-Vaughn Co. 1992

9. Norma H. Dickey, Editor in Chief. ***Funk & Wagnalls New Encyclopedia.*** Rand McNally & Co. 1988.

9b. Ibid. ***Hammond World Atlas***. World History Section. New York: Funk and Wagnalls, Inc. 1988.

10. Hans Hofer & A Horn, Ed. ***Czech and Slovak Republics: Insight Guides***. Boston: Houghton Mifflin 1993.

11. Angus Baxter. ***In Search of your German Roots.*** Baltimore, Maryland: Genealogical Publishing Co. Inc. 1987. ISBN 0-8063-1200-9.

12. ***Encyclopedia Britannica***. Vol 2, p 629 - Capetian; p 253 - Black Death; Vol 4, p 304 -The Enlightenment; p 920 - France; Vol 5, pp 210-11 - Germany; pp 213-5 - Languages; pp 218-10 - History; Vol 8 - Napoleon; Vol II, p 427 - Swabia; and many more references indicated in the superscript notes.

12. ***Encyclopedia Britannica. Macropedia*** Vol 24, pp 748-755 - Napoleon; Vol 25, pp 930-946 - Poland. More volumes from both Micropedia and Macropedia are cited with page numbers identified in the text.

13. Friedrich Heer, editor. ***Milestones of History***. **_Vol 2: The Fires of Faith, 150 to 1204 AD_**. New York: Newsweek Books. Second edition, 1973.

14. Mike Corbishley. ***Time Link: The Medieval World***. New York: Peter Bedrick Books. !993.

15. The Editors. ***Quest From the Past.*** Pleasantville, New York: Reader's Digest Association, Inc. 1984.

16. ***Everybody's Complete Encyclopedia***. A very old one-volume publication, printed before 1939, which provided much valuable, succinct but vivid information. Many dates came from this book.

17. Arthur Cotterell. Editor. ***Penguin Encyclopedia of Classical Civilizations***. Harmondsworth, Middlesex, England: Penguin Books.1993. Ancient civilizations 600 BC- 600 AD - Greece, Rome, Persia, India, China.

18. Barbara A. Hanawalt. ***The Late Middle Ages: An Illustrated History.*** New York and Oxford: Oxford University Press. 1998.

19. Ibid. ***The Middle Ages: An Illustrated History.*** New York and Oxford: Oxford University Press. 1998.

20. Colin Platt. ***The Atlas of Medieval Man***. New York: Crescent Books. 1979. An exceptionally fine resource on the architecture and relevant history of five centuries.

21. The Editors. ***Light of the East:*** **_Time Frame AD 1000-1100._** Alexandria, Virginia: Time-Life Books Inc. 1988, second printing 1990.

21b. Tony Allan, Editor. ***The Divine Campaigns:*** **_Time Frame AD 1120-1200._** Alexandria, Virginia: Time-Life Books Inc. 1988.

21c. Ibid, Editor. ***The Mongol Conquests***: **_Time Frame AD 1200-1300._** Alexandria, Virginia: Time-Life 1989.

21d. Ibid, Editor. ***Age of Calamity***: **_Time Frame AD 1300-1400._** Alexandria, Virginia: Time-Life Inc. 1989.

21e. Richard Humble. Editor. ***The Seafarers: The Explorers.*** Alexandria, VA: Time-Life Books Inc. 1978.

21f. The Editors. ***Voyages of Discovery***: **_Time Frame AD 1400-1500._** Alexandria, Virginia: Time-Life 1989.

22. R.J. Unstead. ***Living in a Crusader Land***. A & C Black, Reading, Mass: Addison-Wesley Publishing, 1971.

23. Xavier Barral 1 Altet, Series editor: Henri Stierlin. ***Taschen's World Architecture. The Early Middle Ages:*** **_From Late Antiquity to AD 1000._** 1997. English Translation - New York: Lory Frankel. Printed in Germany. See excellent pictures of early Greek and Roman architecture. ISBN 3-8228-8261-5.

24. Edward Norman. ***The House of God: Church Architecture, Style and History***. London, England: Thames and Hudson, Ltd. 1990. Vaults p.306; **gargoyles** (figures of evil spirits on water spouts or freestanding) p 64.

25. Gayla Visalli, Ed. ***After Jesus: The Triumph of Christianity.*** New York; Montreal: Reader's Digest 1992.

26. James H. Acland. ***Medieval Structure: The Gothic Vault***. Toronto and Buffalo: U of Toronto Press. 1972.

27. Adam Bajcar. ***Poland: A Tourist Guide***. Warsaw: Interpress Publishers. 1977

28. Krzytof Dydynski. ***Poland: a Travel Survival Kit.*** London: Lonely Planet Publications. 1993.

28b. David Simonis, et al. ***Spain.*** Melbourne: Lonely Planet Publications. 1999.

29. Henri Stierlin, Editor. ***Architecture of the New World, Italy and Central Europe***. English translator - Carol Brown. Lausanne: Compagnie du Livre d'Art, S.A.

30. Enzo Orlando, Editor. ***The Life and Times of Napoleon: Portraits of Greatness.*** C.J. Richards Translator. Curtis Publishing Co. 1967.

31. Claude Mignot. ***Architecture of the Nineteenth Century in Europe***. Fribourg, France: Office du Livre, 1983. Translator D.Q. Stephenson. New York: Rizzoli International Publications, 1984. **Note**: Fribourg is near the former home of Johann Schneider I and II, who migrated about 1805, to Warsaw, Poland.

32. Michael Gibson. ***Spotlight on the Age of Revolution***. Hove, E Sussex, UK: Wayland Publishers.1985.

33. Robert Johnson. ***A Trip Through Poland in 1814***. Vancouver: _Wandering Volhynians_. Vol 4 No 1, Mar 1991, pp 13-31

34. Nadine Slavinski. ***Germany By Bike: 20 Tours Geared for Discovery.*** Seattle, Wash, USA: The Mountaineers, 1994. Map p 6. Rhine Borderlands - Black Forest to Baden-Baden - pp 111-120, 231; Rhineland Vineyards and Spires - pp 121-135; Rhine valley - Tier to Bingen - pp 136-144; Danube tour - p 232

35. Paul Hetherington. ***Byzantine & Medieval Greece: Churches, Castles & Art***. London: John Murray. 1991.
36. Monica Dambrosio and Roberto Barbieri. ***The Early Middle Ages.*** English translation by Star Language Centre. Accuracy review by Dr. Imre Bard. Austin, Texas: Raintree and Steck-Vaughn Co. 1992
37. Matthew Holden. ***The Crusaders.*** A Sentinel Book. Hove, Sussex, UK: Wayland Publishers. 2 nd ed 1980.
38. Peter Gay. ***Age of Enlightenment***. New York: Time Life Books. Revised 1969. Reprinted 1976.
39. Alan Palmer, Editor. ***Milestones of History: Vol 8: Age of Optimism, 19 th Century***. New York: Newsweek Books. Second edition 1974.
40. Myrtle Macdonald. ***Roots and Branches: Ancestors and Descendants of Johann Schneider and Christian Mielke.*** Chilliwack, B.C. To be published 2017.
41. Paul Kennedy. ***The Rise and Fall of the Great Powers: Economic Change and Military Conflict***. New York: Random House. 1987.
42. ***Fodor's 95: Europe The Best of 31 Countries***. New York and Toronto: Random House Inc. Fodor's Travel Publications Inc. 1995.
42b. ***Fodor's*** 04: ***Spain.*** New York and Toronto: Random House Inc. Fodor's Travel Publications Inc. 2004.
43. David W. Paul. ***Czechoslovakia***: ***Profile of a Socialist Republic at the Crossroads of Europe***. Boulder, CO: Westview Press. 1881
44. Neal Ascherson. ***Struggles for Poland***. New York: Random House.1988; England: Michael Joseph. 1987
45. Henry H. Halley. ***Bible Handbook***. Grand Rapids, Mich: Zondervan Publishing. 24th ed, 1995, 25 th 2007.
46. Robert C. Lodwick, editor. ***Remembering the Future***: ***Europe Study***. New York: Friendship Press.1996.
46b. John O. Gooch. ***Leaders'Guide to Europe Study***. New York: FriendshipPress.1995. ISBNO-377-00291-7
46c. Kenneth Ziebell. ***Map'n'Facts: Europe.*** New York: Friendship Press. 1995. Order: FP73024-6
47. David Nicolle. ***Medieval Knights - with Four See-Through Scenes***. Oxford, England: Heinemann Educational Publishers, a Division of Reed Educational and Professional Publishing Ltd.1997.
48. Trevor Cairns. ***Renaissance and Reformation***. Cambridge University Press. 1987.
49. Maurice Ashley, editor. ***Milestones of History: Vol 3. Dawn of a New Era: 1200 to 1400.*** New York: Newsweek Books. 1974.
50. Jo Woestendiek. ***Accent: Comenius***. Winston-Salem Journal. March 1992.
51. Herman R. Steinberg. ***Die Brüder in Polen***. Herrnhut, Germany. 1921.
52. George L. Mosse. ***The Reformation.*** Hinsdale, Illinois: Dryden Press Holt, Rinehart and Winston. 1963.
53. Tory Allan, Series Editor. ***The European Emergence: Time Frame AD 1500-1600.*** Alexandria, Virginia: Time-Life Books Inc. 1989.
53b. Ibid. ***Winds of Revolution: Time Frame AD 1700-1800.*** Alexandria, Virginia: Time-Life Books. 1990.
54. Peter Miller. ***The Face and Faith of Poland***. National Geographic. Vol 161, No 4, Apr 1982, Special Supplement, pp 419A-419B. Includes an essay by Nobel Laureate Czeslaw Milosz.
55. AdamTanner et al. ***Frommer's Eastern Europe on $30 a Day***. New York: MacmillanTravel. Revised 1995
55b. Ibid. ***Frommer's Eastern Europe on $30 a Day***. New York, USA: Macmillan Travel. 1993.
56. Karl Schafer. ***Die Brudergemeinschaften in Polen: Bruder-Almanach***. Herrnhut, Germany. **1878.**
57. J. Taylor Hamilton. ***A History of the Moravian Church or Unitas Fratrum, during the 18th and 19th Centuries***. Bethlehem, PA: Times Publishing Company Printers, **1900**. Reprinted AMS Press Inc: New York 10003, 1971. A remarkably interesting detailed book with five chapters for each decade, covering countries where persecuted Moravians found refuge and established missions. ISBN 0-404-08427-3. Rare. Interlibrary loan - Selkirk College, Castlegar BC. Nil in Moravian Historical Society, Edmonton.
58. Henry Moscow. ***Russia under the Czars***. American Heritage Publishing Co: Horizon Caravel Book. 1962.
59. John King & Richard Nebesky. ***Prague: City Guide***. Hawthorn, Victoria, Australia: Lonely Planet. 1994.
60. Neville Williams, Editor. ***Milestones of History: Vol 4. Expanding Horizons: 1415 to 1516.*** New York: Newsweek Books. 1974.

61. Ewald Wuschke, ***Editor's Notes***. Wandering Volhynians (WV). Vol 7, No 4, Dec 94, p 3.
62. Max Grossert. ***The Schulzendorferand Hollandrys in Posen***. WV Vol 8, No 3, Sep 95, p 12-15, 19-20.
63. Ewald Wuschke. ***Die Schwaben und die Kaschuben***. WV Vol 6, No 3, Sep 93, pp 20-21.
64. Ibid. ***Editor's Comments: Poland.*** WV Vol 4, No. 1, Mar 91, p 13.
65. Ibid. ***Editor's Comments: Volhynia***. WV Vol 8, No 4, Dec 95, pp 8-10
66. Adolf Kraft. ***The Hollandrys of the Vistula Warthe Regions***. WV Vol 8, No 3, Sep 95, pp 15-18.
67. Ewald Wuschke. ***The Hollandry: the first democratic village government in Europe***. WV Vol 6, No 1, Mar 93, p 20
68. Ewald Wuschke, Editor. ***St. Petersburg Lutheran Church Records***. WV Vol 7, No 1, Mar 94, p 4.
69. Cecil Stockman. ***The Stockman-Schneider Family Histories***. WV Vol 3, No 3, Sep 1990, pp 10-11.
70. George P. Fisher. ***History of the Christian Church***. New York: Charles Scribers Sons. 1896.
71. Kurt H.Vitt. ***The Founding of the Moravian Church in Western Canada*** and ***The Andreas Lilge Story***. Edmonton: Canadian Moravian Historical Society, 2304 - 38 Avenue, Edmonton AB T6L 4K9. 1983.
72. ***Daily Texts of the Moravian Church: Annual***. English version. Bethlehem PA, printed in 26 languages.
73. Clement Hoyler. ***The Semi-Centennial of Bruderheim and Bruederfeld:*** 1895-1945. Edmonton: Canadian Moravian Historical Society, 2304 – 38 Avenue, Edmonton AB, T6L 4K9.
74. Alan Palmer, Editor. ***Milestones of History: Vol 9. Nations and Empires,*** 1854-1900. New York: Newsweek Books, revised 1974.
75. Fiona Macdonald. ***Everyday Life: The Middle Ages***. London; Sydney: Silver Burdett Company. 1984, 87.
76. James Laver, Keeper of Victoria and Albert Museum. ***The Arts of Mankind: The International Pictorial Treasury of Knowledge.*** Englewood Cliffs, New Jersey: International Graphic Society: Esco Publishing. 1962.
77. Kenneth Scott Latourette. ***A History of Christianity***. New York: Harper Brothers Publishers. !953.
78. Andrew Beattie. ***Visitor's Guide: Czechoslovakia***. Ashbourne, Derbyshire, UK: Moorland Ltd. 1991.
79. Haig Babian. ***The Middle East: Old Problems and New Hopes***. Atlanta, Dallas, Glenview, Palo Alto and Oakland NJ: Scott, Foresman and Company. 1963.
80. H.A.R. Gibb. ***Mohammedanism: An Historical Survey***. London, Oxford and New York. Oxford University Press. Second edition. 1970. [Very good book, but wrong to add "ism" to Mohammed. The correct term for the religion is Islam and the people are Muslims].
81. R.W.F. Wootton. ***Understanding the Sects of Islam***. Worthing, West Sussex, UK: FFM. Revised 1992.
82. Kenneth Cragg. ***The Call of the Minaret***. Ibadan, Nigeria: Orbis Books, Maryknoll, New York. Second edition, 1985. First edition published 1956 in England: Oxford University Press, Inc.
83. Helen and Richard Leacroft. ***The Buildings of Early Islam***. London, Leicester, Sydney and Auckland: Hodder & Stoughton, and in the USA: Addison-Wesler Publishing Company.
84. Clement Hoyler, rediscovered by William G. Brese, ed. ***Pioneering in Western Canada*** or ***Sowing and Reaping in Home Mission Field***. 1995. Moravian Historical Society: 2304–38 Avenue, Edmonton. T6L4K9. Photo on cover is of Moravians arriving in Edmonton, Edmonton Journal, July 6, **1894**.
85. Ron Neuman. ***Sompolno to Strathcona: Lippert Family History***. Edmonton AB: Technical Graphics with Moravian Historical Society. 1984.
86. Earl A Schneider, ed. ***From Bush to Bushels: A History of Bruderheim & District.*** Bruderheim, Alberta, T0B 0S0. Published by Bruderheim Historical Society. 1983. 45 miles NE of Edmonton. ISBN 0-88925-340-4
87. Dennis P. Fjestad, ed. ***South of the North Saskatchewan River***. Published by: Josephburg History Book Committee, Box 3252, Fort Saskatchewan, Alberta, Canada. 1984. [SW of Bruderheim; east of Edmonton].
88. Editorial Committee. ***South Edmonton Saga.*** Published by Papaschase Historical Society, 9233 96 Street, Edmonton, Alberta, T6C 3Y5. 1984. ISBN 0-88925-462-1
89. History Book Committee. ***Each Step Left It's Mark: A History of Hay Lakes and Surrounding Area.*** Hay Lakes History Book Committee, Box 158, Hay Lakes Alberta T0B 1W0. 1982. ISBN 0-88925-334-X

90. Adrian Franck and Pearl Gregor, Editors. ***New Sarepta: Looking Back. 1900-1980.*** Published by the New Sarepta Historical Society, New Sarepta, Alberta.
91. Melville Belle Grosvenor, Editor-in-Chief. ***The Renaissance: Maker of Modern Man.*** Washington DC: National Geographic Society Publishers.
92. Karl Stumpp. ***The German Russians.*** Translated by Joseph S. Height. Lincoln, Nebraska: American Historical Society of Germans from Russia. 1971, reprinted 1978.
93. Joseph S. Height. ***Homesteaders on the Steppe:*** 1804-1945. Bismarck, North Dakota: North Dakota Historical Society of Germans from Russia. 1975.
94. Arthur Cotterell, ed. ***The Penguin Encyclopedia of Classical Civilization***. Hammondsworth, Middlesex, England: Penguin Books Ltd. Excellent source 600 BC to 600 AD of Greece, Rome, Persia, India and China.
95. Rodney Castledon. ***World History: A Chronological Dictionary of Dates***. New York: Shooting Star Press, Inc. ISBN 156924 213-5. <u>If you know the date of an historical event, you can find a succinct sentence about it</u>.
96. Mark Honan. ***Vienna***. Hawthorn, Victoria, Australia: Lonely Planet Publication. 1998.
97. Norman Davies. ***Heart of Europe: A Short History of Poland.*** Oxford: Oxford University Press. 1986.
98. Joan Evans, Editor. ***The Flowering of the Middle Ages***. London: Thames and Hudson Ltd. 1988.
99. Euan Cameron, Editor. ***Early Modern Europe***. Oxford, England: Oxford University Press. 1999.
100. Bob Dent. ***Hungary: Blue Guide***. London, UK: A&C Black; New York: WW Norton. 2nd ed, 1998.
101. Nicola Williams. ***Romania and Moldova***. Hawthorn, Victoria, Australia: Lonely Planet Pub. 1998.
102. Ronald Hingley. ***The Tsars: 1533-1917.*** New York, NY: The Macmillan Company. 1968.
103. Emil Roleder. ***Faith Under Four Flags.*** Published privately. Contact Edwin Roleder, 6709 North 28 th Street, Tacoma WA 98407, Phone 253-759-7099 or c/o Lutheran Retirement Homes, Tacoma WA.
104. Interview with Milan Opočenský. ***Faces of Faith.*** Toronto, Canada: <u>Presbyterian Record</u>, Jan 1999, p 30.
105. Ewald Wuschke. ***German Settlements in Poland and Volhynia.*** <u>American Historical Society of Germans From Russia</u> (AHSGR) Journal. Winter 1990, pp 50-53.
106. H.L. Peacock. ***Modern European History*** 1789-1980. London: Biddles Ltd. Third edition, 1987.
107. Knowledge Network Series. ***St. Petersburg: the Hermitage***. TV Channel 9, 1998-9.
108. Klaus Granzow. ***Pommern in 1440 Bildern***. Verlag Gerhard Rautenberg, Leer.1986. ISBN3-7921-0327-3 Remarkable pictures and maps of prewar Pommerania and Posen (Poland); buildings dating back to the Middle Ages. A fascinating book found in a second hand store.
109. Edmund De Schweinitz, S.T.D. ***History of the Church Known as the Unitas Fratrum or Unity of Brethren***. Bethlehem, PA: Moravian Publication Concern. Lectures - Moravian Theological Seminary, **1876**-77; 87.
110. Marvin Scott. ***Of Many Times and Cultures:*** Teacher book - grades 6 to 12. Portland Maine: J. Weston Walch. 1993.
111. Michael Worth Davison, ed. ***Everyday Life Through the Ages.*** New York: Reader's Digest. 1992.
112. J.J. Sharp. ***Discovery in the North Atlantic: 16th-17th centuries.*** Halifax, NS: Nimbus Publishing. 1991.
113. Marzieh Gail. ***Life in the Renaissance***. A Landmark Grant. New York & Toronto: Random House Inc, and New York: Chanticleer Press. 1968.
114. Pierre Miquel. ***The Age of Discovery 1450-1600.*** <u>Silver Burditt Picture Histories</u>. London: the Hamlyn Publishing Group Ltd. 1978.
115. Neil Grant. ***The Renaissance***. New York: Franklin Watts Inc. 1971.
115b. John R. Hale. ***The Renaissance***. New Jersey. Time Line Inc. 1965, 1975.
116. ***Exploration.*** World Book TM. 1999. Chicago: World Book Inc. <u>Computer CD.</u>
117. Stephen Neill. ***The Story of the Christian Church in India and Pakistan***. Madras: Christian Literature Society: The Diocesan Press. 1972.

118. University of Alberta. Alumni Association Travel Brochure. ***Fall Foliage on the Hudson River***. Edmonton, AB: University of Alberta. 2001.

119. Kenneth H. Pearson, Editor-in-Chief. ***Encyclopedia Canadiana***. Toronto: Grolier of Canada. 1977.

119b. Ibid_______, ***Encyclopedia Canadiana***. 1968 edition.

120. James H. Marsh, Editor-in-Chief. ***Canadian Encyclopedia***. Toronto: McClelland & Stewart Inc. 2000.

121. Ibid_______. ***The Canadian Encyclopedia***. Edmonton: Hurtig Publishers. 1988, 1985.

122. Chaim Potok. ***Wanderings***. New York: Fawcett Books. 1990. Jewish history for 2000 years. Outstanding.

123. ***Webster's*** ll*:* ***New Riverside Dictionary***. 1984. Boston: Houghton-Mifflin Co.

124. Victor A Shepherd. ***So Great a Cloud of Witnesses***. Mississauga, ON: Light and Life Press. 1993.

125. ***World Book***. Chicago: World Book Inc. 2001.

126. Canadian Broadcasting Company. ***Canada: A People's History***. Episodes 2 to 4. CBC Television. August 30, 2001. Sponsored by Bell Canada Enterprises and Sun Life Insurance Co.

127. Lister B. Sinclair. ***Hands Across Time: The Vintage Year*** 1685. CBC Radio "Ideas". August 31, 2001.

128. Art Downs, ed. ***Pioneer Days in British Columbia***. Surrey, BC: Heritage House Publishing. 1975-79.

129. Ervin Austin MacDonald. ***The Rainbow Chasers***. Vancouver/Toronto: Douglas & McIntyre. !982, 2 nd ed 1985. ISBN 0-88894-408-x(pbk)

130. Michael H. Tomyn, ed. ***Vegreville in Review***. Vegreville Historical Society. 1980. ISBN 0-88925-109-6. 2 Volumes.

131. Daniel Francis, editor. ***Encyclopedia of BC.*** Madeira Park, BC: Harbor Publishing House. 2000.

132. Pat Jepson & Ron Denman, editors. ***Down Country Roads: Chilliwack's Agricultural History***. Chilliwack, BC: Rotary Club and Chilliwack Historical Society.

133. Howard G. Hageman in collaboration with Ruth Douglas See. ***That the World May Know***. Covenant Life Curriculum. Richmond, Virginia. CLC Press. 1965.

134. J.E. Hutton. ***A History of the Moravian Church***. Second edition, revised and enlarged **1909**. London, E.C.: 32 Fetter Lane. Available from Douglas Library, Queens University, Kingston, ON. 39083001192302. Can be downloaded from web site: http://everdaycounselor.com/hutton/i9.htm. An outstanding book.

135. Myrtle Macdonald. ***Lutheran and Moravian Interrelations for 500 Years***. To be published

136. John Lawrence. ***A History of Russia***. Second revised edition. 1969. London: George Alen and Unwin Ltd. Hard cover or paperback: New York: A Mentor Book.

137. James Laver, Keeper. ***The Arts of Mankind: International Pictorial Treasury of Knowledge***. 1962. Englewood Cliffs, New Jersey: Esco Publishing Co.

138. Daniel Francis, Ed. ***Encyclopedia of British Columbia***. Madeira Park, B.C: Harbour Publishing. 2000.

139. Michael Worth Davison, ed. ***Everyday Life Throughout the Ages***. New York: Readers Digest 1992.

140. Margaret McNaughton. ***Overland to Cariboo***. Vancouver, B.C.: J.J. Douglas Ltd., **1896**. 1973 edition.

141. T.F. Jeletzky, ed. ***Russian Canadians: Their Past and Present***. Collected Essays by the Chekov Society of Ottawa. Ottawa: Borealis Press. 1983.

142. Jo Ann Kuhr. ***Clues***. American Historical Society of Germans from Russia. Lincoln, Neb, 68562-1199.

143. ***British Columbia: A Century of Progress***. Official Centennial Record. 1858 -1958. Vancouver: Evergreen Press Ltd.

144. J.G. MacGregor. ***Edmonton: A History***. Encyclopedia. Hurtig Publishers. 1967, second edition 1975.

145. ***Loyalists Under the Army Flag***. The War Cry. The Salvation Army. July 5, 1997.

146. Kneifl. ***The Lutheran Church,*** 1555 - 1939. 1976.

147. Daniel Francis, Editorial Director. Horizon Canada. St. Laurent, Quebec: Journal by The Centre for the Study of Teaching Canada Inc., non-profit. Purpose: to promote and publish historical research on Canada.

148. Charlotte Gray. ***Sisters in the Wilderness***. Founders Canadian Literature. CBC Television July 20, 2004.

149. Fazlur Rahman. ***Islam***. 1966. 2nd ed. Chicago: University of Chicago Press. 1966. ISBN:0-226-70281-2.
150. ***Canadian Social Studies Atlas***. Toronto and Vancouver: J.M. Dent and Sons (Canada) Ltd., with Edinburgh: John Bartholomew & Sons Ltd, the Geographic Institute. Revised ed 1958.
151. John B. Carver Jr., Chief Cartographer. ***The Territorial Growth of the United States***. Washington, D.C.: National Geographic Society, the Cartographic Division. Sept. 1987.
152. Charles W. Thayer. ***Life World Library: Russia***. New York: Time Inc. Maps by Rand McNally. 1965.
153. Howard Palmer. ***Alberta, a New History***. Edmonton: Hurtig Publishers. 1990. ISBN 0-88830-340-8.
154. William L. Allen, ed. ***The Roman Empire: Greatest Extent, the Time of Trajan,*** *AD 117.* Historical Italy. Washington DC: National Geographical Society, Cartographic Division. Insert - Feb 1995.
155. Pierre Burton. ***Settling the West -*** 1896-1914. Toronto: McClelland and Stewart Ltd. 1984.
156. George Smith. ***Life of William Carey***. Christian Classics Ethereal Library. First issue **1909**. Reprinted 1913 and 1922. http://www.biblebelievers.com/carey/Carey4.html. Especially chapters 10 and 12.
157. Peter Partner. ***Two Thousand Years: The First Millennium: the Birth of Christianity to the Crusades***. London, England: Granada Media. 1999. Contains a wealth of pictures illustrating living conditions.
158. Ibid. ***Two Thousand Years: The Second Millennium: From Medieval Christendom to Global Christianity***. London, England: Granada Media. 1999.
159. Patrick K. O'Brien, General Editor. ***Atlas of World History: From Origins of Humanity to Year 2000***. Institute of Historical Research. University of London: Oxford University Press. 2000, 2002.
160. Maitland A. Edey, editor et al. ***Atlas of the World***. Life and Rand McNally. New York:Time-Life. 1966.
161. Adam Giesinger. ***From Catherine to Khrushchev***. Lincoln, Nebraska: American Historical Society of Germans from Russia. 1974, sixth printing 2002.
162. Alfrted P. Aquilina. ***The Mackenzie: Yesterday and Beyond.*** North Vancouver, BC: Hancock House Publishers ltd. 1981. 1SBN 0-88839-083-1.
163. Marvin Lyons, edited by Andrew Wheatcroft. ***Russia: In Original Photographs* 1860-1920.** London and Henley: Routledge & Kegan Paul Ltd. 1977. ISBN 0 7100 8653 9
164. Margaret Aston. ***The Fifteenth Century: The Prospect of Europe.*** London: Thames and Hudson. 1968. "The historian paints with words and the painter with his pencil." Fascinating from cover to cover; 153 illustrations; 216 pages; paperback.
165. Kenneth Scott Latourette. ***Christianity Through the Ages.*** New York: Harper and Row. 1965. Sterling Professor of Missions and Oriental History and Fellow of Berkeley College, Emeritus, of Yale University.
166. Steve Hrynew, ed. ***Pride in Progress: Chipman, St. Michael, Edna/Star and Districts***. Chipman, Alberta: Alberta Rose Historical Society. 1982. ISBN 0-88925-369-2.
167. Ben Dupré. ***Where History was Made: Landmarks of History from Thermopylae to Ground Zero***. Oxford 2008, Quereus www.quereusbooks.co.uk. ISBN 978-1-84724-255-6.
168. J.M.S. Careless. ***Canada: A Story of Challenge***. New York: St. Martin's Press. Toronto: Macmillan 1963.
169. Wells N. Oliver. ***The Chilliwacks snd Their Neighbors***. Vancoucer: Talon Books. 1987.
170. U of Leiden and U of Leuven. ***Historical History***. Belgium and Berlin.

171. History 3000 BC to Today. WWW.runningreality.org.

172. For updates on current anthropological and historical research, information can be found on the internet through Google. Wickipedia and the BBC are valuable resources.

Appendix A: INDEX and CATALOGUE OF EVENTS

Items Dates Pages

802-11 Nicephorus I; 803 recognized independence of Venice; 811 died invading Bulgaria;
812-13 Michael I sent embassy to congratulate Charlemangne as Holy Roman Emperor; was deposed;
813-20 Leo V an Armenian, ruled; 820-29 Michael II Phrygian Dynasty started; 826 Arabs plundered Greek Islands; In 838 sacked Marseilles, settled S Italy;
829-42 Theophilus; 842-67 Michael III drunkard;
See Italy: 845-875 Carolingian Dynastry Italian Branch;
843-855 Lothar ruled Aix-la-Chapelle, Lombardi(N Italy), Rome (central Italy) Frisia (Netherlands); Austrasia (named Lotharingen) Lorraine in French; map 20;
855-75 Louis II king of Italy 13;18; Milan capital; other sons/cousins ruled Lorraine, Provence and Burgundy;
861 Russian northmen attacked Constantinople;
See Italy: 867-1095 Byzantines reconquered Sicily/Italy;
867-886 Basil I Macedonian Dynasty ruled Byzantium (Eastern Roman Empire) & part of the Balkans;
880 reconquered Italy from Arabs;
886-912 Leo VI in 900 Constantinople still first city in the world; 904 Russians attacked; 910 paid Magyars tribute;
911 Carolingians died out: 911-918 Saxon king Conrad 18;
918-36 Henry I enlarged Saxon (Saxony) kingdom 18;
912-959 Constantine VII; 917 Symeon of Bulgaria invaded Thrace & Macedonia , named himself Czar of Bulgars and Greeks; 924 invaded again;
919 Romanus I co-regent with Constantine VII extended Byzantine Empire to Euphrates and Tigris;
936-73 Otto I king of Saxons, Franks & Italy (from Lombardi wife); crowned Holy Roman Emperor; 961 ended chaos in Rome 18; revived West Roman Empire; friction with Eastern; gave bishops rich estates; monastaries 21; maps 10, 20;
959-63 Byzantine Romanus II; 961 reconquered Crete;
963-69 Nicephorus II defeated Arabs and Bulgarians; recovered Cyprus; 968 took Antioch;
969-76 John I drove Russians out of Balkans;
973-83 Saxon Otto II married highly educated daughter of Byzantine emperor Theophano; brought culture 18;
976-1025 Basil II 14; 23 drove Romanians across Danube; fought off many invasions by Bulgars; powerful Greek soldier-farmers ignored Basil. He preserved Greek knowledge 13; his sister Ann married Kiev Vladimir 23;
982-3 Saxon Otto II defeated Saracens & troops of Basil II in S Italy 18; 983 regent Theophano 996-1002 Otto III;
1002-24 Henry II last Saxon king united German states;
1004 ruled north half of Italy, 1014 Holy Roman Emperor; 1022 took Byzantine S Italy 18; 21; map 20;
1018-22 Basil II controlled Macedonia, parts of Syria & Iraq from Muslims & Armenia from Persians;
1025-28 Constantine VIII; daughter Zoe co-emperor with
1028-34 Romanus III; 1034-41 Michael IV with Zoe;
1041-2 Michael V; 1042-54 Constantine IX with Zoe;
1050 Empress Zoe died aged 70; older sister Theodora shared throne with Constantine IX; 1053 Frank Robert Guiscard founded Norman empire in S Italy 21;
1054 East Orthodox/ West Roman church split 23;

Items Dates Pages

1055-6 Theodora ruled alone; 1056-7 Michael VI Macedonian dynasty overthrown by rebels;
1057-59 Isaac Comnenus founded new dynasty;
1059-67 Constantine X; Hungarians seized Belgrade; his widow ruled with him 1067-71;
1067-71 Romanus IV blinded in 1071 by Seljuk Turks;
1970 Seljuks stopped Christian pilgrims taking relics 23;
1071 St. Mark Cathedral was completed in Venice 34; See Venice; 1071-78 Michael VII;
1072 Frank/Norman Robert Guiscard conquered Palermo capital of Sicily & last Byzantine possessions in S Italy;
1078-1081 Nicephorus III a soldier; See Muslims;
1081-1118 Emperpor Alexius Comnenus, in 1095 asked Pope Urban to protect Constantinople from Muslims 23;
1081 Robert invaded the Balkans; 1085 he died;
1081 German Norman Henry IV invaded Italy 23; 1084 sacked Rome; Robert died 1085; Roger succeeded 21; Norman pilgrims, knights & mercenaries on both sides
1088 Patzinak Turks settled in Balkans 23;
1091-1154 Roger Guiscard I & II ruled Sicily; attacked Malta 21; 1095 Hungarians took Croatia & Dalmatia;
1101 Roger II count of Sicily; 1130-54 king; at Palermo Al-Idrisi wrote ***Book of Roger*** geography 36;

Byzantium: 1095-1453 **Crusades/Frank/Greek Rule**; Most Crusaders were unwashed and illiterate; Muslims had an advanced civilization with vast philosophical, literary, medical and scientific knowledge 81;
1095 Pope Urban II proclaimed Crusades 23;
1095-1272 Crusades led by Godfrey Duke of Lorraine and Trancrad, nephew of Frank Robert Guiscard, map 24;
1095 world's first university founded at Salerno, Italy;
1101-54 Roger II Count of Sicily; 1127 claimed Italy;
1106-25 Henry V succeeded Henry IV 23;
1118-1143 John II Comnenus; defeated Patzinaks & Serbs in Balkans; with Saxony Lothair II, drove Roger II back;
1143-80 Manuel I paid Venetians to resist Roger II;
1145-7 the 2 nd Crusade failed;
1149-1272 Franks influence/ruled Byzantine empire 32; With Venice fought Holy Roman Emperor Frederick I Barbarossa 27; 1159 Arabs took back land in N Africa;
1154-66 William succeeded Roger II; 1166 William II;
1180-83 Alexius II; 1183-85 Adronicus; map 38;
1185 Norman army attacked Byzantine empire;
1185-95 Isaac Angelus II; 1195-1203 Alexius III;
1189 3rd Crusade; 23-25; 1190-1197 Swabian Henry VI ruled north Italy and Sicily through his wife 27; map 27;
1194 Almost a century of Normal rule in Italy ended;
1197-1250 Swabian Frederick II ruled Sicily and Naples;
1202-4: 4 th Crusade; Venice took half the booty; uneducated Franks & Romanians took Constantinople; ruled 50 years; Baldwin IX of Flanders > Baldwin I of Byzantium; Greek nobles fled; set up dutchies in Nicea, Trabzon, Thessalonica, Epirus & Agean islands 25; 32;
1212 5 th Crusade, Children's; died/sold as slaves 25;
1228 6 th Crusade; scholarly Swabian Hohenstaufen Frederick II won back Jerusalem 25; 27; founded university of Naples and medical school at Salerno;

Items Dates Pages

1604-6 **Champlain** twice further explored Atlantic coast and Acadia; see Explorers of American Atlantic Coast; See Huguenots/French Protestants; fled Inquisition;

1608 commissioned by Sieur de Monts Champlain established a trading post named Quebec (river narrows); the Iroquois were gone; a few Algonquin nomads 69;

1608-15 Champlain explored lakes Champlain & Huron map 70, built a vast fur trading network and alliance of Hurons & Algonquins; Iroquois favored the English 69: He chose Recollect priests (humble Franciscans) 70;

1610-33 Étienne Brûlé explored GreatLakes; spoke Huron;

1600-11 **Henry Hudson** explored Hudson Bay and James Bay; died in mutiny. Earlier explored Hudson River; his discoveries were basis of English claims on Canada 72;

1611-35 king Henry IV named Champlain Commandant (Governor) of New France; Ship building; textile industries, mining began; named Ile St Hélène for his wife 69;

1621 King James I named Nova Scotia, granted to Scotch poet Sir Wm Alexander; contested by French 71; 96;

1625 Jesuits came to Canada, stopped protestant immigration; mission with Hurons on Georgian Bay 72;

1628 Acadia &Fort Quebec fell to English David Kirke 72;

1628 Acadia French=Nova Scotia English 72; 96; French to English several times; 1630-70 Loire French colonists;

1629, 1634 Champlain sent Jean Nicolet via rivers/Huron/Nippissing/lakes to build trading forts on Great Lakes & Fox/Illinois rivers &Wisconsin 70; 74; had Indian wives; Michilimackinac at north top of Lake Michigan 107, 96;

1635 Champlain died: known as Father of New France; was a map maker and writer of note 73;

Canadian History after Champlain

1639 Ursiline Sisters built Quebec Hôtel Dieu Hospital 72;

1642 Governor Paul de Chomedy(Sieur de Maisonneuve) started settlement of Mont Royal (Montreal) 73;

1645 Jeanne Mance Montreal Hôtel Dieu Hospital 73;

1649 Jesuit Father Brébeuf martyred by Iroquois 72;

1653 Marguerite Bourgeoys brought brides; 1658 started school for French and native girls in Montreal 73;

1663 Governor Maisonneuve appointed Surpician priests as Seigneurs (feudal lords) of Montreal Island 73; Seigneurial system 73; 105; 125; see Montreal;

1665 Missions & fur trading on Mississippi 70-76; 98;

1665 Radisson & Groseilliers were fined by French Governor of Quebec 70, for trading furs since 1658 without a licence on Lakes Michigan & Superior, so sailed from Boston to England, met Prince Rupert; were likely instrumental in application for the HBCo.:

1665-72 Jean Talon Intendant (under Governor) claimed entire Great lakes, North West & Mississippi for Louis XIV; sent fur traders via Ottawa River/Great Lakes to rival HBCo; had Louis Joliet/Jesuit priests Dablon & Marquette to establish settlements on Mississippi 74-75;

1670 Hudson Bay Co Charter in Rupert's Land;

1670-74; 84-87 Radisson & Groseilliers in HBCo 74; French Sulpician RC missions on Lake Ontario;

1670-82 La Salle built ships on lake Ontario; reached mouth of Mississippi, named Louisiana 75; 98; map 97;

1672-82 Governor Frontenac established Cataraqui up the St. Lawrence (Kingston) and more forts 96 ; 1675-82 with Intendant Duchesneau; both recalled to France;

1682 French Campagne du Nord hired Raddison to rival English; 1684 HBCo rehired him; 1687 fled to England to escape French price on his head 74;

1689-98 Frontenac reinstated to fight Iroquois 74; 96;

1690-92 Henry Kelsey explored from Hudson Bay/Manitoba/Saskatchewan River to Alberta for HBCo 107-8;

1713 After the War of Spanish Succession 95; Treaty of Utrecht ceded Acadia & Newfoundland to British. Then Canadian French Courier de Bois (Scot-French-Indian voyageurs) built forts along Great Lakes/Ohio/Mississippi rivers blocking New England expansion west 103; France stopped sending ships into Hudson Bay 107;

1726, 1731-8 Sieur La Verendrye string of forts from Lake Superior to Red River, Forts Rouge (Douglas/Gary/Winnipeg) Assiniboine/Missouri Rivers maps 117, 121;

1743 claimed the Dakotas for France maps 97,108; sons/nephew explored Nebraska, Wyoming & Montana 98;

1732 Moravian missions began in West Indies 100; 135; 1733 in Greenland/Labrador; 1734 Georgia/Carolinas; 1736 to Pennsylvania (1681William Penn founded) 73;

1754-5 Anthony Henday first white man saw the Rockies; established trade with Blackfoot tribe 107;

1750-3 Charles II of England sponsored Huguenot settlers in Lunenberg, Nova Scotia 96;

Canadian History: British Rule Began

1754-63 French & Indian War on Great lakes map 104;

1755 French Acadians were deported 96; 104; 110; many remained in Louisiana, called Cajuns 96;

1759 James Cook mapped St.Lawrence/Labrador 105;

1756-63 Seven Years' War 103-105; Treaty of Paris gave all New France territories to England. The Ohio valley assigned to Canadien French; New England angry 106; Huguenots (French Protestants) were welcomed;

1759 English Gen Wolfe defeated French Montcalm; Governor Murray granted freedom of religion, French language rights & jury membership, which angered Montreal Scot/American merchants 105;

1763 after Seven Years' War fur-bearing animals declined so traders moved to Montreal, joined NorthWest Co.

1764 2000 French Acadians returned to New Brunswick and 1783 2000 more 116; immigrants from Ireland 110;

1770-72 Samuel Hearne **to Arctic** Coppermine River 108;

1774 Rivalry of HBCo & NWCo. 74; 107-108; 124; NorthWestCo Métis Voyageurs 107; 117; map 121;

1774 HBCo began building posts inland like NWCo 124;

1774 Quebec Act confirmed French rights of land, law & religion. This including Wisconsin and Ohio 111, causing increased demand for independence;

1775 Spanish Bodego Quadra explored Pacific coast, reached Alaska 109; 1776-79 James Cook (1728-79) third voyage discovered Hawaii; surveyed/mapped 88 Pacific coast of N America Oregon to Bering Sea 109;

1777-78 Peter Pond built HBCo forts Lake Athabasca/La Loche/Chipewyan;1788 NWCo RC forts/missions 109;

Items	Dates	Pages

60 BC Julius Caesar elected consul; formed first triumvirate; 58-50 BC Caesar annexed the whole of Gaul, west of Rhine; 55BC invaded Britain; 46 BC dictator in Rome; 46 BC Julian calendar with leap year adopted;
44 BC Caesar assassinated; 2 nd triumvirate with Mark Anthony; 31 BC Egypt a Roman province;
42 BC Brutus and Cassius defeated;
30 BC-14 AD Octavian (Augustus Caesar) Emperor;
30 BC-124 AD Pantheon built; Pax Romano (2 centuries peace) but taste for violence with animals & gladiators);

Italy: 14 BC-312 AD **Expansion/Roman Emperors** xiii; 2;
14 BC-37 AD Tiberius emperor; followed for short reigns;
6 BC Judea annexed; 4 BC Herod died; Judea divided among Herod's 4 sons; crucifixion for anarchists;
37-42 Caligula; 42-54 Claudius; 54-68 Nero; 62 Paul in Rome under house arrest; 63 fire destroyed half the city of Rome; Nero began rebuilding wide straight streets;
68-9 Galba; 69-79 Vitileus; 70 Roman troops destroyed the temple and city of Jerusalem; 79 Mt Vesuvious errupted, buried Pompei; 79-81 Titus; 81-96 Domitian; 90 celebrated opening of Colosseum with gladiators fighting wild animals; 30,000 Huns and 40,000 horses treked from west from Asia due to drought and epidemic of anthrax; Malaria epidemic at Rome; 96-98 Nerva; High aquaducts brought fresh water; underground catacombs were many-layered graves; later for refuge;
98-116 Trajan: the empire reached its largest, map xiii; excellent housing for courts/military in every province; 106 Roman rule in Dacia (Romania), colonization/ assimilation 2; 114 annexed Armenia;116 Assyria;
118 Rome's populaton exceeded a million, map xiii;
117-138 Hadrian; Hadrian wall N Britain xviii; 1-2; Tacitus wrote History (commentary about tribes) 2;
132 Jupiter shrine built in Jerusalem temple;
138-161 Antonius Pius; 161-180 Marcus Aurelius;
180-192 Commodus; 193-211 Septimius Severus ruled in N Africa built unique beautiful architecture;
177 persecuted Christians hid in catacombs in Rome;
189 plague killed 2000 people a day in Rome;
211-217 Emperors Caracalla; Roman citizenship given to every free born subject in the empire;
218-222 Heliogabalus; Goths invaded Asia Minor & Balkan Penninsula; 222-235 Alexander Severus;
235-8 Maximus; 238-244 Gordian I, II & III;
244-9 Philip the Arabian; 249-251 Decius;
253-60 Valerian; 260-8 Gallienus; 268-70 Claudius II;
257 Visigoths & Ostrogoths invaded Black Sea area;
250 Franks settling up rivers in Gaul;
258 Allemani, Suevi & Burgundians xv-xvi; 4; map 6;
268 Goths sacked Athens, Sparta & Corinth;
270-75 Aurelian defeated Goths & Marcomanni; rebuilt walls of Rome; took Greek Palmyra in Sicily; Greek culture in S Italy since 700BC; see Greece/Agean Islands;
276-82 Marcus Aurelius Probus; 282-83 Carus;
284-305 Diocletian; 285 Empire divided: West & East;
312-337 Emperor Constantine reunited west & east empires; built great capital in the village of Byzantium 3;

Items	Dates	Pages

Italy: 312-476 **Roman Empire: Capital Constantinople**;
312 Constantine (306-337) ruled east & west halves of empire map xvi; 324-30 built beautiful capital in Byzantium named Constantinople 3; thousands of Roman officials in marble/mosaic porticoes/gymnasia/stadia 7-8; His three sons succeeded; Constantine II died;
340 Constans ruled west; Constantius II east map xvi;
351 Huns invaded Balkans (east) 3; 379 Visigoths invaded;
361-3 Julian east Emperor;
364-375 Valentinian I ruled west Caledonia (Britain) to N Africa; 364-378 Valens east to Persian border; Visigoths impatient for land promised, killed Valens & 2/3rds of Roman army 3; 375-392 child Valentinian II; regent Gratianus; 388 co-emperor Theodosius I: 379-395 east & west reunited; resettled Visigoth cavalry in Balkans south of Danube; 395-408Arcadius ruled fromConstantinople;
395 Honorius ruled at Milan, closed Roman Colosseum;
374-397 Bishop Ambrose built Milan cathedral 7;
400 Vandals, a Germanic tribe, gradually moved west in central Gaul; 406 settled in Spain 3; 5; maps xv, xvi.
401-410 Huns and Visigoths invaded Italy, plundered Rome 3; maps xiv, xv; 407 Romans withdrew from England to defend Rome;
416 Visigoths drove Vandals south in Spain;
408-450 east Theodosius II, sister regent; fought/bought off Huns 3; from Constantinople ruled Europe south of Danube, Macedonia, Greece, N. Africa 4; 5; 8-9; xvi; compiled laws; kept Huns out of Rome 3-4, so Huns moved on and crushed Worms, Burgundy; Venice founded by refugees/mercenaries 4;
416 Visigoths conquer Vandal kingdom in N Spain;
425-54 west Valentinian III minor; mother regent;
428 Vandal King Gaiseric led 80,000 to occupy N Africa;
429-454 Aetius was Roman chief minister/virtual ruler;
430 Saint Augustine killed in Hippo 3; 439 Vandals took Carthage; wealthy in grain exports 4; maps xiii, xiv;
450-457 east Emperor Marcian; 451 Salian (west) Franks helped Rome defeat Huns; 451-750 Gallo-Romans jntermarried; French dialects evolved 4;

Italy: 433- **Tribal Rulers in North**
433-493 Saxon Odoacer ruled north Italy 4-5;
455 Vandals from N Africa sacked Rome; anarchy 4; xv;
461-5 Roman Emperor Severus held court in Carthage;
467-72 Anthemius Emperor in Rome central Italy; 468 destroyed half of Roman fleet of 1000 ships;
473-4 Glycerius; 474-5 Julius; 475-6 Romulus;
466-74 East Byzantine Leo I defeated Huns in Dacia;

Italy: 476 **Last West Roman Emperor Romulus Deposed;** by Saxon Odovacar, pensioned in Naples; since 454 Italy protected by Germanic tribes; 476 bought Sicily from Visigoths; 476-565 Byzantine Emperors still Roman speaking 4; had educated Ostrogoth Theodoric;
474-491 East Emperor Zeno; educated Ostrogoth Theodoric; 480 hired Bulgars to fight east tribes; 482 tried to resolve West-East Rome differences; 487 helped Ostrogoths invade Italy 4; maps xiv-xvi;
488-493 Ostrogoth Theodoric took Ravenna xiv;

Items Dates	Pages

Moravia and Bohme 925-1306 **Premysl Dynasty:**
925-29 Wenceslas (Vaclav) ruled; capital in Prague; 927 built St. Vitus cathedral 35; was forced to accept Holy Roman Emperor Henry I of Saxony 15; murdered by brother Boleslav 15; canonized 15;
935-967 Boleslav I in Bohemia controlled Moravia 15;
967-999 Boleslav II magnificient cathedral, churches and forts 15, 35; 1035-55 Bretislav 29; 35;
1085 Vrastislev II; 1096-1299 involved in Crusades 29;
1140-73 Vladislav II; 1198 Otakar I
1230-53 King Wenceslas; 1253-78 Otakar II added Austria & Hungary; silver mines; German settlers;
1278-1305 Wenceslas (Vaclav) II ruled Bohemia, Moravia and two-thirds of Poland 29-30;
1306 Wenceslas III, last Premsyl was assassinated 30;

Moravia 1310-1437 **Luxemburg-Bohemia Dynasty:**
1310-46 John of Luxemburg king of Bohemia; married daughter of Wenceslas III, Holy Roman Emperor 40;
1347-78 king Charles IV; 1355 Holy Roman Emperor; Prague the cultural focus of Europe; trade crossroads; magnificent buildings 47;
1348 Charles University founded;
1347-51 bubonic plague killed one third of Europe, but not land-locked Bohemia & inland parts of Poland;
1377-1453 England/France Hundred Years' War 43-46; Anne, daughter of king Wenceslas married Richard II of England; Czech nobles studied under Wycliffe;
1398 Jon Hus professor Charles University v; 52; 1400 ordained priest; taught/expanded Wycliffe's doctrines;
1402-1414 preached in 3000 seat Bethlehem Chapel; composed hymns; 1403 became Rector 40; 1409 elected Chancellor 52;
1378-1419 Wenceslas IV & part to Sigismund half-brother, king of Hungary/Holy Roman Emperor 52; 1411 Wenceslaus gained from sale of indulgences, so opposed Hus 52; 1412 excommunicated; still preached; most of Bohemia-Moravia provinces followed Hus 52;
1414 Holy Roman Emperor Sigismund summoned Hus to Council at Constance; 1415 burnt to stake as heretic 52; "Storm of Protest" by both working classes and wealthy, petition signed by 450 nobles 82;

Moravia/Bohemia (Bohme) 1419-1526 **Hussite Majority**;
1419-1437 Hussite War against Sigismund 52-53; 55;
1420 Protestant Hussites split between radical Taborites and a majority of moderate Ultraquists; in Bohemia/ Moravia/Slovakia. Nobles and common people elected:
1452-71 king George of Podebrad; suggested a European Council to solve international problems by diplomacy, not war. The pope refused; other nations not ready; 1457 **Unitas Fratrum** (Unity of Brethren, Moravian church) founded at Lititz, 100 miles east of Prague; refused to carry arms & take oaths 15; 53; 1467 for Apostolic Succession, bishop ordained 82; by Waldensean priest 27; 53; 1501 hymn book printed;
1471-1526 Jagiellon Hungarian kings ruled Bohemia and Poland; were tolerant, reformation spread 64;

Items Dates	Pages

Moravia/Bohemia (Bohme)1526-1806 **Hapsburg Rule:**
1515-56 Charles V Hapsburg: Holy Roman Emperor all Spain/Netherlands/Austria; 1555 split Spain & Austria;
1526-1548 Ferdinand I Hapsburg of Austria ruled huge Austria/Bohemia/Moravia/Hungary/Silesia; resided ln Prague, Bohemia due to magnificient buildings 61; 1546 Ferdinand called protestants to war with Saxony; Two protestant denominations evolved: Ultraquists obeyed, pacifist Unitas Fratrum (Unity of Brethren) 65 refused; 2000 expelled; settled in Lissa (Lezno)Poland;
1523-1571 Unitas Fratrum bishop Jan Blahoslav composed /published 743 hymns and chorales, scholarly grammar, translated New Testament and parts of Old; printed in six columns four languages (Czech, Greek, Latin, German, grammar and exposition) 62;
1531-1548 Ultraquist John Augustus became bishop 61;
1564-76 Emperor Maximillan II, persecution eased but churches went underground; Inquisition 62;
1576-1612 Emperor Rudolf II lived in Prague 62; prospered; Counter-Reformation/persecution 63; tolerated Ultraquists/Calvinists and Lutherans 76; 1593 scholarly Czech ***Kralice Bible*** printed 62; 1602 Holy Roman Emperor Rudolf II intensified persecution, especially of Moravian Brethren 62;

Moravian/UnitasFratrum/UnityBrethren:1618-1726
See Moravia 1310-1437 Luxemburg-Bohemia Dynasty
1415 John Hus martyred; 1457 pacifist Unitas Fratrum;
See Moravia/Bohemia (Bohme)1526-1806 Hapsburg Rule;
1546 Unitas Fratrum expelled; refuge in Lissa Poland
1618-48 Thirty Years' War: as 200 years before, protestant clergy banned; teacher/Bishop Jan Comenius & 36,000 Unitas families found refuge in Saxony/Silesia/Poland/ Dresden/Berlin/England 76-7; many **Brüder Gemine** (midweek studies) were established; schools in Lissa;
See Czech (Bohemia);

Moravian Unitas Scholars: England/Europe 1641-1732;
1641-2 Comenius invited to England as consultant on teaching methods; his early textbooks were printed in English. Next invited to France; revised curriculum taught in Hungary, Romania, Sweden, Holland 77;
1650-4 in Calvin College NE Hungary; wrote picture textbook ***Orbis Pictus*** in vernacular & Latin 83;77; all children, girls & boys, to enjoy, not dread school.
1655-60 Sweden plundered Poland-Lithuania, Lissa college & town; killed protestants, a third of the population of 10 million 80; the Church of England and Prince Rupert funded repairs at Lissa. Comenius wrote books in Amsterdam;
1660-1741 Bishop Daniel Jablonski, born in Danzig, educated in Frankfurt an der Oder & Oxford, England; with Leibnitz was cofounder & director of Academy of Sciences, Berlin 1693 88; 90;
1415-1775 waves of persecuted Moravians to Saxony/ Poland/England; Cennick (Kunik) family 77; 82; 101; 1746 John Cennick studied at Herrnhag 77; 101;
1641-42 Comenius education reformer; guest in UK of Samuel Hartrib; book published 77; see Comenius;

Items Dates	Pages

1642 Civil war in England; 1653-9 Cromwell ruled 71;
1657-60 Archbishop of Canterbury approved Unitas 77;
1657 brothers Paul and Adam Hartman and Paul Cyrill, ordained ministers from Lissa Poland raised support in England for exiled Moravians; Prince Rupert, Oliver Cromwell and Archbishop assisted 77;
1673 Bishop Adam Hartmann, Oxford DD degree 77-78;
1660-1741 Jablonski, Daniel and Peter 77-78; 88;
1733 Theologians Spangenberg of Jena and Oettinger from Tübingen taught Theology to Zinzendrof 100;

Moravian Herrnhut, Saxony: Count Zinzendorf 1722;
1722-60 Pietist Count Zinzendorf (born 1700 in Dresden, Saxony) 78; Christian David brought ten persecuted Moravian families to Zinzendorf's estate; settlement named Herrnhut; built choirs (industrial schools) 99;
1726 Count Z found ***Ratio Disciplinae*** by Comenius in a library and was impressed; saw the refugees had similar values. 1727 there were 300 various German & Czech refugees, some contentious 99, Just 26 years old, he joined their nightly worship as their feudal lord hoping for better relations. They covenanted a non-stop Prayer Watch that lasted 100 years; resusitation began.
1728 Daily Texts (with an Old and New Testament scripture, hymn & comments) written and later printed.
1727 Zinzendorf was decorated by the king of Denmark. He saw Eskimos from Greenland 100; started weekly classes on geography and other cultures; sent them two by two to Silesia/Hungary/Swizerland/England; began midweek Diaspora fellowships (Brüder Gemine) within state churches, to strengthen them 65;76-7; 83; 101 remained members of Lutheran churches;
1728 at a special day of prayer 26 single men volunteered to serve overseas 100;
1730 Anna Nitschmann led women's education choir;
1731 population grew to 600 mostly from fleeing the inquisition by Jesuits. Christian David did many high risk evangelistic tours in Bohemia-Moravia;
1732 the traditional Easter Sunrise Service began with horns, trumpets and violins. More hymns were composed, some by Count Z 100;
1733 Theologians Spangenberg of Jena & Oettinger from Tübingen taught Theology to Zinzendrof 100;
1734 en route to America Spangenberg and 9 other Moravians ministered in England, received a government land grant; became a British citizen 100;
1737, 1743 Archbishop of Canterbury praised Zinzendorf; advised ordination as bishop 101;
1738-40 Wesleys returned from America discouraged, worshipped with Moravians 101;
1738 Printer James Hutton, Fetter Lane 101;
1739 Peter Böhler preached in Oxford in Latin; was taught English by Wesleys 101-103;
1808 Seminary at Fulnek England; named for Bohemian (Moravian) Fulnek 135;

Moravian Brethren World Missions Began 1732- present:
1732 mission to Huguenots refugees in Danish West Indies; by Dolber & Nitschmann to black slaves 100;

Items Dates	Pages

1732 Christian David: high risk tours in Bohemia 100;
1733 Greenland by Matthew & Christian Stach and Christian David as carpenter 101;
1734 in S America: Guyana (Surinam) and 1739 Guiana;
1735 Zinzebdorf (Z) began Settlement school in Holland; David Nitschmann consecrated first Bishop 100;
1734 Spangenberg and 9 others: stopover in England for land grant. 1736 in Georgia/cleared it/crops/school for Indian children. Spangenberg became a British citizen.
1736 Bishop Nitschmann & 23 Moravians, the Governor and John & Charles Wesley sailed to Georgia 100;
1736 Spangenberg led some, approved by William Penn to Pennsylvania 100; industrial Settlement buildings begun;
1739 Synod at Gotha; Resusitated Unity of Brethren to build churches only in new locations; to be a leaven in existing churches in midweek Brüder Gemine 101;
1739 Z (Zinzendorf) in Danish West Indies gained release from prison of two missionaries 101;
Mission in Dutch Guiana S America;
1732-36 David Nitschmann, (3 had same name) 99-100; martyr in Moravia, carpenter and bishop 104;
1745-1808 David Zeisberger 63 yrs among Delawares & Iroquois; dictionary, translated scripture; industries 102; 104; 113; driven west by New Englanders 106;

Moravian Herrnhaag Headquarters: 1736-47 **Frankfort on Main: exiled** Zinzendorf **served Baltic/UK/America**;
1736 Saxony Government exiled Zinzendorf as a heretic, since fellow noblemen disapproved of ordination of a nobleman; rented/renamed Marienborn castle Herrnhaag; had 56 Jewish/ Gypsy squatter families, 30-40 old Brethren refugee families from Moravia province of Bohme and multiethnic scholars/seekers 100; 102;
1736 December at Herrnhaag first Synod of Resuscitated Unity of Brethren. Delegates: England/all Europe 101; decided Bishops' Role: spiritual not administrative 112;
1746 English John Cennick drawn to Moravians studied in Herrnhaag; discovered he descended from a refugee from Bohemia 100 years before 76-77; 101;
1736-49 Academic and theological education and hymn writing flourished; his wife/son lived there & he toured:
1736 July Z encouraged Brüder Gemine (non-denominational diasporas) at universities Magdelburg & Jena 101;
1736 at Königsberg, Prussia he started printing the Bible in Livonian; wrote to Frederick William I regarding suffering Austrian refugees on Baltic land, so he invited Z as a guest in his hunting lodge for 3 days 102;
1737 Jan -March Z in England ministered to German business men & encouraged Moravians already working there; the Archbishop of Canterbury wrote open letters recognizing the church as Episcopal; urged Zinzendorf to be ordained a Bishop 101; in May Bishops Jablonski & Nitschmann consecrated him as Bishop. Congratulations came from Canterbury/Prussian king/others 101;
1738 Jena professor Peter Böhler was consecrated Bishop by Zinzendorf ; 101-103;
Moravian owned ships carried colonists, missionaries and industrial products for sale;

Items Dates Pages

Items Dates Pages

Appendix B: LIST OF HISTORIC MAPS

Inside Back Cover: **Surprising Information for Book Distributors and the Website**

A comprehensive yet concise history of Europe and America, from prehistory until after 1913, was assembled by Myrtle Schneider Macdonald. Dates appear at the beginning of sentences, as a visual aid. Significant findings missing in other histories have been included and documented accurately. A major reason for interrelating the histories of European countries, and later of America, was to stimulate awareness of waves of migration back and forth through the centuries. Most Canadians and Americans have Celtic, Frank, Gothic, Germanic, Norse, Viking, Rus and Slavic ancestors who migrated up the rivers of Europe and Russia. National boundaries kept changing. Using **Systems analysis,** an unusually broad approach, simultaneous events in the whole of Europe and America are interrelated. Human interest bits featuring ethnic, social, political and religious movements, are interwoven to correct racism and insularity, as well as regional and ethnic bias.

Boredom, very common in students is dispelled. The author found surprising interconnections such as of Eleanor of Aquitaine, both a minstrel and sophisticated French queen, who participated in the Crusades. Her second husband was Richard I the Lion Heart of England; her sons Kings John (Magna Charta) and Henry III.

Another amazing correlation was of Richard II who married Princess Anne of Prague, Bohemia, a grandchild of *Good King Wenceslas* (of the familiar Christmas carol) and sister of Wenceslas III (Vaclav). At that time John Wycliffe translated the Bible into English. Czech-Bohemians studying under him at Oxford University, took protestant faith back to Jon Hus, the Chancellor of Charles University, Prague. He started the reformation.

Content is chosen **to appeal to a broad spectrum of academic interest and disciplines**. Academics and students around the world can benefit from this internationally interrelated study of history. Using this as a textbook, people throughout the Americas, Europe, Russia, Middle East and North Africa can gain fresh appreciation of their own history and that of other cultures. The author is Canadian with much experience overseas. Peace-keeping Canadians often have the function of promoting mutual understanding and tolerance.

This work **fills in serious gaps in the history of important people groups**. For example, few people know that educated **Huguenots** (French Protestants) were scattered during ***the Inquisition*** to England, Prussia, the West Indies, Acadia (Canada), New England & South Africa where they established shipbuilding, viniculture, silk production and business. **Jacques Cartier, Samuel de Champlain and many early explorers** were Huguenots. Horrible blood-baths of Huguenots, Moravians and other **non-conformists** were under-reported in text books, probably due to embarrassment to either church or state. They are reported here in a sensitive manner, briefly. Scholars concerned about ***ethnic cleansing*** could benefit from this book.

Historians barely mention the **Moravian Church** (Unitas Fratrum=Unity of Brethren=Brũder Gemine), though their influence has been great ever since Jon Hus began reformation a hundred years before Martin Luther, and was martyred in 1415. Persecuted Bohemian-Moravians spread in waves for centuries into Saxony, Africa, Switzerland, Poland, Russia, England and America. Educators can benefit from the scholarly, practical books of Bishop **Comenius** (1592-1670) [p 77]. He was among thousands expelled from Bohemia-Moravia during the 30 Years' War (1614-48). They found refuge in Lisa (Lezno) Poland. He was invited to teach at Harvard College (later University) but chose to accept invitations to reform education of boys **and girls** in Poland, Sweden, Denmark, Hungary, Romania, Holland and England. He added pictures to primers.

Few Lutherans realize their church was revived through the thousands of *diasporas,* small mid-week fellowships (*Brũder Gemine*) of *Moravians* in Europe, the Baltic States and Volhynia (now Ukraine). Because they refrained from sheep-stealing and church-planting, they did not keep membership statistics. East Europeans are aware of the continuing influence of *Brũder Gemine* today but not of the name Moravian church. They are still numerous in the West-Indies and east and south Africa. Moravian missions began in the Danish Caribbean 1732, Greenland 1733, Georgia (America) 1734 and Pennsylvania 1736. John and Charles Wesley sailed to Georgia with them and when they returned to England disillusioned, they worshiped for a time with Moravians in London. They then began the Methodist movement.

During the *Great Awakening* in England, Ireland and America, Moravian influence was great. They did not believe in taking up arms during the many wars in Europe and later in the American War of Independence and Civil War, but their well-built schools and industries were often occupied by troops from either or both sides. European armies required much food and care of the injured, and conscripted their young men.

This work is **not** biography or family history, but **some personal bits are included so as to bring to life the abstract or obscure**. The information is accurate, chronological and of value to secular academics and students in a variety of disciplines, as a textbook or reference book. Genealogists also will find it useful.

Made in the USA
Charleston, SC
19 December 2016